HISTORICAL DIMENSIONS OF
NATIONAL SECURITY PROBLEMS

NATIONAL SECURITY STUDIES SERIES

Sponsored by the National Security Education Program of New York University, in cooperation with The National Strategy Information Center

Editorial Board

Donald G. Brennan, Hudson Institute
Klaus Knorr, Princeton University
Laurence W. Martin, University of London
Ernest R. May, Harvard University
Charles C. Moskos, Jr., Northwestern University
Fred A. Sondermann, Colorado College

HISTORICAL DIMENSIONS OF NATIONAL SECURITY PROBLEMS

edited by
Klaus Knorr

Published for the
NATIONAL SECURITY EDUCATION PROGRAM
BY THE UNIVERSITY PRESS OF KANSAS
Lawrence/Manhattan/Wichita

© Copyright 1976
by the National Security Education Program
of New York University

Standard Book Number 0-7006-0143-0
Library of Congress Catalog Card Number 75-41842

Printed in the United States of America
by Allen Press, Inc., Lawrence, Kansas

Permissions have been granted by the publishers for quotations from these works:

Albertini, Luigi. *The Origins of the War of 1914*, translated and edited by Isabella M. Massey. Vol. 1, 1952. Oxford University Press, Oxford.
Beloff, Max. *The Foreign Policy of Soviet Russia, 1929–1941*. Oxford University Press.
Brinton, Crane. *A Decade of Revolution, 1789–1799*. Copyright © 1934 by Harper & Row, Publishers, Inc.
Burn, A. R. *Alexander the Great and the Hellenistic Empire*. Macmillan Publishing Co., Inc., 1948.
Bury, John Bagnell. *The Invasion of Europe by the Barbarians*. London: Macmillan & Co., Ltd., 1928; reissued, New York: Russell & Russell, 1963.
Butow, Robert J. C. *Tojo and the Coming of the War*. Stanford University Press.
Challener, Richard D. *Admirals, Generals, and American Foreign Policy, 1898–1941*. Copyright © 1973 by Princeton University Press.
Clausewitz, Karl von. *On War*, edited and translated by Michael Howard and Peter Paret. With commentaries by Peter Paret, Michael Howard, & Bernard Brodie. Princeton University Press, 1976.
Deutscher, Isaac. *Stalin*. Oxford University Press.
Fairbank, John K., and Teng, Ssu-yü. *China's Response to the West*. Harvard University Press. © 1954 by the President and Fellows of Harvard College.
Gilbert, Martin, and Gott, Richard. *The Appeasers*. Copyright © 1963 by Martin Gilbert and Richard Gott. Houghton Mifflin Company.
Hamilton, J. R. *Alexander the Great*. Hutchinson Publishing Group Ltd. and the University of Pittsburgh Press.
Hemming, J. *The Conquest of the Incas*. Harcourt Brace Jovanovich, Inc.
Holborn, Hajo. *A History of Modern Germany*, vol. 3: *1840–1945*. Copyright © 1969 by Hajo Holborn. Alfred A. Knopf.
Howard, Michael. *The Franco-Prussian War*. © Michael Howard, 1961. Macmillan Publishing Co., Inc.
Hussey, J. M. *The Byzantine World*. Hutchinson Publishing Group Ltd. and Harper Torchbooks.
Iriye, Akire. *Across the Pacific*. Harcourt Brace Jovanovich, Inc., copyright © by Akire Iriye.
Kennan, George F. "Europe's Problems, Europe's Choices," *Foreign Policy*, no. 14 (Spring 1974). © 1974 by National Affairs, Inc.
Lafore, Laurence. *The End of Glory*. Text copyright © 1970 by Laurence Lafore. Maps copyright © 1970 by J. B. Lippincott Company.
Lafore, Laurence. *The Long Fuse*. Copyright © 1965 by Laurence Lafore. J. B. Lippincott Company.
Oakley, Stewart. *A Short History of Denmark*. Copyright © 1972 by Stewart Oakley. Praeger.
Robinson, Charles A. *Alexander the Great*. Copyright 1947 by E. P. Dutton & Co.; renewal © 1975 by Charles Alexander Robinson, Jr.
Rolo, P. J. V. *Entente Cordiale*. St. Martin's Press, Inc.
Rowse, A. L. *Appeasement: A Study in Political Decline, 1933–1939*. Copyright © 1961 by A. L. Rowse. W. W. Norton & Company, Inc., New York, N.Y.
Schmitt, Bernadotte. *The Annexation of Bosnia*. Cambridge University Press.
Taylor, A. J. P. *The Origins of the Second World War*. 1st American edition. New York: Atheneum, © 1961.
Truong Buu Lam. "Intervention versus Tribute in Sino-Vietnamese Relations," in *The Chinese World Order*, edited by John K. Fairbank. Harvard University Press. © 1954 by the President and Fellows of Harvard College.
Utley, Robert M. *Frontier Regulars*. Copyright © 1973 by Robert M. Utley. Macmillan Publishing Co., Inc.
Utley, Robert M. *Frontiersmen in Blue*. © 1967 by Robert M. Utley. Macmillan Publishing Co., Inc.
Wedgwood, C. V. *The Thirty Years War*. Yale University Press.
Wohlstetter, Roberta. *Pearl Harbor: Warning and Decision*. Stanford University Press, 1962.
Young, G. F. *The Medici*. Random House, Inc.

Foreword

This volume is the sixth in the National Security Studies Series sponsored by the National Security Education Program of New York University in cooperation with the National Strategy Information Center, Inc. Under the general editorship of Professor Frank N. Trager of New York University, the Series has attempted to provide the academic community with texts, bibliographies, and other materials suitable for research and classroom use.

Historical Dimensions of National Security Problems will provide students with a sense of the recurrent nature of diplomatic and military problems. While they do not present a cyclical view of history, the essays in this volume do underscore the fact that the basic issues of national defense can be found in many states at many points in time. This seldom-explored view of national security should be of interest to the general reader as well as to the student.

Other volumes in the National Security Studies Series include:

1. *National Security and American Society: Theory, Process, and Policy*, edited by Frank N. Trager and Philip S. Kronenberg (1973).

2. *American Defense Policy Since 1945: A Preliminary Bibliography*, compiled by John Greenwood and Robin Higham, edited by Geoffrey Kemp, Clark Murdock, and Frank L. Simonie (1973).

3. *Congressional Hearings in American Defense Policy, 1947–1971: An Annotated Bibliography*, edited by Richard Burt and Geoffrey Kemp (1974).

4. *Nuclear Proliferation: Phase II*, edited by Robert M. Lawrence and Joel Larus (1974).

5. *Modules in Security Studies*, edited by Alden Williams and David W. Tarr (1974).

Preface

The plan for this volume was generated by widespread concern over the neglect of history in the study and teaching of national-security and related problems in international relations. I consulted a number of younger scholars, political scientists, and historians, especially those assembled at the National Security Educational Seminar held at Colorado Springs in the summers of 1972 and 1973. Two meetings were held at the offices of the National Security Program in the Graduate School of Public Administration, New York University, in January and April 1973. Those who participated were: Donald Kagan (Yale), Peter Karsten (now University of Pittsburgh), Klaus Knorr (Princeton), Benjamin Lambeth (now at RAND), Allan Millett (Ohio State), Capt. Richard Sinnreich (West Point), Frank N. Trager (NYU)—our host, and Paul Wolfowitz (now at the Arms Control and Disarmament Agency). The purpose and structure of the volume were determined at these conferences.

I would like to thank these participants, as well as the contributors who were subsequently recruited, for their collaboration. I want to record especially my gratitude to Professor Frank N. Trager, whose National Security Program gave generous financial support and whose friendly advice on all aspects of the enterprise was invaluable. Finally, I wish to express my appreciation to Frank Simonie, then Professor Trager's assistant, who was extremely helpful on administrative matters.

Klaus Knorr

Princeton, New Jersey
June 1, 1975

Contents

Foreword vii

Preface viii

Introduction: On the Utility of History
   Klaus Knorr 1

What Happened? The Problem of Causation in International Affairs
   Allan R. Millett and William B. Moreland 5

Military Strategy and Civilian Leadership
   Russell F. Weigley 38

Threat Perception
   Klaus Knorr 78

Response to Threat Perception: Accommodation as a Special Case
   Peter Karsten 120

War-Limiting
   Charles H. Fairbanks 164

Alliances, 1815–1945: Weapons of Power and Tools of Management
   Paul W. Schroeder 227

Technological Change, Strategic Doctrine, and Political Outcomes
   Bernard Brodie 263

The Moral Basis of National Security: Four Historical Perspectives
   Thomas L. Pangle 307

The Authors 373

Introduction: On the Utility of History

Klaus Knorr

This volume of essays was designed to serve two purposes. One is to contribute to the understanding of a number of substantive problems. The other is to demonstrate that the study of historical experience can greatly benefit the study of national-security problems in the contemporary world. It is hoped that this demonstration will help to bring about an end to the present neglect of history. The substantive findings of this book can stand on their individual merits. Its pedagogical purpose is the subject of this Introduction.

To some of us whose teaching and research engages such problems as peace and war, national and international security, it has seemed for some time that both student and faculty interest in acquiring and using historical knowledge has greatly diminished during the past ten years or so, and that this trend has reached the point at which lack of competence, if not sometimes trained incapacity, forecloses any widespread consultation of historical materials for throwing light on present-day problems and policies.

This decline can no doubt be attributed to many factors, including lesser attention to, and a lower quality of, history teaching at American high schools. The somewhat naïve endeavor at the universities to make historical research "scientific" has led to the endless proliferation of highly specialized monographs that are of interest only to the fellow specialist. This sort of output is meant to be consumed by the "professional," and is scarcely calculated to evoke the interest of nonprofessionals. The eruption of the "counter-culture" on the academic scene in the second half of the 1960s added a positive antihistorical impetus. People who find the present wholly unacceptable will naturally reject its antecedents. Indeed, if one wants to do away with the present, one wants to be unique and to be working toward a future that is unique. Knowledge of the past is apt to cast doubt on the easy claim to uniqueness; it may also be suspected of restraining, if not shackling, us in the attempt to build a bright new society and world. This suspicion rejects the often-quoted dictum that "those who do not know history are condemned to repeat it." Instead, to paraphrase, it suggests that those who do *know* history are condemned to repeat it.

Moreover, there are many social scientists who see "modernity"—the product of the industrial and scientific revolution—as a process that is essentially unlike anything that preceded it. Historical experience, they conclude, is irrelevant to the study of what is now happening to mankind.¹ At the same time, other social scientists, like many young historians motivated by the ideal of "hard science" and often trained in little else than statistical method, try to generate and test hypotheses claiming transtemporal validity by quantifying what in most instances resists quantification. While they do turn to history, their objective is to find "facts" fitting dubious statistical indicators of things that obviously elude numerical comprehension. In most cases, these people do not seriously study history; rather, they ransack it in their quest for suitable "data."

This editor reaffirms the older belief that historical study can enrich the social sciences, and vice versa, even when such cross-fertilization can not produce definitive results by the standards of hard science. The social scientist who turns to history does not, of course, ordinarily become a historian and write history. Focusing on the problems of the present, and perhaps even cultivating prediction, he wants to tap historical knowledge in order to exploit transtemporal as well as transspatial comparison for generating and testing hypotheses. He consumes rather than produces historical studies. His use of history looks like abuse to some historians, who consequently resent it, while social scientists, on the other hand, are generally delighted when their concepts and propositions are employed by historians; after all, the historian's use of the social sciences makes historical studies more accessible and useful to the social scientist.

There is, however, also the hoary question in the minds of many historians of whether historical events are essentially iterative enough to permit the generalizations to which social scientists are devoted. Are there universal as well as particular events and experiences?² Many historians have asserted that all events are essentially unique and that history is capable of qualitative change that precludes or at least greatly limits comparison over time. Others have claimed that there are recurring invariants in human experience across the ages, even if these invariants occur under unique sets of circumstances and, in fact, have to be inferred from the complex concatenation of historical events. Like the concepts of social scientists, these "constants" are intellectual constructs.

The question of "universals" versus "particulars" touches on the significance of the following essays in two related ways. If one takes the position, as this editor does, that past events are both unique and universal, one obviously has to be careful not to compare what is incomparable; one must not forget that constants recur in richly differing contexts; and one should not underestimate the job of discovering levels of analysis on which transtemporal comparison can be fruitfully undertaken. As total events, the Peloponnesian War, the Thirty-Years' War, and the Second World War were utterly different from one another. Yet surely, all these wars were preceded by threats; all involved threat perception in their genesis; and all provoked responses that were in a sense typical. Different societies often face similar circumstances and react to them in similar ways. Neither circumstances nor responses are exactly identical. But they often are similar enough to justify the construction of "universals." Similarity makes for a measure of comparability.

The second and related way in which the problem of "universals" and "constants" impinges on our enterprise concerns the question, already mentioned, of whether the history of mankind is continuous—with the same set of universals always recurring—or is given to the emergence of qualitative change so fundamental that transtemporal constants are precluded. It seems to us that this question is informed by a dichotomization that courts sterility. Of course, qualitative change does take place. But it does not preclude essential similarity of events. The Industrial Revolution was a truly revolutionary qualitative change in the life of the human race, and certain phenomena that it generated (e.g., population densities permitted by skyscrapers and high-speed transportation) cannot be founded in preindustrial ages. But that does not mean that in the fifth century B.C. comparative production advantages did not tend to bring about and structure intersocietal trade, as they did in the 1960s. And even though nuclear weapons did not exist in the nineteenth century, certain relationships between military technology and strategy were then quite similar to what they are now. Arms races are recurrent phenomena, and so are problems of civilian-military relationships.

We conclude that the understanding of past events and problems can be part of a learning process that assists us in understanding present events and problems. Without knowing how past societies coped with problems similar to our own, the options they considered, the choices they made, and the consequences entailed by these choices, we can only arrive at a flat, poorly instructed understanding of present problems.

To use the study of the past as a source of learning brought to bear on comprehending the present is not, of course, easy. Historians who read this volume may well find prime examples of the difficulties in the chapters contributed by social scientists. The latter are not trained in how one should use historical materials properly. While they rarely go to primary source materials, they may find it difficult to be critical in the evaluation of secondary works (although they can consult the critical reviews of historical studies by professional historians). Another difficulty arises from the fact that historians of equal technical competence often disagree in the explanation of past events. This is not surprising in view of the ambiguity of all reality, past and present. Perhaps the greatest difficulty results from the necessarily selective focus that historians apply in studying the past. The social scientist turning to historical works does so with a question or a set of questions that may not have inspired historians. For example, when I was seeking historical experiences with the perception of international threats, I found numerous books, many of them excellent, about the genesis of numerous wars. But one problem—*my* problem— that historians were seldom interested in was that of threat perception and its difficulties. Under these circumstances, the curious political scientist, finding at best only incidental attention paid to his question, faces the unfortunate choice of making do with very little or of going to primary materials that he is unprepared to consult properly. These difficulties are not, of course, prohibitive. As in this volume (I hope!), they may account for blemishes but do not vitiate the entire enterprise.

Since our purpose was in part pedagogical, we were not out to find final answers or even so much to arrive at novel hypotheses (although some of the latter emerged). Nor did we only want to show how recourse to historical knowledge can elucidate contemporary problems, as all the chapters indeed do. We also sought to demonstrate how the study of the past leads us to formulate questions that apply to the present. In some cases, it is left to the reader himself to puzzle out some of the questions suggested by the historical material.

As they stand, the following essays exhibit diverse ways of bringing historical knowledge to bear on contemporary issues. This, to be frank, was more the fruit of serendipity than of careful planning. Some authors studied a few historical cases, some only one in correspondingly greater detail, while others referred to numerous historical events. Some chapters are profuse in the use of quotations from historical works, while others are not. It is hoped that these differences in organization, style, and texture are themselves instructive and stimulating.

Notes

1. There are, to be sure, historians who assume history to be discontinuous. For example, Michael Foucault believes that the modern mind is not the result of a gradual historical process but was the precipitate of two great and sudden discontinuities, the first occurring in the mid-seventeenth and the second at the beginning of the nineteenth century, and that these revolutionary transformations obstruct transtemporal understanding. George Huppert, "Divinatio et Eruditio: Thoughts on Foucault," *History and Theory* 13 (1974):191–207.
2. For a recent discussion see Adrian Kuzminski, "The Paradox of Historical Knowledge," *History and Theory* 12 (1973):269–80.

What Happened? The Problem of Causation in International Affairs

Allan R. Millett and William B. Moreland

Making any sense from the seeming chaos of international affairs is a difficult and time-consuming task. Consider, for instance, that in one brief two-month period in 1974 a U.S.–U.S.S.R. summit meeting took place; at least five national governments fell from power and were replaced; one new country emerged; India joined the nuclear club by detonating its first atomic device; a new dedication of the NATO Charter was signed; a South American coup d'état took the life of an elected Marxist president; a devastating famine continued in the northern states of Africa; the combatants in the October 1973 Middle East war signed disengagement accords; the French conducted their latest round of atmospheric nuclear tests; Turkey lifted the domestic ban on cultivation of the opium poppy; the U.S. and the U.S.S.R. conducted several subsurface nuclear tests; the Greeks and the Turks engaged in a bloody war over the fate of Cyprus; and the U.S. agreed to help develop nuclear-power generating plants in Egypt as well as in Israel. The list could be continued.

These events are at best only distant disturbances to the daily existence of millions of people. Yet each also has the potential to change or to end the lives of millions of other people. It is for this latter reason that an understanding of the consequences of international activity for national security is important.

It is the thesis of this chapter that foreign-policy and defense officials operate in and are affected by a context of political constraints that includes commonly understood partisan politics and domestic social and governmental tradition as well as foreign events. This essay explores and illustrates some of the models that might be used by analysts in their thinking about international relations; it also discusses some of the lessons that these abstractions can provide in describing the complex phenomena of international affairs.

Theoretical Perspectives on International Relations

The number of viewpoints that might be useful in understanding the events and interactions of international politics is neither small nor fixed. There are 140-odd national governments that pursue quite independent interests; there are several hundred international organizations and multinational corporations that, to some extent, have other than national interests in mind; and there are several thousand organized political and economic interests that engage in activities that sometimes come in conflict with the national policy of one country or another. If we are to make sense of the sheer volume of events, some method of sorting out these perspectives is required.

Both the practitioner of foreign-policy-making and the analyst of foreign policy give meaning to the reality of world relations by imposing order on their observations through the use of mental constructs—preconceived images based upon previous experience and training. Graham Allison suggests that three types of these mental constructs are: (1) a "rational" actor category; (2) models of organizational politics; and (3) models of individual politics in a bureaucratic setting.[1] Another model that is popular with democratic and Marxist thinkers alike is that foreign-policy actions are the outputs of domestic political events and social structure.

The Nation as Actor

When viewed from an American or any other national perspective, the events of our two-month period of 1974 might be interpreted as expressing some order or meaning. As Henry Kissinger has observed, "In the traditional conception, international relations are conducted by political units treated almost as personalities."[2] It seems easier, almost compelling, to give meaning to the actions of governments, as if they were the actions of individuals, particularly if we make the assumption that nations engage in international relations for a purpose. This shorthand notation allows us to divorce the messy internal politics among numerous domestic factions within a single country from the making of foreign policy. Nations can act rationally, whereas individuals are necessarily involved with processes of bargaining and compromise that are (or appear to be) somewhat less than rational. It is almost reassuring, furthermore, to analyze international events as the purposeful acts of great "statesmen." Even if their acts are irrational, the student can understand the acts in logical fashion. Hans Morgenthau asserts that international politics can be conceived of as old-fashioned power politics between nation-states acting in their own self-interest. This view "provides for rational discipline in action and creates [for the observer] that astounding continuity in foreign policy which makes American, British, or Russian foreign policy appear as an intelligible, rational continuum . . . regardless of the different motives, preferences, and intellectual and moral qualities of successive statesmen."[3]

Studies that start with the assumption that nations act rationally take as a given that all behavior in the international arena is purposeful and chosen as a result of a conscious appraisal of national self-interest. Under this conception, national actors are treated as unitary decision-makers that exhibit the classic abilities of a rational economic man. First, all nations have a known or at least a knowable ordering of both internal and external priorities. Second, nations possess the ability to deduce the consequences of all future activities they undertake. And, finally, nations make rational choices. When faced with a choice among alternatives, a nation that behaves rationally will always choose the option that ranks highest on its list of preferences. The acts of nation-states are thus motivated by conscious self-interest.[4]

The utility of this conception quite obviously derives from its ability to reduce substantially the number of behaving (and potentially threatening) political units to a relatively small group of nation-states. For both the practitioner and the analyst it is far easier to follow and understand 140-odd countries and their activities than it is to monitor the thousands of potentially important political and economic groups among the nations of the world. Furthermore, while individuals and organized groups may have an impact upon international events, their activities are relatively less important per se than the decisions and activities of the national government of a country. Individuals may commit acts of violence (which may be threatening to another government), but when the same acts are committed by an organized group that is directed by another country, the consequences may be far different.[5]

In addition, the unitary-actor mode of explanation has been part of the Western intellectual tradition in writing about international affairs for at least three centuries (when it began to replace divine explanations); it coincided with the rising power of the national state. Even if the acts of states (particularly those that went to war) appeared in their consequences to be irrational, the conventional pre-Marxist interpretation of international affairs was that nations acted according to some relatively dispassionate notion of national interest. Although national interest has proved as elusive as most terms in the hands of academics and politicians, it can be usefully understood as the preservation of the state as a physical and politically sovereign entity; it may also provide for the state's economic and physical expansion, the preservation of its domestic institutions and culture, and the continuation of the nation's internal political processes free of foreign manipulation.

To illustrate the unitary-actor and other explanations of international events, we can usefully examine three historical events which span three centuries, include highly disparate actors, and involve complex relationships of diplomacy, war, and national survival. These events are the Thirty Years' War (1618–1648), the coming of the American Revolution (1763–1775), and the successful Japanese attack on the United States naval base at Pearl Harbor (December 7, 1941).

Although it was fought at a time when the European state-system was still highly fragmented (especially in the hundreds of polities of central Europe that were loosely referred to as "Germany"), unstable, and shaped by the attitudes and practices of feudalism and the universal church, the Thirty Years'

War still appears as an international event basically caused by dynastic rivalries and national aspirations. As one recent historian describes the conflict:

> As religion was still the pivot of men's political thoughts and social activities, and as even secular ideas found expression most commonly in biblical and ecclesiastical language, arguments of statecraft and political propaganda readily appeared in the guise of religious or theological controversy. There is no doubt, however, that all decisions of consequence were taken in the cool light of what at the time became known as *raison d'état*.[6]

Even if the analysts choose to emphasize different international aspects of the war, they still organize their explanation around the unitary-actor model. A distinguished French historian saw the war as a struggle waged by the Habsburg dynasties of Spain and the Holy Roman Empire against the emergent Bourbon dynasty of France's Louis XIII; an equally noted Czech historian believes that the struggle was an even deeper one between the emerging concept of proto-democratic, middle-class, capitalist-mercantile statehood, developed in the Netherlands, and the concept of autocratic dynastic statehood, championed by both the Catholic Habsburgs and the Protestant German princes.[7] Because coreligionists among the soldiers often faced and slaughtered one another on the battlefields of the Thirty Years' War, because the shifting coalitions of belligerent states often included Protestant and Catholic rulers on both sides, and because the spoils of war were the cities and countryside of Germany, the war is ideally suited for unitary-actor analysis.[8]

Although its roots extend back to the Reformation and the fragmented condition of the Holy Roman Empire (the "Empire" contained over three hundred autonomous political units, of which thirty or more were sufficiently populous and wealthy to be important actors), the Thirty Years' War was caused immediately by the succession of a Habsburg prince, Ferdinand of Styria, to the throne of Bohemia in 1617 and then his selection as Holy Roman emperor in 1619. In retaliation for Ferdinand's orders to restore Church property to the religious orders in Bohemia (a militantly Protestant nation), the Bohemian Czech nobility rebelled and replaced Ferdinand with a new king, the elector palatine Frederick V. Frederick's own lands, which bordered on Bohemia, were limited and vulnerable to attack from rival Bavaria and the Habsburgs' Austrian lands, but he counted on support from other German princes or from the other European powers. None came. By 1622 the Bohemian rebels were defeated, executed, exiled, and dispossessed by a pro-Habsburg coalition which included Spain, Bavaria, and Protestant Saxony. The victors occupied not only Bohemia and other rebel territories, but also the Palatinate.

Despite their defeat, the Bohemians in exile continued the war from northern Germany with a mercenary army and drew some other Protestant north-German princes into the war. They were also supported by the United Provinces of the Netherlands, which feared any increase in Habsburg power and was on the verge of renewing its war with the Spanish Netherlands, or what is now Belgium. Denmark also entered the war as part of the anti-Habsburg coalition. The war, however, turned in favor of the Holy Roman emperor as his allies and his own newly formed army (commanded by a Bohemian military entrepreneur named Albrecht von Wallenstein) swept northward to the Baltic. By 1629 the Habsburg coalition was in the ascendancy from northern Italy to the borders of France and Hungary and to the Baltic.

Ferdinand's war of conquest, marked by a plundered countryside and ravaged cities, came to an abrupt halt in 1630, when Sweden, subsidized by France, sent an expeditionary force to Germany. Led by the expansionist warrior-king Gustavus Adolphus, the Swedes destroyed a major Imperial army at Breitenfeld (1631) and then "liberated" much of northern Germany while drawing Saxony and some of the other smaller states into its new coalition. Ferdinand was disheartened, for he had announced in 1629, in the Edict of Restitution, that Church lands throughout Germany should be returned to the prelates and orders that had held them before 1555. Now the Swedes and their allies had ruined not only his plans for a more centralized, more militantly Catholic empire, but also had invaded the heretofore undamaged lands of Bavaria and of the House of Habsburg. Even though Gustavus Adolphus died in action in the Swedes' next major victory (Lützen, 1632), the anti-Habsburg coalition maintained enough cohesion and enough military strength to keep the war going in central Germany. A crucial factor was that France declared war on Spain in 1635, which reversed a Swedish defeat at Nordlingen in 1634. With France at war against them in the Low Countries and along the Rhine, the Habsburgs were unable to regain enough military initiative to drive the Swedish-German armies to the Baltic or to defeat France. Abetted by plague and famine, the war continued for thirteen more years, until the belligerents finally negotiated a settlement (the Peace of Westphalia) in 1648. Although the major belligerents received some lands or some other form of indemnification, the peace treaties essentially restored the *status quo ante bellum*, less the several hundreds of thousands of lives and the enormous wealth that the war had consumed.

Although the Thirty Years' War may seem too far removed in time and place to be worth analyzing in any manner, even American and British schoolchildren "know" that the coming of the American Revolution was brought about by two unitary actors—the patriots of Britain's North American colonies and the British government of George III and Parliament. The

Declaration of Independence tells us so, and even in two centuries of retelling, the war is seldom discussed (outside academic circles) as anything other than a tragic clash of inalienable colonial rights and liberties with the nonnegotiable principles and rights of the unwritten but real British constitution.

Faced with a staggering war debt and an expanded empire in 1763, Great Britain attempted to tax the colonials in order to pay for the costly business of protecting the colonies and running an imperial administration. Within the North American colonies (Canada excluded), groups of American political and business leaders rallied the populace to oppose taxation as an abridgment of the right of Englishmen to have a voice in their own governance. (One wonders whether the colonials really would have accepted taxation *with* representation.) Through written and spoken protest, through urban mob violence, and through refusals to sell imported goods or to use tax stamps, the colonials thwarted a series of revenue measures imposed from 1764 to 1773. Faced with growing illegal resistance, George III and his ministers concluded that the very life of the British Empire and indeed their ability to govern at home were threatened by the Americans. Reluctantly, they turned the royal government in North America into a military occupation (especially in militant New England) and tried to restore the crown's authority through progressively more repressive restrictions on colonial self-government.

In the face of growing intransigence in London, the Americans organized secret groups, known variously as "Sons of Liberty" or "committees of correspondence," to co-opt the colonial assemblies and the militia. By 1774 the potential rebels were in virtual control of most local governments, and they began to store arms and to train select militia companies for military resistance to the crown. When Maj. Gen. Thomas Gage, the British military commander in North America and the royal governor of Massachusetts, attempted to arrest some patriot leaders and confiscate colonial military stores, the militia clashed with the British army at Lexington and Concord and then drove the "redcoats" back into Boston, which the colonials then besieged. Similar outbreaks shortly followed along the Eastern seaboard, all the way from Canada to Georgia, and the American War for Independence had begun.[9]

Even though emotional and moralistic rhetoric about the causes of the American Revolution has been largely abandoned by both British and American historians, analysts find it most comfortable to view the coming of the war as a struggle between two unitary actors—even though they know that before and during the war there were substantial amounts of both loyalism and apathy in the colonial population. Yet whether one's perspective starts from London or Philadelphia, the analysis is essentially framed by rational-actor assumptions. As one student of British politics explains:

The eighteenth-century conflict between the North American Colonies and Great Britain was a clash of rights. Neither side possessed a monopoly on love of parliamentary institutions or civil liberties. Both firmly grounded their arguments in a common political heritage. Britain was committed to the principle of parliamentary supremacy as the only safeguard against absolute monarchy. Americans asserted they were not to be taxed for revenue except by their own representative assemblies. The failure to reconcile these two positions would mean the destruction of the first British Empire.[10]

Even though the events that led Japan to attack the American fleet at Pearl Harbor on December 7, 1941, are probably more complex and more compressed in time than the events that brought on the American Revolution, an analyst might produce a plausible, factually acceptable explanation of the Pearl Harbor attack within the model of the unitary rational actor. For one thing, by World War II the central governments of nation-states were more fully in control of both the articulation and the execution of foreign and military policy than the governments of the seventeenth and eighteenth centuries. More importantly, the political legitimacy and administrative effectiveness of the twentieth-century nation-state meant that the actions of the central government could and did commit the entire population (their lives, their fortunes, and their sacred honor) to the policies that those governments followed—even if those policies in concert meant World War II.

Although the Imperial Japanese government had for generations dreamed of driving the Europeans from Asia and replacing their influence with Japanese political and economic hegemony, it was not until 1941 that Japan could honestly anticipate that a war for this purpose would succeed. The German invasion of Western Europe in 1940 had driven most of the European colonial powers to the brink of national extinction, but not until the German invasion of Russia in 1941 was the penultimate threat to Japan removed. The Japanese rejected a German proposal for a joint war on Russia (the two nations were linked by a mutual nonaggression pact), for the Japanese government was predisposed to avoid war at that time against the Soviet Union. Japan was, in fact, already deeply involved in a war with Nationalist China. The Japanese government, however, quite logically concluded that the time was ripe for extending its influence into resource-rich and weakly defended Southeast Asia. It first made Vichy France's colony of Indochina a military base and protectorate; then it looked covetously at Burma, Malaya, the Dutch East Indies, and the Philippines. Only the possibility of American intervention and the need for military preparation deterred the Japanese.

The United States administration of Franklin D. Roosevelt watched the Japanese government with alarm. Committed to sustaining the Allies with aid short of actual belligerency, the American government recognized that the Asian colonies contributed to the war against Germany and guarded the routes from Australia and New Zealand to the battlefields of the Middle East and Africa. Moreover, the United States was interested in supporting the Nationalist Chinese war effort, which would be impossible without access through Burma and India. In 1941, with the national elections behind it and the Allies and the Chinese skirting defeat, the Roosevelt administration imposed a series of economic sanctions against Japan, which were accompanied by proposals for Japanese withdrawal from China and Indochina and for further negotiations with regard to peaceful economic cooperation and non-aggression in the Pacific. Japan, however, believed that the United States would never agree to dismantle the European hegemony in Asia or to allow Japanese economic exploitation of the area. At the same time, the United States appeared to be edging (as it was) into the war against Germany. The Japanese assumption was that the war for Europe was more crucial to the United States than saving the corrupt Nationalist regime in China or maintaining the European empires in Asia. This was a conclusion that the American government also shared, but it could not ignore the consequences of Japanese expansionism.

In the summer of 1941, despite several abortive attempts at diplomacy, the Japanese government committed itself to a daring, ambitious, and complex simultaneous attack on every significant American and Allied base in the Pacific. This surprise attack on enemy air and naval strength was to be followed by rapid land conquest. The Japanese military planners concluded that their armed forces could accomplish these missions if their enemies received no prompt reinforcements. There remained, however, the American battle fleet in the naval base at Pearl Harbor, a fleet at least potentially poised to sail to the rescue of the beleaguered territories in the western Pacific. Planning for a quick conquest and an equally stubborn defense of those conquests from its island bases in the central and southwest Pacific, the Japanese mounted a skillful naval attack by carrier-based aviation on Oahu's airfields and fleet anchorages. Catching the Americans by surprise, the Japanese navy eliminated the battle fleet and the immediate threat of interference to its government's plans for the conquest of Southeast Asia.[11]

Of course, the attack on Pearl Harbor had enormous consequences which made the Japanese plans seem horribly short on political intelligence. Unified by the attack, the American people supported entry into a war against both Japan and Germany, a war in which a massive American military effort defeated Japan and, in concert with Great Britain and Russia, destroyed Nazism almost simultaneously. But the attack had been from the first a calculated risk, an exercise in realpolitik which simply went astray for the Japanese and rebounded to America's advantage.

Organizations as Actors

A second kind of model that is used to order how nations interact is derived from a different set of assumptions. Modern government is made up of a conglomerate of organizations, each of which specializes in different yet overlapping sectors that are important to the maintenance of the country. The growth of these bureaucracies is attended by a parallel growth in the society's dependence upon these organizations for expert guidance and advice. Thus the bureaucracy takes on an identity of its own, with an obvious interest in maintaining its own existence.

Foreign and defense policy, as well as domestic policy, result from a process of pulling and hauling between different parts of the government.

> Each organization attends to a special set of problems and acts in quasi-independence on these problems. But few important issues fall exclusively within the domain of a single organization. Thus government behavior relevant to any important problem reflects the independent output of several organizations, partially coordinated by government leaders. Government leaders can substantially disturb, but not substantially control, the behavior of these organizations.[12]

One reason that control of "the bureaucracy" is so difficult is that it requires the control of single individuals who work within an organization. Large numbers of people working on complex problems must share a common understanding of the purposes of the organization—which may or may not mean the country as a whole—if they are to be effective and efficient. Standardized operating procedures—rules of expected behavior—are adopted and regularly announced by the organization's leadership through various formalized means to ensure that subordinates will handle the day-to-day problems of the bureaucracy with consistency, regardless of individual experience or position within the hierarchy of the organization.

The policies and activities of a government, then, are the aggregate *outputs* of governmental routines that are controlled and directed by organizational entities. Individuals come and go, and political styles may change. But the organization and its methods of handling the day-to-day business of government change more slowly. In the long run, so the argument goes, if you wish to understand how and why a government takes actions in the international sphere, you should develop an understanding of that country's bureaucratic organizations and standardized bureaucratic practices.

Although the academic emphasis upon the policy influence of governmental organizational behavior is a relatively recent phenomenon, there are innumerable historical examples of such behavior and its policy implications. Again, the Thirty Years' War, the coming of the American Revolution, and the attack on Pearl Harbor illuminate the impact of organizational politics on international relations.

In the early stages of the Thirty Years' War, German mothers would threaten their children with the warning that Mansfeld would come for them if they did not behave. Ernst von Mansfeld, a mercenary general in the service of Frederick of Bohemia, admitted that his soldiers were a plague beyond his control:

> Neither they nor their horses can live by air. . . . All that they have, whether it be arms or apparel, weareth, wasteth and breaketh. If they must buy more they must have money, and if men have it not to give them, they will take it where they find it, not as in part of that which is due unto them, but without weighing or telling it. This gate being once opened unto them they enter into the large fields of liberty: . . . they spare no person of what quality so ever he be, respect no place holy so ever, neither Churches, Altars, Tombs, Sepulchres nor the dead bodies that lie in them.[13]

Any modern student who has read the German classics *Wallenstein* by Schiller and *Simplicissimus* by Grimmelshausen or has seen Bertolt Brecht's play *Mother Courage and Her Children* knows that Mansfeld's description does scant justice to the pillaging during the Thirty Years' War.

Both the length and the destructiveness of the Thirty Years' War are closely related to the structure of seventeenth-century European armies and their behavior in the field, behavior beyond the control of their princes or their generals. Essentially, the belligerent rulers of the Thirty Years' War did not have enough money to pay the armies that they sent against one another. Their tax-collecting policies and tax-collecting organizations were inadequate to support skilled standing armies. Therefore, the rulers offered lands and promises of other revenues to general-entrepreneurs who would subcontract with mercenary colonels for troops. The result was the creation of polyglot armies of many religious faiths and nationalities which had little attachment to either cause or country. Even Sweden and Bavaria, which entered the war with small national armies, incorporated alien mercenaries into their ranks rather than introduce conscription, and Ferdinand II had no Austrian army at all, relying on Spanish troops and those raised by Wallenstein in return for lands and titles. Although the warring princes might placate Wallenstein, Tilly of Bavaria, Bernard of Saxe-Weimar, Mansfeld, and the Swedish marshals with royal patronage, they could not meet their needs for supplies and pay. The generals understood this from the first, but with the exception of Wallenstein, who organized his own central German lands into highly efficient production for war, they relied on taxation and confiscation from occupied cities and rural areas. Even Gustavus Adolphus, whose army was better supported and disciplined than those of his enemies, followed the policy "that war must support war."[14]

When the armies grew to one hundred thousand or more, they became more difficult to feed and control, and the problem was complicated by the fact that armies were accompanied by as many or more noncombatants as soldiers. It was common at the time to estimate that there were at least twice as many camp followers (of all sexes and ages) as soldiers; and in one army, officers were allowed between five and eighteen servants. Such forces moved slowly across Germany during the campaigning season, often "racing" one another to unspoiled lands, where they might find winter quarters among the population. Since the lands of the belligerent princes were often distant or already ravaged, they often settled on "neutral" areas, which spread the war's destructiveness and sometimes forced the "neutrals" to enter the war in search of protecting allies. Opposing armies marched away from each other in search of food as often as they closed with one another for battle. As these armies took on a life of their own, so did the war; for military service and the ability to pillage became as sure a means of survival for the common people as minding one's farm and awaiting the soldiers and the plague. As the war dragged on, the indiscipline of the armies increased, and the Germans could not escape their grasp. The city of Marburg was occupied ten times, and the city of Magdeburg was besieged eleven times. When Tilly's Bavarians stormed Magdeburg in 1631, they massacred thirty thousand Saxons, and later sieges and sackings were measured by whether or not they were worse than Magdeburg. The result was that the war ended only when so many had died and so much had been consumed that all the armies of the belligerents were in a state of mutinous collapse or threatened (as was the case in France and Spain) to drag their monarchs into penurious decline.[15]

Although the organizational behavior of the agencies of the British government in North America, 1763–1775, pales in comparison with the impact of the armies on the Thirty Years' War, the executors of colonial reform did their inadvertant share in alienating the Americans from the mother country. As part of its efforts to regularize administration and increase the colonial contribution to supporting the cost of empire, George III's government attempted to increase the effectiveness of its varied agents of policy, and in doing so, it unconsciously contributed to the disillusionment of its American subjects.

One major problem was the governance of the trans-Appalachian frontier. After its victory over the French in 1763, the British government assumed that to keep the peace on the frontier, it should increasingly monopolize the

Indian trade and protect the tribes from colonial settlement. But this extension of authority could not be separated from the entrepreneurial activities of the two British commissioners for Indian affairs—Sir William Johnson and John Stuart—and their agents. Both Johnson and Stuart ran affairs with the Indians in a highly personal manner, both because the tribal leaders understood and respected only that sort of leadership and because there was no bureaucratized administrative agency to perform their duties in a more effective manner. The British army might have developed this skill, but it was largely driven from the frontier by Pontiac's Rebellion (1763–1765). As a result the colonial traders who were not part of the Johnson-Stuart faction protested that the organization for Indian affairs was designed for personal profit, not government policy. As the British government increased the authority of its frontier officials to exclude colonial traders and settlers, the Americans protested that the management of Indian affairs was another example of Parliament's efforts to deprive one group of Englishmen of an inalienable right to make money while it favored another group.[16]

On the North American seacoast the British agencies most responsible for tax-law enforcement—the customs service and the vice-admirality courts—found that their own improved administration was interpreted as Royal repression. The same reforms that made these two agencies less prone to corruption and patronage made them suspect in colonial eyes. Two British reforms—broadening the jurisdiction of the customs service and establishing a new vice-admirality court at Halifax—were especially provocative, although both were designed only to speed tax collections and the processing of a wide range of maritime cases. For both agencies their normal procedures ran counter to colonial expectations and desires, and as resistance to Royal administration grew, both the customs service and the vice-admirality courts became targets of patriot harassment. Virtually any attempt to collect taxes and to enforce maritime regulations passed in London became a *casus belli*.[17]

As resistance mounted to the normal civil agencies of colonial administration, the British government increasingly turned over the functions of Royal government in North America to the British army and the Royal Navy. Neither was well prepared to assume civil duties, and British army and navy officers were especially obtuse in dealing with the colonials. Both groups were ignorant of civil law and colonial commercial practices; both groups were noted for their lack of tact and their ill-concealed contempt for the colonials. Reflecting the distaste for the colonials that characterized both their services, British officers were insensitive to the colonial reaction to normal British military practices. When the army and navy attempted to track down their own deserters in Boston, their actions were interpreted as military repression of civil liberties and as interference in the normal life of the city. In the case of the army, the standard practice of posting sentries near Royal offices exposed single soldiers to mob harassment. One such incident turned into the Boston Massacre in 1771. And the very presence of military forces to support Royal governors allowed the most militant patriots to argue that the crown was committed to establishing a military "dictatorship" over the colonies, although this alternative was applied only in Boston and then only in 1774. Yet by the time the Revolution entered its shooting phase in 1775, both civil and military officials of the crown had, in simply following normal organizational practices, unwittingly helped to alienate the colonials and bring on the Revolution.[18]

Perhaps no international phenomenon has been as carefully examined for the impact of organizational behavior as the successful Japanese attack on Pearl Harbor. Assuming that either individual incompetence, criminality, or administrative inefficiency allowed the Japanese fleet to attack the navy's key Pacific base, the United States Congress in 1944 conducted a searching investigation of the debacle. The investigation uncovered many examples of administrative practices that in accumulative fashion provided the Japanese with an opportunity to achieve strategic and tactical surprise, but two examples will suffice—the fundamental defects in the joint army-navy defense plans for Oahu and the mishandling of clues to the attack by the military's cryptographic operation "Magic."

Traditionally the United States Army and the United States Navy had before 1941 resisted the concept that there should be a common commander for joint army-navy operations (e.g., an amphibious landing) and the same highly institutionalized outlook affected the plans for the defense of the navy installations on Oahu. Reflecting traditional coast-defense doctrine, the army had the responsibility for protecting the island from enemy surface attack and invasion, although the army assumed that the navy would stop any enemy fleet before it closed Oahu. Reasoning from such assumptions, the army maintained air patrols only above the island itself, while the navy was responsible for long-range over-ocean air patrols. As a result the army early-warning radars and air patrols were insufficient to give more than a half-hour's warning to the anchored fleet. The navy officer who might have provided adequate long-range reconnaissance patrols, however, had five superiors and did not have operational control over the planes he needed, most of which were assigned to training missions. In addition, this officer was not well informed on the possibility of war, at least not so alarmed that he was willing to fight through the bureaucratic maze at Pearl Harbor for enough planes to give Oahu a 360° long-range reconnaissance patrol. Lulled by the navy high command's aura of infallibility and supposed superior knowledge of fleet operations, the army did not question either the navy's air-reconnaissance operations or its intelligence-analysis operations, both of which were sadly defective at Pearl Harbor.[19]

The local commanders at Oahu were, moreover, not well served by the intelligence-collecting and -analysis operations of their parent services. In Washington the problem was too much information and the too-parochial use of the raw data collected by the "Magic" system of intercepting and decoding Japanese radio messages. At least partially because the State Department was the only agency that would sponsor cryptography in its infant development after World War I, the experts of the Army Signal Intelligence Service and the navy's Communications Security staff of the Office of Naval Intelligence (ONI) had broken the Japanese diplomatic code ("Purple"), but not the operational codes of the Imperial Japanese Navy. Knowing how to decipher "Purple" gave the American government an enormous advantage in its relations with its allies and in its negotiations with Japanese diplomats, but it did not permit the government to follow Japanese naval units when the Japanese fleet itself adopted radio silence. When the fleet went quiet (as it did when it left home waters for Hawaii), the only source of information on its location and plans would have come (theoretically) from messages sent from naval headquarters in Japan, messages which were still not decodable. In the meantime, the "Purple" intercepts were closely controlled by a handful of army and navy officers in Washington, who were servicing their own high commands, the State Department, and the president with information on Japanese cabinet meetings and diplomatic instructions.

Yet, on several occasions during the last weeks before Pearl Harbor, the "Magic" system picked up information that indicated that the Japanese might be planning an attack on Pearl Harbor. A Japanese ensign assigned to the consulate at Honolulu sent reports in diplomatic code on United States fleet movements, berthing locations, and air defenses; and his messages were intercepted. Similarly, the Japanese Foreign Ministry also sent messages to its officials that included clues that the Japanese navy intended to strike Pearl Harbor. Yet the "Magic" operation was so tightly run that these clues were not available in Hawaii (where they might have forwarned the local commanders), and in Washington they were largely ignored because they had been sent in diplomatic code between Foreign Ministry offices, not by the Japanese military establishment. Knowing that their own services would not use the State Department's communications system for operational purposes, army and navy intelligence officers did not recognize the importance of these messages, and thus missed an opportunity to identify the attack on Pearl Harbor.[20]

Even if the cryptographers had been alert to the Pearl Harbor "signals" and had properly interpreted them, it is unlikely that they could have convinced their immediate superiors of the significance of those signals. Even though the Office of Naval Intelligence had more influence on naval planning than the Military Intelligence Division (MID) had on army war planning, neither of the intelligence offices had much influence on prewar operational matters. The army's MID concerned itself with collecting raw data of a limited sort and with preparing operations against subversives, spies, and saboteurs. For much of its information on international relations it depended on the summaries of ONI, which the navy passed to it in irregular fashion. The Office of Naval Intelligence seldom sortied into the troubled seas of predicting international events, and when it did, its analyses were most noted for their lack of specificity and their tendency to mirror the current opinions of the Office of the Chief of Naval Operations as the intelligence officers understood those opinions. Since neither service paid much attention to intelligence experts and looked upon them as peripheral participants in war-planning, it is understandable that an intelligence prediction of an attack on Pearl Harbor would not have received much attention. When one army colonel raised the possibility of such an attack, his fears were dismissed out of hand by his superiors.[21]

From the Japanese side the organizational behavior of the Imperial Army and Imperial Navy also clearly influenced both the decision to go to war in the Pacific and to ensure American entry into the war by striking Pearl Harbor. Both services tended to see international relations as a strategic problem in which the European states encircled Japan, opposed its conquest of China, and deprived it of natural resources, resources necessary to maintain not only the civilian economy but also the military establishment. Oil and minerals were especially important to the latter. Even though they had internal differences, the military and the naval staffs also regarded the European allies (with the exception of Russia) as essentially the same threat. Convinced that Japan faced slow economic strangulation if it did not dominate Southeast Asia, the military staffs shouldered aside those civilian officials who either wanted to avoid war or who regarded Russia as the primary threat. With Gen. Hideki Tojo as premier, the military viewpoint was institutionalized as the dominant view in the cabinet in October, 1941.

Although the Japanese military establishment assumed that war with the European powers (less Russia) was inevitable months before Pearl Harbor, the army and naval staffs had great trouble agreeing on a common strategic plan, a development that helped prolong negotiations with the United States. Eventually the Japanese high commanders settled on the only plan that both the army and the navy could agree upon—a simultaneous attack upon the Asia colonies of the European powers, including the Philippines, and a naval attack upon the American fleet at Pearl Harbor. Indoctrinated in the concept "command of the sea" and viewing the U.S. Navy as its traditional enemy, the

Japanese naval staff insisted that the plan of conquest would be unduly endangered if the American Pacific Fleet was allowed to go untouched. Since the Japanese army could assign only about one-fifth of its ground and aviation forces to the attack on Southeast Asia (the remainder were committed to China and the defenses against Russia), Imperial Army headquarters accepted the navy's estimate. In any event, the army staff generally held the United States military in contempt and knew little about American public opinion. Even though Adm. Isoroku Yamamoto, commander of the Combined Fleet, warned that the United States might not negotiate a quick peace with Japan, the chauvinistic military staffs did not accept the possibility that the Untied States might regard the war with Japan as equally "total" as the German challenge. Misled by the logic of their contingency planning and deaf to any contrary evidence that the United States could be kept out of war or, if attacked, prevented from waging total war against Japan, the army and the navy staffs pointed the navy's fast carrier striking force toward Oahu.[22]

The Individual as Actor

A third sort of mental construct in the analysis of external events continues the theme of understanding bureaucratic practices but includes in the description the role of individuals acting from a bureaucratic base. While events of international politics can be viewed from a national perspective, and while bureaucracies (large numbers of people operating with unseen hands) do handle the interchange among nations through regularized practices, individuals operating in organizational "leadership" roles do make, or fail to make, the decisions.[23] These individuals may attempt to act rationally (in the formal sense), but the national interest and the goals of foreign and defense policy may not be uniformly perceived by all those concerned.

The understanding of external events is likely to be quite different for a minister of defense as compared to a minister of the treasury or a minister of foreign affairs. These individuals may share a consensus on the broad, vaguely defined goals of an ideology—the right of an individual to express dissenting opinions or a belief that the state will wither away when "true" socialism is achieved—but when it comes down to the hard facts of a specific decision, these individuals will be conditioned in their view of the world, in part, by the parochial view of the organization they serve. These leaders are intelligent men and women, however, who constantly question and probe the activities of their organization and, moreover, do not blindly accept the recommendations and opinions offered by the organization. Leaders (almost by definition) take an active part in shaping how the bureaucracy interprets events, and they take an active role in expressing their organization's viewpoint to leaders of other organizations. In short, they convince themselves that their organization's view is correct—or mostly nearly correct—before taking action.

But sources of information (external intelligence), past experience, and past administrative practices differ among organizations. Organizational perspectives as well as an individual leader's viewpoints come in conflict and must be resolved through processes of mutual cooperation, bargaining, and compromise. It is the leaders of the organization, operating from a bureaucratic base, and sometimes from a political base outside the organization, that engage in negotiations and make the *inter*organizational compromises.

Furthermore, regardless of the outward form of the government—democratic or totalitarian—leaders act within a setting where accommodation among differing viewpoints is not unusual but essential. Even within authoritarian countries where a supposedly iron hand guides the activities of bureaucrats, ideology and the party line are neither so clearly defined nor understood that differences of opinion among people in positions of operational control do not occur. Although less visible, perhaps, these squabbles are worked out through mechanisms similar to those operating in more open societies.[24]

Bargaining and compromise might remain an academic exercise in explaining how things get done in international politics if it were not for the continuous flow of new (potentially threatening) situations and events, as well as the press of deadlines. Policy-makers are forced to operate in real time; busy people do not have time to contemplate each decision in isolation from other decisions. Complex issues and contingencies may warrant detached, scholarly study, but they seldom receive this kind of focused attention. Rather, the practical man operates in a world where interim solutions are sought.[25] He tries to find workable short-run approximate solutions that will allow him to minimize his likelihood of error and allow him to take remedial steps if an error does occur. The participants know also that different viewpoints and decisions may come in conflict, but that the issue probably will be raised again. And while their viewpoint or solution may not "win" this time, they will almost always have the opportunity to exercise influence again in the future.

The individual-politics model of international affairs is difficult to describe in the breadth of its complexity; it is even more difficult to apply for purposes of analysis or control. There are thousands of individuals and groups who are in a position to affect the foreign policy and defense posture of a single country. What is perhaps more disturbing is the realization that actions on the part of nations are not always deliberate steps in a well-ordered and thoughtfully considered plan. Rationality is a goal and not an actuality. Policy-making and policy execution from the individual perspective is a messy business that involves piecemeal, patchwork decisions on the part of numerous actors.

Activity is a product of nondecision as much as decision. And there is always the possibility of serious mistakes.

The Thirty Years' War offers several examples of the power of the individual perspective upon the decisions of crucial leaders of that conflict. At the height of the Habsburg successes in 1628, Ferdinand II began to consider seriously a dramatic internal reform urged upon him by his Jesuit confessor and his allies, Maximilian of Bavaria and the lesser Catholic German princes. This policy was to return Church lands which had been seized and administered by secular princes over a period of seventy-five years. This policy meant a dramatic challenge to the terms of the Peace of Augsburg (1555), which had established the principle that a German prince could require all his subjects to adopt his religion, whether Catholic or Lutheran. Where German states had become Protestant, the Church's property had been surrendered to the Protestant prince and his followers. Ferdinand, as a devout Catholic, patron of his family's fortunes, and leader of the pro-Habsburg forces, decided that the program of restitution would strengthen his dynasty and his military coalition. He could not, however, get a council of the German princes (Catholics and Protestants alike) to accept his plan, so in 1629 he issued the Edict of Restitution which would return Church lands to Catholic overlords of his choosing. A direct blow at the power of much of the German nobility, the edict was not popular with Pope Urban VIII, and it alarmed the Catholic German princes. Its enforcement eventually added to the turmoil of the war and so angered the pro-Habsburg princes that they demanded and received Wallenstein's removal from the command of Ferdinand's armies. It also tightened the French-Swedish alliance against the Holy Roman Empire. Overly attentive to his conscience and his kin, Ferdinand denied to his cause the victory that his armies had already won.[26]

By redefining the Thirty Years' War as another phase of the Counter-reformation, Ferdinand II complicated the policies of his most successful general, the ambitious, erratically brilliant Albrecht von Wallenstein. Organizer of the most effective army south of Sweden and north of Spain, Wallenstein built his force on a cadre of officers for whom religion was no barrier to advancement. Moreover, he had administered his own expanded lands and other conquered territories efficiently enough to give his army an independent economic and political base. Strict enforcement of the Edict of Restitution directly threatened the maintenance of his army, and Wallenstein both protested to Vienna and failed to enforce the edict in either the spirit or letter that Ferdinand intended. Counseled by his immediate advisors, who represented the pro-Spanish and militantly Catholic faction in his court, Ferdinand removed Wallenstein in order to hold his Spanish kin and their armies and to placate his German allies. As a result, Wallenstein was absent from command when the Imperial forces lost the first crucial battles against the Swedes. Although he returned to his army to face Gustavus Adolphus, Wallenstein never returned to his former power. Yet fearful of Wallenstein's hold upon his soldiers and lands and concerned that he might negotiate a separate peace with the anti-Habsburg allies, Ferdinand engineered a mutiny in Wallenstein's army and had the general murdered by his own officers in 1634. Wallenstein's destruction was in part a Habsburg response to the general's too-ardent defense of his own self-interest and the welfare of his army.[27]

For another giant of the Thirty Years' War the need to answer the imperatives of military command and dynastic fortune was equally fatal. Gustavus Adolphus entered the war in the same fashion that he and his forebearers had faced the Danes and Poles—at the head of the Swedish army. For a Swedish monarch not to have done so would have been unthinkable, and by 1630 Gustavus already had an enviable and deserved reputation as a battlefield leader and military reformer. Although he was admirably served by his chancellor, Axel Oxenstierna, and his generals, Gustavus was the embodiment both of the Swedish state and of the anti-Habsburg coalition. His presence in the field also ensured that his German allies would serve against the imperial armies and that the French connection to Richelieu's treasury was firm, whereas at the same time Sweden's role in the war was not captive to French policy. Gustavus could not surrender his role of battlefield leader (there is no evidence that he ever considered otherwise), and after the victory at Breitenfeld his prowess as a general reached legendary proportions. Yet his effectiveness as a diplomat and as an organizer of war was probably more important to the anti-Habsburg cause than was his tactical ability. Captive of both military tradition and his ability to command an army whose loyalty was largely personal, the Swedish king died leading a cavalry charge at Lützen in 1632, thus depriving his army and his cause of its moving spirit.[28]

Although George III never considered field command an essential ingredient of kingship, the English monarch was not a passive bystander in the politics of the coming of the American Revolution. Rather than being the despot portrayed in patriot propaganda, George III was a thorough constitutionalist and a strong supporter of parliamentary authority. He viewed his monarchical role as being that of defender of the British constitution, and he worked closely with a succession of ministries to strengthen the empire and the right of Parliament to pass laws for the governance of that empire. That he also preserved the concept of the crown as the symbolic cement of that empire and furthered the fortunes of the House of Hanover is undeniable, but George III resisted every attempt by both colonials and pro-American factions in England to override the parliamentary acts that angered the Americans.

As an ardent English patriot and a believer in parliamentary authority, the king found that he could not separate his Royal responsibilities from the acts of his ministers, and he refused to see the colonial challenge as essentially different from the attacks on the Parliament and the crown from such domestic radicals as John Wilkes. Instead George III, abetted by ministers like Lord North, interpreted the American protest movement as a misguided attempt to subvert the very foundation of British government and law. In addition, the king was aware that the solvency of the British government depended on its ability to raise sufficient revenue to support an army and a navy that would be strong enough to protect the empire from a resurgent France and Spain. Yet, George III allowed the Parliament to back down in 1766 and 1769 from the strict enforcement of colonial revenue laws rather than risk a disruption of parliamentary government. Although he was saddened by the misbehavior of his American subjects, the king saw no alternative to coercion after 1770, because he identified the future strength of the British government with its ability to administer the American colonies without challenge. His loyalty, not only to his crown, but also to Parliament and Whitehall, led him to support those ministers who were most anxious to use force in order to bring obedience to British law. This loyalty was almost unfathomable to American patriots, who believed that any reasonable man could see that the mother country could not survive economically without her North American colonies. The king and the "King's Friends" refused to accept such an argument, for as men of principle (however conservative) they could not brook any challenge to their conception of the linkage between crown and Parliament. From their perspective, to have adopted the constitutional arguments of the patriots would have been to accept institutional suicide.[29]

In 1941 President Roosevelt and his civilian and military advisors faced a similar problem of perspective in a world even more fraught with danger, and their special definition of their country's foreign-policy difficulties created the environment that helped make Pearl Harbor possible. None of them was anxious to provoke a war with Japan (as they did not), but their unique perspectives blinded them to the possibility of a Japanese attack on the Pacific Fleet. They communicated this lack of awareness to their commanders on Oahu.

From the point of view of the American military commanders the most frustrating problem they faced in 1941 was the need to reconcile the conflicting demands of the Allies for war matériel and assistance in the war against the German U-boats, the rush to mobilize and rearm America for a series of contingencies, and the obvious need to reinforce the vulnerable Philippines. They were not unaware of the possibility of a Japanese attack on Pearl Harbor (they, in fact, worried about it in 1940), but the more they analyzed Japanese policy, the more they became convinced that the most likely Japanese attack would be into Southeast Asia. In a political sense their reasoning was perceptive. The army and navy chiefs of staff and their war planners recognized that the

United States was the only formidable barrier to Japanese expansion, but they wondered whether the Roosevelt administration would risk going to war to help defend the Dutch East Indies and Malaya when public opinion seemed so divided about aiding the Allies in the much more significant European war. Strategically, they concluded that Japan, however, could not risk a southern attack unless the American naval and air bases in the Philippines were eliminated. In a Joint Army-Navy Board study completed in 1941, the planners identified an attack on the Philippines as the most likely direct Japanese threat to the United States, and thereafter they sent what reinforcements they could to Gen. Douglas MacArthur's Philippine command and to the Asiatic Fleet. By dispatching heavy bombers and submarines to the Philippines, they believed that they might deter Japan until at least 1942, while at the same time they husbanded the bulk of their forces for continental defense and possible intervention in the European war. The army and navy chiefs were, in fact, concerned that the economic sanctions imposed by Roosevelt in 1941 would provoke the Japanese, and they counseled the president and Secretary of State Cordell Hull to continue negotiations at all cost in order to keep the Japanese out of the war as long as possible. As information of Japanese troop and fleet movements poured in during October and November 1941 the military chiefs were united in their expectation that war was near, but that the opening attacks would fall upon the Allies in the western Pacific.[30]

The military's conviction that the Japanese would strike (if and when they did) at bases in the western Pacific was shared by President Roosevelt and Secretary of State Hull. Their definition of the probable Japanese strategy was not substantially different from that of their military advisors, although there were men in both the White House and the State Department who thought either that the Japanese would not enter the war or that, if they did, it would be against the Soviet Union. Outside the federal executive branch, there were still vocal and substantial critics of any American intervention in either the war in China or the war in Europe, and Roosevelt spoke to this audience with fine-honed ambiguity. Both publicly and privately, other American policymakers wondered whether the president had any clear idea of what the United States was going to do, and this uncertainty helped reinforce the conviction that the Japanese would not directly attack American possessions and thus ensure American entry into a Pacific war. Although the military was convinced that the United States would not commit any overt hostile acts (a policy that they themselves approved), they were uncertain whether Roosevelt could react quickly and decisively within America's military limitations to support the Allies in the Pacific. Roosevelt himself was equally uncertain, but he hoped that the deployments to the Philippines and the permanent basing of the Pacific Fleet at Pearl Harbor would deter the Japanese. The military leaders hoped that these deployments would perform this role, but they feared that the Philippine bases might be too strong to be ignored and too weak to resist the Japanese if they attacked. The president was perfectly aware of their view, but he allowed Hull to play out the diplomatic charade with the Japanese on the slight chance that the war could at least be postponed. All eyes were, however, on the Philippines.[31]

Army Chief of Staff George C. Marshall and Chief of Naval Operations Harold R. Stark were in constant communication with their subordinates on Oahu, and they communicated their concerns about the Philippines to them. In fact, much of the military activity on Oahu was the training and forwarding of reinforcements to the Philippines. This local tendency to focus upon the likelihood of war in the western Pacific was reinforced by considerable doubt about the technical ability of the Japanese navy to strike Pearl Harbor without warning, but the crucial factor was the conviction on Oahu that the Japanese would strike first in Southeast Asia. Although the local commanders of the army and navy saw and shared only a fraction of the intelligence information provided Washington, they adopted the same assumptions as their superiors and their president. Rather than concentrate on their own local defense problems, they shared the global concerns of their government and were lulled into defenselessness by their assumptions about Japanese intentions.

So pervasive and intense was the government's fixation on the Japanese moves in the western Pacific that when the first message of the Japanese attack on Pearl Harbor arrived in Washington, the secretary of the navy assumed that there had been a mistake in transmission and that the message was really from the Philippines.[32]

DOMESTIC POLITICS

The last model emphasizes the role of the individual decision-maker operating in a competitive yet largely institutional setting. There is, however, no clear distinction between where a government ends and the governed populace begins, for there are quasi-official representatives of what might be called "private" interest groups that influence foreign and military policy. These representatives may be agents of an organized lobby (in the sense of being paid spokesmen), or they may be agents for an ideological position that is widely held but unorganized within the larger civilian population. Indeed, these individuals can spring to prominence as spokesmen for an issue of the moment and just as quickly disappear as the issue fades from public view. In short, a significant number of persons and issues within the larger population of a country compete along with governmental actors to have their voices heard on some aspect of governmental activity in foreign affairs.[33]

The methods of competition engaged in by these groups and individuals are as diverse and complex as the groups themselves. Some methods emphasize gaudy public controversy with as wide a dissemination of views to as large an audience as possible. Other techniques depend upon quiet persuasion in small private meetings with government officials. The techniques of manipulation used to influence decisions are truly too numerous to catalogue. The important point is that private interests exercise some control over how a nation's foreign activities and policies are carried out, if only in the sense that policy-makers themselves feel constrained to pay attention to and seek support from the groups whose voices are raised outside the official family.

These observations apply equally as well to closed, authoritarian societies. Although the competition is somewhat muted, and certainly far less visible, domestic factions within these authoritarian regimes frequently attempt to draw attention to their position to influence the leadership in various ways. On the other side of the coin, the leadership is often aware of these subtle pressures and responds to them if only to give themselves and their actions a semblance of legitimacy.

A more comprehensive variant of the domestic-politics model includes not just these unofficial activities that are purposely designed to affect foreign policy (e.g., lobbying for an increased tariff), but also those domestic events that impinge upon the conduct of foreign policy, however inadvertently. Usually such events are not the random acts of individuals or small groups, but movements or events of such magnitude that they influence how a nation's government behaves in the international arena. Such domestic events are not hard to identify. In American history, for example, they would include the Civil War and the Great Depression of the 1930s. The important thing to remember is, however, that even in the absence of such cataclysmic events as a civil war or economic collapse, it is not unusual for foreign-policy-makers to be constrained or encouraged to act in certain ways by conditions within their own state that may have little initial, direct international significance. For the pursuit of foreign policies that demand substantial financial and manpower resources, the ability of governments to mobilize these resources is often limited by public reluctance or opposition that may or may not relate to the merits of the foreign policy concerned.

The impact of domestic constraints on foreign-policy decision-makers is easily demonstrated by the experiences of major actors in the Thirty Years' War, the coming of the American Revolution, and American entry into World War II. For the Thirty Years' War, the French case is illustrative, because the government of Louis XIII and his First Minister, Cardinal Richelieu, faced such severe internal problems that active military intervention in the war was unthinkable before 1635. Even then, French entry was against only Spain and was strategically limited to the lands immediately bordering the realm, again because the

French government feared the domestic strains of a more ambitious strategic plan. Yet Richelieu had viewed the war, almost from its origins, as a serious challenge to the integrity of the French state, the stability of Louis XIII's reign, the health of Catholicism in Europe, and the development of the doctrine of royal absolutism. Although he was fearful that the Habsburg coalition of Spain and Imperial Germany would eventually encircle France, Richelieu was, nevertheless, prevented from entering the war by internal problems.[34]

The three groups that imperiled the French monarchy were the Calvinist Huguenots, the powerful nobility (*les grands*), and the peasantry. All three groups were motivated by a complex mixture of concerns, including religious conviction, national political power, regional loyalty, and economic self-interest. Of the three groups the Huguenots, some 10 percent of the French population, posed the greatest threat, for they were led by nobles of considerable ambition and military talent, such as the Duc de Rohan. Moreover, the Huguenots, since the Edict of Nantes (1598), had enjoyed political privileges that made them virtually a state-within-a-state. In addition, they had ties with both England and the Netherlands, both of whom used the Huguenots to discomfit the French monarchy.

The Huguenot menace had a major constraining impact on Richelieu's early efforts to close the pass of the Val Telline between Austria and Italy to Spanish troops that were redeploying to Germany and the Spanish Netherlands. While Richelieu was deep in major diplomacy and minor military maneuvering in northern Italy, a Huguenot revolt forced him to abandon his plans and his own subsequent siege of the Calvinist stronghold of La Rochelle. At a critical time in the development of the Thirty Years' War (1625–1629) when Ferdinand II and his allies were conquering much of Germany, France was paralyzed by a civil war. Richelieu, in fact, made peace with the Huguenots on terms that angered the militant Catholic nobility (the *dévots*) because he could not postpone his efforts to shore up the anti-Habsburg coalition. This he did by supporting the Swedish intervention, an alliance with "heretics" which further outraged the *dévots*.

Although Richelieu neutralized the Huguenots with force and conciliation (he, in fact, brought some of their leaders into the French military service), he was plagued by conspiracies against both Louis XIII and himself. From 1626 until 1632 these plots also limited France's ability to act internationally. The plots usually centered on the person of Gaston d'Orléans, the king's brother and the heir to the throne until the birth of the future Louis XIV in 1638. Although Gaston was the symbolic center of plots by the nobility, the leadership came from powerful nobles and clerics of the *dévot* faction, such as members of the Montmorency and Guise families and Michel de Marillac, who were aided by ambitious courtiers, Spanish agents, and even Huguenot nobles. Since the plots involved Gaston, Queen Anne, and the queen mother, Marie de Médicis, as well as some of the most powerful regional nobles in France, Richelieu could neither ignore them nor crush them out of hand, for fear that he would only stimulate increased resistance to his centralizing policies and ambitious plans for taxation. The result was that these plots further inhibited French diplomatic action, while at the same time they made a more aggressive foreign policy imperative. As Richelieu clearly recognized, the series of conspiracies was encouraged by the possibility of Spanish intervention, and when France declared war on Spain in 1635, the declaration of war justifiably cited Spanish meddling in French politics as a *casus belli*. Yet until Louis XIII's monarchy was on firm ground and the army and bureaucracy were clearly under Richelieu's control and were ascendant over the nobility, France could not risk war with its major antagonist.

Further constraints upon French diplomacy were the fear and the reality of regional peasant revolts. Although the monarchy crushed these revolts with sheer military force, it was forced to put down two major upheavals which affected a quarter of France from 1636 to 1639. These uprisings dramatized another constraint upon French policy and upon the policies of the other belligerents. War meant increased central control and taxation, but loyalty to the crown and the effectiveness of its administrators and military forces were not yet great enough to deter outbreaks of violence in areas pressed by economic hardship and heavier taxation.

The successive ministries that served George III from 1763 until 1771 were no more free from domestic political constraints than was Richelieu's. Thus, England's internal governmental problems contributed to the coming of the American Revolution. Faced with the severe financial problems associated with the Seven Years' War, George III pressured Parliament to make the colonial administration more rational. George's intervention into parliamentary politics became an issue in itself, and factions polarized between the "King's Friends" and old-line Whigs who were determined to maintain parliamentary traditions. The result was a high degree of ministerial instability, which helped make the crown's policy appear weak and vacillating. In an effort to create parliamentary unity in 1766, George appointed the great war leader William Pitt to head the third government in three years, but Pitt undermined his own authority by accepting a peerage and becoming a recluse. The factionalism continued unabated, and one result was that three different sets of colonial revenue measures were revoked by 1769. Although colonial opposition to these taxes alarmed Parliament, the British government's own instability made it especially vulnerable to any determined opposition and gave pro-American members an influence that was greater than their numbers warranted.[35]

Another domestic constraint upon Parliament that encouraged the colonials to see the British government as ready for coercion was the Wilkes Affair. John Wilkes, a London editor and member of Parliament, had developed a popular following as a sharp-tongued critic both of the crown and of parliamentary corruption. Between 1763 and 1769 Wilkes was arrested and jailed twice on charges that were not sustained by the courts, and was three times denied a seat in Parliament, to which he had been elected. His imprisonments set off mob violence in London in which Royal troops shot several rioters; coroner's juries found the soldiers guilty of murder. The Wilkes Affair had, however, a chastening effect on the Whigs who had opposed George III's political activism and colonial policies. Faced with possible revolt at home as well as in America, the Whig majority fell in line with the "King's Friends" in the 1770s in order to bolster both the authority of the crown and the influence of Parliament. The new near-consensus in Parliament gave the North ministry the authority to follow an increasingly intransigent policy toward both the domestic radicals and the colonial malcontents. The latter, outraged by the new parliamentary militancy, soon rebelled.[36]

Although the Roosevelt administration did not face domestic rebellion over its foreign policies in 1941, the American government was alternately constrained and encouraged by internal public opinion as it faced the Germans and Japanese in the second year of World War II. Ever conscious of his vulnerability in Congress and stung by his failures to reverse the Neutrality Acts of 1935–1939, Roosevelt, in the year before Pearl Harbor, acted with characteristic indirection and disingenuousness. His lack of candor, however, was not simply a personality flaw.

After the fall of France made aiding Great Britain both imperative and controversial, a number of pressure groups and lobbies organized to push American foreign policy in the direction that they preferred. The noninterventionists rallied to a variety of groups. Traditional pacifist groups and religious organizations opposed intervention, as did, predictably, crypto-fascists such as the Silver Shirts, the German-American Bund, and the anti-Semitic Christian Front of Father Charles E. Coughlin. Until the invasion of Russia in June 1941, the American Communists and their sympathizers opposed assisting the "imperialistic" Allies. While these groups were a considerable nuisance, the most formidable check on the administration was the America First Committee, a group constituted predominately of midwesterners connected with big business. Advocating hemispheric defense and noninvolvement, the America First Committee had close ties with such influential senators as Robert A. Taft, Arthur H. Vandenberg, William E. Borah, Burton K. Wheeler, and Hiram W. Johnson. Well-financed and skilled both in lobbying and in public propaganda, America First helped to make every major administration proposal in 1941 a battle. During that year the administration had to use all its guile and all its political credit in order to enact Lend Lease, to arm merchantmen, to extend its Atlantic naval patrols, to extend Selective Service, and to repeal the restraints of the Neutrality Acts. On the votes on some foreign-policy issues, the Democratic defections ran as high as one-quarter of the membership of the House and Senate, while the majority of the Republicans voted against the administration. America First helped make this opposition to intervention effective.

Concerned by the isolationists' strength, the administration encouraged and assisted another set of prointerventionist lobbies: the Committee to Defend America by Aiding the Allies, the Century Group, and Fighting for Freedom. These lobbies, as did America First, emphasized the crucial nature of the European war and undervalued the Japanese threat, but they were a valuable antidote to isolationist propaganda. The interventionist lobbies, however, approved of the administration's efforts to assist China and to help defend the Allies' colonies in Asia as part of the struggle against Hitler.[37]

In crude terms, perhaps the lobbies canceled one another out, but they helped prevent any sort of national consensus on foreign policy in 1941, and they encouraged a procrastinating president to temporize. Roosevelt was probably even more impressed by the results of the Roper and the Gallup public-opinion polls, which he studied like an ancient Roman pondering the entrails of geese for omens. The polls were not much help in divining the future course of policy. In 1940 the polls showed that a majority of Americans believed that if France and Britain fell, Germany would attack the United States. The same majority expected the United States to go to war, and it advocated more assistance to the Allies. But a small minority favored declaring war, and a large majority at one time in 1940 actually said that it preferred peace to a defeat of the Axis that would involve American participation. As late as the autumn of 1941, the polls showed that only one-quarter of the American people were ready to declare war against Germany or Japan. In the face of such ambiguous collective advice, Roosevelt probably could not have taken a more open, forthright position on belligerency; but his apparent vacillation angered both the isolationists and interventionists, and it probably encouraged the Japanese to strike in 1941.[38]

A further constraint came from the political debate about America's rearmament program. Although both the interventionists and the isolationists generally approved of a greater defense effort, there were other substantial interest groups that inhibited the government's ability to arm and to conduct more convincing diplomacy. If one disregards the considerable interbureaucratic fighting over mobilization policies, the most important opposition came from corporation and labor leaders, from racists, and from the civil-rights movement. Correctly perceiving that the massive rearmament program involved the economic welfare and the political power of millions of Americans, labor leaders (especially John L. Lewis of the United Mine Workers) and civil-rights organizers (especially A. Philip Randolph) were unwilling to accept the rhetoric of sacrifice from big business and from political conservatives, who said that internal arguments over wages and civil rights were wounding the rearmament program. In 1940 Lewis urged his miners to vote against the president, and in 1941 Randolph organized thousands of blacks for a march on Washington, a march that was called off only after Roosevelt promised to establish a fair employment practices program that would prevent defense industries from using discriminatory hiring practices. In addition, the Congress was restive enough about production problems and the plight of small businessmen to establish a special investigating committee under Senator Harry S. Truman to monitor the administration's defense programs. As part of a pattern of growing congressional militancy, the Truman Committee added to the domestic disarray that inhibited presidential activism in conducting foreign policy.[39]

It is difficult to argue that any of the domestic constraints of 1940 and 1941, viewed retrospectively, were decisive in bringing on the Japanese attack on Pearl Harbor. Most of the policy debate, in fact, centered on the war in Europe. Nevertheless, Roosevelt as a consummate popular politician was concerned enough about internal divisions to carry on his diplomacy with such indirectness that both isolationists and interventionists were angered by what they viewed as duplicity. Without some sort of national consensus (which Roosevelt believed imperative before taking a democratic society to war), American diplomacy did not have the international authoritativeness it required in order to make deterrence in Asia work.[40]

Models of Reality: An Assessment

A multitude of viewpoints are possible and potentially useful to an understanding of the making of both foreign and defense policy. The four perspectives illustrated in this essay were chosen because they represent different levels of analysis (international, national, organizational, and individual) and different behaving units: for example, the nation, as it interacts with other nations in international politics; national bureaucratic organizations, as they carry out standardized routines; and groups and individuals, as they operate in a political matrix that includes other individuals as well as other organizations. Other models of behavior could have been included. For instance, we might interpret international affairs from the perspective of foreign-policy events,[41] international-integration theory,[42] national attributes,[43] or international-systems theory,[44] among others.

The point of these examples is to demonstrate that multiple approaches to explanation are possible and that multiple viewpoints can highlight aspects of international behavior that might otherwise be overlooked. Models are abstractions, however, that may not re-create reality; models focus attention (whether they are intended to or not) upon only a limited number of relationships. For instance, although we know that rationality is an ideal that is seldom observed in practice, the comparison of empirical reality to this ideal serves a useful purpose. The process of ordering our observations and ranking our preferred options from several perspectives may make clear some previously unknown alternative course of action. The test of the utility of a model to a policy-maker is not, after all, whether it somehow "fits" with some theoretical reality, but whether the model provides useful information that can be acted upon.

While the decisions of defense- and foreign-policy officials may not be rational in the strict economic sense, the process of bargaining and compromise described by our third model does ensure that multiple viewpoints—political as well as interpretive—will be represented in the outcome. After all, without perfect knowledge about the state of the world one is less likely to make mistakes when more, rather than less, information informs the process of decision. Likewise, the larger the number of participants, the more likely it is that a "correct" solution will be found, although the psychologist Irving Janis has recently argued the opposite viewpoint.[45] Also, because the pursuit of foreign policies involves advantages and sacrifices that will not be distributed evenly over society, the push and pull of politics is apt to make the definition of the national interest more representative in societies that cannot, by their very structure, be unitary actors.

We began this essay by noting that analysts give meaning to the complex of international affairs by imposing their own interpretation in the form of mental constructs—abstractions based upon previous training and experience. We have presented four of these models as if they were independent of each other. It is a fair assumption, however, that hybrid mental images based upon some combination of parts of these and other models will be used at different times and under different circumstances.[46]

The important point to remember as we try to reconstruct what happens in international affairs is not that this particular model or that particular approach was used. Rather, elements of the different approaches are applicable to an explanation of what occurred. For instance, it is important to remember that different bureaucracies in a single country, as well as groups of individuals within a single bureaucracy, view the goals of defense policy and foreign policy differently. Because perceptions of events differ and because foreign-policy goals are seldom understood in quite the same way by all of those concerned, in some situations, notably noncrisis situations, a process of competition emerges in which an individual attempts to press his viewpoint as "the" correct interpretation of events. This competition results in a subdued yet constant political war within the bureaucracy.

Despite the theoretical implications of the rational-actor model, every bureaucracy contains differences of opinion on most issues. Policy-makers of one nation can often find at least partial support among the divided bureaucratic factions in another nation's government. This often provides a starting point for international bargaining that may lead to political compromise at a higher level.

Notes

1. Graham T. Allison, *The Essence of Decision* (Boston: Little, Brown, 1971), chap. 1. The executive functions of national government (whether they are performed in the name of a prime minister, president, or premier) are carried out by semi-autonomous yet integrated organizations commonly called bureaucracies.
2. Henry Kissinger, "Domestic Structure and Foreign Policy," *Daedalus* 95 (Spring, 1966):503–29.
3. Hans Morgenthau, *Politics among Nations* (5th ed.; New York: Knopf, 1970), p. 6.
4. The basis for rational choice among political alternatives is explored in Anthony Downs, *An Economic Theory of Democracy* (New York: Harper & Row, 1957), and in James M. Buchanan and Gordon Tullock, *The Calculus of Consent* (Ann Arbor: University of Michigan Press, 1962). Rationality in an international setting is explored by Morton Kaplan in *System and Process in International Politics* (New York: John Wiley, 1967). A considerable amount of work on theoretical rationality is outlined in the writings on game theory and decision theory. See particularly the references on these subjects in David Sills, ed., *International Encyclopedia of the Social Sciences* (New York: Macmillan, and Free Press, 1968), vols. 1 and 13. Rational behavior in an organizational setting is discussed by Anthony Downs, *Inside Bureaucracy* (Boston: Little, Brown, 1967). Downs's work derives from an older literature, extending back into the 1950s. See particularly, James March and Herbert Simon, with Harold Guetzkow, *Organizations* (New York: John Wiley, 1958), and Herbert Simon, *Administrative Behavior* (New York: Macmillan, 1947).
5. The reader is alerted that the treatment given this model is much more extensive in other literature. See, for example, Morgenthau, *Politics among Nations*.
6. Sigfrid H. Steinberg, *The Thirty Years War and the Conflict for European Hegemony 1600–1660* (New York: Norton, 1966), p. 2.
7. Georges Pagès, *The Thirty Years War, 1618–1648* (New York: Harper & Row, 1970); Josef V. Polisensky, *The Thirty Years War* (Berkeley & Los Angeles: University of California Press, 1971).
8. See, for example, Carl J. Friedrich, *The Age of the Baroque, 1610–1660* (New York: Harper & Row, 1952), pp. 161–96; Hajo Holborn, *A History of Modern Germany*, vol. 1, *The Reformation* (New York: Knopf, 1959), pp. 305–60; E. A. Beller, "The Thirty Years War," in *The New Cambridge Modern History* (14 vols.; Cambridge; Eng.: Cambridge University Press, 1958–1970), 4:306–58. The most detailed account in English is C. V. Wedgwood, *The Thirty Years War* (New Haven: Yale University Press, 1939).
9. Lawrence Henry Gipson, *The Triumphant Empire: The Rumbling of the Coming Storm, 1766–1770* (New York: Knopf, 1965), and *The Triumphant Empire:*

Britain Sails into the Storm, 1770–1776 (New York: Knopf, 1965); Cecil Headlam, "The Constitutional Struggle with the American Colonies, 1765–1776," in *The Cambridge History of the British Empire*, ed. J. Holland Rose et al. (8 vols.; Cambridge, Eng.: Cambridge University Press, 1929–1936), 1:647–84; Don Higginbotham, *The War of American Independence* (New York: Macmillan, 1971), pp. 29–56.

10. Charles R. Ritcheson, *British Politics and the American Revolution* (Norman: University of Oklahoma Press, 1954), p. vii.
11. Herbert Feis, *The Road to Pearl Harbor* (Princeton, N.J.: Princeton University Press, 1950), which is a classic unitary-actor analysis. See also Louis Morton, "Japan's Decision for War," in *Command Decisions*, ed. Kent R. Greenfield, Office of the Chief of Military History, Department of the Army (Washington, D.C.: Government Printing Office, 1960), pp. 99–124.
12. Allison, *Essence of Decision*, p. 67.
13. Quoted in Wedgwood, *Thirty Years War*, p. 133.
14. J. W. Wijn, "Military Forces and Warfare, 1610–48," in *The New Cambridge Modern History*, 4:202–25; Michael Roberts, *Gustavus Adolphus* (2 vols.; London & New York: Longmans, Green, 1953, 1958), 2:169–271.
15. Wedgwood, *Thirty Years War*, pp. 16, 132, 147, 167, 293, 316, 350–52, 384, 421, 435, 475, 497. For the destructiveness of the war, see Theodore K. Rabb, "The Effects of the Thirty Years' War on the German Economy," *Journal of Modern History* 34 (March 1962):40–51.
16. Jack M. Sosin, *Whitehall and the Wilderness: The Middle West in British Colonial Policy, 1760–1775* (Lincoln: University of Nebraska Press, 1961); John R. Alden, *John Stuart and the Southern Colonial Frontier* (Ann Arbor: University of Michigan Press, 1944); James T. Flexner, *Mohawk Baronet: Sir William Johnson of New York* (New York: Harper & Row, 1959).
17. Thomas C. Barrow, *Trade and Empire: The British Customs Service in Colonial America, 1660–1775* (Cambridge, Mass.: Harvard University Press, 1967), pp. 186–257; Carl Ubbelhode, *The Vice-Admiralty Courts and the American Revolution* (Chapel Hill: University of North Carolina Press, for the Institute of Early American History and Culture, Williamsburg, Va., 1960).
18. John Shy, *Toward Lexington: The Role of the British Army in the Coming of the American Revolution* (Princeton, N.J.: Princeton University Press, 1965); Neil R. Stout, *The Royal Navy in America, 1760–1775* (Annapolis, Md.: Naval Institute Press, 1973).
19. Roberta Wohlstetter, *Pearl Harbor: Warning and Decision* (Stanford, Calif.: Stanford University Press, 1962), pp. 5–70.
20. Ibid., pp. 170–227; Ladislas Farago, *The Broken Seal* (New York: Random House, 1967), pp. 158–61, 224–33, 262–78.
21. Wohlstetter, *Pearl Harbor*, pp. 279–338.
22. Robert J. C. Butow, *Tojo and the Coming of the War* (Princeton, N.J.: Princeton University Press, 1961), pp. 154–227, 310–63; John Toland, *The Rising Sun: The Decline and Fall of the Japanese Empire, 1936–1945* (New York: Random House, 1970), pp. 89–208.
23. As it is used here, the term *leadership* denotes a process of involvement of an organization in a substantive arena and not the more formal meaning usually attached to a high-echelon appointment. This usage includes both high- and low-level positions; leadership is sometimes more evident at the lower levels of a bureaucracy than among the formally responsible officials.

24. Under some circumstances, however, the conflict can be resolved more quickly in an authoritarian regime. A bullet in the neck assures that the replacement for a dissident leader understands the limits of his expected conformity. The equivalent situation arises in a democracy when a leader is forced to resign or is publically fired.
25. Simon, *Administrative Behavior*, calls this strategy "satisfysing" (sic). And Charles E. Lindblom refers to a variant of this approach as "The Science of 'Muddling Through,'" *Public Administration Review* 19 (Spring, 1959):79–88. See also David Braybrooke and Charles Lindblom, *A Strategy of Decision* (New York: Free Press, 1963).
26. Wedgwood, *Thirty Years War*, pp. 239–66.
27. Francis Watson, *Wallenstein* (New York: D. Appleton-Century, and London: Chatto & Windus, 1938).
28. Roberts, *Gustavus Adolphus*, 2:774–89.
29. Stanley Ayling, *George the Third* (London: Collins, 1972), pp. 104–71; Jack M. Sosin, *Agents and Merchants: British Colonial Policy and the Origins of the American Revolution, 1763–1775* (Lincoln: University of Nebraska Press, 1965); Richard Pares, *King George III and the Politicians* (Oxford, Eng.: Clarendon Press, 1953).
30. Samuel Eliot Morison, *The Rising Sun in the Pacific, 1931–April 1942*, vol. 3 of *History of United States Naval Operations in World War II* (Boston: Little, Brown, 1950), pp. 48–95; Louis Morton, *United States Army in World War II: The War in the Pacific: Strategy and Command: The First Two Years* (Washington, D.C.: Government Printing Office, 1962), pp. 92–127; Forrest C. Pogue, *George C. Marshall*, vol. 2, *Ordeal and Hope, 1939–1942* (New York: Viking, 1966), pp. 120–231.
31. James MacGregor Burns, *Roosevelt: The Soldier of Freedom, 1940–1945* (New York: Harcourt Brace Jovanovich, 1970), pp. 132–67; Julius W. Pratt, *Cordell Hull* (2 vols.; New York: Cooper Square, 1964), 2:476–519.
32. Burns, *Roosevelt*, p. 162.
33. In other words, the rough-and-tumble of domestic politics extends into the area of foreign policy as well. The "pluralist" school of political theory has provided the most thorough description of this kind of competition. The effects of domestic individuals and groups in the making of foreign policy is also explored by Richard C. Snyder, H. W. Bruck, and Burton Sapin, "The Decision-Making Approach to the Study of International Politics," in *International Politics and Foreign Policy*, ed. James N. Rosenau (rev. ed.; New York: Free Press, 1969). This same point of view is taken by Raymond Bauer, Ithiel de Sola Pool, and Lewis Anthony Dexter, *American Business and Public Policy* (New York: Atherton, 1963).
34. Geoffrey R. R. Treasure, *Cardinal Richelieu and the Development of Absolutism* (London: Adam & Charles Black, 1972), pp. 81–147; William F. Church, *Richelieu and Reason of State* (Princeton, N.J.: Princeton University Press, 1972), pp. 173–205, 283–339.
35. Denys A. Winstanley, *Lord Chatham and the Whig Opposition* (Cambridge, Eng.: Cambridge University Press, 1912); John Steven Watson, *The Reign of George III, 1760–1815* (Oxford, Eng.: Clarendon Press, 1960), pp. 94–195; Ritcheson, *British Politics*, pp. 68–135.
36. George Rudé, *Wilkes and Liberty* (Oxford, Eng.: Clarendon Press, 1962).
37. The domestic debate is summarized in the following works: Selig Adler, *The Isolationist Impulse* (London & New York: Abelard-Schuman, 1957), pp. 274–319;

Wayne S. Cole, *America First: The Battle against Intervention, 1940–1941* (Madison: University of Wisconsin Press, 1953); Mark L. Chadwin, *The Hawks of World War II* (Chapel Hill: University of North Carolina Press, 1968); H. Bradford Westerfield, *Foreign Policy and Party Politics* (New Haven, Conn.: Yale University Press, 1955), pp. 130–35; Robert A. Divine, *The Illusion of Neutrality* (Chicago: University of Chicago Press, 1962), pp. 286–335.

38. Nobutaka Ike, ed., *Japan's Decision for War: Records of the 1941 Policy Conferences* (Stanford, Calif.: Stanford University Press, 1967), pp. 21, 44, 153, 238.
39. Richard Polenberg, *War and Society: The United States, 1941–1945* (Philadelphia: Lippincott, 1972), pp. 5–36, 73–106, 154–59; Donald H. Riddle, *The Truman Committee* (New Brunswick, N.J.: Rutgers University Press, 1964).
40. Burns, *Roosevelt*, pp. 98–153.
41. The events data movement springs from various theoretical perspectives. See, for instance, Charles F. Hermann, *Crises in Foreign Policy* (Indianapolis, Ind.: Bobbs-Merrill, for Center of International Studies, Princeton University, 1969). Also, Charles A. McClelland, "Action Structures and Communication in Two International Crises: Quemoy and Berlin," in Rosenau, *International Politics*, pp. 473–82. See also James N. Rosenau, "Pre-theories and Theories of Foreign Policy," in *Approaches to Comparative and International Politics*, ed. R. Barry Farrell (Evanston, Ill.: Northwestern University Press, 1966), pp. 27–92.
42. Karl W. Deutsch, *The Analysis of International Relations* (Englewood Cliffs, N.J.: Prentice-Hall, 1968).
43. The International situation itself may determine what kind of decision process is followed. Charles Hermann has characterized the decision process according to three dimensions: the degree of the sense of threat, the time available for decision, and the degree of anticipation of the situation. See his "International Crises as a Situational Variable," in Rosenau, *International Politics*, pp. 409–21, for an extremely interesting treatment of this topic.
44. Rudolph Rummel, *The Dimensions of Nations* (Beverly Hills, Calif.: Sage, 1972).
45. Irving Janis, *Victims of Groupthink* (Boston: Houghton Mifflin, 1972).
46. Kaplan, *System*; and Oran R. Young, *A Systemic Approach to International Politics*, Research Monograph no. 33 (Princeton, N.J.: Center of International Studies, Princeton University, June 30, 1968).

Military Strategy and Civilian Leadership

Russell F. Weigley

The most frequently quoted generalization about war may well be Karl von Clausewitz's dictum that "War Is a Mere Continuation of Policy by Other Means."[1] Although it is quoted so often that the earliest beginner in the study of national-security problems can scarcely be unaware of it, to repeat this apothegm somehow is still taken as a mark of sophistication—as when critics of United States involvement in Indochina readily scored debating points by claiming that what first went wrong was that America lost sight of the political ends of war. In order to demonstrate a properly sophisticated knowledge of national-security affairs today, to be sure, it is necessary to affirm also that not only war but the maintenance and use of military force short of war ought to be tailored to political ends.

It may appear strange, then, that although the English-speaking world has been familiar with the writings of Clausewitz for nearly a century, the harmonizing of military force and political purpose—in practice as distinguished from Clausewitzian theory—should still remain an often intractable problem. The imprecations of the soldiers against the "frocks" when civilian leadership sought to restrain military strategy in World War I might be dismissed as representative of a generation of military men not yet schooled in anything but waging war.[2] So might David Lloyd George's misunderstanding of the strategic problems of the Western Front in the same war, or Woodrow Wilson's amazing indifference to military problems even while he was a war President, be taken as symptoms of a statesmanship that was new to military affairs after a century predominantly of peace in the Western world. But after another half-century of continuous immersion in international political problems that were inseparable from their military dimensions and of considerable schooling of foreign relations specialists and soldiers in each others' specialties, the "frocks" and the soldiers seem still to be perpetually at odds during military crises. We have not come far from the period 1914–1918 when soldiers of the Vietnam War say that civilian "leaders were responsible for prolonging the war also through the indecisive use of our military power" and while civilian commentators, even inside the Department of Defense itself, rejoin contemptuously that "the 'hawks,' of course, were primarily the military."[3]

As notable as the persistence of unresolved tensions between soldiers and civilian policy-makers, and thus between war and the policy that it is supposedly a continuation of, has been the ubiquity of such tensions in every kind of political system. Parliamentary democracy, authoritarian monarchy, fascism, and communism have all been unable to render war, or the military strategy of waging it, into a disciplined tool of policy rather than an autonomous force. They have also been able to rely on subordinating military leadership to civilian leadership. The clashes of the Great War of 1914–1918 between "frocks" and soldiers plagued imperial Germany as well as republican France and parliamentary Britain. If the contests appear slightly more subdued in Germany, it was only because there the civilian leadership was more docile about abnegating itself and national policy to the importunities of soldiers and strategy. Since World War I, the questions of how to subordinate war to policy and soldiers to civilians have been as puzzling to the Communist powers as to the United States. From the time of Joseph Stalin's purge of Marshal M. N. Tukhachevsky and other soldierly comrades of the Bolshevik armies (1937) through the period of Marshal G. K. Zhukov's rise to power and prestige in World War II, his postwar decline, his rise again in partnership with Khrushchev, his subsequent new decline, and the Soviet Army's participation in the political elimination of Khrushchev in order to find a new foothold of power for itself (1964), the history of military-civil relations in the Soviet government traced the pattern of a roller coaster, attaining no stable level of military subordination to civilian policy and leadership. Rather the search for a proper balance between their military strategy and their party doctrine and policy has been the consistent theme. Similarly, such drastic expedients as the abandonment of customary military ranks have not saved the People's Republic of China from the tensions between their national policy and leadership and their supposedly subordinate military instruments.

Moreover, such phenomena are scarcely confined to recent history. During the whole history of the modern state, the only occasions on which civilian leadership and military strategy have been thoroughly in harmony have occurred when the two forces have been combined in a single individual, such as Frederick the Great or Napoleon. Under all other political circumstances or systems, military leadership and strategy have tended to depart from subordination to national policy and civilian leadership in direct proportion to the magnitude of the military threats that have been perceived as confronting a state, regardless of the nature of that state's nonmilitary institutions, whether they were democratic or authoritarian. The heyday of modern militarism—when military strategy shaped rather than served policy in every Continental European power— occurred after the victories of militaristic Prussia in 1866 and in 1870 and 1871 convinced all the powers that they could have no security unless they subordinated every aspect of their political and social lives to military expediency as Prussia had done. In every European great power during this era, the civilians abdicated to the military a major share in the direction of the state, in hopes that their military could then assure that they would not suffer the same fate as Austria in 1866 and France in 1870, that it could instead win for them victories comparable to those of Prussia. Furthermore, no modification of the professional conditioning of the military by the circumstances and traditions of any particular political system offered assurance that the military would not grasp the opportunity to elevate strategic concerns above those of policy when the statesmen offered them that opportunity.

When this era of militarism reached its climax in the Great War, the supreme threat apparently posed by militaristic Prussia-Germany drove even Great Britain to place herself and her government at the disposal of her generals and admirals. However, when the military failed to repay the abrogation of civilian policy and leadership with a suitable reward in renewed national security, but rather led every belligerent country into a blood bath and a decline in national security, disillusionment set in. In the midst of the Great War itself, despite the rule that military ascendancy tends to grow in proportion to the severity of the military crisis, David Lloyd George in Britain and Georges Clemenceau in France began the process of reasserting the primacy of civilian leadership and national policy. This disillusionment became universal. In Germany—despite the protective covering of the stab-in-the-back legend—the war of 1914–1918 discredited the military so much that Adolf Hitler was able to achieve a remarkable subordination of the soldiers to himself and his party before World War II. Indeed, at no time during World War II did the military predominate in any great Western power to the extent that they had during World War I. Nevertheless, the tendency that strategy is likely to break loose from policy in the cauldron of war still operated. From 1941 to 1945 Stalin had to undo many of the effects that the great purges had had upon the Red Army. He also had to restore the military to a power and prestige that, upon the return of peace, he made haste to try to reduce—with anything but complete success. In the United States, too, the military reached such a pinnacle of power that, according to many historians, military strategy came to shape national policy; and many citizens believe that this is still the case. In Great Britain, Winston Churchill habitually sacrificed the long-run interests of empire, as well as such decades-old policies as his own enmity to communism, for short-run advantages of military strategy. And although Churchill never had to circumvent the soldiers' power by subterfuge in World War II, as Lloyd George had had to do in dealing with Sir Douglas Haig in World War I, it was also true that Churchill's perceptions were so militarized that, with him, civilian leadership was no longer as civilian as it had usually been in modern Britain. The militarizing of the perceptions of civilian leaders themselves, so that the very guardians of policy against the primacy of military strategy become the apostles of strategy, indeed appears to be far from infrequent. The most conspicuous case in recent history has been Hitler, who sought military success far more eagerly than his more cautious generals. The historical record suggests that institutional arrangements of civilian-military relationships cannot guarantee the subordination of strategy to policy. Historically, every type of political system and every arrangement of institutions has instead subordinated policy to strategy whenever a crisis of national security has seemed severe. And even if the political institutions of a state so strongly protect civilian control of the military that civilian control can exert itself directly both at the top and far down the chain of military command, during national-security crises the civilian leadership itself tends to sacrifice policy to the exigencies of war.

Historical experience offers no clear guidance, then, toward assuring that Clausewitz's dictum will be observed, that war will be a mere continuation of policy, and that civilian leadership will control military strategy in the interests of policy. Without reliable institutional safeguards of the primacy of policy and with no assurance that in military crises civilian leadership itself will retain civilian perspectives, we must fall back on the quality of leadership—on persons rather than on institutions—to find some hope that civilian policy and civilian definitions of national interest will outweigh military strategy. History can at least provide instances—albeit rare—of how a capable civilian leadership has tried in practice to hold national policy and military strategy in their normatively proper relationship despite the immense contrary pressures that war appears inevitably to generate.

Much of this paper will be given over to one case study of the efforts of a wise and capable civilian leader—wisdom and capability in civilian leadership being the elements, however elusive and uncertain they may be, that are required to assure that war will not become utterly autonomous and that guiding policy will not be lost in its flames. The case study will provide, in turn, a background for a more detailed examination of the recent historical record, which will lead us finally back to Clausewitz's dictum, in order to reassess that dictum. The case study is drawn from American history, and so are most of the other historical instances that will be offered; but American problems of reconciling military strategy with policy are representative of those of every modern great power.

Soon after World War I, a British soldier, Colin R. Ballard, influenced by that war's conflicts between soldiers and "frocks," and between strategy and policy, published a book called *The Military Genius of Abraham Lincoln*. Ballard thought that in the American Civil War, President Lincoln had solved the problems of civilian control of the conduct of war by the expedient of becoming a master strategist himself—"the Strategist of the North . . . the forerunner of that which we now call the High Command."[4] Ballard's view of Abraham Lincoln has now become commonplace. It has been echoed most notably in mid-twentieth century by one of the preeminent academic historians of the American Civil War, T. Harry Williams, in *Lincoln and His Generals*.[5] Unfortunately, as Ballard had to point out, if Abraham Lincoln had in fact been a military genius, he would fail to provide a model for other civilian leaders who want to control the direction of war, because civilians that muster such qualifications are in short supply. (So, of course, are military professionals of genius, but professional expertise is a compensating quality.)

Fortunately, Lincoln's record as a war leader does include other elements more pertinent to the problems of civilian statesmen who find themselves obliged to exercise leadership over military strategy but who may not be blessed with the possession of military genius. Whether or not the Ballard-Williams interpretation of Lincoln's military capacities is correct, and whether or not Lincoln was a great captain who wore a frock coat, Lincoln like any head of government of a modern great power in wartime carried far too many other burdens, and faced too many varied problems, to spend much of his time practicing the art of military strategy. Obscured by the question of how well he conducted himself on those occasions when he did personally essay the role of military strategist is his ability to choose generals whose military strategy harmonized with the civilian leadership's conception of the purposes of the Civil War. The ability thus to orchestrate military strategy and national policy does not require genius, but it does offer guidance to statesmen of ordinary mortal attainments.

President Lincoln's conception of the war aims of his government, and in a somewhat less well defined fashion the conception held within the Union administration and Congress more generally, passed through two major stages. In the early part of the Civil War, Lincoln and probably most Northern congressmen hoped to end the war by conciliating the South until a peace of reunion became possible, even while they felt obliged to take up arms against the South's claim to independence. In the latter part of the Civil War, Lincoln based his conduct of the war upon a conclusion that the congressmen of his political party had largely reached before he did, but that he accepted only reluctantly—namely, that conciliating the Southern political leadership had proven impossible, and that restoring the Union would require the extinction of the Confederate government's pretensions to sovereignty by the utter defeat of the armed forces supporting those pretensions. Not the least of Lincoln's claims to distinction as a war statesman, but one not often clearly stated, is that in each of these two major stages of policy the president employed a general in chief of the United States Army whose military strategy accorded thoroughly with his government's policy—Maj. Gen. George B. McClellan for the first stage, and Lt. Gen. Ulysses S. Grant for the second.

When Lincoln took office as president on March 4, 1861, he confronted secession and the Confederate States government at Montgomery as fully accomplished facts. The Confederacy had drawn on the resources of the almost-sovereign nineteenth-century American states, and upon many of the federal institutions that it found operating within its borders, to emerge full-blown with all the paraphernalia of sovereignty—postal service, courts, and, most pertinently, an army. In deciding how to deal with this formidable polity, the president of the United States hoped to restore the Union and yet avoid war by buying time and, with time, a gradual erosion of the popular support for secession. He would uphold the claims of United States sovereignty in the Confederacy, but he would do so in such a way that there need be no armed collision between the Union government and the secessionists. In upholding the Union, he said in his inaugural address: "There needs to be no bloodshed or violence; and there shall be none, unless it is forced upon the national authority." He would hold the property and places in the South belonging to the federal government; but these areas were on the periphery of the Confederacy, such as Fort Sumter, in the harbor of Charleston, South Carolina. He would also collect the duties and imposts belonging to the United States—but in fact he was planning to do so as inoffensively as possible by utilizing naval vessels cruising offshore, not by forcing customs officers into Southern cities. "Beyond what may be necessary for these objects," he said, "there will be no invasion—no using of force against, or among the people anywhere."[6]

The rock on which this conciliatory policy foundered proved, of course, to be Lincoln's conviction that in order to avoid a sacrifice of the principle of continued Union and eventual reconciliation, he would have to retain the federal property in the South that was not already in secessionist hands when he took the oath of office. This conviction led to the outbreak of war at Fort Sumter on April 12, 1861, because the Confederate government of President Jefferson Davis, urged on by the state of South Carolina, believed equally that recognition of the principle of secession, as well as the practicalities of commerce, demanded that the United States flag should no longer fly over a fortress guarding the principal harbor of the state that was most fervently secessionist.

Despite the commencement of war at Fort Sumter and despite Lincoln's immediate call for 75,000 militia, he persisted in the hope that restoration of the Union might be accomplished less by armed force and bloodshed than by conciliation. In his very call for troops, he assured the South: "I deem it proper to say that the first service assigned to the forces hereby called forth will probably be to re-possess the forts, places, and property which have been seized from the Union; and in every event, the utmost care will be observed, consistently with the objects aforesaid, to avoid any devastation, any destruction of, or interference with, property, or any disturbance of peaceful citizens in any part of the country."[7] Lincoln still believed, as he stated in his message to the special session of Congress assembled July 4, 1861, to deal with the crisis, that "it may well be questioned whether there is, to-day, a majority of the legally qualified voters of any State, except perhaps South Carolina, in favor of disunion." He therefore believed that undermining the Confederate government through conciliation should still be possible.[8] Congress supported his conciliatory interpretation of the nature and purpose of the war when the House adopted the so-called Crittenden Resolution on July 22, and the Senate adopted a similar statement on July 25.

For many months, Lincoln adhered to the policy of conciliating the South even while he waged war against the secessionist governments. When his military commander in the Department of the West, Maj. Gen. John C. Frémont, and the secretary of war, Simon Cameron, sought to depart from Lincoln's promise to maintain Constitution and laws inviolate and threatened to assault the peculiar Southern institution of slavery—Frémont by proclaiming the liberation of slaves of rebellious owners in Missouri, and Cameron by proposing that black men be enlisted as soldiers and then be emancipated—the president quickly repudiated Frémont and Cameron. In his annual message to Congress on December 3, 1861, he reemphasized his policy, even while recognizing that war has a tendency to generate a momentum of its own toward accelerated and remorseless violence. "The war continues," he said. "In considering the policy to be adopted for suppressing the insurrection, I have been anxious and careful that the inevitable conflict for this purpose shall not degenerate into a violent and remorseless revolutionary struggle." "The Union must be preserved," Lincoln said elsewhere in the same message, "and hence, all indispensable means must be employed. [But] we should not be in haste to determine that radical and extreme measures, which may reach the loyal as well as the disloyal, are indispensable."[9]

The military leader chosen by Lincoln to wage war while preventing its degeneration into a remorseless revolutionary struggle was General McClellan. Called to Washington to revitalize the army encamped around the capital, to assure the city's safety, and to prepare for a new offensive after the Union debacle at the first Battle of Bull Run in July 1861, McClellan had commended himself first to Lincoln's attention because he was credited with a successful campaign to carry the banners of the Union back into western Virginia. He soon commended himself further, however, by favoring a method of waging war that was consistent with Lincoln's conciliatory policies. Far from trying to free slaves in the manner of Frémont and Cameron, McClellan favored the return to their owners of fugitive slaves who reached his lines. By consorting in the capital with Democratic politicians who were known for their sympathies toward slavery and toward a still more lenient policy with regard to the South than the president's, McClellan promptly earned the distrust of a faction of the Republican congressional delegation that was increasingly inclined toward punitive policies. But the general's attitudes—combined though they were with an arrogant disdain for the civilian officers of the War Department and even for their civilian superior in the White House—did not prevent Lincoln from appointing McClellan general in chief of all the armies of the United States, in addition to his immediate responsibilities for his field army, when the ancient Brev. Lt. Gen. Winfield Scott retired at the beginning of November.

When McClellan's field force, the Army of the Potomac, invaded Virginia, McClellan summarized his own policy toward the citizens of invaded areas by writing to a Virginia gentleman whose property had been injured by his forces:

> Without pausing to inquire or desiring to learn whether you are friend or foe to the cause I have the honor to serve, it was my intention to do all in my power to alleviate in your case the sufferings caused by the inevitable exigencies of this unhappy war.
>
> Permit me here to state that it has ever been, and ever shall be, my constant effort to confine the effects of this contest to the armed masses and political organization directly concerned in carrying it on.
>
> I have done my best to secure protection to private property, but I confess that circumstances beyond my control have often defeated my purposes.
>
> I have not come here to wage war upon the defenseless, upon noncombatants, upon private property, nor upon the domestic institutions of the land. I and the army I command are fighting to secure the Union and maintain its Constitution and laws, and for no other purpose. I regret to learn you have suffered, and the inconvenience you have endured. . . .[10]

In another document that was eventually to become publicized and controversial, taking its name—the Harrison's Bar Letter—from the Virginia river landing where he wrote it, McClellan ventured to offer policy advice to President Lincoln. The general said that conciliatory methods of war-making must be persevered in:

> The time has come when the government must determine upon a civil and military policy covering the whole ground of our national trouble. . . .
>
> This rebellion has assumed the character of war; as such it should be regarded, and it should be conducted upon the highest principles known to Christian civilization. It should not be a war looking to the subjugation of the people of any State in any event. It should not be at all a war upon population, but against armed forces and political organizations.

Neither confiscation of property, political executions of persons, territorial organization of States, or forcible abolition of slavery should be contemplated for a moment. In prosecuting the war all private property and unarmed persons should be strictly protected, subject only to the necessity of military operations. All private property taken for military use should be paid or receipted for; pillage and waste should be treated as high crimes; all unnecessary trespass sternly prohibited, and offensive demeanor by the military towards citizens promptly rebuked.[11]

McClellan's military strategy was attuned to this line of policy. During the era of the Civil War, most European and American soldiers regarded Napoleon I both as the greatest general of all history and as the model for all strategists, with a consequent dedication to decisive battle as the supreme goal of war—the grand, climactic, thunder-stroke battle that could win a war in a single day, the Austerlitz victory. But McClellan avoided pitched battles. A Napoleonic battle, whose object was the destruction of an enemy army, or at least of its ability to fight, in a single sledge-hammer blow, was likely to be horrendously costly to both armies—especially because rifled weapons had been introduced since Napoleon's own day. It was likely to nourish among both the vanquished and the victors a bitterness that would stand in the way of the desired peace of rapid reconciliation. Thus, whenever possible, McClellan sought to seize geographical objectives, not by battles, but by sieges in the formal style of eighteenth-century limited war. Hoping to avoid direct collision with the main Confederate army in front of Washington, he turned it out of its prepared defenses by moving his army by water to the Virginia peninsula southeast of Richmond. His principal strategic objective was not the destruction of the enemy army in Napoleonic fashion but the capture of the Confederate capital, Richmond, whose fall he hoped would cause the South to fear the power of the Union's military stick enough that the carrot of his and the president's conciliatory policy would be able to restore peace.

Unfortunately for McClellan, for Lincoln, and for the prospects of a harmonious peace, though McClellan was in many ways a soldier of respectable abilities, he was not a good enough general to achieve his designs either in strategy or in policy. A superabundant caution repeatedly delayed the commencement of his offensive from Washington toward Richmond, until Lincoln lost patience with him enough that on March 11, 1862, the president relieved him as general in chief of the armies and confined him to the command of the Army of the Potomac. By July 7, when he wrote the Harrison's Bar Letter, McClellan had led that army to within sight of the church steeples of Richmond, only to be rolled back from the city by the opposing Confederate force, the Army of Northern Virginia, under a formidable general in the Napoleonic style, Robert E. Lee. Lee hoped to achieve his own Austerlitz victory over McClellan's army, and in the Seven Days battles around Richmond, from June 25 to July 1, 1862, he might have succeeded had his own army not been hampered by inexperience in staff work and in divisional command. Nevertheless, Lee pinned McClellan to a narrow foothold on the Virginia peninsula along the James River, whence a new Union general in chief, Maj. Gen. Henry Wager Halleck, decided that the Army of the Potomac had to be withdrawn because opportunities for offensive action required a new start from a new base of operations. While the Army of the Potomac was in the process of withdrawing from the peninsula by sea, Lee defeated segments of it—together with another Union army, Maj. Gen. John Pope's Army of Virginia—in northern Virginia, at the second Battle of Bull Run. Then Lee invaded Maryland. McClellan, who was given Pope's army along with his own, there confronted Lee along the Antietam Creek, and thus halted the invasion. But despite having an overwhelming superiority in numbers over Lee and despite the great good fortune of having come into possession of much of Lee's plan of campaign, McClellan could accomplish no positive results. It would not be enough for the North to drive Southern armies from Northern soil in a war in which the Union's object had to be conquest. McClellan fought the battle of Antietam with a tactical ineptitude that had become all too familiar a concomitant of his considerable strategic abilities, and Lincoln consequently felt obliged to remove him from command.

McClellan had possessed strategic abilities and most especially a recognition of the need to tailor military strategy to fit national policy. He was followed at the head of the Army of the Potomac by a series of generals, most of whom had no higher tactical abilities than he, and none of whom equaled him in the ability to match military strategy to the Union's war policy. The dreariness of the middle period of the Civil War for the armies of the Union in the eastern theater of war was not caused only, however, by military commanders whose combination of Napoleonic ambitions and limited talents caused them to look to the next battle in search of an Austerlitz (rather than toward a strategy to end the war) and then to lose their would-be Austerlitz battles at that. Another cause was that in the middle period of the war, Lincoln himself failed to supply his strategists with war aims and policy that were well enough defined to permit strategy and policy to mesh.

Well before he removed McClellan, Lincoln had begun to abandon his hope that the Union could be restored by conciliating and fighting the South simultaneously. Lincoln's hopes that a deep well of Union loyalty in the South would spring free to drown the Confederacy were proving illusory, and Confederate resolution was proving too stout to be undermined by a policy in which the harnessing together of conciliation and war tended to cause each purpose to lame the other. Lincoln's disillusionment with McClellan had developed not only from disappointment with his military accomplishments but also from growing differences over policy. As early as March 6, 1862, Lincoln suggested to Congress that preventing the degeneration of the conflict into remorseless revolutionary struggle might be impossible:

> In the annual message last December, I thought fit to say "The Union must be preserved; and hence all indispensable means must be employed." I said this, not hastily, but deliberately. War has been made, and continues to be, an indispensable means to this end. . . . If, however, resistance continues, the war must also continue; and it is impossible to foresee all the incidents, which may attend and all the ruin which may follow it. Such as may seem indispensable, or may obviously promise great efficiency towards ending the struggle, must and will come.[12]

The specific issue immediately in question was, in McClellan's phrase, "the domestic institutions of the land." On March 6, Lincoln was calling for congressional subsidies to compensate slaveowners in any state that might voluntarily choose gradual abolition; but he was also warning that more drastic measures might have to follow in order to strike at the root cause of the war. And a direct attack on slavery would constitute not only waging war "upon noncombatants, upon private property," in contravention of General McClellan's views of proper policy; it would also amount to the initiation of social revolution in the South—of a "remorseless revolutionary struggle."

Not that Lincoln was yet ready to go so far. He told Horace Greeley that he wanted any steps toward emancipation to be urged "*persuasively*, and not *menacingly*, upon the South."[13] On May 19 he revoked an order of Maj. Gen. David Hunter's, commanding the Department of the South on the coasts of South Carolina, Georgia, and Florida, in which Hunter essayed to follow in Frémont's footsteps and to emancipate the slaves in his military district. But that he found the movement of events carrying him away from such restraints the president again indicated in his very announcement of the revocation, saying to slaveowners: "You can not if you would, be blind to the signs of the times."[14]

The president indicated the new direction of his policy, and its divergence from McClellan's, yet more forcefully in a letter written during July 1862, the same month that McClellan offered his reassurance to the Virginia gentleman whose property had been injured and his policy advice to Lincoln in the Harrison's Bar Letter. Reverdy Johnson of Maryland, who was sent to New Orleans by the federal government in order to investigate certain complaints against Maj. Gen. Benjamin F. Butler's allegedly harsh occupation regime there, dispatched a complaint made by Louisiana citizens against the activities of a Brig. Gen. John Wolcott Phelps, who was proposing to enlist black soldiers:

It seems the Union feeling in Louisiana is being crushed out by the course of General Phelps [Lincoln responded to Reverdy Johnson]. Please pardon me for believing that is a false pretense. The people of Louisiana—all intelligent people every where—know full well, that I never had a wish to touch the foundations of their society, or any right of theirs. With perfect knowledge of this, they forced a necessity upon me to send armies among them, and it is their own fault, not mine, that they are annoyed by the presence of General Phelps. They also know the remedy—know how to be cured of General Phelps. Remove the necessity of his presence. And might it not be well for them to consider whether they have not already had *time* enough to do this? If they can conceive of anything worse than General Phelps, within my power, would they not better be looking out for it? They very well know the way to avert all this is simply to take their place in the Union upon the old terms. If they will not do this, should they not receive harder blows rather than lighter ones?[15]

By this time, Lincoln had prepared and submitted to the cabinet a preliminary draft of an emancipation proclamation. By this time, McClellan's offensive against Richmond had clearly been a failure, and the hope of enticing the South back to its old allegiance by sparing noncombatants and private property also gave no indications of success. If the South could not be conciliated, then the only alternative policy would be to destroy the institutions that spawned and supported the Confederacy—slavery and the Confederate armies. "I am a patient man," Lincoln told Reverdy Johnson, "—always willing to forgive on the Christian terms of repentance; and also to give ample *time* for repentance . . . but it may as well be understood, once for all, that I shall not surrender this game leaving any available card unplayed."[16] "What would you do in my position?" he asked another Louisiana complainant two days later. "Would you drop the war where it is? Or, would you prosecute it in future, with elder-stalk squirts, charged with rose water? Would you deal lighter blows rather than heavier ones? Would you give up the contest, leaving any available means unapplied[?]"[17]

Secretary of State William H. Seward persuaded Lincoln not to issue an emancipation proclamation immediately, because with the Union armies in defeat, a proclamation might look like a desperate government's cry to the black man for rescue. By checking Lee's invasion of Maryland at the Antietam in September, however, McClellan won, if not a satisfactory victory, still enough of a success to overcome Seward's objection and to warrant Lincoln's announcement on September 22 that slaves would be emancipated in rebel areas that did not submit to the Union by January 1, 1863. McClellan thought emancipation a hateful as well as a misguided policy. "Help me to dodge the nigger—we want nothing to do with him," the general wrote to his Democratic friends. "*I* am fighting to preserve the integrity of the Union and the power of the Govt—on no other issue. To gain that end we cannot afford to mix up the negro question—it must be incidental and subsidiary."[18] Much about McClellan's attitudes can be inferred from his comment about one of those friends: "Mr. [W. H.] Aspinwall is decidedly of the opinion that it is my duty to submit to the President's proclamation and quietly continue doing my duty as a soldier. I presume he is right, and am at least sure that he is honest in his opinion."[19] It signified a turning point in the Civil War when Lincoln put McClellan on the shelf on November 5, 1862, somewhat over a month after the Emancipation Proclamation. In military strategy and in policy alike, Lincoln was abandoning the effort to wage war using elder-stalk squirts, charged with rose water.

Though it was the slavery issue that most acutely threatened to transform the war into remorseless revolutionary struggle, Lincoln was changing his conciliatory policy in other areas as well. During the summer he had countenanced proclamations made by General Pope of the Army of Virginia that Robert E. Lee and other Southerners considered barbarous. Pope directed his army to live off the invaded country; his authorized officers were to requisition supplies and to reimburse loyal citizens. He announced that Virginia communities must pay compensation for any damage done by marauders or guerrillas within their limits, and he threatened to destroy any house from which a Union soldier was shot. In a step that was highly dubious under the laws of war, he ordered the administering of an oath of allegiance to all disloyal male citizens within his lines, and he directed the expulsion beyond the lines of any such citizen who refused to take the oath, threatening the death penalty to any who returned after expulsion or to any person who from within his lines communicated with the enemy.[20]

While Lincoln was becoming disposed to embrace such harshness, however, through 1863 his policy on the central issue of the abolition of slavery continued to vacillate. Before January 1, 1863, he seemed even to be willing to depart from his Emancipation Proclamation, by suggesting in his annual message to Congress on December 1, 1862, a plan for federal compensation for states that would adopt a program to free their slaves by January 1, 1900. In fact, of course, he issued his final Emancipation Proclamation on January 1, 1863, and thereafter as the Union armies advanced southward, they apparently brought freedom to the slaves in any areas that the rebels had controlled at the beginning of the year. But the constitutional foundation of presidential emancipation was doubtful, and Lincoln gave no aid to an organized abolitionist movement to assure abolition by a congressional statute or, better, by a constitutional amendment. Furthermore, in the "ten-percent plan" for reconstruction of the seceded states, which he announced to Congress on December 10, 1863, and in his policies toward such states as Louisiana, Tennessee, and

Arkansas that in large part fell to Union arms, Lincoln seemed to be veering back toward generous offers of a return to the *status quo ante bellum*, complete with a restoration of certain politicians of prewar Southern prominence. His motive here, however, was probably for the most part a desire to undermine loyalty to the Confederacy, not to establish a permanent program for political reconstruction. These uncertainties of presidential policy accompanied, not surprisingly, an uncertain direction of military strategy and a musical-chairs series of changes of generals during late 1862 and throughout 1863.

Yet while there were presidential vacillations during 1863, there was also a continuing tendency rising above the vacillations—the tendency symbolized by the removal of McClellan, and persisted in because no other direction of policy could any longer offer substantial hope of ending the war. To those who criticized his movement toward a clearer program of freedom for black men, hesitating though that movement was, he argued on August 26, 1863, that the meaning of the war now demanded black freedom, even to the extent of arming black men:

> I thought that in your struggle for the Union, to whatever extent the negroes should cease helping the enemy, to that extent it weakened the enemy in his resistance to you. Do you think differently? I thought that whatever negroes can be got to do as soldiers, leaves just so much less for white soldiers to do, in saving the Union. Does it appear otherwise to you? But negroes, like other people, act upon motives. Why should they do any thing for us, if we will do nothing for them? If they stake their lives for us, they must be prompted by the strongest motive—even the promise of freedom. And the promise being made, must be kept.[21]

At least as significantly for his thoughts on the conduct of the war, Lincoln said in the same message:

> You desire peace; and you blame me that we do not have it. But how can we attain it? There are but three conceivable ways. First, to suppress the rebellion by force of arms. This, I am trying to do. Are you for it? If you are, so far we are agreed. If you are not for it, a second way is, to give up the Union. I am against this. Are you for it? If you are, you should say so plainly. If you are not for *force*, nor yet for *dissolution*, there only remains some imaginable *compromise*. I do not believe any compromise, embracing the maintenance of the Union, is now possible. All I learn, leads to a directly opposite belief. The strength of the rebellion, is its military—its army. . . . No word or intimation, from that rebel army, or from any of the men controlling it, in relation to any peace compromise, has ever come to my knowledge or belief.[22]

The course of military events in 1863 had not been altogether one of indecision comparable to Lincoln's uncertainty of policy. In the western theater of war, the year had assured the preeminence among the Union commanders beyond the Alleghenies of a general whose capacity to win almost unbroken success had emerged with the capture of Forts Henry and Donelson on the Tennessee and Cumberland rivers as early as February, 1862, but which for a time had been obscured by jealousies within the army. U. S. Grant, commanding the Army of the Tennessee, had solved the difficult puzzle of finding a way to dry ground on the east bank of the Mississippi around Vicksburg, and in July, 1863, had captured the Confederate citadel, opening the entire length of the Mississippi River to Union control and cutting off the Confederate east from the provender of the trans-Mississippi West and from the European supplies arriving by way of Mexico. Elevated thereafter to command all the western armies of the Union, Grant had gone on in October and November to break the Confederate siege of Chattanooga and open the way for a Union advance against Atlanta which would bifurcate the Confederacy still again. Grant, moreover, was a general whose view of the appropriate strategy for the winning of the war harmonized with Lincoln's increasingly firm conviction that in war policy no compromise was possible, that only the outright defeat of the Confederacy would suffice to restore peace, and that the defeat of the Confederacy required specifically the destruction of its armies, on which the whole Confederate political structure depended.

Grant had begun the war like Lincoln and McClellan, hoping that a quick and dramatic military success would soon open the way to a peace of conciliation; but earlier than Lincoln or McClellan he had felt obliged to discard reliance on elder-stalk squirts and rose water, writing:

> Up to the battle of Shiloh [which he fought April 6–7, 1862] I, as well as thousands of other citizens, believed that the rebellion against the Government would collapse suddenly and soon, if a decisive victory could be gained over any of its armies. Donelson and Henry were such victories. An army of more than 21,000 men was captured or destroyed. Bowling Green, Columbus and Hickman, Kentucky, fell in consequence, and Clarksville and Nashville, Tennessee, the last two with an immense amount of stores, also fell into our hands. The Tennessee and Cumberland rivers, from their mouths to the head of navigation, were secured. But when Confederate armies were collected which not only attempted to hold a line farther south, from Memphis to Chattanooga, Knoxville and on to the Atlantic, but assumed the offensive and made such a gallant effort to regain what had been lost, then, indeed, I gave up all idea of saving the Union except by complete conquest. Up to that time it had been the policy of our army, certainly of that portion commanded by me, to protect the property of the citizens whose territory was invaded, without regard to their sentiments, whether Union or Secession. After this, however, I regarded it as humane

to both sides to protect the persons of those found at their homes, but to consume everything that could be used to support or supply armies.[23]

The Union was to be restored by means of "complete conquest." Everything that could be used to support armies was to be destroyed, and the primary object of military strategy would be to crush the Confederate armies themselves: such was Grant's conception of waging the Civil War well before the beginning of 1864. In response to Grant's victories in the West in 1863, Congress passed a bill reviving the full rank of lieutenant general, unused since George Washington's day. Lincoln signed the bill on February 29, 1864, the next day nominating Grant to receive the newly recreated rank. Succeeding Halleck as general in chief, Grant resolved: "My general plan now was to concentrate all the force possible against the Confederate armies in the field."[24] To Maj. Gen. George G. Meade, commanding the Army of the Potomac, which was still the principal Union field force in the East, Grant dispatched orders: "Lee's army will be your objective point. Wherever Lee goes, there you will go also."[25] To Maj. Gen. William Tecumseh Sherman, who took Grant's former place as commander of the western armies, Grant gave similar orders to move against the Army of Tennessee, the principal Confederate field army in the West. Grant's mode of strategy was a strategy of annihilation, based on agreement with Lincoln's judgment that "the strength of the rebellion, is its military—its army," and having as its primary objective the destruction or capture of the two principal enemy armies.

While emulating Napoleon as a strategist of annihilation, however, Grant abandoned the pursuit of the climactic Austerlitz battle, the specifically Napoleonic method that Lee had followed, for a campaign that would "fight it out on this line if it takes all summer"[26]—or longer—a strategic outlook that recognized realistically the staying power of modern mass armies and the indecisiveness of single battles in the age of rifled weapons. Concerning his purpose of annihilation and his patient method of achieving it against Lee's Army of Northern Virginia—in the campaign that he began in the spring of 1864, by prolonged direct contact and combat with the enemy army—Grant was to write in his memoirs:

> Soon after midnight, May 3d–4th, the Army of the Potomac moved out from its position north of the Rapidan, to start upon that memorable campaign, destined to result in the capture of the Confederate capital and the army defending it. This was not to be accomplished, however, without as desperate fighting as the world has ever witnessed; not to be consummated in a day, a week, a month, or a single season. The losses inflicted, and endured, were destined to be severe; but the armies now confronting each other had already been in deadly conflict for a period of three years, with immense losses in killed, by death from sickness, captured and

wounded; and neither had made any real progress toward accomplishing the final end. . . . The campaign now begun was destined to result in heavier losses, to both armies, in a given time, than any previously suffered; but the carnage was to be limited to a single year, and to accomplish all that had been anticipated or desired at the beginning in that time. We had to have hard fighting to achieve this.[27]

"The criticism," Grant also said, "has been made by writers on the campaign from the Rapidan to the James River that all the loss of life could have been obviated by moving the army there on transports. . . . [But] to get possession of Lee's army was the first great object. . . . It was better to fight him outside of his stronghold [Richmond] than in it."[28]

The fit between Grant's and Lincoln's current strategic thinking was exact. The previous September, Lincoln had written to General Meade concerning the proper use of the Army of the Potomac:

> To avoid misunderstanding, let me say that to attempt to fight the enemy slowly back into his intrenchments at Richmond, and there to capture him, is an idea I have been trying to repudiate for quite a year. . . . My last attempt upon Richmond was to get McClellan, when he was nearer there than the enemy was, to run in ahead of him. Since then I have constantly desired the Army of the Potomac, to make Lee's army, and not Richmond, it's objective point.[29]

When his war policy had begun to harden, Lincoln had also warned the Southern people: "If they can conceive of anything worse than General Phelps, within my power, would they not better be looking out for it?" With Grant and Grant's chosen lieutenants, he gave the South something considerably worse than General Phelps; for Grant not only sought to destroy enemy armies, he also remained firm in the resolve formed after Shiloh to destroy everything in the South that could support enemy forces. When in the summer of 1864 Lee sought to divert the Union from its persistent pressures upon his Army of Northern Virginia by detaching a force to the Shenandoah Valley to raid toward Washington from there, Grant responded by creating a new Army of the Shenandoah under Maj. Gen. Philip H. Sheridan. Its instructions were of the usual sort: "To follow him [the enemy] to the death. Wherever the enemy goes let our troops go also."[30] But in addition, to assure that the Shenandoah Valley should cease being a granary and a corridor of invasion for the Confederacy once and for all, Grant wanted Sheridan's troops to "make all the Valley south of the Baltimore and Ohio Road a desert as high up as possible . . . to eat out Virginia clear and clean as far as they go, so that crows flying over it for the balance of this season will have to carry their provender with them."[31] Sheridan embraced these instructions, with the conviction that "death is popularly considered the maximum of punishment in war, but it is not; reduction to poverty brings prayers for peace more surely and more quickly than does the destruction of human life."[32] He eventually announced that indeed "a crow would have had to carry its rations if it had flown across the valley."[33]

Sheridan's destruction of crops, livestock, barns, mills, and often houses in the Shenandoah Valley proved to be the prelude to Sherman's devastation of still wider areas of the Confederacy in his famous marches through Georgia and the Carolinas in the late autumn of 1864 and the winter and spring of 1865. Having weakened the Confederate Army of Tennessee until he believed that he needed to detail only a portion of his own armies to deal with it, Sherman set out first from Atlanta to the sea, and thence from Savannah into the Carolinas. These campaigns were aimed, not at the Confederate armies directly, but at the destruction of all that could support them through a broad swath of territory and, more importantly, at the destruction of the will of the Southern people to sustain their armies and the war. "I attach much importance," said Sherman, "to these deep incisions into the enemy's country, because this war differs from European wars in this particular: we are not only fighting hostile armies, but a hostile people, and must make old and young, rich and poor, feel the hard hand of war, as well as their organized armies. . . . My aim then was, to whip the rebels, to humble their pride, to follow them to their inmost recesses, and make them fear and dread us."[34]

Grant and Sherman, in correspondence, together devised the plan for Sherman's marches; Grant gave the orders for Sheridan's program of devastation in the Shenandoah Valley. And although the Army of the Potomac, with which the general in chief himself chose to travel, concentrated on the more directly military objective of destroying Lee's army rather than giving itself over to depredations against property and to terrorization, Grant's friend Adam Badeau nevertheless was essentially right when he said in his biography of Grant that the general had developed the new methods of "American war":

> But above all, he understood that he was engaged in a people's war and that the people as well as the armies of the South must be conquered, before the war could end. Slaves, supplies, crops, stock, as well as arms and ammunition—everything that was necessary in order to carry on the war, was a weapon in the hands of the enemy, and of every weapon the enemy must be deprived.[35]

As another early commentator put it, Grant recognized "that it was the mind of the South we had to conquer, not alone fortifications and territory."[36]

Lincoln, of course, was not addicted to vengeful statements about making people fear and dread him and his cause (though as we have seen, he could offer warnings graphically enough). Still, all his words and conduct indicate his thorough approval of Grant's, Sherman's, and Sheridan's activities in a course of war that was utterly different from what he had sponsored when McClellan was his general in chief. And among the promises of malice toward none and charity for all in his second inaugural address, Lincoln offered also a grimmer observation:

> Fondly do we hope—fervently do we pray—that this mighty scourge of war may speedily pass away. Yet, if God wills that it continue, until all the wealth piled by the bond-man's two hundred and fifty years of unrequited toil shall be sunk, and until every drop of blood drawn with the lash, shall be paid by another drawn with the sword, as was said three thousand years ago, so still it must be said "the judgments of the Lord, are true and righteous altogether."[37]

Whether or not Abraham Lincoln possessed military genius, in wartime he was a masterful civilian commander in chief, who chose generals whose own policies and strategies were consistently attuned to the war policies of his government. In the early stages of the Civil War, when Lincoln hoped primarily to conciliate the South—at the same time showing enough military force to warn the South that rejection of his conciliatory overtures was futile—he supported as his general in chief George B. McClellan. McClellan combined obvious conciliatory intent on his own part (which was expressed in studied protection for private property and aversion to emancipation) with a strategy of maneuver and siege (which was aimed at achieving with a minimum of bloody and embittering battle the capture of the political objective of the enemy capital). McClellan's departure from command coincided with Lincoln's conclusion that conciliation would not restore the Union. In the middle phase of the war, Lincoln groped to find a proper policy, and Union military strategy groped fitfully for overall direction and coherence as well. Lincoln was well aware that war has a logic of its own (contrary to Clausewitz, who stated that war has its own grammer but not its own logic);[38] he felt acutely, as he stated, that often he did not control events, but that events controlled him,[39] and that the natural direction of events in war is likely to be toward "remorseless revolutionary struggle." He hoped to find a way to avoid that outcome in the Civil War, but he failed. The war became a social revolution. Once Lincoln acquiesced in that result, and concluded finally that only the utter destruction of the Confederate armies, war resources, and will to fight would restore the Union, he chose and supported, in Grant and Sherman, generals whose strategy fitted the new, and now ruthless, design of the war.

It reflects much concerning the history of such American civilian-military relationships as have involved the yoking of military strategy to national policy, and also much about American historians' approach to such issues, that assessments of Lincoln and his generals have rarely linked the development of

Lincoln's war policies to the evolution of Civil War military strategy so as to offer the perspective just summarized. Historians of Lincoln and the Civil War have focused either upon the political dimensions of the Lincoln administration or upon Lincoln the commander in chief as military strategist. Rarely have they united the two to portray Lincoln as builder of the arch connecting strategy with policy. Colin Ballard's book exemplifies the latter approach; its argument that Lincoln mastered his military problems explores only in the most limited degree the relationship between Lincoln's strategic insights and his political designs for restoring peace. The military Lincoln rather than the political-military Lincoln also is the subject of such historical studies as T. Harry Williams's *Lincoln and His Generals* and Kenneth P. Williams's *Lincoln Finds a General: A Military Study of the Civil War*, the five-volume uncompleted work that is the most detailed history of Union command. Both deal favorably with Lincoln's contributions to fighting the war but do not venture far from the military history of the war to explore how Lincoln the strategist complemented Lincoln the statesman and politician.[40]

American historians here follow the historically customary attitudes of American soldiers and civilians, to which Lincoln was a conspicuous exception. Until at least as late as the 1920s, American textbooks on military strategy treated the subject almost exclusively as a military one, devoid of political implications.[41] The first systematic American writer on strategy, Henry Wager Halleck, was a noted legal scholar as well as a soldier; he was also an authority on international law and a principal author of the first constitution of the state of California. Nevertheless, his breadth of interests was insufficient to make his *Elements of Military Art and Science*—which was first published in 1846 but attracted greater attention after he became general in chief of the Union armies—more than a technical military treatise, except for an introduction justifying the study and practice of war. Halleck's definition of strategy was a standard military one, based on the works of the French-Swiss interpreter of Napoleon, Antoine Henri baron de Jomini: "*Strategy* is defined to be the art of directing masses on decisive points, or the hostile movements of armies beyond the range of each other's cannon."[42] Halleck's chapter entitled "Strategy" is for the most part a Jominian discussion of the merits of various kinds of lines of operations, in the geometric vein that was characteristic of the nineteenth-century strategic studies of the school comprising Jomini and his followers. The rest of Halleck's book deals largely with tactical issues. Nor did Halleck prove able to harmonize military strategy with national policy in practice; his tenure as Civil War general in chief was an ineffectual one between McClellan and Grant, when neither Union strategy nor Union war policy showed much coherence and Halleck was unable to rescue either one from uncertainty and confusion.

Subsequent American military writing through the rest of the nineteenth century and into the twentieth followed the pattern established by Halleck: on the one hand, American military studies at their greatest breadth of conception—that is, in their discussions of strategy—remained apolitically military to the point of abstraction from the real world; on the other hand, even such breadth as the study of strategy entailed was rare in American military writing. As late as the first two decades after the establishment of the Army War College in 1903, for example, papers in the college archives whose titles make them appear to be strategic studies prove in fact to be concerned primarily with tactics.[43] Until the First World War, considerations of what the twentieth century would call national strategy or grand strategy—the integration of military strategy into the larger service of national purposes—rarely entered American military writing.

To be sure, American military writing of the late nineteenth and early twentieth centuries included the works of Rear Adm. Alfred Thayer Mahan, and a more comprehensive view than the ordinary one was to be found therein. But while in appointing Mahan to lecture at the Naval War College the founder of the college, Rear Adm. Stephen B. Luce, hoped to discover in him a naval Jomini, and while Mahan's reputation is generally that of a strategic writer, surprisingly little about military strategy turns up in Mahan's multitudinous books and articles. Especially in Mahan's histories, the bulk of the pages prove to be taken up with military history on its familiar tactical level. As for strategy, Mahan's thought can be summed up in his emphasis on the necessity to build a concentrated battle fleet to defeat or overawe the enemy fleet and achieve command of the sea—whence all that is valuable in naval power flows—and in a subsidiary Jominian concern with lines of communication, which command of the sea renders secure. When Mahan was not writing about tactics, what he offered was not so much strategic study as a prescription for national greatness: command of the sea achieved by a strong battle fleet made Great Britain the greatest of the world powers, with the commerce, markets, and raw materials of all the world available to her; therefore, sea power, he suggested, can do much the same to enhance the greatness of other powers, including the United States. Mahan's journalistic writings on international problems elaborate on this theme with specific prescriptions for the United States, such as the value of an isthmian canal and of overseas coaling stations and bases.[44]

Thus Mahan approached bringing strategic study into harness with a design for national policy, but he did not quite reach that result; his strategic dogmas tended to remain on too lofty a level of generalization to provide immediate guidance either to strategists or to policy-makers. American naval writers of the late nineteenth and early twentieth centuries were prolific, in fact, in offering suggestions, much like Mahan's, that expansion both of American sea power and of American commercial activities overseas could mutually reinforce one another. The pages of the *Proceedings* of the United States Naval Institute are filled with articles expatiating upon this theme, which is after all one that does not require any special acuity of vision. A hasty scanner of the *Proceedings* might in fact conclude that naval officers of Mahan's era were predominantly economic determinists, so much did the contributors discuss economic rivalry as the taproot of those international quarrels that made maintenance of naval power necessary. Yet a more careful reading of the *Proceedings*, and of other naval writings, leaves the naval officers' estimate of the importance of economics, and particularly of business enterprise, as a factor in national greatness so ambiguous that two recent painstaking historians of naval attitudes have reached opposite conclusions about the matter. Peter Karsten, in *The Naval Aristocracy*, speaks of the naval officers' "ability to identify American trade or investments with America's 'national interest.'" He also writes that "'political' and 'strategic' motives for war were given due consideration and treatment, to be sure," in the officers' views of war, "but these factors were put in proper perspective, which is to say that they were related and subordinated to economic stimuli."[45] Richard D. Challener, on the other hand, states in *Admirals, Generals, and American Foreign Policy, 1898–1914*:

> It is, indeed, by no means an untenable hypothesis that many of the economic arguments put forth by the Navy were deliberately phrased in such manner because naval spokesmen thought that this was what their civilian superiors wanted to hear and also that it was the best way to make their case before Congress and the public. In the industrialized America of 1900, in which business interests predominated and were worried about the economic future, what could be more logical than to try to advance the Navy's credibility by arguing that the job that the Navy could do best was the advancement of American overseas commerce?[46]

The United States Army, as Challener notes in the same book, did far less than the navy to bring its strategic thought into the service of national policy: "There were relatively few Army officers, as compared with their naval colleagues, who concerned themselves with the world scene. The Army was still on the periphery of world politics. Its tradition was purely Continental," that is, concerned with the defense of the United States and with policing the continent against marauding Indians.[47] The military writer who has been called "the army's Mahan," Bvt. Maj. Gen. Emory Upton, wrote about neither strategy nor world policy, but only about tactics and military organization.[48]

The institutions of American government throughout the nineteenth century and into the twentieth reflected the vagueness of the predominant ideas about relationships between military strategy and national policy. No institutional machinery existed for coordinating military strategy with national policy. Any coordination depended upon the relationships established among themselves by individual personalities in the civil and military branches, as in the fortunate rapport that Lincoln achieved by choosing generals in chief whose strategy reflected his policies; but the institutional arrangements impeded even that. Until the beginning of the twentieth century, the command structures of the army and the navy almost prohibited coherent direction of the armed forces even for the most exclusively military purposes, let alone their coordination with the civil branches of government.

Only the president, as commander in chief, gave unity to both army administration and the operations of the army, and he customarily was too busy and too inexpert militarily to perform this task well. The secretary of war might have seemed to be the president's deputy for military purposes and the most direct embodiment of the principle of civilian control over the military. For a time in the early years of the Republic, through the War of 1812, the secretary had in fact often commanded the operations of the army as well as administered the army bureaucracy. By 1821, however, the role of the ranking professional officer had evolved into that of general in chief of the army, and army regulations came to charge the secretary merely with administration and the general in chief with command of operations. To the extent that the regulations were interpreted literally, civilian control over military operations was almost nullified. In practice, throughout the nineteenth century, secretaries of war and generals in chief quarrelled chronically over the boundaries between their responsibilities, and two generals in chief, Winfield Scott and W. T. Sherman, practically ceased communicating with the secretaries of war, leaving direction of the army in utter disarray.[49]

The command structure of the navy became, if anything, worse. There, during the initial period the small infant navy was actually controlled by the secretary of the navy, who was advised from 1815 to 1842 by a professional Board of Navy Commissioners. This gave way in 1842 to the "bureau system," whereby five to eight separate bureaus administered various facets of naval activity, each bureau reporting directly to the secretary. Only the secretary could have given unity to the work of all the bureaus, but this civilian cabinet member lacked the naval expertise to do it. The Navy Department became a congeries of autonomous kingdoms, in which it was difficult to coordinate the design of the ships with their proposed functions, or with anything else. The bureaus, furthermore, dealt primarily with logistics; operational command was left in a nether world with nobody except the inexpert secretary to control it.[50]

The worst of these command and administrative problems began to be tackled by civilian and military reformers after the Spanish-American War of 1898 had revealed some of the inadequacies of the military departments for the service of a newly assertive world power. The pressures created by the Spanish-American War and by the new directions of American foreign policy at the opening of the twentieth century coincided with the drive of the Progressive Era toward infusing governmental administration in all its branches with the new managerial efficiency that was presumed to have been developed by corporate business.[51] The effect was to produce the Elihu Root reforms in army administration and rather less effective but still noteworthy improvements in navy administration. Secretary of War Elihu Root designed and in 1903 secured from Congress the establishment of an army general staff, which was to be a "directing brain" for the army, an agency to plan and to see that plans were executed.[52] Heading the general staff was to be a chief of staff, who would also be the principal professional adviser to the secretary of war. The office of general in chief was eliminated; command authority over all the army would flow from the president through the secretary, as constitutionally it should; and in place of the former rivalry between the secretary and the principal professional officer, it was hoped that there would develop—and there frequently did—a symbiotic relationship between the civilian head of the War Department and his professional adviser, his chief of staff.

Many naval reformers desired a navy general staff similar to that of the army, but all they got in the first years of the twentieth century was the General Board, an advisory body, which managed to give a certain central direction to naval administration through the prestige and wisdom of its first president, Adm. of the Navy George Dewey, but which left the bureaus as autonomous and the secretary of the navy as overburdened as before. No secretary of the navy in the early twentieth century was an Elihu Root, and the secretaries actually preferred what one of them, Josephus Daniels, called a "calculated policy of dispersion,"[53] because however inefficient it was in requiring the secretary to oversee too many subordinates directly, this system did keep the reins of power finally in the secretary's hands, free from interference by any one powerful professional figure. Working behind Daniels's back, the reformist professionals secured congressional creation of the office of chief of naval operations (CNO) in 1915; but Daniels contrived to dilute the reformers' intentions, leaving the CNO in charge of the operations of the fleet, subordinate to the secretary, but otherwise leaving the bureau system essentially intact.[54]

For that matter, the general staff of the army proved a less formidable improvement than Root had intended. In trying to ensure that the general staff would be free enough to be a directing brain that would be able to think and plan unburdened by administrative routine, Root left it with so little control over the special-staff bureaus that actually administered the army, such as Quartermaster, Ordnance, and Engineers, that the War Department, like the Navy Department, tended to go its accustomed administrative ways, little affected by the new agency at the top. For a time it appeared that the adjutant general, through whom orders passed from the War Department to the army, might elbow aside the chief of staff as principal professional officer; and while in 1911–1912 the dynamic Maj. Gen. Leonard Wood won that battle for himself as chief of staff, World War I proved that the ascendancy of the chief of staff over the army was not yet assured. New and hasty organizational reforms had to occur in the War Department and in the general staff itself in the midst of the war in order to permit reasonably effective management of the army's war effort; and acting as the principal headquarters in the European theater of war, Gen. John J. Pershing's American Expeditionary Force spent the war as yet another autonomous kingdom.[55]

The World War I president, Woodrow Wilson, felt a distaste for war so acute that it verged on pacificism. His distaste for involving himself with the command of armies was similarly so strong that he had Secretary of War Newton D. Baker give Pershing broad instructions that left the A.E.F. commander only dubiously subordinate to the chief of staff. Then Wilson and Baker communicated with Pershing so little that the chief of the A.E.F. alone spoke for the United States in Europe on many issues where military affairs impinged upon interallied diplomacy, as well as on matters of strategy. Wilson's coordination with his military strategists was in no way comparable to Lincoln's. So limited was Wilson's comprehension of the exigencies of military planning that twice before the entry of the United States into World War I, he had recoiled in horror from the knowledge that the general staff was engaged in strategic contingency planning. He did so first when, amidst his Mexican crises, he learned from General Wood that the army actually had in its GREEN plans a set of designs for waging war against Mexico; he did so again when, amidst growing tensions with Germany, he learned of the BLACK plans for a German war.[56] Some historians believe that Wilson led the United States into World War I, not so much in response to the German campaign of unrestricted submarine warfare, which was the ostensible cause, as to ensure a role for the United States in the diplomacy that would shape the postwar world. If so, Wilson nevertheless regarded military strategy and national policy as occupying separate compartments, with policy-making virtually adjourned—the secret treaties among the Allies, for example, were not to be discussed while war persisted—until military strategy had completed its work of drawing the fangs and claws of the German armies. Only then would diplomacy recommence its own work of fashioning a world in which henceforth—in an expectation significant of Wilson's whole perception of the discreteness of war, on the one hand, and diplomacy, on the other—international relationships could unfold with no further recourse to war as a means of resolving disputes.

The Senate rejected Wilson's particular blueprint for this postwar world, but American policy in the 1920s and 1930s offered little more guidance to the planning of military strategies in the service of policy than Wilson's dreams of a warless world might have implied. Inevitably, after the experiences of 1917–1918, the United States Army's thinking about the likely shape of future war was governed by its recollections of the Western Front, of the one great overseas campaign it had thus far fought. Because it had fought on the Western Front briefly enough to escape the dreadful casualties of the other major belligerents, it did not even feel obliged to seek a substitute for infantrymen's bodies as an instrument with which to break through enemy defenses similar to those of 1918; and while maintaining a doctrine of the offensive as the key to victory in war, it paid little attention to the technology or theory of tanks and tactical aviation. Because the most difficult problem for the American army in World War I had been to procure sufficient quantities of the matériel of war, army planners devoted much of their energy to designs for industrial mobilization in the next war. But a national policy that denied any intention of returning mass American armies to European battlefields on the model of 1917–1918 made army plans for either the tactics or the industrial support of mass war apparently irrelevant to policy.[57]

The Joint Board, a coalition of planners from the army's general staff and the navy's general board, which had first been instituted under the aegis of Elihu Root, was now revived after a period of supension during the inhospitable Wilson years. It could pursue, among such exercises as the RED plans for a British war and the MAROON plans for a Canadian war, the ORANGE plans for a war that even at the height of Wilsonian pacifist optimism seemed not unlikely to occur—a Pacific Ocean war against Japan. But here, too, national policy and military stategy were in little harmony: the ORANGE plans envisioned a Pacific war as beginning with a Japanese assault against the Philippine Islands. So slight were the means provided the armed forces for defense of that archipelago that, by the mid-1930s, army planners favored the abandonment of any pretense of a capacity to guard the Philippines, preferring a withdrawal of America's defensive perimeter in the Pacific Ocean to the triangle made by Alaska, Pearl Harbor, and Panama. Yet American policy not only continued to claim that the Philippines would be defended, but also, at the beginning of the 1940s, it applied against Japan economic sanctions that courted—and eventually provoked—the ORANGE war, for which the American forces were not ready.[58]

By that time the Anglo-American tradition of distrust of the military— as always a potential threat to representative government and the American constitutional principle of civilian control—had nurtured in turn a tradition of armed forces so monastically divorced from politics and policy that army leaders never clearly presented to the civil government their misgivings about challenging Japan in the western Pacific until the course of challenge was already firmly set. Instead, during the 1920s and 1930s they considered it their duty to continue laboring upon versions of the ORANGE plans. They went on pretending that there was a useful defense to be made in the Philippines— holding a base there until the navy's battle fleet could fight its way across the Pacific to bring supplies and reinforcements—even though the specific details of the plans increasingly mocked such conclusions. The United States Army had not always been so studiously apolitical; General McClellan, advising Lincoln on war policy in his Harrison's Bar Letter had spoken candidly about the inseparability of military strategy and national policy in defense and war. More forthright advice from the armed forces about the vulnerability to Japanese attack of both the Philippines and other American positions in the western Pacific would not have been likely to alter substantially President Franklin D. Roosevelt's policy of challenging Japan; but a belief that the divorcement of the military from policy-making required plastering over the truth about the military vulnerability of the islands certainly carried apoliticism to excess.

It has grown commonplace to argue that with the entrance of the United States into World War II, the opposite excess promptly prevailed, that President Roosevelt became disproportionately dependent upon his military advisers in wartime policy-making as well as in military strategy, that under the guidance of military strategists who were unsophisticated in international or domestic politics, the United States thereupon consistently sacrificed its national political interests to the expediency of military strategy during World War II. It is true that by executive order of July 5, 1939, in recognition of the imminence of war in Europe, the president gave the chief of staff of the army and the chief of naval operations immediate access to himself in the realms of "strategy, tactics, and operations," and that subsequently the engulfment of the United States into the world crisis gave a strategic cast to practically every international question, opening the way for President Roosevelt and his military chiefs to have intimate consultations about almost everything.[59] It is also true that under the conditions of war, Roosevelt's civilian advisers, especially Secretary of State Cordell Hull, suffered a diminution of influence relative to that of the military chiefs. The magnitude of this process can easily be exaggerated, however; for it was lack of personal rapport between Roosevelt and Hull, more than the existence of war, that separated the secretary of state from the president. Indeed, Roosevelt was always such an inveterate collector of diverse counsel that his dependence on a variety of civilian confidants remained absolutely high all through the war, even while it exhibited a relative decline because of the growing influence of the military. Harry Hopkins, Henry Morgenthau, Averell Harriman, Henry L. Stimson, and James Forrestal —the latter two, although they were armed-forces secretaries, by no means merely represented professional service views—are examples of prominent civilian leaders who were highly influential with the impressionable president during the Second World War.

It is also not true that Roosevelt became so dependent upon his military advisers—who were reorganized early in 1942 as the Joint Chiefs of Staff—that he overruled them only twice in the whole course of the war, though for a time that notion was another historical commonplace. As Kent Roberts Greenfield, long the chief historian of the army, put it:

> Of the cases noted in which F.D.R. overruled his military chiefs, more than half of the twenty-odd (instead of [Robert E.] Sherwood's two) can be cited as having occurred in 1942, 1943, and 1944 [at the height of the war]. And this reckoning does not include the cases in which the Joint Chiefs of Staff probably refrained from proposing a plan which represented their best military judgment, because they knew that they could not get Mr. Roosevelt to support it.[60]

More to the point than any counting of occasions of disagreement was the circumstance that for a United States that was still new to the comprehensive global exercise of its power, considerations of military strategy often inevitably outweighed global political interests that had not yet been fully defined. Referring to allegations that American wartime planning lacked the focus upon political objectives that Prime Minister Churchill is reputed to have insisted upon in British planning, Forrest C. Pogue, the biographer of Gen. George C. Marshall, the army chief of staff, observes: "The Americans saw clearly enough the political advantages Churchill might gain for Britain by his policies. But if these did not serve American interests, the U.S. Chiefs of Staff preferred to deal in terms of military advantages."[61]

Still more to the point, the central feature of America's alleged waging of World War II mainly in terms of military strategic expediency—namely, the pursuit of a military victory as complete as possible by means as direct as possible—better served the purposes of American policy than any other strategy could have done. The resistance of American policy-makers and strategists alike to the British effort to draw the principal thrust of the Western Allies into the Mediterranean and southern Europe was based simultaneously upon the American strategists' belief that it was a strategic error to strike against the enemy's periphery rather than against decisive objectives in his heartland, and upon the policy-makers' belief that no American interests proportionate to the likely military investment lay scattered along the periphery. As Brig. Gen. Albert C. Wedemeyer, a principal army planner who was himself acutely conscious of postwar stakes vis-à-vis the Soviet Union, approvingly quoted Secretary of War Henry L. Stimson with regard to British efforts early in 1942 to draw the Americans into the Egyptian campaign: "The Middle East is the very last priority of all that are facing us, we have foreseen for months that the British would be howling for help here that we really should not give them, and I think now is the time to stand pat."[62] The political danger of the British strategy in the Mediterranean, as soldiers such as Wedemeyer and civilians such as Stimson saw it, was that it would postpone an Anglo-American invasion of northwestern Europe across the English Channel so long that it would be the armies of the Soviet Union that would overrun all of Germany itself, perhaps penetrate even into the Low Countries and France, and thus leave little of the industrial heartland of Europe for Anglo-American liberation or conquest. The best way to assure maximum American influence in postwar Europe, and thus to serve best the interests of American foreign policy, was to thrust Anglo-American military power directly at Germany across that industrial heartland and thus to end the war with Anglo-American troops occupying as much as possible of the most politically and economically important part of the Continent. Similarly, the best way to assure maximum American influence in the postwar Far East was to thrust American military power as directly and rapidly as possible toward the Japanese home islands—to put them under American occupation.[63]

Yet while strategy and policy could fortunately coincide for the United States during World War II, the wartime relationship between the military chieftains and the president and his civilian advisers nevertheless revolutionized the attitudes of the American military toward their duties to the civilian branches of the executive and toward their divorcement from politics. Drawn by the president into continual discussion of strategy and policy together, they lost nearly all the inhibitions that before the war had restrained them even from candid strategic consideration of the Philippine defense problem when policy indicated that they must attempt to hold the archipelago against Japanese attack:

> The military attitude toward civilian control changed completely during the war [says Samuel P. Huntington in his classic *The Soldier and the State*].... One would hardly recognize the cowed and submissive men of the 1930's in the proud and powerful commanders of the victorious American forces. Civilian control was a relic of the past which had little place in the future. "The Joint Chiefs of Staff at the present time," Admiral [William D.] Leahy said quite frankly and truthfully in 1945, "are under no civilian control whatever." And the Chiefs made it clear that they wanted to perpetuate this situation. "There was one point upon which all of us agreed," to quote Admiral Leahy again. "We felt the Joint Chiefs

of Staff should be a permanent body *responsible only to the President* and that the JCS should advise the President on the national defense budget."[64]

Both Leahy and Huntington exaggerated. As the quotation from Kent Roberts Greenfield implies, Franklin Roosevelt was a president whose interests in military activities and whose conception of his duties as commander in chief resembled Abraham Lincoln's conception much more than Woodrow Wilson's. There was in fact never any question that Roosevelt controlled the military. The extent to which the American forces became committed against their own wishes to a Mediterranean strategy beginning with Operation TORCH—the invasion of North Africa—is a major index to Roosevelt's control. For while the American military disagreed with Churchill and the British strategists about the desirability of TORCH, the president did not, and his way of course prevailed. The effect was to postpone for a year the most cherished desire of the American military strategists—the invasion of northwestern Europe across the English Channel. After the war, furthermore, the various statutes that federated the armed forces under a Department of Defense also created, in the secretary of defense, a civilian deputy to the president for military affairs who proved at least as powerful an embodiment of day-to-day civilian control over the military as the secretaries of war or of the navy had been—a fact that Secretary Robert S. McNamara especially was to demonstrate. With advanced late-twentieth-century modes of communication added to the constitutional and legal principles and mechanisms of civilian control of the military by the time of the Vietnam War, President Johnson could exercise even a tactical control of military operations from the presidential command center in the White House.

All of which should not, however, obscure the drastic changes in the American civil-military balance, and particularly in the relationship between national policy and military strategy, that did occur during and after World War II and that Huntington rightly pointed out. The military lost their habit of self-effacement. More important was the militarization of the perceptions held by the civilian heads of government.[65] The military power that was generated by the United States during World War II and was largely maintained after the war was so immense, and government leaders' awareness of it was so acute, that the temptation to apply military means as a possibly swift solvent of otherwise intractable problems was constant and sometimes irresistible. Accounts of John F. Kennedy's administration depict, even among that sophisticated president and his advisers, a militarization of perceptions such that "toughness" had become an index of merit, and willingness to employ military force almost routinely as an instrument of policy had become the gauge of toughness. Once again in American history, the kind of orchestration of military strategy to the service of national policy that Lincoln had once achieved was abandoned—not now because the civilian leaders of government cut themselves off from military strategy, as they had done throughout most of the American past, but for the reverse reason—that policy now tended to serve strategy.[66]

Yet the record of the American past is not unique. Not the United States—not any other major power either—has found the awesome might of modern military forces readily adaptable and controllable by the civilian leadership as a mere instrument of national policy. Particularly when states have gone to war, all leaders have found that the momentum of war creates its own logic, as well as its own grammar.

The tendency of the United States during World War II to deal in military advantages was itself far less singular, and far less an evidence of naïveté, than is often alleged. Hitler and the German war and industrial machines represented a most terrifying combination of menaces; and during World War II all the great powers that were allied against Hitler postponed the pursuit of policy advantage in a post-Hitlerian world in order to assure themselves that Hitler would indeed be defeated, persisting in such postponement as long as the most minuscule chance of a German victory remained—long after, the perspective of hindsight now informs us, the tide of war had turned firmly against the Nazis. Winston Churchill asserted that if Hitler should invade hell, the prime minister would surely say a good word in the House of Commons for the Devil himself. Therefore, Chuchchill, the veteran anti-Communist, embraced Stalin and the Soviet Union for the sake of military success in the anti-Hitler war; and in order to ensure against his fears of a Nazi-Soviet separate peace, Churchill in wartime dealt generously with Stalin in offering to consign much of eastern Europe to eventual Soviet domination.[67]

Churchill's famed insistence on a military strategy of peripheral attacks against the Nazi empire was itself not the policy-based effort to limit the postwar Soviet sphere in southern and southeastern Europe that the Prime Minister and his admirers after the war claimed that it had been. Rather, it was mainly a strategy of military expedience, which was aimed at limiting the military dimensions of the war to proportions commensurate with Britain's limited military strength. Those proportions could be retained in campaigns fought through the narrow land masses of the Mediterranean littoral, but not in a great land war fought across the north European plain. When Churchill did give thought during the war to considerations of postwar British policy, he cherished the hope of restoring a strong and independent France, so as to afford Britain a partner in facing the Soviet Union after the anticipated postwar departure of the United States from Europe. But Churchill's persistent efforts to postpone the cross-channel invasion of France, as well as his attempts to renege even after the decision for the invasion had been made, threatened to undercut the one military strategy that would best have served his postwar policy—because during the war he followed the star of British military expediency, not that of postwar policy advantage.[68]

Because the American insistence on the cross-channel invasion did plainly serve American national policy as well as the military designs of the American strategists, it was the United States much more than Great Britain—Roosevelt much more than Churchill—whose method of fighting the European war accorded with policy interests. But Stalin may well have sacrificed policy advantage to the pressures of military strategy more than did either of the Western Allies. At the Teheran Conference of the Big Three Allied leaders in November 1943, Churchill's opposition made the cross-channel invasion —Operation OVERLORD—in the spring of 1944 still doubtful until Stalin threw his weight firmly alongside the Americans' in behalf of OVERLORD. In doing so, Stalin sacrificed the Soviet political advantage, evidently urged on him by some of his advisers, that was to be gained from encouraging the Anglo-Americans to entrap themselves in inhospitable blind alleys by pursuing Churchillian adventures into the rugged mountains of northern Italy and the Balkans. Instead, Stalin wanted the Anglo-American armies to invade France, at whatever cost to his postwar prospects in northern, industrialized Europe, because his immediate overriding concern was the military one of ensuring the defeat of Hitler. Similarly, Stalin neglected to exploit the wartime accretions of strength enjoyed by the Communist parties of occupied western Europe, preferring instead to enjoin those parties to tame subservience to Anglo-American directives, lest he jeopardize his military alliances while the peril from Hitler remained only incompletely abated.[69]

All modern political leaders have found it extremely difficult to harness military strategy to the service of policy. War does have a logic of its own as well as a grammar: the logic that impels civilian leaders to the sacrifice of policy in favor of strategy under the imperatives of war, the logic that drives war toward remorseless revolutionary struggle. The immensity of the difficulties of harnessing war into an appropriately subordinate role to statecraft, and the cumulative and accelerating loss of control by statesmanship over war and the military power that occurred in the greatest state of modern continental Europe—these after all form the grand themes of the most monumental single historical work on the relationship between military strategy and civilian leadership, the four volumes of Gerhard Ritter's *Staatskunst und Kriegshandwerk: Das Problem des "Militarismus" in Deutschland,* translated into English by Heinz Norden as *The Sword and the Scepter: The Problem of Militarism in Germany.*[70] "The problem of militarism," said Ritter, elaborating upon his title, "is the question of the proper relation between statesmanship as an art and war as a craft."[71] "Militarism," he said, "is the exaggeration and overestimation of the military, to a degree that corrupts that relation. Militarism is encountered whenever the pugnacious aspects of diplomacy are one-sidedly overemphasized and the technical exigencies of war, real or alleged, are allowed to gain the upper hand over the calm considerations of statesmanship."[72]

Pointing to Clausewitz's dictum that "War is the continuation of diplomacy by other means," Ritter asked: "How explain all these conflicts" between the art of statesmanship and the craft of war, "if diplomacy (as a struggle for power) and war are basically one and the same thing?"[73]

The core of Ritter's answer lay in his affirmation that "what Clausewitz failed to see or at least to acknowledge is that war, once set off, may very well develop a logic of its own because the war events themselves may react on and alter the guiding will; that it may roll on like an avalanche, burying all the initial aims, all the aspirations and apprehensions of statesmen."[74] War has demonstrated a scarcely controllable tendency to override diplomacy; for "of the two opposing concepts, diplomacy and war, only one is unequivocally definable —namely, war, the clash of arms," while "diplomacy is in truth not a clear-cut thing. It carries a dual meaning with which the mysterious demoniac quality that hovers over all political history is closely associated."[75] The ambiguity, the intangibility, and in the end the frequent ephemerality of diplomacy and statecraft as opposed to war, the mysterious demoniac quality underlying even diplomacy—all rise out of the basic warlike nature of the state: "Wherever the state makes its appearance in history it is first of all in the form of a concentration of fighting power."[76]

But Clausewitz, despite his less than adequate perception that war has its own logic, also told us why war tends to run away from policy. "The main idea underlying the state," he wrote to August Count von Gneisenau, "is defense against the enemy without": military defense is the essence of the state. In quoting this less-well-known line from Clausewitz, Gerhard Ritter disapprovingly saw Clausewitz as himself succumbing to militarism and helping to lay the foundation for the later tragedy of German militarism: here was a Clausewitzian idea, said Ritter, to which the elder Field Marshal Helmuth von Moltke subscribed but which the statesman Bismarck could never have endorsed. Yet Ritter himself also had to imply that in this statement Clausewitz struck closer to the root of the problem of reconciling policy with strategy, statesmanship with war, than he did in his more famous dictum.[77]

War is not simply the continuation of policy by other means. For one thing, once war is accepted as a means toward serving policy, the desirability of winning for the sake of future purposes of deterrence or aggressive threat-making tends to be added to the original objective. But beyond that, as Ritter points out, war also is too closely bound up with the nature of the state itself. It lends, in Ritter's word, a mysterious demoniac quality to all statecraft. It forever threatens to break free of rational policy-making restraints into remorseless revolutionary struggle. This essay has praised Abraham Lincoln as a rare and outstanding example of the civilian leader who could nicely adjust military strategy to his policy. But Lincoln had first yoked strategy to the service of policy in order to prevent the degeneration of war into remorseless revolutionary struggle, and in this one of his aims, after all, despite all his vision and skill, he failed.

Notes

1. Carl von Clausewitz, *On War*, trans. J. J. Graham (3 vols.; New York: Barnes & Noble, 1968), 1:23.
2. Numerous examples of this military attitude are offered in Alfred Vagts, *A History of Militarism: Civilian and Military* (rev. ed.; New York: Meridian Books, 1959), especially pp. 237–45. Less well known but almost equally valuable is the same author's *Defense and Diplomacy: The Soldier and the Conduct of Foreign Relations* (New York: King's Crown Press, 1956).
3. Maxwell D. Taylor, *Swords and Plowshares* (New York: Norton, 1972), p. 407; Neil Sheehan et al., *The Pentagon Papers as Published by the New York Times* (New York: Bantam Books, 1971), p. 524.
4. Colin R. Ballard, *The Military Genius of Abraham Lincoln* (Cleveland, Ohio: World, 1952), p. 4; originally published by Oxford University Press in 1926.
5. Thomas Harry Williams, *Lincoln and His Generals* (New York: Knopf, 1952). The breadth of the acceptance of this view is suggested also by its frequent reiteration, albeit with the guarded acknowledgment that Lincoln was after all a civilian and not a soldier, in the numerous Civil War histories written by Bruce Catton.
6. Abraham Lincoln, *The Collected Works of Abraham Lincoln*, ed. Roy P. Basler (9 vols.; New Brunswick, N.J.: Rutgers University Press, 1953–1955), 4:266.
7. Ibid., 4:332.
8. Ibid., 4:437.
9. Ibid., 5:48–49.
10. *The War of the Rebellion: A Compilation of the Official Records of the Union and Confederate Armies* (4 series, 70 vols. in 130 vols.; Washington, D.C.: Government Printing Office, 1880–1901), ser. 1, vol. 11, pt. 3, p. 316. Hereafter cited as *O.R.*; all citations refer to Series 1.
11. George B. McClellan, *McClellan's Own Story* (New York: Webster, 1887), pp. 487–88.
12. Lincoln, *Collected Works*, 5:145–46.
13. Ibid., 5:169 (March 24, 1862).
14. Ibid., 5:223.
15. Ibid., 5:342–43 (July 26, 1862).
16. Ibid., 5:343.
17. Ibid., 5:346 (July 28, 1862).
18. Allan Nevins, *The War for the Union* (4 vols.; New York: Scribner, 1959–1971), 1:304; from S. L. M. Barlow Papers, Henry E. Huntington Library.
19. McClellan, *Own Story*, p. 655.
20. *O.R.*, vol. 12, pt. 2, pp. 50–53, for Pope's policy. For discussions, see Douglas Southall Freeman, *R. E. Lee: A Biography* (4 vols.; New York: Scribner's, 1934–

1935), 2:263–64; Kenneth P. Williams, *Lincoln Finds a General: A Military Study of the Civil War* (5 vols.; New York: Macmillan, 1949–1959), 1:253–54. Under the laws of war, oaths administered under duress could not be regarded as binding. Pope soon ameliorated his order for his troops to live off the country; *O.R.*, vol. 12, pt. 3, p. 573.

21. Lincoln, *Collected Works*, 6:409. In the terms of Charles Fairbanks's essay in this collection, in his emancipation policy, Lincoln turned an end into a means, as is especially evident in the phase of the policy that involved the arming of freedmen.
22. Ibid., 6:406–7.
23. Ulysses S. Grant, *Personal Memoirs of U. S. Grant* (2 vols.; New York: Webster, 1885–1886), 1:368–69.
24. Ibid., 2:129.
25. Ibid., 2:135n; *O.R.*, vol. 33, p. 828. For the similar orders to Sherman, see Grant, *Memoirs*, 2:131n; *O.R.*, vol. 32, pt. 3, p. 246.
26. Grant, *Memoirs*, 2:226; *O.R.*, vol. 36, pt. 2, p. 627.
27. Grant, *Memoirs*, 2:177–78.
28. Ibid., 2:140–41.
29. Lincoln, *Collected Works*, 6:467 (September 19, 1863).
30. *O.R.*, vol. 37, pt. 2, p. 558.
31. *O.R.*, vol. 37, pt. 2, p. 301.
32. Phillip H. Sheridan, *Personal Memoirs of P. H. Sheridan* (2 vols.; New York: Webster, 1888), 1:488.
33. Mark Mayo Boatner, III, *The Civil War Dictionary* (New York: McKay, 1959), p. 746.
34. William T. Sherman, *Memoirs of General William T. Sherman by Himself* (2 vols.; New York: Appleton, 1875), 2:227, 249.
35. Adam Badeau, *Military History of Ulysses S. Grant* (3 vols.; New York: Appleton, 1868–1881), 3:643.
36. A. D. Wales, "Grant: His 'Majesty' and Genius," *Journal of the United States Military Service Institution* 39 (1906):5–6.
37. Lincoln, *Collected Works*, 8:333.
38. Clausewitz, *On War*, 3:122.
39. Lincoln, *Collected Works*, 7:282 (April 4, 1864).
40. For citations, see notes 4, 5, and 20 above. For all that, the portraits of Lincoln by the two Williamses must be praised as among the most well rounded available. The principal scholarly biography of Lincoln, James G. Randall, *Lincoln the President* (4 vols., vol. 4 with Richard N. Current; New York: Dodd, Mead, 1945–1955) is disturbingly weak on anything concerning military affairs. Randall was an outstanding American historian, but as a Civil War "revisionist" of the disillusioned post–World War I era who regarded "war" as merely a euphemism for "mass murder," he allowed his aversion to the phenomenon to reflect itself in a slipshod handling of military topics that he would not have tolerated in his treatment of such specialities of his as constitutional history.
41. My rather tedious experience in reading American textbooks on military strategy written during the nineteenth and early twentieth centuries leads me to submit as the first book that took a reasonably broad view linking strategy with diplomacy George J. Meyers's *Strategy* (Washington: Byron S. Adams, 1928). More typical examples of the genre, in addition to those mentioned later in this essay, are James Mercur, *Elements of the Art of War, Prepared for the Use of the Cadets of the United States Military Academy* (2d ed., rev. and corrected; New York: Wiley, 1889); Jo-

seph M. Califf, *Notes on Military Science and the Art of War* (2d ed.; Washington, D.C.: Chapman, 1891); John Bigelow, *The Principles of Strategy, Illustrated Mainly from American Campaigns* (New York: Greenwood, 1968), which was originally the second revised and enlarged edition, published by Lippincott in 1894; James S. Pettit, *Elements of Military Science, For the Use of Students in Colleges and Universities* (rev. ed.; New Haven, Conn.: Tuttle, Morehouse & Taylor, 1895); Arthur L. Wagner, *Strategy. A Lecture Delivered by Colonel Arthur L. Wagner, Assistant Adjutant-General, U.S.A., to the Officers of the Regular Army and National Guard at the Maneuvers at West Point, Ky., and at Fort Riley, Kansas, 1903* (Kansas City, Mo.: Hudson-Kimberly, 1904); G. J. Fiebeger, *Elements of Strategy* (n.p., [1906?]); William K. Naylor, *Principles of Strategy, with Historical Illustrations* (Fort Leavenworth, Kans.: General Service Schools, 1921).

42. Henry Wager Halleck, *Elements of Military Art and Science: Or, Course of Instruction in Strategy, Fortification, Tactics of Battles &c* (3d ed.; New York: Appleton, 1862), p. 37; first edition published in 1846. For Halleck's career, see Stephen E. Ambrose, *Halleck: Lincoln's Chief of Staff* (Baton Rouge: Louisiana State University Press, 1962).

43. I examined much of this material, with frustrating results, while preparing my *The American Way of War: A History of United States Military Strategy and Policy* (New York: Macmillan, 1973). For a guide to the material, see Benjamin Franklin Cooling, ed., *A Suggested Guide to the Curricular Archives of the U.S. Army War College, 1907–1940*, Special Bibliographic Series, No. 8 (Carlisle Barracks, Pa.: U.S. Army Military History Research Collection, 1973). These curricular archives are the property of the National Archives and are currently in the custody of the U.S. Army Military History Research Collection at Carlisle Barracks.

44. The principal histories are Alfred T. Mahan, *The Influence of Sea Power upon History, 1660–1783* (Boston: Little, Brown, 1890), *The Influence of Sea Power upon the French Revolution and Empire, 1793–1812* (2 vols.; Boston: Little, Brown, 1892), and *Sea Power in Its Relation to the War of 1812* (2 vols.; Boston: Little, Brown, 1905). Among the collections of essays, *The Problem of Asia and Its Effect upon International Politics* (Boston: Little, Brown, 1900) and *Naval Strategy, Compared and Contrasted with the Principles and Practice of Military Operations on Land* (Boston: Little, Brown, 1911) are especially relevant to the discussion at hand. Mahan discussed the origins of his ideas in his reminiscences, *From Sail to Steam: Recollections of Naval Life* (New York: Harper, 1907). For a bibliography, see William E. Livezey, *Mahan on Sea Power* (Norman: University of Oklahoma Press, 1947), pp. 301–11. For selections, see Allan Westcott, ed., *Mahan on Naval Warfare: Selections from the Writings of Rear Admiral Alfred T. Mahan* (new ed.; Boston: Little, Brown, 1941). Among critiques, see especially, Richard Hofstadter, *Social Darwinism in American Thought* (rev. ed.; Boston: Beacon, 1955), chap. 9, especially pp. 184–92; Peter Karsten, *The Naval Aristocracy: The Golden Age of Annapolis and the Emergence of Modern American Navalism* (New York: Free Press, 1972) passim, especially chap. 7; Walter LaFeber, *The New Empire: An Interpretation of American Expansion, 1860–1898* (Ithaca, N.Y.: Cornell University Press, for the American Historical Association, Cornell Paperbacks, 1967), pp. 85–93, and "A Note on the 'Mercantilistic Imperialism' of Alfred Thayer Mahan," *Mississippi Valley Historical Review* 48 (March 1962):674–85; Julius W. Pratt, "Alfred Thayer Mahan," in *The Marcus W. Jernegan Essays in American Historiography*, ed. William T. Hutchinson (New York: Russell & Russell, 1958), pp. 207–26; Margaret Tuttle Sprout, "Mahan: Evangelist of Sea

Power," in *Makers of Modern Strategy: Military Thought from Machiavelli to Hitler,* ed. Edward Mead Earle (Princeton, N.J.: Princeton University Press, 1943), pp. 415–45. Mahan is one military subject who has not been neglected by American historians.
45. Karsten, *Naval Aristocracy,* pp. 187, 221.
46. Richard D. Challener, *Admirals, Generals, and American Foreign Policy, 1898–1914* (Princeton, N.J.: Princeton University Press, 1973), pp. 410–11.
47. Ibid., pp. 23–24.
48. Richard C. Brown, "Emory Upton: The Army's Mahan," *Military Affairs* 17 (Fall, 1953):125–31. On Upton, see also, Stephen E. Ambrose, *Upton and the Army* (Baton Rouge: Louisiana State University Press, 1964); Peter Smith Michie, *The Life and Letters of Emory Upton, Colonel of the Fourth Regiment of Artillery, and Brevet Major-General, U.S. Army* (New York: Appleton, 1885); Russell F. Weigley, *Towards an American Army: Military Thought from Washington to Marshall* (New York: Columbia University Press, 1962), chap. 7. In addition to his tactical manuals, Upton wrote *The Armies of Asia and Europe* (New York: Appleton, 1878) and *The Military Policy of the United States* (Washington, D.C.: Government Printing Office, 1904).
49. The organizational problems of the army can be followed in Russell F. Weigley, *History of the United States Army* (New York: Macmillan, 1967). For the special difficulties of Scott (whose collision was with Secretary of War Jefferson Davis) and Sherman, see Charles Winslow Elliott, *Winfield Scott: The Soldier and the Man* (New York: Macmillan, 1937), pp. 648–58; and Lloyd Lewis, *Sherman: Fighting Prophet* (New York: Harcourt, Brace, 1958), pp. 608, 615, 622. Much about the demarcation between the civilian and the military spheres in the nineteenth-century War and Navy departments can be learned from the relevant chapters of Leonard D. White's excellent volumes on the administrative history of the federal government to 1901: *The Federalists: A Study in Administrative History* (New York: Macmillan, 1959); *The Jeffersonians: A Study in Administrative History, 1801–1829* (New York: Macmillan, 1959); *The Jacksonians: A Study in Administrative History, 1829–1861* (New York: Macmillan, 1954); *The Republican Era, 1869–1901: A Study in Administrative History* (New York: Macmillan, 1958). For the experiences and views of a professional soldier who served both as secretary of war and as general in chief, see John M. Schofield, *Forty-six Years in the Army* (New York: Century, 1897), pp. 406–11, 419–23, 467–82.
50. Still the standard work despite its age—it originated as articles written in the early twentieth century—is Charles Oscar Paullin, *Paullin's History of Naval Administration, 1775–1911: A Collection of Articles from the U.S. Naval Institute Proceedings* (Annapolis, Md.: U.S. Naval Institute, 1968). There is much about naval administration as well as naval policy in Harold Sprout and Margaret Sprout, *The Rise of American Naval Power, 1776–1918* (Princeton, N.J.: Princeton University Press, 1939).
51. Progressivism as a search for efficiency and order is explored especially in Robert H. Wiebe, *The Search for Order, 1877–1920* (New York: Hill & Wang, 1967).
52. U.S., War Department, *Annual Reports of the War Department for the Fiscal Year Ended June 30, 1902,* vol. 1: *Report of the Secretary of War and Reports of Bureau Chiefs* (Washington, D.C.: Government Printing Office, 1903), p. 43. For the Root reforms, see especially Paul Y. Hammond, *Organizing for Defense: The American Military Establishment in the Twentieth Century* (Princeton, N.J.: Princeton

University Press, 1961), pp. 10–48; this study by a political scientist ought to be consulted regarding all the organizational developments in the War, Navy, and Defense departments that are touched on in the remaining portion of this essay. See also U.S., Congress, Senate, *Creation of the American General Staff*, by Maj. Gen. William H. Carter, 68th Cong., 1st sess., *Senate Documents*, vol. 2 (serial 8254), no. 119 (Washington, D.C.: Government Printing Office, 1924); Philip C. Jessup, *Elihu Root* (2 vols.; New York: Dodd, Mead, 1938), especially 1:240–68. Root's statements of policy are collected in Robert Bacon and James B. Scott, eds., *The Military and Colonial Policy of the United States: Addresses and Reports by Elihu Root* (Cambridge, Mass.: Harvard University Press, 1916); and his reports as secretary of war, in U.S., War Department, *Five Years of the War Department* (Washington, D.C.: Government Printing Office, 1904).

53. Samuel P. Huntington, *The Soldier and the State: The Theory and Politics of Civil-Military Relations* (New York: Vintage Books, 1964), p. 250; Huntington's interpretative study contains much information as well as controversial insights concerning all the changes in the twentieth-century American military system. See also Raymond G. O'Connor, "Origins of the Navy 'General Staff,'" in *American Defense Policy in Perspective: From Colonial Times to the Present*, ed. Raymond G. O'Connor (New York: Wiley, 1965), pp. 139–44.

54. William Reynolds Braisted, *The United States Navy in the Pacific, 1909–1922* (Austin: University of Texas Press, 1971), in addition to exploring the specific subject of its title in painstaking detail, contains an excellent brief discussion of Daniels as secretary of the navy and of the events leading to creation of the office of Chief of Naval Operations, based on the primary sources, pp. 176–84. See also Josephus Daniels, *The Cabinet Diaries of Josephus Daniels, 1913–1921*, ed. Edmund David Cronon (Lincoln: University of Nebraska Press, 1963).

55. The early trials of the general staff can be followed, mostly through printings of the documents, in Maj. Gen. Otto L. Nelson, Jr., *National Security and the General Staff* (Washington, D.C.: Infantry Journal Press, 1946), pp. 58–186. For the Wood-Ainsworth battle over the supremacy of the chief of staff over the adjutant general, see, for a dispassionate account from the latter's perspective, Mabel E. Deutrich, *Struggle for Supremacy: The Career of General Fred C. Ainsworth* (Washington, D.C.: Public Affairs Press, 1962), chap. 8; and for a eulogistic treatment of Wood, see Hermann Hagedorn, *Leonard Wood: A Biography* (2 vols.; New York: Harper, 1931), vol. 2, chap. 5. Henry L. Stimson was serving his first tour as secretary of war when the Wood-Ainsworth controversy reached its climax, and his support for the chief of staff was decisive; see Elting E. Morison, *Turmoil and Tradition: A Study of the Life and Times of Henry L. Stimson* (Boston: Houghton Mifflin, 1960), pp. 150–61, and Henry L. Stimson and McGeorge Bundy, *On Active Service in Peace and War* (New York: Harper, 1948), pp. 33–37. The World War I chief of staff told the story of his trials in Peyton C. March, *The Nation at War* (Garden City, N.Y.: Doubleday, 1932), a book written in anger in response to the aspersions against the general staff in John J. Pershing, *My Experiences in the World War* (2 vols.; New York: Stokes, 1931). See also Edward M. Coffman, *The Hilt of the Sword: The Career of Peyton C. March* (Madison: University of Wisconsin Press, 1966), and Daniel R. Beaver, *Newton D. Baker and the American War Effort, 1917–1919* (Lincoln: University of Nebraska Press, 1966). Much can be learned about the deficiencies of the World War I general staff from the description of logistical difficulties in U.S., Department of the Army, Quartermaster Historian's Office, Office of the Quartermaster

General, *Quartermaster Support of the Army: A History of the Corps, 1775–1939*, by Erna Risch (Washington, D.C.: Government Printing Office, 1962), chap. 14.

56. For the latter incidents, see Hagedorn, *Leonard Wood*, 2:144; Frederick Palmer, *Newton D. Baker: America at War* (2 vols.; New York: Dodd, Mead, 1931), 1:40–41.

57. There is no altogether satisfactory history of the development of armored-force doctrine in the United States Army; an early approach is Mildred Hanson Gillie, *Forging the Thunderbolt: A History of the Development of the Armored Force* (Harrisburg, Pa.: Military Service Publishing Co., 1947). On aerial doctrine, see Robert Frank Futrell, *Ideas, Concepts, Doctrine: A History of Basic Thinking in the United States Air Force, 1907–1964* (2 vols.; Maxwell Air Force Base, Ala.: Aerospace Studies Institute, Air University, 1971). On economic mobilization planning, see U.S., Department of the Army, *History of Military Mobilization in the United States Army, 1775–1945*, by Marvin A. Kreidberg and Merton G. Henry (Washington, D.C.: Government Printing Office, 1955), chaps. 12–15; R. Elberton Smith, *United States Army in World War II: The War Department: The Army and Economic Mobilization* (Washington, D.C.: Government Printing Office, 1959), chaps. 1–3; Harry B. Yoshpe, "Economic Mobilization Planning between the Two World Wars," *Military Affairs* 15 (Winter, 1951):199–204; 16 (Summer, 1952):71–96. For an overview of the period see Maurice Matloff, "The American Approach to War, 1919–1945," in *The Theory and Practice of War: Essays Presented to Captain B. H. Liddell Hart*, ed. Michael Howard (London: Cassell, 1965), pp. 213–43.

58. For army and navy planning for an ORANGE war, see Russell F. Weigley, "The Role of the War Department and the Army," and Waldo H. Heinrichs, Jr., "The Role of the United States Navy," in *Pearl Harbor as History: Japanese-American Relations, 1931–1941*, ed. Dorothy Borg and Shumpei Okamoto (New York: Columbia University Press, 1973), pp. 165–88, 197–259; Louis Morton, *United States Army in World War II: The War in the Pacific: Strategy and Command: The First Two Years* (Washington, D.C.: Government Printing Office, 1962), pp. 24–44, and "War Plan ORANGE: Evolution of a Strategy," *World Politics* 11 (January 1959):221–50; Mark Skinner Watson, *United States Army in World War II: The War Department: Chief of Staff: Prewar Plans and Preparations* (Washington, D.C.: Government Printing Office, 1950), pp. 412–17.

59. *Federal Register*, vol. 4, July 7, 1939, p. 2786; cited in Huntington, *The Soldier and the State*, p. 319.

60. Kent Roberts Greenfield, *American Strategy in World War II: A Reconsideration* (Baltimore, Md.: Johns Hopkins Press, 1963), p. 56. Greenfield refers to a myth established by Robert E. Sherwood, *Roosevelt and Hopkins: An Intimate History* (rev. ed.; New York: Harper, 1950), p. 615 (which actually speaks of the *few*, not precisely two, occasions when Roosevelt overruled the joint chiefs), and perpetuated by Huntington, *The Soldier and the State*, p. 329.

61. Forrest C. Pogue, *George C. Marshall: Organizer of Victory, 1943–1945* (New York: Viking, 1973), p. 11.

62. General Albert C. Wedemeyer, *Wedemeyer Reports!* (New York: Holt, 1958), p. 155.

63. Chester Wilmot, *The Struggle for Europe* (New York: Harper, 1952), is a vigorous British-oriented account by an Australian journalist who takes the opposite view to the one stated here: Wilmot holds that the British policy-maker–strategists were politically astute and that their American counterparts were politically naïve.

This same now-familiar view received one of its most influential American expressions in Hanson W. Baldwin, *Great Mistakes of the War* (New York: Harper, 1950).

64. U.S., Congress, Senate, Committee on Military Affairs, *Hearings*, Admiral Leahy speaking before the Committee on Military Affairs, Senate, on S. 84, 79th Cong., 1st sess., 1945, p. 521, and William Leahy, *I Was There: The Personal Story of the Chief of Staff to Presidents Roosevelt and Truman. Based on His Notes and Diaries Made at the Time* (New York: Whittlesey House, 1950), p. 239; both quoted in Huntington, *The Soldier and the State*, pp. 335–36.

65. "Militarization" and "militarism" are terms used so frequently and loosely that they are in danger of being drained of meaning. I refer to Gerhard Ritter's definition on page 70 below.

66. David Halberstam, *The Best and the Brightest* (New York: Random House, 1972), portrays vividly, even if with somewhat gossipy tendencies, the characters and atmosphere of the Kennedy administration as it approached involvement in Vietnam. Portrayals with much kinder intent do little, in retrospect, to soften the picture: Arthur M. Schlesinger, Jr., *A Thousand Days: John F. Kennedy in the White House* (Boston: Houghton Mifflin, 1965), and Theodore C. Sorensen, *Kennedy* (New York: Harper & Row, 1965). A brief but acute analysis of the course of involvement is contained in Bernard Brodie, *War and Politics* (New York: Macmillan, 1973), chaps. 4 and 5.

67. Raymond G. O'Connor, *Diplomacy for Victory: FDR and Unconditional Surrender* (New York: Norton, 1971), depicts Churchill's wartime diplomacy of cajolement of the Soviets in a manner affording a useful corrective to Churchill's own *The Second World War* (6 vols.; Boston: Houghton Mifflin, 1948–1953).

68. For a skillful British exposition of the argument that British Mediterranean strategy was a strategy, not of political farsightedness, but of military expediency, see Michael E. Howard, *The Mediterranean Strategy in the Second World War* (New York: Praeger, 1968).

69. Stephen E. Ambrose, "Applied Strategy of World War II," *Naval War College Review* vol. 12, no. 9 (May 1970), p. 62; Gabriel Kolko, *The Politics of War: The World and United States Foreign Policy, 1943–1945* (New York: Random House, 1968), for Stalin and the Communist parties of the West, especially pp. 14–18, 35–37.

70. Gerhard Ritter, *Staatskunst und Kriegshandwerk: Das Problem des "Militarismus" in Deutschland* (4 vols.; Munich: R. Oldenbourg, 1954–1968); Gerhard Ritter, *The Sword and the Scepter: The Problem of Militarism in Germany*, trans. Heinz Norden (4 vols.; Coral Gables, Fla.: University of Miami Press, 1969–1973). (In the Norden translation, the first volume is a translation of the third, the 1964, version of the volume in the German original; the second volume is a translation of the second, the 1965, version; the remaining volumes are translations of the first editions.)

71. Ritter, *The Sword and the Scepter*, 1:5.
72. Ibid.
73. Ibid., 1:6.
74. Ibid., 1:65.
75. Ibid., 1:7.
76. Ibid.
77. Ibid., 1:212, 260; the quotation is from p. 212.

Threat Perception

Klaus Knorr

Ever since mankind became organized in separate states, to threaten others or be threatened by them has been a recurring experience. While international systems have been systems for cooperation, they have also been threat systems—if by systems we mean relationships structured by the ability of each sovereign state to choose between cooperation and conflict. The choice of conflict has been frequent over the millennia. It has been a threatful world, and it still is.

State-actors can threaten foreign societies by other means than military violence. The threatening action may be economic, ideological, or politically subversive. But these other means are usually far less effective in producing coercion than the military threat. The military threat has been the classic threat, and it is the subject of our exploration.

If a state-actor is or feels threatened by another, he anticipates—with some degree of probability—the loss of something of value, such as territory and population, restriction or loss of sovereignty, economic assets, and political constitution. This is on top of having lost freedom from threat and of having to cope with that threat in one way or another. Indeed, war itself, and the value losses it is apt to entail, rather than defeat, may be feared. And so may be the need for larger defense efforts. In any case, this chapter concentrates on threats to major values, such as territorial and political integrity.

A threat that is addressed by one actor against another is an instrument of coercion. It may be more or less determinate. It can be precise and substantive, as in the case of an ultimatum; and it can be vague, to be inferred from less definite acts—for example, veiled verbal statements and increases in armed forces. In either case, we call this an *actual* threat. Of course, state *A* may not perceive an actual threat from *B* even though *B* and third parties are aware of it. Conversely, state *A* may feel threatened contingently by state-actor *B*, even though the latter has issued no threat whatever. As dictionaries explain, one can feel threatened by something which by its very nature or relation to oneself (e.g., a river in a flood area) threatens one's welfare. Similarly, *A* may feel threatened by *B* simply because the latter has the capability of making an actual threat. We call this the perception of a *potential* threat.

In one of the most famous documents of statecraft dealing with threat perception, Eyre Crowe, a British official, referred in 1907 to the potential German threat as follows:

So long, then, as Germany competes for an intellectual and moral leadership of the world in reliance on her own national advantages and energies England can but admire, applaud, and join in the race. If, on the other hand, Germany believes that greater relative preponderance of material power, wider extent of territory, inviolable frontiers, and supremacy at sea are the necessary and preliminary possessions without which any aspirations to such leadership must end in failure, then England must expect that Germany will surely seek to diminish the power of any rivals, to enhance her own by extending her dominion, to hinder the co-operation of other States, and ultimately to break up and supplant the British Empire.

Now, it is quite possible that Germany does not, nor ever will, consciously cherish any schemes of so subversive a nature. Her statesmen have openly repudiated them with indignation. Their denial may be perfectly honest, and their indignation justified. . . .

But this is not a matter in which England can safely run any risks. . . . It would not be unjust to say that ambitious designs against one's neighbours are not as a rule openly proclaimed, and that therefore the absence of such proclamation, and even the profession of unlimited and universal political benevolence are not in themselves conclusive evidence for or against the existence of unpublished intentions. . . .

Meanwhile it is important to make it quite clear that a recognition of the dangers of the situation need not and does not imply any hostility to Germany.[1]

Perception of actual or potential threats involves the estimate of probabilities about whether the anticipated harm will materialize. Even an actual threat which is precise and substantive may be a bluff. There is always a question of credibility. Potential threats by definition refer to a possibility. They may or may not become actual. Their actualization will be regarded as more or less likely.

There is still another threat of which state-actors are cognizant. It is not experienced vis-à-vis a particular other state. Historical experience has made state-actors aware of the fact that the intentions and capabilities of states to do harm to others can change abruptly. Today's friendly neighbor may become dangerous tomorrow, because, for example, he has acquired additional territory or superior technology or a strong ally or a different government. The observation that interstate changes in intentions and capabilities can unpredictably lead to dangerous threats follows from the very structure of the international system in which each unit is militarily sovereign. We call this, therefore, the *systemic* threat. It means that, over the longer run, no state-actor can ever be certain of its security. It is for this reason that, throughout history, nearly all states have maintained armed forces even when they perceived no threats, actual or potential, and did not themselves choose to make threats. State-actors know that threats may arise more rapidly than it is possible to develop "from scratch" the capabilities for deterrence and defense.

The Eyre Crowe memorandum referred to this threat, which is inherent in the constitution of the international system: "A maritime State is, in the literal sense of the word, the neighbour of every country accessible by sea. It would, therefore, be but natural that the power of a State supreme at sea should inspire universal jealousy and fear, and be ever exposed to the danger of being overthrown by a general combination of the world."[2] Thomas Hobbes referred to the systemic threat when he said that the state of nature is a state of war against all; Machiavelli, Locke, Montesquieu, and Kant understood its deep challenge.[3]

As a matter of statecraft, threat perception is not only concerned with whether or not a threat exists, but also with its character, especially the quality and magnitude of the implied peril. Strictly speaking, this is a question of threat assessment. But the two operations are so closely intertwined that they are treated as one in the following.

With this conceptual introduction we are ready to turn to historical experience in order to study the problems of international threat perception. We begin with two cases from the relatively recent past.

In the peace treaty of Versailles, the victors of World War I not only imposed large territorial losses on Germany; they also restricted her army to 100,000 men without heavy artillery, tanks, and aircraft, and they demilitarized much of the Rhineland. During the 1920s and early 1930s, sharp political divisions made for weak German governments. In 1933, Hitler, the leader of the fascist Nazi movement, came to power and established dictatorial rule. He began to rearm Germany; he remilitarized the entire Rhineland in 1936, annexed Austria in 1938, and took full control of Czechoslovakia in 1939. World War II also broke out in 1939, when Germany invaded Poland.

No one of consequence in 1934, let alone in 1932, foresaw the imminence of an enormously destructive war, as, indeed, no one of consequence had foreseen in 1912 the protracted bloodiness of World War I. Neither Hitler nor any other government leader wanted to bring about the kind of war that World War II turned out to be. Major wars evidently have low predictability. But what interests us most in the years preceding World War II is the inability of British statesmen to perceive the kind of threat that was imminent in the behavior and capability of Nazi Germany. Why did they believe that appeasement would work? We present excerpts from several historical studies. Martin Gilbert and Richard Gott wrote:

> The legacy of the Treaty [of Versailles] was bitterness in Germany and a sense of guilt in Britain.

J. M. Keynes said the Treaty was filled with clauses "which might impoverish Germany now or obstruct her development in future." Many Englishmen read, and accepted, his criticisms. Ashamed of what they had done, they looked for scapegoats, and for amendment. The scapegoat was France; the amendment was appeasement. The harshness of the Treaty was ascribed to French folly. But nobody could deny that Britain had supported France. France was blamed for having encouraged Britain in an excess of punishment. Justice could only be done by helping Germany to take her rightful place in Europe as a Great Power.

Appeasers turned to Germany with outstretched arm, hoping for a handshake. But the Germans hesitated. The war had embittered them too. . . . The more reluctant Germany proved to accept an Anglo-German rapprochement, the guiltier the appeasers felt. They wanted German friendship, and resented Germany's unwillingness to consider it. . . .

Appeasers ignored the Nazi record, and made Anglo-German relations seem more capable of successful evolution than the record gave reason to suggest. Many were revolted by stories of Nazi brutality. But those who considered Anglo-German friendship a vital interest were willing to close their eyes to excesses. Such men sought excuses for the barbarism of 1933, and tried to move closer to Germany in the years that followed. Sometimes the evils of the new régime were condoned, sometimes ignored, sometimes wished away. . . .

Diplomats challenged the appeasers from the first weeks of the Hitler régime. They denied that the Germans would make excellent friends, or allies. Two months after Hitler had come to power Sir Horace Rumbold, British Ambassador in Berlin, reported that . . . the régime would prove as aggressive abroad as it had already shown itself at home. Even before he met Hitler he wrote, "Germany's neighbours have reason to be vigilant." He claimed that the need for vigilance was urgent. Hitler would turn against his neighbours "sooner than they may have contemplated."

A. C. Temperley, one of the English delegates at the Disarmament Conference, insisted that disarmament was impossible while Germany continued to rearm. . . . "There is a mad dog abroad once more and we must resolutely combine either to ensure its destruction or at least its confinement until the disease has run its course." . . .

Vansittart, the most vociferous of anti-Germans, was Permanent Under-Secretary for Foreign Affairs. He noted "his entire agreement" with Temperley's memorandum. . . . He deplored the growing English tendency to divorce German domestic brutality from possible aggression abroad. Nazism he claimed, knew no such division.

> From the very outset of the regime I have felt, with all deference to those who with more sweet reasonableness were disposed for at least a little to wait and see, that there was no doubt whatever about the ultimate intentions of the Nazis. . . . It is an open secret that anything peaceful said by Hitler is merely for foreign consumption and designed to gain time. . . . Nothing but a change of heart can avert another catastrophe; and that change of the German heart is unlikely to come from within, for the true German nature has never changed.

Here was crude racialism. Though it offended many, it found sympathizers.[4]

A. L. Rowse wrote:

> Chamberlain, Simon, Halifax, Hoare—the Big Four as Sam Hoare delighted to call them—they were the men who forced it [appeasement] through, against all opposition, within their own government, or outside. . . .
>
> What was characteristic of this inner group . . . ? There were several things that united them. They were "men of peace," *i.e.* no use for confronting force, or guile, or wickedness. That they did not know what they were dealing with is the most charitable explanation of their failure; but they might at least have taken the trouble to inform themselves. There were plenty of people to tell them, but they would not listen. They all shared a Non-conformist origin, and its characteristic self-righteousness—all the more intolerable in the palpably wrong. These things are more important than people realise; to the historian they are significant elements. One way or another they had none of the old 18th-century aristocracy's guts—they were middle-class men with pacifist backgrounds and no knowledge of Europe, its history or its languages, or of diplomacy. . . .
>
> There is a further consideration of some interest for political thought. . . . In this story we see the decadence of British empiricism, empiricism carried beyond all rhyme or reason. In general I am in sympathy with empiricism in politics; I much prefer it to doctrinairism. The practical way of looking at things, not looking too far in advance, (*pace* Amery), not rocking the boat, and other clichés that do duty for thinking ahead, may serve well enough in ordinary, normal times. But our times are not "normal" in the good old Victorian sense, and never will be again. And this habit of mind in politics will certainly not serve in times of revolution, perpetual stress and conflict, war, the reshaping of the world. This conventional British way of looking at things was simply not equal to the times, and it caught these men out badly.
>
> Even so, the empirical habit of mind, that considered itself so much more practical . . . need not have equated itself with ignorance. Not one of these men in high place in those years ever so much as read *Mein Kampf*, or

would listen to anybody who had. They really did not know what they were dealing with, or the nature and degree of the evil thing they were up against. To be so uninstructed—a condition that arose in part from a certain superciliousness, a lofty smugness, as well as superficiality of mind—was in itself a kind of dereliction of duty.

They would not listen to warnings, because they did not wish to hear. And they did not think things out, because there was a fatal confusion in their minds between the interests of their social order and the interests of their country. They did not say much about it, since that would have given the game away, and anyway it was a thought they did not wish to be too explicit about even to themselves, but they were anti-Red and that hamstrung them in dealing with the greater immediate danger to their country, Hitler's Germany.[5]

Laurence Lafore said:

All these men, and the others of the group, shared a peculiar moralistic outlook. They abominated war (Simon, indeed, had opposed World War I) but they rather admired strength. They were passionately patriotic and in old-fashioned ways both chivalrous and insular. Foreigners seemed remote and rather unreal to them. They loathed violence and cherished human life.[6]

A. J. P. Taylor wrote about the period when, after the destruction of Czechoslovakia, Hitler began to turn on Poland, and the British government reconsidered its posture of appeasement:

The British ministers did not fear defeat in war, though they naturally dreaded war for its own sake. They supposed that the defensive position of Great Britain and France was absolutely secure; they further supposed that, if Great Britain and France went to war with Germany, they would win; they even supposed that Hitler also recognised this. What they feared, with some justification, was that Hitler would count on their standing aside.

[Even at this time, the British ministers saw no need for negotiating an alliance with the Soviet Union in order to stop Germany.]

The British had a poor opinion of the Red Army.... No doubt they were also relieved not to be associated with Bolshevik Russia.... The British were unshakably convinced that Soviet Russia and Nazi Germany were irreconcilable enemies. Hence there was no need to pay a price for Soviet friendship.[7]

What do these historical researches tell us about the problems of threat perception? The British appeasers were obviously wrong about their perceptions of the threat to peace resulting from German behavior. Evidently, this threat was something contingent, something that could happen and then produce fearful events, even though their exact probability and shape was unpredictable. Indeed, under all circumstances, a threat is something conditional, potential, hypothetical. Even an ultimatum may be a bluff, and marching troops can be ordered to stop. The crucial point is that a threat is usually not observable. It is a cognitive construct. But unless it is a product of psychopathology, this construct is derived from things which, in principle, can be observed—that is, the behavior of governments and the capabilities of states. Unfortunately, these observable realities rarely have unmistakable meaning. They are ambiguous, and also they change over time.

These properties indicate two intrinsic intellectual difficulties. First, threat perceptions rest on estimates of the past and the present. These estimates are inferences from usually fragmentary, opaque, and contradictory bits of information. Second, these perceptions concern the future, and there can be no reliable information about the future. Throughout history the future has confronted rulers with truly surprising turns of events. For instance, one perception of the British appeasers seemed to be backed by irrefutable evidence of past behavior. This was the assumption that Communist Russia and Nazi Germany were irreconcilable enemies. These countries had been behaving as such. That Hitler and Stalin would conclude a nonaggression pact, as they did, thus enabling Germany to concentrate her military forces against the West, was inconceivable to the British government before it happened. When it did happen, it came as a complete surprise.

Why, specifically, did the British appeasers underestimate the German threat to peace? To begin with, as Rowse and Lafore explain, they were men who did not have sharp intelligence and extensive knowledge in foreign affairs. They were insular in outlook. And their smugness was one factor that prevented them from listening to their critics, many of whom were professionally trained in foreign affairs. This suggests that intelligence and pertinent knowledge and training are among the requisites of accurate threat perception. National leaders, however, may get to the top on the basis of other qualifications, such as domestic political influence, class position, and party loyalty. If they do, they may not be aware either of the pitfalls of international threat perception or of the need to be served by people of compensatory competence.

In view of the usual inadequacies of available information and the limited predictability of foreign behavior and future events, even high intelligence and analytical competence cannot, of course, assure correct threat perception. As the historical record discloses, these difficulties are greatly and often fatally compounded by the intervention of emotions and predispositions. Thus, as Gilbert and Gott point out, guilt feelings about the harsh peace treaty of Versailles induced many British statesmen to perceive Hitler's initial steps to break the "shackles of Versailles"—then a favorite German phrase—as only the righting of a previous wrong. It is also clear that strong anti-Communist feeling and fears of Bolshevist Russia caused the British appeasers to want a strong Germany as a bulwark against Soviet penetration into central Europe and to refrain, until it was too late, from seeking an understanding with Moscow on joint resistance to Nazi aggression.

Above all, as Rowse, Lafore, and Taylor suggest, their strong fear of war made the appeasers ignore, belittle, or misconstrue any evidence that seemed to render the preservation of general peace precarious, if not hopeless. In order to avert the danger of war, they stoutly clung to pursuing rapprochement with Germany, always hoping that one more concession (at the immediate expense of other countries) would do the trick. Their wishfulness made them accept only shreds of intelligence that fitted into what they wanted to achieve. The greatest dangers to realistic threat perception do not inhere in the intellectual difficulties resulting from poor evidence and future uncertainty. The perceiver can gain an awareness of these problems and can make allowances for them. The greater danger lies in rigid preconceptions and attitudes of which the perceiver is unaware, or not aware enough. Such predispositions make him desire to see certain things happen, and to make what he wants to do seem justified. And the push and pull of underlying emotions that are attached to the values at stake in international affairs, and that are attached also to foreign actors in such forms as hatred and contempt, can lead the perceiver astray. These intervening preconceptions and attitudes produce selectivity in the receipt and use of information; they therefore contribute to a distorted image of reality and to false expectations.

These pitfalls characterize the threat perception not only of individuals but also of groups, whether political or bureaucratic. Relevant groups find it convenient and comfortably reinforcing to share working assumptions that are based on preconceptions regarding foreign threats or absence of them. They tend to engage in what has been called "group think."[8] Challenges to collective preconceptions tend to lead—as Gilbert and Gott observed about the British appeasers—to a hardening of positions that can become obsessional, and hence less receptive to corrective interpretations and insights.

The British example also demonstrates that it is easy for governments, bureaucrats, elites, and larger publics to disagree on matters of threat perception. Before the imagery of the British appeasers finally and suddenly collapsed when Germany invaded Poland, British opinion was already strongly, indeed almost evenly, divided on the merits of appeasing Hitler. Disagreement is natural in view of the intrinsic difficulties of threat perception in international affairs, conflicting appreciations of the values at stake, and different sets of emotions and attitudes.

There were also various misperceptions of relative military capabilities. The British underestimated Germany's capacity for waging general war.[9] They thought mistakenly that both France and Britain were basically secure if general war came.[10] On the other hand, they felt that Britain was extremely vulnerable to bombing from aircraft. And even on relatively technical matters, it is far from easy, before the test of war, to arrive at correct estimates of relative forces. According to Taylor:

> It was the universal belief that there was no defence against attack from the air. Baldwin expressed this when he said: "The bomber will always get through." It was expected that every great city would be levelled to the ground immediately on the outbreak of war; and the British government, acting on this assumption, made preparations for more casualties in London alone during the first week of war than in fact the entire British people suffered during five long years. The only answer was supposed to be "the deterrent"—a bomber-force as large as the enemy's. Neither Great Britain nor France claimed to possess such a force in 1936 or even in 1939; hence, in large part, the timidity of their statesmen. All these calculations turned out to be wrong. The Germans had never planned for independent bombing. Their bomber-force was an auxiliary for the army on the ground, and they had to improvise the air-attack on Great Britain in the summer of 1940. The Germans were answered and defeated not by British bombing, but by fighter-command, which had been despised and comparatively neglected before the war. . . . The pre-war years ran their course under the shadow of hideous mis-apprehension.
>
> . . . .
>
> Wars, when they come, are always different from the war that is expected. Victory goes to the side that has made fewest mistakes, not the one that has guessed right. In this sense, Great Britain and France did not prepare adequately. The military experts gave the wrong advice and pursued the wrong strategy.[11]

British statesmen were by no means alone in misjudging the relevant events that preceded World War II. In fact, all important actors were more or less wrong. The French appeasers were less doctrinaire and consistent than their British counterparts, but their fear of war and their reluctance to spend more on defense preparations induced them to underestimate the German threat.[12]

Soviet governments before World War II were extremely wary of external threats to their country's security. According to Lenin, "History suggests that peace is a breathing space between wars."[13] His analysis of imperialism envisaged capitalist societies as being completely antagonistic to socialist rule everywhere and the chief capitalist states as being an inevitable threat to the rest of mankind.[14] The military interventions in the Russian civil war, half-hearted though they were, reinforced this belief. Stalin and his advisors had no illusions about the predatory and dangerous character of the Nazi government in Germany, and, especially in 1938 and 1939, had indicated Soviet readiness to form an anti-German coalition, offers that the British and French governments rejected. Feeling unready militarily and being fearful also of a Japanese attack on Siberia, Stalin concluded, in August 1939, a nonaggression pact with Germany. Here is how an official Soviet historian explains this step:

> This treaty delivered, for some time at least, the Soviet Union from the threat of a war on two fronts without allies. It gave the USSR time to strengthen its defence capacity. . . .
>
> Naturally, it [the Soviet Government] did not for a moment count on the nazis honouring their commitments. But it was apparent that nazi Germany would not attack the USSR in the immediate future.[15]

However, when in 1941, after the defeat of France, Germany made unmistakable preparations to attack the Soviet Union, Stalin disbelieved the signals. The official historian briefly acknowledges Stalin's mistake:

> The aggressive designs of the Hitler clique and its intention to attack the Soviet Union were apparent to the Soviet Government and the leadership of the Soviet Armed Forces. But an error was made in determining the time of this attack. Stalin mistakenly believed that in the immediate future Hitler would not venture to violate the treaty of non-aggression without a pretext. He kept postponing vital precautionary military measures for fear of giving Hitler such a pretext.[16]

According to Isaac Deutscher, a Stalin biographer, "[Stalin] now committed one of those errors to which the over-cunning are sometimes liable. He dismissed all ill omens and was confident that he, by himself, with his tactical skill and flair for sharp political turns, could retrieve the situation."[17]

In May 1941, Stalin made several moves that were calculated to placate Hitler, but he received no German sign of appreciation. On June 14, exactly one week before the German invasion, Stalin made one more attempt, by authorizing the official news agency to issue a statement soundly criticizing the British ambassador for spreading rumors of an "impending Russo-German war."

Deutscher observes:

> It would be difficult to find, even in the diplomatic records of the Second World War, anything quite as pathetic. And yet this bizarre statement, where Stalin praised before the whole world those who next week were to unmask themselves as Russia's mortal enemies and taunted those who next week would be her only allies, this bizarre statement was not wholly false. It was true, as Stalin claimed, that Germany had made no demands on Russia. He evidently expected Hitler to raise demands over which it would be possible to bargain. German attacks on Austria, Czechoslovakia, and Po-

land had indeed been preceded by open claims and loud threats. Stalin apparently thought that Hitler would act according to precedent. Because he did not see the usual danger signals he refused to admit the imminent danger. In his statement he invited Hitler, in that devious manner which Hitler understood so well in March 1939, to put forward his claims and to start negotiations. Hitler did not take the hint.[18]

When Hitler's armies struck, the Soviet Union suffered dangerous initial reverses, which resulted in part from Stalin's desire not to "provoke" Hitler by fully mobilizing and deploying the Soviet forces.

Stalin had received plenty of correct warnings from various sources, including the governments of Britain and the United States, of the impending German attack. Not unreasonably, he distrusted warnings from people who had an interest in provoking war between Germany and Russia. Evidently, Stalin wanted more time to prepare the Soviet Union militarily, and this wishfulness led him to disregard even the strongest indications of an impending German attack and to misjudge Hitler's potential range of behavior. This is the element of wishfulness. Furthermore, the Germans practiced deception.[19] Finally, preconception, based on the study of the past, played an important part. Soviet intelligence had noticed that Hitler had previously made exorbitant demands prior to initiating military aggression. He had done so vis-à-vis Austria, Czechoslovakia, and Poland. Stalin expected this pattern to persist, and he felt safe as long as Germany did not present him with a new set of demands; but in the end, he found that, this time, Hitler did not repeat the pattern. Preconception as well as wishfulness and deception misled Stalin.

The historical record is full of instances of how intelligence officials relied on the persistence of previous patterns of conduct and were proved wrong when these patterns were broken. Thus, for several weeks in 1962, despite much evidence to the contrary, American intelligence discounted information that the Soviet Union was deploying intermediate-range ballistic missiles in Cuba. These officials did so because a close study of past Soviet behavior indicated a consistent record of avoiding "adventurist" military moves. They simply could not believe that the Soviet government would do anything as imprudent and flamboyant.[20] But it did. Egypt and Syria achieved surprise in attacking Israel in October 1973. The previously efficient intelligence apparatus of Israel misread a number of key indicators, because it *assumed* that the Arabs would not attack.[21] This assumption was based in part on the belief, derived from plenty of previous experience, that the Arab countries were incapable of maintaining political and military secrecy, which is a prerequisite of achieving surprise. This time, however, the Arab governments had the capability. In July 1974, when civil strife had broken out in Cyprus, Turkey threatened to invade unless a satisfactory settlement was achieved at once. American officials were apparently surprised by the actual landing of Turkish troops, because on similar occasions in 1964 and 1967, Turkey had made the same threat and had assembled troops only to stop short of landing in Cyprus.[22] It is natural for intelligent threat perception to study an actor's past behavior with great care. But as many historical examples show, it is dangerous to project analytical conclusions into the future without serious qualifications and hedging. To do so is to court surprise. The past does not repeat itself automatically.

On the whole, Hitler was scarcely more realistic than his counterparts in matters of threat perception. He clearly did not want the general war that his actions precipitated, and this alone amounts to a colossal blunder. Before every aggressive step he took, the German military advised him against it. They feared that war might break out and that Germany would once more suffer defeat. Every time until 1939 he proved right in calculating on the unwillingness of Britain and France to go to war. Thus, he became overconfident of his ability to predict the moves of his foreign opponents. But it is doubtful that he had been shrewdly realistic in his assessments earlier on. Snell says that "the foreign policy of Nazism was often based upon doctrinaire fixations rather than upon a realistic assessment of international power relationships. To set the illusory character of Hitler's foreign policy apart from Bismarck's and for want of a better name, the spirit of the Nazi program might be called one of 'romantic *Realpolitik.*' "[23] This suggests that Hitler's intuition was affected by doctrinaire assumptions about foreign statesmen. In his earlier predictions, he may have been right, in part at least, for the wrong reasons. It is also clear from Snell's account that the Nazi leaders, sharing a common habit, were unwilling to accept intelligence reports that contradicted their preconceptions. The Nazi leaders rejected information they received from Germany's foreign service when it conflicted with their preconceptions. The cautions thus received were "discounted as expressions of personal conservatism, weak nerves, or even disloyalty. Thus the makers of doctrinaire and illusory policy strengthened their own illusions. This was to be one cause of blunder in Hitler's conduct of foreign policy in 1939."[24]

The United States was much more remote from the events leading up to World War II, and it was not until it was under way—and especially after the fall of France, Belgium, the Netherlands, Denmark, and Norway—that the question of threat perception became an issue. At the beginning of 1940, the bulk of the American public was still bound to an isolationist posture. The internationalists feared that Hitler's conquest of Europe would create a world power that would threaten the survival of the United States as a free and democratic society. In June a Gallup poll showed that about two out of three people felt that if England and France fell, Germany would eventually attack the United States; five out of eight expected their country eventually to go to war against Germany; and three out of four believed that the United States was not giving enough aid to Britain and France. However, only one out of fourteen favored a declaration of war on Germany:

> Although the American public sensed danger in June, 1940, it remained in great part bound by the continentalist, anti-European, and pacifist ideas which had prevailed for two decades. Major ethnic minorities still were torn between old and new allegiances. Many in the American interior continued to believe their civilization safe from any external threat. The danger to America was not yet direct enough or of sufficient duration to convert public opinion from one extreme, isolation, to the other, intervention. Thus is was that by the beginning of June, 1940, no American leader had publicly demanded war.[25]

What stands out clearly in his American example is that national threat perception can be very divided and contentious, sharply constraining the government. Disagreement in the United States was no doubt facilitated by the fact that an Axis victory in Europe presaged no direct or immediate threats to the security of this country. To infer such threats, over the longer run, demanded analytical competence and imagination. Also interesting is the strong conditioning by ideals and slogans (e.g., pacifism, neutralism) and by emotional attachments that were anchored in ethnic identifications and animosities. Americans of Anglo-Saxon descent and American Jews tended to identify with Britain and France and to support the interventionist cause. Americans of German and Irish descent tended to support isolationism.[26]

Our second major case concerns threat perceptions between the United States and Japan. Following the Russo-Japanese War and the establishment of Japanese control over Korea, Willard Straight was among those who sounded the alarm. What seemed most serious to him was not

> simply Japanese domination over Korea, but the likelihood of Japanese suzerainty over Asia and the subsequent rise of all Asia against the West. That is why he constantly returned to the theme of incompatibility between East and West. Because of the very incompatibility, the West must strive to prevent the revolt of the East under Japanese domination. What Straight was expressing was a notion of the "yellow peril." Japan's successful war against a Western power was a spectacle which had been forecast by some since the 1890's but which had not seemed a real possibility. Here was the East rising against the West, Orientals against Occidentals.
>
> In its crudest form this anti-Orientalism was expressed as an anti-Japanese movement on the west coast of the United States. . . . As the San Francisco *Examiner* put it, "Once the war with Russia is over, the brown stream of Japanese immigration" would inundate California. The kind of Japanese that Straight had found in Korea—uncultured, uneducated, uncouth

—would "invade" the west coast, creating all varieties of problems, ranging from labor competition to sexual crimes. The result would be a "complete Orientalization of the Pacific Coast," and it would cease to be truly American.[27]

President Theodore Roosevelt shared the belief that Japanese civilization, modes of thought, and motivation were different from their Western counterparts and that Orientals were at least anti-Occidental.[28] The first serious perception of Japan as a danger not only to American interests in the Far East but eventually to the United States itself was evidently conditioned by the racial concepts and vulgarized Darwinian thoughts that, around the turn of the century, were widespread in this country and in Europe. But Western observers were also alarmed by the military prowess displayed by industrializing Japan. The latter had suddenly become a great power and was conspicuously eager to imitate the ruthless imperialist expansion in which Western powers were engaged. The thought of a possible clash across the Pacific at some future time was not fanciful under the circumstances. Considerations of major war were commonplace among the other great powers at the time.

Reciprocal fears were expressed in Japan:

> It is revealing that the Japanense navy, which had earlier eschewed continentalism and pan-Asianism lest these should create trouble with the United States, now came to view Japanese-American relations as critical and heading toward a showdown. The continued anti-Japanese agitation in the west coast and the opposition of the United States to Japanese policy in Asia were driving the naval strategists in Japan to a fatalistic view of their relations with the American navy. One of them wrote in 1913, "The sudden emergence of the California question, coupled with the China question, impels us to action and gives us a great opportunity to promote a great union of Japan and China." The espousal of such a pan-Asianist view by a naval spokesman revealed a fundamental change in the Japanese view of America. Four years later, in 1917, although the two nations were now allies against Germany, the Japanese navy formally adopted the policy of viewing the United States as the most likely enemy. . . . In February 1918, a staff officer of the Navy General Staff urged a Siberian expedition in order to prevent the United States from controlling Siberia, since it could then close in on Japan from the north, west (China), east (Hawaii, Guam), and south (Philippines). Should the United States oppose a Japanese expedition to Siberia, Japan should not hesitate to go to war with it.[29]

Of course, neither in Japan nor in the United States was there agreement on regarding the other power as a potential threat. But significant groups did so in both countries. As these views greatly strengthened American sympathy with China and also created opposition to Japanese designs in China, so Japanese anxieties helped to fuel aggressive expansionism on the Asian mainland. It often happens that threat perception begets aggression aimed at strengthening one's position; such aggression, in turn, evokes hostile reponses in the outside world and, in a continuing vicious circle, further threats are perceived as a result.

A degree of amity returned to Japanese-American relations by the early 1920s. But this rapprochement evaporated quickly when Japan seized Manchuria in 1932–1933 and invaded China proper in 1937, thus causing world peace to seem to be as threatened in the Far East as it was in Europe. A major factor in this development was the romantic attachment to China which had been growing in he United States. However, vis-à-vis the troubles brewing in Europe, isolationist attitudes at first muted the American response to Far Eastern events. Only in 1939 and 1940 did more and more of the American elite reorder their perspectives on how world developments were threatening American security and other interests. The new focus was no longer concentrated on the fate of China. According to Iriye:

> There still exists the myth, shared by many scholars in the three countries, that the United States and Japan went to war over China, and that, whether for moral, economic, or other motives, the United States was determined to prevent Japanese domination of China....
>
> Some contemporaries in the United States, China, and Japan, however, clearly saw the key issues in the late 1930's. In America, there is no doubt that, beginning in 1938, the conviction grew that the East Asian crisis was no longer an isolated phenomenon but was part of a developing world crisis. Italy and Germany had revealed their intention of altering the status quo by force even before 1936, but there was a time lag between these developments and the realization in the United States of the seriousness of the crisis....
>
> In the minds of American policy makers, a clear link was established between the developments in Europe and in East Asia. There emerged the possibility, as they saw it, that the aggressive nations, in particular Germany and Japan, might band together and collectively menace the status quo and peace in the whole world. It seemed imperative to respond to the challenge if America's security and its concomitant, peace in the world, were to be maintained. Aggression in Asia must be resisted to discourage lawless action in Europe. Moral globalism was given official status by security considerations....
>
> It did not matter whether the aggressor or the victim of aggression was in Europe or in Asia, a democracy or a socialist state. What mattered was the distinction between the party of order and that standing for forceful alteration of the status quo.[30]

The new perspective which restructured American threat perception—and which led ultimately to the United States intervention in Vietnam—was not regional but global. American security was now seen as requiring a particular world order which could be maintained only by the global commitment of American power to the preservation of the status quo. American threat perception became increasingly focused on the Axis powers, which were identified as aggressor states. Japan was one of them. She was perceived as being bent on upsetting existing international order as much by her drive toward southeast Asia as by her attempt to subjugate China.

To advance southward was a basic Japanese policy after 1938. The addition of British, French, and Dutch colonies, which were rich in natural resources, to the Japanese empire would make Japan more self-sufficient, and especially less dependent on American oil and iron. Iriye wrote:

> By 1940, when southern advance was made a national policy, top naval circles had also come to the conclusion that Japanese action in southeast Asia would bring about conflict not only with Britain but also with the United States. This was because of the view, held by the navy, that Britain and America could not be separated; once Japan struck at British colonies, the United States would be bound to intervene. The question, therefore, was whether war with these two powers justified the policy of southern advance. By late 1940 section chiefs of the Navy Ministry and the Naval General Staff came to the belief that since war with America was sooner or later inevitable, Japan should take the initiative and advance into southern Indochina and the Dutch East Indies to secure naval bases and strategic raw materials. Circular reasoning here is notable. For naval strategists, the policy of southern advance would make conflict with the United States inevitable; since war was bound to occur, Japan should advance southward to prepare itself for the conflict.[31]

Japan's aggressive imperialist push, which, according to Iriye, made Japan an enemy in American eyes, was apparently motivated, in large part at least, by Japanese anxieties over an eventual clash with the United States and, hence, by the need to make the Japanese empire more self-sufficient economically. This is another telling example of the spiraling of mutual threat perception between two opponents. *A* perceives a threat in *B*'s behavior. *B*, perceiving *A*'s reaction as a threat, continues with the behavior that is bound to increase *A*'s threat perception. It is easy for the perception of threats to be self-fulfilling. Even if it is doubtfully justified at first, the undoubting perception of threats can make them indubitable. Apprehension on either side can invoke apprehension on the other. This is very different from the cautious style of the Eyre Crowe memoranda which correctly regarded threat estimates as hypotheses that could turn out to be false. Indeed, to the view of perceiving Germany as menacing Britain and her interests, Crowe offered an alternative that was also capable of explaining German behavior but did not require the British government to regard Germany as very threatening.³²

The Japanese military and civilian leaders who eventually decided on war against the United States were governed by various misperceptions, even in the area of their professional competence. For example, army leaders, who had badly underestimated Chinese resistance, assumed that Germany and Italy would be victorious in Europe. Navy leaders failed to understand the importance of the aircraft carrier and of amphibious landings, so they stuck to the battleship, which represented an obsolescent technology.³³ Threat perception that focuses on the capabilities of an external actor relative to one's own capabilities becomes easily distorted by overestimating or underestimating one's own strength for one reason or another, usually predispositional. The Japanese planners could hardly ignore the material superiority of the United States. But in their eyes, American material superiority was offset by Japanese moral superiority. The United States was assumed to be a country of low morale, unable to put up with a prolonged struggle.³⁴ In this connection, there was also a predisposition to project past success into the future.

Robert Butow observes:

> In fairness it must be said that the mind-over-matter factor had demonstrated its value again and again throughout Japanese history—the most recent example, and the one most often cited in the Japan of the 1930's, being the Russo-Japanese war of 1904–1905. . . . As General Kojiro Sato had remarked some years later, in explaining how ten thousand Japanese could defeat fifteen thousand Russians: "To divide 4 by 2 and obtain 2 is an ordinary material judgment. But if we should obtain 3, an invisible coefficient (the Japanese spirit) must have been multiplied by the visible quotient."³⁵

The example suggests how an actor's treasured self-image can interfere with correct situational perception.

We conclude this case study by asking why American leaders and intelligence officers were surprised by the Japanese attack on Pearl Harbor on December 7, 1941. It was certainly not for want of relevant information. An American cryptanalyst had broken the Japanese diplomatic code used for dispatches between Tokyo and Japanese embassies abroad. Cryptanalysts had also succeeded in deciphering codes employed by Japanese agents in American cities. By analyzing radio traffic, the navy had been able to deduce the location and composition of Japanese fleets. Competent political analysis had been supplied by Ambassador Grew and his staff in Tokyo. Two changes in the call signs of Japanese warships on November 1 and December 1 caused some delay in radio analysis but indicated that something unusual was afoot. As early as January 1941, a rumor originating with the Peruvian embassy in Tokyo stated that the

Japanese were preparing a surprise attack on Pearl Harbor, but this was regarded as fantastic.[36]

Why, then, were American officials not expecting an attack and why had they failed to put American forces on a cautionary alert? One reason was that no single person or agency ever had all the incoming information at any given moment. But the principal reasons were those analyzed by Roberta Wohlstetter:

> First of all, it is much easier *after* the event to sort the relevant from the irrelevant signals. After the event, of course, a signal is always crystal clear; we can now see what disaster it was signaling, since the disaster has occurred. But before the event it is obscure and pregnant with conflicting meanings. It comes to the observer embedded in an atmosphere of "noise," i.e., in the company of all sorts of information that is useless and irrelevant for predicting the particular disaster. . . .
>
> In short, we failed to anticipate Pearl Harbor not for want of the relevant materials, but because of a plethora of irrelevant ones. . . .
>
> . . . .
>
> For every signal that came into the information net in 1941 there were usually several plausible alternative explanations, and it is not surprising that our observers and analysts were inclined to select the explanations that fitted the popular hypotheses. . . . Apparently human beings have a stubborn attachment to old beliefs and an equally stubborn resistance to new material that will upset them. . . .
>
> A third factor that served to increase the natural noise level was the positive effort made by the enemy to keep the relevant signals quiet. The Japanese security system was an important and successful block to perception. It was able to keep the strictest cloak of secrecy around the Pearl Harbor attack and to limit knowledge only to those closely associated with the details of military and naval planning. . . .
>
> In addition to keeping certain signals quiet, the enemy tried to create noise, and sent false signals into our information system by carrying on elaborate "spoofs." False radio traffic made us believe that certain ships were maneuvering near the mainland of Japan. . . .
>
> A fifth barrier to accurate perception was the fact that the relevant signals were subject to change, often very sudden change. This was true even of the so-called static intelligence, which included data on capabilities and the composition of military forces. In the case of our 1941 estimates of the infeasibility of torpedo attacks in the shallow waters of Pearl Harbor, or the underestimation of the range and performance of the Japanese Zero, the changes happened too quickly to appear in an intelligence estimate. . . .
>
> To these barriers of noise and security we must add the fact that the necessarily precarious character of intelligence information and predictions was

reflected in the wording of instructions to take action. The warning messages were somewhat vague and ambiguous. Enemy moves are often subject to reversal on short notice, and this was true for the Japanese. They had plans for canceling their attacks on American possessions in the Pacific up to 24 hours before the time set for attack. . . . The fact that intelligence predictions must be based on moves that are almost always reversible makes understandable the reluctance of the intelligence analyst to make bold assertions. Even if he is willing to risk his reputation on a firm prediction of attack at a definite time and place, no commander will in turn lightly risk the penalties and costs of a full alert. . . .

Last but not least we must also mention the blocks to perception and communication inherent in any large bureaucratic organization, and those that stemmed from intraservice and interservice rivalries. The most glaring example of rivalry in the Pearl Harbor case was that between Naval War Plans and Naval Intelligence.[37]

Four factors stand out in explaining this underestimate of a threat. First, bureaucratic structures and proclivities cause decentralization, inertia, and rivalry. Second, information is ambiguous and contradictory, subject to alternative interpretation partly because the opponent practices deception. The information, which, in retrospect, was clearly correct, is intermixed with misinformation. Warning is seldom clear-cut. Third, intelligence people are reluctant to make a firm prediction of a course of action that could be reversed. While the second factor is situational, the other two are dispositional. But the weightiest dispositional factor is the fourth: "human attention is directed by beliefs as to what is likely to occur."[38] Since threat perception involves inferences from usually fragmentary and ambiguous information, predetermined expectations and beliefs permit people to sustain the interpretation that fits. "Wishfulness in conditions of uncertainty is natural and is hard to banish simply by exhortation."[39]

That the United States was surprised by the attack on Pearl Harbor is far from an exceptional experience. A little earlier, the Japanese had made a surprise attack on the British at Singapore, which Wohlstetter describes:

The stunning tactical success of the Japanese attack on the British at Singapore was made possible by the deeply held British faith in the impregnability of that fortress. . . . Yet the defenses of Singapore were rendered useless by military surprise in the form of an attack from an unexpected, northerly direction.

More recently, the Korean War provided some striking examples of surprise. The original North Korean attack was preceded by almost weekly maneuvers probing the border. These regular week-end penetrations built up so high a level of noise that on June 25, 1950, the actual initiation of hostilities was not distinguished from the preceding tests and false alarms.

The intervention of the Chinese, at a later stage of the Korean War, was preceded by mass movements of Chinese troops and explicit warnings by the Chinese government to our own, by way of India, that this was precisely what they would do if we crossed the 38th parallel. Nonetheless, in important respects, we were surprised by the Chinese Communist forces in November, 1950.[40]

For another example, we have noted earlier that despite a flood of telling signals in the summer of 1941, the German attack on the Soviet Union achieved total surprise. Facing a complex and changing real world, the peculiar mind-set of the perceiver makes attention selective. Various attitudes drive men to underestimate or overestimate threats. Man, it seems, not only tends to be a prisoner of his perceptions, his perceptions also are slaves to his predispositions.

The two cases we have examined in considerable detail indicate the major objects of anxiety regarding which threats may be sensed or anticipated by governments, elites, and publics. Historically speaking, the principal objects of concern have been: first, war itself and all the costs it entails even if defense succeeds; second, the very need to maintain or increase forces for deterrence and defense; third, defeat (including defeat of allies or friendly societies) and its various consequences in terms of losses of territory, population, allies and empire, economic assets, independence or autonomy, the future capacity for deterrence and defense, and so forth; and fourth, the breakdown of international order and the attendant expectations that war, defeat, and the loss of various external assets are becoming more likely than before. Moreover, since the capacity for deterrence and defense remains crucial as long as threats—whether actual, potential, or systemic—persist, changes in the capabilities of one's own state in comparison to the capabilities of other states tend to become matters of concern.

The practitioners of statecraft commonly understand these things. Two other things they understand far less well. One is that the behavior of one's own country can increase the possibility of war and defeat, as well as the collapse of international order; in other words, that one can be indirectly a threat to oneself by appearing threatening to others. Proper threat perception should include this dimension. The other is the astonishing failure to understand what is so easily observed historically, namely, that international threat perception is rarely done well. It is nearly always more or less defective, often grossly so. This seems to be one of the most primitive areas of statecraft. Yet everybody seems to assume that threat perception is easy. One notices the absence of procedural rules for minimizing error.

Our two case studies illuminate the difficulties involved in international threat perception. We have classified these difficulties as *intrinsic,* or intellectual, and *predispositional.* They are intrinsic when the international environment is, objectively speaking, hard to understand because information is poor or because it is hazardous to project the past or present into the future. They are predispositional when the actor's perception is distorted by intervening attitudes.

The course of history does not suggest that the intrinsic difficulties of threat perception are invariant. Such perception can be situationally, experientially, and strategically easy—or, rather, relatively easy. Threat perception can be *situationally easy* when the opponent's behavior is confidently known and leaves no doubt about acute danger. In 490 B.C. the Greeks *knew* that the Persians were coming to attack them. In the spring of 1588 the English *knew* that the Spanish armada was on its way to invade England. Of course, even in such situations the actual attack may fail to materialize for one reason or another. The deployment of a force poised to strike may have been a bluff. Or there might be second thoughts at the last moment, so that a planned strike might be called off. But the expectation of attack will be high. The perception of contingent threats is facilitated during periods when general state behavior in a system is highly aggressive. For European states during the seventeenth and eighteenth centuries, war was evidently commonplace. It broke out easily. Similarly, although there had been no continent-wide conflagration since the Napoleonic wars, European statesmen were generally aware of a high danger of general war around 1900. However, while it is relatively difficult during such periods to underestimate threats, is it also easy to *overestimate* them. The situational effect tends to be asymmetrical.

Threat perception is *experientially easy* for societies, especially weak ones, that have been subject to repeated attack and military pressure. They are naturally sensitive to the signs of danger or to its sudden eruption. Thus, in view of what has been happening to them over more than a century, threat perception is easy for contemporary Iran and Turkey. Powerful societies, however, can recover from error and muddle through. For materially weaker societies, the margin of survivable error is small, and historical experience produces alertness. Experience also tends to affect the time perspective. At the present time, many observers find it hard to understand why the Soviet leadership senses keenly a threat from China. After all, they reflect, China is only a fledgling nuclear power, whose nuclear capabilities are far inferior to the enormous ones of the U.S.S.R.; the Soviets are likewise superior in conventional military forces. The explanation lies in the long time horizon that is characteristic of Russian thinking in these matters. Russia has suffered (as well as undertaken) repeated invasions, some of which have come from the East; therefore the threat perceptions of her leaders have a long range. Given a long time horizon, the absence of immediate threat is not necessarily reassuring.

Threat perception, finally, is *strategically easy* when societies are prepared to see a threat in any state whose military strength is either great or growing relative to their own, even when that state exhibits no present indication of hostile intent. The crude strategy for survival is to strike at once. Threat perception is then facilitated, because it is easier to estimate the capabilities of states than their intentions. Thus, writing about the genesis of the Peloponnesian War, Thucydides stated: "The real but unavowed cause I consider to have been the growth of the power of Athens, and the alarm which it inspired in Lacedaemon; this made war inevitable."[41] Indeed, what finally alarmed the latter was when Athens, which already possessed a superior navy, built a wall to protect itself from assault on land. The Lacedaemonians begged Athens to refrain from doing so; but the Athenians refused.

The Romans acted on similar considerations, as Balsdon points out:

> Indeed, in the first two stages of the expansion, the conquest of Italy and the acquisition of the Western Empire, it is difficult to find any driving impulse other than that of simple fear, however much that fear may have involved (and, later, have been replaced by) a lust for power. Conquest was first the only alternative to being conquered and made subject—by the Etruscans, by the Gauls, by the Samnites.[42]

Thus, after Carthaginian advances on Sicily had led Rome to the first Punic War and to victory in 241 B.C., the Romans became suspicious when, after having been defeated and having made a peace treaty, Carthage built a new powerful army.[43]

According to Plutarch, Marcus Cato, the famous Roman statesman, visited the Carthaginians. Upon his return

> he acquainted the senate that the former defeats and blows given the Carthaginians had not so much diminished their strength, as it had abated their imprudence and folly; and that they were not becoming weaker, but more experienced in war. . . . that the peace and league they had made was but a kind of suspension of war which awaited a fairer opportunity to break out.[44]

Moreover, Cato was worried lest past success had caused Rome to become corrupt and debilitated:

> It seemed a perilous thing to Cato that a city which had always been great, and was now grown sober and wise, by reason of its former calamities, should still lie, as it were, in wait for the follies and dangerous excesses of the ever-powerful Roman people; so that he thought it the wisest course to have all outward dangers removed, when they had so many inward ones among themselves.[45]

However, while these three factors make threat perception *relatively easy*, they do not insure realistic estimates. They only raise the probability that fairly realistic expectations will emerge.

Certainly, historical experience is not a sure guide to correct perception in the present. Such experience may generate the belief that the specific past will repeat itself. For example, after more than a century of intermittent war between France and Austria, Metternich—the famous Austrian statesman—simply and wrongly concluded that France would remain Austria's potential enemy in the future:

> Metternich's foreign policy rested on the assumption that western affairs were primary: French aggression, he supposed, was the main threat to the Vienna settlement, and the security of Germany and Italy his main problem. The assumption was wrong: France had passed her zenith and would never again seek to dominate Europe. The threat to Austria's existence, which finally destroyed her, came from Russia, not from France, and the deepest Austrian problem was the Eastern Question.[46]

Threat perception can become stereotyped as a result of historical experience.

Our case studies have repeatedly shown the risk of simply projecting past experience into the future. The risk is magnified whenever "group think" (e.g., in bureaucracies) becomes expressed in rigid operational doctrines, or even in formal ideologies (as in the case of Leninism). Rigid self-indoctrination occurred in the United States government after the early 1950s, when the at first pragmatic perception of aggressive Soviet moves in eastern Europe and the Middle East[47]—which may have been inspired in part by Soviet anxieties about Soviet security—gradually hardened into the routine assumption that there was a world-wide monolithic and ever-aggressive Communist movement, and thus induced excessive threat perception. One factor in this development was America's determination not to repeat the mistake of "Munich," where British and French appeasement led to an agreement (in 1938) that in effect gave Hitler a free hand in Czechoslovakia. The Munich Agreement was seen in retrospect as having encouraged Hitler to continue with the aggressive moves that led to World War II. The lessons of Munich were: "Appeasement does not pay"; "Better to nip aggression in the bud"; and so forth.[48]

Even when threat perception is situationally easy, relatively speaking, mistakes are hard to avoid, because conflicting predispositions lead the clearest signals to be ignored, as we have seen in Stalin's case in 1941. Furthermore, awareness of a heightened danger of war in a regional system, and consequent alertness, does not preclude misperceptions on the precise nature and timing of threats to a particular country. Threat perception was situationally easy during the three decades preceding World War I. Awareness of danger was generally high. Nevertheless, uncertainties abounded. French leaders were conscious of

Germany's larger population and economic production, so they sought to restore the balance by building a colonial empire and, especially, by acquiring powerful allies. But they were by no means united about the priority to be accorded to defense in the allocation of resources. Those who wanted increased social outlays tended to downgrade the threats to French security.[49] The British, who had been preoccupied with the preservation of their colonial empire and had held aloof from European affairs, around 1900 recognized their isolation as a liability. According to Laurence Lafore:

> The British now accurately appraised the perils of standing alone and in every sphere hastened the policy of disengagement, of transferring or sharing responsibilities. In the West, the transfer of power to the United States was sealed in the Hay-Pauncefote Treaty, by which the British conferred, as it were, their legal rights to construct a canal across the Central American Isthmus upon the United States. In 1902, Great Britain made an alliance with Japan, a vigorous, newly westernized state, the only modern and wholly independent power not governed by Europeans. Japan was to serve as a counterweight to Russian scheming in Manchuria. British isolation officially ended.[50]

After 1906 the British foreign service focused on Germany as the threat to Britain. What was expressed tentatively in Eyre Crowe's famous memorandum soon became an article of faith. Crowe's memorandum was then "the statement of a creed, and it became a test of orthodoxy."[51] The result was the Entente Cordiale with France and Russia. In France, Théophile Delcassé and others had been ready to conclude an alliance with the United Kingdom:

> When he took over the Foreign Office, Delcassé's views on foreign policy were clearly and definitely formed. Talking to Paléologue on 29 December 1898 he said, "for Russia, as for France, England is a rival, a competitor whose proceedings are often very disagreeable; but she is not an enemy and certainly not THE ENEMY! ... Ah my dear Paléologue if only Russia, England and France could be allied against Germany!" He confessed to being "haunted" by the notion of an Anglo-French alliance. Its achievement was his mission.[52]

The relations between the great European powers were bedeviled by frequent misunderstandings and miscalculations. Two examples may be cited briefly. The naval race between Germany and Britain played an important part in exacerbating relations between the two countries. Beginning in 1897, Germany decided to become a naval power, thereby challenging Britain's "two-power standard"—that is, a British fleet as strong as the two next-largest navies. In retrospect, it is fairly clear that in building a navy, German leaders had no aggressive designs on Britain, but wanted the navy as a badge of great-power-hood, as a status symbol. The British were misled by extremist chauvinist statements in some of the German press: they never understood German motivations on this matter. Conversely, the Germans failed to comprehend that naval superiority was the unquestionable symbol of security to the British. The British public was not very much interested in foreign affairs; but it was united on one question: "the maintenance of naval superiority was known to be a matter of life and death to an island Power, dependent upon imported foodstuffs."[53]

The establishment of the Entente Cordiale was a surprise to Germany, whose leaders had assumed that Anglo-French and Anglo-Russian differences of interest could never be satisfactorily solved. Blusteringly, they put pressure on France—for example, by fomenting a crisis over French designs on Morocco—in the hope that lack of British and Russian support would sow distrust between the countries. The Germans only succeeded in solidifying the Entente Cordiale.[54]

In the end, the arms race that immediately preceded World War I was a dangerous overreaction to threat perceptions; and the overreaction served to sharpen anxieties. According to Albertini:

> The armaments race, which between 1912 and 1914 characterized the policy of all the European Great Powers, had as its object the security of each one of them; but "instead of a sense of security (writes Grey) there had been produced a sense of fear which was yearly increasing. Europe was afraid of the German Army.... Preparations for war had produced fear, and fear predisposes to violence and catastrophe." On 29 May 1914, Colonel House, Wilson's emissary in Europe wrote from Berlin to the President: "The situation is extraordinary. It is militarism run stark mad. Unless someone acting for you can bring about a different understanding, there is some day to be an awful cataclysm. No one in Europe can do it. There is too much hatred, too many jealousies."[55]

There still is no complete agreement on the causes of World War I, though most historians share the conclusion that the leading powers blundered into a kind of war that none of them wanted to precipitate. One factor that facilitated its outbreak was the gross misperception on the part of all major belligerents about what sort of war it would be, should it not prove avoidable. Everywhere, diplomacy was based on the belief that a war, if it came, would be short. As L. L. Farrar, Jr., has written:

> Most European leaders assumed a short war. This assumption may have been essential to their decision for war. Few of them would have opted for the war if they had foreseen a protracted, revolutionary or unsuccessful conflict. They assumed that a short war would be decisive, limited and productive. The assumption was therefore made because it was desirable and not because any evidence made it likely.[56]

This case demonstrates once more the power that wishful thinking has on threat perception. It was widely argued that industrialization and, especially, economic interdependence among the major powers had rendered a long war unfeasible. Military planners had planned for a brief and decisive war. But clearly, desire was father to the belief, even though war aims envisioned changes in the status quo so large as to be incompatible with everything but an all-out effort.

Finally, even when threat perception is relatively easy strategically because it is limited to monitoring comparative changes in the national military strength of states, it is often far from easy absolutely speaking. As Michael Howard points out:

> In the summer of 1870 the kingdom of Prussia and her German allies totally destroyed the military power of Imperial France. For nearly eighty years the defeated nation had given the law in military matters to Europe, whereas the victor, ten years earlier, had been the least of the continent's major military powers. Within a month Prussia established a military preeminence and a political hegemony which made the unification of Germany under her leadership a matter of course, and which only an alliance embracing nearly every major power in the world was to wrest from her half a century later.
>
> There was little precedent in the history of Europe for so dramatic a reversal. . . . In 1870 the Prussian army had to its credit the brilliant campaign of 1866 against Austria, but this was only one in the long series of defeats which the Hapsburgs had suffered at the hands of Prussia and France since the days of Eugene of Savoy. The completeness of the Prussian success in 1870 thus astounded the world. The incompetence of the French high command explained much: but the basic reasons for the catastrophe lay deeper, as the French themselves, in their humiliation, were to discern. The collapse at Sedan, like that of the Prussians at Jena sixty-four years earlier, was the result not simply of faulty command but of a faulty military system; and the military system of a nation is not an independent section of the social system but an aspect of it in its totality. The French had good reason to look on their disasters as a judgment. The social and economic developments of the past fifty years had brought about a military as well as an industrial revolution. The Prussians had kept abreast of it and France had not. Therein lay the basic cause of her defeat.[57]

Changes in the relative military strength of countries can take place very swiftly and for reasons that are not always easy to discern. After the Austrian-Prussian War of 1866 the French were aware of the growth of Prussian military power. So they enlarged their army and improved its armament:

> By the standards of its past campaigns the French army *was* ready; ready, as Trochu was later to write, "as it had been for the Crimean War, for the

Italian War, for the Mexican adventure, for all the military enterprises of that era; that is to say, ready to fight successfully and sometimes with brilliance against armies constituted and trained like itself." It was the tragedy of the French army, and of the French nation, that they did not realise in time that military organisation had entered into an entirely new age.[58]

The Prussians had understood the military implications of industrial development. Assisted by a brilliant general staff (itself a major innovation), their military planners perceived that the railroads, which then constituted a new and revolutionary system of transportation, permitted both speed of mobilization and the employment of large forces which could be concentrated quickly and overwhelmingly at the decisive points for decisive battles.[59] The French misunderstood the nature of the military threat confronting them. Their underlying misperception was largely an intellectual failure.

Such misperceptions are far from rare. Only some sixty years earlier, before the utter and ignominious rout of their army by the French at the battle of Jena (1806), the Prussian leadership had been totally ignorant of the revolutionary innovations in military doctrine, recruitment, and tactics that France had introduced during the French Revolution and that Napoleon had perfected. On the other hand, in 1914, French armies suffered heavy initial defeats by Germany because French military leaders, again misunderstanding military technology, had prepared for an offensive war of quick thrust, which the newest weapons, especially the machine gun, inhibited. Before World War II, French military leaders had opted, with equal fervor and more disastrous consequences, for a strictly defensive posture anchored in the Maginot line of fortification. As the Germans had well understood, the newest military technology then favored a fast war of movement that would rely on the shock effect of concentrated tanks and aircraft. The blitzkrieg was over in a matter of weeks.

As these examples suggest, the perception of relative military strength involves factors other than the things that are easily counted, such as military manpower, military budgets, and numbers of weapons. These other factors are the quality of military leadership, qualitative differences in arms and other matériel, the training and morale of troops, and the magnitude of military potential. These are things that make it difficult, even in the absence of distorting predispositions, to estimate the precise nature of military threats.

Indeed, after looking at circumstances that render international threat perception relatively easy—though not, as we have established, easy absolutely speaking—we must now inquire into conditions that make correct perception especially hard. Situational problems obviously multiply when societies are strange to one another. It is not surprising, for instance, that before the Russo-Japanese war of 1904–1905, the Russian leadership vastly underestimated Japanese military capabilities. This was the first time, after the industrial revolution had expanded significantly, that a European power had fought a Far Eastern one that had only recently begun to modernize. The Russian forces were defeated both on land and on the sea.[60] Strangeness between societies has often been extreme in the course of history. Thus, the Aztecs and Incas were utterly unprepared to cope with the Spanish conquistadors.[61] When Pizarro struck out into the Incan empire in 1532, his eventual success was no doubt facilitated by the facts that the Incas were engaged in dynastic warfare and that an epidemic had killed many thousands of people, including some of the leaders. But his force was tiny—62 horsemen and 106 foot soldiers; and when they reached Cajamarca in the high Andes, they found themselves in the midst of a large Inca army, the size of which filled the Spaniards with confusion and trepidation. Hemming has described this event:

> Despite their experience, Pizarro's 150 men had marched into an impasse and were now thoroughly frightened and desperate. All that they could decide during that anxious night was to employ the various tactics and advantages that had proved successful in the Caribbean. They could use surprise, attacking first without provocation, and take advantage of the novelty of their appearance and fighting methods. . . . They had in mind the tactic that had succeeded so well in the conquest of Mexico: the kidnapping of the head of state.[62]

They managed, indeed, to capture the chief by means of trickery:

> The Spaniards immediately asked the glaring question: Why had a ruler of Atahualpa's experience and power walked into such an obvious trap? The answer was quite clear. The Inca had totally misjudged and underestimated his opponents. . . .
>
> The Inca . . . could not conceive that, with the odds so completely in his favour, the Spaniards would be the first to attack. Nor could he imagine that an attack would come without warning or provocation, before he had even held his meeting with Governor Pizarro.
>
> The Spaniards themselves had acted in terror and desperation, and could scarcely believe the crushing success of their ambush. "Truly, it was not accomplished by our own forces for there were so few of us. It was by the grace of God, which is great."[63]

To explore another case of political and cultural strangeness, it is interesting to ask how the Chinese and Japanese perceived the threat that the imperialist Western powers presented to them, beginning in the middle of the nineteenth century, and why it took the Chinese so much longer than the Japanese to understand the full nature of this threat.

During the eighteenth and nineteenth centuries, Chinese emperors firmly refused the sort of regular diplomatic relations that were practiced in Europe.

The traditional concept of relations with "barbarians" (i.e., people not of Chinese culture) was a system of tributary but nonexploitative relations. Since China was regarded as the center of the universe, other states could not be conceded equality of status. Only patron-client relations were conceivable.[64] The majority of mandarins regarded foreign affairs as a lowly, if not unworthy, occupation. The tardiness with which the Chinese government and elite came to comprehend the threat of sea-borne imperialist power can be attributed in part to the facts that no official Chinese mission was sent to the West until 1866 and that regular diplomatic relations were not established until 1877.[65] Their traditional disposition inhibited the systematic gathering of information.

The appearance of hostile foreigners at the Chinese boundaries was not, of course, a novel experience. Such threats had come from Central Asia repeatedly over the millennia. Beginning in the sixteenth century, moreover, the Chinese were affected by Russia's drive into Siberia, and they dealt with this threat by defense and diplomacy in fairly realistic fashion.[66] They were nevertheless totally unprepared for dealing with maritime Western aggression. That they were facing a hostile threat was clear to them after the Opium War. What they did not understand until much later were the precise nature of the threat, the copious sources of power behind it, and the immense inferiority of their ability to deter and defend. The slow process of increasing perception went through three phases.

After China's defeat by British arms in 1840, it took the Chinese rulers and elite two decades before they acknowledged the need to study the West—a necessity that the Japanese had understood before Commodore Perry's arrival in 1853. This was the first phase.[67] There were a few scholar-officials—such as Lin Tse-hsu and Wei Yuan—who recognized the need to study the things that made Western forces militarily superior, namely, modern warships, firearms, and military training. They advised that China could only protect itself by adopting these innovations and by simultaneously practicing a diplomacy that would set one barbarian against the other. But the Manchu dynasty was more concerned with securing its domestic rule, especially after the outbreak of the Taiping Rebellion, than with preserving the territorial integrity of China.

The second phase began after British and French troops had fought their way into Peking in 1860. This shock induced a change in the court's attitude and in its policy.[68] The prototype of a foreign office was set up. A "theory of self-strengthening" emerged. One of the most perceptive scholars, Feng Kuei-fen, invented the concept. To quote from one of his studies:

> The largest country on the globe today, with a vast area of 10,000 *li*, is yet controlled by small barbarians. . . . We are shamefully humiliated by those four nations [Britain, Russia, US and France] in the recent treaties—not

because our climate, soil, or resources are inferior to theirs, but because our people are really inferior. . . . Why are they small and yet strong? Why are we large and yet weak? We must try to discover some means to become their equal, and that also depends upon human effort. Regarding the present situation there are several major points: in making use of the ability of our manpower, with no one neglected, we are inferior to the barbarians; in securing the benefit of the soil, with nothing wasted, we are inferior to the barbarians; in maintaining a close relationship between the ruler and the people, with no barrier between them, we are inferior to the barbarians; and in the necessary accord of word with deed, we are also inferior to the barbarians. The way to correct these four points lies with ourselves, for they can be changed at once if only our Emperor would set the general policy right.[69]

It was widely recognized, during this phase, that Western pressure could not be resisted by simply introducing better ships and guns while leaving the traditional Chinese system intact. The need was to study both Western technology as a whole and Western science, which had bred it, and to start with the industrialization of the country. Appropriate schools and arsenals were established, and some modest administrative reforms were undertaken. But the reform movement began to stagnate before long. On the surface, this resulted from bureaucratic conservatism, inertia, and incompetence. But the essential cause was the failure of even the most perceptive Chinese to see that the foreign threat could not be resisted by some sort of synthesis of the traditional regime and Confucian principles, on the one hand, and Western arms, technology, and science, on the other. To grasp the impossibility of this was no mean intellectual problem, for this demanded the startling recognition that traditional China, with its core values, was not viable in the face of these new external threats. For Chinese society to survive as an autonomous body, it had to give up what its elite treasured most.

The third phase[70] began after China's defeat by Japan in 1895, which was regarded as particularly humiliating, and the Boxer uprising of 1898. Japan's shattering victory over the new Chinese army and navy—which was the result of a generation of effort at modernization—made it clear that modernization in China had been too superficial. The Boxer uprising sealed the fate of the corrupt Manchu dynasty. Now a large proportion of the scholar-official class realized that the existing political structure was incompatible with China's survival, and some now perceived the ultimate bases of Western power and, therefore, the need for the most profound transformation of Chinese society. An example is Yen Fu. Benjamin Schwartz represents his views thus:

> The fundamental thesis is stridently proclaimed. The ultimate source of Western power—of the difference between East and West—lies not merely in weapons and technology, not simply in economic or even political orga-

nization, or in any institutional arrangement. The ultimate source is an entirely different vision of reality. It is to be sought in the realm of ideas and values.[71]

Yen Fu came to believe that the Western idea of the freedom of the individual

> means the free exercise of all human capacities and functions—the creation of conditions which release and condition constructive human energies. . . . The motive power of these energies is the enlightened sense of self-interest in the individual. . . . The energies which ultimately account for the wealth and power of the social organisms of the West are energies latent in the individual.[72]

Yen Fu, in other words, saw in the modern ethos, which had inspired Western man since the Renaissance, the mainspring of the explosion of power that, in however acquisitive and aggressive a form, hit the Far East at this time. Hence, he was able fully to perceive the Western threat.

Three facts stand out especially in the slow evolution of Chinese threat perception. First, cultural strangeness made the task intellectually difficult. Second, the Chinese elite was divided in its threat perceptions. Third, the dispositional factor was predominant. To perceive threat perception as Yen Fu and his associates did was to infer the obsolescence of the Chinese political, as well as its social, system. This was obviously difficult to recognize for the class of scholar-officials who were the beneficiaries of traditional structures.

Why was Japan's reaction to the challenge of the West so prompt, purposeful, and sure? Why did it comprehend the nature of the threat with only a minimum of hesitation? The initial Japanese response to the preindustrial colonial powers (e.g., Portugal and the Netherlands) was the seclusion policy of the traditional Tokugawa rule. But when the modern West struck forcefully, in 1853, the danger was as acute to Japan as it was for China. When Commodore Perry and his "black ships" forced the opening of Japan to Western commerce and initiatives, he set in motion a chain of events that brought the Tokugawa regime down in ruins. Perception of the Western threat played a key role in the revolutionary transformation that led to the Meiji restoration in 1868. The revolutionary leaders knew that the external crisis could not be met by the existing political and economic structure. They quickly set Japan on its course of political, economic, and military modernization, but without making Japan a passive object of "Westernization."

The existing historical literature does not furnish a completely satisfactory explanation of why, despite cultural strangeness, the Japanese were so realistic in their perception of the threat represented by the Western powers. The fact that China was the first target of the Westerners gave the Japanese another fifteen years and the opportunity to ponder on what was happening on the Asian mainland. Also, unlike the more self-contained Chinese, the Japanese had a long tradition of borrowing from abroad such things as technology and forms of art and of incorporating the borrowings successfully into their own culture. In addition, the Japanese elites were more attuned to military matters than were the Chinese mandarins. But the crucial factor was probably that the traditional Chinese system continued on for about six decades after the first definite defeat (in the Opium War), whereas the Japanese almost immediately managed a political revolution, which brought to power a new elite which was sensitive to the foreign threat, understood its implications, and set out on rapid modernization. This political transformation was greatly facilitated, if not largely brought about by, the fact that the crumbling Tokugawa regime had become increasingly inefficient for purely domestic reasons as well. But the correct estimate of external threat played a significant part.

The historical material suggests then that, in addition to the problem of strangeness—essentially an intellectual problem to overcome—dispositional factors obstructed realistic threat perception in China to a much greater degree than in Japan. If the full recognition of an acute external menace points up the need for revolutionary change in the threatened country, it is not surprising that governing elites are reluctant or subconsciously unwilling to assess realities that doom their privileged status. Given such dispositional constraints, situational strangeness is very helpful in making delay acceptable.

As we have seen, situational strangeness in the past was often the result of geographic isolation. This condition will be much less significant in the future; it may disappear altogether. We have nonetheless dwelled on these historical cases because strangeness generated by other conditions will remain important in the future. Obviously, situational strangeness also results from vast international differences in political, economic, cultural, and ideological systems. Nazi Germany was politically strange to the British appeasers. Though France was hardly an unknown entity to her neighbors when the French Revolution broke out, the nature of this revolution was not understood for some time; neither were its implications to international power relationships. Crane Brinton has written:

> The European war which began in 1792 and which was to last until 1815 is in one sense a successor to previous great wars, a product of rivalries and tensions of long standing. Yet even here the French Revolution brought something new. Though the governments who made the first coalitions against France were seeking simply to manipulate the balance of power in their own favor, they came to regard themselves as defending a European order, a social system based on the continuing power of the successors to the warrior and priestly classes of the Middle Ages. Talleyrand later found

them a word for it—Legitimacy. France was not only trying to upset the balance of power, to gain her "natural frontiers"; she was freeing the peoples of Europe from kings, priests, and nobles, preparing them for self-government.

. . . .

> The truth is that . . . the conservative powers of central Europe did not want to go to war with France to restore legitimate monarchy and repress the menace of a world-wide revolution. French rhetoric, at the time and since, coupled with the misleading analogy of the Bolshevik Revolution, makes it easy today to consider the war as from the first an attempt by European conservatives to stamp out a social revolution that threatened to spread through all Europe. The men in power in eighteenth-century Europe, however, had no such prescience. To [them] . . . the French Revolution meant simply that for a while at least France could be counted out of the game. Internal difficulties, ran the axiom, incapacitate a country in foreign affairs. . . . It is unreasonable to expect these sensible, successful statesmen of routine to realize . . . that the French Revolution was a religious movement, that it aspired to universality, and that this aspiration could be illogically centered on the geographical entity France to make national France far more successfully aggressive than dynastic France had ever been. These statesmen were used to the realities of a struggle for power in which moral ideas were deliberately, and usually without success, employed to deceive one's opponent. They were quite incapable of understanding the workings of democratic nationalism, in which moral ideas enable private citizens as well as statesmen very successfully to deceive themselves. . . . Catherine, in 1792, thought France so weakened that a corps of 10,000 men would be sufficient to traverse it from one end to the other. It is difficult to get people to exert themselves against a danger they simply do not see to be a danger.[73]

Another factor in the situation was the eagerness of the radical wing of the French revolutionaries to misrepresent the threat to the Revolution from the legitimate courts of Europe. In fact, the Girondist party wanted war in order, by invoking foreign danger, to oust more conservative collaborators and thereby radicalize the Revolution.[74] Not only did the other European governments fail to comprehend the challenge to their countries' political regimes that was loosened by the French Revolution, they also did not recognize its military implications. They assumed that violent revolution was debilitating, as, indeed, it had often been. They failed to see, as a result of political strangeness, that the new mobilizing force of nationalism brought advantages in morale, élan, and military promotion that were to make French armies extremely formidable for some time to come.

The kind of political strangeness that revolutionary change suddenly brings to the international scene naturally makes threat perception situationally difficult. Although the passage of time brings the opportunity for better comprehension, this opportunity may not be fully seized if the revolutionary state is regarded not only as a foreign enemy but also as the source of an international revolutionary appeal to which other states are not domestically immune. Ideological hostility is then apt to distort threat perception. We noted this in the case of the British appeasers vis-à-vis the Soviet Union. Yet even if such ideological constraints do not operate, it will be hard to assess the intentions and capabilities of societies that are politically and culturally alien. This is one reason why it is difficult at this time for the governments and intelligence services of the United States, the Soviet Union, and China to engage in realistic threat perception vis-à-vis one another. There is, moreover, the additional difficulty of comprehension in the case of states that are closed systems in the sense that their governments control and restrict intercommunication between their societies and other societies. They do not afford the easy penetration by press, scholars, tourists, and so forth, that is permitted by capitalist societies. Political and cultural strangeness is already a barrier to correct threat perception; the deliberate closedness of a state is another.

Obviously, threat perception is also relatively difficult situationally when relevant foreign actors practice deception, as Hitler did with reference to his foreign counterparts. Furthermore, the intrinsic difficulty of threat perception may be aggravated when foreign governments, for one reason or another, misrepresent foreign threats to their own public. During the period of the Cold War, for instance, United States governments tended to exaggerate the Soviet threat to American security in order to assure sufficient domestic support for what they regarded as realistic foreign and defense policies.[75] Such a gap between public rhetoric and real official assumptions, which also prevailed in the Soviet Union at times,[76] magnifies the ambiguity of information that is available to foreign actors. Information may also be ambiguous because the foreign actor is not a unitary person; he speaks with separate and often distinct voices. Take a student of current Soviet foreign policy, for example. During any one period, he will find differences, substantial or in nuance, among the statements made by members of the Politburo, by members of the armed services, and by editorialists in the main Soviet newspapers. A Soviet student of American policy would find similar discrepancies. In most instances, these discrepancies are not engineered to confuse or dupe foreign audiences. Usually they are the normal result of different people speaking in divergent contexts, with different audiences and purposes in mind. Furthermore, foreign statements may be ambiguous or misleading because their authors have not settled on their own plans. In early 1950, for example, the statements of American officials, including Secretary of State Acheson, gave the impression abroad that the government of the United States was not deeply committed to fight for the survival of South Korea.[77] This impression may well have led to the Korean War. Decision-makers in North Korea, perhaps also in the Soviet Union, probably assumed that all relevant American statements were carefully designed to express United States interests—which they were not. To exaggerate the rationality of a foreign government is indeed a frequent tendency in threat perceptions.[78] If one finds the usual untidiness of government intolerable, one may try hard to superimpose careful design on ambiguous behavior. Finally, these intellectual difficulties will be compounded when the perceiver is under time pressure. The cognitive materials used in the risky business of forecasting are then apt to be especially fragmentary, and there may be little or no opportunity to gather additional information in order to reduce the ambiguities of available materials.

Making the best of ordinarily inadequate information on the probable intentions and capabilities of other states is only one of the intrinsic problems of threat perception. Scientists map reality with precision only where structures are simple and structural variety is limited.[79] In matters of threat perception, however, reality is complex and varied; the governments of different states are not simple structures, nor are they alike. Poor information adds ambiguity.

The act of threat perception creates an image of reality; it is a device, a hypothesis.[80] Indeed, this holds true of all perception. All human awareness is a personal construct, something that we organize. It is a set of assumptions that deals with the outside world selectively, focusing on some components while screening out others. We continuously "bet" about the nature of reality.[81] Pre-existing assumptions (i.e., theories) about the outside world help us to select our "bet." But for this very reason, they hinder, as well as help, perception.

The other intellectual difficulty vis-à-vis threat perception is that it concerns the future, and often not just the immediate futures. There is no information whatever about the future. The political and social phenomena that are objects of threat perception change over time. Even if we knew what is true today, we could not know what will be true tomorrow. As historical accounts demonstrate again and again, state behavior is highly unpredictable. It can change suddenly; surprise is frequent and not rarely dramatic. All we can do is to speculate on the shape of future events by studying the relevant (especially the recent) past. The mere projection into the future of what we have learned about the past is, as has already been pointed out, extremely hazardous.

Although international threat perception is intellectually difficult, and hence easily subject to error, the historical material demonstrates or suggests time and again that it is intervening predispositions that, coming on top of the inherent intellectual difficulties, make perhaps even more for the proliferation of misperceptions. In the following section, we will identify the principal predispositions encountered in historical cases, by concentrating first on the individual perceivers and then on the perceivers operating in a bureaucracy.

The facts that all perception is fundamentally selective and that selection is normally governed by working assumptions, or beliefs, about the outside world permit predispositions to intervene in the act of threat perception. One such predisposition is inertia, that is, a preference for escaping the rigors and puzzles of continuously monitoring the environment and of modifying existing schema if the signals do not fit, or of deliberately experimenting with different sets of assumptions. People tend to defend their assumptions by means either of selective attention or of inattention to ambiguous information. As a result, preexisting assumptions remain unquestioned for too long, although they tend to become obsolete over time even when they were fairly realistic originally. The easy and lazy thing is to predict today what you predicted yesterday.

Emotional factors obviously can also predispose, as in the case of the psychopathic personality (Stalin? Hitler? President Wilson?). More generally, the perceiving actor may be misled because he hates or despises another actor, harbors guilt feelings toward him, or has formed positive attachments. Ethnic, religious, and ideological identifications or hostilities often generate these intruding emotions. But historical experience can also do so. Thus, we noted the feelings of guilt that the British appeasers had toward Germany after World War I.

Third, threat perception may be dominated by ideological preconceptions, that is, by more or less formalized belief systems that pretend to define reality authoritatively, usually by emphasizing certain parts of reality, such as certain motivations or goals, while belittling or ignoring others. Thus, Marxism-Leninism defines the nature and consequences of capitalist societies. Racial conceptions that, in a form of vulgar Darwinism, were prevalent in Western societies toward the end of the nineteenth century and in Nazi Germany in the 1930s are other examples of ideologist thinking. Ideologies have other functions than to describe reality—that is, to judge it normatively and to change it—and this may subvert the descriptive function; it can also be highly misleading when applied to complex, ambiguous, and changing realities. Less formal ideologizing tends to distort threat perception between international actors that find themselves locked in an intense and prolonged competition for regional or world influence. This happened, for example, to the United States and the Soviet Union after World War II. The Cold War led both sides to develop beliefs whose function it was to emphasize the differences between the two societies, each side stereotyping the other as evil, aggressive, and so forth. These sorts of quasi-ideological beliefs are apt to mislead each side's perception of the other.[82] One's intentions toward an object influences one's perceptions about it.

Fourth, and perhaps most pervasive, is the intervention of wishes. We know from experiments in social psychology that desirability affects the subjective assignment of probability to a future event. As we saw, the British appeasers of Hitler did not want war, and the French appeasers did not want to spend more on defense; hence, both downgraded the German threat. The Chinese mandarins during the middle of the nineteenth century did not want to comprehend the nature of the Western imperialist threat because there would be no place for mandarin privilege in a modern China that was capable of coping with the Western threat. The actor wants to do something—raise or lower the defense budget, go to war or evade it, or whatever—and he interprets his environment in conformity with his wishes. The effective consciousness shuts itself off from parts of reality that do not fit in with what one wants to do.

Finally, more subtle and harder to define, the deliberate misrepresentation of foreign threats may lead to self-deception, especially on the part of political leaders. This factor calls for more extensive exploration. Deliberate misrepresentation of external threats—whether overestimates or underestimates—has been practiced throughout recorded history. We need only refer to three typical and familiar situations. First, whatever the exact nature of political systems, domestic struggles for power and authority may lead the incumbents and the challengers to misrepresent international threat perception. Weak governments have often sought to bolster their authority by overestimating or inventing foreign threats in order to divert attention from domestic problems or to benefit from the unifying predispositions that have been built into political culture as a reaction to external danger. Domestic weakness can also induce governments to ignore and play down foreign threats. Opposition leaders and critics may seek to establish an identity and an attractive policy alternative by differing with the incumbents on matters of threat perception, even if the difference calls for misrepresentation in one direction or another. Second, domestic competition over the use of national resources, in particular over whether to increase or cut allocations to military purposes, tends to generate differences in threat perception, either by way of wishful thinking or by deliberate misrepresentation. Third, threat misrepresentation may serve purposes of foreign policy, for instance, to attract and support allies or, alternatively, to abandon or discourage them. From our point of view, threat misrepresentation is important because many people find it psychologically difficult to sustain deliberate misrepresentation. To say one thing while believing another may be feasible for some, but social psychologists tell us that for many it results in uncomfortable feelings of dissonance that demand resolution.[83] Quite often, the misrepresenter resolves the problem by believing, genuinely, partly, or wholly, what at first he only pretended to believe.

While all perception is ultimately the act of individuals, threat perception as a task of statecraft takes place in collective groups, especially in organizations.

The intervening predispositions that we have discussed also characterize the behavior of bureaucracies. Organizations have, of course, certain advantages in mapping the external environment of the state. Compared with the effort of individuals, that of organizations benefits from superior resources, including specialists, for procuring and processing information. But organizations, especially large ones, need to coordinate their work, and the set of assumptions or preconceptions that guides perceptual activity often plays this role. This tends to make these assumptions routinely rigid and resistant to revision, even though they are likely to obsolesce over time because reality is always in flux. This is not to say that bureaucracies do not learn and modify their working assumptions—or that organizations do not vary in this respect—but self-indoctrination results from basic organizational needs, and this makes for rigidity. Moreover, if any potential ideology is officially obligatory, members of government organizations will find it difficult to deviate from built-in perceptual constraints.

The usual structure of rewards leads to the intervention of additional predispositions in the act of perception. It is hard for a member to break away from the beliefs of his group or to express views that are known to be unwelcome to superiors. The incentive is to tell superiors what they want to hear. It is also difficult in such collective settings to confess ignorance or uncertainty or to take an agnostic stand on threat perception. Finally, bureaucracies may have interests of their own that conflict with objective threat perception. The military, for instance, tend to overestimate foreign military threats, since they may get more resources if the outside world looks threatening. Other bureaucracies may have the opposite interest.

All these dispositional factors enjoy easy entry into the business of threat perception, because the intrinsic intellectual difficulties render such perception hypothetical and hence permissive. Nobody can be logically compelled to accept any one answer as correct. This makes it easy for bias to creep in.

Our case studies—and much other historical material we could add—gives the impression that international threat perception is rarely done right, especially if one assumes an interest, not only in the fact or possibility of a threat, but also in its nature and timing. There are, of course, kinds of international relationships that do not raise the problem of threat perception—cooperative relationships, for instance. Even when threat perception is relevant, it is situationally easy between countries that are dependably peaceful or friendly, and when capability restrictions preclude threat-making. There is, however, always the question of how long these conditions will last. Threat perception is also relatively easy situationally when countries are already at war or when they receive an ultimatum type of threat or when agreements preclude threat-making, at least for the time being, as is the case between allies. But these are not the critical cases. They come about when the capabilities of foreign states permit aggressive action and when their intentions are uncertain. The fact that, historically speaking, correct threat perception is exceptional—resting perhaps on luck or intuitive judgment, that is, on unreliable resources—stands in sharp contrast to the common assumption that threat perception is easy. Most people on record speak in these matters with great confidence. They may disagree among themselves, but all seem to be sure when—in view of the intellectual difficulty and the risk of predispositional bias—they should be unsure.

As a result of this curious failure to recognize the true difficulties of the task, statecraft has developed few remedial measures. The only notable remedy is resort to worst-case assumptions, particularly in military planning. This practice rests on the knowledge that it is more difficult to assess (let alone predict!) the intentions of foreign actors than their capabilities to do harm to others. What is merely possible is important when the consequences of actual occurrence would be grave. But such a strategic assumption, which is prudent insurance, must not be confused with the estimate of a threat. In practice, unfortunately, such confusion is not rare.[84] From postulating that an event is hypothetically possible it seems easy to slip into the assumption that it is probable; and if one's behavior is based on the assumption of probability, it may act like a self-fulfilling prophecy. The authorities of the object state may become alarmed, increase their military forces, and so forth. If we read the historical record correctly, then it seems extremely important that this record become known, so that the fateful problems of international threat perception are taken more seriously. The world would be better off if international threats were neither overestimated nor underestimated.

Notes

1. George P. Gooch and Harold W. V. Temperley, eds., *British Documents on the Origins of the War, 1898–1914* (London: His Majesty's Stationery Office, 1926–1938), 3:407.
2. Ibid., 3:402.
3. See Thomas Pangle's chapter in this book, pp. 338–43, 347, 361.
4. Martin Gilbert and Richard Gott, *The Appeasers* (Boston: Houghton Mifflin, 1963), pp. 3–4, 6, 9, 13, 15, 18–19.
5. Alfred L. Rowse, *Appeasement* (New York: Norton, 1961), pp. 18–19, 116–17.
6. Laurence Lafore, *The End of Glory* (Philadelphia: Lippincott, 1970), p. 192.
7. A. J. P. Taylor, *The Origins of the Second World War* (New York: Atheneum, 1962), pp. 206, 208.
8. Irving L. Janis, *Victims of Groupthink* (Boston: Houghton Mifflin, 1972).
9. Basil H. Liddell Hart, *History of the Second World War* (New York: Putnam's, 1971), p. 10.
10. Taylor, *Origins*, p. 206.
11. Ibid., p. 116. See also, Lafore, *End of Glory*, p. 194.
12. Cf. Taylor, *Origins*, p. 117.

13. Jane Degras, ed., *Soviet Documents on Foreign Policy* (London: Oxford University Press, 1951), 1:59.
14. Cf. V. I. Lenin, *Imperialism: The Highest Stage of Capitalism* (New York: International Publishers, 1939), pp. 9–11.
15. B. Ponomaryov et al., eds., *History of Soviet Foreign Policy, 1917–1945* (Moscow: Progress Publishers, 1969), pp. 383–84.
16. Ibid., pp. 421–22.
17. Isaac Deutscher, *Stalin* (New York & London: Oxford University Press, 1949), p. 454. See also, Max Beloff, *The Foreign Policy of Soviet Russia, 1929–1941* (2 vols.; London & New York: Oxford University Press, 1947–1949), pp. 376–84.
18. Deutscher, *Stalin*, pp. 454–55.
19. Barton Whaley, *Codeword BARBAROSSA* (Cambridge: Massachusetts Institute of Technology Press, 1973), pp. 241–45.
20. Klaus Knorr, "Failures in National Intelligence Estimates," *World Politics* 16 (1964):455–67.
21. *New York Times*, December 10, 1973, pp. 1, 18.
22. *New York Times*, July 21, 1974, p. 21.
23. John L. Snell, *Illusion and Necessity: The Diplomacy of Global War, 1939–1945* (Boston: Houghton Mifflin, 1963), p. 8.
24. Ibid., p. 9.
25. Cf. Mark L. Chadwin, *The Hawks of World War II* (Chapel Hill: University of North Carolina Press, 1968), p. 31.
26. Ibid., p. 20.
27. Akira Iriye, *Across the Pacific* (New York: Harcourt, Brace & World, 1967), pp. 104–5.
28. Ibid., p 106.
29. Ibid., p. 131.
30. Ibid., pp. 201–3.
31. Ibid., p 208.
32. Gooch and Temperley, *British Documents*, pp. 414–16.
33. Robert J. C. Butow, *Tojo and the Coming of the War* (Princeton, N. J.: Princeton University Press, 1961), p. 418.
34. Ibid.
35. Ibid., pp. 418–19.
36. Roberta Wohlstetter, *Pearl Harbor: Warning and Decision* (Stanford, Calif.: Stanford University Press, 1962), pp. 382–85.
37. Ibid., pp. 387, 393–95.
38. Ibid., p. 397.
39. Ibid.
40. Ibid., pp. 398–99.
41. Thucydides, *The History of the Peloponnesian War,* ed. Richard Livingston (New York: Oxford University Press, 1960), p. 46.
42. John P. V. D. Balsdon, *Rome: The Story of an Empire* (London: World University Library, Weidenfeld & Nicolson, 1970), p. 24.
43. Ibid., p. 25.
44. Plutarch, *Lives of the Noble Romans*, ed. Edmund Fuller (New York: Dell, 1959), p. 145.
45. Ibid.
46. A. J. P. Taylor, *The Habsburg Monarchy, 1809–1918* (new ed.; London: Hamilton, 1948), p. 36.

47. Cf. John Lewis Gaddis, "Reconsiderations: Was the Truman Doctrine a Real Turning Point?" *Foreign Affairs* 52 (January 1974):386–90.
48. Ernest R. May, *"Lessons" of the Past: The Use and Misuse of History in American Foreign Policy* (New York: Oxford University Press, 1973), chap. 2.
49. Luigi Albertini, *The Origins of the War of 1914* (3 vols.; New York: Oxford University Press, 1952–1957), 1:551–54.
50. Laurence Lafore, *The Long Fuse* (Philadelphia: Lippincott, 1965), p. 108.
51. Ibid., p. 132. See also, P. J. V. Rolo, *Entente Cordiale* (London: Macmillan, 1969), pp. 276, 279.
52. Rolo, *Entente Cordiale*, p. 81.
53. Ernest L. Woodward, *Great Britain and the German Navy* (Oxford, Eng.: Clarendon Press, 1935), p. 11. See also, pp. 12–53, and Lafore, *The Long Fuse*, pp. 131–32.
54. Rolo, *Entente Cordiale*, pp. 274–77.
55. Albertini, *Origins*, p. 550.
56. L. L. Farrar, Jr., *The Short-War Illusion: German Policy, Strategy & Domestic Affairs, August–December 1914* (Santa Barbara, Calif.: ABC Clio, 1973), p. 148.
57. Michael Howard, *The Franco-Prussian War* (New York: Macmillan, 1961), p. 1.
58. Ibid., p. 39.
59. Ibid., pp. 2–5.
60. William L. Langer, *Explorations in Crisis* (Cambridge, Mass.: Harvard University Press, 1969), pp. 28–42.
61. Cf. Miguel Leon Portilla, ed., *The Broken Spears: The Aztec Account of the Conquest of Mexico* (Boston: Beacon, 1962); John Hemming, *The Conquest of the Incas* (New York: Harcourt, Brace, Jovanovich, 1970).
62. Hemming, *Conquest*, pp. 36–37.
63. Ibid., pp. 44–45.
64. Immanuel C. Y. Hsü, *China's Entrance into the Family of Nations* (Cambridge, Mass.: Harvard University Press, 1960), p. 12.
65. Immanuel C. Y. Hsü, *The Rise of Modern China* (New York: Oxford University Press, 1970), pp. 356–67.
66. Cf. Mark Mancall, *Russia and China* (Cambridge, Mass.: Harvard University Press, 1971).
67. Cf. Ssu-yü Teng and John K. Fairbank, *China's Response to the West: A Documentary Survey, 1839–1923* (Cambridge, Mass.: Harvard University Press, 1954), chaps. 3 and 4.
68. Cf. ibid., chaps. 5 and 6.
69. Ibid., p. 53.
70. Ibid., chaps. 9 and 10.
71. Benjamin I. Schwartz, *In Search of Wealth and Power: Yen Fu and the West* (Cambridge, Mass.: Harvard University Press, 1964), p. 43.
72. Ibid., pp. 59–60.
73. Clarence Crane Brinton, *A Decade of Revolution, 1789–1799*, vol. 12 of *The Rise of Modern Europe*, ed. William L. Langer (New York: Harper, 1934), pp. 65, 83–84.
74. Ibid., pp. 86–87. Also: Robert R. Palmer, *The Age of the Democratic Revolution* (2 vols.; Princeton, N. J.: Princeton University Press, 1959–1964), 2:12–21.
75. Gaddis, "Truman Doctrine," p. 386.
76. Ibid., p. 388.
77. Glenn D. Paige, *The Korean Decision* (New York: Free Press, 1968), pp. 66–69.

78. Cf. Raymond A. Bauer, "Problems of Perception and the Relations between the United States and the Soviet Union," *Journal of Conflict Resolution* 5 (September 1961):225–26.
79. Marc J. Roberts, "On the Nature and Condition of Social Science," *Daedalus* 103 (Summer, 1974):52.
80. Joseph H. de Rivera, *The Psychological Dimensions of Foreign Policy* (Columbus, Ohio: Charles E. Merritt, 1968), pp. 20–21.
81. Robert E. Ornstein, *The Psychology of Consciousness* (San Francisco: W. H. Freeman, 1972).
82. Cf. Bauer, "Problems of Perception," pp. 227–28.
83. Cf. Leon Festinger, *A Theory of Cognitive Dissonance* (Stanford, Calif.: Stanford University Press, 1962).
84. De Rivera, *Psychological Dimensions*, p. 28.

Response to Threat Perception: Accommodation as a Special Case

Peter Karsten

In the preceding chapter, we encountered the problem of threat perception. We may now explore questions relating to the *responses* offered by states that perceive real or potential threats from other states.

As demonstrated in the preceding chapter, *mis*perception is frequent and hence an important dimension of threat perception. We will obviously have nothing to say of *un*perceived threats, as they elicit no reaction, but misperception has two other forms: (1) deliberate misrepresentation, by which we mean a manufactured, contrived, purposive "perception" of a nonexistent threat (e.g., Bismarck's "perception" of a French "threat" in 1875),[1] designed to justify and excuse policies for which a foreign "threat" is deemed necessary; (2) the erroneous perception of a threat from a quarter that either does not, in fact, offer any threat, be it real or potential, or *does* offer a threat, the nature of which is not fully understood. (It may be argued, of course, that if state actors perceive a threat from another state, then a potential threat may be said to exist. But there are clearly order-of-magnitude differences in the threats inherent in the state system. All threats threaten, but some threaten more than others. And whenever disagreement exists in the state erroneously perceiving the threat, we may prefer to call such a process "erroneous perception" rather than "potential threat perception.") Herein, cases of the latter sort (2) will be treated in the same fashion as accurate perceptions of real or potential threats, for here we are concerned with behavior, responses, reactions, and results; and misperception that leads to uncalled-for confrontation or accommodation can take the same form and evoke the same response as would "true" threat perception.

The spectrum of responses is familiar and easily identified: One responds to a threat by surrendering, accommodating, deterring-defending, allying, rearming, offering counterthreats, or actively attacking; one may also respond by using a combination or sequence of two or more of these.[2] Behavior on the latter end of the spectrum (deterring-defending to actively attacking) is relatively well reported. One may increase and modernize one's armed forces (as Britain did in 1859, facing a new French capability—steam-driven steel warships; or as Japan did in the 1880s and 1890s, facing Western powers that were anxious to "penetrate" Japan).[3] One may engage in a "preemptive strike" (as Sparta did when she perceived that Athens, a potential enemy, was growing so powerful as to imperil Sparta's security in the easily foreseeable future).[4] One may scan the horizon for new allies (as Bostonians did in 1774; Chinese, in the 1890s; British, in the first decade of the twentieth century; and Soviets, in 1938).[5]

To illustrate the point, let us briefly consider the case of China in the 1890s, when, because of the destruction of China's new navy by Japan, a growing sense that Britain could not be counted on to aid her, and a growing fear of Germany and France, as well as Japan, China turned to Russia. Liu K'un-i, the Imperial Commissioner of Liang-Chiang, said to the court:

> Your minister notes that diplomatic relations between Chinese and foreigners have continued for thirty years until the present day, when the matter is even more difficult to handle. China's use of hard and soft policies should stress their modification according to the times. The chances of all countries being friendly or hostile to us are guided by circumstance. After the war in Annam, when China failed to handle the issue properly, we were considerably despised by all countries. This time, when we negotiated peace with Japan, we made too many compromises which encouraged the gradual inception of a waylaying policy—glaring at us like tigers, all the various powers seek to find a plump spot to bite into us. We estimate that our power is inferior to theirs, so we must quickly make an international alliance as a means of seeking assistance.
>
> According to your minister's humble understanding, the impending disaster from other countries is still slow in coming, but that from Japan is imminent. This is because she is close to us; after she has obtained Taiwan and Liaotung, the way for her entrance will be even more convenient, as if her army could start directly from our pillow and mat—it can invade any part of our territory at will. . . . But Russia does not want Japan to be strong, and Japan's invasion of our Three Eastern Provinces (Manchuria) makes Russia even more jealous. Thus, by the Sino-Japanese peace treaty (of Shimonoseki) we had already ceded Liaotung to Japan, but Russia, France, and Germany compelled her to return it to China. Is Russia doing this especially for us? She is, at the same time, working for herself. If we take this opportunity to establish close relations with her, for mutual assistance, and also give her some concessions, Russia will surely be glad to comply. Even though this move cannot protect our various coastal provinces, Japan certainly will not dare to covet the territory of the Three Eastern Provinces, which are close to Russia. . . . If these provinces were lost, how could the dynasty maintain its foundation, and how could our Emperor face his ancestors? That is why, whenever your minister thinks of this, he cannot keep his heart from palpitating and his muscles from twitching.

[A similar memorial was made by Chang Chih-tung.]

To save the critical situation today, nothing is better than the conclusion of a secret treaty of alliance with a strong power for assistance. From ancient times, whenever nations have opposed each other, as if with horns, they usually have used the policy of allying with a distant country to attack an enemy nearby. With regard to the Sino-Japanese situation today, this policy is even more suitable. China's power today can never oppose simultaneously all the nations in the East and West. . . .

I understand that the tendency of foreign countries in recent years has been to establish particularly close relations with one or two others among all the countries which have general relations. In time of peace they make secret treaties in advance, and in wartime they aid one another with military provisions and armaments. If there is no secret treaty, then when something happens they remain neutral and will not interfere.

Now if we wish to make a treaty, and to have a bond for mutual assistance, naturally Russia is most convenient for us, because England uses commerce to absorb the profits of China, France uses religion to entice the Chinese people, Germany has no common territorial boundary with us, and the United States does not like to interfere in others' military affairs. It is difficult for all of these nations to discuss an alliance with us. It is known that Russia, as China's neighbor, has kept treaty agreements with us for more than two hundred years, and that she has never embarked on hostilities; she is different from other countries who have frequently resorted to warfare with us. Moreover, her behavior is grand and generous, and cannot be compared with that of the Europeans. For example, in the church case at Tientsin in 1870, in which all the countries were busy making a clamor, Russia did not participate; and in the treaties over Ili (1879 and 1881) our nation completely refused and then modified the eighteen articles, and Russia generously consented. This time she has demanded the return of the territory of Liaotung for us; although she did it for the sake of the general situation in the East, yet China has already actually received the benefit. Japan's spearhead has been slightly blunted by this. In comparison with other countries who acted as bystanders, putting their hands in their sleeves, and covertly planning for commercial profits, Russia shows a great difference.

It is just the right time for us to take this opportunity and work vigorously for an alliance, deepening our friendship and making a secret treaty with her. In everything concerning Russian commercial affairs and boundary matters, we should make some compromises. If Russia resorts to warfare in the East, we should aid her navy with coal and food, permitting her war vessels to enter our dockyards for repairs. On land we must permit her to use our roads, supply her with resources, food, vehicles and horses; in accordance with her reliance on our supplies we should offer her coöperation and subsidy according to our means. But we should have it settled in the contract that in case China is attacked, Russia will have to help us with armed forces, of which the most important is the navy. We must also make a decision during our conference with Russia concerning the method of compensating her, because Russia is very suspicious that England dominates the situation in the East. If China and Russia form an alliance, English influence will be considerably curbed; and Russia would be willing to accommodate us.[6]

The Sino-Russian treaty was, as Chang Chih-tung indicates, a secret one. Needless to say, the *deterrent* value of *secret* treaties is slight. But such treaties may still be of some *defensive* value. In any event, let it suffice to say that one may take any one of a number of familiar steps to *confront* a threat. We will have little more to say of confrontation, as we wish to focus on a response located on the less familiar end of our spectrum—namely, accommodation.

When we speak of accommodation, we do not have in mind a posture adopted out of sympathy or affection; where there is no perception of threat, no sense of danger, there can be no accommodation—at least none in our sense of the meaning of the word. The passages offered in the preceding chapter suggested that some British leaders felt sympathy for Germany in the 1930s; another account goes further and points out that there was a substantial amount of outright affection for Hitler among British and French conservatives.[7] To the extent that there is truth in these arguments, it may be said that a number of policy-makers in Britain and France found Hitler to be nonthreatening; their policies would then have to be regarded as something other than those of accommodation. The same may be said of the Norwegian pro-Nazi Vidkun Quisling and his associates.[8]

We want ultimately to focus on one-sided, unidirectional forms of accommodation, and we will consider accommodative relationships between relatively equal powers and between relatively unequal powers. It is certainly true that major powers that feel threatened by one another sometimes engage in what might be styled detente, rapprochement, or mutual accommodation. The Prussian and French resolution of differences over the status of Luxembourg in 1867 is one example of this process. The transformation of Russian and Manchu policies in the late seventeenth century from those of confrontation to those of accommodation is another.[9] Another involves the mutual accommodation of Nazi Germany and the Soviet Union in 1939. Hajo Holborn wrote of Germany's motivation:

> Apparently a new refusal by the Japanese in early August to enter into an anti-Soviet treaty arrangement with Germany and Italy convinced Hitler that if he wanted to immobilize the Soviet Union he would have to make a deal with the Soviet rulers. That the price would be exorbitant Hitler knew, and he authorized Ribbentrop to offer the Russians even more than they eventually demanded. But while the rulers of the Kremlin did not ask for the Turkish straits, they received more than the lion's share in the par-

tition of Eastern Europe, which was contained in the secret supplementary protocol of the nonaggression pact. Finland, Estonia, and Latvia came into the Russian sphere of interest. In addition, the Soviet Union was free to appropriate Bessarabia. Poland was to be divided along the Narew, Vistula, and San rivers. Hitler had empowered Ribbentrop to grant the Russians control even of the Turkish straits if need be, but the Russians remained silent on the issue. The lavish concessions which Hitler made to the Russians revealed his determination to reach agreement with the Soviet rulers under any conditions. He wanted to make sure that Poland would not receive assistance from the Soviet Union, and more than that he hoped that a pact with the Soviet Union would convince England and France of the hopelessness of supporting Poland.[10]

The official Soviet history had this to say about Stalin's motivation:

> In the course of the negotiations with Britain and France the Soviet Government lost all hope of reaching a satisfactory agreement.
>
> It took into account the Munich betrayal, France's contravention of her allied commitments to Czechoslovakia and, in effect, to the USSR as well, the betrayal of the Spanish Republic by the Western powers and the Anglo-Japanese compact. When the talks with Britain and France reached a deadlock because of their reluctance to co-operate with the USSR and reports began to filter through to the effect that Germany and Britain had entered into secret negotiations, the Soviet Government became convinced that it was impossible to secure co-operation with the Western powers. Nevertheless, it did not give its consent to the German proposal to begin talks on an agreement. Neither did it react to a telegram from the German Government of August 15, requesting that the German Foreign Minister should be received in Moscow for talks. In the three-day period from August 15 to 17 it became glaringly apparent that no understanding would be reached with the British and French military missions. On August 20 Berlin again asked if the Soviet Government would receive Ribbentrop. The situation forced the Soviet Government to agree, and the talks that followed his arrival in Moscow ended on August 23 with the signing of a Soviet-German Treaty of Non-Aggression. This treaty delivered, for some time at least, the Soviet Union from the threat of a war on two fronts without allies. It gave the USSR time to strengthen its defence capacity....
>
> [On August 27, 1939] K. Y. Voroshilov held a press conference at which he debunked a Reuter report quoting him as telling the British and French missions that since a Soviet-German Treaty had been signed the Soviet Government considered as pointless any further negotiations with Britain and France. "The military negotiations with Britain and France," he said, "were broken off not because the USSR signed a non-aggression pact with Germany. This pact was signed because, among other circumstances, the military talks with Britain and France had entered a deadlock by virtue of

insuperable differences." In this situation the Soviet Union could not expose the country to a mortal risk by turning down the German proposals.

Naturally, it did not for a moment count on the Nazis honouring their commitments. But it was apparent that nazi Germany would not attack the USSR in the immediate future. Even a short postponement was of the utmost importance in view of the delicate and unfavourable situation which emerged in the summer of 1939, when war would have caught the USSR at a disadvantage, for it would have had to fight in isolation on two fronts —against Germany and against Japan.

By postponing its involvement in the war the USSR was able to build up its armed forces and improve their combat training and armaments. Unfortunately, this period was not used fully from the military point of view. But the gain was very great from the standpoint of foreign policy. The international situation was such that when in 1941 the Soviet Union was forced to enter the war it was no longer threatened by political isolation, as was the case in 1939. Britain was now fighting Germany, and the imperialist contradictions between the USA, on the one hand, and Germany and Japan, on the other, had reached a point of tension where the possibility of a compact between them was unrealistic. The objective requisites were on hand for an anti-fascist coalition of the major world powers—the USSR, the USA and Britain.[11]

Max Beloff, described the extent of Soviet accommodation by 1941:

"I am under the impression," wrote Schnurre on 15 May 1941, "that we could make economic demands on Moscow which would even go beyond the scope of the treaty of January 10, 1941, demands designed to secure German food and raw-material requirements beyond the extent now contracted for. The quantities of raw materials now being contracted for are being delivered punctually by the Russians, despite the heavy burden this imposes on them, which, especially with regard to grain, is a notable performance."

Schulenburg left Moscow for Berlin on 13 April. On 28 April, before returning to his post he had an interview with Hitler in which he endeavoured to explain all Russia's recent actions as dictated entirely by apprehensions for her own security, and declared that in his view Stalin had no intention of going over from the side of the Axis powers to that of Great Britain. On the contrary, he was convinced that Stalin was prepared to make even further concessions. It had been intimated that if the Germans applied in due time, the Russians could supply up to five million tons of grain in the following year.[12]

The behavior of France and Britain in the years between the Fashoda Affair (1898) and the Entente Cordiale (1904) might be regarded as another example[13] (though in this case both felt threatened by Germany as well as by one another, and their mutual accommodation must be viewed in this light as an alliance-building form of defense-deterrence). Needless to say, some mutual accommodation, or detente, can occur on one level of interaction between powers while confrontation continues, or even begins, on another level. The same may be said of unilateral accommodation.

Nothing more will be said about mutual accommodation in this chapter; our attention will be focused on those acts of one-sided concessions that are taken in order to preserve a part of what is threatened, to avoid war, to avoid making increased provisions for deterrence-defense, or to win "clients." Such acts we will define as accommodative acts. We are especially interested in acts of accommodation in which A gives up something of value to state B in order to safeguard what remains or in order to secure some new interest. To be sure, one rarely finds a case of "pure" accommodation, unadulterated by a measure of defense-deterrence sufficient to constitute a "threshold" over which a threatening power must cross. But we can isolate and examine some thirty-five cases of clear and pronounced accommodation, which are listed in table 1.

Before examining these cases, let us consider one that we are not including because the accommodative actions are thoroughly mixed with other less accommodative actions and because the resulting vector does not point clearly in an accommodative direction. We have in mind Sweden's relations with Germany during World War II.

To be sure, Sweden did, on at lease two occasions, accommodate Germany. The first time was during the summer of 1940, when she allowed German troops and war material to pass from the port of Göteborg into Norway on sealed trains. But she did so only after the last major Allied position in Norway, the port of Narvik, had fallen to the Nazis. Until that point in time Sweden had steadfastly resisted German demands that she allow the transit of troops and supplies over her territory. Moreover, throughout the war, Sweden provided the Norwegian underground with monies, food, and refuge; she released ten interned British ships in early 1942, ignoring stern German protests; and she helped several hundred downed allied aviators return to Britain.

The second act of accommodation occurred in June of 1941, when Sweden allowed a German division to pass over Swedish territory to Finland, en route to the Eastern front. The Swedish premier, Per Albin Hansson, initially opposed Germany's demand that the division be allowed to transit Sweden. But Hansson wanted to "avoid a split in the cabinet, which might well have resulted in the formation of a more appeasement-minded body." Thus, when King Gustaf expressed his own willingness to accede to the German demands, a willingness to give up something in order to save the rest, Hansson and the Council of Foreign Relations gave their consent "on the condition that the coalition cabinet in the future would unanimously refuse all German demands for similar transport of troops." This was clearly an act of accommodation, but it was a measured and conditional one, clearly designed to buy time, and it was followed by less accommodative behavior: visas granted to tens of thousands of Hungarian and Danish Jews; reception of over two hundred thousand war refugees, many of whom were fleeing Nazi authorities; unambiguous messages to Germans who were eying Swedish iron ore fields, to the effect that any German intervention would result in Swedish destruction of power plants that were vital to the ore operations; refusal to grant credits to Germany (unlike Switzerland, Sweden maintained a favorable balance of trade with Germany throughout the war); and the continued development of what Premier Hansson called "an extensive military establishment adjusted to our judgment of the requirements."[14]

Sweden did engage in two acts of accommodation, in order to avoid war and to gain time. But she also engaged in other much less accommodative activities, and, on balance, we are not satisfied that her relations with Germany during World War II constitute accommodation as we understand it. The thirty-five historical cases listed in table 1 do.

Table 1 represents these cases in order of the relative strengths of the accommodating and accommodated parties, strengths that we estimated by using the concepts of military power offered in the writings of Klaus Knorr. Alternatively, we might have organized the cases in terms of the degree of threat perceived to a state's interests. But were we to have done so, the lists would not appear terribly different, for (not surprisingly) the "serious threats" column would include *no* cases in which the accommodating party was militarily stronger than the party accommodated, and, with only two exceptions (Florence/France/1494 and Kgama III/Britain/late nineteenth century), the "minor threats" column would include *only* those cases in which the accommodative party was militarily stronger than the party being accommodated.

Inasmuch as this chapter constitutes little more than a preliminary survey of the historical record of accommodative acts, the reader is cautioned that the generalizations that I will offer are based on a rather modest sample and must be regarded as tentative ones. But with that caveat in mind, I submit that the generalizations may be of some value as suggestive hypotheses for some future scholar's more exhaustive research.

Let us now raise some questions regarding the nature of accommodation, questions that we can bring to our little data base. Why do some states choose accommodation as a posture when they perceive threats? Are there any characteristics of such states, state-actors, or state systems that might explain accommodative behavior? Are weak states more likely to accommodate than strong ones? Are minor threats more likely to be met with accommodative gestures than serious threats? Is accommodation a largely irreversible process—

Table 1

Thirty-five Historical Examples of Accommodation

Accommodator Stronger Than Accommodated (12)	Accommodator Weaker Than Accomodated (10)	Accommodator Not Obviously Stronger or Weaker Than Accommodated (13)
Accommodator/ Accommodated/Date	Accommodator/ Accommodated/Date	Accommodator/ Accommodated/Date
Philip of Macedon/ Athens/339 B.C.	Alexius Comnenus I/ his enemies/late eleventh century A.D.	Carthage/Rome/second century B.C.
Alexander/Persians and Greeks/328 B.C.	Michael VIII/his enemies/ late thirteenth century A.D.	Theodosius/Goths/ fourth century A.D.
China/The Mongols/Han dynasty, second century B.C.–first century A.D.	Florence/France/1494	Frisians, English, and French/Vikings/ ninth century A.D.
China/Vietnamese/late seventeenth century A.D.	Holland/her enemies/ eighteenth century A.D.	Aztecs/Spanish/1520s
Britain/American Colonies/1769	Turkey/Russia and France/ 1829	Britain, Prussia, Russia/France/1831
Britain/Barbary States/ late eighteenth century A.D.	Kgama III/Britain/late nineteenth century A.D.	France/Britain/1839
U.S./S.E. Indian tribes/ 1853	Denmark/Germany/1914	Austria/Britain/1853
Union/Confederacy/1865	Norway/Britain/1915	Britain/Germany/late nineteenth century A.D.
Prussia/Austria/1866	Switzerland/Germany/1942	Russia, Serbia/ Austria/1909
U.S./Powder River Indians/1868	Finland/Soviets/1949	Austria/Turkey/1909
Austria/Montenegro/ 1909		Britain/Germany/1938
Germany/Denmark/1940		France/Germany/1938
		Wang Ching-wei faction/Japan/1938

that is, does the fact that a state at time t chooses an accommodative posture imply that it will be accommodative once again when it perceives a new threat at time $t + 1$? And, finally, when can we say that accommodation "succeeds" or "fails"? Let us look at the data.

The more obvious examples of accommodation are those of weak or declining states confronted by aggressive, stronger powers (the declining Byzantine Empire, eighteenth-century Netherlands, the decaying Ottoman Empire, mid-nineteenth-century China, the American Indian tribes, the Italian city-states in the age of Charles VIII, Denmark in 1914, Switzerland in World War II, Finland since World War II). The Ottoman Empire became very accommodating in 1829, agreeing to the independence of Greece, but only after experiencing military setbacks in the Balkans at the hands of Russia and after witnessing the appearance of a French naval squadron in the Aegean.[15] Treaties signed to stave off total defeat are clearly cases of accommodation. So also are instances of "Byzantine" diplomacy, a phrase given to the elaborate and flexible network of accommodative arrangements made by Byzantine rulers with Turks, Normans, Bulgars, Serbs, Magyars, Venetians, Genovese, and numerous other real or potential enemies. Alexius Comnenus I was most adept at such diplomacy in the late eleventh century.[16] So was Michael VIII in the late thirteenth century, but while in 1090 Alexius I possessed substantial military capabilities, by 1260 Michael VIII did not. J. M. Hussey has written:

> The problem of the Byzantine government after 1261 was, then, one of diminished and totally inadequate material resources. Without the backing of proper military and naval defence it found that diplomacy alone was of no avail; unable to enforce its authority within its own territory, it had no option but to suffer, and in the end to rely on, the virtually independent land-owners and local governors. Internal difficulties such as these were increased by long periods of civil war during the fourteenth century and by the continuous pressure from without from 1261 onwards, particularly from Charles of Anjou, from Serbia, and finally from the Ottoman Turks.

> For a short time the deceptive brilliance of Michael VIII disguised the essential weakness of the restored Empire. He neatly staved off a dangerous situation by adroit diplomacy. Charles of Anjou had recently established himself in the kingdom of Sicily, where he had defeated the Hohenstaufen in 1266. Charles wished to extend his authority to Greece and the Byzantine Empire, and he built up an alliance against Michael VIII. He was supported by the Papacy and the former Latin Emperor of Constantinople, Baldwin II, and William of Villehardouin (who had been defeated by Michael VIII in the Morea)—clearly a dangerous alliance. The Byzantine Emperor cleverly used the Golden Horde and the Mongol Khan Hulagu against Bulgaria and Rum, and Hungary against Serbia, thus countering his enemies in Asia Minor and the Balkans. He held out the advantages of a friendly alliance to Charles' brother Louis IX, who was contemplating a crusade. He subsidized the Sicilians who were bitterly hostile to their Angevin ruler, with the result that they successfully revolted and gave the crown to Peter of Aragon with whom he came to an understanding. He also thought it wise to win over the Papacy with the promise of ecclesiastical reunion at the Council of Lyons in 1274.

> Michael thus broke up Charles' plans, but at great cost, both financially and in other respects. His approach to Rome roused bitter opposition in

neighbouring orthodox countries, for instance, Bulgaria where there was strong feeling against Constantinople. It was equally bitterly opposed at home. When mass was celebrated in the imperial chapel in Constantinople on 9 January 1275 the epistle and gospel were chanted in both Greek and Latin, and commemoration made of Gregory, "the chief Pontiff of the apostolic Church and oecumenical Pope." But the feeling of one and all was voiced by the Emperor's sister, who is reported to have said, "Better that my brother's Empire should perish than the purity of the Orthodox faith." This offer of union between Rome and Constantinople became a well-worn imperial gambit during the Palaeologian period, but after 1204 many Byzantines preferred submission to the infidel rather than the abandonment of what they regarded as the long venerated traditions of their Church. And as their enemies closed in, the Byzantines clung all the more to the Orthodox Church whose authority and prestige steadily increased.

The international position won under Michael VIII could not be sustained. This was not because of the ineffectiveness of individual Byzantine rulers some of whom, as Andronicus II or John Cantacuzenus or Manuel II, were certainly outstanding and gifted men, but was due to the impossibility of restoring firm central control in the face of increasing feudal separatism and to the complete lack of adequate resources with which to counter the Serbian enemy in the Balkans and the Ottoman enemy in Asia Minor.[17]

If the accommodative postures of Carthage, the late Roman Empire, Byzantium, the Aztecs, and the Manchus may be said to have been damaging to their interests (and I think that we may clearly say this), then we may also say that accommodation is unlikely to preserve interests or to stave off disaster if it is offered as a long-term policy by weak or undynamic states that are confronted by numerous aggressive enemies. Nonetheless, accommodation made a good deal of sense at the time to these states, and we ought not try to second guess them with our advantage of hindsight; after all, given their sense that a confrontation of the threat facing them was either too costly or too risky, accommodation was a perfectly reasonable way to buy time. One could never know what might happen to alter the situation.

Another instance of a weaker state accommodating a stronger one is that of the Florentine accommodation of France in 1494. Pietro Medici had allied Florence with Naples against Milan in the struggle for power within the Sforza dynasty. When Charles VIII of France invaded Italy on behalf of the Milanese Sforzas, Pietro was placed on the horns of a dilemma. George F. Young described the problem thus:

> By this time Charles's army was entering the borders of Tuscany and laying siege to its frontier fortresses, which were defended by such mercenary troops as Pietro had been able to collect; but these troops being quite unfit to cope with such an army failed to arrest the French. The frontier for-

tress of Sarzana, which Charles attacked at the end of October, was soon captured; and the French King continued his advance. Pietro had now only two courses open to him. He has been spoken of with contempt by all writers for his action in this crisis, but whether this view is correct seems open to question, as it would appear to have scarcely sufficiently considered the problem before Pietro. On the fall of Sarzana the only two alternatives possible to him were, either to be prepared to sustain a siege of Florence by the French army, or to endeavour by a partial surrender to induce the French King to pass peaceably through Tuscany, avoiding the capital. The first course meant, inevitably, in view of the complete disparity in military power between the organised army which Charles commanded, and Florence's mercenary levies, the assault and sack of Florence by foreign troops. Had the French King been attempting to conquer Tuscany the matter would have been different, and Florence would have been bound to resist to the end and to fall with honour. But this was not the case; the French King had no special quarrel with the Florentine State; so that the sack of the city would have been endured on behalf of another State which had no claim upon Florence for such a sacrifice, and which, though principally concerned, had sent no force to join with her in opposing the French King.

Pietro, therefore, chose the second course, and in order to persuade Charles VIII to accept terms and pass without further aggression through Tuscany by the coast road which avoided Florence, went off in person to the camp of the King of France to try and achieve this by a personal interview. He there saw for the first time what a regular organised army was like, and, if he had not done so before, must have realised at once how futile would be any opposition which Florence could offer to such a force, and that it could only have a result which he was bound at all costs to prevent. The French King agreed to pass peaceably through Tuscany, but would not consent to avoid the capital, and required, as the condition on which Florence should be spared from assault and her territory from devastation, that Pisa, and the fortresses of Sarzana, Sarzanello, Ripafratta, and Pietrasanta should be held by him until the conquest of Naples had been completed. Most of these places were already in Charles's possession, while it was only a question of days before all would be so; and he had power to hold them for as long as he chose; so that Pietro in agreeing to these terms did not make any great concession.

Pietro returned to Florence on the 8th November in expectation that the citizens would be thankful, under the circumstances, for what he had achieved. But the seed so assiduously sown by his cousins at last bore fruit; the citizens had not seen Charles's army, and did not know their own weakness and the French King's strength; their pride was wounded by the idea of the surrender of fortresses; and the combined result brought matters to a climax. Pietro was met by a storm of indignation; the measure of his unpopularity was now full; and there was a general clamour for his banishment and that of his whole family. The Signoria assembled, and promptly passed a decree banishing the Medici permanently from the state of Florence (9th November 1494).[18]

But the policy of Pietro Medici soon became the policy of the Signoria itself. Charles VIII and his army were admitted to the city; his terms were precisely those he had offered to Pietro. Once within Florence, however, Charles VIII had to become somewhat accommodating himself, for Florence retained some defense and deterrent capabilities. Young continued:

> The [French] army was quartered about the city on the unwilling inhabitants, and Charles proceeded to the despoiled and dismantled Medici Palace, where he took up his abode. There next day he summoned the Signoria before him to hear the humiliating terms which he intended to impose on the city. But the ancient spirit of Florence was as strong as ever, and when these terms were read out to them the members of the Signoria utterly refused to accept them. Whereupon the King flew into a rage and swore that if the treaty he had dictated were not forthwith signed they should have war; that he would sound his trumpets, call out his troops, and sack the city. Upon this one of the senators, Piero Capponi, gave that answer which has passed into a Florentine proverb: "If you sound your trumpets we will sound our bells." Charles knew what that meant, for he had on the day before seen a brief example of it in connection with a false alarm; he knew that it meant the ringing of the great bell, "La Vacca," which hung in the tower of the Palazzo della Signoria, and which when it sounded out over Florence would call out into the streets the whole male population of the city, armed and ready to fall on the French troops, scattered in their various quarters, and before they could offer any collective resistance. He would find himself in a hornets' nest. Charles reflected for a moment, and then passing the matter off with a bad joke gave in, and Florence was saved. A less humiliating treaty was drawn up and agreed to, though it was not a whit more satisfactory for Florence than that for agreeing to which Pietro the Unfortunate had incurred such a storm of indignation from the same men.[19]

Denmark's accommodation of Germany in 1914 (she sealed the Baltic with mines to forestall German actions designed to accomplish that goal, which actions might well have resulted in hostilities between Germany and Denmark) is also worth citing,[20] as is Norway's accommodation of Britain in 1915. Norway wanted to sell fish to both Britain and Germany, but was pushed by Britain into a "Fish Agreement," in which she promised to deliver no less than 85 percent of her catch to Britain at mutually agreeable prices. She later acceded to Britain's demand that there be no further deliveries of copper ore to Germany. In the words of Nils Örvik, Norway was simply "too weak to resist" and "consequently had to yield." She wanted to avoid a costly and bloody war. This she did:

> But she also wanted to carry on her economic life as an independent sovereign nation and make decisions for herself. This she could not do. She was forced to accept such terms as she could get.
>
> Because war as an instrument of practical politics was out of the question, Norway was left with one alternative: to keep peace at the sacrifice of her full sovereign status. She had to take what she was given, and what little bargaining power she had did not prove sufficient to preserve her the right of self-determination in her economic life.[21]

A third case from Scandanavia is that of Finland's accommodation of Russia, a recurrent twentieth-century phenomenon. Juho Kusti Paasikivi, one of the foremost Finnish statesman to espouse accommodation of the Soviet Union, began his political career to the pre–World War I era as a member of a "group of conservative politicians who had been convinced that the national identity of the Finnish people could be preserved only through prudent appeasement of the strategic interests and prestige of the Russian Empire." He continued to lobby for accommodation in the era of Stalin, as did his countryman Urho Kekkonen, head of the Agrarian party. On two occasions—once just before, and the other during, World War II—the Finns found themselves at war on the Soviets. But by 1944 they were returning to accommodation. In 1945 the Finnish delegation to the Paris Peace Conference was instructed by President Paasikivi "always to bear in mind that the maintenance of good relations with the Soviet Union had overriding importance and that nothing was to be done in Paris that might give rise to the suspicion that Finland was plotting with the Western Powers against the Soviet Union." This kind of accommodation has now been given the label "Finlandization."

Paasikivi's desire to avoid giving any sign that Finland sought to create a new "cordon sanitaire" was justified. The Soviet foreign minister, Molotov, made the Soviet position quite clear. In private talks between the Finnish and Soviet delegations this warning was put more brutally. Molotov's deputy, Vyshinsky, told Prime Minister Pekkala: "Just try to move the frontier closer to Leningrad with the aid of the Western Powers and you will see what happens to you."

The Finnish government tried and imprisoned several of their own World War II leaders to avoid seeing the Soviets intervene for this purpose. They also declined the offer of Marshall Plan aid, again to avoid offending their Soviet neighbors. They entered into a mutual defense treaty with the Soviets. And they appear to have avoided naming anti-Soviet politicians to high office in order to avoid confrontation. In exchange, the Soviets have returned the port of Porkkala and parts of the province of Karelia to Finland.[22] Max Jakobson, a Finnish scholar, describes the Paasikivi way to "Finnish neutrality":

> Paasikivi offered a new concept of Finnish-Soviet relations that not only was tailored to fit the prevailing facts of power but also was designed to restore the faith of the Finnish people in an independent future. He had always argued that the Russian interest in Finland was primarily strategic and defensive. It was to make sure that the city Peter the Great had built would be safe from attack through Finland. This, according to Paasikivi, was a "legitimate interest," a subtle phrase which, like a shorthand symbol, conveyed both the direction and the limit of his policy of appeasement. It was designed to assure the Soviet Government that its need for security would be satisfied, while serving notice that Finland was not prepared to yield to demands that went beyond the legitimate—ideological demands for instance. By convincing the Soviet leaders that Finland would in no circumstances turn against them, Paasikivi believed, the Finns could secure their own independence and way of life.

> Paasikivi may well have recognized his own thinking in what Winston Churchill wrote in his chapter on Munich in *The Gathering Storm*: "Those who are prone . . . to seek sharp and clear-cut solutions of difficult and obscure problems, who are ready to fight whenever some challenge comes from foreign power, have not always been right. On the other hand, those whose inclination is to bow their heads, to seek patiently and faithfully for peaceful compromise, are not always wrong. On the contrary, in the majority of instances, they may be right, not only morally, but from a practical standpoint."[23]

A final example of a weaker country's accommodation of stronger ones is that of Switzerland in World War II. Neutral Switzerland, to be sure, has generally preferred policies of defense or deterrence to those of accommodation, and it had always retained the capability to punish an invader. General Guisan, the Swiss chief of staff, braced the army's will to resist in 1940. Several pro-German officers who provided the Axis with state secrets were shot for their treason in 1942 and 1943. But the Swiss found themselves entirely surrounded by the Axis, and they appear to have "adjusted to realities" and altered their policies in at least three ways. In the first place, in order to avoid border incidents with Axis troops, they proceeded to turn away Jewish refugees. In the second place, they agreed to Axis demands that they black out the country in November 1940, in order to prevent Allied bombers from using Swiss cities as nighttime navigational aids. In the third place, in 1941 they extended substantial credits to Germany and agreed to export only such goods as were approved by the Axis.[24] Until August 1944, when the Allied forces reached the Swiss borders and it became evident that the Axis power was declining, Swiss exports to the Axis (including many key strategic products) were substantial. (see graph 1).

Graph 1
Exports to the Allies and to Germany, 1938–1945
(in millions of Swiss francs)

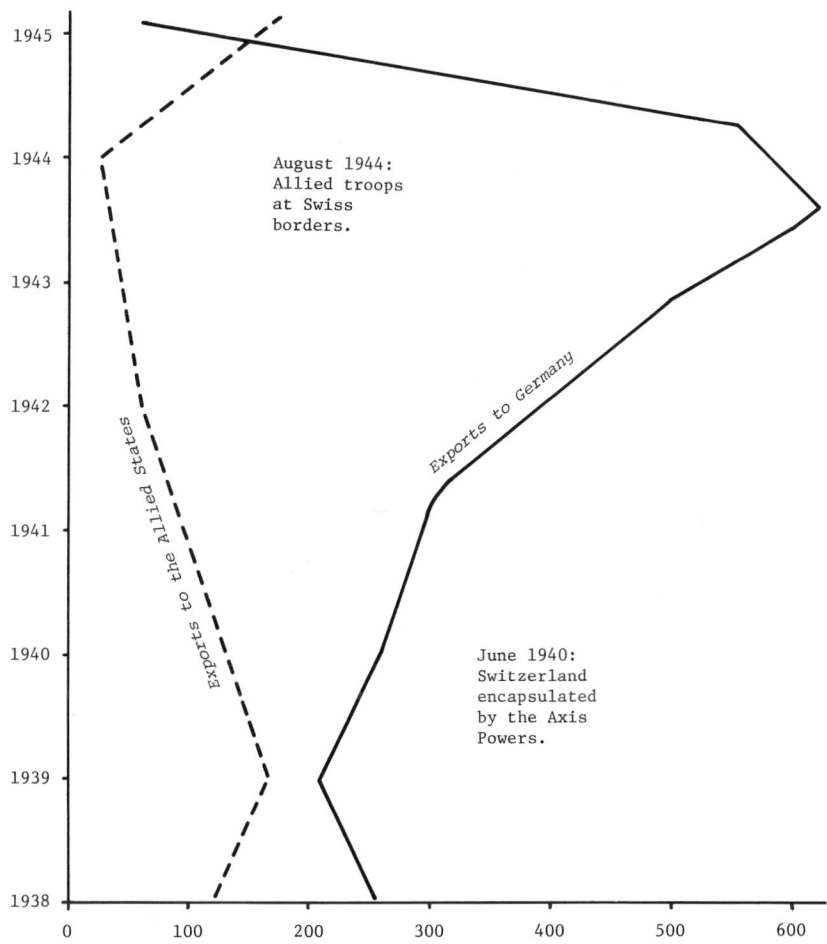

Source: *Die Schweizerische Kriegs-Wirtschaft 1939–1948. Bericht des Volkswirtschaftsdepartementes* (Bern, 1950), table on p. 65.

Weaker states, then, are known to have behaved in an accommodating fashion towards stronger powers. But are these the *typical* acts of accommodation? Probably not. In any event, it is certain that weak states are not the *only* ones to have responded to threats with acts of accommodation. George Kennan recently argued that a substantial withdrawal of American forces from Western Europe would not result in a process of "Finlandization" (accommodation of the Soviet Union by Western European states):

> Most small or militarily-inferior nations are sensible enough to recognize that there is nothing to be gained by yielding to blackmail of any sort from stronger ones, because the demand acceded to today will merely be followed by another one tomorrow; and if one is going to enter on this path, one must expect it to end with the total loss of national independence. In this case, it is obviously preferable to make one's stand on the first demand, when you still have a chance, than on the last one. So obvious is this that a study of the behavior of governments in the face of a large disparity in military power would probably reveal that as a general rule the smaller and weaker the country, the more sensitive its government to any hint of military pressure being applied against it, and the more ready its resistance to anything that smacks of pressure or blackmail from the stronger power.[25]

Our analysis of these thirty-five acts of accommodation offers some support for Kennan's hypothesis.[26] Only ten of the thirty-five (29 percent) were the acts of weaker powers. Thirteen were the acts of relative equals, and twelve the acts of *stronger* powers. Kennan's remarks may describe adequately the reasons that weaker powers generally try to avoid assuming accommodating postures (though we would not know that, of course, until we had calculated ratios of accommodative acts to confrontative acts of weak and strong states that had perceived threats). But why do stronger powers sometimes assume such postures towards weaker ones?

In order to understand this phenomenon we must keep in mind that in responding to a perceived threat, a nation-state, whether systematically or not, ordinarily engages in some assessment of the nature of the threat, then estimates the prestige, treasure, manpower, and other resources that it will have to spend in order to counter or eliminate that perceived threat. It may then decide that it wishes to purchase such defense or deterrence, or it may decide that it does *not* wish to engage in such expenses—that it will take its chances with the perceived threat, or that it will engage in what it deems a less immediately expensive accommodative gesture. If the perceived threat is deemed to be relatively small, and the costs of and/or the risks involved in confrontation or deterrence are deemed to be great (relative either to the level of the threat or to the resources available), then the stronger power may prefer accommodation to confrontation. A few examples: British payment of "protection" money to Barbary states in the eighteenth and early nineteenth centuries; later Han accommodation of certain Mongol tribes on the borders of the empire; late-seventeenth-century Chinese accommodation of certain successful Vietnamese insurgents; Prussian accommodation of a defeated (but useful) Austria in 1866; Lincoln's accommodative posture towards former rebels in 1865; Parliament's repeal of the Stamp Act and Townshend Acts in 1765 and 1769.[27]

Threatening states generally threaten in two ways: they demand something of value, and they add that they are willing to go to war in order to attain their objectives. The threatened state may want badly to retain the thing of value that is threatened, but it may be even more anxious to avoid a costly war. If deterrence fails, defense may work, but only after one surrenders something that one values—peace. One may successfully defend that which is threatened, but only if one first relinquishes one's desire to remain at peace.

War is an expensive, often unpopular, destabilizing, risky business, even (indeed, in some ways especially) for rich and powerful states. Hence, threats emanating from lesser powers are often dealt with via accommodation. A twentieth-century example: Austria-Hungary's accommodation of Prince Nicholas's Montenegro in 1909 as a result of Austria's annexation of Bosnia, which Bernadotte Schmitt describes thus:

> During these months, the relations between Austria and Montenegro had been anything but satisfactory. Instead of responding cordially to [the Austrian Foreign Minister] Aehrenthal's overture of 7 October, Prince Nicholas protested against the situation of his country, declared that he would no longer be bound by Article 29, presented a note of protest to the Austrian minister, and asked for a rectification of frontier with Herzegovina. Not content with this, the prince issued a fiery proclamation to his people and allowed a demonstration against the Austrian legation. He also despatched a note of protest to the Powers. Finally a partial mobilization was ordered, though it was explained as being only for defensive purposes.
>
> Aehrenthal did not at first take these outbursts seriously and, knowing the greed of the prince, offered him 500,000 crowns, as well as the modification of Article 29, in return for a correct attitude. But when Nicholas continued defiant, a sharp communication was sent to Cetinje [the capital of Montenegro]. Austria would consent to modification of Article 29 and would accord large economic advantages; the prince would be appointed to the honorary command of an Austrian regiment and invited to visit Francis Joseph, provided Montenegro abandoned her hostile attitude. But she had to make the choice "between the advantages of our friendship and the weight of our hostility.". . .
>
> When on 22 January Prince Nicholas summoned the foreign representatives in Cetinje, except the Austrian minister, and asked them to telegraph to their governments a fiery protest against the Austrian miliary preparations, Aehrenthal evidently thought the time had come to act. So the consul in Scutari was instructed to pay out money to the principal agent in Albania [a hostile neighbor of Montenegro's] and to make arrangements for the landing of arms in the event of war.

When, however, [the Russian Foreign Minister] Izvolsky, decided to abandon Serbia and communicated to Cetinje a copy of the note addressed to Belgrade [whereby Russia had warned Serbia that she must yield to Austria], Montenegro's position was hopeless. Aehrenthal accordingly attempted a new overture, for which a recent summons of the Austrian minister to the konak provided the entering wedge. The offer was made in general terms, but Aehrenthal promised to show "the greatest possible spirit of accommodation," provided the offer was accepted promptly; if he feared the opposition of his people, the prince could declare that he had to follow the advice of the Powers.[28]

Prince Nicholas agreed this time, after having rattled his saber as loudly and as long as he dared. In the process, he did gain some concessions from Austria that Baron Aehrenthal was willing to grant rather than to risk a potentially destabilizing use of force.

Stronger powers can also behave in an accommodative fashion towards weaker powers during or after hostilities, in order to neutralize the slight, but still annoying, threat they may still pose, or (more positively) in order to win them over as allies or clients. A few examples: First, Philip of Macedon's generous treatment of Athens and others of the Greek city-states after the battle of Chaeronea. We offer two accounts. The first is by A. R. Burn:

> Philip was far too good a politician to have any ideas of holding down the whole of an unwilling Greece by Macedonian garrisons at all strategic points. It is a remark which he might easily have made himself, that you can do anything with bayonets, except sit on them. Philip had no desire for such a throne. Nor would the man-power of Macedonia have been sufficient. On the contrary, Philip tried all his life to placate all Greeks who could be placated, and he sought for himself nothing more nor less than the Captaincy of such a League, to carry Greek arms into Persia, as Isokrates and many others had so long proposed. On the morrow of the battle [of Chaeronea], his political emissaries were already busy making overtures for the formation of a League of United Greek States.
>
> At the same time, with an eye to the short as well as to the long run, he was at pains to divide Athens from Thebes, by imposing such peace terms as should placate the former—a city which Philip had always respected and in which there was a strong peace party—while firmly holding down the latter, a state which was both unpopular among its neighbours and physically easier for a Macedonian garrison to hold. Thebes had to see a Macedonian garrison installed on her citadel, which implied control of her government. The two cities at opposite ends of Boiotia, Plataia and Orchomenos which Thebes had destroyed, were to be restored. Their inhabitants could be trusted to pursue a good anti-Theban policy, and, the most cunning stroke of all, Thebes was made to cede to Athens the border

territory of Orôpos, the bone of contention in endless border wars. As "compensation" for this bounty, Philip required Athens to surrender her holdings in the Gallipoli peninsula, which Philip required as jumping-off ground for the next act on his programme. . . .

For the rest, Philip showed towards Athens an astonishing generosity—and saw to it that it was well publicised. He restored his Athenian prisoners without ransom (not, we must suppose, immediately, but as part of a peace treaty by which Athens entered into formal alliance with him); and he sent back ashes of their dead, after honourable cremation on the battlefield, accompanied by a military guard of honour under Antipatros and Alexander. . . .

Philip himself marched on with his army through western Attica to Corinth and the Peloponnese. Most of the secondary cities of central Greece had felt the weight of his hand at Chaironeia. The others, those which had taken the Macedonian side from the start, were congratulating themselves on their foresight and on their correct judgment of Philip as a good and generous Hellene. With every state Philip made a separate treaty; there was no general treaty between Philip and the Greeks, which might have assisted the discontented in any efforts to form a common front against him. Only Sparta, proud as ever, though now impotent in her corner of the Peloponnese, still stood out and refused to negotiate. Philip marched down through Arcadia and into the plain of the Eurôtas, his army reinforced by allied contingents of Argives, Messenians, Arcadians—all Sparta's old enemies. Sparta's territory was ravaged and disputed border lands taken from her and given to her neighbours. It is not clear whether in the end Philip took the trouble to make peace with her at all. Certainly he never considered outraging Greek feeling by destroying, as he could have destroyed, that unbeautiful, unwalled, untidy city, which, almost as much as Athens, had become a pan-Hellenic institution. Moreover, it would have been unlike Philip not to calculate that Argos, for example, was much more likely to remain a good ally so long as she not only had the debatable land of Kynouria to cultivate, but a vindictive and unforgiving Sparta against whom to hold it.

The separate treaties with each state were the basis of Philip's predominance. Meanwhile, Greek feeling, ever sensitive, as Philip well knew, was to be placated by the spectacle of free and equal membership for all, in a League which was to put an end to the eternal and fratricidal border wars, and which had a positive common object—a thing the lack of which has contributed to the unsuccess of many another League in history—in the prosecution of national, imperialistic and frankly predatory war against Persia. Revenge for the outrages committed by Xerxes, was the cry. Privately, poor men thought of well-paid service as mercenaries, of good farms as colonists, of good openings in business or posts under the government:

and many rich men thought, if we may judge by Isokrates, what a good thing if all these formidable mercenaries and hungry proletarians could be drawn off elsewhere.

The negotiations at Corinth were protracted. Philip must have worked hard, giving endless audiences and using his famous charm upon potentially useful or troublesome politicians and condottieri.[29]

The second account is by J. R. Hamilton:

> The punishment of Thebes was severe, as befitted an ally of Macedon which had defected. The leaders of the anti-Macedonian faction were executed or banished, and an oligarchy of 300 pro-Macedonian exiles was set up, supported by a Macedonian garrison in the Cadmeia, the citadel of Thebes. The Boeotian League was dissolved and orders were given for Plataea, Ochomenus, and Thespiae, destroyed by Thebes, to be restored. Theban prisoners, if not ransomed, were sold into slavery. Athens deserved punishment no less than Thebes, and expected it. Preparations were made to resist, but Philip expressed his willingness to negotiate and offered lenient terms. Athens was to disband her confederacy and give up her claim to the Chersonnese, but to retain her possessions in the Aegean and to recover Oropus from Thebes. She was to become an ally of Macedon, and Philip undertook not to send troops into Attica or warships into the Piraeus. Athenian prisoners were to be restored without ransom. Philip's offer was readily accepted, and Athenian relief and gratitude were expressed in the grant of citizenship to the king and his son and in the erection of a statue to Philip in the Agora.
>
> Athens had fared much better than Thebes. No doubt the difficulty of besieging a city which could be supplied from the sea weighed with Philip, and admiration for the cultural achievements of Athens may perhaps have had some influence. But the most important consideration was undoubtedly the Athenian fleet, now numbering over 350 ships, which he required for his expedition against Persia, soon to be made public.[30]

Philip died before he could launch his planned invasion of Asia, but his accommodation of Athens served his son Alexander well when the invasion took place. And Alexander had learned the art of statecraft well; he, too, could accommodate Greek and Asian alike to serve his interest and conserve his strength, according to Charles A. Robinson:

> After the battle [of Arbela, in Persia, when Alexander crushed Darius III] Alexander was proclaimed king of Asia, and made magnificent sacrifices to the gods and rewarded his friends with wealth and estates. And being desirous of honor among the Greeks, and to emphasize that this had been a Panhellenic campaign of revenge, he wrote the Plataeans that he would rebuild their city, because their ancestors had fought so nobly during the

Persian Wars. He sent also to the people of Croton in Italy a portion of the spoils, honoring the zeal and valor of their athlete Phayllus who, when the rest of the Greeks in Italy refused to help their brother Greeks during the Persian Wars, fitted out a ship at his own cost and sailed with it to Salamis, that he might have some share in the peril there.

When Alexander approached Babylon, the people came out to meet him en masse and surrendered their citadel and money. Entering the city, he commanded the Babylonians to rebuild all the temples which Xerxes had destroyed, and especially that of Marduk; and he himself sacrificed to Marduk and performed whatever other religious rites the Chaldaean seers directed. With the same tolerance and wisdom that he had already shown in Egypt, Alexander made Mazaeus, the Persian who had fought so well against Parmenio at Gaugamela, satrap of Babylon, but again he was careful to separate the civil, military and financial powers; Macedonians were appointed as military commandant and financial superintendent.

After a month's halt in Babylon, Alexander started for Susa, the administrative capital of the Persian empire, and on the way received a letter from Philoxenus, whom he had sent on immediately after the battle, telling him that the city had surrendered and that all the money was safe. . . .

Now Alexander made ready to crush Spitamenes. One decision of the utmost importance, however, had been forced on Alexander by all this warfare. If he really meant that he was to be king of the barbarians, as well as of the Macedonians, he must permit the barbarians to enter into full responsible partnership with him and have their own stake in his success. He therefore took the dramatic step of adding large numbers of Bactrians, Sogdians and other Asiatics to the army. His confidence was fully rewarded, for it was these Asiatic soldiers who pressed the enemy so hard that they cut off Spitamenes' head and sent it to Alexander. Alexander carried his policy of cooperation with the barbarians even further, when a few months later at Bactra he ordered that 30,000 native youths should be taught the Greek language and trained in the use of Macedonian weapons. These decisions, not to mention some of his other ideas and the Oriental dress that he wore occasionally, did not however, delight the Macedonians.[31]

One final example of accommodation of a weaker power by a stronger one during wartime: Hitler's initially accommodative occupation of Denmark (from 1940 to 1943). Denmark was occupied, to be sure, but the German demands were relatively modest, and the Danes retained a considerable "nuisance" capability of which the Germans were fully conscious. Stewart Oakley describes this event:

> While bombers flew threateningly overhead, the German envoy informed the government that Denmark would be "protected" for the duration of the

war, but promised that there would be no interference by German military authorities in the country's internal affairs; any further resistance would, however, be answered with an aerial bombardment of the capital. Stauning [the Danish prime minister] and his colleagues were in no position to make more than a verbal protest and ordered an immediate cessation of hostilities to prevent unnecessary bloodshed.

As had been promised, the occupying forces behaved, at first at least, with "correctness," and the initial public alarm caused by their arrival subsided; the lives of most Danes were little changed. Shortages of certain items made themselves felt, some more foodstuffs had in time to be rationed, and some others, such as tea and coffee, disappeared altogether, but no real hardship was suffered. Prices rose as the National Bank increased its note issue to compensate suppliers for the growing debt incurred by the Germans for goods which they in effect requisitioned. But the government imposed price controls, and inflation was kept in check. Inflation and German orders indeed helped to speed the wheels of industry, and unemployment, which had been high at the beginning of 1940, was somewhat reduced. Hitler decided to try to make of Denmark a "model protectorate" to demonstrate that peoples who did not oppose the formation of the "New Order" in Europe had nothing to fear. He also needed Danish agricultural produce, supplies of which might be interrupted if the Danes were given serious cause for complaint.[32]

Initially, the Danish response was one of mutual accommodation. The elderly diplomat Erik Scavenius, who had negotiated the accommodation of Germany in the opening days of World War I as foreign minister, was named to that post again. He was not a Nazi, but he believed that Danes must learn to accept the "New Order" (which, after Dunkirk, seemed to have come to stay) and that they should adopt a cooperative attitude towards the representatives of German power in their country. But many Danes did not agree, and by 1941 a resistance movement was gaining momentum. Hitler became annoyed, but when Scavenius emerged as prime minister, Hitler continued to soft-pedal, in the hope that the Danish Nazi party would emerge as the leading party in the land. Stewart Oakley adds:

> For a time tension was relaxed. The accommodating attitude of the new German plenipotentiary Werner Best eased Scavenius's task, and in March 1943 it was felt that circumstances warranted the holding of elections. In spite of strong German support, the Danish Nazis failed to increase their representation in the *Folketing*; the occupation had done nothing to shake the Danish electorate's allegiance to the old parties.[33]

In this instance, accommodation did not help to achieve the end for which it was the means. But this failure may be accounted for by Hitler's failures on the battlefields of Europe. In effect, by 1944 (when the resistance grew to such proportions that Hitler ordered an end to "gentleness"), Germany was no longer overwhelmingly stronger than Denmark.

Another sort of accommodation of weak by strong is that of co-optation,[34] a strategy often utilized by great powers that are less ambitious or expansionistic than those we have just considered (Philip, Alexander, Hitler). Co-optation was employed by the Han emperors "to use barbarians to check [or attack] barbarians" (*i-i-chih-i* [or *i-i-fa-i*]).[35] It was the strategy employed by Roman emperors for years, and by the Eastern Emperor Theodosius (himself a co-optated Spaniard) against the Visigoth invasion of Thrace in A.D. 382. But there was a difference between what Theodosius did and what others had done before him. Arnold Jones writes:

> Beyond the frontier the Roman government had always tried to create an outer protective screen by making treaties with the neighbouring barbarian chieftains, whereby they undertook to refrain from raiding the provinces themselves and provided forces to protect it. In return they received protection against their neighbours and often a subsidy. In some areas the chieftains came to value imperial recognition and took pride in the titles and royal insignia conferred upon them. On the desert frontier of Syria, Arabia and Palestine a regular system was built up, whereby the Roman government appointed paramount chiefs or phylarchs over the Saracen tribes adjacent to each province. In Africa the system was developed yet further, Roman prefects being substituted for native chiefs over the nearer and more settled tribes. Barbarian tribes thus allied to the empire (*foederati*) might be called upon to supply contingents for distant operations. Thus we find Mavia, a Saracen queen, sending a force of Bedouin from the Syrian desert to defend Constantinople against the Goths in 378.
>
> Such barbarian contingents were harmless and useful so long as they were sparingly used and went back to their homes beyond the frontier when the campaign was over. The situation was entirely changed when Theodosius I, after long and indecisive warfare with the Goths whom Valens had received into the empire in 376, gave the entire tribe of the Visigoths lands in Thrace, allowing them to remain a federate people under their own king. The Visigoths were ultimately settled in Aquitania under the same conditions, and various other barbarian groups which had forced their way into the empire, such as the Burgundians and the Alans, were given similar terms. Such federate bands were highly unreliable, since their chiefs naturally exploited their position to blackmail the government and to win larger and better territories and increased subsidies for their tribesmen. The Roman government was impelled to use them since they were there, and would, if left idle, be even more dangerous to the internal peace of the empire.[36]

And J. B. Bury says:

> The Visigoths were induced, through the successes and skilful dealings of Theodosius, to become subjects of the Emperor—not regular provincials and Roman citizens, but allies on a footing of freedom and semi-independence, still remaining a nation but owing definite obligations to the Emperor. Lands in the province of Lower Moesia, the modern Bulgaria, were assigned to them—the same region in which Constantine had settled their Christian fellow-countrymen whom Wulfilas had led out of Dacia. They were to pay no tribute for the land; they were to receive certain pensions from the government; but they were to serve the Empire when needed as federate soldiers under their own chief. The capitulation was concluded in October 382. . . .
>
> Theodosius fully appreciated the dangers of the Gothic problem, and he pursued unremittingly a policy of conciliation and friendship. He cultivated the friendship of the Gothic chiefs, whom he used constantly to entertain in his palace, and he secured devoted adherents among them. . . . There seemed a chance that if this policy were pursued the Goths might gradually become enervated, lose their old restlessness and national pride, and reconcile themselves permanently to the provincial state. But if under the panic inspired by the Hun and the dexterous dealings of Theodosius they seemed to have declined from their old independent spirit, this spirit was far from being yet extinct; and though some of them were fully reconciled to the privileges of belonging to the Empire, there were others who thought otherwise. . . .
>
> The Goths had followed Theodosius in his campaign against the usurper Eugenius, but when the great Emperor died, and was succeeded by two very young princes, they reconsidered the position. It proved to be a turning-point in their history. The parliament of the people met and deliberated. Two motives, so we are told, operated. One was dislike and distrust of the new Emperors or rather of their advisers; the other was the apprehension that if they continued as they were they would become enervated and would decline. In any case it was felt that preparation must be made for emergencies; and that the best preparation was unity and a leader. Accordingly the Visigoths chose a king. They had a family marked out to furnish a king whenever a king should be chosen, the Balthas or Bolds, and their choice fell on Alaric the Bold.[37]

A particular set of circumstances—the death of Theodosius, the weakness of his successors, the victory of Gothicism, and the rise of Alaric—doomed that particular co-optative act to failure.

A more successful example of the strategy of co-optative accommodation is that of the late-eighteenth-century Manchu court's handling of Vietnamese civil strife, a peripheral threat to its hegemony. Here, as in the other cases, mutual accommodation seemed preferable to war. According to Truong Buu Lam:

> Although [Chinese imperial] troops were massed at the frontier, orders to move them never came. For this inaction there seem to have been three reasons.
>
> The first is related to an earlier experience of an unsuccessful campaign against Burma. From 1766 to 1770 China undertook several expeditions designed to bring Burma under control, but all resulted in disaster. The [imperial] court's explanation was that the Chinese soldiers were exhausted by Burma's climate and by the diseases they had contracted there. The implication was that the same thing could happen in Vietnam, where climatic conditions were similar.
>
> The second reason given by the court was that the Vietnamese people were rebellious. An expedition would be costly of men and money, and the best that could come of it would be the annexation of Vietnam. But then, what would China profit from the conquest of a country impossible to control, unless, as in Sinkiang, the imperial government should send there a large number of officials and troops? . . .
>
> Third, the court felt that even if China could control Vietnam directly it would be necessary to appoint a viceroy to administer the country. With this in mind, an imperial decree noted that in such a case, there would be no difference between a Ch'ing viceroy and Nguyên Huê [the rebel], for the new Vietnamese ruler might now be viewed as an imperially appointed official. The Chinese emperor had indeed been entrusted by Heaven to administer the entire world and he delegated officials to take care of the internal affairs of the various distinct territories. The notion underlying this view was that "Heaven divided the territories but not the people."
>
> Thus the court was in no hurry to send Chinese troops into Vietnam. The Ch'ing now felt no overriding obligation toward the [deposed] Lê king because by twice fleeing from Hanoi he had shown himself to be an unworthy ruler. Peking, therefore, was now ready for a peaceful settlement of the Vietnamese problem. The court hoped that the appointment of a famous military leader to settle it would intimidate Nguyên Huê and induce him to offer his submission.
>
> Nguyên Huê, on his part, was no less ready for a peaceful solution. Even before launching his attack against the Chinese expeditionary forces, he had been worried about China's subsequent vengeance. His worry was exacerbated by the fact that the Siamese, incited by the survivor of the former Nguyên princes, Nguyên Anh (who eventually was to unify and rule over Vietnam under the reign title of Gia-long), were threatening his new kingdom from the south and west.

Thus the way was paved for negotiations. A few days after Fu-k'ang-an's arrival on the frontier, an important embassy bearing tribute arrived from Hanoi to offer Nguyên Huê's submission. It was exactly what both the court and Fu-k'ang-an had expected. The court, as we have seen, had desired a peaceful settlement, whereas Fu-k'ang-an was particularly eager not to antagonize the court because he had been involved in irregularities in his former post. Moreover, Vietnamese documents state that the governor-general was not indifferent to the numerous presents offered by Nguyên Huê.

In addition to all this, Nguyên Huê's submission and apologies were perfectly acceptable. The tone of his petition was respectful and obedient, as were the manners of his envoys. Nguyên Huê stressed many times that his attack on the imperial army had been nothing but an accident; it had occurred because in the early hours of the morning his soldiers could not distinguish the Chinese from the local forces. In other words, he would not have dared to attack the imperial troops. Thus Chinese prestige was saved.

It is not surprising that Fu-k'ang-an imposed only two conditions for peace: all Chinese prisoners were to be handed back to China and Nguyên Huê himself was to come to the Chinese capital to offer his apologies and submission. Nguyên Huê accepted these conditions with one slight modification: he would come to the capital only in the following year in order to participate in the celebration marking the emperor's eightieth anniversary. In the meantime he sent an important embassy to Peking, headed by his nephew, to present tribute.

The Vietnamese crisis was thus virtually over, and the only condition to be fulfilled was Nguyên Huê's visit to Peking [which condition was ultimately fulfilled].[38]

Two final examples of this co-optative phenomenon may be worth consideration.[39] They deal with the efforts of some U.S. officials to accommodate American Indian tribes of the Southwest and the Powder River region (the northern Plains) in the mid-nineteenth century. Secretary of War Conrad summed up the case for accommodation in 1851: "It would be far less expensive to feed them [the Indians] than to fight them." Robert Utley describes the efforts of Indian agent Robert S. Neighbors in the mid-1850s to accommodate the Indians of Texas and the Arizona Territory:

> The nomadic way of life itself stood in imminent peril. To arranging an accommodation that would end the shedding of his countrymen's blood at the same time that it secured rights and property to the Indians, [Indian Agent Robert S.] Neighbors dedicated himself with tireless energy.

> As Neighbors and his superiors saw it, the solution lay in guaranteeing land to the Indians. At first the idea was to draw a line separating the

settlements from the Indian country—the old idea of a permanent Indian frontier. The Indians would be compelled to stay on one side, the whites on the other. As the impossibility of imposing such a restriction became increasingly apparent, this solution gave way to another: set aside reservations for the Indians and let the oncoming settlements flow by, leaving behind islands of Indians in a sea of whites. On the reservations the Indians would be taught to support themselves as farmers rather than as huntsmen, and the federal Intercourse laws would protect them from white rapacity. Neighbors repeatedly urged this plan, but the federal government could do nothing until Texas made available the land. This the legislature finally did, after six years of federal prodding, early in 1854. The act of February 6 authorized federal officials to survey no more than twelve leagues (53,136 acres) of unclaimed state land for occupancy by the Indians of Texas.

Neighbors and Captain Marcy explored the headwaters of the Brazos the following summer and marked out two reservations. One, on the upper Clear Fork of the Brazos, was for the Southern Comanches. Genuinely alarmed by the approach of the settlements and influenced over the years by the counsel of Neighbors, they professed readiness to settle down and try their hand at farming. The other reservation, on the Salt Fork of the Brazos just below Fort Belknap, was for the Anadarkos, Caddos, Tawakonis, Wacos, and Tonkawas. Semisedentary and loosely confederated tribes, they had been caught in a tightening vise of settlements on the one side and roving Comanches on the other. They greeted the innovation with relief and brought to it a considerably firmer grounding in agriculture than the Comanches. By the middle of 1855 both reservations, each with its own agent under the supervision of Neighbors, were in operation and exhibiting encouraging results.[40]

But the effort did not solve the entire problem. Congress "refused to pay more than a token price" for land acquired in the process and refused "to sanction more than token issues of food to a people reluctant to learn new ways of supporting themselves." Agent Neighbors was assassinated by frontier whites, and the accommodative posture soon gave way to a more aggressive one.

Later the process was repeated in the Powder River region. There, throughout the 1860s, Sioux and Blackfeet resisted the army's advance and demanded the abandonment of Forts Phil Kearney and C. F. Smith, the main defense outposts on the Bozeman Trail. Unwilling to fight a war whose costs seemed destined to outweigh any accruing benefits, the government acquiesced. Robert Utley later says:

> For the army, it was an unpalatable but not indigestible prescription. The forts had cost a great deal of blood, toil, and treasure, and to hand them over to Red Cloud's torch-bearing warriors was deeply humiliating. Such

abject surrender, furthermore, could not help but inspire them—and by example their brethren of the southern Plains—to further resistance. Besides, strategists contended, the forts were needed to keep the Indians off the railroad and to serve as offensive bases when the time of reckoning came. Yet top officers had to admit that with available resources the road could not be made safe for travelers, and the withdrawal would free a full regiment of infantry for more mobile use along the railroad. And they conceded the obvious truth that every mile the Union Pacific advanced toward the shorter Salt Lake City–Virginia City route made the Bozeman Trail that much more obsolete.

The treaty laid before the Indians at Fort Laramie also defined a reservation on which to concentrate the Sioux and other northern tribes—nearly all of present South Dakota west of the Missouri River. It granted hunting rights on the Republican River and in Nebraska and Wyoming north of the Platte. And, a further necessary concession to the Red Cloud people, it reserved the Powder River country as "unceded Indian territory" on which no white might trespass without Indian consent. . . .

. . . .

Shepherding the Platte and Powder River Sioux to General Harney's reservation turned out to be an undertaking of several years' duration. But from most appearances the Fort Laramie Treaty could be counted a success. It ended the Red Cloud War. Red Cloud submitted himself to Indian Bureau paternalism, and although he remained a maddeningly disruptive influence for the next forty-one years, he never again took the warpath. Many of his people chose the same course, and a state of comparative tranquility settled on the northern Plains.[41]

Eventually the pressure of grazers, farmers, and miners on the unceded land provoked confrontation with those Indians who were unwilling to submit to reservation life, however, and army units (among them George Custer's Seventh Cavalry) were dispatched to force the Indians to leave the land. Accommodation was only deemed appropriate under very particular circumstances. In no way did it preclude a policy of confrontation once the circumstances had changed. Thus Bismarck displayed an accommodating attitude toward the Ottoman Empire throughout the crises of the late 1870s, because, as he put it himself, he did not think the Balkans to be "worth the bones of a single Pomeranian Grenadier." Since Bismarck was anxious to hold together the League of the Three Emperors (Austria, Germany, Russia), he sought to avoid any divisive Balkan war. Later, during the Bosnian crisis of 1908, another German chancellor, Prince Bülow, would urge Austria "to show herself as accommodating as possible [towards Turkey] in economic matters and in questions affecting the state finances."[42] But circumstances had changed; Germany no longer urged on Austria a policy of *total* conciliation in the Balkans. Russia had by now entered into the Triple Entente, and there was "a generally growing conviction in Berlin that Germany's only reliable ally must be shored up, no matter what the cost. What this meant was the underwriting of Austria-Hungary as a Great Power, which meant in turn not merely the defense of its frontiers but the support of such aggressions as it might wish to take." Austria wanted to annex Bosnia? Germany would support her. Prince Bülow told his ambassador in Vienna that "the consideration of our alliance relationship imperatively demands that with Baron Aehrenthal we avoid all that might be capable of crossing him in this so vital question for Austria-Hungary."[43] According to Laurence Lafore:

> There was no doubt that all this represented the culmination of a gradual change in the attitude of the Germans, which had once been one of caution in supporting Austrian ventures. The Near Eastern Question was now seen in Berlin as well worth the bones of the entire German Army. Nor was there any doubt that this abandonment of Bismarck's precept and dictum was the consequence of the evolving insecurity of the Habsburg Monarchy in the face of the "centrifugal" pressures of an aroused Slavdom and, at the same time, of Germany's encirclement.[44]

We have examined cases of accommodation of the strong by the weak and of the weak by the strong. It remains for us to examine those cases of accommodation in which the parties involved may be said to be of relatively equal strength, the one not *obviously* stronger than the other. Under these conditions, why does accommodation occur?

Much depends on perception. A sense of powerlessness may dispose a state to accommodate, whether this powerlessness is accurately perceived or not. If a government *feels* that it lacks sufficient physical resources, manpower, and/or allies, it may choose accommodation, even though its people may still in *fact* possess the ability to resist. A state possessing sufficient resources and manpower may choose accommodation if its leaders lack nerve. The Aztec empire in the Age of Cortez may be an example of this phenomenon. Aztec sources report that Montezuma was unable to sleep or eat, thinking that "everything he did was in vain." He was "lost in despair, in the deepest gloom and sorrow," "filled with terror," and "conquered by despair."[45] Montezuma appeared to have feared that the Spaniards might have been vengeful messengers of the gods, or gods themselves. His fear led him to offer various gifts to the Spanish and to open the gates to them. This form of accommodation, based on excessive fear, may also be seen in the French response to Munich in 1938. Laurence Lafore says:

> The crumbling of the French determination took place partly for a reason of the utmost significance which only much later came to light. Bonnet (the French foreign minister) was ... an excessive realist. His offense was to lose hope. He did not destroy France as a great power; rather he exag-

gerated the fact that it had ceased to be one. He was a trained economist and a former ambassador at Washington, and these qualifications helped him to see, as clearly as anybody else in Europe, that the only way to preserve a system which had depended on the fading illusion of French greatness was to invoke the power of the United States. In September of 1938 he acted on his certainty and secretly pled with Roosevelt for promises of military support in the war he knew would follow the honoring of the alliance with Czechoslovakia.

Bonnet's reasoning was based partly on the pessimism of the French generals, much heightened by the horrifying tales spread that September by Charles Lindbergh about German air power, which reduced the French air force to the verge of tears. Lindbergh, after a visit to Germany, was convinced it was irresistible. He passionately sought to persuade the British and French that resistance was suicide. He presented fabulous figures (8,000 planes) on the German air force and German plane production. They were terrifying, although completely incorrect.

The logic of such a strategic situation was formidable. The Soviet Union had no common frontier with the beleaguered Czechs or with Germany, and the governments of Poland and Rumania, which lay between, were fanatically averse to allowing Red troops on their territories. France had no common frontier with the Czechs, and the estimate of German power and the strength of the Siegfried Line, much overrated by the French generals, seemed to assure that Czechoslovakia would be doomed and France itself threatened and its cities laid waste. It seemed possible that Italy and Spain would join Germany. Most significantly, *the French General Staff had made no plans at all to march into Germany to assist the Czechs.* Still, Bonnet had been willing to risk war if France could be assured of American aid. . . .

Roosevelt promptly rejected Bonnet's solicitations. There was then nothing left, the Frenchman despairingly concluded, except to follow Britain's initiative, and thereafter he exceeded the British in his zeal for a general settlement which would, if necessary, concede Hitler anything he wanted east of the Rhine. . . .

Much of the French press was stridently opposed to a strong stand. . . . As one headline put it in April 1938, "Must three million Frenchmen die to keep three million Germans under Czech rule?" The French skill at epigram concealed a much more pertinent and difficult question: should an incalculable number of French lives be risked to prevent the Nazi state from dominating Europe? Bonnet and Daladier, informed men, might reject the false premises of the first question; the second they dared not answer.[46]

Our other cases do not represent such blatant instances of fear or overestimation. Indeed, several (the accommodation of France by the other members of the Holy Alliance in the Belgian Crisis of 1831, the French accommodation of Britain over Syria and Egypt in 1839, the Austrian accommodation of Turkey in 1909, the French and English accommodation of the Vikings in the ninth and tenth centuries) appear to have involved thoughtful threat assessment and cost evaluation and could be styled successes. The Danegeld (payments to Viking raiders to forestall further pillaging) were expensive and embarrassing, but they were clearly less distressing to those nobles in power than the alternative thought of the centralization of royal power that was clearly required if one were to mount any effective counteroffensive.[47] Similarly, the Turkish demand for compensation from Austria for the loss of Bulgarian tribute in 1908 was annoying, but when it was supported by an effective Turkish boycott of Austro-Hungarian goods, Baron Aehrenthal sheathed his rattling saber. Further jockeying was useless. According to Bernadotte Schmitt, Aehrenthal

> proceeded to consult the governor of the Bodenkreditanstalt about "a payment to Turkey" and then took up the matter with the Austrian and Hungarian premiers and the joint minister of finance, who was also entrusted with Bosnian affairs. Although the ministers were of opinion that it was not compatible with the dignity of the Monarchy to "buy" (*abkaufen*) Turkish good will, Aehrenthal himself was convinced that there was no other course, an opinion in which he was doubtless confirmed by the intensification of the boycott, the damaging of the Austro-Hungarian arms on an establishment in Beirut, and the demand of Achmed Riza for the restoration of the *status quo ante* on the ground that financial compensation would be "only humiliating" for Turkey! For the moment, because of the opposition of the two premiers, he could not do more than offer an Austro-Hungarian loan of 50–60,000,000 francs; but since he thereby professed to meet Kiamil's demand for "a material concession on the part of the Monarchy which could be made effective and available independently of the consent of the other signatory Powers," he did at long last concede the principle asserted by the Porte from the beginning.[48]

In each of the four instances of accommodation cited above the process succeeded because both sides were satisfied with the arrangement; neither sought to disturb the status quo in any fundamental way. But there *were* moments in history in which aggressive, expansionistic states *did* seek to alter fundamentally the balance of power. When other states, relatively equal to these imperialistic ones in power, sought to accommodate, the end result was an alteration of the balance of power to the disadvantage of the accommodating state. This type of accommodation, which is generally due to the misperception by the accommodating state of the ultimate intentions of the threatening state, is what we now call appeasement. As Hans Morgenthau puts it: "Appeasement is a foreign policy that attempts to meet the threat of imperialism with methods appropriate to a policy of the status quo."[49] This may describe the steady loss of power experienced by Carthage at the hands of Rome and her allies from 212 B.C. to 149 B.C. (when Carthage reversed itself and went down fighting). It certainly describes the policies adopted by Britain's Chamberlain government towards Hitler's Germany. Turn back to the words of A. L. Rowse, cited on pages 82–83 of the preceding chapter, for a clear assessment of that government's misperception of Hitler.

In between those acts of accommodation that result in minor adjustments to the status quo and are not destabilizing and those acts of appeasement that fundamentally alter the balance of power and *are* destabilizing, there are a number of more ambiguous cases of accommodation—ambiguous because one could not be expected to predict with ease the final outcome of the power balance on the basis of evidence concerning the behavior of either party at the time of the initial act of accommodation. While the experience of accommodation may transform an accommodated state that was not bent on fundamental change into one that *is* bent on such change, it may also transform an accommodating state into one that confronts and resists both threats and demands in the future. In short, the first act of accommodation of a threat does not lead inevitably to new threats or additional acts of accommodation.

To be sure, the accommodation of a threat may well lead the threatening power to offer new pressure and to demand additional concessions. When Austria sought to accommodate Britain and France in 1853, British (and French) demands increased. Paul Schroeder says that

> Austria's policy . . . became steadily more pro-Western, and Clarendon acknowledged the fact. "I have always and at all times thought that Austria and England were natural allies," he assured Westmorland on July 19; the whole Cabinet had "the warmest feelings" toward her. Yet the more Austria cooperated, the less London really seemed to be satisfied; new demands were raised, pressure and complaints abounded not merely in regard to Russia, but also concerning Italy, Switzerland, Bosnia, Serbia, Montenegro, the case of the Hungarian refugee Martin Koszta, and the treatment of British travelers. A climax was reached in late July when, just as Austria was ranging herself with the West against Russia far more closely than Clarendon had earlier thought possible, British leaders identified her with Russia and denounced her as treacherous and hostile. Clarendon wrote Berlin on July 26, "The moment is good for emancipating Prussia from the thraldom of Austria exercised through the king which of course is that of Russia."[50]

But such demands may well provoke a reversal of the accommodative behavior. The failure of the efforts of the Italian city-states to stem the French tide through a policy of accommodation inspired these states to unite more effectively in the future to resist sixteenth-century French efforts to acquire hegemony in that part of Europe. A similar shift also appears to have occurred in British policy towards Germany and France at the *fin de siècle*, shifts described in Eyre Crowe's memo:

> From 1884 onward, when Bismarck first launched his country into colonial and maritime enterprise, numerous quarrels arose between the two countries. They all have in common this feature—that they were opened by acts of direct and unmistakable hostility to England on the part of the German Government, and that this hostility was displayed with a disregard of the elementary rules of straightforward and honourable dealing, which was deeply resented by successive British Secretaries of State for Foreign Affairs. But perhaps even more remarkable is this other feature, also common to all these quarrels, that the British Ministers, in spite of the genuine indignation felt at the treatment to which they were subjected, in each case readily agreed to make concessions or accept compromises which not only appeared to satisfy all German demands, but were by the avowal of both parties calculated and designed to re-establish, if possible, on a firmer basis the fabric of Anglo-German friendship. To all outward appearance absolute harmony was restored on each occasion after these separate settlements, and in the intervals of fresh outbreaks it seemed true, and was persistently reiterated, that there could be no further occasion for disagreement.[51]

After citing several examples of German aggressiveness and British accommodation (in Southwest Africa, the Cameroons, Samoa, New Guinea, and Zanzibar), Eyre Crowe notes:

> On this and other occasions England's spirit of accommodation went so far as to sacrifice the career of subordinate British officials, who had done no more than carry out the policy of their Government in as dignified a manner as circumstances allowed, and to whose conduct that Government attached no blame, to the relentless vindictiveness of Germany, by agreeing to their withdrawal as one of the conditions of a settlement. . . .

> . . . And when shortly after the outbreak of the South African war, Germany threatened the most determined hostility unless England waived the exercise of one of the most ancient and most firmly-established belligerent rights of naval warfare, namely, the search and citation before a Prize Court of neutral mercantile vessels suspected of carrying contraband, England once more preferred an amicable arrangement under which her undoubted rights were practically waived, to embarking on a fresh quarrel with Germany. The spirit in which this more than conciliatory attitude was appreciated at Berlin became clear when immediately afterwards the German Chancellor openly boasted in the Reichstag that he had compelled England by the display of German firmness to abandon her absolutely unjust claim to interference with the unquestioned rights of neutrals, and when the Emperor subsequently appealed to his nation to hasten on the building of an

overwhelming German fleet, since the want of superior naval strength alone had on this occasion prevented Germany from a still more drastic vindication of Germany's interests.

. . . There is one road which, if past experience is any guide to the future, will most certainly not lead to any permanent improvement of relations with any Power, least of all Germany, and which must therefore be abandoned: that is the road paved with graceful British concessions—concessions made without any conviction either of their justice or of their being set off by equivalent counter-services. The vain hopes that in this manner Germany can be "conciliated" and made more friendly must be definitely given up. It may be that such hopes are still honestly cherished by irresponsible people, ignorant, perhaps necessarily ignorant, of the history of Anglo-German relations during the last twenty years, which cannot be better described than as the history of a systematic policy of gratuitous concessions, a policy which has led to the highly disappointing result disclosed by the almost perpetual state of tension existing between the two countries. Men in responsible positions, whose business it is to inform themselves and to see things as they really are, cannot conscientiously retain any illusions on this subject.

Here again, however, it would be wrong to suppose that any discrimination is intended to Germany's disadvantage. On the contrary, the same rule will naturally impose itself in the case of all other Powers. It may, indeed, be useful to cast back a glance on British relations with France before and after 1898. A reference to the official records will show that ever since 1882 England had met a growing number of French demands and infringements of British rights in the same spirit of ready accommodation which inspired her dealings with Germany. The not unnatural result was that every successive French Government embarked on a policy of "squeezing" England, until the crisis came in the year of Fashoda, when the stake at issue was the maintenance of the British position on the Upper Nile. The French Minister for Foreign Affairs of that day argued, like his predecessors, that England's apparent opposition was only half-hearted, and would collapse before the persistent threat of French displeasure. Nothing would persuade him that England could in a question of this kind assume an attitude of unbending resistance. It was this erroneous impression, justified in the eyes of the French Cabinet by their deductions from British political practice, that brought the two countries to the verge of war. When the Fashoda chapter had ended with the just discomfiture of France, she remained for a time very sullen, and the enemies of England rejoiced, because they believed that an impassable gulf had now been fixed between the two nations. As a matter of fact, the events at Fashoda proved to be the opening of a new chapter of Anglo-French relations. These, after remaining for some years rather formal, have not since been disturbed by any disagreeable incidents. France behaved more correctly and seemed less suspicious and inconsiderate than had been her wont, and no fresh obstacle arose in the way which ultimately led to the Agreement of 1904.

Although Germany has not been exposed to such a rebuff as France encountered in 1898, the events connected with the Algeciras Conference appear to have had on the German Government the effect of an unexpected revelation, clearly showing indications of a new spirit in which England proposed to regulate her own conduct towards France on the one hand and to Germany on the other. That the result was a very serious disappointment to Germany has been made abundantly manifest by the turmoil which the signature of the Algeciras Act has created in the country, the official, semi-official, and unofficial classes vying with each other in giving expression to their astonished discontent. The time which has since elapsed has, no doubt, been short. But during that time it may be observed that our relations with Germany, if not exactly cordial, have at least been practically free from all symptoms of direct friction, and there is an impression that Germany will think twice before she now gives rise to any fresh disagreement. In this attitude she will be encouraged if she meets on England's part with unvarying courtesy and consideration in all matters of common concern, but also with a prompt and firm refusal to enter into any one-sided bargains or arrangements, and the most unbending determination to uphold British rights.[52]

An act of accommodation, then, is not generally part of an irreversible process, though it puts one, at least momentarily, on "the slippery slope." It may well inspire the accommodated party to exert new pressure, but the act itself is virtually always opposed at the time by officials who are anxious about the future or annoyed at the loss of whatever is being sacrificed. Eyre Crowe's memo provided evidence of such anxiety and annoyance. Another act of accommodation, involving different parties, also resulted in a steeling of will within the accommodating state. The need to accommodate Austria in 1909 was an important cause of both Serbia's and Russia's ultimate confrontation with Austria some five years later. When Serbia and Russia were informed of the Austrian annexation of Bosnia—a step supported by pressure from Berlin, Russia and her allies were unprepared to challenge this alteration of the status quo. Sir Edward Grey was "of opinion that to risk Serbian territorial claims a war which might eventually involve the greater part of the continent of Europe must even from the Russian point of view be out of all proportion to the interests at stake." Russia and Serbia consequently accepted the change and made little protest over the heavy-handed Austrian treatment of Slavic politicians or Austria's flaunting of forged documents "purporting to show the complicity of the Serbian government" in subversive activities. But Austria's victory was an expensive one. Laurence Lafore says:

The Serbs, now violently and permanently inflamed and, also, painfully humiliated, organized still more secret societies, including one called "The People's Defense" (*Narodna Obrana*), which was to prove particularly energetic in provoking the Austrians. Terrorism, propaganda, and conspiracy proliferated. Austria-Hungary was now universally regarded by Serbs as a deadly and implacable enemy. The government, itself expansionist, began to be violently attacked by the secret societies for being insufficiently so. And in Russia, the degree of animosity was scarcely less great. Izvolsky, although his reputation had been formally saved by conceding the German demands, still suffered from the disgrace of his surrender and his ineptitude. But the disgrace was felt to be a national one; and it was determined by many persons in high places that there must never again be such a surrender of Russian interests or such a betrayal of Russia's client Serbia.[53]

Serbia and Russia were not the only powers to reassess their policies in the light of this "humiliation" of Russia (which, in the words of Bernadotte Schmitt, "she burned to revenge and which profoundly affected her policy in the years to come").[54] Britain read in this humiliation further evidence of German ambition, and perceived a German threat to British interests. According to Bernadotte Schmitt:

> Bülow also admitted, in 1913, what others believed in 1909: "The German sword had been thrown into the scale of European decision." Because of that fact, other swords were sharpened. The British naval scare of 1909, precipitated by rumours of secret and accelerated German shipbuilding and terminated by a doubling of the British programme, was doubtless influenced by the diplomatic action of Germany in the Balkan crisis. Equally important from the German point of view was the decision of Russia to undertake the reorganization of her army on a grand scale, and this was actually begun before the end of 1909. These British and Russian measures lay in the logic of the situation, for, as the Russian ambassador in Paris expressed it, when the news leaked out of the secret ministerial council at which the Russian ministers declared that Russia could not wage war,
>
>> such a public exposure of our weakness has made a most painful impression on our friends and must encourage our opponents to present the most impossible demands to Russia in the firm conviction that we shall yield. The cabinets of Paris and London have therefore drawn the conclusion that Russia, France and England must pay more attention than ever to action in common and at the same time must take the military measures necessary to convince their opponents that they have to deal with a political combination which knows how to insure respect for itself and will carry through its demands.[55]

Accommodation of a threat on one day, then, does not necessarily imply that a similar threat will be accommodated in the same fashion tomorrow. One power may accommodate another temporarily if it feels that it is "not ready" at the moment to resist, if it wants to buy time.

One final point: often political realities are substantially responsible for the accommodative posture assumed. A few examples: the French Radical politician Joseph Caillaux appears to have hitched his career to a star of accommodation towards Germany, both in 1911, while premier, and in the war years themselves.[56] Neville Chamberlain did the same in the 1930s.[57] Kgama III of the Ngwato (a Tswana tribe of the Bechuanaland Protectorate) was most accommodating to British imperial agents throughout his reign, giving up some of his local prerogatives in order to gain others and to protect the rest from threats and incursions by the Boers, rival Ngwato leaders, other Tswana tribes (the Ndebele and the Kwena), the British South Africa Company, and, ultimately, the South African federation.[58] To be sure, Kgama's relations with Britain were of alliance proportions, but Kgama also sensed *some* degree of threat from Britain itself, and he consciously offered elaborate obeisance and relinquished several controls over his subjects and domains. His situation was clearly comparable to that of other African leaders in the late nineteenth century, though there were important variations, reflecting different degrees of external and internal threats.[59]

Another example of accommodation born of domestic rivalries is that of China, facing Japanese invaders in the 1930s. Gerald Bunker writes:

> The basic policy that the Kuomintang government adopted to deal with the Japanese menace was the traditional imperial policy of barbarian taming—resistance in the last extremity, but wherever possible using diplomacy and superficial concessions to prevent a contest of military force in which China could only be the loser, and using time bought to build China's strength, garner foreign support, and wherever possible, to tighten up on the concessions previously offered.
>
> The Japanese threat and the Chinese methods adopted to meet it necessitated a diplomatic and conciliatory leadership surrogate which would appear to alternate with a hard-line patriotic policy. The instrument of this seeming "soft" policy would necessarily have to endure intense popular opprobrium. Wang's desire for personal sacrifice and his history of genuine rivalry for the power of the state made him ideally suited for this role.[60]

Wang Ching-wei's primary objective was to end the war between Japan and the Kuomintang in order to redirect Kuomintang (and hopefully Japanese) military efforts against the Chinese Communist armies. His secondary objective may have been to wrest the leadership of the Kuomintang from the hands of Chiang Kai-shek. The Japanese were not as willing to cooperate as Wang had hoped, but by 1943 his *chi-mi* policy (that of accommodating "the barbarians") began to bear fruit:

> Wang met with Prime Minister Tojo in Tokyo on December 21 and 25 and, agreement having been reached, the Nanking government declared war upon the United States and Great Britain on January 9, 1943. The declaration was carefully phrased to make the move appear consistent with Chinese nationalism and to avoid hostilities with Chungking....
>
> This time the Japanese carried through on their promises. During February and March agreement was reached for the rendition of various Japanese concessions and the subjection of Japanese residents in China to Chinese taxes. The Vichy government agreed to formally retrocede French concessions and extraterritorial rights. Tojo told the Diet on June 15 that Ambassador Tani had been instructed to begin negotiations for revising the "basic treaty." Finally on August 1 the Nanking government celebrated with patriotic fervor what it represented as a great victory for Chinese nationalism, the take-over of the Shanghai concessions. At last Japan allowed the "blue-sky white-sun" flag to fly, unencumbered by the yellow pennant, all over occupied China.[61]

These were substantial concessions, but they were inadequate and late in coming:

> Wang did not falter in his efforts to tame the barbarians, even expressing to them how he was "striving to make manifest the virtue of the emperor." Finally, five years after the Jukodo, Japan made the public commitments that she had promised in the Konoye statement of December 22, 1938. In a protocol to the new treaty of alliance signed on October 30, 1943, Japan agreed to withdraw her troops from China as soon as peace was restored; further, Japan even renounced her rights under the Boxer Protocol to station troops in north China. It had been Wang's endeavor for all these years to bring Japan to make public the private promises which had caused him to leave Chungking. Now that Japan was on the road to defeat, these promises no longer had any political meaning.[62]

Whether Wang succeeded or not is ultimately of little importance to us here, however. What concerns us is the motive behind Wang's accommodative policy. He was willing to surrender some Chinese sovereignty to Japan, at least temporarily, in order to terminate the war and to redirect Japanese and Kuomintang energies on the "Western" Communist enemy. Internal Chinese political disputes and a Confucian ideology precipitated Wang's accommodative gesture.

In summation, accommodation occurs when the leadership of a state perceives a real or potential threat to the state's interests and decides that they must surrender or forego something in order to preserve other things of value, or in order to gain time, or in order to avoid additional defense expeditures or a risky war. And here it is worth repeating that the threat to which the accommodator responds need not be one that imperils one's territory, prestige, independence, or trade. A refusal to give obeisance to or to collaborate with a stronger power may be viewed by the stronger power as threatening from the point of view of its interest. It may respond by sweeping the recalcitrant state aside. But such a move might require a shifting of forces deemed useful elsewhere, and it may also lead to any number of unknowns—a coalition of new enemies who come to the aid of the recalcitrant state, a protracted guerrilla war, dissension within the stronger power's own councils, or even a series of military setbacks. Hence (as we have seen) the stronger power may prefer to be accommodating. For this reason we must conclude that the relative strengths of the threatened and threatening states are not predictable. Given the right circumstances, strong states are just as likely to be accommodative as weaker ones.

Accommodation is very much a product of circumstance and setting. It may owe much to the existence of domestic political strife. It may occur because of the immediate military or alliance aims of one or the other of the parties. Or it may simply occur because the leaders have lost their nerve.

The fact that a state has in the past assumed an accommodative posture is a poor indicator of that state's future behavior when its interests are again deemed to be threatened. Some states engaging in acts of accommodation are simultaneously taking steps to increase their capabilities to deter or defend in the future. As we have said, pure accommodation, unadulterated by other responses to threat perception, is a relatively rare phenomenon. To be sure, the state being accommodated may choose to apply new pressure in the future, basing its expectations on the success it attained in the past, but it appears to be generally true that a state that has engaged in an act of accommodation experiences a steeling of the will after the fact and is not likely to follow such a course in the future. As we have said, accommodation is not usually part of an irreversible process. Of course, at times it does become part of such a process. Some states, especially those with basic, nonremedial weaknesses, do accommodate without recourse to alternative strategies. And the future postures of such inherently weak states are reasonably predictable.[63]

The patterns that we think we have discerned are, of course, based on a small, quite circumstance-specific sample of observed cases, each of which themselves appear quite opaque on the historical record. But if we have not revealed any dazzling new laws of international relations as a result of this exploratory survey, we can probably agree that the historical record is the place to begin in searching for such principles.[64]

Notes

1. Erich Eyck, *Bismarck and the German Empire* (London: Allen & Unwin, 1950), pp. 213–23.
2. An example of such a "mix" of accommodation, deterrence-defense, rearmament, and maneuvers is that of U.S. policy towards Japan in the wake of the vigorous Japanese reaction to the San Francisco school segregation controversy of 1906–1907. The cruise of the White Fleet in 1908–1909, aimed partly at Japan, was coupled with new battleship construction, federal pressure on the San Francisco school board to reconsider its policies, and warm apologies and assurances of friendship offered to Japan. See Thomas A. Bailey, *Theodore Roosevelt and the Japanese-American Crises* (Stanford, Calif.: Stanford University Press, 1934), pp. 59, 81–83, 91–93, 121–22, 141, 222–301.
3. Michael J. Salevouris, " 'Riflemen Form': The War Scare of 1859–1860 in England" (Ph.D. diss., University of Minnesota, 1971); William G. Beasley, *The Modern History of Japan* (New York: Praeger, 1963), pp. 135–37.
4. Thucydides *The Peloponnesian Wars* 1. 23. 6, 1. 33. 3, 88.
5. Richard D. Brown, *Revolutionary Politics in Massachusetts: The Boston Committees of Correspondence and the Towns, 1772–1774* (Cambridge, Mass.: Harvard University Press, 1970), pp. 38–41, 94–95, 149–50, 167–79; Ssu-yü Teng and John K. Fairbank, *China's Response to the West* (Cambridge, Mass.: Harvard University Press, 1954), pp. 127–29; Eyre Crowe memo of January 1, 1907, reprinted in George P. Gooch and Harold W. V. Temperley, eds., *British Documents on the Origins of the War, 1898–1914* (10 vols.; London: His Majesty's Stationery Office, 1926–1938), 3:398–403; Hajo Holborn, *A History of Modern Germany*, vol. 3: *1940–1945* (New York: Knopf, 1959), 3:792.
6. Teng and Fairbank, *China's Response*, pp. 127–29.
7. Margaret George, *The Warped Vision* (Pittsburgh, Pa.: University of Pittsburgh Press, 1965).
8. Paul M. Hayes, *Quisling* (Newton Abbott, Eng.: David & Charles, 1971), passim.
9. René Albrecht-Carrié, ed., *The Concert of Europe* (New York: Walker, 1968), pp. 235–36; Mark Mancall, *Russia and China* (Cambridge, Mass.: Harvard University Press, 1971), passim. I am indebted to Sterling Kernek for suggesting the Albrecht-Carrié volume.
10. Holborn, *History*, 3:793.
11. B. Ponomaryov, ed., *History of Soviet Foreign Policy, 1917–1945* (Moscow: Progress Publishers, 1969), pp. 382–84.
12. Max Beloff, *The Foreign Policy of Soviet Russia, 1929–1941* (2 vols.; London & New York: Oxford University Press, 1947, 1949), 2:378. I thank Nicholas Fedoruk of the Hudson Institute for this citation.
13. P. J. V. Rolo, *Entente Cordiale* (London: Macmillan, 1969), passim. Cf. Jerald A. Combs, *The Jay Treaty* (Berkeley: University of California Press, 1970), p. 47 and passim.
14. H. Gunnar Hagglöf, "'A Test of Neutrality,'" in *The Theory and Practice of Neutrality in the Twentieth Century*, comp. by Roderick Ogley (New York: Barnes & Noble, 1970), pp. 164–65; David Hinshaw, *Sweden: Champion of Peace* (New York: Putnam, 1949), pp. 122, 143, 156–59, 173–74; Oscar F. Ander, *The Building of Modern Sweden* (Rock Island, Ill.: Augustana Library, 1958), pp. 230–31.
15. Albrecht-Carrié, *Concert*, p. 114.

16. J. M. Hussey, ed., *The Cambridge Medieval History* (Cambridge, Eng.: Cambridge University Press, 1966), vol. 4, pt. 1, pp. 213–17.
17. Joan M. Hussey, *The Byzantine World* (3d rev. ed.; London: Hutchinson University Library, 1967), pp. 72–73.
18. George F. Young, *The Medici* (New York: Modern Library, 1933), pp. 230–32.
19. Ibid., p. 246.
20. See Stewart Oakley, *A Short History of Denmark* (New York: Praeger, 1972), pp. 206–7; and Palle Lauring, *A History of the Kingdom of Denmark* (Copenhagen: Høst, 1960), p. 236.
21. Nils Örvik, *The Decline of Neutrality* (Oslo: J. Tanum, 1953), pp. 60–61 and passim.
22. Max Jakobson, *Finnish Neutrality* (New York: Praeger, 1969), pp. 25, 28, 32, 33, 59, 77–78, and passim.
23. Ibid., pp. 34–35.
24. "Sans doute, les concessions jugées indispensables ont-elles crée des situations douloureuses et entrainé des décisions contestées. Désireuses de ne pas multiplier les incidents avec les troupes de l'Axe qui encerclaient la Suisse, les autorités ont, a plusieurs reprises, donné l'ordre de refouler des fugitifs et persécutés notamment juifs qui demandaient la droit d'asile." Jean Rohr, *La Suisse Contemporaine* (Geneva, 1972), p. 13. Roderick Ogley, comp., *The Theory and Practice of Neutrality in the Twentieth Century* (New York: Barnes & Noble, 1970), pp. 144–48. I am indebted to Daniel Ben-Yaacov of the World Institute in Jerusalem for the reference to the table on Swiss exports.
25. George Kennan, "Europe's Problems, Europe's Choices," *Foreign Policy*, no. 14 (Spring, 1974), pp. 14–15.
26. Thus I disagree with Ray Gastil's critique of Kennan (*Foreign Policy*, no. 16 [Fall, 1974], pp. 188–89), at least with regard to Gastil's claim that small nations have in the past tended disproportionately to accommodate.
27. See, for example, Charles A. Robinson, *Alexander the Great* (New York: Dutton, 1947), pp. 130–31, 160; Ying-shih Yu, *Trade and Expansion in Han China* (Berkeley: University of California Press, 1967), pp. 12–15; Truong Buu Lam, "Intervention versus Tribute in Sino-Vietnamese Relations, 1788–1790," in *The Chinese World Order*, ed. John K. Fairbank (Cambridge, Mass.: Harvard University Press, 1968), pp. 173–74; Holborn, *History*, p. 188.
28. Bernadotte E. Schmitt, *The Annexation of Bosnia* (New York: Fertig, 1970), pp. 234, 236; originally published in 1937.
29. Andrew R. Burn, *Alexander the Great* (new, enl. ed.; New York: Collier, 1962), pp. 42–44.
30. J. R. Hamilton, *Alexander the Great* (London: Hutchinson University Library, 1973), pp. 36–37.
31. Robinson, *Alexander the Great*, pp. 130–31, 160.
32. Oakley, *Short History*, pp. 225–27. Cf. Erich Thomsen, *Deutsche Besatzungspolitik in Dänemark, 1940–1945* (Düsseldorf: Bertelsmann Universitätsverlag, 1971).
33. Oakley, *Short History*, p. 227.
34. Obviously, one might also describe Philip's, Alexander's, and Hitler's policies as co-optative, inasmuch as some Greeks, Persians, or Danes, respectively, *were* being drawn into the power circles. But the expansionistic major power is less committed to a co-optative policy than the static major power, for the former has more aggressive options available to him than has the latter.
35. Yu, *Trade*, p. 14.

36. Arnold H. M. Jones, *The Decline of the Ancient World* (New York & London: Longman's, 1966), p. 215.
37. John B. Bury, *The Invasion of Europe by the Barbarians* (New York: Russell & Russell, 1963), pp. 60–63; originally published in 1928 in London.
38. Truong Buu Lam, "Intervention versus Tribute in Sino-Vietnamese Relations," in Fairbank, *Chinese*, pp. 173–74. Cf. Frank N. Trager, *Burma: From Kingdom to Republic* (New York: Praeger, 1966).
39. Perhaps another example, Bismarck's accommodation of Austria after her defeat in 1866, is worth mention in a note. Hajo Holborn comments on Bismarck's lenient treatment of Austria: "Bismarck had to overcome King William's strong objections to his attempt not only to make peace with Austria speedily before the European powers might intervene but also in a form that would allow him in the future to reestablish cooperation with Austria in international affairs. William I wanted to inflict penalties in the form of territorial cessions from almost everyone who had fought against Prussia. Only reluctantly did the king give in to the arguments which Bismarck presented with passionate vigor in stormy meetings.

"Bismarck warned the king not to alienate the feelings of the South German states, which he considered immediate allies against France and future members of a German federal state. For that reason he did not wish to take land from them." Holborn, *History*, 3:188.
40. Robert M. Utley, *Frontiersmen in Blue: The United States Army and the Indian, 1848–1865* (New York: Macmillan, 1967), pp. 56, 76–77.
41. Robert M. Utley, *Frontier Regulars: The United States Army and the Indian, 1866–1891* (New York: Macmillan, 1973), pp. 134–37.
42. Schmitt, *Annexation*, p. 115.
43. Laurence Lafore, *The Long Fuse* (Philadelphia: Lippincott, 1965), p. 161.
44. Ibid., p. 162.
45. See Miguel Leon-Portilla, ed., *The Broken Spears: The Aztec Account of the Conquest of Mexico* (Boston: Beacon, 1962), pp. 17, 29, 31, 35, and passim.
46. Laurence Lafore, *The End of Glory* (Philadelphia: Lippincott, 1970), pp. 219–21. A later epigram: "Why die for Danzig?"
47. Holger Arbman, *The Vikings* (New York: Praeger, 1961), pp. 74–81, especially 80. In this sense, King Alfred's effective mobilization of Anglo-Saxons in England stands out in sharp contrast to the policies of Frisians, Saxons, and Frenchmen before and after him.
48. Schmitt, *Annexation*, pp. 100–124, especially 116. Cf. Albrecht-Carrié, *Concert*, pp. 62–78, 132–34.
49. Hans J. Morgenthau, *Politics among Nations* (New York: Knopf, 1959), p. 59. Compare Quincy Wright, *A Study of War* (Chicago: University of Chicago Press, 1942), 2:853n: "When commercial-minded leaders have to deal with military-minded leaders, their effort to appease may precipitate war."
50. Paul W. Schroeder, *Austria, Great Britain, and the Crimean War* (Ithaca, N.Y.: Cornell University Press, 1972), p. 50 and passim.
51. Gooch and Temperley, *British Documents*, pp. 408–411.
52. Ibid., p. 419.
53. Schmitt, *Annexation*, pp. 157–58, 164; Lafore, *Long Fuse*, pp. 162–63.
54. Schmitt, *Annexation*, p. 207.
55. Ibid., pp. 252–53.
56. Richard M. Watt, *Dare Call It Treason* (New York: Simon & Schuster, 1963), pp. 47–51, 138–45.

57. Alfred L. Rowse, *Appeasement* (New York: Norton, 1961), pp. 21, 117–18.
58. Louis W. Truschel, "Accommodation under Imperial Rule" (Ph.D. diss., Northwestern University, 1970), pp. 31–37, 45–51, 102–3, 127–29, 410–21.
59. Ibid., pp. 410–20.
60. Gerald Bunker, *The Peace Conspiracy: Wang Ching-wei and the China War, 1937–1941* (Cambridge, Mass.: Harvard University Press, 1972), pp. 11–17.
61. Ibid., p. 272.
62. Ibid., pp. 275–78. Cf. John H. Boyle, *China and Japan at War, 1937–1945: The Politics of Collaboration* (Stanford, Calif.: Stanford University Press, 1972), pp. 89, 91–93, 212, 336, 355.
63. We cannot say anything stronger than "reasonably predictable" because of the many variables involved (type of political system, quality of leadership, effect of public opinion, available resources, state of existing defense-deterrent capabilities, nature of crisis, type of threat, intentions and capabilities of threatening power, etc.). Carthage, after all, finally did decide to resist in 149 B.C.
64. I acknowledge with gratitude the bibliographical advice of Professor Cho-yun Hsu and Evelyn Sakakida Rawski of the University of Pittsburgh and Sterling Kernek of Western Illinois University; the many thoughtful comments and suggestions of Professor Klaus Knorr of Princeton University; and the wise suggestions of the Fifth National Security Education Seminar, Colorado Springs, 1975.

War-Limiting

Charles H. Fairbanks

Introduction

The intention of this study is to use historical evidence in order to illuminate the problems of war-limiting. In this subject more than others it is important to return to the testimony of history, because the discussion of limited war in our time has been overwhelmingly dominated by the cases of Vietnam, Korea, and Algeria. Our investigation will demand particularly close attention to the details of military and diplomatic events, so that we can follow the precise relationship between the actions of the adversaries in limiting or in expanding the war. We need to follow events closely enough to see both the motive for and the result of actions. For this reason, I have chosen to concentrate on one case of limited war, the Italo-Turkish war of 1911–1912, for the principal narrative and to discuss other historical cases of war-limiting when the processes they illustrate appear in the account of the war. I will present the events of the war; on the basis of these events, I will analyze some of the processes involved in war-limiting. But the small historical sample that can be surveyed in one chapter necessarily limits the conclusions that can safely be drawn. I have seen it as my main task to uncover some of the processes that are at work in war-limiting, without attempting to define completely the conditions under which these processes can operate or to draw lessons for policy. I have tried to present the evidence even where I drew no analytical conclusions from it, in the hope that other students of limited war may draw their own conclusions without being tied to the present analysis.

Why I am discussing here "war-limiting" rather than "limited war" ought to be explained. Our contemporary concern with limited war stems in part from the limited wars of our times, but it stems also from the experience of the "total" wars of this century. War-limiting is something that took place, whether more or less successfully, in the wars we call "limited" and that failed in the "total" wars. It is therefore at least as important to study war-limiting in the cases where it failed on a massive scale—the "total" wars— as in the "limited wars" narrowly considered. Our awareness of the problem of total war springs above all from the experience of the First and Second World Wars. In these wars the military means used by each side to win were so unlimited—in space, in time, and technologically—that they hurt the ends for which the wars were undertaken, namely, the welfare or security of the nation and its people.

History suggests that although this kind of problem has appeared many times before, its peculiar salience is characteristic of our own times.

It appears, then, that the problem of limited war is to a large extent coextensive with the problem of war aims. Provisionally we could say that limited wars are fought because in an expanded war the use of certain means would contradict the aims for which the war is fought. Until very recently, war aims have tended to be studied very little. This is most easily seen in the scholarly treatment of the First World War. The great collections of diplomatic documents ended with 1914 and began again with 1919; the diplomacy of the war itself was not of interest to those who compiled them.[1] It is striking how many decades had to elapse before scholarly studies of the war aims of the opposing sides were undertaken; these studies still remain very inadequate. The subject of the origins of the First World War has virtually monopolized the attention of scholars. Yet the origins of the First World War would be of no more interest than the origins of the Franco-Prussian War if the war had been won in a few weeks, as was expected, and it had been concluded by a moderate peace treaty. It was the vast expansion of war aims during the course of the war, as well as the expansion of the means (including the temporal prolongation of the war) to achieve these ends, that made the consequences of the war so momentous. Seen in this light, war aims and their relation to the means by which the war was fought ought to be the primary focus of interest for conflicts such as the First World War, and the diplomatic origins of the war should be an important but secondary topic of inquiry.

There was a failure of war-limiting in the First World War because the pursuit of the means to achieve the original war aims destroyed far more important underlying aims. The problem of war aims is thus a problem of the relation between means and ends, and so is the problem of war-limiting. If war-limiting is in its broadest sense a problem of the relation between ends and means, it is of great interest to the political theorist as well as to the student of foreign policy.[2] In war the ordinary kind of means-ends rationality is not often found; the relationship between ends and means is there particularly problematic. War-limiting comes to light as one of the most interesting aspects of this question: to what extent can rationality dominate human life? One final implication of this inquiry should be noted. One could define technique or technology as the totality of means that are most efficient to achieve any human ends and that are arrived at purely with a view to those ends.[3] Technology has, of course, a great impact on the success of war-limiting; but the very attempt to limit rationally the means in war is itself a case of technique or technology in the broadest sense.

These simple observations about the ramifications of the problem of war-limiting will enable us to broaden our historical discussion. The term "limited war" is most often applied to situations where external constraints (e.g., neutrals threatening to intervene or geographic conditions) narrow the choice of specific *means* by which the defeat of the enemy may be sought. There are also well-known cases of limitation of the means by internal constraints, such as those of domestic politics. These familiar cases supply two elements in a typology of kinds of war-limiting: wars externally and internally limited with respect to means.

A much rarer type of war-limiting is seen in wars that are limited with regard to their means *in general*—that is, cases where all possible means towards the usual immediate end of war, the enemy's defeat, are restrained. In these rare cases, one side actually courts partial "defeat" for reasons of policy. Here general "victory" is no longer seen as the key to the specific political aims of the war. With some sacrifice of precision, such wars can be called internally limited with regard to their *ends*. The complications of this usage need to be explored briefly. Of course, the ends are always limited in war. This was true even in World War II, where the total-war outlook on the Allied side culminated in the demand for "unconditional surrender"—apparently an extreme case of forgetting the specific ends in the single-minded concentration on the means. Yet everyone understood that "unconditional surrender" did not mean, for Germany, the fate of Carthage. This sort of limitation of ends is, however, trivial in comparison with the unfamiliar type of war-limiting that we have called above "limitation of the ends." It is useful to give some examples of this, because it is the opposite extreme from the means-dominated total wars of our time.

A striking example (on a narrow scale) of a war in which the ends are limited in this way is cited by Admiral Mahan:

> England and Spain were allies in Toulon in 1793, when the excesses of Revolutionary France seemed to threaten the social order of Europe; but the Spanish admiral told the English flatly that the ruin of the French navy, a large part of which was there in their hands, could not fail to be injurious to the interests of Spain, and a part of the French ships was saved by his conduct, which has been justly characterized as not only full of firmness, but also as dictated by the highest political reason.[4]

A much more important case was the conduct of Austria at the end of the Napoleonic Wars. When Austria joined the European coalition against Napoleon in 1813, Metternich's broadest aim was the destruction of French domination over Europe and the reconstruction of a balance-of-power system in its place. The very success of this endeavor, however, brought with it a new danger: the domination of the Continent by Russia. In population, revenues, and armed forces Russia far exceeded any of the other powers except Britain and the expanded Napoleonic France.[5] Achievement of the specific Russian war aims in Poland would have brought Russia into the heart of Europe and given

Prussia an indefensible frontier, while redirecting Prussian energies into Germany (and therefore against Austria). Prussia was at the time acting as the faithful supporter of Russian policy, and Britain was likely to withdraw into isolation. Russian ambitions extended to the little-known attempt to place a Russian client—Bernadotte, Royal Prince of Sweden—on the throne of France.[6] The menace to Austria was indeed great, and great skill was required of Austria in limiting the war against France in order to prevent Russian hegemony. This danger became ever greater as the extent of allied victory over Napoleon became clearer. In January 1814 Metternich emphasized in diplomatic dispatches that victory was not necessarily good: "The sole remaining evil . . . is an excess of riches. We are protected against this . . . only by moderation. . . . I need not tell you that I am as much embarrased by the plenitude of success as heretofore by the plenitude of disaster."[7] Metternich's response, in the words of Henry Kissinger, was to "attempt to substitute hesitation in military operations for French resistance." He sent orders to Prince Schwarzenberg, the Austrian commander, to advance only "cautiously" and to "utilize the desire of the French common man for peace by avoiding warlike acts."[8] Finally, on 16 January, orders were issued to halt the movements of the Austrian army entirely. Eventually, operations against Napoleon were resumed, but only after Castlereagh had joined Metternich in resisting the ambitions of Russia.

Metternich's policy during the War of Liberation is a case of the strict control of the military means by deliberately limiting the war aim—to the point of courting partial "defeat." It is thus possible to describe Metternich as fighting a war that was internally limited with regard to its ends. In the very same campaign the opposite stance was visible in Emperor Alexander of Russia, who insisted that war aims not be defined until complete victory over France had been achieved. Metternich's management of the 1813–1814 war appears as an example of perfect means-ends rationality. The question that needs to be kept in mind throughout this study is to what extent rationality can control the means in war, so that the aims are achieved without unwanted side effects.

These cases of wars that are limited internally with regard to ends are taken from wars fought by allies with differing aims. But not all wars that are limited in this way are alliance wars. The 1911–1912 war between Turkey and Italy was also distinguished by an ususual degree of limitation of *ends*.

The decaying Ottoman Empire—the "Sick Man of Europe"—had been losing peripheral provinces to independence movements and acquisitive foreign powers throughout most of the nineteenth century. On September 28, 1911, the Italian government suddenly demanded in a diplomatic note that Turkey consent to military occupation of the province of Tripoli (present-day Libya) by Italy. The conciliatory Turkish reply was judged to be unsatisfactory, and war was declared the following day. It lasted until October of 1912. Various incidents were given as excuses for the ultimatum, but it was in fact a classical case of a "war of aggression." Italy was in the mood for colonial expansion, and Italian statesmen had earlier extracted from the great powers an acknowledgment of Italian special interest in Libya. On the basis of these promises, Italian statesmen expected that Libya would fall to them when the Ottoman Empire disintegrated. These promises were linked to Italian support for French dominance in Morocco. In the summer of 1911, France was in the process of absorbing Morocco; this made many Italians think that the last opportunity had come for cashing in on the promises concerning Libya. There are considerable suspicions that the timing of the attack was heavily influenced by the desire of the prime minister, Giovanni Giolitti, to distract attention from some difficulties that his legislative program was undergoing internally.[9]

While Italian statesmen wanted Libya, they did not want it enough to sacrifice other foreign-policy aims. This fundamental fact was the basis of the Italian intent to fight a limited war for Libya. The war that emerged was indeed exceptionally limited for a modern Western state; it included such archaic features as a safe-conduct for Turkish troops to cross the Italian-dominated Mediterranean.[10] The war on which Italy had embarked was, in the first place, deliberately limited with regard to its *ends*. Even if the other powers would have permitted it, Italy would not have wished the overall defeat of Turkey. This undoubtedly would have led to the breakup of the Ottoman Empire. Given the limited power of Italy relative to the other major European states, the resulting redistribution of territory would not have been favorable to Italy. In any case, the dissolution of the Ottoman Empire would have been likely to set off a general war, which was not in Italy's interest. For this all-important reason, the Italian war aim could not be "victory." Several other motives also required restraint. Italy did not wish to see its economic interest in Turkey and its maritime trade suffer, even temporarily. As San Giuliano, the Italian foreign minister, expressed it later in the year: "Interruption of Dardanelles would be as disadvantageous to Italy as to other powers, as she is partially dependent for grain supplies on Black Sea trade, as also for important Russian market for Italian oil and vegetable produce."[11]

Both internal and external conditions restricted the military means used by Italy. Internally the extent of the effort that could be undertaken to gain Tripoli was limited by two factors: One was the desire to maintain the domestic political and economic situation on a near-peacetime footing. This precluded large expenditures on the war. The second was the desire not to interfere with military readiness for other conflicts, particularly war with Austria.[12] This dictated that only a fraction of the army be used in the Libyan war and that only a minimum of military supplies be dissipated.

But it was the external limits on Italian military means that were the most pressing. In general, all the European powers were anxious not to have their interests in the Ottoman Empire disrupted by extensive military operations. In this sense the semicolonial subordination of Turkey to the powers was a blessing to the Empire. It conferred a certain measure of protection. The most important external obstacle to the extension of the war was the restraint that Austria could exercise by virtue of the Triple Alliance among Germany, Austria, and Italy. Since 1887 the Triple Alliance treaty had included the following provisions (part of Article VII in the 1891 revision):

> If, in the course of events, the maintenance of the *status quo* in the regions of the Balkans or of the Ottoman coasts and islands in the Adriatic and in the Aegean Sea should become impossible, and if . . . Austria-Hungary or Italy should find themselves under the necessity of modifying it by a temporary or permanent occupation on their part, this occupation shall take place only after a previous agreement between the two Powers aforesaid, based upon the principle of reciprocal compensation for every advantage, territorial or otherwise, which each of them might obtain beyond the present *status quo*.[13]

While this article was ambiguous, it was interpreted by Aehrenthal, the Austro-Hungarian foreign minister, to rule out any military operations without Austrian approval in the territory specified. Quite apart from these obligations, Italy had a motive not to give Austria-Hungary any excuse to discard the article. Italy feared Austrian occupation of parts of the Balkans—an event that was far more likely than occupation by Italy.

To serve these motives for limiting the war, the Italians planned a conflict that was bounded in several ways. First, and most important, the war was to be limited *geographically* to Libya. Second, it was to be limited *temporally*. Giolitti seems to have hoped that the Turks would yield in a few weeks to the *fait accompli* after troops landed, or even that they would yield to the ultimatum itself—which the Turkish cabinet did consider.[14] Finally, Italy planned to limit the war by eschewing certain traditional "weapons," such as economic warfare, in return for their not being used by Turkey against Italy. Trade between the two countries was to continue; it was not until November 27, 1911, that Turkey declared a 100 percent tariff on Italian imports.[15] Most of the belligerent coasts were not blockaded, and for a time no merchant vessels were seized.[16]

Because of the Italian need to minimize foreign interference and Turkish economic or social retaliation, it was essential to communicate the intention to fight a limited war. The following official statement was issued on October 2:

1. The various rumours of the landing of Italian troops in other parts of the Ottoman Empire than in Tripoli and Cyrenaica are categorically denied.
2. Italy has not the remotest intention of landing troops in any part of the

Ottoman Empire except in Tripoli and Cyrenaica. A categorical denial in advance is given to any similar reports that may come to hand later.
3. The naval operations which the Royal Navy is compelled to carry out in European waters are exclusively directed towards protecting the Italian coasts, Italian open towns, the military expedition to Tripoli, and Italian merchant ships in the Adriatic and Ionian Seas from contemplated Turkish raids.[17]

The Italian aim seems to have been to seize the important part of Libya quickly. Since Italian naval superiority assured that Libya could not be reconquered by Turkey, a peace agreement could be expected to follow shortly. We could define the Libyan war, as planned, as a *forcible limited war*, rather than the coercive limited war that is the focus of Schelling's analysis.[18] That is, the Italian leaders began the war without anticipating any need to play on Turkish wishes by threats. The Italian government thus intended a limited war in which ends and means were to be in perfect equilibrium. The positive aim—acquisition of Tripoli—was to be achieved without incurring any of the costs that war usually brings. The means were to achieve the end, but nothing beyond it.

Turkey found itself fighting a limited war for very different reasons. The Libyan war was, for Turkey, a limited war because Turkish means were limited externally through lack of power. Turkey was so weak that it had to fight on the ground chosen by the Italians. Turkey had a second reason for limiting the war: the importance of Libya was not as great as that of the European parts of the Empire that might be threatened by an expanded war against Italy. Thus, in spite of the great differences in the motives of the two belligerents, they had very important interests in common: above all, that there be no upheaval in the Balkans.

Before turning to the narrative of the war, we should consider briefly some of the differences between Italy and Turkey that affected war-limiting. Italy and Turkey possessed armies of comparable size, but that of Turkey was poorly organized and equipped. More important, only about 3 percent of the Turkish army was in Libya, and there was no way to reinforce it: there was no effective navy. Indeed, the geographical separation of Libya was the precondition of Italy's plan for limited war. Only this fortunate fact made it possible to isolate the main theater of war from the others.

While the location of the theater of war was supremely advantageous for the Italian plan, the character of it was not. Libya is a desert sprinkled with oases; the two limited areas of rain-fed agriculture—the Jabal Nafusah and the Jabal al-Akhdar—are slightly inland and were not reached by the Italians in the course of the war. Almost all supplies had to come from Italy, and the desert terrain was unfavorable to the infantry-dominated warfare of 1911. Finally, the Arab and Berber population turned out unexpectedly to be hostile toward the Italians, and furnished the bulk of the forces that Turkey employed. It gives some indication of the military difficulties facing Italy in Libya to note that the whole territory was not finally conquered until 1931,[19] although this was partly due to accidental developments and to the temporary abandonment of the effort.

The asymmetry in naval power was very important. It meant not only that the theater of war could be isolated, but also that Italy and the Italian colonies were virtually invulnerable to Turkish attack. On the other hand, the coasts and island possessions of Turkey were extremely vulnerable. The military asymmetries were compounded by the difference in financial resources. While Italy had a substantial reserve of money available to fight the war, Turkey ran a large deficit every year. There was not enough money to mobilize the entire army, and this was a pressing motive for limiting the war.[20] These Italian advantages were only partly compensated for by the fact that Turkey had diplomatic protection due to its semicolonial status. This gave the other European powers the "right" to protect their commercial interests in Turkey, and this involved some protection to Turkey itself. Italy lacked this diplomatic advantage. Turkey also held important hostages in the more than sixty thousand Italian residents and in the Italian commercial interests there. Italy did not have on its own territory anything through which Turkey could be hurt in a comparable way.

Turning to the domestic structure of each country, Italy was nominally a parliamentary democracy, but one in which electoral manipulation by the government played a vital role. At the time of the war, Giovanni Giolitti, the master manipulator, was prime minister. Since Giolitti was the most important Italian political figure of the epoch, the executive power was relatively strong. But Giolitti had achieved his preeminence only by continuously compromising. He had to worry about the political groups opposing him and about public opinion. The latter was generally favorable to the Libyan venture, but was unaccustomed to limited war.

The domestic structure of Turkey was clearly very different, although it is not well understood.[21] Three years after the overthrow of Sultan Abdul Hamid's autocratic rule Turkish politics were in flux. Formal power was shared by the cabinet, which was largely composed of members of the old bureaucracy who were accustomed to accommodating Western demands, and the Parliament. The Parliament was chosen in elections that were rigged by the chauvinist Committee of Union and Progress, which, during most of this period, was the single most important political force.[22] But this party was weakly organized and proved unable at the decisive points to control its members in Parliament. The third important political factor was the army, which was in the background until the summer of 1912. The army itself was divided into factions that supported both the committee and its opponents. The most important feature in all this is the absence of any fixed rules by which decisions were made or rulers chosen; the deciding political factors fluctuated wildly every few months. Beyond this unstable political system lay the opinion of small elites, which was very hostile to yielding Libya but was accustomed to waging limited wars.

It is easy to see how unequal were the two powers engaged in the war. In these circumstances it evidently depended largely upon the Italians whether the war was kept limited or whether it was expanded. Turkey was not, however, without ways of expanding the total inventory of means used in fighting the war. The Ottoman Empire was unable to expand the war geographically, as Italy could, except perhaps in the Red Sea area. But Turkey could expand the war internally, by hurting Italians within her own borders. She could also expand the war diplomatically by bringing third parties into the conflict on her side. Finally, Turkey could extend the war in *time*. Temporal limitation and expansion is an important dimension of war. Of course, temporal expansion of war is important because it almost always increases the various costs of waging it.

War termination is a particular problem in limited war, as we shall see. This problem has come to light, for example, in constructing scenarios of limited nuclear war. For the present, it suffices to note that temporal extension of the war offers itself as a way out for states that find a limited war imposed on them by a stronger power. This was well stated by Azzam Pasha, secretary general of the Arab League, after the 1948 war with Israel: "We have a secret weapon which we can use better than guns and machine guns, and this is time. As long as we do not make peace with the Zionists, the war is not over; and as long as the war is not over there is neither victor nor vanquished. As soon as we recognize the existence of the state of Israel, we admit by this act that we are vanquished."[23]

The Italian statesmen had hoped to keep the war limited—even in time—by relying on the geographical separation of Libya from the rest of the Ottoman Empire. But it is quite possible that the war was *lengthened* by this isolation.[24] This effect is quite visible in overseas colonial wars. Peru and Spain did not officially end their state of war until 1871, when Peruvian independence was acknowledged. The war between Portugal and Holland in the East Indies and elsewhere lasted from 1600 until 1663 with only brief intervals of peace.[25] This was not untypical of the overseas wars of that age. In all these cases, war can go on almost indefinitely, precisely because it does not touch the homelands of the countries engaged. It may be that the greater the geographical isolation of the theater to which the war is limited, the greater the likelihood that the war will be quite unlimited temporally.

Meditation on these historical cases might have cast some doubt on the Italian plan: a "forcible" war of territorial acquisition, narrowly limited both geographically and temporally. Such quick strokes have often been attempted, but they have rarely succeeded as planned. An analogous case is the Spanish seizure of Sardinia and Sicily from Austria and Savoy in November 1717 and July 1718. Although the islands were too isolated to be defended by their sovereigns, an alliance quickly formed against Spain. This led to widespread war and eventually to Spain's evacuation of the islands. The only successful case that comes to mind is Louis XIV's seizure of districts in the geographically isolated Spanish Netherlands in 1683.

Neutral Restrictions on the War: Albania

In view of Italy's intention to restrict the war to Libya, it is somewhat surprising to find that the first military encounters took place off the coast of Turkish Albania. In peacetime, six small Turkish torpedo boats were stationed there. They now formed a potential, if very weak, threat to Italian shipping. Prior to the outbreak of war, the duke of Abruzzi had been sent to this coast with two cruisers, a battleship, and several destroyers under Biscaretti, with orders to prevent the enemy from going out to sea.[26] The orders did not state *how* the enemy was to be prevented from going to sea in peacetime; the duke of Abruzzi telegraphed back that he would use force if necessary. When, one hour after the declaration of war on September 29, two of the Turkish torpedo boats put to sea from the port of Preveza, they were met off the coast by Biscaretti's squadron. In the ensuing engagement one torpedo boat was sunk, and the other was driven back into Preveza. The next day the Italians took action that strained even further their proclaimed intention to fight a war limited to Libya. Italian destroyers entered the harbor of Preveza, sank two more Turkish torpedo boats at anchor, and captured a yacht moored at the quay. When fired on from the shore, the Italian ships fired back.

Austria was enraged by these actions. Austrian protests charged that they violated Article VII of the Triple Alliance as well as the original Italian promises to keep the war limited; Russia was also concerned.[27] To give point to these threats, Austria began to take measures preparatory to mobilization. This crisis between the allies was particularly dangerous since important groups in Austria, headed by the chief of staff, Conrad von Hötzendorff, wished to use the Libyan war as an excuse to make war on Italy; violations of promises to limit the war would provide an excuse.

The civilians responsible for directing the war on the Italian side thus felt that unauthorized attacks made by Abruzzi's command had placed the nation in great danger. They were the more outraged when it shortly became apparent that both attacks had been carried out before Abruzzi's fleet had received notice of the declaration of war.[28] The duke of Abruzzi intended at this point to demand the surrender of the Turkish ships still at Preveza and to bombard the fortifications if they were not turned over. The Italian government, however, was now frightened and ordered him not to open fire against enemy territory. The duke was to withdraw his fleet "once the coast was cleared of Ottoman ships." How this was to be achieved with the restraining order in effect was not stated. Immediately afterwards, the duke received two further orders. One told him to obtain the surrender of the ships by threat of bombardment, but not to carry out this threat. The other urged him to stop the unloading of arms in Albania; it was again left unclear how this was to be done. Abruzzi cabled back that an empty threat would not work. Finally, on October 5, Biscaretti sent a boat under a white flag into the Albanian harbor of San Giovanni di Medua to check for possible unloading of arms. When the boat was fired upon, Biscaretti bombarded the fortifications. Giolitti, the prime minister, telegraphed that Biscaretti had disobeyed formal orders and that "it is deplorable that personal vanity compromises the vital interests of the country."[29] Accordingly, new orders were sent to the duke of Abruzzi to abandon surveillance entirely in "the Adriatic basin." Abruzzi tried to evade these orders by construing "Adriatic basin" narrowly, but he was corrected, and his fleet was ordered elsewhere. At this point, then, Italy had yielded entirely to Austrian pressure to limit the war more than Italy had intended.

We have discussed these operations at some length because they give a good introduction to the difficulties of the military-civilian relationship in limited war. Two things are most striking. First, we have seen the difficulties created for Italian military men by the flood of contradictory, vague, and impractical orders sent from Rome. The confusing character of these orders must have been connected with inevitable indecision and debate among civilian policy-makers working under the pressure of Austrian protests and threats. The other important fact revealed here is the consistent military dissatisfaction with limited war. Biscaretti and the duke of Abruzzi often twisted or broke orders that required the limiting of hostilities.

The unhappiness of military men with limited war is often very strong; it can override pressing motives of prudence and bureaucratic interest. This is most clearly seen in the attitude of the United States Air Force toward counterforce and other forms of limited nuclear war from 1960 to the present. The air force has never advocated any of these doctrines wholeheartedly and has sometimes resisted their implementation. Yet throughout this period the air force had important reasons to favor ideas of limited nuclear war. These doctrines were the best way of answering minimum deterrence and other strategic notions that would give a dominant role to the navy and its less vulnerable deterrent force. Doctrines of limited nuclear war could also save the manned strategic bomber, which was seriously endangered in the early sixties and is also today. Yet neither these motives nor the strong political and military arguments for a policy of limited nuclear war have been sufficient to put the air force solidly behind it.

Military resistance to limited war has increased with the professionalization of military life, but it is a very old phenomenon. In the Bible the Hebrew captains of the host, or generals, are consistently depicted as seeking extremes of violence that went beyond the orders of the kings. When Absalom, the son of David, rebelled, David ordered his general Joab to spare his life; that is, he sought to limit the war in this respect. But after the defeat of Absalom's army, Joab completed the victory by personally killing Absalom.[30]

Why are military men so resistant to limited war? We might provisionally give four answers: 1. Military men realize better than civilians the operational difficulties of limited war.

2. Experts, or practitioners of a technique, never like to see the means that it specifies interfered with by considerations external to that expertise. This is reinforced by the fact that military officers are not only experts but, usually, members of a distinct social group with its own conventions and its own solidarity.

3. It is uncomfortable for military men to hazard their lives, or to think of themselves as doing so, for a goal that is limited. This emerges very clearly in Joab's reproach to David for limiting the war against Absalom. When David mourned Absalom,

> Joab came into the house to the king, and said, Thou hast shamed this day the faces of all thy servants, which this day have saved thy life. . . . In that thou lovest thine enemies, and hatest thy friends . . . for this day I perceive, that if Absalom had lived, and all we had died this day, then it had pleased thee well. Now therefore arise, go forth, and speak comfortably unto thy servants: for I swear by the Lord, if thou go not forth, there will not tarry one with thee this night.[31]

4. The education of military men emphasizes the concentration of force and, more generally, the importance of complete victory over opposing military forces.

5. Finally, there is the "vanity" that Giolitti attributed to Biscaretti. Limiting a war often cuts off the opportunities for distinction and, therefore, for promotion. Often limited war requires operations that are inglorious or unsuccessful. Histories of Africa have given a considerable role in the pushing forward of colonial frontiers during the period 1884 to 1900 to the ambition of officers who could not attain any distinction in peaceful Europe.

Attempts to Limit the War by Formal Agreement

The Austrian veto on operations along the Albanian coast led directly to an Italian proposal for exclusion of this area (and somewhat later of the

Red Sea) from the war by formal agreement with Turkey.[32] The proposal for formal neutralization was a sensible move on the part of Italy. Italy could thus get rid of the only two possible sources of Turkish attacks on Italy or her colonies, without having to recede from the intended policy of limited war and without having to anger third parties. Neutralization by agreement would remove the tension between normal military operating procedures and the political limitations on the war. Given the one-sidedness of this proposal, it is not surprising that the Turks responded coldly. They proposed instead a neutralization agreement that was equally beneficial to Turkey: that the territories of both countries be neutralized entirely, except for Libya. This would have foreclosed any future geographical expansion of the war by Italy. Paralyzed by these incompatible interests, the idea of formal neutralization died; within a month the Italians were no longer pursuing it.

This attempt at formal neutralization suggests an expansion of our typology of kinds of war limitation. Wars may be limited (a) by some consensual, interactive process between the two sides or (b) by one or both sides acting separately. In the latter category belong wars in which the ends are limited (discussed above) and wars that are limited by disproportion in power between the participants (e.g., Turkey and Italy). "Consensual" limitations may be (a) by formal written agreements, public or secret; (b) by the informal exchange of assurances; (c) by tacit bargaining. The latter two categories are difficult to differentiate historically. Finally, a rough division of the formal agreements can be made into (a) general and continuing limitations on war (e.g., the Geneva Convention, diplomatic immunities, the Truce of God in the Middle Ages) and (b) ad hoc formal limitations on war. The attempted neutralization of possible theaters of war in 1911–1912 is an example of an attempted ad hoc formal limitation; the safe-conduct given to Turkish troops to cross the Mediterranean from Port Said to Constantinople is an attempt that was carried out.

General and continuing formal limitations have tended to be of peripheral importance in determining the outcome of wars. Ad hoc formal limitations might be more important. One might think that formal limitations would be the most dependable and least ambiguous way of limiting war, and that they would therefore be fairly frequent. Recent history, however, contradicts this expectation. Few attempts at formal ad hoc limitation of war have been made: the Italo-Turkish war and the attempt of Germany and Belgium to exempt central Africa (the "conventional Congo basin") from hostilities in 1914 are the most prominent recent cases. In most cases where the attempt has been made—and in both the cases just cited—agreement could not be reached. In the few instances throughout history in which a formal agreement was

reached, it often broke down. Herodotus gives a case from the sixth century
B.C., when Argos and Sparta went to war over Thyrea, a border district:

> The Argives having advanced to save their land from being cut off, both parties held a conference. They agreed that three hundred men on each side should fight, and that whichever side prevailed [*perigenontai*] should have the lands. They also agreed that the bulk of each army should withdraw to their own country, and not remain during the contest, lest, if the armies were present, either side, seeing their own men beaten, should come in to help them. Having agreed to these terms, the armies withdrew, and the picked men on each side remaining behind engaged. They fought with such equal success that, of the six hundred, three men were left alive: of the Argives, Alkenor and Chromios, and of the Lacedaemonians, Othryades . . . The two Argives, thinking themselves victorious, ran to Argos; but Othryades, the Lacedaemonian, having stripped the corpses of the Argives, and carried their arms to his own camp, remained at his post. The next day both armies, having been informed of the event, met again in the same place, and for a time both said that they had won. One side alleged that the greater number of their men survived; the other side pointed out that those survivors had fled, and that their countryman had kept the field and stripped their dead. At length, the dispute ended so that they fought and when many had fallen on both sides, the Lacedaemonians obtained the victory.[33]

What accounts for the marginal importance of formal ad hoc war-limiting agreements in history? In the case of Sparta and Argos, the terms of the formal agreement were not precise enough to cover all contingencies. These are the kinds of contingencies that can (in the absence of a formal agreement) be adjusted through tacit bargaining. The result will be a somewhat different state of mutual limits. Tacit bargaining can in the same way deal with "violations" of the preexisting limits. If, on the other hand, the terms of an agreement are formal and known to even a small public, inevitable ambiguities can be used easily by opponents of limitation to attack the agreement; it is easy to say that the other side is cheating. Before a formal limitation is actually agreed upon, its formality and relative publicity give an opportunity for endless arguments as to whether the terms benefit the two sides "equally." It might be suggested that the very need for a formal agreement shows that the factual basis for such an agreement in the interests of the two sides is insufficient. Finally, formal limitations run against the most common emotional attitudes toward war much more blatantly than less visible methods of war-limiting.

The War in Libya: Limitation and Military Failure

We turn now to the main theater of war—Libya. The core of the Italian war plan was to send an expedition to occupy Libya and then to hold it until peace. It was felt that this was not a problem; General Pollio, the chief of staff, told Giolitti that it could be done with twenty thousand men.[34] The purely military task was therefore subordinated to the effort to limit the war diplomatically, to prevent it from becoming an international diplomatic question. This could be avoided by presenting potentially hostile powers with a *fait accompli*: a swift declaration of war and the swift attainment of military dominance in Libya.[35] War was accordingly declared (September 29) long before Italian mobilization was complete (about October 10).[36] The military movements ordered were governed not by standard military procedures but by the attempt of the civilian planners to create this *fait accompli*. At the very beginning, for example:

> At midnight 28–29 [October], when war was not yet declared, the Minister of Foreign Affairs, Marquis di San Giuliano, insisted in a telephone call to the Minister of Marine that at any cost Admiral Aubry be requested to hasten the bombardment of Tripoli; and he added that it was extremely urgent because of the difficulty of controlling for long the international political situation.[37]

Eventually it was decided to occupy the capital city of Tripoli with a light detachment of sailors on October 5, rather than to wait for the army convoys arriving on October 12. All this was in the service of an important type of war-limiting: limitation of the diplomatic expansion of the war (involvement of neutrals) by the temporal limitation of military action against the enemy.

As Luigi Albertini points out, the premature occupation of the city of Tripoli may have created a *fait accompli*, but it also compelled the abandonment of the Italian commander's plan for a sudden pincer attack, once the whole expeditionary corps had arrived, that would have secured the entire Tripoli oasis.[38] The twelve hundred sailors, outnumbered by the Turkish garrison, were able to occupy only the city and its immediate outskirts, from which the army had subsequently to fight its way out in the course of trench warfare. The tiny area of the sailors' occupation also afforded the Turks and Arabs the covered positions from which they were to attack the Italians on October 23, 1911.

What were the military effects of these measures to limit the war? In late October, serious setbacks overtook the Italian effort to seize Tripoli. The most difficult moment in this crisis was the battle of Sciara Sciat (Shara Shatt, or Sharashett) on October 23. In this engagement the Turkish troops and the Arab irregulars attacked the Italian lines, accompanied by a rear attack by infiltrators and Turkish sympathizers in the occupied area. The attack succeeded in breaking through the Italian lines and surrounding two companies of Italian troops. The Turkish attack was finally contained and repulsed, but it had drastic consequences. The attack was followed by panic among the Italian troops and by the massacre of Arab civilians behind the lines, creating considerable outrage in the neutral press.[39] Further Turkish attacks followed, leading to the temporary abandonment by the Italians of about one-third of the area originally occupied in the Tripoli oasis.

The reverses of late October caused consternation in Italian public opinion, which became quite discouraged during November and December,[40] and in the Italian government. Giolitti addressed the following telegram to General Caneva, the commander of the expeditionary force at Tripoli:

> 29 October 1911
> In Italy it produced a very grave impression that even the number of dead of the 23 [October] and the 26 is not officially known. Also, yesterday foreign ambassadors observed to me that such a lack of news produces abroad grave impressions that could create a belief either in the most serious losses or in a lack of organization.[41]

The strength of this reaction in Italy, which might seem disproportionate to the losses or to the importance of the military setback, has to be seen as the result not only of the battles but of the whole situation that had developed by the end of October. Italy had begun the war with the expectation of creating a *fait accompli* by swift military action that could be kept isolated from Turkish retaliation or from foreign diplomatic intervention. When the military problem was solved, the Italians expected that Turkey could somehow be brought to make peace quickly. But Turkey had not decided to make peace, and the Italian army had been unable to move beyond the suburbs of a few coastal cities. The engagements of 23–26 October had made it seem that the Italian position was insecure even in these few sanctuaries, where the army was protected by the Italian fleet. Sciara Sciat had shown that the Arabs would not easily accept the Italian occupation, as had been expected. When added to the difficulties of terrain and climate, this made an eventual Italian occupation of the whole province much harder to imagine. The publicity given internationally to Italian atrocities created a hostile climate of opinion abroad, a difficulty that earlier colonial ventures had not had to face.[42] As an English diplomat had already noted, it was likely that the sympathy of the European press would "encourage Turkey to expect material support and prolong and possibly extend the area of the war."[43] In short, it was probably at this time that it began to seem to some both in Turkey and in Italy that the result of the war was not a foregone conclusion. This realization came as a tremendous shock to the directors of Italian policy; it deserves to be called "the crisis of late October."

The crisis of late October evidently stemmed not only from miscalculating Turkish resistance, but from the very endeavor to fight a limited war. We have seen how this interfered with the military operations in Libya. And there were no victories in other theaters that could have served to distract attention from minor reverses in Libya; this too was a consequence of the Italian leaders' policy of limited war. To the public it seemed clear that Giolitti's intention to fight a limited war was largely responsible for the military difficulties. The military means, limited by Giolitti's policy, had proved insufficient. It was easy to infer that the limitation was the cause of the failure. This inference is one that is always likely to be made in limited wars. The charge that Giolitti's restraint was producing failure in the war was quickly made, particularly by the Nationalists who threatened Giolitti's political position.[44]

In these ways Giolitti became involved in the cycle so familiar in limited wars, where the attempt to limit war results in military failures, whether important or unimportant, and these failures in turn make it more difficult to maintain a policy of limiting the war. This process is helped along by the administrative demands of limited war. In the modern context, limited war tends to demand centralized and detailed civilian control of military (and diplomatic) operations, which Giolitti and San Giuliano tried to exercise. But, in the modern context, these civilian political leaders tend to lack technical expertise in the military field. It is thus likely that for the sake of limiting war they will order ineffective or technically difficult military operations. It would seem that Giolitti and San Giuliano did not understand the difficulties of an attack on Tripoli before the forces were prepared, or of holding the city of Tripoli with naval forces alone, or of cordoning off the 180 miles of sea between Crete and Cyrenaica with four ships.[45] It was only the weakness and passivity of Turkey that prevented Giolitti's unrealistic orders from having more serious consequences than they did have. Of course, these mechanisms by which war-limiting generates pressures against itself can be reinforced by the effects on the adversary. Military success given to the enemy by a strategy of limited war may impel it to expand the war in some way. Even in the case we are considering, where a severely limited war was forced on Turkey by its own weakness, this took place to an extent. Sciara Sciat and the Italians' failure to establish themselves solidly at the beginning of the war encouraged Turkey to continue the war indefinitely, expanding it in a temporal sense.

How did Giolitti and his associates respond to the late October crisis, which was seen (in part correctly) as the consequence of his attempt to fight a limited war? On November 5, 1911, Giolitti submitted for the royal signature a decree proclaiming the full sovereignty of Italy over Libya. This annexation decree was the most important diplomatic event between the outbreak of the war and the peace treaty; it affected in a fundamental way the limited character of the war. Giolitti decided on the decree of annexation against the advice of San Giuliano and the other officials of the Italian foreign office, who pointed out how much more difficult this step would make a negotiated settlement. Why did he take this step which was apparently so foolish?

Documentary evidence has only recently become available that enables us to see the inner history of Giolitti's response to the late October crisis. Consider the following two telegrams:

Victor Emmanuel III to Giolitti, 25 October 1911

> Yesterday I saw General Robilant and I was impressed by his opinion that Turkey will draw out things, especially because she is persuaded that the stand of the Powers will prevent Italy from carrying out that decisive blow which alone could mean the end of the war. If, in view of the lengthening of the present situation, the Government decided on an action in the Aegean, it is naturally necessary . . . that adequate means be prepared in time.

Giolitti to Victor Emmanuel III, 25 October 1911

> In view of the latest events at Tripoli I believe we ought to pursue the following course: to make now every effort to destroy as quickly as possible nuclei of Turkish forces existing in Tripolitania, in order to prove to the world that the conquest is definitive. After that, to proclaim the absolute sovereignty of the Kingdom of Italy over Tripolitania and Cyrenaica. After making ready the fleet or troops that might be necessary to occupy several islands, we will decide which actions of occupation or blockade might be necessary to force the Turks to peace. In the event of these possible further steps, we ought to consider the international difficulties which one or the other means of action might provoke. The Minister of Foreign Affairs and I have just now given Ambassador [to Germany] Pansa instructions, above all upon the point of Italy's requirement that she have full and complete sovereignty.[46]

This telegram contains the first mention that I have seen of a proclamation of annexation. It shows that the annexation decree was a direct response to the defeats of late October, rather than something decided upon separately, whether for internal reasons or otherwise. It reveals that Giolitti responded to this crisis, and to the political pressure that it generated, with a three-fold program: (1) further military action in Libya; (2) proclamation, while the war was still in progress, of the "absolute sovereignty" of Italy over Libya; (3) extension of the theater of war in order to compel Turkey to make peace.

The last two items in Giolitti's program propose a partial dissolution of the limitations that had hitherto been placed on the ends of the war (by proclaiming Italian sovereignty over Tripoli) and on the means by which these ends were pursued (by expanding the theater of war). We will therefore discuss these two proposals, the reasons for them, and their actualization at some length.

The geographical expansion of the war constitutes a familiar response to the ineffectiveness of the means in limited war. The annexation decree is more difficult to understand. We may discern in the evidence the following reasons for the Italian decree of annexation. First, a decree of annexation would serve to deflect internal criticism of lack of success in the war by making it clear that the government was fully committed to the acquisition of Libya. Second, on the international level, the lack of military success, culminating in the defeat of Sciara Sciat, gave an opening to pressure from third countries that necessarily favored a settlement that would preserve their standing both in Italy and in Turkey. Given the legitimization of international meddling by the other powers' interests in Turkey, mediation by the powers in a sense hostile to Italy now appeared possible.

Prior to the outbreak of the war, and during its early stages, Italian statesmen had voiced no demand for formal sovereignty over Libya. They had apparently been willing to control the province under nominal Turkish sovereignty, the arrangement made when Bosnia, Crete, and Egypt had changed hands earlier.[47] After the early military successes, Italian diplomats began to speak of full sovereignty as well as of more partial solutions.[48] But now, given the declining prospects of military success, the expectation was likely to arise that Italy was abandoning her preferred war aims because of the lack of means to achieve them. Both inside and outside of Italy, this would have looked like an abandonment of Italian interests and an acceptance of humiliation.

In any case, the effect of the decree of annexation was to forestall possible hostile mediation by closing off Italian options. Once the decree was issued, neither the powers nor Turkey could pressure Italy, since the Italian position had become rigid; it could not be changed even by a subsequent Italian loss of will, except in the unimaginable case of a complete defeat. Looking at the annexation decree from the Turkish side, the now more favorable military situation would have made Turkey less willing to make peace on any terms acceptable to Italy. But the annexation decree forced the decision on Turkey; it compelled her to take the initiative.

A more analytical formulation of the purpose of the annexation decree, as seen in Giolitti's telegram to the King, would be this: to compensate both internally and externally for a decline in the apparent effectiveness of military means with an assertion of *will*—by making the war aims extreme and rigid. In other words, the Italian decree of annexation is an example of the use of *ends* (the war aims) as a *means* to winning the war. This type of expansion of war deserves an important place in the discussion of war-limiting. The increase in the extent of Italian war aims after a partial Italian defeat is the opposite of what usually occurs. We are more familiar with cases where "victory" leads to expanded aims, and "defeat" to diminished ones. In the

Korean war, for example, the original American war aims involved only the restoration of the status quo prior to the North Korean invasion. Once United Nations forces had crossed the thirty-eighth parallel and found themselves occupying North Korea with little resistance, American leaders began to think in terms of the reunification of Korea.

In order to understand the relationship between the changing military means and the changing ends of the war, which was the reverse of what usually happens, we must make some distinctions between various kinds of war aims. To begin with, a distinction can be drawn between positive and negative war aims. A positive war aim exists when the war is being fought, in whole or in part, to procure some good. A negative war aim, on the other hand, is the prevention of some evil. In the case of the war over Libya, the dominant aim was positive for Italy—the acquisition of Libya—and negative for Turkey, which fought the war to prevent the loss of Libya.

A more important distinction, cutting across these categories, is that between *actual* and *latent* war aims. We will call "actual war aims" the conscious motives a nation's leaders have for going to war or for waging war at any particular time under discussion. "Latent war aims" are those ends that national policy-makers are not striving for at the time in question, but ones that they would care about if it should seem that they might be brought about by the war. These terms may also be applied to any element in a nation that influences or attempts to influence policy with regard to war aims.

The distinction between actual and latent war aims is historically very important. World War I is the modern case that illustrates this most impressively. In general terms, the war was embarked on for relatively narrow aims belonging to traditional balance-of-power diplomacy; but in the course of the war the ends swelled enormously on both sides. Negative war aims, latent at the beginning of the war, came to include for almost all the major participants the loss of their status as great powers and, in the case of Austria-Hungary and the Ottoman Empire, their disappearance as nations. Latent positive war aims that emerged in the course of the war included, for Germany, hegemony over Europe. On the Allied side, a new aim somehow emerged of transforming the international system into one based on nationality as the criterion for statehood, on elimination of conflict among nations through international organization, and on universal adoption of liberal-democratic institutions. The specific example of German war aims toward Belgium is particularly striking. Prior to the war, and in the discussion immediately preceding the decision to go to war, there is no sign whatever of any German desire to acquire rights in Belgium. But the lists of official war aims adopted during the war almost always include aims in Belgium, ranging from commercial privileges to complete control over the country and partial annexation of it to Germany.

The importance of latent war aims seems to be due to two principal factors: first, to human beings' different conceptions of what sort of aims are proper in peace and in war, and second, to the effects of means on ends. The latter factor concerns us here. Wars are perhaps more precisely undertaken as means to ends than are most human activities. In war, however, the ends seem to shift with the effectiveness of the means much more than in most human activities, because the variations in the effectiveness of the means are both enormous and largely unpredictable. Any large change in what the available means can do tends strongly to awaken latent ends. An unexpected increase in the power of the means, as in Korea, usually activates positive latent ends. Latent negative ends are activated by a decline in the power of the means, by "defeats." This gives to one side a greater power to inflict harm on the other in a way that was not expected originally. To counteract this threat requires either abandonment of the war or an increase in the means of waging it. If the war has been significantly limited at the beginning, an easy way to strengthen one's military means is to remove some of the limitations on the war. Part of the English response to the disasters of 1940, for example, was to carry the war to the enemy's homeland by aerial bombing of civilian targets, something neither side had systematically engaged in before. This is obviously one of the most important reasons why wars do not remain limited, even when they were carefully planned as limited wars. It is also probably *the* most frequent factor defeating attempts to limit war. Other difficulties depend on specific social structure or diplomatic environment, while this factor operates at all times and in all places.

In the case we are examining, Giolitti saw the defeats of late October as a threat to latent ends that had not been at issue previously: the maintenance of Italian prestige, a short and cheap war, the diplomatic isolation of the war. In response, Giolitti sought to strengthen the military means by abolishing some of the limits on the war: namely, by expanding the war geographically. He also responded by taking away some of the previous limitation on the *ends* of the war. With the annexation decree, Giolitti made the Italian war aims much more extreme and entirely rigid. In doing this, Giolitti was using what had been the ends of the war as a means.

When Giolitti made the Italian war aims less limited, he was responding to a crisis created in large measure by his original decision to wage a narrowly limited war. Using ends as a means is a particularly great temptation in limited wars. In cases such as the Tripoli war, where the ends as well as the means are openly limited, the ends offer themselves for tampering with, since they are not at or near the maximum. To relax the limits on means always requires expenditure of resources, while relaxing the limits on the ends often requires only talk. In many conflicts, the expansion of the means is more likely to cause trouble with neutral powers. This prospect is important when, at the start, the means were limited in order not to offend third parties, as was the case in the Libyan war. As the naval actions off Albania showed, many of the ways in which Giolitti could have expanded the means would have gotten him into trouble, whereas to expand the ends offered an easier way out. Given that limitations on ends are ultimately more fundamental than limitation of means, one may say that this externally limited type of limited war has within it a certain self-destructive tendency: the very need to keep the war limited provokes the dissolution of the limits. All these forces acting to destroy limits on war aims are reinforced by the fact that "regularizing" the war will often please the military and public opinion.

There are many other cases in history where states did what Giolitti did in response to the difficulties of late October 1911: to increase war aims as a means to winning the war. A similar sort of process probably affected Allied war aims in the First World War. This was not a case of limited war in the traditional sense, but it is a very important example of the failure of war-limiting. The course of Allied policy on war aims through the war is not well understood, and contradictory views were held by different statesmen of the same country at the same time. It is, however, possible to speak in a rough way of the general movement of Allied war aims, and this is contrary to what we might have predicted. From 1917 to the summer of 1918, the Allies were in general faring badly in the war: the disastrous Nivelle offensive, the subsequent mutinies in the French army, the defeats at Ypres and Caporetto, the collapse of the Russian front, and finally the great German 1918 offensive in the West brought a deepening spirit of gloom. But the general movement of Allied war aims during this period was not, as one might expect, in the direction of greater restraint; on the contrary, the war aims expanded. The case of Austria-Hungary is particularly instructive. Russian war aims had threatened the integrity of Austria-Hungary from early in the war, but it was by no means clear that its division into petty states would benefit the Western allies. Such a division might have strengthened Germany by the absorption of German Austria—something that the final peace treaty was explicitly intended to prevent—and it might have created a power vacuum in the Balkans that would probably have been filled by Germany. By decreasing the number of weak great powers, the elimination of Austria-Hungary contributed to the process by which countries such as France and Italy ceased to be great powers. Many of these considerations were recognized in the position papers on war aims that were prepared in the Allied cabinets during the earlier part of the war; the majority of the studies that have been published recommended that Austria-Hungary not be dissolved.

It was precisely during the darkest period of the war for the Allies that the disruption of Austria-Hungary on grounds of ethnic self-determination became a public policy of the Allies and that this disruption was made inevitable by official recognition of the Czechoslovak secessionist committee. The reasons for this great transformation are not clear, but it has been ably argued that in their greatest desperation the Allies grabbed at the national conflicts in Austria-Hungary as an important method of hampering the war effort of the Central Powers, and thus of avoiding defeat in the war.[49] If this interpretation of the events is true, the expansion of Allied war aims in a period of defeat resembles Giolitti's annexation proclamation: it is a use of ends as means. The activation of latent negative ends by the possibility of defeat again drew forth this reversal of the normal relation of ends and means.

A final historical parallel to Giolitti's response to the late October crisis is the British response to the fall of France in 1940. British war aims during the period of the "phony war" were not precisely defined, but they surely did not exclude the possibility of a negotiated peace with the Hitler regime on the basis of the restoration of Poland. After the German conquest of Norway, Denmark, the Low Countries, and France, and after the loss of the British army's weapons and vehicles, there no longer seemed to be any means by which Britain could hope to win. The country was exposed both to destruction from the air and to invasion. In these circumstances, one would normally expect the war aims to contract with the contraction in the means available for forcing British war aims on Germany. What actually happened is well known. As Churchill stated in a speech to Parliament on June 18, 1940, a day after the capitulation of France: "We abate nothing of our just demands; not one jot or tittle do we recede. Czechs, Poles, Norwegians, Dutch, Belgians have joined their causes to our own. All these shall be restored."[50]

Indeed, in the course of the fall of France, British war aims expanded. No thematic study of war aims was prepared within the British government at this time. But in Churchill's private memoranda the expressed war aims actually became more and more sweeping as the crisis went on. On May 28, 1940, Churchill wrote of Britain's "inflexible resolve to continue the war till we have broken the will of the enemy to bring all Europe under his domination."[51] Finally, by August 3, 1940, after the French capitulation, Churchill was writing in connection with a Swedish offer to communicate German terms for ending the war that Britain would continue to fight "until Hitlerism is finally broken."[52] At this point the destruction of the Nazi regime within Germany, which had not been at issue earlier, had become the ultimate aim of the war.

Churchill thus expanded British war aims in response to defeat. More striking was the way in which he made them more rigid, as Giolitti did, by specifying not only Britain's preferred war aims but also how these war aims would be altered by changes in the effectiveness of the British means. The absolute rigidity that Churchill tried to give to British war aims is most eloquently expressed in his famous speech after Dunkirk:

> Even though large tracts of Europe and many old and famous States have fallen or may fall into the grip of the Gestapo and all the odious apparatus of Nazi rule, we shall not flag or fail. We shall go on to the end, we shall fight in France, we shall fight on the seas and oceans, we shall fight with growing confidence and growing strength in the air, we shall defend our Island, whatever the cost may be, we shall fight on the beaches, we shall fight on the landing grounds, we shall fight in the fields and in the streets, we shall fight in the hills; we shall never surrender, and even if, which I do not for a moment believe, this Island or a large part of it were subjugated and starving, then our Empire beyond the seas, armed and guarded by the British Fleet, would carry on the struggle.[53]

Taken in conjunction with the statements already quoted, this stakes out a very extreme position: that the ultimate aim was to change the enemy's domestic structure and to make the enemy disgorge all his conquests, and that in pursuit of this aim Britain would continue the war even past the point where the country had lost its independence. Finally, Britain would not, if the war seemed hopeless, make peace with Germany even on terms that would largely concede British demands.

The specific formulation of British war aims and the circumstances in which they would hold is of course a response to the needs of speaking to a broad audience. But it is essentially the same position taken by Churchill in private and actualized in British diplomacy. In fact, the most extreme of all Churchill's statements of rigid war aims was addressed to Reynaud, the French prime minister:

> The Allies must maintain an unflinching front against all their enemies.... The British government were prepared to wage war from the New World, if through some disaster England herself were laid waste.... It would be better far that the civilisation of Western Europe with all its achievements should come to a tragic but splendid end than that the two great democracies should linger on, stripped of all that made life worth living.[54]

This may, of course, have been partly bluff. But the same basic position guided British diplomacy. Churchill instructed British diplomatic representatives to have no communication with the Germans about terms of peace, even though Hitler had declared his desire for a compromise peace.[55]

The policy adopted by Churchill in response to the crisis of 1940 is in a certain sense absurd. It represents the use of ends as means and the insistence on pursuing the means (the war) even when these means had ruined the end for which they were undertaken (the well-being of the British people).

But this is precisely why it is so useful to compare the case of Churchill with that of Giolitti: Britain in 1940 shows that the use of war aims as a means to winning the war is not always a mistake. As we shall see shortly, it was a serious error in Giolitti's case, in which it had the results that one would predict. Churchill doubtless chose to make these declarations of war aims to give the British a sense of purpose and to heighten their morale; to convince both Germans and neutrals, through an assertion of will, that Britain's military position was stronger than they would otherwise have thought; and perhaps also to limit the flexibility of his possible successors in the event of further disaster. From contemporary accounts it is clear how much Churchill's defiant stance lifted the morale of the British in comparison with the half-hearted commitment made by Chamberlain to the war.

Consequences of the Annexation Decree

No one today would deny that Giolitti's annexation decree was a mistake. As Denis Mack Smith writes, "The unexpected result was that a war intended to last a few weeks at a negligible cost dragged out in fact for over a year and seriously depleted Italian strength."[56] The annexation made negotiations almost impossible, since it proclaimed beforehand that the Italian and Turkish terms were irreconcilable. It is likely that Giolitti himself came to regret the proclamation of annexation; certainly Italian diplomats did. As Sir Edward Grey, the British foreign secretary, remarked in the spring: "I was sure the Italian government would like to find some way of ending the war, if they could get around their Decree of Annexation of Tripoli. They had themselves said in general terms that they would be prepared to receive suggestions."[57] The decree clearly decreased Turkish willingness to make peace. Bompard, the French ambassador in Constantinople, wrote that "the decree of annexation has caused peace to lose its last partisans, and there is no one today in Constantinople who dares to speak of subscribing to the Italian conditions."[58]

The ultimate effects of the annexation decree may have been far-reaching. As we have seen, it lengthened the war. The prolongation of the war led to the demand, and eventually the need, to expand the war in order to end it. The expansion of the theater and the military means used brought tension with Austria and France; it also enormously increased expenditures. These were among the outcomes that Giolitti had sought to avoid by fighting a limited war. More important, the expansion of the war led to the expulsion of Italians from the Ottoman Empire. Turkey's long absorption in the war enabled the Balkan coalition to form against Turkey; it also created the preconditions for Turkey's defeat in the Balkan Wars. The Balkan Wars increased the influence of Austria and Russia, as opposed to that of Italy, in the Balkans and may have led to the First World War—a titanic chain of consequences that was not sought by Giolitti. He had been tempted by the very effort to fight a limited war and by the problems that this created to use less limited war aims as a means to win the war. This reversal of the normal means-ends relationship in turn made the war still more difficult to finish, and then made it even less limited.

The annexation decree may have achieved its internal purposes at the time, although it ultimately prolonged the war and thus increased discontent with the way Giolitti was waging it. The decree was also successful externally in its negative intent—to create conditions that would make unfriendly mediation by neutral powers impossible. But this result was only good on the assumption that the positive aim—to force Turkey to make the decision to end the war—could be achieved. This did not happen. Friendly third-party pressure for a Turkish decision was decreased by the decree, since the Powers were offended by Italy's sudden and unilateral decision to annex. A purely Turkish initiative was not likely. It is much harder to force a decision to act (above all publicly) than to force a decision to abstain from acting. Since to end a declared war requires a formal public decision, the inherent tendency of such wars is to be temporally unlimited unless an end is in some way brought about through military action. Giolitti may have thought that the war would not drag on because the military situation would improve. If so, he again exhibited one of the other problems of limited war: that the centralized civilian control it requires is likely to lead to false assumptions about technical military matters.

It was particularly unreasonable to expect the annexation decree to result in a Turkish decision to end the war, because of the specific form of the Italian action, which demanded that the Turks yield not only the substance (possession of Libya) but also the form (Italian sovereignty). This was the most difficult thing to get, because it required the most open and public decision to put an end to the war; it ruled out, for example, suggestions that were made to end the war by an indefinite armistice. More important, the decision for peace was hard to get, because it was the form, not the substance, that the Turks most cared about. The actual loss of Libya would not have been very painful. The province was so poor that it required an annual subsidy from Constantinople, not only to pay the expenses of administration, but also to feed the inhabitants. It was largely desert, and a large portion of the populated area was not administered by Turkey.[59] Far greater than the loss of actual control over Libya was the blow to the prestige of the empire through the formal relinquishing of sovereignty.

Giolitti does not seem to have thought about this, or about the consistent pattern of extreme tenacity in defense of formal rights that had been shown by the Ottoman Empire in the previous hundred years. Whenever Turkey had lost territories, it had refused to admit the fact and had clung to the trappings of sovereignty as long as possible. In 1911 Turkey still claimed Massaua and Tunisia, which had been occupied by Italy and France in 1885 and 1881 respectively. Although in 1911 Egypt had not been ruled from Constantinople for over a hundred years, Turkey still insisted on the formal recognition of its suzerainty and the symbols of that suzerainty, such as flying the Turkish flag and the use of Turkish army uniforms.[60] This same pattern is seen in the treatment of tribal incursions: when, in 1913, the Saudis expelled the Turks from El Hasa, the Turkish reaction was to appoint Ibn Saud as governor of the lost province.

This clinging to formal authority is not peculiarly Turkish, but is a consistent pattern of behavior among certain types of states. It is seen also in the behavior of China toward its dependencies, or in the insistence of Bukhara on minting its own coins, an Islamic symbol of sovereignty, long after it had passed under Russian control.[61] The cases that come most readily to mind are those of major states, premodern and autocratic in their structure, that are declining drastically in power. But this pattern has a wider distribution; it also characterizes, for example, the Arab states in their dispute with Israel. What these states share is a position of weakness, which results in an inability to secure foreign-policy objectives in substance. If the form is still maintained, however, this demonstrates some apparent strength and can perhaps be exploited in the future.

These tendencies have a general importance, because limited wars (in the common sense of limited) are more likely to be fought between very unequal powers than between those having comparable power. It is easier to keep a war limited if it is limited for one side by inescapable facts, if the decision for limited war has to be taken by one side rather than two. But in this situation one cannot assume that similar types of concessions are equally reasonable for both sides. If, owing to its tradition or to asymmetry of strength, one side cannot yield on some issues that seem less important to the stronger side, the latter should not include them in its war aims. Giolitti, by failing to consider the asymmetries between Italy and Turkey, forced Turkey into a position of die-hard resistance that then had to be overcome by further military efforts. This was one of the factors that made it difficult for him to keep the war limited.

Attempts to Expand the War

We will now take up the second part of Giolitti's response to the crisis that his limited-war project faced in late October. This was the expansion of the war beyond Tripoli. Before commenting on the processes at work, we must review the history of the threats to extend the war geographically in

October–November 1911, the means by which these threats were communicated, the Turkish response to them, and the outcome.

Very quickly after the reverses in Tripoli an Italian diplomat who was still in Constantinople remarked to a German diplomat (known to be very close to the Turks) that Italy might have to occupy Salonika. The same day the semiofficial newspaper *Tribuna* said that Italy might have to take action outside Libya.[62] The Russian embassy in Rome heard on October 30 that Italy was considering striking at Turkey in the Red Sea, and on the following day that the Italian foreign minister had asked expert advice on how to strike a decisive blow and been told to destroy the Turkish fleet in the Dardanelles.[63] On the day of the annexation decree, the Austrian ambassador reported from Rome that naval action was being planned against Salonika, the Dardanelles, or Smyrna. Afterwards the flood of Italian threats continued. The Italian ambassadors in St. Petersburg and in Paris avowed that Italy would have to strike a decisive blow, although it was not yet decided where, and similar reports continued to come from Rome.[64] On November 12 it was reported that Italy would refrain from forcing the Dardanelles, but would attack Rhodes instead, while on November 20 this was reversed: Italy wanted to act now, but would choose a more important target than the Aegean islands.[65]

Thus, at the time of the annexation decree, reports were abroad that the Italians might strike in four different places on the coast of the Ottoman Empire. These reports could be read by the Turks in Italian newspapers and were doubtless transmitted to them by the ambassadors in Constantinople. The actual threats made by Italy were of course compounded by rumors. On November 6 the French ambassador in Constantinople reported that Italian warships had been seen near Smyrna, although none were in fact there.[66] Slightly later, a military journal remarked about this period: "No further naval action appears to have been taken by the Italians outside Libya, although rumors frequently arrive of expected seizure of islands in the Aegean sea, attacks on Syrian coast towns and even of the forcing of the passage of the Dardanelles."[67] Rumors will be an important factor in whether any limited war can be controlled by one side and whether it can be kept limited. As the Tripoli case illustrates, the overwhelming majority of these will be rumors that the war is being expanded, not that it will be kept limited.

The Turks took the threats and rumors of a wider war very seriously. The uncertainty of the Italian action required defense at many points. For example, by November 6, 450 extra troops had been sent to the island of Samos to deal with a possible Italian *coup de main*, although the Italians had not directly threatened this point.[68] A force equal to about half the peacetime army was mobilized, mainly from reserve (*Redif*) divisions, to defend Albania, Salonika, the Dardanelles, and the Aegean islands.[69] The cost of this mobilization was a heavy strain on Turkey. Thus, at first sight, the Italian threats to extend the war served two functions: They pressured neutral powers to intervene to force peace on Turkey, and they subjected Turkey to financial attrition prior to any attack.

The immediate Turkish response to these threats was to defend the coasts and to try, in turn, to use neutral powers to prevent the extension of the war. Between November 8 and November 10 Turkey asked Germany, Austria-Hungary, and Britain to intervene diplomatically with Italy. Shortly after this the Turks discovered how to manipulate the interests of the powers in order to stop the Italians from expanding the war. On November 13 the Turkish ambassador in Paris informed the French that two Italian warships were off Jidda (the port of Mecca) and that this threat to the Holy Cities was likely to cause riots among "overexcited Muslims."[70] This was an obvious attempt to stir French fears of discontent among its Muslim subjects in case the Italians expanded the theater of war. The Turkish tactic had succeeded when France expressed its concern to Italy. The Italian foreign minister then assured the French that no attack would be made on Jidda, but he hinted that the Italians might be forced to act at Akaba.[71] In any case, no operations would be undertaken in the Red Sea while the king of England was passing through on his way to India.[72] In fact, the day before the English king reached Port Said, two Italian cruisers bombarded Akaba, as San Giuliano had hinted that they would.[73] Already on November 3, the day that the first threats to extend the war to the Red Sea were made, a cruiser had sunk a Turkish gunboat at Akaba.[74] Immediately after the English king had passed through the Red Sea, Sheik Said in Yemen was bombarded.[75] The Red Sea thus became the first and, as we shall see, the only area beyond Libya to which Italian operations were extended in 1911.

By protesting possible operations near Mecca, the Turks had been able to produce French diplomatic intervention against the extension of the war. Turkey had thus found out how to turn the Italian threats in order to extend the war against Italy. Pursuing this discovery, on November 18 the Turks sent an *aide-mémoire* to the powers, pointing out the likelihood of Italian naval action against Ottoman "ports and coasts" and stating that defense against this might require arresting "for an indefinite period the movement of ships of any flag and thus paralyzing general commerce."[76] This was a very thinly veiled threat to close the Dardanelles to neutral shipping. The Turkish note went on to state that before undertaking any such measures the Turks would ask the neutral powers to obtain from Italy an undertaking not to extend the hostilities.

What was going on at this point was well described by the British foreign secretary, Sir Edward Grey: "It was obvious that each party to the war hoped that, by making neutral Powers uncomfortable, intervention on its behalf could be brought about."[77] It is remarkable to find two adversaries, both trying to get neutrals to work in their behalf by playing on the same issue and both believing that this technique could work. All the major powers indeed had an interest in pleasing either Turkey or Italy through intervention: the unstable balance of foreign influence at Constantinople, so productive of commercial concessions, prestige, and military help, could be upset in favor of one side. On the other hand, Italy could be held in the Triple Alliance or drawn out of it by friendly intervention. The unusually strong international interest in keeping open the straits (and to a lesser extent in preventing restlessness among Muslim subjects) also provided an unusual *opportunity* for neutral intervention. It was thus not unrealistic for either Turkey or Italy to hope for intervention. The question was whether the complicated situation would result in neutral intervention for Turkey or for Italy.

Responses to the Turkish counterthreat were strong. Russia and Britain, in particular, were very disturbed by the threat to their commerce.[78] The English reaction was clear: "Treaty or no Treaty I think our interest in the grain trade and commercial shipping connected with the Black Sea is such that we could not stand the Black Sea trade being stopped by this wretched war."[79] It was at first unclear whether the alarm of the powers at the prospect of the straits being closed would be turned against Turkey or Italy. Fairly soon, however, it became clear that the powers would take no action to pressure Turkey into ending the war. Indeed, Austria responded favorably to the Turkish request for intervention:

> Count von Aehrenthal spoke . . . to-day of the Turkish proposal that the Powers should take steps to prevent Italy from taking action in the Dardanelles. He said that he thought demand of Turkish Government unjustifiably unreasonable, but that before replying to it he would consult the European Powers. Meanwhile, he was having the treaties and conventions with Turkey searched to see if any stipulation could be found in them which would justify Powers taking action in this matter.[80]

At the same time, Russia began a campaign of the powers to make representations at Rome and Constantinople against any blockage of neutral trade. Since it was an Italian action that initially would pose such a threat to trade, this ostensibly even-handed move was really favorable to Turkey. Russia's desire to do a favor for Turkey at this point sprang from the hope to obtain the opening of the Dardanelles to Russian warships in return for protection. The failure of Italian threats to expand the war was thus related in part to the nature of limited war, which tempts neutral powers to exploit the situation. In any case, the Russian proposal was accepted by Germany and Austria-Hungary before the march of events made it obsolete.[81]

This favorable response of the powers to the Turkish threat only reinforced the attitude that they had shown from the start toward the new Italian program of expanding the war. None of the powers had put any pressure on Turkey to end the war. As we saw, France had warned Italy against operations near Mecca. The French also sent a cruiser to the coast of Syria, ostensibly to protect French interests against disorders that might result if the Italians attacked.[82] Most unyielding of all had been the attitude of Austria-Hungary. As early as November 4, the day of the annexation decree, Austria-Hungary had declined to accept the extension of the war to the Aegean:

> Until now we have maintained a friendly attitude. . . . But if the Italian fleet were to be sent into the Aegean, I [Aehrenthal] am determined to regard any step beyond a simple (naval) demonstration, for instance, aiming at even only a temporary occupation of an island, as contrary to Article VII of the Treaty. . . . Thus, should Italy actually proceed even to the temporary occupation of an island in the Aegean, a precedent (Präjudiz) would thereby be created which I could not tolerate and I should, in that case, be obliged to emphasize that we should have to ask ourselves what value, in those circumstances, the further retention of Article VII can have for us.[83]

In reply, Italy had assured Austria-Hungary immediately that it would adhere to all the articles of the Triple Alliance.[84]

The final result of the pressure that was brought on Italy by the neutrals came when Italy promised the other powers on November 22, 1911, that for the time being the war would not be extended.[85] This declaration put a formal end to the Italian attempt to extend the war, although the content of the promise was not entirely clear. Immediately after this declaration of November 22, Italy began one last secret effort, requesting Germany to ask Austria whether it would permit any operations in the Aegean if they were outside of Europe. These inquiries were unrewarding, and finally, on December 16, Italy asked Germany to drop them.[86] This marked the conclusive defeat of the first Italian effort to extend the war.

The only area that the Italian declaration of November 22 apparently did not cover was the Red Sea. The Red Sea was, after all the talk, the only new theater of war. Although there seem to have been no major operations in December, many bombardments were undertaken in January and February. This front continued to be active through most of the war. On January 7 the largest naval engagement of the war took place when Italian cruisers destroyed eight Turkish gunboats at Kunfidah off the coast of Arabia. On the twenty-first, Italy declared the blockade of part of the Yemen coast.[87] This burst of activity in January may have come in response to the final abandonment of hopes to extend the war to the Aegean in December. The Red Sea theater of war obviously needed to be kept much more carefully limited than the Libyan theater. Giolitti states that "these operations in the Red Sea, calling for very special manipulation behind the scenes, were controlled by the ministry of the Interior under my personal direction."[88]

Why was the Red Sea the only place where Giolitti's program of expanding the war was actually carried out? The most important reasons seem to be that here Turkey was vulnerable, with only a small Italian expenditure of resources, and that the interests of neutral powers were small. There were no international waterways that could be closed by the Turks, no foreign investments (except the beginning of a French railway in the Yemen), and no Christian minorities that were protected by the Powers. Thus, neutral objections to the extension of the war, which proved fatal to action in the Aegean, did not interfere with Italian operations against Turkish Arabia. The only neutral objections made were by France: the warning about Jidda, already referred to, and later a protest against the bombardment of the French railway workings at Hodeida. Both of these protests were easily dealt with.

Turkey was particularly vulnerable in Arabia, where its communications (beyond Medina) were by sea and where Turkish control was already very shaky because of the revolts of the Imam Yahya in Yemen and Sayyid Idris in Asir. Idris, in fact, cooperated with the Italians in fighting the Turks.[89] In Arabia it was easy to worry the Turks, but it was impossible to strike a blow that would have decisive consequences. The Italian attacks in Arabia did cause some diversion of Turkish military effort and some losses, but it does not seem to have had any serious effect on the Turks: none of the Italian attacks ever provoked Turkish retaliation or led to any change in Turkish policy.

There are other reasons why the Red Sea did not become a sanctuary area, like the rest of the Ottoman Empire, at this point. The Red Sea was the area, apart from Libya and perhaps Albania, where Italian and Turkish forces and territory were in closest proximity. Turkey had three divisions on the Red Sea coast, as well as about a dozen gunboats. The Italian colonies of Eritrea and Somalia—not yet completely subdued—were near Turkish Arabia and were defended by fewer troops.[90] The Italians were thus able to claim that the extension of the war to the Red Sea was defensive; this is a standard justification for dissolving some of the limits in a limited war.

Finally, it was easier for the Italians to expand the theater of war to include the Red Sea because hostilities had already taken place there, without neutral protest, before the extension of war became an issue. Immediately after the war began, on October 2, Italian warships had met a Turkish torpedo-gunboat at sea, engaged it, and followed it to Hodeida, which was then shelled.[91] It is difficult to draw a line excluding "hot pursuit" in fighting a limited war. It is indeed possible that the Italian defensive claim was correct, that the Turks were hoping to extend the war to the Italian colonies from a base in Turkish Arabia. There is a small amount of ambiguous evidence that might suggest this.[92] This was certainly the only way in which Turkey could have avoided having a one-sided limited war imposed on it. But this aim, if it existed, never achieved any results. It would have taken truly extraordinary vigor and cleverness to overcome Turkey's lack of naval power. In the absence of this, Turkey was forced to wage a war of attrition, hoping that Italy would eventually grow tired.

It is not clear whether the Italian threats to extend the war were signs of a real intent to take military action or whether they were merely bluffs intended to bring about neutral pressure against Turkey. Neutral diplomats tended to interpret the Italian threats in the latter way.[93] Italy did have important reasons of its own, apart from neutral pressure, for not attacking the straits. The Italian undersecretary of state for foreign affairs pointed out, when Italy finally withdrew the threats, how harmful the interruption of trade with Russia would be. There is other important evidence, however, that Italy did seriously consider making an attack. For instance, the Italian government asked Count Bosdari, their ambassador to Bulgaria, what repercussions an Italian naval action against Salonika or against the Dardenelles would have in the Balkans.[94] This suggests that serious thought was being given to extending the war, as long as it would still remain limited with regard to the participation of the Balkan powers. The most reliable Italian witness confirms the seriousness of his country's threats.[95]

It might seem at first glance that it does not make a difference whether the Italian threats were an attempt to create neutral pressure on Turkey, genuine threats against Turkey, or the signs of an actual plan to act, since the same threat effects result from following each of these approaches. Further reflection reveals that this is not so. If the Italians actually intended to widen the theater of war, or even to make their threat to do so as plausible as possible to the Turks, it was foolish to mention the Dardanelles as one of the possible points of attack. An attack against the Dardanelles was the attack that would inevitably arouse the greatest neutral opposition. It was the attack that was calculated to bring not only Austria-Hungary, but also Britain and Russia, into the diplomatic lists against any expansion of the war. Above all, it was only a threat against the Dardanelles that enabled Turkey to bring to bear its effective counterpressure against Italy through the neutrals: the claim that an effective defense of the straits required their closing to neutral commerce. In fact, in the ensuing diplomatic struggle the damage to neutral commerce through any closure of the straits was used (except by Austria-Hungary) as the reason against *any* Italian expansion of the war. If the Italians did intend to make a threat that would act on Turkey directly, it was a mistake not to limit the Italian threat from the start by specifically excluding the straits. The Italian threat was excessive, with the result that it lost credibility and became self-destructive.

On the other hand, if the best hope for ending the war was to work through neutral diplomatic pressure, the threat to act against the straits was probably essential, and the threats to strike elsewhere in the Aegean blurred the Italian communication to the neutrals. In this case, the requirements of direct military coercion and of indirect diplomatic coercion proved to be mutually contradictory. The Italian statesmen probably wished to keep their options open until the further unveiling of the diplomatic context within which they would have to work. They wanted to hold a strategy in reserve in case the narrow confines of an externally limited war excluded their first choice. But they might have done better to decide which course was the more promising at the beginning and then publicly to close off the other option.

This discussion suggests a hypothesis about limited wars, or at least certain types of limited wars, that could only be affirmed after further research. It may be that "limited" wars, as opposed to "total" wars, tend to be characterized by a certain rigidity, in the sense that, in order to fight them well, more available alternatives have to be closed off at an earlier point and more irrevocable commitments have to be made to courses that may fail. Perhaps one can generalize that limited wars need to be more carefully planned than other wars, although many of the most important types of limited wars, such as colonial wars, were historically not at all well planned. This need for careful planning requires centralized decision-making, which is also necessary for other reasons. The rigidity of at least some limited wars, which we have been discussing, is masked by the frequent use of the word "flexibility" with regard to limited war.

The fundamental reason that Italy did not expand the limited war in the fall of 1911 was that the neutral powers would not allow it. An increased opportunity for neutral pressure was provided by the Italian attempt to be flexible in fighting the limited war. The danger to neutral interests that was posed by Italy's threats to expand the war could have resulted either in pressure on Italy to keep the war limited, which happened, or in pressure on Turkey to end the war. Why was the former, not the latter, the consequence of the Italian threat? Some of the reasons for this have been explored in the narrative. Another part of the answer might be this: the object of pressure on Italy was to keep the status quo, but the object of pressure on Turkey would be to force Turkey to take a very difficult decision in public. The neutral task in forcing such a decision had been made much harder by the annexation decree. Under these circumstances, the neutrals took the easier course—pressure on Italy to keep the war as limited as before. This course was also easier in the sense that there was a moral barrier to the other course. To say that Turkey should make peace so that neutrals would not be inconvenienced by an Italian expansion of the war would be to deny to Turkey the right to defend herself.

Responses to Continued Limitation of the War

After Italy finally abandoned these attempts to extend the war, a long period of inactivity followed during the winter. Only in Libya and, on a minor scale, in the Red Sea did operations continue. Because direct assaults against the Turkish positions in Libya had proved rather unrewarding, attention turned to interfering with the supply line of the defending forces. In late December, transports set out for Zuara, the city that controlled the caravan route from Tunisia into Libya. Bad weather kept the Italians from landing, and the expedition was finally abandoned on January 14.[96] The consequence was that Italy could only act against Turkish supply lines through pressure on neutral powers —England in Egypt and France in Tunisia—not to permit the passage of contraband to Libya. Already in November, shortly after the crisis of late October, the Italian government and public opinion had become very concerned about the passage of contraband. On November 20 a diplomat at Rome wrote that the Italian press was "beginning to occupy itself with this question with a bitterness that grows day by day."[97] After the neutral powers had vetoed the expansion of the war in the autumn, it must have seemed particularly intolerable that they also refused to take the measures that would discourage Turkish resistance in the one major theater where Italy was allowed to fight.

The failure to expand the war thus did not reconcile Italian public opinion to slow operations in Libya; rather it created pressure for a different kind of expansion of the conflict: the cutting off of neutral supply routes to the Turks. For this purpose an Italian warship stopped and conducted into an Italian port the French steamship *Carthage* in mid-January. The Italians claimed that this ship was carrying an airplane to Tunis for the Turks. But Poincaré, head of the new chauvinist French government, denied the Italian right to stop the ship and demanded the return of the airplane in strong terms. A grave international incident was thus created. When Italy attacked Libya, and when Italy wished to extend the war to the Adriatic and the Aegean, it was inevitable that at least a potential clash of interests with Austria-Hungary, Russia, and Britain would arise. But there had hitherto been no trouble with France, which had been generally sympathetic to Italy's designs on Libya. These good relations with France were important if Italy was to continue to poise herself between the Triple Alliance and the Entente. Realizing this, Giolitti yielded to the French demands almost immediately, though not before bad communications had resulted in the seizure of two other French ships, the *Manouba* and the *Tavignano*.[98] The incidents were settled when Italy yielded, but the bad blood between Italian and French public opinion remained. We will soon see the far-reaching consequences of this diplomatic transformation.

The mistaken seizure of two additional ships is another of numerous incidents that show how technical difficulties interfere with the central civilian management that is desirable in modern limited wars. In premodern limited wars, bad communications helped to keep wars limited, because news of an expansion would often not arrive in the capital for months. But, in general, the existence of rapid modern communications, combined with their occasional failure, creates serious difficulties.

Public Opinion and Limited War

In the preceding narrative the reader will have noticed the impatience of Italian public opinion with the continued limitation of the war. At this point it is useful to discuss the issue thematically. Italian public opinion in the Libyan war seems to have seen the war as a matter of victory or defeat, rather than of pursuing certain political goals without harming other goals. On the whole, Italian public opinion seems to have wished to expand the limited means that were being used to obtain Libya; it also was happy with the expansion of the ends of the war beyond the mere control of Libya. The annexation decree, as we saw, was profoundly satisfying to Italian public opinion.

Why was Italian public opinion so hostile to war-limiting? Turkish public opinion was generally against peace on compromise terms and in favor of expanding the war where possible (e.g., by the expulsion of Italians). But the question was not really posed for Turks at this time, since Turkey was compelled to fight the war in a limited way if the war was to be fought at all. Turkish opinion tolerated the fighting of World War I—a war that was "total" for Italy—in a highly limited manner. For example, the Turks resisted German pressure to remove the director of the Banque Ottomane, a British national, even though he was controlling the currency supply in a manner that was injurious to Turkey's war effort.[99] The Turkish motive was fear that the bank could hurt them after the war. The Turks were able to keep their eye *both* on peacetime goals and on the goal of victory; they displayed more perfect means-ends rationality than the Western democracies.

This contrast tempts us to consider that the Italian public's hostility to war-limiting might be something characteristic of modern liberal (or capitalist) democracy, which existed in Italy at least formally.[100] This hypothesis is strengthened by reflecting on parallel cases of democratic impatience with war-limiting (e.g., World Wars I and II, Korea, Vietnam) and nondemocratic toleration for it (e.g., Russia and Japan on the Manchurian border, 1938–1939). Are there any reasons to expect that public opinion in modern liberal democracies will be peculiarly intolerant of war-limiting?

To begin with, in any *republican* regime, policy issues—such as how to fight a war—tend to become issues of partisan political debate. Given that the public has latent war aims, the opposition can play on these latent goals by attacking the limitation of the war. Ronald Cunsolo has argued that Giolitti's Nationalist opponents tried to use his strategy of limited war in Libya to weaken his domination of Italian politics; they succeeded to a considerable degree.[101] Republican regimes also press against limited war because they engage the citizens' sense of honor. In autocracies, as Tocqueville remarks, the citizens are likely to regard the government as an invading army camped in their midst, which they must somehow cope with. In a regime with citizen participation, on the other hand, the self-respect of the citizen is much more bound up in what the government does. If the citizens feel that their individual pride is at stake in a victory or defeat in war, they will become more reluctant to accept the kind of careful means-ends rationality that is necessary in order to fight limited war.

Another characteristic belonging specifically to *egalitarian democracies* is what Tocqueville called the "tyranny of the majority": the power of an excited majority to sweep aside the preference of a minority, which, within a different social structure, would be a politically significant pressure group. The majority within a democracy holds this unprecedented power because the majority controls both the government, in all its branches, and public opinion. It thus has both a "physical" and a "moral" power, and a minority has no body—such as the nobility, the clergy, or the commons—to which it can resort for protection against another such body. In a *liberal* (enlightened or nontraditional) democracy this effect will be compounded by the tendency of the atomized citizenry, distrusting traditional guidance, to turn to public opinion for their beliefs and standards.

Modern total wars probably provide the strongest examples of the tyranny of the majority in the *political* sphere (as opposed to the tyranny of the majority over the intellect, which is much more pervasive). In both the First and the Second World War an unquestioned orthodoxy formed against any limitation of the war. As we noted earlier, in the case of World War I there were many, particularly within the governments, who thought the war should be stopped or its aims restricted. They were *unable* to state their views publicly; Lord Lansdowne, who did state them, was instantly destroyed after forty-seven years at the summit of English politics. As a contemporary notable put it:

> [Lansdowne] got somewhat *out of touch with public opinion*, and published in the *Daily Telegraph*, in Nov. 1917, a letter in which, to the general surprise, he strongly advocated a negotiated peace instead of the policy of Thorough, on which the ministry and the Empire were set. His ideas received hardly any support save from the small pacifist section.

In subsequent years he took little or no active part in politics [italics mine].¹⁰²

This unanimity contrasts strikingly with the vigorous debate about war aims and a negotiated peace during the War of the Spanish Succession (1701–1714); unanimity on total-war aims in major wars seems to be a distinctively modern phenomenon.

The orthodoxy that crystallizes about war aims and that is defended with all the force of the tyranny of the majority is likely, for other reasons that we will discuss, to crystallize against a limited conception of the war. But in any case the tyranny of the majority tends to prevent interest groups from acting publicly in favor of a limited war. One would expect that demands to limit a war would be somewhat more likely to come from minorities (classes, ethnic groups, and, particularly, economic interests), while demands to expand a war would come somewhat more often from the public as a whole. There are many cases in history where special interests have kept a war limited in some respect. During the War of the Spanish Succession, for example, Dutch shipping interests contributed to the fact that Holland continued to trade with France and Spain, although it was at war with these countries.¹⁰³ The tyranny of the majority makes such interests go underground, where it is more difficult for them to act. It might seem that the influence of the tyranny of the majority would run counter to the political strife that republican politics exhibits. This is to some extent true, but the situation that tends to result is this: a general orthodoxy crystallizes about the ends of the war—most often, simple victory—while partisan controversy rages about whether the proper means are being used. In these circumstances the most frequent demands will be that these means be increased or that the war be abandoned because its ends are not total.

A further feature of specifically modern democracies is the combination of efficient, rapid communications with some freedom of the press to publish news. This has the consequence that the public knows the extent to which the war is limited, something that in earlier times was often known only by those at the scene of war and perhaps by the central government. At the same time, the public often does not know *why* the war is limited. Impatience with limited war is likely to result from this combination of circumstances. This occurred in the Italo-Turkish war. The Italian public knew that the war was being restricted to Libya; but Giolitti could not tell the public the foremost reason for this—the threats made by Austria. Had these threats been exposed, Italian public opinion would have shattered the Triple Alliance, an essential part of Italian foreign policy. In this respect, the existence of modern communications tends to press against the limitation of war.

Democracy, and especially modern liberal democracy, is also the rule of those who are relatively unfamiliar with the complexity of political interactions, particularly of international relations. The democratic citizen finds his country going to war with another country over some issue. Not realizing the character of international relations, where there is no common judge to restrict the scope of conflicts, he is likely to assume the relationship between these countries to be one of general "hostility," as opposed to "friendship." It will be difficult for him to feel that even in wartime the interests of nations are partly opposed and partly compatible. Thus the democratic man will lack the intellectual basis for acceptance of war-limiting. Perhaps a more important outcome of the democratic man's tendency to see international relations in domestic terms will be the tendency to see one's international adversaries as violators of obligations, in a quasi-legal sense. Therefore the war against the adversary will be seen as a kind of punishment, and punishment is in ordinary usage an act largely divorced from means-ends rationality. Even the war for Libya, one of the simplest cases of an acquisitive war in history, was regarded by a large segment of Italian public opinion as a punishment for Turkish tyranny and misrule in Libya. This creates profound difficulties for war-limiting.

To this must be added a characteristic of modern liberal democracies that is not shared by ancient or medieval democracies: the citizens of modern liberal democracies do not have a personal taste for war. Their ordinary lives are lived in the pursuit of comfort, entirely apart from fighting and the risk of death; they are not accustomed to violence as a means. The other aspect of this is the gentler character of the democratic man, until he becomes a soldier. Tocqueville ascribes this to equality of condition: the democratic man is more compassionate than members of other societies because he can see himself in the place of other men more easily. When a war is fought with citizen armies, as the Tripoli war was, the unwarlike soldiers need a strong reason both to overcome their gentleness and—more vitally—to commit themselves to danger. In limited war, the true goal is often secret or incomprehensibly complicated. Where the main goal is clear and open, as in Libya, it is still unpleasant for the newly made soldier to believe that he is risking his life in a limited endeavor, that he must expend all his energies and stake all when the government itself is not using every means toward the winning of the war. There were, in fact, very serious problems of morale among the Italian troops in Tripoli.[104]

These two aspects of democratic character conduce to peacefulness or pacifism. The practical consequences extend in two directions: unwillingness to fight, or total war for unlimited goals in order to overcome this unwillingness. The latter outcome nullifies efforts to limit war; the former is ambiguous. It can, indirectly, help to limit war through the dislike of warlike measures; it can also make a war unacceptable or unsuccessful. In general, all the factors discussed above tend to make it psychologically uncomfortable for democratic men to fight limited wars; this discomfort can result either in expansion of the war or in not fighting it. In our own time, when militarism has become less popular, the second outcome has become more frequent; in 1911-1912 the balance turned toward expanding the war.

Responses to the Problem of Public Opinion

How can a government that desires to fight a limited war deal with the reluctance of democratic public opinion to fight such a war? The pressure exerted against war-limiting can be satisfied most easily in one of two ways: by actually expanding the war, or by rhetoric. An expansion of the war can be either real or illusory; in the latter category belong actions that merely *seem* to hurt the enemy, such as the Red Sea bombardments or the naval attack on Beirut (to be described shortly).

The rhetorical response to dissatisfied public opinion is particularly important, because it seems to offer a way of dealing with the public while the government continues to fight the limited war that it wishes. The object of the rhetoric in this case is to convince the public that the government is not pursuing the war half-heartedly. This can be done by a public statement of expanded war aims. We have seen that rhetorical assuagement of the public discontent with limited war gave Giolitti one of his principal motives for the annexation decree. Proclaiming major goals, however, does not need to be done in such a definite way; one can say, as semiofficial Italian sources did during the war, that by means of the war Italy intended to extend the civilizing mission of Italian culture. To present a war as a kind of crusade is a very easy way of meeting the need for public commitment to the war.

A second type of rhetorical response to popular discontent with limited war was that taken by the Italian government when international difficulties prevented it from extending the war in the fall of 1911:

> Italian opinion, which had followed with enthusiasm the happy beginning of the Tripoli war, begins to be marked by a certain impatience at the almost complete halt to military operations and the postponement of the naval action very often announced but which has never come true. The government, in order to stop the criticism of opposition papers, had to claim energetically the right to direct as it wishes the course of operations and to choose the hour and the place where it is convenient to it [the government] to carry its effort against the enemy.[105]

Here the Italian government made up for not expanding the war by declaring that it maintained the Italian *right* to expand the war, that limited war was not forced on it externally. The implication was perhaps that the government did not extend the war for military reasons or for other reasons that had to be kept secret—but not because it was not free to extend the war.

These two rhetorical strategies for combating popular resistance to limited war create, in turn, new problems. If a government asserts its willingness and its right to expand the war, it creates the expectation that this right will be used in the future. After the Italian government asserted its right to expand the war, criticism of the limited war was diminished only momentarily. By the spring of 1912 criticism was growing stronger and stronger, and the government could not at this point explain all the reasons in favor of keeping the war limited; this would have been a retraction of its earlier claim of freedom to extend the war.

If criticism is halted rhetorically by expanding the war aims, this tends to create the expectation that the means will also be expanded to secure the larger ends. This is equally true if the aims of the war, as expressed, are vague rather than specific. One should not fight a crusade with limited means. Moreover, the expansion of the vague aim of the war is likely to be reflected eventually in expansion of the specific war aims. Thus, the disinclination of the public in modern liberal democracies toward limited war tends to invite a rhetorical response, which itself leads to further pressure on the limits of the war. Stated most generally, in wartime statesmen often become prisoners of their own rhetoric.

The First World War is perhaps the most classic case in which statesmen, in attempting to maintain somewhat limited war aims, were unable to escape from their rhetoric about the transcendent importance of the war. This was, perhaps, the most important factor in the process by which Allied war aims became more sweeping as the war went on. By the end of the war, actual policy decisions demanded a sweeping reconstruction of Europe and of international politics—as seen in the decisions at the peace conference—which corresponded to the sweeping character of Allied propaganda. At the beginning of the war the specific changes advocated in private governmental memoranda were much more restrained. In explaining how the real (private) war aims changed, a massive role would have to be given to the public Allied statements of why the war was being waged, which were extremely far-reaching from the very beginning. For instance, Sir Edward Grey, the British foreign secretary, said in November 1914 that the peace treaty must secure "an end of militarism for ever and for reparation to ruined Belgium" while not permitting "continuance or recurrence of an armed brute power in central Europe."[106] Such rhetoric, provoked by the (perhaps subconscious) need to provoke full commitment to the war and by the desire to attract neutral support, obviously made it much more difficult for British leaders to turn toward a negotiated compromise peace.

Expanding the War in 1912

In February 1912 rumors that Italy would extend the war to a new theater once more began to spread. These rumors were the signs of serious concern within the Italian leadership about the course of the war. From February 7 to February 18, General Caneva, the commander of the Italian troops in Tripoli, was recalled to Rome for conversations with the government. Giolitti's account of this meeting is revealing as regards the role of civil-military conflicts in limited war:

> In my communications with General Caneva, I made it very clear that I had no intention of giving him orders or directing military operations from my study, leaving him full responsibility and liberty of action in that respect, and assuring him that I would confine myself to drawing his attention to the general aspect of the war. Caneva, after having sent Lieutenant-Colonel Giardino to Rome to explain the reasons for the slow progress of military operations, arrived himeself early in February.... He appeared to lack initiative and not to realise sufficiently the reasons of foreign policy which demanded more rapid action, so as to avoid complications which might arise at any moment in a war which brought so many other interests into play. General Caneva, on the contrary, fixed his attention almost exclusively on the local military situation.
>
> In our conversations, he explained to me with great clearness the military situation and the difficulty of decisive action, convincing me that much of the criticism directed against his operations was unfounded, but I pointed out to him the urgency for political reasons of terminating the war as speedily as possible.... I had always in mind the possibility of the powers intervening to bring about peace, and realised that when such negotiations are entered upon it is inevitably on the basis of results obtained.[107]

What emerges most clearly from this account is how technical military problems in winning the war in Tripoli forced the extension of the war. Giolitti was not really able to argue when he was told that conditions rendered a speedy victory impossible. This inability of the civilian leadership to control the military operations with a view to its limited war strategy arose in this case from the kind of operations that were being conducted. Here it was a question of land warfare, at a distance, with the armies in continuous contact, and with rather poor communications. Under these circumstances, the operations did require more immediate, on-the-spot exercise of the commander's discretion than were required by purely naval operations or the disjointed operations in the Red Sea—which, as we have seen, Giolitti controlled more tightly. The essential fact was that the best weapons and forces for limited war were not the weapons and forces that could be used in the theater to which it was hoped to keep the war limited.

Caneva seems to have "told the Cabinet his opinion, that months would be necessary in order to conquer Tripolitania and Cyrenaica, and years for the complete pacification of their populations."[108] Giolitti considered such a long war impossible both diplomatically and in terms of public support. The conference with Caneva thus made it an absolute necessity to abandon some limits and to expand hostilities in order to coerce a decision for peace.

What were the various possibilities for coercive attacks on Turkey? Direct attacks could take place in the Red Sea, Syria, Cilicia, or in the Aegean, where several targets were offered: the Dardanelles, Salonika, Smyrna, the Aegean islands. Some attacks could be carried out largely by naval forces, whereas others called for a substantial army. The latter approach was difficult for Italy, because about half the Italian army was now tied down in Libya; the very sparse forces remaining in Italy could scarcely be further weakened in view of the possibility of war with Austria or France. If major land operations were to be avoided and mere bombardments were judged insufficiently coercive, the two most attractive targets were the Dardanelles and the Aegean islands. At these two points, major loss could be caused to the Ottoman Empire through naval action.

One final possibility was to exercise indirect coercion on Turkey by stirring up, subsidizing, and supplying the Balkan states. The opportunity is indicated in a dispatch (March 28) of the British minister to Serbia: "It would seem that Servia and Bulgaria are longing for Italian action against Turkey in Europe and I was told and begged to keep the information secret, that the Italian Minister here has on more than one occasion been unofficially approached with offers of assistance in Macedonia in case Italy should desire combined action."[109] Serbia and Bulgaria, acting under the patronage of Russia, did in fact conclude, in March 1912, a treaty envisaging a joint attack on Turkey. Italy's ability to expand the war by using the forces of others was thus restrained only by neutral interests and by her own limited war aims with regard to the Balkans.

The Italian government, concluding from Caneva's testimony that the war could not be won in Libya, appears to have immediately chosen one of these opportunities to expand the war.[110] On February 20, two days after Caneva's departure from Rome, an Italian squadron left for Beirut. Having arrived there on the twenty-fourth, it demanded the surrender of the Turkish naval vessels in the harbor, the ancient ironclad corvette *Avni-Illah* ("Help from God") and the torpedo boat *Ankara*. When this was not immediately granted, the Italians sank the Turkish ships by gunfire and torpedo. The virtually defenseless Turkish warships tried to secure sanctuary for themselves by sheltering in the inner harbor, among neutral ships and in the heart of the Western quarter of the city.[111] Consequently, many Italian shells fell in the city, killing civilians. The sequel reveals the basis for neutral restraints on Italian attacks. "The engagement caused a panic in the town and an arms depot was plundered by the mob"; martial law had to be proclaimed.[112]

Because the warships at Beirut posed no danger to any Italian enterprise, the attack has to be understood as a sop to public opinion or as a threatening demonstration. It showed Turkey that Italy could act outside Tripoli. The Turkish government certainly seems to have regarded the Beirut attack as a trial run for the rumored Italian move in the Aegean. For several days prior to the Beirut attack, Turkey had been warning the neutral Powers that it would respond to an Italian extension of the war, or to the appearance of the Italian fleet before the Dardanelles, by closing the straits to neutral commerce or by expelling Italian residents. Turkey responded immediately to the naval attack on Beirut by ordering the expulsion of Italian nationals from Syria within fourteen days.[113] A general expulsion of Italians from the whole empire was probably the ultimate sanction that Turkey possessed against Italian expansion of the war. By using this sanction in a partial form to respond to the first Italian attack of the war outside Tripoli or the Red Sea, the Turkish government showed how seriously it took the attack. The partial expulsion communicated to Italy that any attack that was not a mere demonstration would be met by a general expulsion. Turkey thus declared where her threshold of response lay. Here was an attempt to nip the expansion of the war in the bud.

The cycle of threat and counterthreat was broken at this point; the Italians did not do anything to retaliate specifically against the Turkish expulsion order. Thus, nothing was done to discourage the Turks from meeting a further Italian expansion of the war with an expulsion. Perhaps the arsenal of Italian opportunities for expanding the war did not include anything suitable as a reply; there were available only minor actions that would not hurt—such as another Red Sea bombardment—or major attacks, with serious consequences for Italy, which would only be decided on as worthwhile in their own right and not as preventive retaliation. In this case also, flexibility was denied to the Italian pursuit of limited war. To wage effective coercive warfare, it would seem to be necessary to know from the beginning whether one has available a sufficient range of threats to "trump" the various enemy responses; very careful planning is required.

Thus the outcome of the entire Beirut incident—naval attack and expulsion —was somewhat negative. The expulsion hurt Italian interests more than the loss of the old warships hurt Turkish interests. Moreover, neutral Powers reacted badly to the Beirut attack. France, "painfully surprised," delivered an official protest and sent a cruiser to Beirut to watch over French interests. Austria also protested, while Britain feared violence against Christians in Syria.[114]

At this point, the diplomatic climate had become more favorable to Italian expansion of the war than it had been in 1911.[115] The real decision as to whether Italy could strike a serious blow at Turkey lay, as before, with Austria-Hungary. During February, negotiations seeking to obtain Austrian permission to expand the war were in progress. Italy again tried to persuade Austria by acting through Germany. Germany saw the difficulties between France and Italy over the seized ships as a chance to revitalize the Triple Alliance, if only Austria-Hungary would drop its opposition to Italian action in the Aegean. Finally the Germans persuaded Berchtold, the new Austro-Hungarian foreign minister. After having made it clear that he would not permit any attack on the Dardanelles or the Balkan coast of Turkey, he told the Italians on April 15 that they could seize the three Aegean islands of Stampalia (Astropalaia), Carpathos, and Rhodes.[116] This, then, was the coercive stroke chosen by the Italians—or rather by Austria for them—to speed the end of the war.

In the meantime the constant rumors of Italian action in the Aegean had produced their effect on Turkey. On March 5/6 the Turks had forbidden neutral shipping to pass through the Dardanelles at night. This normal defensive measure doubtless also served to underline the Turkish threat to close the straits entirely in the event of Italian activity nearby. On the tenth, the Turks actually began laying mines in the straits.[117]

When Berchtold finally gave his permission to seize three islands, the Italian fleet had already sailed for the Aegean. One squadron bombarded Turkish positions in the Aegean islands (Chios, Samos) and on the mainland (Tchesme), also cutting the cable between Rhodes and the mainland.[118] But another squadron, to Berchtold's astonishment, struck first, not in the southern Aegean, but at the Dardanelles. Italian warships bombarded the outer forts for two hours on April 18, the day of the opening of the newly elected Turkish Parliament. The Turks immediately closed the straits to all shipping.[119]

The reasons for this attack at the very center of neutral concern remain unclear. In reply to the swarm of protests from neutrals, embarrassed Italian diplomats gave conflicting explanations for the bombardment. At first it was presented as a demonstration of Italy's freedom of action to the new Turkish Parliament, a sop to public opinion, and an "attempt to bring Russia, directly menaced in its exports, to act actively."[120] The next day, Italian diplomats averred that the exchange of gunfire was not intended and that the commanding admiral had exceeded his instructions.[121] Albertini, a contemporary witness as well as an astute historian, concludes that the attack on the straits was undertaken on the initiative of the navy, without the knowledge of the Foreign Office.[122] It seems likely, on the basis of the evidence, that Giolitti accepted either a plan to simply sail near the straits or one proposed to him by an admiral to decoy Turkish warships out of the straits and then attack them. In any case, the plan was not to include any action against the Turkish forts.

The admiral in command, however, either decided to undertake the bombardment on his own or sailed so close to the forts that they opened fire on him. He was then "compelled" to return their fire in order to defend his ships.[123]

This incident, which nearly wrecked the government's plan for extending the war to the Aegean islands, is a good example of the difficulty that the inevitable autonomy of military forces in the face of the enemy creates for war-limiting. It was easy for the Italian commander to place his fleet where it would be fired upon by the Turks. At that point the admitted justification of self-defense permitted him to fire back. A commander who is dissatisfied, for whatever reasons, with the limited character of the war can dissolve, by a kind of "salami tactics," the restraints that his government has imposed on the war. This again points out how contingent was the limited character of the war. If Italian forces everywhere had been as exposed to the Turkish forces as they were at the straits and in Libya itself, the defensive rationale for expanding the war would have been powerfully strengthened, and the balance between military and civilian control of operations would have inclined much more towards the military.

It remains to discuss the Turkish response to the bombardment of the Dardanelles. When the Italian foreign minister had confessed the accidental character of the attack, he insisted that this not be told to Turkey:

> Position of Italy is as follows: She had not intended any attack on Dardanelles at present time; she must reserve to herself liberty to attack Turkey in any way to her advantage, and Turkish apprehensions on account of Dardanelles are an asset to her; but in practice such an attack is not likely to be realised either soon or at any time.[124]

It was probable, therefore, that the attack on the straits appeared to Turkey, not as an isolated act, but as a planned step of "coercive diplomacy." In a limited war, unintentional or unauthorized acts are apt to be regarded as part of a plan. Thus, communications between belligerents on the limits of the war can easily become confused. Italy, in this case, wished to deceive the Turks, to make a bluff. Italy did not consider taking the course of communicating to the Turks that the attack had been inadvertent. This has sometimes been suggested as a means of communicating that the military is not under control, that there is an element of incalculable risk in continuing a war. The Turks thus remained with the impression that the Italian bombardment was a planned act of coercion. Yet it was followed by no further attacks on the Dardanelles. The combination of implicit communication and failure to act further seemed to imply that this was the maximum act of coercion against the Dardanelles that the neutral powers would allow. The attack may eventually have caused the Turks, not "apprehension," but reassurance.[125]

If the attack was intended to threaten Turkey into making peace on

Italian terms, it was evidently a failure. The immediate Turkish response, besides closing the straits, appeared in the reply to an even-handed mediation effort by Russia which had been in progress since January. The reply, dated April 23, expressed the most unyielding position ever taken by Turkey. Turkey insisted on a formal Italian renunciation of sovereignty over Libya, together with "integral and effective" maintenance of the Sultan's sovereign rights.[126] This statement of peace terms contrasts vividly with the effective control over Libya that many Turkish statesmen were willing to concede to Italy in the autumn. It was partly the consequence of a temporary resolution of internal conflicts; the chauvinist Committee of Union and Progress had vanquished its foes by securing the dissolution of the old Parliament and by packing the newly elected one in the "big-stick election" of 1912.[127] In any case the Italian attack, which was "coercive" in form, produced not accommodation but (if anything) greater resistance.

The bombardment of the Dardanelles was a mistake in a second sense. It enabled Turkey to return to the tactic used in the autumn: interrupting or threatening to interrupt neutral commerce in order to induce the neutral powers to act against any Italian expansion of the war. Turkey took the position that the straits ought to remain closed as long as there was Italian action, or the danger of it, anywhere in the Aegean. Ultimately this tactic did not succeed, because strong Russian protests forced the Turks to promise, on May 1, to reopen the straits. But Turkey had kept the straits closed long enough to legitimize such action in the event of a real Italian attack there and to strengthen the impression that Great Britain and Russia would not, therefore, stand for such an attack.

We turn now to the serious extension of the war that had been actually planned by the Italian government. On April 23 the Italians occupied the island of Stampalia for use as a naval base in the Aegean. On May 4 Italian troops landed on Rhodes; by the twentieth the other islands of the Dodecanese had been taken. The Italians had thus taken twelve islands, instead of the three to which they had promised Austria they would restrict themselves; Austria was quick to protest.[128] Italian seizure of the Dodecanese served the following purposes. First, it threatened a further extension of the war to more vital areas of the empire. Second, it hurt Turkey in the present through loss of prestige and by giving secessionist hopes to the Greek population of the Aegean islands. Third, it encouraged Turkey to make a quick peace by threatening the loss of the islands if the war were prolonged. The French ambassador to Rome reported a fourth reason: "Above all," by seizing the islands, Italy would "acquire gages for future exchange, which would permit the Turks to find an honorable pretext to evacuate Tripolitania."[129] Here, then, was at last a way of dealing with the underlying problem of the Italian limited war: that the Turks had no reason to incur the tremendous loss of prestige through ending the war without getting something (either a positive benefit or the removal of some harm) in return.

Were these purposes achieved through the Italian extension of the war? It may be, as we shall see later, that the attack did have some effect on Turkey's eventual willingness to negotiate. But Turkey certainly did not make peace after the attack. Albertini judges the effect on Turkey to have been "very modest." The French ambassador predicted at the time that the new attack would not move the Turks to make peace.[130] Why did the Italian act of coercion not work as it was intended to?

To begin with, the occupation of the Aegean islands was only a very small application of the power to hurt, since the temporary loss of these islands was no more than an annoyance to Turkey. The threat of permanent loss was much more serious; but still, the loss of these Christian islands was less undermining than the surrender by the Caliph of Muslim Libya. Most effective, perhaps, was the demonstration of Italian will to attack more vital parts of the empire if peace were not concluded. In conjunction with later threats and rumors, the actual attack in the Aegean frightened the Turks enough to make, during the summer, the largest effort yet to defend against attacks in the Aegean. In mid-June, for example, "in expectation of an Italian attack, the Turkish infantry division in Smyrna was reinforced by another division from Constantinople and by the *Redifs* [reserves] of the '84 and '89 year classes from the Konia, Ushak, Aidin, Smyrna, and Denizli Divisions . . . this force amounted to 80,000 men, under Mahmud Muktar Pacha."[131] Thirty thousand men were gathered at the Dardanelles. But the threat of further Italian attack was not enough to make Turkey decide for peace. This may have been due to an apparent Italian mistake: the attack in the Aegean was made all at once, not gradually. After May 20, no further military actions in the Aegean were undertaken, except for a raid on the Dardanelles in July. The Turks thus may have received the impression that Italy had extended the war to the utmost limits imposed on Italy by neutral powers. This impression was largely correct. At the end of May, Giolitti wished to take Samos and Chios (at the mouth of the Gulf of Smyrna). These moves were stopped by Austria-Hungary, France, and Russia.[132] It might have been wiser for Italy to begin with one or a few islands and then proceed gradually up to the foreseeable maximum. This was the method pursued, in a nonwar context, when the European Powers undertook in 1905 a naval demonstration to force Turkey to make reforms in Macedonia. The composite fleet was ordered to seize islands even closer to the Dardanelles, according to a preestablished schedule, until Turkey yielded.[133]

Of course, there was a strong reason why Italy did not take this course of graduated violence. As at the beginning of the war, Italy wished to isolate her military action from diplomatic intervention by limiting the time in which it took place. Otherwise Austria would have put a stop to the extension of the war beyond the three islands originally permitted. This demonstrates how it is not only the demands of the military sphere that interfere with the proper management of limited war but also the demands of the diplomatic sphere.

An important part of the coercive purpose of the seizure of the Aegean islands apparently was to threaten the Turks that these islands would not be returned unless Turkey made peace quickly. But as Schelling has pointed out, such a tactic requires both a threat (that the islands might not be returned) and an *assurance* (that they would be returned if Turkey cooperated).[134] It is a very delicate matter to make the threat without destroying the assurance. The Italians took steps to assure the credibility of the threat. In late June, for example, the Italian ambassador in London asked Great Britain to contradict a rumor "that we [the British] had assured the Turks that they need not be anxious about the Aegean islands, as these would revert to Turkey unchanged after the war."[135] But Italy did not provide the assurances that should have gone with their threat. In the Italian press there were insistent demands, particularly from the Nationalists, for the annexation of the Dodecanese. Neutral powers feared that Italy would retain the islands, and some Italian diplomats encouraged these fears.[136] The king of Italy himself, in conversation with the French ambassador at the time of the attack, hinted in this direction:

> Victor Emmanuel III spoke to me of the island of Rhodes, which he knows very well. He insisted on the richness of this region. He considers that its economic value is not less than its geographic importance, and that "it could be a good thing for exchange [*base d' echange*] when the moment comes." The King added that the occupation of Stampalia itself is not without advantage, because "it possesses one of the best anchorages in the Archipelago."[137]

Here, notions of coercive diplomacy are mixed up with a desire to keep the islands.

The failure of Italian diplomacy to conform to Schelling's prescription points to underlying difficulties in carrying out limited war. The very fact that an extension of the war has been carried out makes assurances difficult. The demonstration of increased military means in extending war encourages latent ends, such as annexation of the islands, to become actual. Even if the government is not affected by these new hopes—and Giolitti does not seem to have shown any interest in retaining the islands—their sprouting will confuse communication with the enemy. Giolitti could not control either public opinion, particularly when it was the opinion of his political opponents, or the king, his nominal superior. The emergence of latent ends had, of course, the additional effect of increasing public pressure for harsher peace terms; in this sense the coercion that was intended to end the war also prolonged it. Moreover, the impressive and rapid success in the Aegean increased the irritation with the slow methods that were being pursued in Libya, and thus the success generated some new pressures to expand the war.[138]

Efforts to Expand the War on Turkey

The outcome of the Turkish reaction to the seizure of the Dodecanese is well known. On May 20 Turkey decreed that all Italian nationals (with minor exemptions) be expelled by June 3 (later extended to June 18). As Giolitti remarks, "This was a very serious reprisal on her part, as there were at least twenty thousand Italian subjects at Constantinople and fifty thousand in other parts of the Turkish Empire."[139] While the net balance of action and reaction was probably more injurious to Italy than to Turkey, the nearly total expulsion of Italians was the ultimate expansion of the war that was available to Turkey for deterring future Italian coercive attacks. In this case, Turkey seems to have judged correctly, for the Italians carried out no more major expansions of the war.

The other dimensions of the Turkish response are obscured by insufficient evidence. The occupation of the Aegean islands clearly had a great impact on Turkish opinion, which seems to have embodied two contradictory impulses —to compromise and to pursue the war more fiercely. On June 1 the personnel of the Turkish fleet, which was anchored in the Dardanelles, demanded to be led against the enemy.[140] This would have utterly contradicted Turkey's own limited-war policy: the fleet, which was useless against Italy, needed to be saved for the ever-present possibility of a war with the Greeks, against whom it might achieve something. In this instance the Turkish military showed the same kind of attitude toward limited war as the Italian military did, in spite of great cultural differences.

The occupation of the islands may, on the other hand, have made the Turkish government somewhat more willing to negotiate.[141] Italy at this point was also more anxious to negotiate. Giolitti followed the coercive occupation with peace feelers; in early June he sent emissaries to talk with the Turkish government. Most of the important members of the Turkish cabinet indicated great interest in an "honorable" peace. A Turkish peace proposal—not accepting the annexation decree—was worked out, and negotiators were appointed. On July 12, negotiations actually began at Lausanne. But it immediately appeared that the discussions were hopelessly deadlocked. According to the chief Italian delegate, Fusinato, it became clear that the Turkish delegation had no definite instructions.[142] In any case, the terms of the two sides appeared to be far apart. On July 28, the Lausanne negotiations were suspended. It is thus quite doubtful that the coercive occupation of the Dodecanese moved the Turks toward peace. Negotiations did begin after the occupation, but at most times during the war, Turkey would probably have been willing to negotiate on the basis of the abandoning of the annexation decree. Given Italian unwillingness to compromise on this issue, it is not clear how serious the negotiations were. For the Turks they served the useful function of diverting neutral pressure for peace and of making additional Italian attacks less likely. The fact that the Italian government planned no more coercive attacks for four and one-half months lends some support to the view that the attack on the Dodecanese did not achieve its purpose. Giolitti himself seems to have felt at this point that such attacks were counterproductive; he says that "wishing as far as possible to aid the work of the Turkish government, I gave orders to suspend operations of a warlike nature in the Aegean."[143]

Why was a coercive attack so ineffective in achieving a negotiated settlement of the limited war? First, as we have observed, the occupation of the islands could affect Turkey mainly as a threat. But further action of the same kind was strongly discouraged by neutrals; this the Turks knew. This impasse was not entirely accidental. There is a tendency for limited war to impede its own operation, since it gives an opening to neutral powers to limit the war. If Turkey and Italy had been comparable powers engaged in a "total" war, no one would have questioned Italy's right to attack the straits; the logic of self-defense would have been acknowledged.

The state of Turkish internal politics was another reason that negotiations did not progress as a result of the occupation. Coercion in limited war tends to rely on the enemy being one actor who can come to a rational decision, trading peace (in this case) for an end to pressure. This is never entirely true in any state where faction plays an important role; it is least of all true for states like Turkey at that time, in which there is no fixed mechanism for making political decisions. In April, Turkish policy had temporarily come under unified control as a result of the triumph of the Committee of Union and Progress in the "big-stick election." But explosive discontent developed, particularly within the army, in reaction to the domination of the committee. In May a military conspiracy—the "Savior Officers," which aimed at the overthrow of the committee—began to form. This threat brought about the resignation of the cabinet on July 17 and the formation of a new cabinet, which was largely made up of opponents of the committee. This, however, did not end the political strife, which culminated in the coup d'état of the Committee of Union and Progress on January 23, 1913. This political instability made it very difficult for Italian coercion to be effective or for Turkey to make peace at all. Although the competing factions all privately expressed some interest in ending the war, any group that actually carried out such a decision would have been open to a devastating attack.[144] The ordinary tendency to let things drift rather than make a decision is immensely exacerbated by this kind of domestic conflict.

For these reasons, negotiations did not resume until August 13, even though the new government, in the words of one of its members, saw that its chief tasks were "to liquidate the Tripoli venture" and "to provide for the needs of the treasury, whose distress was perhaps without precedent."[145] The latter task reinforced the former, since the financial crisis was due in large measure to the war. In the middle of June, war expenses required a 25 percent increase in taxes and a 3 percent levy on the salaries of all officials. General mobilization would have bankrupted the Ottoman Empire.[146] This situation was the more dangerous because of the storm clouds that were gathering in the Balkans. By the beginning of August it was becoming clear, even from the European press, that Serbia and Bulgaria had come to some kind of agreement against Turkey, while Albania had been in revolt for some time. To deal with the threatening situation in the Balkans, it was essential for Turkey to make peace with Italy.

The general situation was thus moving in a direction that would have assisted Italy in forcing peace on Turkey if there had not been such domestic difficulties. The situation was complicated, however, by the fact that the impending upheaval in the Balkans also made peace more necessary for Italy. Serious consequences would have ensued if Italy had found itself fighting alongside the Balkan states against Turkey. When a conference of the Powers was called to settle the war, Italy was likely to find itself the object of the conference's work rather than a participant.[147]

During the long summer and fall period of intermittent negotiations there were no further expansions of the war. The only apparent exception was a night raid on the Dardanelles by Italian torpedo boats under Captain Millo on July 19. The torpedo boats passed up the Dardanelles in an attempt to torpedo the Turkish fleet, but they were stopped by cables at the narrows. This attack was, like the bombardment in April, unauthorized by the civilian government, and the attack involved the government in diplomatic difficulties. As the French ambassador remarked, "the initiatives of local authorities put in question the policy of the government."[148] The consequences of this adventure for the participants shed light on the Italian government's difficulties in maintaining centralized control of policy at this time and on military motives for going beyond limited war:

> Every man in the Italian flotilla was highly rewarded for this gallant expedition. Captain Millo was promoted to the rank of Rear-Admiral, passing over 25 officers who were senior to him, and he was appointed Chief Inspector of Torpedoes. All the lieutenants in the flotilla were promoted

to the rank of Capitaine de Corvette (Lieutenant Commander). Distinguished-service medals were presented in person by the King.[149]

Final Negotiations

On August 13 new peace negotiations were begun at Caux (later they were held at Ouchy).[150] The Turks continued to be unwilling to make peace on the basis of Italian annexation, but Giolitti would not sacrifice his decree, as other Italian officials wished him to do. As for a long time previously, this was the greatest obstacle to peace. Finally the Italian and Turkish negotiators arrived at a compromise, through which Turkey would give up sovereignty over Libya by granting the Arabs there "independence," without formally admitting Italian sovereignty in the province.

The government in Constantinople, however, did not approve these terms for three weeks, and then only with significant changes. Giolitti's response (October 2) was to give the Turks an ultimatum to sign before October 10; he threatened to take naval action in the Aegean and to interrupt the passage of Turkish troop transports reinforcing the Balkans. These were serious threats, for the only rail line to Macedonia was inadequate and could be shelled from the sea. Giolitti thus returned to threats to expand the war for the first time since the occupation of the Dodecanese in May. These threats were effective; on October 4 the Turkish cabinet approved the agreement that had been worked out by their negotiators. What accounted for the higher effectiveness of threats to expand the war at this point?

First, these threats were called upon to achieve less: only to overcome the resistance to specific terms that had already been approved by the Turkish negotiators. Italian threats were more credible, because the imminence of peace had decreased the legitimacy of neutral restrictions on expanding the war. The neutrals wanted to get the Libyan war out of the way before the Balkan states declared war (they had mobilized on September 30). The neutrals finally began to put pressure on Turkey. Above all, the nearness of war in the Balkans gave Italy, for the first time, a threat that was, on the one hand, truly dangerous and, on the other hand, practicable with small forces: namely, naval attacks on the Turkish supply line to Macedonia. All in all, it is fairly likely that the Italo-Turkish war would have continued indefinitely had it not been for the war in the Balkans. The British ambassador to Turkey remarked after the peace: "Italy would certainly not have obtained peace on the same terms were it not for the action and sacrifices of the Balkan States and some of their representatives here have the feeling that Italy has left them in the lurch."[151] This again indicates some of the difficulties of limiting war. Because the war was limited otherwise, it tended to be unlimited temporally. Under ordinary circumstances, no coercive means were available to the Italians to overcome this tendency.

At this point, domestic divisions within Turkey again wrecked the peace negotiations. Giolitti writes:

> On the 8th, we were informed from Constantinople that when the Council of Ministers assembled to discuss the peace with Italy, a great demonstration had taken place around the Sublime Porte, and the people had demanded the continuation of the war and the resignation of the cabinet which had made peace. Military action was feared, and martial law had been proclaimed. The minister for Foreign Affairs had been threatened with death, and was very frightened and depressed.[152]

The cabinet at Constantinople now decided to change the terms that it had approved (October 11). Italy gave another ultimatum, which was to expire October 15, and ordered the fleet to prepare a strike against Smyrna or against the railroad to Macedonia. The Turkish cabinet, which met on the fourteenth, agreed once more to sign if certain additional changes were made, most of which were agreed to by Giolitti. The internal difficulties seem to have had the effect of giving Turkey a slight advantage in the arguments over the precise terms of peace. At last, on October 15, a few hours before the Italian deadline, the Turkish delegates signed the preliminary articles of peace. After twelve and one-half months the Italo-Turkish war was over. The terms of peace included a complicated charade by which the Sultan proclaimed the "autonomy" of Libya without admitting Italian sovereignty. Turkey was to remove her troops from Libya, and Italy was to restore the Dodecanese to Turkey. Neither of these provisions was fully carried out. Some Turkish officers remained behind, to lead the Arabs against Italy in World War I. Thus, Turkey continued the war in a still more limited fashion. Italy, in turn, used both this nonfulfillment of the treaty and the Balkan Wars to prolong her occupation of the Dodecanese. Eventually, the islands were annexed, just as Victor Emmanuel had hinted that they would be. The complex and awkward treaty, and its violation by both sides, testify to the difficulties of controlling war once it has broken out.

Conclusion

In the course of this study, some tentative hypotheses have been advanced about war-limiting; but it is not possible to repeat all of these here. It will be enough to conclude with a look at the costs and benefits of the Italo-Turkish war, which was fought as a limited war, to each of the participants, and then with a brief summary of the reasons for this outcome. The aims of Turkey in the war were entirely negative: Turkey sought to avoid the loss of Libya with its accompanying decline in prestige, to avoid the expenditure of resources, and above all to avoid the further dismemberment of the Ottoman Empire in the Balkans. None of these aims was really achieved. In considerable measure this was due to the huge Italian superiority in strength. It was also due to the inability of Turkish statesmen to make the decision to trade the loss of Libya for a reduced chance of losing the European part of the empire. The loss of the European areas in the Balkan War of 1912 might not have occurred if Turkey had not been at war with a European power for such a long time. It was only after Libya had been invaded that negotiations among the Balkan states began, and the war with Italy sapped Turkey's financial strength. The Balkan War was a crowning disaster for Turkey: it removed the most prosperous part of the national territory, it shattered irrevocably the integrating ideology of "Ottomanism," and it humiliated the country in the eyes of Muslims everywhere far more than any defeat by a great power would have. To the extent that Turkish management of the war with Italy produced the Balkan collapse, it has to be considered very unsuccessful.

The positive end sought by Italy in the war was the acquisition of Libya. This was achieved at least formally, although peace with Turkey did not mean actual control of the country. The negative ends that Italy sought to avoid by waging a limited war were these: casualities, expenditure of resources, a long war, expulsion of Italians from Turkey, interruption of trade with and through Turkey, complications in general Italian foreign policy, neutral interference in the war, and war in the Balkans. Italian expenditures of resources and casualities were moderate, although they were much greater than expected. The war cost half a billion to a billion lire, and the expenditure of military supplies caused the Italian army to be caught short in 1914. Casualties were only 1,432 killed and 4,250 wounded; Turkish casualties were not vastly more than this.[153]

War-limiting thus achieved, for Italy, the aim of minimizing financial and human costs. But this very success contributed, as has been the case in other limited wars, to lengthening the war: losses were not great enough to motivate either side to peace. None of the other negative aims that are sought in fighting limited wars were achieved. The Italian economy was affected adversely.[154] The war invited trouble with France and Austria-Hungary, and it caused the expulsion of Italians from Turkey. Finally, it probably produced the defeat of Turkey in the Balkan War. While it was a disaster for Turkey, this was also a misfortune for Italy. It has been argued that the Balkan War led to the First World War. More immediately, its result was to strengthen Russian influence in Serbia, Austrian influence in Bulgaria, and German influence in Turkey; and an Austrian client state was set up in Albania, which had been the object of Italian ambitions. None of this was compensated for by results that were advantageous to Italy. Thus in the Italo-Turkish war the means remained substantially limited, even though they were expanded several times in the effort to end the war. But the negative *results* of the war, to avoid which the means were limited, did not remain limited as planned.

Why did the limited war planned by Giolitti and his colleagues not work out as intended? The following major problems of war-limiting seem uppermost. In the first place, Giolitti did not realize the impatience with war-limiting that the military and the public would show in a country such as his. Nor had he reflected sufficiently on the kind of concessions that Turkey could make to end the war. Perhaps Giolitti mistakenly thought that a country that is better able to win a war with its opponent is also better able to endure that war. Throughout the war, Giolitti faced the difficulty of forcing a formal decision for peace on Turkey in spite of domestic divisions in Turkey. War-limiting relies heavily on a rational weighing of costs and benefits by the adversary. But in a factional fight, a policy can be retained that no leader or group actually favors, because no one can take the initiative in abandoning it.

Giolitti also ran into a related problem: the lack of flexibility of coercive limited war, and perhaps of limited war in general. Versatility is a virtue often claimed for "latent violence" as opposed to pure force. It is true that limited war can potentially be a means to many ends for which "total" war would not serve. But versatility is not the same as flexibility. We saw how flexibility and ad hoc planning had unfortunate effects for the Italians during the threatened expansion of the war in 1911 and in the expansion that was actually carried out in the spring. One tentative hypothesis that has emerged from this study is that coercive limited war, if it is to work well, requires more careful prior planning than more "total" forms of war.

In Giolitti's original approach to the war, limitation of means went along with limitation of the ends: the *only* end sought was the acquisition of Libya. It soon appeared, however, that this limitation of means interfered with the very means intended to achieve the limited end. The restraints on military action produced setbacks in military operations. These setbacks produced in turn a further chain of consequences. With the partial failure of the means, what we have called latent war aims came to the surface. New issues, beyond Libya, threatened to be affected by the war. Latent war aims were a problem in war-limiting throughout the war, both after defeats in the early fall of 1911 and after the Dodecanese success in 1912. In response to the emergence of latent ends, Giolitti tried to expand the war, in order to coerce Turkey, and he expanded the formal war aims, using means as ends.

These latter problems could be called problems of "feedback," a central difficulty in war-limiting. Again and again Giolitti and his associates found that an action that was taken in order to limit the war had unintended effects that made it more difficult to limit the war. Or a decision to expand the war in a limited fashion would in turn lead, as a side effect, to its expansion in still different ways. For example, the original decision to limit the war geographically probably made it less limited temporally. The limited expansions of the war that were planned as "coercive diplomacy" awakened latent war aims in the Italian public and thus made war-limiting harder. The elements of the environment in war are often interconnected in such a way that when the war is pressed down in one place, it billows out somewhere else. For all these reasons, means and ends rarely remain in the perfect balance that war-limiting seeks.[155]

Notes

1. Cf. A. J. P. Taylor, *The Origins of the Second World War* (2d ed.; Greenwich, Conn.: Fawcett, 1966), pp. 13–14.
2. The relations between ends and means in human affairs is perhaps the foremost subject of Plato's political philosophy, where it appears in the discussion of the arts (*technai*) and their use as a standard for the whole of human life; see especially the *Republic, Gorgias,* and *Hipparchus.*
3. This definition will be recognized as a variant of Jacques Ellul's *The Technological Society,* trans. John Wilkinson (New York: Knopf, 1964), p. xv.
4. Alfred T. Mahan, *The Influence of Seapower upon History, 1660–1783* (New York: Sagamore, 1957), p. 139.
5. See the figures in the *Almanach de Gotha* for 1813.
6. See the dispatches of Castlereagh to Liverpool, January 22, January 30, February 16, and April 4, 1814, in Sir Charles K. Webster, ed., *British Diplomacy, 1813–1815* (London: Bell, 1921), pp. 133, 137, 138, 148, 174; also Clemens von Metternich, *Memoirs of Prince Metternich, 1773–1815,* trans. Mrs. Alexander Napier (5 vols.; London: Bentley, 1880–1882), 1:225–30.
7. Quoted in Henry Kissinger, *A World Restored,* Universal Library edition (New York: Grosset & Dunlap, 1964), p. 111.
8. Ibid., p. 112, quoting August Fournier, *Der Congress von Chatillon* (Vienna, 1900), p. 51.
9. Giovanni Giolitti, *Memoirs of My Life,* trans. Edward Storer (London: Chapman & Dodd, 1923), pp. 234, 244.
10. Telegram, Defrance (Cairo) to de Selves, November 12, 1911, in Commission de Publication de Documents Relatifs aux Origins de la Guerre de 1914, *Documents Diplomatiques Françaises* (Paris: Imprimerie Nationale, 1929), 3d ser., vol. 1, no. 97; hereafter cited as *Documents Diplomatiques.*
11. Rodd (Rome) to Grey, December 1, 1911, in George P. Gooch and Harold Temperley, eds., *British Documents on the Origins of the War, 1898–1914* (London: His Majesty's Stationery Office, 1933), vol. 9, pt. 1, p. 339; cited hereafter as *British Documents.*
12. Agostino Gaibi, *Manuale di storia politico-militare delle colonie Italiane* (Rome: Provveditorato Generale dello Stato, 1928), p. 297.
13. Luigi Albertini, *The Origins of the War of 1914,* trans. and ed. Isabella M. Massey (3 vols.; London: Oxford University Press, 1952–1957), 1:52.
14. M[ahmud] Muhtar Pasha, *La Turquie, l'Allemagne et l'Europe depuis le Traité de*

Berlin jusqu'à la guerre mondiale (Paris: Berger-Levrault, 1924), pp. 138–39. Muhtar Pasha was a member of this cabinet and favored yielding to the ultimatum.
15. William C. Askew, *Europe and Italy's Acquisition of Libya, 1911–1912* (Durham, N.C.: Duke University Press, 1942), p. 89 n28.
16. William H. Beehler, *The History of the Italian-Turkish War* (Annapolis, Md.: By the Author, 1913), pp. 26–27.
17. See Sir Thomas Barclay, *The Turco-Italian War and Its Problems* (London: Constable, 1912), p. 96 n1.
18. Thomas C. Schelling, *Arms and Influence* (New Haven, Conn.: Yale University Press, 1966), pp. 1–3.
19. For the stages of conquest see Angelo Piccioli, ed., *La Nuova Italia d'oltremare* (Milan: Mondadori, 1933), p. 287.
20. Beehler, *History*, p. 82.
21. The best account is Feraz Ahmad, *The Young Turks* (Oxford, Eng.: Clarendon Press, 1969).
22. See "Les courants politiques dans la Turquie," *Revue du Monde Musulman* 21 (December 1912): 202, 214.
23. Quoted by Nadav Safran, *From War to War: The Arab-Israeli Confrontation, 1948–1967* (Indianapolis, Ind.: Bobbs-Merrill, 1969), p. 39.
24. The only contemporary source I have seen that takes account of this is "Un Temoin," *Histoire de la guerre italo-turque, 1911–1912* (Paris/Nancy: Berger-Levrault, 1912), p. 60.
25. Charles R. Boxer, *The Portuguese Seaborne Empire, 1415–1825* (New York: Knopf, 1969), p. 113.
26. Giovanni Roncagli, *Guerra Italo-Turca (1911–1912): Cronistoria delle operazioni navali* (Milan: Ulrico Hoepli, 1918), pp. 82–83; pp. 82–130, is the best source for all of these events off the Albanian coast.
27. For these protests see Albertini, *Origins*, 1:346; Roncagli, *Guerra*, pp. 107–16.
28. The duke of Abruzzi did not receive notice of war until the morning of October 1. Roncagli, *Guerra*, pp. 102, 104.
29. Claudio Pavone, ed., *Quarant'anni di politica italiana: dalle carte di Giovanni Giolitti* (Milan: Feltrinelli, 1962), 3:63–66. This is, for the present, the most useful collection of Italian documents for the period; cited hereafter as *Quarant'anni*. Unless otherwise noted, translations are my own; I am grateful to Joan Roth for checking the translations.
30. See II Samuel 18:14–19:8, II Samuel 3, I Samuel 26:6–11.
31. II Samuel 19:5–7.
32. For the neutralization proposals of the two sides and the fate of these proposals, see Askew, *Europe*, pp. 79–80; Giolitti, *Memoirs*, p. 283; telegram, Grey to Rodd (Rome), October 11, 1911, *British Documents*, vol. 9, pt. 1, no. 282 and enclosure; telegram, Bompard (Constantinople) to de Selves, November 8, 1911, in *Documents Diplomatiques*, 3d ser., vol. 1, no. 54.
33. Herodotus 1.82.
34. Giolitti, *Memoirs*, p. 271.
35. The reasons that rapid success was needed are laid out in San Giuliano's memorandum to Giolitti of July 28, 1911, when war was being proposed: *Quarant'anni*, 3:52–53.
36. For the lack of preparedness of the navy at the declaration of war, see Roncagli, *Guerra*, p. 154 (deployment) and p. 77 (bases). For the army, see Albertini, *Origins*, 1:343–44.

37. Roncagli, *Guerra*, p. 156.
38. Albertini, *Origins*, 1:344.
39. Beehler, *History*, pp. 34–35. The fullest account of this engagement and of the ensuing Italian security measures, as well as of neutral response, is Francis McCullagh, *Italy's War for a Desert* (Chicago: F. G. Browne, 1913), pp. 119–298, 347–81.
40. Askew, *Europe*, p. 160.
41. *Quarant'anni*, 3:70–71.
42. Jean-Louis Miège, *L'Impérialisme colonial italien de 1870 à nos jours* (Paris: Société d'Edition d'Enseignement Supérieur, 1968), p. 93.
43. Minute by Louis Mallet, October 1, 1911, *British Documents*, vol. 9, pt. 1, p. 288.
44. Ronald S. Cunsolo, "Libya, Italian Nationalism, and the Revolt against Giolitti," *Journal of Modern History*, vol. 37, no. 2 (June 1965), pp. 195–96.
45. Roncagli, *Guerra*, pp. 248, 258–59.
46. *Quarant'anni*, 3:69–70.
47. See Jagow's telegram from Rome, November 6, 1911, in Albertini, *Origins*, 1:348–49.
48. Askew, *Europe*, p. 91, referring to the French and Russian documents.
49. Leo Valiani, *The End of Austria-Hungary* (London: Secker & Warburg, 1973), pp. 89–90, 143, 150, 170, 173, 204–5, 231–32, 242–44, 264; A. J. P. Taylor, "The War Aims of the Allies in the First World War," in *Politics in Wartime and Other Essays* (London: Hamish Hamilton, 1964), pp. 120–21.
50. Winston S. Churchill, "Their Finest Hour," in *Blood, Sweat, and Tears* (New York: Putnam, 1941, p. 314.
51. Winston S. Churchill, *The Second World War*, Vol. 2: *Their Finest Hour* (Boston: Houghton Mifflin, 1949), p. 91.
52. Ibid., p. 262; for a similar statement of June 16, see p. 196.
53. Churchill, *Blood*, p. 297.
54. Churchill, *Finest Hour*, p. 112. See also Churchill's speech of May 19, 1940 (*Blood*, p. 281).
55. Churchill, *Finest Hour*, pp. 260–62; see Count Galeazzo Ciano, *The Ciano Diaries, 1939–1943*, ed. Hugh Gibson (New York: Doubleday, 1946), p. 277.
56. Denis Mack Smith, *Italy: A Modern History* (Ann Arbor: University of Michigan Press, 1959), p. 277.
57. Quoted in *British Documents*, vol. 9, pt. 1, p. 394, from Siebert-Benckendorff.
58. Bompard to de Selves, November 23, 1911, *Documents Diplomatiques*, 3d ser., vol. 1, no. 202.
59. Great Britain, Naval Intelligence Division of the Admiralty, *Handbook of Libya* (London: His Majesty's Stationery Office, [1917]), pp. 41–42, 48, 62.
60. Barclay, *Turco-Italian War*, pp. 87–94; Earl of Cromer (Evelyn Baring Cromer) *Modern Egypt* (London: Macmillan, 1908), 2:264–69.
61. Seymour Becker, *Russia's Protectorates in Central Asia: Bukhara and Khiva, 1865–1924* (Cambridge, Mass.: Harvard University Press, 1968), pp. 159–62.
62. Askew, *Europe*, pp. 111–12.
63. Ibid., p. 113; for the Dardanelles attack see also the telegram of Lowther to Grey, November 7, 1911, in *British Documents*, vol. 9, pt. 1, p. 322.
64. Askew, *Europe*, p. 113; circulaire from de Selves, *Documents Diplomatiques*, 3d ser., vol. 1, no. 69 (p. 67). For other reports of Italian plans to extend the war see ibid., nos. 54, 65, 92, 138, 165.

65. O'Beirne (St. Petersburg) to Grey, November 12, 1911, in *British Documents*, vol. 9, pt. 1, p. 322; Lowther (Constantinople) to Grey, in ibid., pp. 324–25.
66. Telegram, Bompard to de Selves, November 6, 1911, *Documents Diplomatiques*, 3d ser., vol. 1, no. 32.
67. "The War in the Mediterranean," *Journal of the Royal United Service Institution* 55 (November 1911):1678; henceforth cited as *United Service*.
68. Bompard to de Selves, November 6, 1911, *Documents Diplomatiques*, 3d ser., vol. 1, no. 30.
69. *United Service* 55 (October 1911):1364; 55 (November 1911):1490; and 55 (December 1911):1680.
70. De Selves to Legrand (Rome), *Documents Diplomatiques*, 3d ser., vol. 1, no. 108.
71. Legrand to de Selves, November 14, 1911, *Documents Diplomatiques*, 3d ser., vol. 1, no. 11.
72. Legrand to de Selves, November 15, 1911, *Documents Diplomatiques*, 3d ser., vol. 1, no. 125.
73. Beehler, *History*, p. 47.
74. Giorgio Giorgerini and Augusto Nani, *Gli incrociatori italiani, 1861–1964* (Rome: Ufficio Storico della Marina Militare, 1964), p. 256.
75. Beehler, *History*, p. 47.
76. *British Documents*, vol. 9, pt. 1, p. 324; my translation from the French.
77. Grey to Cartwright (Vienna), *British Documents*, vol. 9, pt. 1, p. 328.
78. For the Russian reaction see *British Documents*, vol. 9, pt. 1, pp. 318, 330, 331; for Britain's, see pp. 331–33.
79. Minute by Sir Edward Grey, November 27, 1911, *British Documents*, vol. 9, pt. 1, p. 332.
80. Cartwright (Vienna) to Grey, November 22, 1911, *British Documents*, vol. 9, pt. 1, p. 326.
81. Askew, *Europe*, pp. 118–19; see also Albertini, *Origins*, 1:353–54.
82. Askew, *Europe*, p. 114.
83. From the Austrian documents in Albertini, *Origins*, 1:353; translated by I. M. Massey.
84. Askew, *Europe*, p. 112.
85. Legrand to de Selves, *Documents Diplomatiques*, 3d ser., vol. 1, no. 186. Cf. Askew, *Europe*, pp. 117–18; Albertini, *Origins*, 1:354. See also Legrand to de Selves, *Documents Diplomatiques*, 3d ser., vol. 1, no. 231; Rodd (Rome) to Grey, December 1, 1911, *British Documents*, vol. 9, pt. 1, p. 339.
86. Askew, *Europe*, pp. 121–22.
87. For subsequent operations in the Red Sea see Beehler, *History*, pp. 51, 52, 60, 81, 90; Askew, *Europe*, p. 189; Giorgerini and Nani, *Gli incrociatori*, pp. 204, 256; *United Service*, 56 (1912):247–48, 416, 710, 736, 1210, 1319.
88. Giolitti, *Memoirs*, p. 306.
89. For the Idris revolt and his cooperation with Italy see Giolitti, *Memoirs*, pp. 306–7; *United Service* 55 (1911):1525, and 56 (1912):736, 1210; Beehler, *History*, pp. 52, 60. The Italians provided Idris with money, ten thousand rifles, and three field batteries with personnel (Giolitti, *Memoirs*, p. 307).
90. For the tenuousness of Italian control over the colonies, see Robert L. Hess, *Italian Colonialism in Somalia* (Chicago: University of Chicago Press, 1966), pp. 95, 128, 140, 146–47; Gaibi, *Manuale*, pp. 151–52.
91. Beehler, *History*, p. 25.
92. Ibid., pp. 47–48.

93. See, in *British Documents*, vol. 9, pt. 1: Grey to Cartwright, November 22, 1911, pp. 327–28; minute by Louis Mallet, November 20, 1911, p. 325; Cartwright to Grey, November 28, pp. 335–36; Rodd to Grey, December 1, p. 339. In *Documents Diplomatiques*, 3d ser., vol. 1, see Bompard to de Selves, November 13, 1911, no. 100; Daeschner (Chef de Cabinet of Poincaré) to de Selves, November 22, 1911, no. 184. See also, Askew, *Europe*, p. 108.
94. Paléologue (Sofia) to de Selves, November 18, 1911, *Documents Diplomatiques*, 3d ser., vol. 1, no. 149.
95. Luigi Albertini, *Venti anni di vita politica* (2 vols.; Bologna: Zanichelli, 1950–1953), pt. 1, vol. 2, pp. 149–53.
96. Lt. Col. André Morier, trans., *La Marine dans la guerre italo-turque* ("traduit de la relation officielle italienne") (Paris: Librairie Chapelot, 1913), pp. 20–21.
97. Legrand to de Selves, November 20, 1911, *Documents Diplomatiques*, 3d ser., vol. 1, no. 170.
98. Albertini, *Origins*, 1:355–56; Albertini, *Venti anni*, pt. 1, vol. 2, pp. 158–59; Askew, *Europe*, pp. 149–56.
99. Ulrich Trumpener, *Germany and the Ottoman Empire, 1914–1918* (Princeton, N.J.: Princeton University Press, 1968), pp. 272–75.
100. The Italian regime of 1912 was in many respects very undemocratic. But it is quite possible that the effects of liberal democracy in transforming the frame of mind of citizens may antedate the full implementation of democracy. Britain during the First World War was a classic case of "tyranny of the majority," although its government still exhibited much aristocratic dominance.
101. Cunsolo, "Libya," pp. 195–96.
102. George Earle Buckle, "Lansdowne, Fifth Marquess of," *Encyclopaedia Britannica*, 12th ed., 31:728.
103. Winston S. Churchill, *Marlborough: His Life and Times* (London: Harrap, 1947), 1:686–87.
104. Z. P. Yakhimovich, *Italo-turetskaya voina, 1911–1912* (Moscow: Nauka, 1967), p. 87; McCullagh, *Italy's War*, pp. 87, 169.
105. Legrand to de Selves, November 20, 1911, *Documents Diplomatiques*, 3d ser., vol. 1, no. 170 (p. 160).
106. Quoted in Taylor, "War Aims," pp. 96–97.
107. Giolitti, *Memoirs*, pp. 292–93.
108. Yakhimovich, *Voina*, p. 88.
109. Barclay to Grey, March 28, 1912, *British Documents*, vol. 9, pt. 1, p. 563 (no. 565).
110. *United Service* 56 (1912):414; Giorgerini and Nani, *Gli incrociatori*, p. 308.
111. See the account of the battle in the Italian official narrative, translated by Morier (see footnote 96 above).
112. *United Service* 56 (1912):415; see also Beehler, *History*, p. 58 and map.
113. Beehler, *History*, p. 58. The Turkish threats were made on February 19 (Lowther to Grey, note in *British Documents*, vol. 9, pt. 1, no. 368), February 20 (note by Poincaré, *Documents Diplomatiques*, 3d ser., vol. 2, no. 69), February 24 (*United Service* 56 [1912]:412).
114. Poincaré to Barrère (Rome), February 27, 1912, *Documents Diplomatiques*, 3d ser., vol. 2, no. 108; *United Service* 56 (1912):416; Giolitti, *Memoirs*, p. 296; Poincaré circulaire, *Documents Diplomatiques*, 3d ser., vol. 2, no. 137.
115. Louis (St. Petersburg) to Poincaré, April 8, 1912; Cambon (Berlin) to Poincaré, May 9, 1912, *Documents Diplomatiques*, 3d ser., vol. 2, nos. 308 and 421 (see also

note 1 for the attitude of Kitchener); British Note, February 29, 1912, *Documents Diplomatiques*, 3d ser., vol. 2, no. 127; Giolitti, *Memoirs*, p. 290.
116. Albertini, *Origins*, 1:359. For the negotiations see Albertini, *Venti anni*, pt. 1, vol. 2, pp. 172–75.
117. Circular telegram, March 7, 1912, *Documents Diplomatiques*, 3d ser., vol. 2, no. 165; Lowther to Grey, March 10, 1912, cited in Editorial Note, *British Documents*, vol. 9, pt. 1, p. 378.
118. For these operations, which were overshadowed by the attack on the straits, see Beehler, *History*, pp. 67–68.
119. Ibid.
120. See Barrère to Poincaré, April 19, 1912, *Documents Diplomatiques*, 3d ser., vol. 2, no. 365 (compare Giolitti, *Memoirs*, p. 360); Jules Cambon to Poincaré, April 20, 1912, *Documents Diplomatiques*, 3d ser., vol. 2, no. 366; Albertini, *Origins*, 1:360 (from Russian and Austrian documents).
121. Paul Cambon (London) to Poincaré, April 20, 1912, *Documents Diplomatiques*, 3d ser., vol. 2, no. 368; Barrère to Poincaré, April 21, 1912, *Documents Diplomatiques*, 3d ser., vol. 2, no. 371; Rodd to Grey, April 19, 1912, *British Documents*, vol. 9, pt. 1, no. 393 (p. 386).
122. Albertini, *Venti anni*, pt. 1, vol. 2, pp. 181–82.
123. This latter possibility is the burden of what San Giuliano told the British ambassador: Rodd to Grey, April 19, 1912, *British Documents*, vol. 9, pt. 1, no. 393 (p. 386). Enticing out the Turkish fleet (together with the seizure of Stampalia) was proposed in the report of Adm. Thaon de Revel after the Beirut attack (February 29) and forwarded to Giolitti by the Minister of Marine on 23 March. See the text in *Quarant'anni*, 3:71–72.
124. Rodd to Grey, April 19, 1912, *British Documents*, vol. 9, pt. 1, p. 386 (no. 393).
125. San Giuliano admitted that "Italian withdrawal after bombardment will be hailed as success by Turkey": Rodd to Grey, April 19, 1912, *British Documents*, vol. 9, pt. 1, no. 394 (p. 387).
126. See the text of the note, *Documents Diplomatiques*, 3d ser., vol. 2, no. 378. Compare Giolitti, *Memoirs*, p. 290.
127. Ahmad, *Young Turks*, pp. 100–104.
128. Avarna made this promise to Berchtold: Albertini, *Venti anni*, pt. 1, vol. 2, p. 175. See Beehler, *History*, pp. 71–76, for a summary of the military events.
129. Barrère to Poincaré, May 10, 1912, *Documents Diplomatiques*, 3d ser., vol. 2, no. 428.
130. Albertini, *Venti anni*, pt. 1, vol. 2, p. 182; see also Jules Cambon to Poincaré, *Documents Diplomatiques*, 3d ser., vol. 2, no. 421 (pp. 445–46).
131. *United Service* 56 (1912):1205.
132. Giolitti, *Memoirs*, p. 303; Albertini, *Venti anni*, pt. 1, vol. 2, pp. 182–83.
133. Lansdowne to Spring-Rice, November 6, 1905, *British Documents*, vol. 5, p. 91.
134. Schelling, *Arms*, pp. 74–75.
135. Grey to Rodd, June 28, 1912, *British Documents*, vol. 9, pt. 1, p. 412.
136. Cunsolo, "Libya," p. 196; Albertini, *Venti anni*, pt. 1, vol. 2, pp. 184–85.
137. Barrère to Poincaré, May 10, 1912, *Documents Diplomatiques*, 3d ser., vol. 2, no. 428.
138. *United Service* 56 (1912):1028.
139. Giolitti, *Memoirs*, p. 303.
140. Beehler, *History*, p. 80.
141. For the negotiations see Giolitti, *Memoirs*, pp. 312–51.

142. Quoted in ibid., p. 318.
143. Ibid., pp. 325–36.
144. For these events see Ahmad, *Young Turks*, pp. 104–20; for the effects on peace with Italy see Lowther to Grey, October 6, 1912, *British Documents*, vol. 9, pt. 1, p. 736.
145. Muhtar Pasha, *La Turquie*, p. 159.
146. Beehler, *History*, p. 82.
147. Albertini, *Venti anni*, pt. 1, vol. 2, p. 196; Rodd to Grey, October 27, 1912, *British Documents*, vol. 9, pt. 1, p. 436.
148. Barrère to Poincaré, July 26, 1912, *Documents Diplomatiques*, 3d ser., vol. 3, no. 224. See also, Albertini, *Venti anni*, pt. 1, vol. 2, pp. 183–85.
149. Beehler, *History*, p. 90.
150. A full, although not necessarily accurate, account of these negotiations is in Giolitti, *Memoirs*, pp. 329–47.
151. Lowther to Grey, October 17, 1912, *British Documents*, vol. 9, pt. 1, p. 431.
152. Giolitti, *Memoirs*, p. 342.
153. Askew, *Europe*, p. 249; Smith, *Italy*, p. 280.
154. Smith, *Italy*, p. 280.
155. I am indebted to the suggestions of various readers of this study, especially Klaus Knorr, Joan Roth, Thomas L. Pangle, David Bolotin, Richard Smoke, and H. Bradford Westerfield.

Alliances, 1815-1945: Weapons of Power and Tools of Management

Paul W. Schroeder

Though the term "alliance" has often been used loosely to mean simply "friendship" or "working partnership,"[1] jurists and theorists have long insisted on a narrower definition, according to which an alliance is a treaty binding two or more independent states to come to each other's aid with armed force under circumstances specified in the *casus foederis* article of the treaty. Whether offensive or defensive, limited or unlimited, equal or unequal, bilateral or multilateral, alliances must involve some measure of commitment to use force to achieve a common goal.[2]

Political scientists by and large adopt this definition as describing not only what technically constitutes an alliance, but also how alliances work and what functions they fulfill. "In concept and in practice," writes one authority, "alliance combines the capabilities of nation-states not simply for the sake of forming associations but essentially to preserve, magnify, or create positions of strength for diplomacy or war."[3] "The purpose of the alliance (treaty of mutual assistance)," writes another, "is to combine the power of the allies against their common enemy."[4] The basic idea of an alliance, another states, "is to assure a preponderance of strength should it come to a contest of capabilities."[5] Alliances, to quote a classic work, are "a necessary function of the balance of power operating within a multiple-state system."[6] Similar statements could be cited almost at will, defining alliances as means of capability-aggregation, collective defense, war, security, and power diplomacy.

The discussion of alliances is not confined to their power-political uses, to be sure. Some political scientists view them as designed only for situations of conflict,[7] or as serving only minor purposes other than capability-aggregation.[8] But most recognize additional purposes of alliance as well—those of legitimating one's own regime or that of an ally, preventing revolution or internal disturbances, spreading an ideology, or enhancing a state's influence and status, for example.[9] Alliances, we know, play a role not only in the balance of power, but also in collective-security or concert systems.[10] The internal rivalries and cross-purposes that all alliances contain are no secret; neither are the negotiations and maneuvering that go on almost constantly between partners in an alliance. None of this, however, invalidates the consensus that alliances are instruments of power politics. The additional purposes and uses of alliances are almost always interpreted as ancillary to those of power and security, and intra-alliance politics are explained as a product of these main purposes, as the result of differing perceptions of the goals, the payoffs, the distribution of burdens, and the strategy and tactics of the alliance.

Despite this consensus, some of the ideas advanced in international-relations theory might lead one to question whether alliances need be primarily instruments of power. Most political scientists do not consider international politics as simply an arena of power conflict; some would even deny that power is the most fundamental reality in it.[11] The central problem for international-relations theory, one often hears, is understanding order rather than power, devising a viable principle of international order for the control and management of conflict.[12] The balance-of-power doctrines with which alliances are generally connected have been challenged on various grounds: whether balance-of-power politics constitutes a real system with identifiable rules and practices,[13] whether that system is stable or tends inherently toward disequilibrium and conflict,[14] and whether historically the balance of power really governed international relations and helped to preserve peace in previous centuries.[15] Everyone knows that alliances in practice do not always serve to increase a nation's power and security, and that allies often clash with each other more than they unite in a common cause.[16] All this might lead one to wonder whether alliances really need to function primarily as weapons of power.

A few writers have in fact gone beyond the power-and-security view of alliances in pointing to their functions as tools of management and control. Richard A. Falk, for example, argues that international violence has been held within tolerable limits in recent decades partly through the control exercised by the great powers, the U.S.A. and the U.S.S.R., over the smaller powers within their alliance systems.[17] Robert E. Osgood writes: "Next to accretion, the most prominent function of alliances has been to restrain and control allies, particularly in order to safeguard one ally against actions of another that might endanger its security or otherwise jeopardize its interests." He further remarks: "Primarily his [Bismarck's] alliances were intended to limit the options of allies while keeping Germany's commitments to them equally limited."[18] Most interesting is the concept of the functions of alliance expounded in the writings of George Liska. In 1962, though still regarding alliances mainly as means of capability-aggregation, he described their goals as: "Always to restrain the adversary and, if and when desirable, *also each other and the scope of a conflict.*"[19] By 1967 he looked on alliances as general means of management in both interstate and imperial systems,[20] and in 1968 he listed a whole series of purposes for forming alliances, the main ones being "aggregation of power, interallied control, and international order or government."[21] Here the power purposes of alliances are not ignored or denied, but they are dethroned, and other functions are emphasized as being equally important.

Compared to political scientists, historians by the nature of their work must pay more attention in detail to the diverse purposes and uses of alliances. Absorbed in digging out the complex motives and calculations behind alliances and in tracing the intricate maneuvers of intra-alliance politics, the diplomatic historian learns very quickly that the unintended functions and results of alliances are often more important than the intended ones. Yet despite the close attention given to the details of forming alliances and to politics, most historians conceive of alliances much as political scientists do—basically as weapons of national security and power, instruments in balance of power politics. Normally, historians do not try to account theoretically for the diversity of purposes of alliances or the phenomena of antagonistic intra-alliance politics. If they do, their answers are likely to resemble those of most political scientists.

Because this essay will argue that a great deal of evidence about alliance politics from 1815 to 1945 suggests a different interpretation of functions of alliances, the question naturally arises, If such evidence exists, why have most historians as well as political theorists missed it or failed to draw the right conclusions from it? Obviously, no very confident answer can be given; the reason could be simply that the majority view is correct. But assuming that this divergent interpretation can be upheld, the answer might lie first in the fact that almost all historians, like political scientists, assume that international relations in modern times have rested fundamentally upon a balance of power. Although there has been debate over whether the balance of power *should be* the basis for international relations, few have disputed that it actually has been; the notion of balance of power is usually taken for granted. This assumption fairly well determines one's conception of the function of alliances as well. If all international relations rest on a balance of power, alliances naturally operate as power instruments in the balance.

Another factor, which is more intangible, may also be fundamental. Both historians and political scientists have concentrated on explaining war and conflict in international relations—historians dwelling generally on the particular causes of particular crises and wars; political scientists, on the general conditions and reasons for international conflict. This emphasis, however natural and understandable, may introduce an insensible bias into the inquiry. The danger is not so much, as some suggest, that power and conflict come to be overrated in international relations, whereas the elements of cooperation, interdependence, and common interests are neglected. It is, rather, that the stress on accounting for war suggests that war is a deviation from the norm, requiring explanation, whereas peace is not. But this assumption is eminently open to challenge. Let us accept what seems quite evident: the fundamental, overriding fact of international politics continues to be the existence of enormous power at the disposal of rival, independent states, with only weak and tenuous restraints upon its use. This very fact means that war is more normal than peace, and that peace (i.e., the restraint of violent international conflict within narrow limits) needs explanation more than war does. This is not merely a theoretical point. It is often more difficult for the historian to explain why war did not break out at a particular time than to explain why it did at another; theorists seem to have more difficulty discerning and defining the general causes of peace than the general causes of war.

Yet, in fact, peace prevails more generally in international relations than does war. Thus the main problem that students have is to account for the theoretically unexpected relative prevalence of peace. This involves determining how various devices of control and management work to keep conflicting national aims and uncontrolled national power from causing more wars than actually happen. The point applies to alliances very directly. One may well assume that their original, normal purposes were and are power-oriented—security, capability-aggregation, gains of various kinds. Yet these purposes serve better to explain why violent conflicts occur rather than how they are avoided. If the latter question comes to be seen as the main one, it leads one immediately to suspect that alliances have perhaps been fulfilling other functions than their original or "normal" ones—functions of the control and management of conflict.

In any case, this essay will attempt, in a rapid overview of the European international system from 1815 to 1945, to illustrate the management and control functions of alliances.[22] It may help to set down here some of the main points that will emerge:

1. The desire for capability-aggregation against an outside threat has not always played a vital role in the formation of alliances. Sometimes powers entered into alliances even though one party or the other (occasionally both) had no need or desire for capability-aggregation. In certain cases, the formation of alliances served to weaken a power's military position rather than to strengthen it.
2. Some alliances, though directed nominally or partly against a particular threat or opponent indicated in the *casus foederis*, had primary aims or targets that were quite separate from those specified in the treaty.
3. All alliances in some measure functioned as pacts of restraint (*pacta de contrahendo*), restraining or controlling the actions of the partners in the alliance themselves. Frequently the desire to exercise such control over an ally's policy was the main reason that one power, or both, entered into the alliance. In every case, the way in which the alliance functioned as a

pactum de contrahendo had an important effect upon the success and durability of the alliance, and on its impact upon the general system.
4. Although alliances were commonly used to try to isolate and intimidate an opponent, alliances were frequently also employed in order to group and conciliate an opponent, in the interest of managing the system and avoiding overt conflict. For example, a group of powers might form an alliance in order to compel an opponent to come into the alliance in order to avoid isolation; or one power might form an alliance with another, in order to compel that ally to become reconciled with its opponent, so that the opponent could in turn be drawn into a wider alliance or a further combination.
5. The perception of a threat from another power might lead a state to try either to form an alliance *against* that power, in order to meet the threat by capability-aggregation, or to ally *with* that power, in order to manage the threat through a *pactum de contrahendo*.

The fundamental European alliance after the Congress of Vienna in 1814–1815 was the Quadruple Alliance of November 1815, which united Austria, Britain, Prussia, and Russia in defense of the peace settlement. Obviously this alliance served the purpose of mutual security against a revival of French aggression and imperialism or against any other threat to the newly established status quo. But no less important for these powers was their general desire to remain allied in order to manage the international system and to solve new problems as they arose. Not only the cataclysms of the previous quarter-century, but also the strains and problems of the final coalition against Napoleon in the period 1812–1814, the conflicts among the great powers that arose during the peace congress, and Napoleon's return from Elba—all combined to convince the great powers that it was vitally necessary for them to make a durable alliance of mutual cooperation and restraint. Significantly, it was Lord Castlereagh, foreign secretary of the least-threatened and "European" of the powers, who sponsored a specific provision for postwar conferences of the great powers in Article VI of the treaty. The same concern for cooperation among the great powers led the allies in 1818 to bring France into the alliance, so that there now existed a Quintuple Alliance to run Europe.[23]

The Holy Alliance of September 1815, which was sponsored by Tsar Alexander I of Russia, also aimed at European concert and mutual restraint on a still loftier plane. The actual treaty was virtually meaningless as an operative instrument, because it contained no *casus foederis* and only a vague statement of aims. Nevertheless, the term "Holy Alliance" denotes a real alliance, one of the most important mutual-security arrangements of the nineteenth century. For the three original signatories—Austria, Prussia, and Russia—formed in fact a very effective union against liberalism, revolution, and territorial and political change. Several times the Holy Alliance sanctioned or helped to execute armed intervention against revolutions (1821 in Italy, 1830–1832 in Italy and Poland, 1846 in Cracow, 1849 in Hungary). In other ways as well, the alliance of these Eastern powers served as a powerful deterrent to war or revolt.

Important as the Holy Alliance was for security purposes, however, it was even more significant and effective as a mutual pact of restraint upon these three powers themselves. Each of them was a jealous rival of the other two at the same time that it shared in a common conservative cause. Each needed and used this alliance to control its partners and to manage intra-alliance rivalries in Germany, Italy, Poland, and the Near East so as to avoid war. Prince Metternich, the Austrian chancellor, demonstrated especially well how the Holy Alliance could be used as a pact of restraint. He recognized that Alexander's original mystical, vaguely liberal dream of a Holy Alliance as a fraternal Christian union among monarchs and peoples might well serve as a cover for expanded Russian influence in Europe, with Russia taking up the cause of moderate political reform. Metternich therefore recast the Holy Alliance treaty into a safe, absolutist form, and then he spent the next decade using his arch-conservative Holy Alliance principles to restrain and manage Alexander I. Much of the diplomacy of the Italian, Greek, and Spanish revolutions from 1820 to 1823 consists of Metternich's efforts to control Russian policy through and within the alliance of the Eastern powers.[24]

The German Confederation of 1815, which was basically a permanent defense league of all the German states, led by Austria and Prussia, similarly served both for mutual security for Germany, especially against France, and as a pact of mutual restraint for controlling the German problem from within. The confederation worked to harmonize the rival claims of Austria and Prussia to leadership and to reconcile these claims of the great powers with the demands for independence of the middle-sized and small states, as well as to protect Germany from outside threats. During the 1820s and 1830s, Metternich used the confederation much more for controlling the internal policies of member states and for managing Austria's junior partner Prussia than he used it for European high politics. His favorite ploy was to insist that Austria could take care of her European interests quite easily without the confederation. Therefore, if the other states did not cooperate with Austria in confederate policy, Austria would pull out and leave them to their fate. This was obviously a bluff, but it was often an effective one.[25]

Metternich never succeeded, despite repeated efforts, in establishing an Italian league that would enable Austria to tie down and manage Italy in similar fashion. Nonetheless, Austria's alliances and dynastic connections in Italy served the same combined security and managerial purposes. The Austro-

Neapolitan secret alliance of June 1815 is a good example of an alliance that gave security to the weaker state and control to the stronger (Naples was forbidden by the treaty to change her form of government without Austria's permission).

In July 1827 the existing combinations of Quadruple, Quintuple, and Holy (i.e., Eastern) alliances were partly broken up by a new partnership when Britain, Russia, and France concluded a convention for joint intervention in the six-year-old Greek revolution against Turkey. Although technically this was not a treaty of alliance, the partners always termed themselves allies, and so they were. Their convention provided for the combined use of force, if necessary, to impose a settlement on Turkey, and it quickly led to a three-power armed intervention, allied destruction of the Turco-Egyptian fleet, a Russian war against Turkey, French occupation of southern Greece, and finally by allied imposition on Turkey of peace terms, which included an independent Greece under an allied protectorate. From our standpoint, the most interesting thing about this significant and powerful alliance is that capability-aggregation and mutual security against a threat that was perceived in common had nothing to do with it. Each of these three powers alone was strong enough to coerce Turkey; each professed (more or less sincerely) to be Turkey's friend and defender and to want to preserve and help her. The alliance, it is obvious, was intended for purposes of management, not power. It grew out of an attempt by the British foreign secretary, George Canning, to form a pact of restraint with Russia in 1826. Fearing that Russia, Britain's chief rival, would eventually, on its own, intervene in Greece, Canning decided to go partners with Russia in order to manage her, to solve the Greek problem, and to advance British interests and prestige in the Levant. The French joined in because they dared not allow Russia and Britain to act without them and thought that France could gain status and influence by participating. The results belied these purposes, to be sure. Instead of a peaceful settlement, the alliance resulted in a war from which Russia, which was supposed to be constrained, made important gains, and which exposed the European system to grave dangers (the collapse of the Ottoman Empire, permanent enmity between Austria and Russia, and the revival of French expansionism). Nonetheless, the alliance still demonstrates the importance—even, in certain instances, the primacy—of management motives in the formation of alliances.[26]

The Russo-Turkish alliance that was signed at Unkiar-Skelessi in July 1833 also demonstrates this. For Turkey, of course, an alliance with its most powerful enemy was purely a desperate security measure to meet the immediate threat of the invading army of Mehemet Ali, khedive of Egypt. As the Turks said, a drowning man will seize hold even of a snake. But the alliance brought no security, in the usual sense, to Russia. The Egyptian army posed no threat to Russia, and from a military standpoint, a Turkish alliance was a distinct liability. Had the Western powers chosen to challenge Russia over this treaty (as the British foreign secretary, Lord Palmerston, was strongly inclined to do), Russia would have found it impossible to defend the Turkish Straits against the navies of the Western powers. The only way this alliance contributed to Russia's security was in helping Russia to preserve and control Turkey, thereby keeping the vital straits from falling into other, more dangerous, hands. The treaty thus gave Turkey free protection (a secret protocol expressly excused her from any military obligation) in exchange for Russian influence at Constantinople and an assurance that the Black Sea would be closed against invaders. Russia had other long-range ambitions in mind as well—gaining more privileges for Orthodox Christians in Turkey and strengthening Russia's special position in the Danubian Principalities (later Rumania). But expansionist aims notwithstanding, this was basicaliy a pact of management and control.

The way in which Russia's main rivals in the Near East—Britain and Austria—reacted to Unkiar-Skelessi and the danger of Russian predominance at Constantinople again illustrates in how many different ways alliances can function. Metternich immediately sought to control Russia through a *pactum de contrahendo*. This was his normal method; besides, Austria needed Russia's support too much elsewhere to challenge Russia openly in the Near East. In the Münchengrätz Agreement of September 1833, Russia and Austria promised to cooperate to preserve the Ottoman Empire and, should it collapse despite their efforts, to act only in concert to meet the problem. Prussia joined this agreement a month later. Having thus enlisted Russia, Metternich tried to bring the Western powers as well into his alliance, in order to control Russia.

Palmerston refused to join. Distrusting Russia and Austria equally, and preferring balance-of-power and confrontation tactics, he promoted a quadruple alliance among Britain, France, Spain, and Portugal in 1834, which was supposed to overawe the Eastern powers and deter them from their supposedly aggressive designs. In reality, for Palmerston's purpose the alliance was both unnecessary and useless. What it actually did was to function as a pact for restraint and management in Western Europe, especially in the Iberian Peninsula. It gave British friendship and support to the insecure regime of King Louis Philippe of France in exchange for considerable British control over French policy in the Spanish and Portuguese civil wars.[27]

The successful settlement of the Belgian question from 1830 to 1839, which culminated in an international guarantee of an independent, neutral Belgium, was more the product of ordinary diplomacy than of alliance politics. One chapter in the story, however, admirably illustrates the principle of allying with one's rival to control his policy. Britain was the power that was most interested in establishing Belgian independence and neutrality; then and later,

Britain considered France the great threat to Belgium. Yet when it became necessary to impose a settlement upon the king of Holland by armed force, Britain signed a convention for this purpose in October 1832 with France. Left alone or allied against, France would cause trouble; within an alliance, France could be used and controlled.[28]

Another alliance over the Eastern Question, the Austro-British-Russian agreement of July 1840, shows another way in which alliances are used for management and restraint. Militarily the alliance was directed against a renewed menace to Turkey from Mehemet Ali, and it succeeded brilliantly in meeting it. By November 1840 Mehemet had been driven back to Egypt and had been forced to submit. But from the more important standpoint of European politics, France, not Mehemet, was the target of this alliance; and its aim (for Austria and Russia, if not for Palmerston) was to bring France back into the Concert of Europe and to force it to conform. Initially, in July 1839, France had joined the other powers in promising help to the sultan and in demanding European control over the peace terms that he would offer to Mehemet. But thereafter France began trying to manage the policy of the concert for its own ends, attempting to save some of Mehemet's gains for him so as to promote French influence in Egypt. The Triple Alliance of July 1840 served as formal notice to France that, unless France got back into line, the other powers would act against Mehemet without France. The European war scare that followed in October/November 1840 derived from French resentment of their own isolation, and their hope to bluff the other powers into allowing France back into the concert without full conformity on France's part. France's joining in the five-power Straits Convention of July 1841 represented France's formal readmission to the concert, as well as a success for alliances as tools of management.[29]

The revolutions of 1848 ended the European stability that had generally prevailed since 1815, producing not only internal upheavals but also international tensions and wars (in Italy, Hungary, and Schleswig-Holstein) which threatened to destroy the existing alliance systems. France became a republic, potentially radical and expansionist, while Italy was swept by revolution and joined in a nationalist war against Austria. This wrecked the conservative entente between France and Austria that had begun to develop before 1848; it also revived their ancient, bitter rivalry over Italy. Both the Holy Alliance and the German Confederation were paralyzed by the revolutions in Central Europe, the German nationalist unification movement, the open rivalry between Austria and Prussia for leadership in Germany, and Prussia's temporary turn to liberalism and an anti-Russian policy.

What is surprising, therefore, is that the main prerevolutionary alliance systems by and large survived the revolutions. Not only did they survive; they actually continued to function for both security and management, indicating how vitally both functions were needed. It was not accidental that when by 1850/1851 all the various efforts to create a more united Germany had run aground, the German governments revived the fallen 1815 confederation. Prince Schwarzenberg, the Austrian premier, expressed the prevailing attitude accurately and without cynicism in remarking that a threadbare cloak was better than none. All the unification efforts, in fact, had been constrained by the fear of destroying Germany's existing bonds and of replacing them with nothing, leaving Germany a prey to Austro-Prussian enmity, French or Russian domination, and internal revolution and civil war. In essence, Holy Alliance principles and restraints had held everyone back from drastic steps from 1848 to 1850— not merely conservatives, but also German nationalists, liberals, and romantics, even the supposedly modern *Realpolitiker* Schwarzenberg (who had taken control in Austria in late 1848) and the new Emperor Francis Joseph. They had had a golden opportunity to confront Prussia and to solve the German question by force in 1850, but they had passed it by—above all because Prussia, though a dangerous rival, was also an indispensable ally against the revolution. Not until Bismarck came to power in Prussia in 1862 would such restraints finally be swept aside.[30]

Holy Alliance principles, as well as fears for Poland, likewise led Tsar Nicholas I to send an army to help Austria crush the Hungarian revolution in 1849. In similar traditional fashion, Nicholas used his mediating position between Austria and Prussia in order to control their policy and manage the German problem, both the general Austro-Prussian rivalry and the conflict between Germany and Denmark over Schleswig-Holstein. His aims were the typical mixture of security, management, and control—preventing war, returning Prussia to conservative paths, and avoiding any unification or strengthening of Germany. Russia, as Nicholas and other statesmen knew, drew great advantages from a confederated Germany and a controlled Austro-Prussian rivalry. The trouble with Russian management in this case was that it was pushed too far, with too arrogant and superior an air. Schwarzenberg, in particular, resented Russian domination and Nicholas's assumption that Austria must follow his lead in the Near East out of gratitude over what he had done for Hungary, and he resolved from the outset to prove himself ungrateful to Russia if the occasion should arise.[31] As for Austria and Prussia, each returned after 1850 to using the unreformed confederation to restrain and manage the other. Prussia even conceded Austria a special three-year defensive alliance in 1851, mainly as a pact of restraint.

Italy in 1849/1850 provides more instances of control and management through alliances. The treaties that Austria concluded with its client states in central Italy in 1849 gave them security against either invasion or externally supported revolt and gave Austria control, thus making sure that the rulers of Tuscany, Modena, and Parma could not again surrender to revolutionary movements. Austria even considered using her control to try to replace Leopold II of Tuscany with a more reliable ruler. The Roman question in 1849/1850 illustrates well the diplomacy of rivals in an alliance. Pope Pius IX, after fleeing from Rome in the face of revolution, appealed to the Catholic powers of Europe, especially Austria, to restore him to power. Schwarzenberg, precisely because he feared French rivalry and ambitions in Italy, resisted Pius's pleas for unilateral Austrian intervention and insisted instead on drawing France into a working partnership in Italy. The French, seeing that such a partnership would strengthen Austria's position, which France wanted to undermine, tried instead to accept the principle of Austro-French partnership in Italy, but to use it in order to prevent any action that would favor the pope. When this policy proved unworkable and some intervention at Rome seemed inescapable, France attempted suddenly to intervene alone, on its own initiative. Austria, however, promptly endorsed France's action, supported the action with Austria's own parallel occupation of other papal territories, and thereby more or less snared France into a partnership against her will.[32]

The Crimean War (1853–1856), which pitted Turkey, Britain, France, and, finally, Sardinia against Russia, tended naturally to promote alliances primarily as instruments of war, security, and capability-aggregation. Yet even in this major conflict, the largest since Napoleon's time, alliances continued to operate in a very important way for control and management. For example, the Anglo-French alliance for war—which was formalized in April 1854, after war had already been declared—actually developed from an entente formed by Britain with France in early 1853 for the purpose of restraining France and managing the Eastern crisis, then in its early stages. France's ambitions at first seemed more dangerous to the British than did Russia's; both powers expected to use their partnership so as to control the other and to better manage the international situation. But as in the period 1825–1827, an alliance that was intended for control resulted in loss of control and war. In a series of moves and developments that is too complicated to relate here, the Western powers—who were struggling to preserve their partnership, to manage one another, and to force Russia to retreat—finally succeeded only in pushing Russia into war and pulling themselves in afterwards. Yet even in wartime, their alliance, which was carefully fitted out with a mutual self-denying clause against territorial aggrandizement, continued to function for control as well as for military victory. Disputes between the allies over war aims and peace terms went on almost continuously. Most French leaders and the French public favored a negotiated peace in the spring of 1855, which Austria was promoting at the Vienna peace conference. Britain opposed a negotiated peace and succeeded in frustrating it. But the next winter, France convinced Britain that the existence of the alliance depended upon reaching peace and, with Austria's help, got Britain to agree to a moderate settlement in March 1856.

An even better example of a *pactum de contrahendo* that was concluded during the Crimean War is the Austro-Prussian alliance of April 1854. Austria sought this alliance partly to get Prussian and German support for Austria's position with regard to the Near East and for Austria's policy against Russia (under the German Confederation, the member states were only bound to defend the Austrian territory that was *within* the confederation against attack, so that Austria's southeastern lands were not protected). In addition, Austria wanted through this alliance to force Prussia and the German states to accept and acknowledge Austria's leadership both in Germany and in European affairs. Thus, from Austria's standpoint, the alliance served both for capability-aggregation and for management. Prussia and the German states, however, agreed to assume further obligations to defend Austria solely in order to restrain it, to prevent Austria, if possible, from allying with the Western powers and either going to war against Russia or provoking Russia to attack Austria. Both Prussia and the rest of Germany assumed that if Austria became involved in the war, they also would be dragged in. The same motives of control and restraint led these states to extend their alliance with Austria in November 1854 and reluctantly to support Austria's peace terms to Russia in 1855 and 1856.

Prussia and Germany managed to escape involvement themselves, but they were not successful in keeping Austria from joining the West. The Anglo-French-Austrian alliance of December 2, 1854, derived from a very complicated mixture of motives, yet it is safe to say that once again the purposes of management and control predominated. The British wanted only an alliance that would get Austria into the war (in fact, they would have preferred simply to hire the Austrian army as mercenaries). Since it seemed unlikely that Austria would actually fight, Britain opposed an alliance with Austria, fearing that it might drag the West into an unsatisfactory peace settlement. The only reason, therefore, that the British reluctantly accepted this alliance was in order to retain control over France; if Britain refused to join, France might, on its own, ally with Austria and thus escape British control. France sought the Austrian alliance in order to produce an irreparable breach between Austria and Russia, destroying the old Holy Alliance once and for all. If this happened, then whether or not Austria actually entered the war against Russia, France would be in a controlling position after the war, able to exploit Austro-Russian hostility and play one off against the other. Austria's motives for this alliance were purely those of management. Only by joining with the Western powers could it hope to both control and end the war before it became revolutionary in its extent and effects. Through this alliance, Austria hoped to force Russia to admit defeat, to moderate Western war aims, to bring both sides to the peace table, and to bring about a negotiated settlement that would check Russia in the Near East, guarantee Turkey, and protect Austrian interests.[33]

One more alliance during the Crimean War illustrates how even a clearly offensive alliance can also serve management functions—Sardinia's alliance with Britain and France in January 1855. For the Western powers, this was simply a means of getting a Sardinian contingent to fight on their side in the Crimea (though an Anglo-French rivalry for control and influence in Sardinia quickly arose from this alliance). Sardinia's entrance into this alliance was not really a matter of free choice; Western and domestic pressures, combined with a general fear of what would happen to Sardinia if it did not act, more or less forced Sardinia into it. Insofar as the Sardinian premier Count Cavour chose to join the West, however, his purposes were those of management rather than security. He wanted to counteract the Austro-French alliance, which threatened to reduce Sardinia to political impotence, to insinuate Sardinia into the West's good graces ahead of Austria, and, if possible, to gain Western support for Sardinia's ambitions in Italy during and after the war.[34]

The final alliance that derived from the Crimean War was the pact of April 1856, which allied Britain, France, and Austria against Russia in defense of Turkey and the recently concluded Peace of Paris. This was clearly an instrument of power and mutual security, yet of the three allies, only Austria took it very seriously in this regard, and the Austrians did so mainly because they had long-range management purposes in mind. Austria's foreign minister, Count Buol, calculated that an alliance guaranteeing Turkey against Russia would compel Britain and France to give general support to Austria, for only with Austrian aid could they protect Turkey. With British and French backing, Austria could afford to brave Russia's and Prussia's anger over Austria's recent policy, and could manage the Italian, German, and Near Eastern problems. As it turned out, this alliance did little for Turkey and nothing at all for Austria.[35]

The Italian crises and wars of 1858–1861, which united Italy, showed again how varied alliance purposes can be. The Franco-Sardinian alliance of January 1859—ostensibly a defensive alignment—really formed part of an elaborate plan concocted by Cavour and Napoleon III in July 1858 to provoke war with Austria and expel Austria from Italy. The coconspirators, however, had quite separate and divergent plans for Italy, each intending to use and control the other. When their plot against Austria began to break down, menacing France with a wider war than Napoleon had bargained for, the emperor used his superior power in the alliance to restrain Cavour and even to force him to postpone or abandon the plan. Only Austria's imprudent ultimatum to Sardinia

239

in April 1859, which touched off the war, kept this basically aggressive alliance from working out to be a pact of restraint, against the wishes of both allies.[36]

The Anglo-French partnership over Italy, which was formed after the Whigs returned to power in mid-1859, was another example of an informal alliance that was formed for control rather than capability-aggregation. Though the British were pro-Italian and anti-Austrian, the main reason the government insisted upon joining with France in support of Sardinia was to control France and thus prevent Napoleon from making territorial gains or acquiring a dominant influence in Italy. In January 1860 Palmerston, now prime minister, and John Russell, the foreign secretary, proposed a formal alliance with France and Sardinia for a final settlement of the Italian question. The three powers would impose terms on Austria (which had just lost half its Italian territory in the 1859 war), and Britain could keep France from taking anything for itself. In other words, in order to curb a dangerous aggressor, avert a threat to the balance of power, and manage an international problem, Palmerston proposed allying *with* the aggressor states against their weakened and vulnerable opponent.[37] The cabinet rejected the proposal out of the usual British aversion to commitments, and soon Napoleon's annexation of Nice and Savoy turned Palmerston violently against France, leading him in turn to seek an Austrian and Prussian alliance against France. Nonetheless, joining with France in order to control France remained a common, almost a standard, British policy, which was followed in connection with France's intervention in Syria in 1861, and even more in regard to the Polish Revolution of 1863. The main reason that Britain did not try harder for joint action with France in 1863/1864 to save Denmark from Prussia and Austria was the British conviction that in this instance France was too likely to escape British control. It was safer to let Prussia aggrandize itself at the expense of Denmark than to risk French aggrandizement on the Rhine.[38]

Although Bismarck's alliances from 1863 to 1870 are mainly examples of capability-aggregation for purposes of expansion, he also devoted much attention and skill to managing his allies. It was not military or security needs that led him to draw Austria into alliance in 1863 against Denmark. The Prussian army was perfectly capable of dealing by itself with both the forces of the German Confederation and the Danish army in Schleswig-Holstein, and Bismarck seems to have had no real fear of foreign intervention. His main reason for drawing in Austria was to commit and compromise the empire, thus ruining its reputation with the Western powers (especially Britain), with the German nationalists, and with the smaller German states, and entangling Austria in a complicated question over which Bismarck might later pick a quarrel with that country. Bismarck's Austrian counterpart, Count Rechberg, also desired control and management. Joint intervention, he hoped, would pin Prussia down to a conservative settlement of the Schleswig-Holstein issue and might serve to restore the old Holy Alliance partnership in Germany. Bismarck easily won the contest for control in this alliance.[39]

The alliance that Bismarck concluded with Italy in April 1866 is an exception to the general rule. It was a purely offensive device, with no other purpose than to wage a joint war on Austria. But this fact also accounts for other unusual aspects of the alliance. Although Italy was eager for war against Austria, the alliance took months to negotiate, because Italy feared betrayal and would not sign until it was reasonably sure that Prussia would actually fight. For the same reasons, Italy agreed to an alliance of only three months' duration, and the alliance lasted even less than that, with Bismarck letting Italy fend for itself once Prussia had defeated Austria.[40] The alliances that Prussia concluded, immediately after this victory, with the South German states of Bavaria, Württemberg, and Baden displayed the more normal mixture of motives. These states gained security, especially against France, while Bismarck sought and gained, mainly, management and control. He expected that these alliances, combined with the German nationalist movement and the economic union of North and South Germany in the Zollverein, would serve to unite these states eventually with the new Prussian-led North German Confederation. For the present the alliances would keep South Germany from gravitating into France's or Austria's orbit, or from forming an independent South German Confederation.[41] The alliances, despite powerful opposition in South Germany to union with Prussia, helped in 1870/1871 to bring these states both into the war against France and into a new German Reich.[42]

In contrast to the shifting and volatile pattern of European alliance politics from 1848 to 1871, the European system and its alliances appear to have been stable during the Bismarckian era, 1871–1890. This stability can be seen equally well as genuine or as deceptive. That is, some scholars have credited the alliances with preserving peace, maintaining a balance of power, and giving Europe a long period of relative calm; but others have interpreted the alliances as both a product and a cause of repeated crises and growing antagonisms in Europe and as the beginning of its division into armed camps.

Both views are partly true. To oversimplify a complicated point: Bismarck's alliances were genuine efforts to give Germany security and to make Europe stable and peaceful, aims that Bismarck recognized to be inseparable. His alliances were therefore both weapons of security and instruments of management. Bismarck was particularly skillful in the latter function, checking opponents, controlling allies, associating antagonistic powers with Germany and thereby with each other, diverting ambitions away from Europe, restraining conflicts within it, and generally managing the system. It is difficult to believe that any other devices would have worked as well as his did; it is still harder to believe, as some scholars suggest, that in the absence of Bismarck's intrigues and domineering management, the European powers would naturally have settled down to peaceful coexistence without serious crises or tensions.

But at the same time, Germany's recent record of aggression and lawlessness, its central geographic location, its unstable, half-hegemonic power position in Europe, and its meteoric rise to that position—all caused strains and fears throughout Europe and raised the constant danger of a hostile coalition against Germany. These fears and strains, added to the normal conflicts and crises of European politics, forced Bismarck into increasingly complex alliance combinations and into expedients that, over the long run, tended to promote tensions and antagonisms rather than to allay them. In short, Bismarck, through his alliances, skillfully managed the European system for peace; but that system was probably unmanageable in the long run, and Bismarck's creation of a powerful Prussia-Germany was partly (though only partly) responsible for this condition of inherent unmanageability.

This interpretation applies well to Germany's first and most basic alliance, the Dual Alliance of 1879 with Austria-Hungary. Capability-aggregation for security undoubtedly was one reason for this alliance, especially for Austria, which gained security against Russia and could hope to attach Germany to Austrian policy in the Balkans. Bismarck, too, had some security concerns, chiefly over the hostility toward Germany that Russia had displayed in 1878/1879 (though plainly Bismarck exaggerated this hostility and even provoked it somewhat in order to sell an Austrian alliance to the pro-Russian Emperor William I). Security considerations were also involved in his desire to tie Austria down, which would prevent Austria from ever joining a coalition against Germany and thus help to keep France isolated. Moreover, geographical and military considerations made this alliance a virtual necessity for both powers. The German-Austrian frontier was so long and exposed that they would either have to be allies or else enemies, constantly armed against each other.[43]

All the same, Bismarck mainly wanted and used this alliance for management and control, of Austria first of all. Bismarck's maxim that every alliance must have one horse and one rider, and that Germany must be the rider, here came into play. He wanted to manage, not only Austria's foreign policy, but even Austria's internal policy and constitution. Austria-Hungary must remain the Dual Monarchy, run by Germans and Magyars, with no experiments in Slav-dominated federalism that would make her an unsafe ally or an incalculable factor in Europe. The reasons for Bismarck's letting Germany assume an unequal share of the burdens of the alliance and for his trying in vain to make the alliance public and permanent under parliamentary sanction were to make any independent policy by Austria more difficult.[44]

The Dual Alliance, moreover, immediately became a tool for managing a power that was even more important to Germany than Austria—namely, Russia. The Eastern crisis of 1875–1878, which had wrecked the revived Holy Alliance of 1872/1873 and had brought Austria and Russia close to war, had presented Bismarck with a dread alternative: either a break with Russia, leaving Russia free to ally with France, or a dangerous, one-sided German alliance with Russia, which would involve the eventual sacrifice of Austria-Hungary, with all the revolutionary consequences that its demise would have, and which would draw the hostility of Britain upon Germany. The Dual Alliance was Bismarck's means of avoiding this impossible choice. By allying with Austria, encouraging an Anglo-French entente, and harassing Russia diplomatically and in the press, Bismarck forced Russia to seek a return to a Holy Alliance relationship as Russia's only escape from isolation. The Dual Alliance also enabled Bismarck to compel Austria to accept a revival of the Three Emperors Alliance with Russia in 1881, and to recognize Russia's interests in the eastern Balkans. In short, Bismarck forced Austria and Russia once again to become allies, because otherwise they were likely to go to war. (Conceivably, though less probably, they might also have worked out their differences and become partners without Germany—which would have represented another kind of danger for Bismarck.) The Dual Alliance thus served directly as a pact of restraint upon Austria; it also became a step toward a wider pact of restraint that would include Russia, with Germany as the manager.[45]

Bismarck's ancillary alliances with Italy (the Triple Alliance, 1882), Rumania (1883), and Serbia (through an Austro-Serb treaty of 1881) fit the same pattern. Security counted most for these states (security for the ruling dynasty from internal dangers as much as state security against foreign threats). Control counted most for Germany. Bismarck never counted on much Italian help in case of war with France; he once remarked that he would be satisfied if one Italian corporal and one drummer boy appeared on the French frontier in response to the *casus foederis*. The Triple Alliance served mainly to control Franco-Italian rivalry, which at this time was acute over Tunisia, and even more to manage the more deep-rooted rivalry of Italy and Austria, which was still more dangerous for Germany. This was why Bismarck insisted upon the Triple Alliance, compelling Italy to pass through Vienna on the way to Berlin. The Austro-Italian alliance from 1882 to 1914 not only worked as a pact of restraint on both sides; it is also the clearest instance of two enemies becoming allies mainly in order to avoid going to war with each other.[46]

Although Bismarck's alliances were the most obvious *pacta de contrahendo* of this period, they were not the only ones. The unwritten "liberal alliance" between France and Britain over Egypt (1876–1882), like the other Anglo-French ententes, was a partnership for mutual restraint and control, especially for Britain. When the Egyptian government began to break down through bankruptcy, the British did not wish to monopolize Egypt; they could not renounce it because of the Suez Canal; therefore, they chose to share with France in dual control. The Egyptian story unfortunately illustrates what may happen when a partnership of mutual restraint breaks down and one partner emerges with the prize. When, through fortuitous events, Britain became sole occupier of Egypt in 1882, this set off a colonial and world rivalry between the erstwhile partners that lasted two decades and brought them close to war more than once, despite repeated sincere attempts on both sides to get back to the "liberal alliance."[47]

The complicated alliance and quasi-alliance arrangements of Bismarck's last years in power illustrate the primacy of control and management in his system, as well as the increasing complexity and fragility of the means that he had to devise for it. He relied more heavily than ever on managing balanced antagonisms in order to preserve peace, even promoting them (e.g., encouraging Russian policy in the Near East by the Reinsurance Treaty of 1887, while he also encouraged Britain, Austria, and Italy to conclude the Mediterranean Agreements to oppose Russia). But these tactics need not be interpreted either as good, skillful balance-of-power politics or as dangerous and deceptive intrigues. They simply indicate that Bismarck's policy of using alliances for control and management was breaking down, forcing him to think of alliances mainly for security. For years he had struggled to avoid choosing between Britain and Russia. But in early 1889 he sought in vain a defensive alliance with Britain, and before his fall in March 1890 he was evidently maneuvering in a complicated and secretive fashion toward a simultaneous coup d'état within Germany and a closer tie with Russia, possibly sacrificing his alliance with Austria. These were desperate expedients; a direct alliance of Germany with either Britain or Russia would have imposed the chief burden of the alliance on Germany and given the other partner more control. The fact that Bismarck not only contemplated these moves but actually began to try them indicates the impending breakdown of his system.[48]

Bismarck was so ingenious, however, that one cannot be certain that he could not have managed Germany's alliance problems at least for a while longer. They quickly proved unmanageable for his successors, and the transformation of European alliances from instruments of management into weapons of security and power proceeded apace. The Franco-Russian alliance that Bismarck had struggled to prevent arose in the period 1891 to 1894 as a defensive treaty directed against the Dual Alliance and tied to its existence. Neither Russia nor France originally had aggressive purposes in the alliance; from a balance-of-power standpoint it was a normal, healthy development. But unlike the Dual Alliance, it was intended only for mutual security, not for the management either of the allies' policies or of general European questions. Equally unlike the Dual Alliance, it contained a military convention and a *casus foederis*, which was supposed to apply automatically in case of an attack or mobilization by Germany or Austria.

Nonetheless, even this alliance worked to some extent as a pact of restraint. Russia made clear that it would not support France in a war of revenge for Alsace-Lorraine; France declined to support Russia against Britain in the Near East or the Far East. Thus the alliance served in practice to keep both partners from adventures in Europe, while freeing them for their individual imperial ambitions in Africa and Asia, which were directed much more against Britain than Germany.[49] In 1899, however, the *casus foederis* was changed to apply, not only to an Austro-German attack or mobilization, but also to any threat to the European balance of power. The French foreign minister, Delcassé, who sponsored the change, expected Austria-Hungary to break up soon, and he wished to use the alliance to keep Germany away from the Adriatic Sea and, if possible, to recover Alsace-Lorraine by diplomacy in the ensuing shuffle. The alliance might thus have been turned more to purposes of general management and control. But actually, Delcassé's basic purpose was to strengthen the alliance as an instrument of French power and security, thus altering the existing balance of power. He hoped to bring Britain gradually into the alliance, to wean Italy away from the Triple Alliance, and to open the way, by the isolation of Germany, to a reversal of 1871—all by peaceful means if possible.[50]

Meanwhile the Triple and the Dual alliances tended to become weaker both as security instruments and as tools of control. Sensing Germany's loss of leadership in the European system, Italy began to demand more support from its own allies for its colonial policy as the price for adhering to the alliance, and at the same time Italy began to loosen its alliance ties. By 1902 it had become clear that Italy would not fight on the side of its allies in a general war. In a paradoxical way, Italy's infidelity made the Triple Alliance even more a *pactum de contrahendo*. The British before 1914 vetoed all proposals for making Italy switch alliances, arguing that Italy's presence in the Triple Alliance served only to restrain Germany, while it constituted no threat to Germany's opponents.

After Bismarck's fall, Germany's turn to world policy led Germany to try to use its alliances more for purposes of extra-European gains, thereby weakening the Dual Alliance as a pact of restraint and as a tool for managing European problems. But there was a countervailing trend that derived from Austria-Hungary's eagerness to avoid war in order to have some chance of solving her critical domestic problems. In order to hold Germany back, Austrian statesmen strove for independence from German control within the alliance; they also dissociated themselves from German *Weltpolitik* and tried to discourage it, especially where it involved such challenges to Britain as the German navy; and in particular, they sought and gained a measure of entente with Russia. Thus the same weakness, vulnerability, and unsolved domestic and foreign problems that, in 1914, finally drove Austria completely into Germany's arms and promoted their joint plunge into war made Austria one of the most important forces for peace, one of the most important bridges between alliances, and one of the most important restraints on Germany during an earlier period, especially from about 1895 to 1907. Austro-Russian cooperation in the agreements of 1897 and 1903 put the most dangerous area in Europe—namely, the Balkans—on ice. An Austro-Russian treaty of neutrality in 1904 gave Russia invaluable security in her rear during the Russo-Japanese War and the abortive revolution of 1905. During the first Moroccan crisis of 1905/1906, Austria tried to restrain Germany, ultimately contributing significantly to a peaceful outcome. All this proves that under certain circumstances even a weaker power can exercise some control and influence over a stronger partner within an alliance.[51]

With the Anglo-Japanese Alliance of 1902, Britain left her "splendid isolation" and entered the alliance system. Her alliances and ententes also served primarily to manage problems—not, however, those of running the European system or of preserving general peace, but those of meeting new challenges to the British Empire. Japan's basic purpose in the initial limited alliance of 1902 was capability-aggregation: if Japan went to war with Russia over the Manchurian-Korean issues, Britain would at least keep France neutral. Britain's alliance goal was to save its Far Eastern commercial, naval, and imperial position—which was threatened by Russia and secondarily by Germany—by devolving some of the burden on Japan. The British had already tried several expedients without success—an Open Door policy, together with the United States; proposals to Russia for a direct understanding; cooperation with Germany. Now the British hoped that Japan would constrain Russia and that the alliance might even make Russia amenable to a direct agreement with Britain.[52]

As it turned out, it required a Russo-Japanese War in 1904/1905, which the British did not desire, and a Russian defeat and revolution, which they did not expect, to bring Britain an unexpected harvest. In 1905 Britain expanded its pact with Japan into a direct defensive alliance protecting India. This wider alliance helped to make Russia, whose government now needed Western financial support in order to survive, amenable to the direct understanding that Britain had sought for a decade. In 1907 the two powers concluded a convention dividing their spheres of influence in Persia and central Asia. Both this agreement and the Japanese alliance served Britain as pacts of restraint. The British consciously used the alliance for the purpose of restraining Japanese commercial and naval competition in East Asia, which was now the most formidable for British interests. As for Persia, by conceding Russia a sphere in the north, Britain protected her exclusive control of the Persian Gulf, curbed Russian penetration of central Persia and Afghanistan, and gained some Russian help in dealing with Germany over the Bagdad Railway. In addition, this entente enabled the British consciously to divert Russia's attention and ambitions toward the Balkans, where Russia would collide with Germany and Austria, rather than with Britain.[53]

The same motive of managing the problems of the British Empire accounts, on Britain's side, for the Entente Cordiale—the Anglo-French agreement of 1904 over Morocco and Egypt which eventually by 1914 had developed into a quasi alliance. While the French, especially Delcassé, had a long-range aim in mind—that of lining Britain up with France and Russia against Germany—the British foreign secretary, Lord Lansdowne, saw the entente as a simple colonial deal exchanging French concessions in Egypt for British cooperation in Morocco.[54] The common view that the main reason for Britain's ending her rivalries with France and Russia and forming ententes with them was to meet Germany's naval challenge and to save the European balance of power is at least very one-sided.[55] This may have been what the British ended up doing, or believed they were doing; it was hardly what they set out to do. As with Lansdowne, the goal of his Liberal successor Lord Grey in strengthening the entente with France and in reaching the 1907 agreement with Russia was to protect Britain's world position by supplanting overseas rivalries with cooperation and partnership, just as Britain had earlier done with the United States. The British knew about Germany's naval program in 1904, of course, but they did not need this entente to meet the challenge. Although eventually the German naval menace came to seem formidable, Germany initially became Britain's main naval rival more through the decline or disappearance of other rivals than through Germany's own efforts.

As for the possibility of German hegemony on the Continent, this certainly worried the British, who never ceased reiterating before 1914 that the existing line-up of powers had to be preserved in order to maintain peace and the balance of power. But the great danger that Britain sought to avert by upholding her friendships with France and Russia was not a Continental war in which Germany would defeat them and emerge predominant. Britain's ententes with France and Russia were not designed to meet this danger; Britain steadily refused to expand them into alliances, and never expected, even if it went to war with Germany alongside France and Russia, to send large land forces to fight at their side. The real danger against which the ententes protected Britain was Franco-German or Russo-German *friendship*—the chance that Germany might break up the Franco-Russian alliance or the Entente Cordiale, that Germany might win Russia over, or that Germany might insinuate itself into the Franco-Russian alliance, thus isolating Britain and exposing her empire anew to French, Russian, and German pressure.[56] This prospect most frightened the British before 1914 and mainly determined Britain's policy in all the prewar crises. Britain used and valued its ententes, not as weapons of power for maintaining the European balance, but as tools for managing imperial problems. They came to have a vital impact on the European system, not simply because Germany tried unsuccessfully to break them up, or because France and Russia tried constantly to exploit them in European power politics, but also because the British themselves, in order to preserve their friendships, sought to maintain a certain salutary rivalry between the Continental blocs. There is nothing intrinsically wrong with such a policy. Britain's resort to balanced antagonisms in 1908/1909 or from 1912 to 1914 was no more reprehensible per se than Bismarck's policy of balanced antagonisms in the periods 1879 to 1881 and 1885 to 1887. The difference is that Bismarck saw that the antagonisms had to be managed if they were to remain balanced, and he therefore undertook to manage them. The British insisted that this was not their problem. In that failure of insight and action lies a certain British responsibility (but their only one) for what happened in 1914.[57]

The final alliance system that was erected before 1914 was the Balkan League of Bulgaria, Serbia, and Greece, which was promoted by Russia in 1912. For the Balkan states, this was strictly an offensive alliance for conquest of Turkish territory and for security from Austrian intervention. Like many alliances for aggrandizement, it held together well in war, and then fell apart over the division of the spoils. But St. Petersburg had promoted this alliance for different purposes—uniting the Balkan states under Russian control, excluding Austria, and managing Balkan affairs to Russia's own advantage. Russian hopes of using this Balkan alliance as a pact of restraint and management were entirely unrealistic, as Russia's friends saw immediately. Even with help from other great powers, Russia could not hold its clients back from war against Turkey in November 1912, and Russia proved equally unsuccessful in trying to settle the Bulgarian-Serbian dispute after the first Balkan War. It was really only Russia's good luck that its bungling attempt to manage Balkan affairs through this alliance ended in a political defeat for rival Austria-Hungary rather than in embarrassment and danger for Russia itself.[58]

The role played by alliances in the origins of World War I has been examined repeatedly, with the verdict often being that the excessive rigidity of the alliance system was an important factor. Had the powers not been bound together in rigid alliances, it is charged, a quarrel between one great power and its small, troublesome neighbor would never have led to war among five great powers. This argument about the excessive rigidity of the alliances needs modification at least. Britain was not rigidly committed to France in 1914 and was not committed at all to Russia. In 1912/1913, Germany was not committed to Austria's Balkan policy, and held Austria back from war against Serbia. Italy was basically uncommitted, despite the Triple Alliance; Rumania had just escaped into neutrality from her alliance with the Central Powers; Balkan alignments were still fluid. One could more easily argue that too much fluidity in alliances, rather than excessive rigidity, helped to bring on the war by raising dangerous fears and hopes in the different camps. Austria was frightened at losing Rumania as an ally and at facing a new Balkan League, whereas France and Russia were encouraged to cap their triumph by creating such a league. Germany feared that Britain might openly ally with France and Russia; yet Germany also hoped that Britain might remain neutral in a Continental war. Germany was afraid that its ally Austria-Hungary might either break up internally or turn to neutrality. Austrian and German leaders hoped that Russia, out of monarchical sentiment, would not actually support Serbia if Austria punished it for the assassination of Archduke Francis Ferdinand.

A more valid connection between alliance developments and the origins of the war lay in the long-term changes that were developing in alliance purposes and functions. The functions of management and restraint had not yet disappeared (Austria and Italy in 1914 were still giving a classic exhibition of allies that were locked in mutual support and rivalry, especially in Albania), but they had receded far into the background. By then, allies usually did not dare to try to control their partners, for fear of undermining the alliances as indispensable weapons of security. Only if this is what is meant by the increasing rigidity of alliances is the charge correct. In 1909 the Austrian general staff (though not the Austrian government) accepted the German Schlieffen Plan, with all its disastrous political implications, in order to commit Germany to support Austria against Russia. In 1912 France stopped trying to hold Russia back in the Balkans and began urging Russia forward instead. Britain did not encourage her friends into forward moves; but neither dared she alienate Russia by trying to restrain her. Most decisive of all, Germany stopped holding Austria back in early 1914, and actually pushed her forward in July. Finally, Austria gave up trying to save herself by staying out of Germany's quarrels and by refusing to join in a struggle for the supremacy of Teuton over Slav. Instead, she decided, in desperation, to gamble her existence on an all-out alliance with Germany and on a joint political and military move to restore her tottering position by a resort to violence.

The story of alliances during World War I is too complicated to allow more than a brief summary here. As one would expect, short-range capability-aggregation for purposes of military victory almost always won out over long-term political management. Yet, even in the furnace of battle, statesmen still paid some attention to how they could manage political problems and to how they could control their allies during the war and after it. Austria negotiated stubbornly with Germany over the fate of conquered Poland and other Eastern territories, mainly in the hope of remaining a great power independent of Germany after the war. Austria and Germany, as rival partners, both tried to control the policy and strategy of their ally Turkey, but they failed.[59] Russia concocted her war aims in Europe not so much for security against a future German threat (this she expected to eliminate) as against a future Anglo-French challenge. Britain and France agreed to Russia's aims in the straits and in the Near East only after assuring themselves of new gains in that area—new positions of strength from which they could confront each other and Russia and from which they could cooperate with each other after the war.[60] Anglo-French relations in the Near East during and after the war represent a long story of rivals in alliance who were working to restrain and use each other.[61] The United States, once it was in the war, tried to control the war aims of its associates.

Postwar alliances continued this pattern. For France, the Anglo-French unwritten alliance in Europe was mainly a means of security against Germany; but Britain used it, as she had used the "liberal alliance" of the nineteenth century, for control, for limiting the alliance to Western Europe, for curbing France's supposed desire for European hegemony, and for trying to keep France from treating Germany too harshly. Britain's policy during the French occupation of the Ruhr, as well as Britain's promotion of the Locarno treaties, clearly illustrates this tendency.[62]

In a similar way, French alliances with Poland and Czechoslovakia combined France's search for security with its desire to manage Polish and Czech policy in the supposed common interest. While hoping to tie Poland and Czechoslovakia tightly to France, the French hoped to remain free in order to promote some sort of Danubian confederation, which would include Hungary and Austria, to strengthen the cordon sanitaire against Germany and Russia. The scheme suited neither Poland nor Czechoslovakia, and Czech foreign minister Eduard Benes countered it with his own alliances with other anti-Hungarian states, namely, Rumania and Yugoslavia (the Little Entente). As for Poland, it was far too independent and ambitious to be controlled by France— witness its quarrels with Czechoslovakia, the Polish offensive against Soviet Russia in May 1920, or the nonaggression treaty with Nazi Germany in 1934.[63]

The alliance network that France, Czechoslovakia, and the Soviet Union erected in 1935/1936 was purely a security weapon against Germany; no other motive could have brought these three states together. Yet the very absence of intra-alliance control and management proved important in this alliance system. Many of its weaknesses were obvious even before it broke down in 1938: the geographical obstacles hindering the stronger powers, especially Russia, from effectively aiding Czechoslovakia, the weakest and most exposed partner; the lack of military conventions or agreements; France's defensive strategy; and internal opposition to the alliance, as well as mutual distrust on all sides. But a major weakness that has gone largely unremarked was the fact that none of these allies could exercise effective influence over its partners on policies that decisively affected the alliance. Both France and the U.S.S.R. tried repeatedly and unsuccessfully to push the other one forward against Germany. France could do nothing to stop Russia from drastically weakening her army in the Great Purge of 1936 to 1938. Russia and Czechoslovakia could not change France's military strategy. Neither great power could help Czechoslovakia meet her minorities problems, especially the Sudeten German one, which threatened to cripple her in a crisis. The allies could not achieve a common policy even on so elementally important a question as how to react to a German Anschluss with Austria.[64]

As for the Anglo-French alliance from 1935 to 1938, the point relevant to our theme is that Britain's appeasement policy toward Germany was in the last analysis an attempt to use this alliance for control and management in the interests of peace, rather than for power and military security.[65] Knowing France's dependence on Britain and France's willingness to have Britain take the lead, British statesmen, especially Chamberlain, tried to solve the Czech crisis and to avert war with Germany by leading their ally France into an agreement and into a wider partnership with the very powers against whom Britain and France were allied—namely, Germany and, to a lesser extent, Italy. Chamberlain hoped to render peace secure, once the Czech-German crisis had been settled at Munich through four-power agreement, by supplementing the Anglo-French alliance with an informal Anglo-German partnership and Anglo-Italian friendship. It is not too fanciful to see this as an attempt to widen a particular alliance into a general European concert (excluding the Soviet Union, to be sure) like that of the nineteenth century. Unfortunately, Hitler was not Alexander I, and Chamberlain was not Castlereagh or Metternich.[66]

After the German occupation of Prague in March 1939 made this form of appeasement impossible, the Western allies turned to security and capability-aggregation against Germany as their prime goal. The German threat now led Britain to extend its commitments in unprecedented fashion—to guarantee the independence of Poland, Rumania, and Greece and to seek an alliance with the Soviet Union. Yet even in these frantic alliance efforts the British still were trying to manage the international problem and to control their allies. A major reason for giving a guarantee to Warsaw was to get Poland to defend Rumania, which the British considered to be more threatened initially than

251

Poland and which they could not protect. Moreover, the Anglo-French alliance with Poland was not really intended to stop Hitler and to preserve the status quo of 1939 at any cost (Poland's independence was guaranteed, but not her existing borders), but to create conditions under which Germany and Poland might reach a negotiated settlement, with Poland making some concessions. Germany's domination of east-central Europe was not supposed to be ended or prevented, but controlled, kept within bounds that were compatible with British and French honor. Germany might still make gains, but not by any more brutal surprises like the takeover of rump Czechoslovakia in March.[67]

The matter of intra-alliance control and management, moreover, helps to explain why no Western-Soviet alliance was formed. One reason, though not the most important one, that neither side tried as hard for an alliance as they might have is that both sides knew that they could not control their partners' actions under the alliance. The Western powers not only had to worry about what the U.S.S.R. would do once it intervened to aid Poland and the Baltic states; they also could not be sure how long and hard the Soviet Union would fight and whether, having got the Western powers involved, it might not make a separate peace with the Germans. The Soviet Union naturally had a similar distrust of the West, especially after Munich; and no assurances or control devices could have removed the distrust on either side. This bolsters the view that a genuine Soviet-Western united front against Germany was never a real possibility in 1939.[68]

Hitler's alliances were mainly intended for capability-aggregation, though he usually ended up exercising a brutal control over those who sided with him. (Franco, an exception, was careful to avoid any real alliance with Hitler.) The Italo-German alliance of May 1939 (the "Pact of Steel") was an overtly offensive treaty in which Mussolini frivolously and fatalistically threw Italy into Germany's arms. Yet even Mussolini attempted to some extent to hold Hitler back through this alliance in August 1939, as he had done earlier, in September 1938. Moreover, Mussolini's determination to keep Italy a great power in the alliance rather than a satellite explains much of Italian policy—the unnecessary seizure of Albania, the attack on France in June 1940, and the disastrous invasion of Greece in October 1940, which ended by reducing Italy to satellite status.[69]

The Axis Alliance that linked Japan to Germany and Italy in September 1940 was, to an even greater degree than the Pact of Steel, exclusively an alliance for capability-aggregation and gain. Ideological ties and sympathies were much less important here than they were between Hitler and Mussolini; Germany and Italy at least had geographical propinquity and some mutual interests, while Germany and Japan had little to offer each other except mutual permission for each to expand at the expense of the other nations. The one area where the two powers might have cooperated, against the Soviet Union, was where political and military coordination was most strikingly absent. There was then hardly any cooperation, management, or control within the Axis Alliance—not much besides cross-purposes, betrayals, and attempts to exploit one's partner. But this explains in good part why the alliance failed so completely both diplomatically and militarily.[70]

The Grand Alliance among Britain, the U.S.A., and the U.S.S.R. in World War II also served primarily as an instrument of power. Victory being the overriding goal of each power, military considerations dominated alliance politics, at least until late in the war. Even questions of great long-range political significance—such as the time and location of a second front, or how much aid to give to which resistance movements, or whether the Western allies should try to land in southeast Europe—were decided mainly on immediate military grounds. The chief strains and problems in the alliance concerned military issues—the delay in the second front, fears of a Soviet separate peace with Germany, the question of Soviet participation in the war against Japan.[71]

Yet long-range concerns over the control and management of problems and allies were always present and active. The vital question for Britain was that of remaining a great power and defending her interests in the company of giants like the U.S.A. and the U.S.S.R., particularly after another world war had drained her resources and undermined her empire. Her only hope was successfully to manage the United States, which involved a number of tasks—such as preserving a special Anglo-American partnership and preventing a Soviet-American one at Britain's expense; securing American long-term military and economic help; curbing the anti-imperialist, anti-British tendencies in American policy; and preserving British economic interests against American encroachment. Rather late in the war, the desire to preserve some sort of balance in Europe by managing the Soviet Union and checking Soviet expansion also became important. Churchill's proposal to Stalin in October 1944 that the Balkans be divided into spheres of influence may be seen as a not very skillful effort to manage a rival within an alliance.[72]

Stalin, although he profoundly distrusted the West, doubtless wanted to maintain the wartime alliance after victory, both for security reasons and in order to get the economic aid that his devastated country needed. But precisely because Stalin preferred that the alliance continue, he was determined to establish positions of strength such that Soviet relations with the West could be based on old-fashioned realpolitik, on principles of *do ut des* and nothing for nothing, with each power free to act as it wished in its own sphere. Stalin, in other words, was determined not to be managed or influenced by the West in this alliance, especially in any way that might affect his power or style of rule in Russia. The Soviet Union had to be given security not so much through the alliance as *against* the alliance; the security Stalin needed was not so much external and military as internal and ideological. This required, along with great new purges and repressive measures within Russia, the establishment of friendly, democratic governments in east-central Europe, as Stalin understood those terms. The Sovietization of east-central and southeastern Europe was neither a case of revolutionary Soviet expansionism, as the orthodox American view used to have it, nor mainly a Soviet response to an American challenge in Russia's sphere, as American revisionist critics contend. It was basically a logical and indispensable requirement for Soviet security as Stalin defined it— the sealing off of Russia from any subversive influences that might undermine his regime. Theoretically speaking, the Western powers could have preserved the wartime alliance with the U.S.S.R., had they resolved from the outset to accept without challenge whatever the Soviet Union did at home or to its neighbors. Stalin would have doubtless given America and Britain the equal freedom to run their countries and control their satellites as they saw fit. But this was incompatible with any conception of a postwar alliance that was entertained in the West, and indeed it was incompatible with any durable alliance relationship at all.[73]

As for the United States, without even trying to summarize the wide-ranging controversy over American policy in the alliance, one can say that it was riddled with contradictions and paradoxes, most of all precisely on whether the Grand Alliance was to be used as a military instrument or as a tool for long-range management and control. On the one hand, the U.S.A., even more than the other two great powers, fought the war simply for total victory. Although less threatened by invasion than either the U.S.S.R. or Britain, the United States was, if anything, even more determined than they to end German and Japanese militarism forever through total victory occupation, drastic control, and sweeping remodeling of their societies. Hence no power was more inclined than the United States to see the Grand Alliance as a military instrument for total victory, to sacrifice or subordinate political to military considerations, and to put off decisions that might jeopardize the military effectiveness of the alliance.

At the same time, no great power fought the war for more grandiose (if inconsistent and confused) aims and ideals for the postwar world. It seems impossible to make a consistent program out of these, either as a liberal democratic program for lasting peace and cooperation or as a sinister imperialist plan to make the world safe for American capitalism.[74] There is no way to harmonize Roosevelt's idea of Four Policemen (policing the world for peace and dividing it into spheres of great-power control) with other American ideas about national liberation, disimperialism, and international control of vital areas, or to harmonize these, in turn, with notions of world peace through capitalist-based economic recovery and development via the Open Door policy. But the point is not whether American ideals were consistent or inconsistent, sensible or unrealistic, noble or sinister. The point is that whether American leaders liked it or not, any hope of achieving such sweeping aims required not merely the total defeat of the enemy but also (among other things), first and foremost, a massive effort by the United States to manage and control its great-power allies while the war was still going on. The United States therefore followed the peculiar policy of refusing in principle to use the Grand Alliance for purposes of intra-alliance management, for fear of ruining it as a military instrument, while entertaining war aims that required that it be used for management purposes on a massive scale. Moreover, despite the American preoccupation with total victory, American leaders did begin fairly early to consider using American economic, political, and military power to manage and control their allies; they increasingly attempted to do so, especially after the development of the atomic bomb. Much of what the United States did in the earlier stages of the Cold War, which is usually interpreted either as an effort to check Soviet revolutionary expansionism or as an American attempt to deprive the Soviet Union of its legitimate wartime gains, is better seen as a belated American attempt to manage the Soviet Union and to bring it back to the American conception of the goals of their alliance.

This survey suggests certain conclusions. The first has already often been mentioned. Technically, alliances are mutual security pacts with a *casus foederis*; for various reasons, this technical definition is useful and should be retained. But functionally, alliances serve many diverse purposes and are best considered as general tools for management and control in international affairs.

If this be so, then analyzing and categorizing alliances according to their types or provisions (defensive or offensive, limited or unlimited, consultative or automatic, with or without military conventions, bilateral or multilateral) are not likely to be very fruitful in describing what alliances really do; nor are attempts to establish statistical correlations between the numbers and types of alliances existing at various times and the corresponding levels of international conflict and tension likely to be very fruitful.[75] Nothing can substitute for the painfully empirical task of functional analysis of particular alliances.

Such analysis should look for other motives and purposes besides the standard ones of mutual security and capability-aggregation—in particular, for the desire to control one's ally, the aim of managing an international problem, and even the hope of avoiding conflict by allying oneself with a rival. In any case, the way in which mutual control or influence is exercised is always important for the durability and effectiveness of an alliance.

Some commonly held ideas about alliances may need to be revised or discarded if these points are valid. For instance, alliance flexibility may not be as useful for peace and stability as balance-of-power theorists generally hold; and alliance rigidity per se may not be as productive of confrontation and war. If an alliance functions as a pact of mutual restraint, it may promote peace to have powers locked tightly into it. It also need not be true, as is often supposed, that powers must have generally harmonious aims and outlooks if they are to become allies and then stay together. In the past, fairly durable alliances and partnerships have been formed that were based on little more than the realization that there was no other means available for managing a dangerous problem and that the likely alternative to an alliance was war. One may fervently hope that this principle continues to work—for example, for the U.S.A. and the U.S.S.R. in the Middle East.

There is no magic formula for using alliances as tools of management for the purpose of promoting international peace and stability. Just as the deceptively simple formulas of balance of power and collective security have often proved inapplicable or counterproductive, so, as our survey illustrates, many efforts to use alliances as instruments of management and control have proved futile, foolish, and even disastrous. Moreover, statesmen can just as well employ alliances as management devices to promote war as use them to preserve peace—witness Palmerston during the Crimean War or Bismarck in the 1860s. Nonetheless, one can make a case that the management potential of alliances offers certain hopeful possibilities for durable peace. Traditionally, the quest for a viable principle of international order has oscillated between two poles—the balance of power versus the integration of nations into an international community. So-called realists see the basic, inescapable reality of international politics as the dispersal of power among essentially independent centers of decision with inherently divergent and potentially conflicting interests and purposes, so that the only way to achieve stability and peace is through balance, checking power with countervailing power. "Idealists," seeing this game either as futile and counterproductive per se or else as having become intolerably dangerous in the present state of arms development, look to various processes and devices of international integration—economic interdependence, world organization, international law, federal and regional movements, and so on—to supplant international conflicts with international community.[76] Neither approach seems to be very hopeful. To put it too simply, balance-of-power politics does not seem to be able to create the needed durable restraints and cooperation among nations; indeed it may often undermine them, whereas movements for integration cannot face or overcome the hard reality of conflicting power and purposes.

It may therefore be more hopeful to seek something in the middle, to search for models in associative-antagonistic relationships in nature and society, to look for devices that specifically unite rivals. Alliances and quasi alliances in international relations are precisely such associative-antagonistic relationships. They normally contain large elements of rivalry as well as cooperation, conflict as well as mutuality of purpose. A knowledge of how they work and survive, therefore, might help in the search for a viable principle of international order. Certainly there is plenty of contemporary material for study. The Western alliance system has been riddled with rivalries and conflicts over intra-alliance control and management, not only between France and the U.S.A., but also between France and Germany, Britain and France, and other members. Yet the alliance has survived till now. In the Warsaw Pact, the struggles over how control is exercised, and by whom, have been less obvious (except where they have broken into the open and been settled by brute force) but no less real. One can conceive of the détente between the U.S.A. and the U.S.S.R. some day developing into a rival alliance, a *pactum de contrahendo* covering at least certain areas of the world and designed to keep peace there in a way that is not too different from that in which the Austro-Russian pact of restraint once kept peace in the Balkans. It is not impossible that Russia and China, once close allies and now enemies, could return to being hostile allies. But to speculate thus is to open up themes even vaster than the subject of this essay.

Notes

1. This usage was particularly common among nineteenth-century European statesmen and publicists.
2. Académie Diplomatique Internationale, *Dictionnaire Diplomatique* (7 vols.; Paris, 1933), 1:109–12.
3. Julian R. Friedman, "Alliance in International Politics," in *Alliance in International Politics*, ed. Julian R. Friedman et al. (Boston: Allyn & Bacon, 1970), pp. 10–11.
4. Wladyslaw W. Kulski, *International Politics in a Revolutionary Age* (2d rev. ed.; New York: Lippincott, 1968), p. 115.
5. Werner Levi, *International Politics: Foundations of the System* (Minneapolis: University of Minnesota Press, 1974), p. 164.
6. Hans J. Morgenthau, *Politics among Nations* (3d ed.; New York: Knopf, 1960), p. 181. Many other textbooks and treatises on international relations, too numerous to list here, use this definition of alliances, as do both the old *Encyclopedia of the Social Sciences* and the new *International Encyclopedia of the Social Sciences*. It seems safe to say that it is the reigning definition.
7. See Steven Rosen, "A Model of War and Alliance," in Friedman, *Alliance*, p. 215; and Christopher Bladen, "Alliance and Integration," in Friedman, *Alliance,* pp. 121–22.
8. Bruce M. Russett, "Components of an Operational Theory of International Alliance Formation," in Friedman, *Alliance*, pp. 238–40, 253–55; Ivo D. Duchacek, *Conflict and Cooperation among Nations* (New York: Holt, Rinehart & Winston, 1960), pp. 372–73, 407–33.
9. E.g., K. J. Holsti, *International Politics: A Framework for Analysis* (Englewood

Cliffs, N.J.: Prentice-Hall, 1967), pp. 110–20; Robert E. Osgood and Robert W. Tucker, *Force, Order, and Justice* (Baltimore, Md.: Johns Hopkins Press, 1967), pp. 78–96.

10. E.g., Inis L. Claude, *Power and International Relations* (New York: Random House, 1962), pp. 89, 115–16, 138–49.
11. See, for example, John W. Burton, *International Relations: A General Theory* (Cambridge, Eng.: Cambridge University Press, 1965), and *Systems, States, Diplomacy and Rules* (Cambridge, Eng.: Cambridge University Press, 1968).
12. Raymond Aron, *Peace and War* (Garden City, N.Y.: Doubleday, 1966), makes the point repeatedly. See also James N. Rosenau, *The Scientific Study of Foreign Policy* (New York: Free Press, 1971), pp. 197–237, in which Rosenau argues for "calculated control" as the central theme and analytic concept in foreign policy and (following Harold Sprout) lists eight means of control, ranging from diplomatic intercourse to total war. Alliance, however, is not among them.
13. For a discussion of various contradictory meanings of "balance of power," see Ernst B. Haas, "The Balance of Power: Prescription, Concept, or Propaganda," *World Politics* 5 (1953):442–77. The rules formulated by Morton Kaplan for a balance-of-power system (*System and Process in International Politics* [New York: Wiley, 1957], pp. 22–36, 52–53, 125–27) have been much debated as to their validity and internal consistency. See, for example, Aron, *Peace and War*, pp. 128–32, and Karl W. Deutsch, *The Analysis of International Relations* (Englewood Cliffs, N.J.: Prentice-Hall, 1968), pp. 136–40.
14. William H. Riker, *The Theory of Political Coalitions* (New Haven, Conn.: Yale University Press, 1962), pp. 168–87. For a reply, see Dina A. Zinnes, "Coalition Theories and the Balance of Power," in *The Study of Coalition Behavior*, ed. Sven Groennings et al. (New York: Holt, Rinehart & Winston, 1970), pp. 351–68.
15. E.g., Richard A. Rosecrance, *Action and Reaction in World Politics* (Boston: Little, Brown, 1963), arguing that the Concert of Europe, not a balance of power, stabilized the European system in the nineteenth century.
16. Ole R. Holsti and John D. Sullivan, "National-International Linkages: France and China as Nonconforming Alliance Members," in *Linkage Politics*, ed. James N. Rosenau (New York: Free Press, 1969), pp. 147–95.
17. Richard A. Falk, "Zone II as a World Order Construct," in *The Analysis of International Politics*, ed. James N. Rosenau et al. (New York: Free Press, 1972), pp. 187–206.
18. Robert E. Osgood, *Alliances and American Foreign Policy* (Baltimore, Md.: Johns Hopkins Press, 1968), pp. 22 and 28.
19. George Liska, *Nations in Alliance: The Limits of Interdependence* (Baltimore, Md.: Johns Hopkins Press, 1962), p. 116, italics mine.
20. George Liska, *Imperial America: The International Politics of Primacy* (Baltimore, Md.: Johns Hopkins Press, 1967), pp. 9–11, 20–21.
21. George Liska, *Alliances and the Third World* (Baltimore, Md.: Johns Hopkins Press, 1968), pp. 24–35.
22. Limitations on space prevent any attempt to prove the case here, of course, and require me to omit many nuances and qualifications that should be included. The notes that follow are more suggestions for further reading than citations of the evidence on which this interpretation rests.
23. Edward V. Gulick, *Europe's Classical Balance of Power* (Ithaca, N.Y.: Cornell University Press for the American Historical Association, 1955); Charles K. Webster, *The Foreign Policy of Castlereagh, 1815–1822* (2 vols.; London: G. Bell, 1934).

24. Maurice Bourquin, *Histoire de la Sainte Alliance* (Geneva: Georg, 1954); Paul W. Schroeder, *Metternich's Diplomacy at Its Zenith, 1820–1823* (Austin: University of Texas Press, 1962).
25. Enno E. Kraehe, *Metternich's German Policy,* vol. 1 (Princeton, N.J.: Princeton University Press, 1963); Heinrich von Srbik, *Metternich, der Staatsmann und der Mensch* (3 vols.; Munich: F. Bruckmann, 1925–1954).
26. Harold W. V. Temperley, *The Foreign Policy of Canning, 1822–1827* (London: G. Bell, 1925); Charles W. Crawley, *The Question of Greek Independence* (Cambridge, Eng.: Cambridge University Press, 1930); Douglas Dakin, *The Greek Struggle for Independence, 1821–1833* (Berkeley: University of California Press, 1973).
27. Charles K. Webster, *The Foreign Policy of Palmerston, 1830–1841* (2 vols.; London: G. Bell, 1951); Charles K. Webster, "Palmerston, Metternich, and the European System 1830–1841," *Proceedings of the British Academy* 20 (1934):125–58.
28. Christopher Howard, *Britain and the Casus Belli, 1822–1902* (London: Athlone, 1974), pp. 44–48.
29. Webster, *Palmerston*; Roger Bullen, *Palmerston, Guizot and the Collapse of the Entente Cordiale* (London: Athlone, 1973); Douglas W. J. Johnson, *Guizot* (London: Routledge & K. Paul, 1963).
30. Friedrich Meinecke, *Radowitz und die deutsche Revolution* (Berlin: E. S. Mittler, 1913); Frank Eyck, *The Frankfurt Parliament, 1848–1849* (New York: St. Martin's Press, 1969); Helmut Rumpler, *Die deutsche Politik des Freiherrn von Beust 1848 bis 1850* (Vienna: Böhlau, 1972); Rudolf Kiszling, *Fürst Felix zu Schwarzenberg* (Graz: Böhlau, 1952).
31. Waltraud Heindl, *Graf Buol-Schauenstein in St. Petersburg und London (1848–1852)* (Vienna: Böhlau, 1970); Kiszling, *Schwarzenberg*.
32. Richard Blaas, ed., *Le relazioni diplomatiche fra l'Austria e lo Stato Pontificio* (3d ser. [1848–1860], vol. 1; Rome: Istituto storico italiano per l'età moderna e contemporanea, 1973).
33. H. W. V. Temperley, *England and the Near East: The Crimea* (London: Longmans Green, 1936); Paul W. Schroeder, *Austria, Great Britain and the Crimean War* (Ithaca, N.Y.: Cornell University Press, 1972).
34. Ennio di Nolfo, *Europa e Italia nel 1855–1856* (Rome: Istituto per la storia del Risorgimento italiano, 1967).
35. Schroeder, *Austria*; Winfried Baumgart, *Der Friede von Paris 1856* (Munich: Oldenbourg, 1972).
36. Denis Mack Smith, *Victor Emanuel, Cavour, and the Risorgimento* (London: Oxford University Press, 1971).
37. Derek Beales, *England and Italy, 1859–60* (London: Nelson, 1961).
38. Stanislaw Bóbr-Tylingo, *Napoléon III, l'Europe et la Pologne en 1863–4* (Rome: Institutum Historicum Polonicum Romae, 1963); Ragnhild Hatton, "Palmerston and 'Scandinavian Union,'" in *Studies in International History*, ed. K. Bourne and D. C. Watt (Hamden, Conn.: Archon Books, 1967), pp. 119–44.
39. Helmut Burckhardt, *Deutschland, England, Frankreich* (Munich: W. Fink, 1970); Andreas Hillgruber, *Bismarcks Aussenpolitik* (Freiburg: Rombach, 1972); Friedrich Engel-Jánosi, *Graf Rechberg* (Munich: Oldenbourg, 1927).
40. Rudolf Lill, "Die Vorgeschichte der preussisch-italienischen Allianz," *Quellen und Forschungen aus italienischen Archiven und Bibliotheken* 42/43 (1963):505–70.
41. Since, in the peace treaty with Austria concluded at Prague later in August, Bismarck

specifically conceded to the South German states the right to form their own confederation, a right that he had already frustrated through these alliances, he hereby managed, as his Saxon opponent Count Beust later remarked, to violate a treaty even before he had signed it.
42. Hillgruber, *Bismarcks Aussenpolitik.*
43. Heinrich Lutz, "Von Königgrätz zum Zweibund. Aspekte europäischer Entscheidungen," *Historische Zeitschrift* 217 (1973):347–80.
44. Martin Winckler, *Bismarcks Bündnispolitik und das europäische Gleichgewicht* (Stuttgart: W. Kohlhammer, 1964); Stephan Verosta, *Theorie und Realität von Bündnissen* (Vienna: Europa, 1971); Hillgruber, *Bismarcks Aussenpolitik.*
45. Besides the works cited in note 44, see W. N. Medlicott, *Bismarck, Gladstone and the Concert of Europe* (London: Athlone, 1956); and Bruce Waller, *Bismarck at the Crossroads* (London: Athlone, 1974).
46. A. J. P. Taylor, *The Struggle for Mastery in Europe, 1848–1918* (Oxford, Eng.: Clarendon Press, 1954). A quotation from a private letter of Austrian foreign minister Count Goluchowski to the Austrian ambassador at St. Petersburg, Count Aehrenthal, on August 16, 1906, shows how clearly the partners understood the nature and purpose of the Austro-Italian alliance: "Now our position toward Italy is of such a nature, that our mutual relations must either assume the character of an alliance (even if not an entirely unreserved one), or the character of a latent enmity which then sooner or later leads to war. However few illusions one may have about the feelings in Italy toward us, the existing Triple Alliance nevertheless secures us against surprises on our southern boundary." Quoted in Verosta, *Bündnisse*, p. 311 (translation mine).
47. Taylor, *Struggle for Mastery*; D. A. Farnie, *East and West of Suez* (Oxford, Eng.: Clarendon Press, 1969); Ronald Robinson and John Gallagher, *Africa and the Victorians* (New York: St. Martin's Press, 1961); Cedric J. Lowe, *The Reluctant Imperialists* (London: Routledge & K. Paul, 1967).
48. Hillgruber, *Bismarcks Aussenpolitik*; Paul Kluke, "Bismarck und Salisbury: Ein diplomatisches Duell," *Historische Zeitschrift* 175 (1953):285–306; Egmont Zechlin, *Staatsstreichpläne Bismarcks und Wilhelms II, 1890–1894* (Stuttgart: Cotta, 1929). See also various essays, especially that by H.-U. Wehler, in *Das kaiserliche Deutschland*, ed. Michael Stürmer (Düsseldorf: Droste, 1970).
49. Taylor, *Struggle for Mastery*; William L. Langer, *The Franco-Russian Alliance, 1890–1894* (Cambridge, Mass.: Harvard University Press, 1929), and *The Diplomacy of Imperialism, 1890–1902* (2 vols., 2d ed.; New York: Knopf, 1956).
50. Christopher Andrew, *Theophile Delcassé and the Making of the Entente Cordiale* (New York: St. Martin's Press, 1968).
51. Fritz Fellner, *Der Dreibund* (Vienna: Verlag für Geschichte und Politik, 1960); Norman Rich, *Friedrich von Holstein* (2 vols.; Cambridge, Eng.: Cambridge University Press, 1965); F. R. Bridge, *From Sadowa to Sarajevo* (London: Routledge & K. Paul, 1972).
52. Max Beloff, *Imperial Sunset*, vol. 1 (London: Methuen, 1969); J. A. S. Grenville, *Lord Salisbury and Foreign Policy* (London: Athlone, 1964); Ian H. Nish, *The Anglo-Japanese Alliance* (London: Athlone, 1966); L. K. Young, *British Policy in China, 1895–1902* (Oxford, Eng.: Clarendon Press, 1970).
53. Nish, *Anglo-Japanese Alliance*; Firuz Kazemzadeh, *Russia and Britain in Persia, 1864–1914* (New Haven, Conn.: Yale University Press, 1968); Briton C. Busch, *Britain and the Persian Gulf, 1894–1914* (Berkeley: University of California Press, 1967); M. B. Cooper, "British Policy in the Balkans, 1908–9," *Historical Journal*

7 (1964–1965):258–79; Peter Lowe, *Great Britain and Japan, 1911–15* (New York: St. Martin's Press, 1969).
54. Andrew, *Delcassé*; P. J. V. Rolo, *The Entente Cordiale* (London: Macmillan, 1969).
55. See, for example, Jonathan Steinberg, *Yesterday's Deterrent* (New York: Macmillan, 1965), pp. 20–21, 29, 205–6.
56. On Britain's use of the Entente in 1911, see Keith Wilson, "The Agadir Crisis, the Mansion House Speech, and the Double-Edgedness of Agreements," *Historical Journal* 15 (1972):513–32.
57. For a specific argument on this thesis, see Paul W. Schroeder, "World War I as Galloping Gertie: A Reply to Joachim Remak," *Journal of Modern History* 44 (1972):319–45. In general on British policy, see Zara S. Steiner, *The Foreign Office and Foreign Policy, 1898–1914* (New York: Cambridge University Press, 1970); George W. Monger, *The End of Isolation* (London: Nelson, 1963); and Samuel R. Williamson, Jr., *The Politics of Grand Strategy* (Cambridge, Mass.: Harvard University Press, 1969).
58. Ernst C. Helmreich, *The Diplomacy of the Balkan Wars, 1912–1913* (Cambridge, Mass.: Harvard University Press, 1938); Edward C. Thaden, *Russia and the Balkan Alliance of 1912* (University Park: Pennsylvania State University Press, 1965).
59. Gerard E. Silberstein, *The Troubled Alliance* (Lexington: University of Kentucky Press, 1970); Ulrich Trumpener, *Germany and the Ottoman Empire, 1914–1918* (Princeton, N.J.: Princeton University Press, 1968); Frank G. Weber, *Eagles on the Crescent* (Ithaca, N.Y.: Cornell University Press, 1970).
60. Clarence J. Smith, *The Russian Struggle for Power, 1914–1917* (New York: Philosophical Library, 1956); Wolfram W. Gottlieb, *Studies in Secret Diplomacy during the First World War* (London: Allen & Unwin, 1957).
61. Jukka Nevakivi, *Britain, France and the Arab Middle East, 1914–1920* (London: Athlone, 1969).
62. Jon Jacobson, *Locarno Diplomacy* (Princeton, N.J.: Princeton University Press, 1972).
63. Piotr S. Wandycz, *France and Her Eastern Allies, 1919–1925* (Minneapolis: University of Minnesota Press, 1962), and *Soviet-Polish Relations, 1917–1921* (Cambridge, Mass.: Harvard University Press, 1969); Marian Wojciechowski, *Die polnisch-deutschen Beziehungen, 1933–1938* (Leiden: Brill, 1971).
64. Joel G. Colton, *Léon Blum* (New York: Knopf, 1966); William E. Scott, *Alliance against Hitler* (Durham, N.C.: Duke University Press, 1962).
65. Martin Gilbert, *The Roots of Appeasement* (New York: New American Library, 1967).
66. Among many recent works using the cabinet papers to discuss British policy, the most important are Ian G. Colvin, *The Chamberlain Cabinet* (London: Gollancz, 1971), and Robert K. Middlemas, *Diplomacy of Illusion* (London: Weidenfeld & Nicolson, 1972).
67. Martin Gilbert and R. S. Gott, *The Appeasers* (Boston: Houghton Mifflin, 1963); Sidney Aster, *1939* (London: Deutsch, 1973).
68. George F. Kennan, *Russia and the West under Lenin and Stalin* (Boston: Little, Brown, 1961); Adam B. Ulam, *Expansion and Coexistence* (2d ed.; New York: Praeger, 1974).
69. Elizabeth Wiskemann, *The Rome-Berlin Axis* (New York: Oxford University Press, 1949); Frederick W. Deakin, *The Brutal Friendship* (London: Weidenfeld & Nicolson, 1962); Norman Rich, *Hitler's War Aims*, vol. 1 (New York: Norton, 1973).
70. Frank W. Iklé, *German-Japanese Relations, 1936–1940* (New York: Bookman,

1956); Paul W. Schroeder, *The Axis Alliance and Japanese-American Relations, 1941* (Ithaca, N.Y.: Cornell University Press, 1958); Johanna M. Meskill, *Hitler and Japan* (New York: Atherton, 1966).
71. John L. Snell, *Illusion and Necessity* (Boston: Houghton Mifflin, 1963).
72. Ernest L. Woodward, *British Foreign Policy in the Second World War* (London: Her Majesty's Stationery Office, 1962).
73. Ulam, *Expansion*.
74. The most important works on the orthodox side of the controversy are probably those of Herbert Feis, beginning with his *Churchill, Roosevelt, Stalin* (Princeton, N.J.: Princeton University Press, 1957) and concluding with *From Trust to Terror* (New York: Norton, 1970), as well as John W. Wheeler-Bennett and Anthony Nicholls, *The Semblance of Peace* (New York: St. Martin's Press, 1972). On the revisionist side, the most important are Gabriel Kolko, *The Politics of War* (New York: Random House, 1968), and Joyce Kolko and Gabriel Kolko, *The Limits of Power* (New York: Harper, 1972). A sensible survey is Gaddis Smith, *American Diplomacy during the Second World War, 1941–1945* (New York: Wiley, 1965).
75. I refer especially to the various studies of J. David Singer and Melvin Small.
76. For evidence that the same realist vs. idealist debate long common in the West is also going on in postwar Japan, see Kei Wakaizumi, "Japan's Dilemma: To Act or Not to Act," *Foreign Policy*, no. 16 (Fall, 1974), pp. 33–35.

Technological Change, Strategic Doctrine, and Political Outcomes

Bernard Brodie

In the last quarter of the twentieth century one need not belabor the point that technological change in the instruments of war, and in all those instruments of peace that are used in war, have had a profound effect on military strategy and hence on the use of war and of threats of war in diplomacy.

It may, however, be important to have some awareness of the actual workings in the past of these processes, because we tend to operate our politics, foreign as well as domestic, in accustomed and sometimes very old-fashioned ways. This means that they may well get dangerously out of phase with the realities of the existing world, especially in matters having to do with something as discontinuous as war.

However, we should notice also that profound changes in ways of making war have occurred even during epochs of virtually static technology. The triggering influences then have to be found in the political and social environments of those times, or possibly in new ways of organizing armies that were independent either of technology or of politics. We have recently become aware also of a contrasting situation, where what may look like extraordinarily important changes in the tools of war or in related technologies may appear to lack significant impact on strategy and politics. It seems fair to say, for example, that recent improvements in nuclear weapons and in the means of delivering them tend to become of diminishing importance as compared with the basic fact of the existence of nuclear weapons in large numbers, even though those improvements may look quite significant to a scientist or to an engineer or to someone paid to be preoccupied with the unthinkable. Similarly, the legendary technical accomplishment of putting two men at a time on the surface of the moon and then retrieving them seems thus far to have been without discernible political or military significance. In short, there seems not to be any direct proportionality between technological change and military-political consequences, even though we acknowledge that historically there has been a close relationship between the one and the other.

Let us therefore consider first an era of great change in the methods and in the whole philosophy of waging war that antedates what we call the technological revolution. The philosophy that we have inherited from the

Napoleonic period, with which that era closed, still prevails today and distinguishes the modern world from that of the eighteenth century and before.

The career of Napoleon ended with the Battle of Waterloo in 1815, at which time the industrial revolution that began with the Watt steam engine had made virtually no dent in the weapons or methods of waging war either on land or at sea. Waterloo followed by exactly a hundred years the death of Louis XIV, which itself represented the close of an era of great change in the methods and uses of warfare in Europe. This Louis was already on the throne of France at the end of the Thirty Years' War in 1648, though he was then only a boy of ten. From the end of the Thirty Years' War to the time of his death, the patterns of waging war in Europe changed in at least three major respects.

First, firearms finally became the dominant weapons on the battlefield in place of the sword and the pike, even though firearms had first appeared over three hundred years earlier. This development can be attributed mostly to the introduction and development of the flintlock musket, but also to the marriage of the socket-clamp bayonet to the musket (the socket fitted around the barrel and thus permitted the musket to be fired while carrying it, which the earlier plug-type bayonet did not) and to the diminished weight and therefore the increased mobility of field guns. A flintlock smoothbore musket was first introduced into the British infantry in 1682, and was modified in 1759 into the famous "Brown Bess," which remained the standard weapon of that service for another eighty years thereafter.

Second, the condottieri—a type of roving mercenary hired for a limited term, that had survived from the Italian Renaissance through the Thirty Years' War—gave way to the standing army, which was still a force of mercenaries but was more decidedly a national army. There might still be foreign regiments or larger units, but increasingly the soldier was also the subject of the king who hired him. Because of the growing wealth of the king (and the continuing poverty of the common man), there was also a movement towards much larger armies in the field.

Third, proceeding partly from the change in the character of the armies, but also from the cultural changes affecting the attitudes of princes, war became decidedly less savage, with all sorts of inhibitions and prohibitions developing that tended to protect the civilian populations from the warring soldiers and the latter from the worst excesses of each other. The condottieri of the Thirty Years' War had to be permitted to plunder the towns they conquered. One such army under Count Tilly sacked Magdeburg in 1631, slaughtering more than thirty thousand civilians of both sexes and all ages. Such an atrocity would have been unthinkable in the latter part of the same century.[1]

These brief remarks may give us some idea of the pattern of war that the eighteenth century opened with and that remained characteristic of that century until its last decade, when the wars of the French Revolution, which were soon to be dominated by the ambitions of Napoleon, changed everything. One has to avoid exaggerated impressions. In the battles of the eighteenth century, armies did not dance quadrilles. The hand weapons of the period being totally inaccurate at any but the nearest ranges, armies would close to those near ranges, sometimes as little as thirty yards, and then pour the most devastating fire into each other's ranks.

There was, besides, a continuation of the medieval cult of valor, as represented, for example, by the tradition in the French army of having officers as high as regimental commanders stand out in front of the ranks and especially of having them insist on letting the enemy fire first in order to impress him with their courage—a practice followed with legendary punctilio at the Battle of Fontenoy in 1745.

Such battles were bound to be devastatingly bloody and costly, but for that reason they were generally avoided. The great general who commanded the victorious French at Fontenoy, Marshal Maurice de Saxe, had already written into his posthumously published *Reflections on the Art of War* a famous and much quoted passage: "I do not favor pitched battles, especially at the beginning of a war, and I am convinced that a skillful general could make war all his life without being forced into one."[2] This general—who was certainly the cleverest of his time except for Frederick the Great, whose career briefly overlapped his—obviously did not live up to his own prescription. And certainly Frederick did not follow it, especially in the early stages of his career, after his accession. However, it is also noteworthy that Frederick, later in his life, did become very dubious about pitched battles, which, he found, were both too costly and left too much to chance.[3]

The modern mind is likely to ask: If not battles, then what? The answer is quite complex, and insofar as we pursue it at all, it is best to do so by comparing the Napoleonic revolution with what went before. We can do that by looking at the change through the eyes of Karl von Clausewitz (1780–1831), whose posthumously published book *On War* (*Vom Kriege*) is, beyond all comparison, the greatest classic on the subject. Clausewitz had enormous personal experience with war, beginning with a march with the Prussian army into revolutionary France when he was an ensign of only thirteen, and ending with Waterloo, twenty-two years later. His experience also included service with the Russian army in 1812, during Napoleon's disastrous march to Moscow and subsequent retreat.[4] Clausewitz was, besides, a keen and careful student of military history. He was dedicated to the modern conception that the knowledge that is basic to theory, whether of war or of anything else, must be empirical. And he believed that for the study of war, historical examples form the whole of one's empirical data—a view that was apt to be more sympathetically received in an age when military technology was virtually static than it sometimes is at present.[5]

To Clausewitz, the most basic of the several fundamental changes that mark the Napoleonic era is not an invention in the so-called art of war but rather a result of the revolution in politics, which of course began in France and which Napoleon was quick to observe and exploit. His enemies, however reactionary they might have been, had to adopt the same system in order to survive. It was a system the most conspicuous characteristic of which was universal conscription, but which involved, on a broader level, the greater mobilization for war of the whole resources of the state. France, being at that time by far the most populous state in Europe except for Russia on the periphery, could not only raise larger armies than its enemies but its generals could also use those armies, if not with abandon, at any rate with an idea that casualties could be replaced.

In Clausewitz's frequent comparisons between the Napoleonic period and the one that preceded it by a generation or more, we learn that the kind of vigor that, for example, he admires in Frederick the Great, who reigned from 1740 to 1786, was likely to be lacking in his opponents. Here is a characteristic passage, from a discussion of the importance of pursuit after victory in battle:

> This is one of the points where recent [i.e., Napoleonic] military experience has opened up a new field of energy. In earlier wars, smaller in scope and more circumscribed, conventions had developed which unnecessarily restricted many aspects of operations and this one in particular. *The very idea, the honor* of victory, appeared to be the whole point so far as the commanders were concerned. Actual destruction of enemy forces was, to them, only one of many means of war—certainly not the main, even less the only one. They were only too ready to sheathe their swords as soon as the enemy lowered his. Once a decision had been reached, one stopped fighting as a matter of course: further bloodshed was considered unnecessarily brutal.
>
> . . . In earlier wars, accordingly, one finds that only the greatest of heroes—Charles XII, Marlborough, Prince Eugene, Frederick the Great—would drive home by vigorous pursuit a victory already decisive enough. Other generals as a rule were content to remain in possession of the field. Contemporary war, which is waged with increased vigor in response to the increased scope of circumstances, has broken these conventional bounds.[6]

The difference, in short, is between the boxer who is intent on a knockout and one who is content to accumulate points. From this difference, various other ones followed. A war that followed the Napoleonic pattern was one in which campaigns were much more closely interconnected than theretofore—if there was need for more than one campaign, which often there was not. From the time that King Frederick William III of Prussia declared war against Napoleon in the autumn of 1806 until his armies were utterly crushed after the disasters at Jena and Auerstadt took less than two weeks, and the peace imposed on Prussia involved no mere detachment of a province or two but a severe curtailment of the size of her army as well as a heavy indemnity. The Prussia whose Frederick the Great had died only twenty years earlier was in effect converted into a vassal state. Not all of Napoleon's wars were so swift from opening to conclusion and so decisive in their results, but that was the pattern that was distinctively his until his enemies defeated him with his own methods.

The military object in this later period was the destruction of the enemy's armed forces, not some secondary gain; and if one campaign did not suffice, then the second was a continuation of the first, and so on until the end was reached. After Napoleon's disaster in Russia in 1812, his enemies joined to close in on him. The campaigns that began early in 1813 on the Elbe in the east and in Portugal in the southwest ended with Napoleon abdicating on April 11, 1814, at which time Austrian, Russian, and Swedish forces were in Paris, and British, Portuguese, and Spanish forces under Wellington had marched through Spain and southern France and had taken Toulouse. The Waterloo campaign of a year later, which ended the "Hundred Days" of Napoleon's return, was the same kind of all-out decisive encounter, telescoped this time into a time frame that was even shorter than that of Jena.

Throughout his long work, Clausewitz takes up again and again the question of whether the opening made by Napoleon into something like "absolute war" would be the invariable pattern of the future, or whether, as a theorist, he should reckon also upon some return of the "incoherence" that, after all, had characterized most of the wars since the times of Alexander the Great. As he says in one place, "When barriers which in fact consisted only in ignorance of what was possible are broken down, it is not easy to build them up again."[7] But he feels also that it would be presumptuous to assume that all wars would henceforward be of the unfettered kind.

Subsequent wars adhered much more closely to the unfettered type, which Clausewitz thought came close to the "absolute" form, than they did to the "incoherent" form of the eighteenth century. Certainly the wars of German unification, which culminated in the Franco-Prussian War of 1870/1871, were of that nature, and in the following century the two world wars were to be much more unfettered in form than Clausewitz could have dreamed. Meanwhile, in America a great civil war had been fought in which the goal and the successful accomplishment of one side was the political extirpation of the other. We should, however, notice that Clausewitz by no means considered the "incoherent" eighteenth-century type of war to be the only alternative to the Napoleonic quasi-absolute type. He was, in fact, one of the first to expound, as having a rational form and objective, what we would now call "limited war," meaning a war having a clearly understood limited purpose for which it is altogether inappropriate to mobilize or to use the full military resources of the state.[8]

Thus, the Napoleonic pattern furnished the experience, and the Clausewitzian theory furnished the philosophic interpretation thereof, with which the world confronted the industrial revolution with regard to the tools of war as well as those of peace.

Technological Revolution in Naval Forces

The flagship *Victory*, on which Admiral Lord Nelson won his victory and met his death at Trafalgar in October 1805, was forty years old on the day of that battle, which means that although most of the timbers had been replaced because of rot, the design of the hull and rigging and the armament were essentially unchanged from the original. The *Victory* was of the type called a "ship of the line" or a "line-of-battle ship," from which comes the modern term "battleship." This meant that she had timbers that were strong enough and armament that was heavy enough to enable her to fight "in the line" against enemy battleships, which lighter naval ships such as frigates or corvettes could not do. The *Victory* was also a "first-rater," which indicated that she had three gun decks, as compared with "second-raters," which had only two. At Trafalgar, incidentally, one of the Spanish ships, the *Santisima Trinidad*, had four gun decks; but this Goliath was among those sunk.

The standard armament for the battleship was the 32-pounder, which was a muzzleloading, smoothbore gun that fired a ball of about that weight and of about 6 inches in diameter. The guns were arranged to fire "broadside," meaning that each side of the ship had half the guns, which were fired through portholes. A first-rater carried a hundred guns or more; and a second-rater, between sixty and eighty. The propulsion was exclusively by sail. The ship was indeed "armored" in comparison with the frigate (which had only a single gun deck and lighter guns, usually 18-pounders in the British navy), but the armor was of heavy oak. About the only technological change that had occurred in the past forty years had been the application of copper sheathing to the bottom, in order that the barnacles, which would otherwise adhere to the hull, would fall off with the slow exfoliation of the copper.

It was with ships like these that British had ruled the seas for over a hundred years, or since the last of the three Dutch wars at the end of the seventeenth century. It was her sea power that enabled her to stay at war with

Revolutionary France and with Napoleon for a twenty-three-year-period, which was interrupted only by the brief Peace of Amiens in 1802. During that time she had blockaded the ports of the Continent; had shipped and supplied an army to the Iberian Peninsula, which had become Napoleon's "Spanish Ulcer"; and had subventioned with money the various coalitions that had formed against Napoleon. In the quick crisis of the "Hundred Days," she had shipped a small but indispensable army to Belgium, which gave backbone to Wellington's unseasoned allied army (including Dutch and Belgians) and which gave Wellington himself status enough to be commander in chief of the army and to deal on equal terms with his Prussian ally Blücher. Together they won at Waterloo. Still, in the main, the effects of sea power had been slow and unobtrusive. Napoleon's brilliant victory at Austerlitz followed by only a few weeks the destruction of his fleet at Trafalgar. And from Trafalgar to Napoleon's first abdication took almost nine years.

The major naval inventions of the nineteenth century, which together totally transformed the appearance and character of the fleet, are four in number: (1) the introduction of steam propulsion; (2) the use of iron (later steel) armor in place of wooden armor; (3) the change to iron (later steel) ship construction in place of wooden construction; and (4) the development of the naval gun from the smoothbore of the *Victory,* which fired spherical solid shot, to a huge, rifled, breechloading weapon that fired elongated projectiles containing high-explosive. We note the distinction between iron armor and iron ship construction. The first French seagoing "ironclad," the *Gloire,* launched in 1859, was of wooden construction with iron plates on its sides, as was the famous *Merrimac* (later renamed the *Virginia*), which fought the *Monitor* in Hampton Roads in 1862. On the other hand, the first British seagoing iron-armored ship, the *Warrior*—which was launched after the *Gloire,* but was completed earlier, in 1861—was of iron construction throughout. It also happened to be the largest naval vessel built up to its time, which was no accident, inasmuch as one of the advantages of iron or steel construction over wood was that it made feasible the building of much larger ships.[9]

It was Clausewitz's contention, which was not shared by some other theorists like his influential contemporary Antoine Henri Jomini, that every important tactical change must automatically have its effect on strategy.[10] On the other hand, it is arguable that adopting iron armor and enlarging the size and power of the ship's guns make for important tactical change without necessarily having profound strategic consequences. The great naval theorist Capt. Alfred T. Mahan, whom we shall discuss below, was certainly of that opinion. On the other hand, such an argument could hardly be put forward concerning a change that made naval vessels independent of wind for their propulsion.

The first steam war vessel, the *Demologos* ("Voice of the People"), was built by Robert Fulton in 1814 for the defense of New York Harbor in the war with England. It had some other novel characteristics, including underwater guns, and because it was not meant to be seagoing at all, it could be far ahead of its time by dispensing altogether with sails. Other seagoing ships, whether of war or of commerce, that adopted steam propulsion also retained sails in order to conserve fuel. The result was a hybrid form of steam-sail ship that continued into the latter part of the nineteenth century. In the British navy there were no armed steamships until 1828, but the first armed steamship to see service in war was the *Karteria*, which was used by the Greek insurgents against the Turks in 1827. The *Karteria* was also the first warship to use in battle the new shell gun invented by the Frenchman Paixhans.

Steam propulsion was, for a long time, confined to smaller warships, because the admirals of the day felt that the equipment for steam propulsion was too vulnerable to be used on the heavier line-of-battle ships. The paddle wheels of the first steamships were extremely vulnerable to shot, and the use of paddle wheels required that the steam boilers be placed above the water line. Oddly, the *Demologos* had solved this problem of vulnerability by putting the paddle in a channelway down the middle of the ship, but this idea seemed to be impractical for seagoing ships. The problem was finally solved by the adoption of the screw in place of the paddle wheel. The screw itself is under water, and its use permits the entire engine, including the boilers, also to be placed below the water line. The first screw-driven warship happened again to be an American ship, the *Princeton*, of frigate size, which was launched in 1843. It was also the first warship to use anthracite coal, which greatly reduced the amount of smoke. During its first year of service in 1844, the *Princeton* was to gain a more undesirable notoriety by being the ship aboard which a new gun was being tested—the 12-inch smoothbore called the "Peacemaker." The gun exploded, killing several high dignitaries of the United States government, including the secretaries of state and of the navy.

However, even after the adoption of the screw, there was no rush to equip with steam propulsion the larger warships of the fleet. The Crimean War (1854 to 1856), however, proved the uselessness thenceforth of any warships not equipped with steam. Some of the line-of-battle ships that were not so equipped had to be towed into action (usually bombarding shore positions) by steam-driven ships. After this war, in 1857, the first lord of the admiralty (the civilian head of the British navy), Sir Charles Wood, read before Commons a statement that said in part: "At this time . . . the sailing vessels ought, almost, to be left out of consideration, for I do not think that except in case of urgent necessity any nation would dream of sending a sailing squadron to sea."[11] One should notice the date, because this means that the rush to steam propulsion on larger warships coincides pretty nearly with the other three major developments mentioned above. If we take the twenty-year period that ended in 1873 with the completion of the British *Devastation*, we find that the instruments of sea power were, during this extremely short period, utterly transformed.

Even before the Crimean War, the introduction of steam propulsion on warships triggered in Britain a series of "invasion panics." The basic fear was expressed in 1845 by Lord Palmerston, then prime minister, who referred to the great land forces of France and warned his countrymen that the Channel was no longer a barrier. "Steam navigation," he declared, "had rendered that which was before impassable by a military force nothing more than a river passable by a steam bridge." The phrase "steam bridge" was to become the watchword of the panic mongers. The economist Richard Cobden later wrote a small book on the subject, entitled *The Three Panics* (London, 1862), which is highly instructive today in illuminating how nations can stir themselves into a frenzy of fear concerning the wholly imaginary intentions and capabilities of a presumed enemy. The panics were interrupted by the British and French going to war, not against each other, but as allies against Russia. After that war, the panics were resumed. Quite apart from the matter of French intentions, the technical arguments to support the "steam bridge" theory were complete nonsense, but they were nevertheless put forward with great seriousness and no doubt with secret pleasure by people whose status made them the official guardians of the state, including the prestigious but superannuated duke of Wellington.[12]

The technical arguments stemmed from the undoubtedly great *tactical* results of steam propulsion, in that the meeting of hostile fleets and the ensuing actions no longer had to be concerned with wind direction and velocity. Previously it had been very important tactically to have the advantage of the "weather gage," which meant to be to the windward side of the enemy. The fleet enjoying the weather gage had the option of pressing an action or of declining one. There were bound to be great strategic changes resulting from so great a tactical change—though not of a kind that warranted the invasion panics—but in addition, there were other direct strategic consequences. The shortest distance between two points on the high seas now became the great-circle route, or something approximating it, which it certainly had not been in days of sail, when prevailing winds much affected the choice of ship routes. A sail ship going from New York to anywhere in South America had first to go eastward almost to Europe before turning into the trade winds. With sail ships there was also a top limit on average sailing speeds, and it was a very low limit. A frigate could sail faster than a ship of the line, but, day in and day out, not a great deal faster. The American *Constitution*, a frigate noted for her fleetness, had a record of 13.5 knots under the most favorable conditions of wind, but in a long voyage at sea she average only about 4.5 knots.

Finally, a strategic as well as political consquence of the greatest importance was that it now became vital to have coaling stations abroad. Britain, in the nineteenth century, happened to be the source of the best maritime fuel in her Welsh Cardiff anthracite coal, but her world-wide empire also gave her coaling stations abroad (and a reason for keeping them), which other great powers might lack. The Russians were to feel this lack keenly in the Russo-Japanese War of 1904/1905. Later, just before World War I, the British Royal Navy had to decide whether to adopt oil as fuel, for Britain had no native sources of oil. The decision was that, inasmuch as Britain had to keep control of the seas in any case in order to survive, she might as well add oil to the list of commodities that had to be imported during wartime; and thus battleships of the *Queen Elizabeth* class were the first to be designed as oil burners.

The resort to iron armor on ships had been triggered initially by the Paixhans shell gun mentioned above, a spherical shell that was fired from a smoothbore gun. If a solid shot stuck in the timbers of a large warship, or if it ricocheted, that was the end of its damage. If it passed through the timbers, it injured or killed only those persons in its direct path. But a shell that lodged in the timbers of a ship would destroy those timbers, and one that penetrated into the gun deck could do enormous damage. The cry went out, "For God's sake, keep out the shell." This could be done only by adopting iron armor, which was in fact applied to some smaller vessels even before the abovementioned *Warrior* and *Gloire* were built.[13] The notion that the *Monitor* and the *Merrimac* were the first ironclads is a complete myth; however, they were the first such ships *to fight each other*. The first ironclads carried wrought-iron plate of some 4 to $4\frac{1}{2}$ inches, the manufacture of which taxed the resources of the iron mills of the time; but the best that the Confederates could do in armoring the *Merrimac* was to lay on two layers of plates of 2-inch thickness each, which weighed as much but were inferior in protection to solid plate such as the *Monitor* carried. The *Monitor* was also the first turreted warship, its two large guns being able to fire in virtually all directions. However, the *Monitor* and the several similar vessels that succeeded her were not seagoing ships.

Undoubtedly the naval gun would have developed in power and range in any case, but the adoption of iron armor was a great stimulus to that development. The most conspicuous change in naval guns, as in land guns, was the adoption of rifling, which began about the middle of the nineteenth century. Rifling gives the projectile a twist in its flight, thus giving it the gyroscopic action of a spinning top. Because it will not tumble in flight, the projectile can now be elongated and given a pointed tip for better cleaving through the air. However, rifling in itself does not enhance the penetrating power of a gun. The 11-inch and 15-inch Dahlgren guns that were built for the federal navy in the American Civil War were built to penetrate armor and were perhaps the most powerful guns of their time, but they were smoothbore guns that fired spherical shot (the original *Monitor* carried the 11-inch variety). Rifling, whether in a hand weapon or any large gun, in the first instance contributes only greater accuracy, mostly because of the tighter fit of bullet or projectile with the gun barrel. However, it can also be exploited to give greater range to the gun, provided the larger mass, and hence the inertia, that comes with the elongated form of the projectile can be overcome by making the gun itself much stronger. If it is strengthened, a rifled gun can be made to give more penetrating power at *longer ranges* than a smoothbore gun.[14]

At any rate, from about the middle of the 1850s until after the end of the century the race was on between the penetrating power of the gun, which also added range and accuracy, and the resistance of armor. Guns changed from wrought iron to steel, then became built-up guns (with outer cylinders shrunk by cooling onto inner sleeves), and then, for a time, wire-wound guns—all to give greater strength. Iron armor had to develop in thickness in order to keep pace with the change, until in the British *Inflexible*—which was completed in 1881, just two decades after the *Warrior,* with its 4-inch armor—it reached a thickness of 24 inches. The *Inflexible* was an "answer" to an Italian ship that housed four 100-ton guns behind a citadel of 22-inches-thick armor. The *Inflexible* had muzzleloading guns that weighed 81 tons each, the last of the muzzleloaders; but by 1884 the British had a breechloading gun of $16\frac{1}{4}$-inch caliber that weighed 111 tons. It was a gun that no ship of the time could comfortably carry and fire.

Later the introduction of smokeless powder, which burned more slowly, made it possible to give a smoother thrust to the projectile in a longer gun, and hence made it possible to reduce its caliber while increasing its range and power. For some time thereafter the maximum caliber of the naval gun was 12 inches. Similarly, by improving the quality of the armor, it was possible to reduce its thickness while increasing its resistance. Nevertheless, the enormous weight and cost of the armor made it necessary to restrict the amount of coverage on the ship, and the huge weight and size of the guns made it necessary greatly to reduce their number and therefore, if possible, to put them in the center of the ship, whence they could shoot to either side. The latter development made necessary first the barbette and then the turret, either of which could be adopted only by doing away finally with any kind of sail rigging. The *Devastation* (of 1873), already mentioned, which had turrets and no sails, was thus the first modern seagoing battleship. Armor could be restricted mostly to the turrets and to the sides of the ship at the water line. The compartmentation made possible by iron or steel construction gave protection to the unarmored portions of armored ships; and unarmored ships (like the present-day destroyer) depended entirely on compartmentation.

The trend to iron or steel construction was somewhat slowed by the fouling problem, because the copper sheathing used on the bottoms of wooden ships could not be applied directly to metal ships. A galvanic action was set up in sea water that prevented the exfoliation of the copper; it also caused corrosion of the iron that the copper touched. However, the advantages of metal construction were so great, and it was so absolutely indispensable in the larger ships carrying both heavy guns and heavy armor, that it was not long before wooden construction for warships was entirely abandoned, while various methods were pursued for dealing with the fouling problem (mostly in the form of antifouling paints, which were being developed even in World War II). The shift from wooden to iron construction of warships has been described as a particular boon for Britain, which had become increasingly dependent on foreign countries for the special kinds of timber required but which was throughout the nineteenth century the world's leading producer of iron and steel.[15]

We are accustomed to thinking of rapid technological change, especially in weapons of war, as being peculiarly characteristic of our own times; but there probably has never been a period of such rapid change in naval architecture and naval armament as the one that occurred in the quarter-century following 1850. During this time it became literally true that a warship was obsolete before it was completed, in the sense that ships that were then already on the ways would easily be able to defeat it in battle. Under such circumstances there was a good deal deal of experimentation but no rush to build up large naval forces. Britain, although still possessing the world's leading navy, had a hodgepodge of types of warships. France, with a comparable hodgepodge, was in second place. For a variety of reasons the United States, after the Civil War, opted to remain entirely outside the race to develop new warship types. Capt. A. T. Mahan, in his memoirs, describes an incident that happened to him when he was in command of an old American warship on the South Pacific station during the mid-1880s. A French naval officer, making a courtesy call, paused on leaving the ship, gazed at the smoothbore guns with which she was armed, and uttered audibly the famous line from the medieval poet François Villon: "Où sont les neiges d'antan?" ("Where are the snows of yesteryear?").[16]

There were several other interesting consequences of the rapid change in this area. One was a large degree of confusion about the future of naval tactics and of the requirements for distinctive types of warships. An example of this is the extraordinary attention that was paid to the ram as an offensive weapon, in the minds of some naval officers the most important of the offensive weapons against armored ships. This odd and aberrant notion developed because of the easy sinking by ramming of the federal ship *Cumberland* by the *Merrimac* on the day before the latter had her famous engagement with the *Monitor*—it being generally overlooked that the *Cumberland* was at anchor at the time; this impression was intensified by some peacetime accidents and also by the sinking through ramming of the Italian flagship (also stationary at the time) by an Austrian ship during the Battle of Lissa in 1866.

The ram seemed to be such a formidable weapon that its advocates forgot to consider how difficult it would be to deliver its blow against a maneuvering vessel, especially if the latter had powerful guns. In a treatise on naval tactics published in 1884, Comdr. William Brainbridge-Hoff declared: "The ram is the most formidable of all the weapons of the ship, and its use requires severe and prolonged practical study," a view that was echoed in the book *Naval Tactics,* published in 1897 (thirty-five years after the *Merrimac*'s triumph) by Vice Adm. S. J. Makaroff of the Russian Imperial Navy, who devoted much space to a detailed discussion of this expedient. The idea of the ram affected the entire architecture of naval vessels, warships being fitted with huge beaks on the prow below the water line—great cumbersome projections that affected the maneuvering qualities of the ship. Designers even experimented with armored but unarmed vessels that could do nothing but ram. The many failures of attempts to ram during the American Civil War and later wars were ignored, as was the increasing ludicrousness of the idea because of the rapidly developing range, accuracy, and power of naval guns.[17] Thus once again we have a historical example of doctrine prevailing over experience, even over plain good sense.

With the rapid developments of the time, the distinction between battleships, cruisers, and lesser warships that had prevailed during days of sail (the frigates being the cruisers of the time) tended to be obscured, and all sorts of hybrid types developed, such as the "armored cruiser," which was a considerable ship but not quite a battleship (the *Maine*, which was blown up in Santiago harbor in 1898, was of that variety, though it is often called a "battleship" in the history books). Acknowledged battleships would be laid down in two sizes, first-class and second-class, as though the latter could be sure of meeting only enemy vessels of their own size. (This odd notion, incidentally, reappeared on the eve of World War II, when the French decided they had to build some "answers" to the German *Gneisenau* and *Scharnhorst,* which were larger than cruisers but smaller than contemporary battleships, the result being the *Dunkerque* class; the United States followed suit with its *Alaska* class, for which it could not even find a suitable designation but finally settled on "large cruiser." Ships of the *Alaska* class had nine 12-inch guns when contemporary American battleships were carrying nine 16-inch guns.)

However, towards the end of the nineteenth century it was clear that with the return of some stabilization in types of warships, great nations that wished to do so could build up their naval power without having to overcome a large lead of a powerful rival, the strength of whose navy would inevitably be expressed mostly in obsolete types. However, after thirty or forty years of preoccupation with technological advance, admiralties also needed renewed clarification of what navies were for, and what the distinctive functions of the various types of warships were. Perhaps also there had to be a certain incentive that had been lacking following the Franco-Prussian War of 1870/1871, in which French naval superiority seemed to count for nothing in warding off rapid defeat. That clarification and a large measure of incentive were to be provided by the writings of Captain Mahan.

The Theories of Alfred Thayer Mahan

In reading Mahan's works today, one might find it difficult to understand why they created such a stir when they first began to appear in the last decade of the nineteenth century and why they had so powerful an effect on the naval aspirations of some of the great powers of the world, including his own United States. They are scholarly works, dealing mostly with the naval history of a remote past; the style of writing is skillful and elegant but hardly exciting. If such works were written today, their authors could not count on having their books widely reviewed. In the 1890s they quite literally shook the world.

Actually, Mahan's first book was a little-noted volume, *The Gulf and Inland Waters* (1883); it formed part of a trilogy describing federal naval operations in the American Civil War, in which Mahan had taken part as a young naval officer.[18] It was no doubt his authorship of this book that marked him for assignment to the new Naval War College in 1885 as "lecturer on naval history and strategy." He developed his lectures and wrote them up. In 1890, when he was fifty and after his work had been turned down by several publishers, he published the best known of his works: *The Influence of Sea Power upon History, 1660–1783*. The dates that form part of the title are usually neglected in referring to the book, but one notices that they lay the scope of the work entirely in what would have seemed, in 1890, to be a vanished age. The first date is that of the Stuart Restoration in England, which was followed by the revival of British sea power, and the latter date is that of the end of the war between Britain and France that had begun with Louis XVI's intervention in the American Revolution. This book was followed two years later by a two-volume work called *The Influence of Sea Power upon the French Revo-*

lution and Empire, 1793–1812; that, in turn, was followed by biographies of Admirals Farragut and Nelson, and subsequently by a continuing flow of works on naval history and strategy until the end of Mahan's life, in December 1914, shortly after the outbreak of World War I. It is rare that one should begin so late in life and then become so prolific and so substantial a writer, but his extraordinary success was undoubtedly a stimulus.[19]

Mahan seems not to have paid much attention to Clausewitz, but he was a disciple of the latter's contemporary Jomini, whom he called "my best military friend." Jomini, unlike Clausewitz, was a firm believer in the fundamental importance of certain "principles" of warfare that have presumably persisted through all sorts of changes in armaments and tactics. One of his most repeated slogans is "Methods change but principles are unchanging." It is therefore not remarkable that Mahan should have thought nothing of deriving from the days of wooden sailing ships some lessons of naval strategy that he felt applied just as well to his own era of steam-driven, heavily armored ships that carried huge rifled guns. As we shall see, his confidence in the unchanging character of strategic principles probably contributed to his making a fundamental error in failing to anticipate the importance of the submarine as a raider on commerce, even though it was already a highly perfected instrument at the time of his death.

The periods that Mahan wrote about in his first two histories (not counting the 1883 work) included the age of such great admirals as Howe, Jervis (Lord St. Vincent), and, above all, Nelson. Men like Jervis and Nelson represented at sea what Napoleon and Wellington represented on land, and in their opinions and conduct they quite anticipated Clausewitz. Both stood for the decisive battle that resulted in the annihilation of the enemy's battle fleet. One of Nelson's statements that Mahan most cherished occurred when Nelson was a captain under Admiral Hotham, who in 1795 failed to pursue vigorously a French fleet that his fleet had engaged and defeated with the capture of two line-of-battle ships. Hotham signaled to the fleet that they had "done well enough," which caused Nelson to say: "If ten ships out of eleven were taken, I would never call it well enough, if we were able to get at the eleventh."[20]

It is always a distortion to attempt to encapsulate into two or three basic ideas the thinking of anyone who wrote so voluminously as Mahan, and yet with him, as with Clausewitz, some ideas are indeed more basic than others. Two closely related themes run throughout Mahan's work. The first concerned the importance of "command of the sea," by which he meant the ability to use the seas and to deny the use of them to the enemy, especially in those maritime areas that were important to the war. The second idea was that command of the sea was achieved only by putting into the maritime areas of dispute a concentrated *battle fleet* that was superior to any that the enemy could bring out. Isolated cruisers might exploit that command through patrol or escort, but only if their operations were covered by a dominant battle fleet composed of battleships.

The battleship type thenceforward enjoyed special attention in design, as well as special prominence in naval budgets. Meanwhile, in the last decade of the nineteenth century and at the beginning of the twentieth, battleships were finally reaching some stability in design, each one then having four large guns in two turrets of two guns each, and four somewhat lesser guns, also in two turrets of two guns each. In the British class called *King Edward VII*, the last of the predreadnoughts, these guns were of two calibers—12-inch and 9.2-inch; also some smaller "quick-firing" guns (of about 3-inch caliber) were being mounted against the "torpedo boats," which had already made their appearance.

For a battleship to have two large but disparate calibers in its primary armament made no sense, and that was finally realized in Britain with the building in 1906 of the famous *Dreadnought*, the first of the "all-big-gun" ships. The *Dreadnought* had ten 12-inch guns arranged in five turrets of two guns each, in addition to its secondary or defensive armament of quick firers.

The *Dreadnought* became thenceforth the standard for all battleships, which changed only by adopting larger calibers of guns (thus becoming "superdreadnoughts") and by achieving greater size and speed as well as by refining their fire-control devices. The naval race between Britain and Germany, which developed out of the German naval laws of 1898 and 1900, became at first a race for battleships and after 1906 a race for dreadnoughts, with the British being determined to keep a superiority of at least 1.6 to 1 in vessels of that type. Their success in doing so assured an overwhelming superiority when the two fleets met off Jutland in May of 1916.

The last of the battleship types, built prior to and during World War II, still adhered to the superdreadnought idea. In the United States Navy they were ships that carried nine 16-inch guns in three turrets of three guns each and were capable of as much as 35 knots, which was as fast as any cruiser of the time. Mounting radar and sophisticated fire-control mechanisms, they could hit unseen targets at distances of more than twenty-five miles. But the advance of technology that had made such powerful vessels possible had also determined their end. Two of the battleships that the Japanese brought to the Battle of Leyte Gulf in October of 1944 carried guns of 18-inch caliber, the largest ever mounted on battleships.[21] American aircraft sank those ships before they had ever fired their huge guns against any enemy ship, a fate that they shared with a substantial number of other battleships of World War II.

The Underwater Revolution

The battleship had indeed been under verbal attack since the beginning of the nineteenth century. As it grew in size and power and thus in cost, it stimulated the search for some means of destroying it with smaller vessels. The latter had to use effective weapons other than guns, for its superiority to other types in a gun duel was what made the battleship. That fact was no doubt one of the primary elements spurring the above-noted enthusiasm for the ram, which, when it could hit home, did so *under* the water line armor protection. But there was another weapon that had the lethal qualities of the ram and was far easier to bring to target—the automotive torpedo. As that weapon was perfected, it became available for use first in small, fast "torpedo boats," later also in submarines, and finally also in aircraft, which could, in addition, use bombs.

Something called a torpedo, which then meant simply an underwater explosive device that could be brought to a ship's hull and perhaps attached to it, dates back at least as far as the American Revolution, when it was in fact combined with a submersible vessel manned by a crew of one. The combination was the invention of David Bushnell, a graduate of Yale College (which commemorates him with a building named Bushnell Hall), and it was actually tried out several times against British warships anchored in the Hudson. All the attempts were failures, partly due to the copper sheathing on the British ships' bottoms, which prevented the submersible from drilling the hole by which the torpedo could be attached.[22]

Robert Fulton subsequently became interested in the submarine, and in 1801 he designed and built one for a crew of four, which he tried to sell to Napoleon, then first consul. Fulton also designed several types of torpedo, which were to be discharged by gunlock on contact. His submarine made several underwater trips in the harbor at Brest, but Napoleon was not interested. Fulton thereupon transferred himself and his experimental instruments to Napoleon's enemy, Britain, whose prime minister, the younger William Pitt, supported some experiments against the French ships blockaded in Bologne. The first of these experiments was carried out on October 2, 1805, with five so-called carcasses. Of the several vessels attacked, one was actually sunk, but the British did not know it. A few weeks later there was another test. This one was a complete failure, but meanwhile the Battle of Trafalgar had taken place. The British felt no further need for Fulton. It is interesting that Admiral Jervis, who had now become Lord St. Vincent and first sea lord, had the insight to remark that "Pitt was the greatest fool that ever existed, to encourage a mode of war which they who commanded the seas did not want, and which if successful would deprive them of it."[23]

There were similar experiments in the War of 1812 and in the American Civil War, not all of which were failures but which today have simply an antiquarian interest. What was necessary in order to make the torpedo an important weapon was for it to become self-propelled and capable of keeping a straight course and a prescribed depth. The first such "automotive" torpedo was designed by the Englishman Whitehead and was tested by the Austrian government in 1867/1868. By 1873 most other significant navies had adopted it and were proceeding to develop it. By 1875 the British navy had already designed a surface boat to carry and discharge the torpedo, and well before the close of the century the torpedo boat, with its special weapon, had stimulated the development of the defensive "quick-firer" gun, already noted, and also of the fast surface vessel called the "torpedo-boat destroyer." The latter then adopted the functions of the torpedo boat and is still with us under the truncated name simply of "destroyer."

The submarine vessel was a harder nut to crack. The ones that we have been describing were all driven by human muscle power and were blind under water. What the submarine needed were good underwater, as well as surface, propulsion and the ability to see and to navigate while submerged. The underwater propulsion was developed with electric batteries in the late 1880s, not surprisingly in France, whose Admiral Aube looked upon the submarine as a means of coping with those "mastodons" which the British were always determined to have in large numbers. Later the gasoline engine was adopted for surface cruising and for recharging the batteries, but that engine was dangerous because of the accumulation of the volatile gasoline fumes in the enclosed craft. A periscope was fitted to the French *Morse* of 1899, which, like the earlier *Gustav Zede,* was made of Roma bronze instead of steel, so that the magnetic compass could be used under water.

Germany at that earlier time was quite uninterested in submarines, Admiral von Tirpitz being of the opinion that this sort of experimentation should be left to wealthier nations. That opinion began to change about 1905. Then, in the year before the outbreak of World War I, the German navy developed the two additional refinements that finally made the submarine vessel a practical warship. These were the adoption of the Diesel engine, which did away with the dangerous fumes of the gasoline engine, and the gyroscopic compass, which was in any case more accurate than the magnetic variety and which could be used within a steel hull at any depth.

Thus, when World War I began, two big question marks troubled the British admiralty and the commander of the British Grand Fleet, Adm. Sir John Jellicoe. The first was: How dangerous were the modern automotive torpedoes against battleships when they were launched from smaller surface vessels like destroyers, which, unlike the slower submarines, were sure to be present in fleet actions. Second, how dangerous would the submarine be against warships, especially when the latter were at anchor. What virtually no one expected or feared at the outbreak of the war was that the German submarine or U-boat (for *Unterseeboot*) would become an important instrument against British and Allied commerce.

It is difficult now, looking back, to understand how the latter danger—or opportunity, depending on one's point of view—could have been so completely overlooked. No doubt, part of the reason lay in the tremendous prestige of the man who was now Rear-Admiral Mahan and of the lessons inculcated by his important works. For, dwelling on the lessons especially of the War of 1812 but also of the American Civil War, Mahan had delivered himself of the dictum that "the *guerre de course* [commerce-raiding] can never be by itself alone decisive of great issues." It is command of the sea that is decisive: "It is not the taking of individual ships or convoys, be they few or many, that strikes down the money power of a nation; it is the possession of that overbearing power on the sea which drives the enemy's flag from it, or allows it to appear only as a fugitive."[24] There are two critical errors in this passage. One is inherent in the reference to "money power" as though it were inevitably inseparable from military power. The federal government in the American Civil War could have its maritime commerce largely swept from the seas by Confederate raiders and yet win the war, especially since it still had access to Europe in foreign ships; but a Britain at war could not tolerate such a loss. The second error was in the phrase "be they few or many." For a nation that is utterly dependent on sea-borne commerce, the scale of losses of commercial shipping is all-important.

The German submarines and surface torpedo-launching vessels turned out to be effective against British warships. Early in the war some important ships were lost to U-boat attacks, and for fear of such attacks, the Grand Fleet was temporarily driven from its anchorage at Scapa Flow. At the Battle of Jutland, in May 1916, the British fleet twice turned away from torpedo attacks by German surface vessels. Although only one British battleship was struck, with a nondisabling hit, the two turn-aways greatly assisted the German High Seas Fleet in making its escape.

The great threats, however, to British—and hence Allied—survival in World War I were the German unrestricted submarine campaigns against British and Allied commerce. When the first one ended as a result of a virtual United States ultimatum after the sinking of the *Lusitania* in May 1915, the British had not yet devised any tools for dealing with submarines. They had no hydrophones and no depth charges.[25] The American diplomatic intervention may well have saved them. When the Germans announced resumption of their unrestricted campaign in February of 1917, they were ready with a much larger number of U-boats than before. The British had meanwhile invented certain elementary devices for attacking submarines, but their losses were nevertheless stupendous. What finally saved them then was the adoption, at the insistence of the civilian prime minister, David Lloyd George, of the convoy system of older times. Admiral Jellicoe, who had left the Grand Fleet and had become first sea lord, had resisted convoying on the grounds that it would not work and that it was anyway too "defensive." But it did work, because it assured that destroyers would be present when submarines found their targets. Jellicoe was sacked. Britain survived. And meanwhile the United States had entered the war as a result of German denunciation of the restrictions undertaken two years earlier in the *Lusitania* crisis.

It took another world war, which began nineteen years after the first, to drive the point home that the kind of surface-fleet domination backed by battleships that Mahan had described was about finished. And this time there was, in addition to the submarine, the combat naval aircraft, whether land-based or carried by that entirely new and distinctive twentieth-century type of warship—the aircraft carrier. Aircraft had been used over the seas during World War I, mostly for reconnaissance, and the aircraft carrier had made its appearance in the British navy just at the close of that war; but the development of both for combat use against sea and land targets was one of the major military-technological achievements of the interwar period and of World War II itself.

The Second World War saw also at sea a remarkable replay of the German U-boat attack against Allied commerce, as well as against warships. Both sides were again unprepared for this contest, the British mostly because they had placed too much confidence in the newly developed ASDIC (later called SONAR), which was a means of detecting not only the presence but also the location of hostile submarines through echo-ranging with ultrasonic (and hence highly directional) sound waves. SONAR proved useful indeed; but nevertheless, it was subject to severe limitations, one being its limited range and another being that it could be used only when the ship carrying it was moving at very low speeds. Also, depth charges, although they had been improved since World War I, still left much to be desired. The Germans, on their part, began the war with an astonishingly small number of submarines. True, they had signed a treaty with Britain in 1935 that limited their submarine fleet; but this had been a voluntary act, and the treaty had provided also for them to build several substantial surface warships, including two large battleships of the *Bismarck* class. The *Bismarck* herself provided some drama in the events leading up to her own sinking in May of 1941, but as compared with what was accomplished by the U-boats, the German surface warships represented strategically just so much wasted resources. The destruction of Allied commerce in the worst period of the war—1942 and early 1943—was comparable to that of the worst periods of World War I, but lasted longer. In

World War II, however, the British had much more assistance from United States naval forces, an assistance that began even before the United States officially entered the war in December 1941. A critical element in the defeat of the U-boat was the conversion of transports into small aircraft carriers—the "jeep carriers"—in order to provide air coverage even in the mid-Atlantic.

Changes in the Technology of Land Warfare after Waterloo

The changes in methods of fighting on land during most of the nineteenth century were less spectacular than those at sea, mostly because, in comparison to the major warship, there was on land no large engine waiting to be transformed. The development of steam-powered railroad transportation both in Europe and America was of immense strategic importance, but its implements were not inherently machines of war. Also, inasmuch as field guns continued to be horse-drawn through World War I, they were obviously subject to a limitation on size that did not apply to naval guns. There was no development in armor that was comparable to that on warships until the coming of the tank in World War I, one hundred years after Waterloo.

The main change in armies was in the volume and accuracy of firepower, from both hand guns and artillery. In the hand gun we naturally think again of the introduction of rifling.

Rifling had appeared in sporting arms as early as the seventeenth century (sporting arms for nobles were always more highly developed than were guns for mere soldiers; that is why the expensive wheel-lock musket never made its appearance at all in mass armies, which went straight from the inexpensive matchlock to the inexpensive flintlock). Rifled hand arms appeared in some armies in the latter part of the eighteenth century. There was the legendary "Kentucky rifle," used by the American woodsman-turned-soldier in the American Revolution, and a weapon called the Baker rifle was used by British troops in the Peninsular War and also in the Waterloo campaign. However, the rifles were confined to a few expert shots, who used them in preliminary skirmishing. The difficulty was not so much that rifles were more expensive to make, which of course they were, but that they took a good deal more time to reload; the bullet had to be hammered home from the muzzle through the twisting grooves. To the hunter, accuracy meant much, and reloading time meant little; but the reverse was true for the soldier.

In 1823 a Captain Norton of the British army invented a type of cylindro-conoidal bullet that could be easily inserted from the muzzle but that expanded on firing so that it would dig into the grooves of a rifled barrel. The invention was enthusiastically taken up in France, where a Capt. C. E. Minié gave his name to it. This new "Minié ball," which was not a ball at all, meant that a rifle could be loaded as rapidly from the muzzle as a smoothbore musket could be, which meant that the latter was finally doomed. Meanwhile, too, beginning about 1820, the flintlock igniter that had prevailed for a century and a half began to give way to the percussion cap, which depended upon the disposition of fulminate of mercury to explode when given a smart hammer blow. Moreover, existing flintlock muskets or rifles could be converted to percussion-cap weapons. This invention increased not only the ease of loading but more especially the reliability of fire in windy or wet weather. By the time of the Kaffir War (1851) and the Crimean War (1854–1856), European armies were using exclusively percussion-cap rifles that fired improved Minié balls.

A concurrent and equally important development was that of breech loading. The first really satisfactory breechloader was developed at Harper's Ferry Arsenal by Christian Sharps, who gave his name to the word "sharpshooter." The perfected 1859 model became the most popular single-shot breechloader during the Civil War. The great initial importance of breech loading was that it permitted reloading as well as firing from a prone position, and hence permitted a much better use of cover, especially for the defense. Breech loading was also far better adapted to the use of rifling, which no longer required an expanding bullet and which invited the use of a cartridge that combined in one piece the bullet, the propelling powder, and the igniter. Within a short period, this in turn made possible the use of the repeater rifle.

The American Civil War was a colossal proving ground for improved weapons of all kinds. For the first time the achievements of the industrial and scientific revolutions were used on a large scale in war, a fact that was bound to be of advantage to the more industrialized North, which in addition had better access to Europe. There were breechloading, rifled cannon for the artillery (and also muzzleloading smoothbores as of old). There were breechloading rifles and, later, repeaters for the infantry and the cavalry. There were also armored trains and land mines. What was especially important, this was the first war to see mass movement of troops by railroad, and the first in which the telegraph was used for military purposes. On the waters there was, as we have seen, the first duel between two ironclad ships, both maneuvering by steam; and there was considerable use of mines and of both free-floating and spar torpedoes, as well as experiments with submarines and spar-torpedo boats. It was the first war to be adequately photographed. Balloons were used (sparingly) for reconnaissance and for signaling messages by means of mirrors. One European observer who watched balloon exercises from the White House lawn with special fascination was Count Ferdinand von Zeppelin, then a young Prussian lieutenant.[26]

The most important effect of the new weaponry was to carry much further a trend that had already been discerned by Clausewitz even in the days of the smoothbore, flintlock musket, and had also been discerned by so superb a tactician as the duke of Wellington. Clausewitz argued at length, to the consternation of soldiers of his own time as well as of ours, that the defensive is the "stronger form" of war, and he applied this both in his strategic and his tactical reasoning.[27] It is obvious throughout *On War* that he disliked the frontal attack, though he seldom discusses the matter directly. Wellington, in most of his major battles and certainly at Waterloo, adopted the defensive stance; and at one point in the latter battle he expressed to a subordinate his contempt of Napoleon's tactics of direct frontal assault. He had expected Napoleon to attempt an envelopment of his right flank, and he had made dispositions against it; but Napoleon disappointed him by proving "a mere pounder after all." At Waterloo as at most of his battles, Wellington took care to put his troops on the reverse slope of the rise that they had occupied, thus minimizing the effect of enemy artillery; and he absorbed attack after attack without counterattacking except with cavalry—until the very end of the battle.[28]

If the tactical advantage was on the side of the defense in that day, how much more was it so when troops could fire in a prone position behind earthworks! The first battles of the American Civil War demonstrated dramatically that the old Napoleonic tactics of mass frontal assault were dead. Both sides speedily learned that a few log-faced earthworks gave them an immense advantage, and the axe and the shovel became nearly as important parts of the soldier's equipment as his rifle. Towards the end of the war, especially in the lines around Petersburg, defensive entrenchments became extremely complex, and their occupation became prolonged. It was a foreplay of what would happen on a much vaster scale in the war of 1914 to 1918. When both Union and Confederate generals occasionally reverted to the Napoleonic frontal attacks, as Lee did at Gettysburg and Grant did at Cold Harbor, the result was almost always a costly failure.

Another change that Clausewitz had discerned occurring in his time and that became pronounced with the weaponry of the Civil War was the diminution in the effectiveness of cavalry used as a shock force. The cavalry attacks at Waterloo had almost without qualification been costly failures; and that at a time when the cavalry had little to fear from musket fire until they had got close to the enemy. When the rifle made the long-range fire of hand arms more deadly, and when the infantry could lie behind breastworks to fire, the function of the army's "shock arm" was virtually abolished. Among the first to see this was the Union cavalry commander Brig. Gen. John Buford, who saw that horses should be used for mobility but that men should dismount when they fought—as his men did in opening the Battle of Gettysburg. Cavalry continued to be effective in reconnaissance and in long-range raids against communications and supplies, but the old-fashioned cavalry charge was a thing of the past—or should have been, if European generals had been ready to learn from the experience of others. The Franco-Prussian War of 1870/1871 had, in its brief duration, a number of old-fashioned cavalry charges, all of which were failures with heavy loss. The one that was considered a success was in the end the most costly of all, because it enabled cavalry generals to point to it for the next forty years as a reason for continuing to use cavalry as a shock force.[29]

Cavalry divisions continued to be maintained even through World War I and were usually kept ready behind the lines during the great "pushes," waiting for the breakthrough that they hoped to exploit but that never came. There were even horse cavalry regiments in World War II, at least in the Polish and the Russian armies, but their utter uselessness finally became apparent to all.

In 1841 the Prussians developed the so-called needle gun, which was the first practical breechloading rifle used by European armies. The "needle" was simply the slender rod that was hit by the hammer at one end and that actuated the primer at the other. The needle gun was supposed to have been decisive in the Battle of Sadowa, which ended the Austro-Prussian, or Seven Weeks' War, of 1866. But the Austrians were also inferior in everything else, most especially in their generalship. That war was less remarkable for the success of the needle gun than it was for the impressive way in which the Prussians used their railroads to mobilize and concentrate their troops.

During the Franco-Prussian War, which came four years later and was the last of the wars of German unification, the Prussians were confronted with an enemy that had an even better hand rifle, the famous French chassepot. However, the superiority that the French had because of this weapon did not begin to make up for their appalling inferiority in generalship.

During this war the French also introduced in combat the Montigny *mitrailleuse* (still the French word for machine gun), which had been designed and built in numbers in unprecedented secrecy under the personal sponsorship of Napoleon III, who, unlike the first Napoleon, was much interested in the development of arms. A machine gun had been designed by Dr. Richard Gatling during the American Civil War, but it was not used in combat, as the *mitrailleuse* was. Both these guns used the principal of multiple barrels, rotating and being fired in turn (the name Gatling was also adopted for an extremely high-speed 20-mm. machine gun mounted aboard American jet fighter craft after World War II, for example on the F-104). The *mitrailleuse* was generally acknowledged to be a failure in the Franco-Prussian War, mostly because it was used as an artillery piece rather than as an integral part of the infantry and because it lacked, among other things, appropriate range for an artillery function. However, because it was mounted on a large-wheeled carriage like a field gun, it could hardly be used in any other way.

The Battle of Plevna in the Russo-Turkish War of 1877/1878 demonstrated to Europeans—had they been willing to absorb the lesson—what the Americans had learned at such cost during the Civil War, namely, that massed attacks are futile, or at least very costly, against infantrymen armed with breechloaders, if the latter are protected by even the most primitive and hastily constructed breastworks. The Turks had an excellent American rifle in the Peabody-Martini. The Russians, who greatly outnumbered the entrenched Turks, attacked three times, and each time they were beaten back with heavy losses. This result was achieved in the absence of any machine guns.

Meanwhile, field artillery was also being improved. The rifling and breech loading that were so successful in the hand arms were applied also to artillery pieces. But, as we pointed out above, the longer projectile permitted by rifling means more mass, and hence inertia; the gun must therefore be made much stronger. In hand arms the differences in mass, and hence inertia, between the ball and the cylindrical bullet were much less significant. The most important of the relevant developments in the mid-nineteenth century was the development by the Krupps of a gun made of steel (in place of cast iron, or the stronger wrought iron, or brass). A Krupp 3-pound muzzleloader of cast steel was displayed at the Great Exhibition in London in 1851 (there was much less secrecy about new weapons at that time); it was considered a marvel for its time in lightness and tensile strength. Later the hooped or built-up principle was applied to field guns, as it had previously been to naval guns.

The next important development in field artillery, as in naval artillery, was the introduction of smokeless powder, which was first developed by the French chemist Vieille in 1874, Alfred Nobel following along with ballistite in 1890, and the British with cordite. Doing away with the smoke was important enough, but, as we noted above, the other great advantage of smokeless powder, not evident in its name, was its slower, more controllable burning. Slower burning meant that more overall thrust could be obtained with lesser maximum pressures in the gun. The larger naval guns lost their beer-bottle shape, with huge thicknesses near the breech, and became longer and more slender; the field guns simply became more powerful for their limited maximum weight.

The final development in making the modern gun—of equal importance to all the others—was the perfection of a suitable recoil mechanism. This meant allowing the barrel to recoil in a slide or trough without moving the wheeled carriage that supported it; it also meant having some device to absorb the shock and to return the barrel to its firing position. If it could be done smoothly enough, reaiming could be minimized or avoided altogether, and the gun could be fired much more rapidly. General Wille in Germany and

Colonel Langlois in France proposed such mechanisms in 1891, and before the decade was out, the French had designed the superb hydropneumatic recoil mechanism of the famous 75-mm. gun that was to be their main field-artillery piece in World War I. Adopted by the Americans upon their entry into that war, it became known to them as the "French 75"; it was still in use in American field-artillery regiments as late as 1930.

The perfection of recoil mechanisms, when applied to smaller arms, made possible the modern machine gun. The Gatling gun and the Montigny *mitrailleuse* had had to be operated by a hand crank. The British inventor Hiram Maxim ended the need for cranking when, in 1885, he devised a gun that used its recoil energy to reload itself, fire, and reject its empty shells. This was the first truly automatic gun, for the gunner had only to squeeze and hold the trigger. The British army adopted it in 1889, and in the Boer War (1899–1902) they were already using a Maxim automatic gun of 37-mm. caliber, which was called a "pom-pom," the ancestor of automatic guns of comparable caliber (up to 40 mm.) used against aircraft in World War II. In the United States, John M. Browning invented, in 1895, a machine gun, later produced by Colt, which used, not the recoil energy, but the high-pressure gases produced by the firing—which were vented through a hole near the muzzle—in order to operate the necessary mechanism. Both the recoil and the gas forms of activation continue to be used today in the most modern forms of automatic and semiautomatic guns and hand arms.

The Boer War at the end of the century provided the first sharp warning of what was to come in World War I, a warning that was to be accentuated in the Russo-Japanese War (1904/1905). In the Boer War both sides were armed with smokeless, repeating rifles. Artillery reassumed the great tactical importance that it had lost after the Napoleonic Wars. The apparent emptiness of the battlefield became the new phenomenon of war. Colorful uniforms gave way to khaki, for better camouflage. Beyond 600 yards, artillery fire was dangerous; within 600 yards, the new small-arms fire was deadly. The big problem was how to cross the last 400 yards against an entrenched enemy. The Maxim machine gun seems to have been tried out in South Africa, but not greatly used; however, in the Russo-Japanese War, there was much more use of machine guns.

An Aberrant Doctrine, and Oceans of Blood

One might think that by the time World War I arrived in the summer of 1914 the cumulative effect of all the inventions that we have been describing would have made a deep impression on the generals who were to do the strategic and tactical planning for that war and then to wage it. On the contrary, they virtually ignored it. It was in the decade and a half before that war that the doctrine of the tactical offensive reached a frenzied apotheosis, especially in France, where Col. Ferdinand Foch at the Advanced School of War (École supérieure de la guerre) published in 1903 his *Principles of War* and gathered round him a group of disciples, including the notorious Colonel de Grandmaison, who directed all their teachings to the glorification of *l'offensive brutale et à outrance*.

In this respect the French were only more vocal and marginally more extreme than their British allies, especially after the first year of the war, when Sir Douglas Haig replaced Sir John French as commander of the British forces in France. The Germans were not far behind in their dedication to the offensive, but far enough to make an enormous difference when the losses could finally be compared at the end of the war. Being considerably occupied in the East, the Germans left it mostly to the Western Allies to hurl offensive after futile offensive against the machine guns and the barbed-wire entanglements of the opponents' unyielding lines. And the Allies paid for it with oceans of blood. They seemed to be incapable of learning from experience, largely because of the unprecedented separation of the high command from the front lines. When Gen. Henri Pétain exclaimed in protest, following the awful agony of Verdun in 1916, "*Le feu tue!*" ("fire kills!"), he was not saying something too trite and banal to be noticed, but rather something that marked him, in the eyes of his colleagues, as unfit for top command. That command went instead, upon the relief of General Joffre, to Gen. Robert Nivelle, who in the spring of 1917 launched the most ambitious of French offensives up to that time, the complete failure of which caused a large-scale mutiny in the French army.

In autumn of the same year the British, who had suffered hideous losses in the futile Somme offensive of the year before, undertook at Ypres, near Passchendaele, a four-months-long attack in a sea of mud. There, as at the Somme, Haig was certain that he was inflicting far heavier casualties on the Germans than his own troops were suffering—which was quite the reverse of the truth—and in his dispatches to the War Office he seemed always to be expecting the enemy to crack under the strain. The miracle is that the British did not crack, though the survivors were left in vast depression. Today there stands at Ypres a momunent to fifty-six thousand British dead whose bodies were lost in the mud and never recovered. Haig was the same commander who in late 1915, after a year of experience that had proved the contrary, delivered himself of the opinion that the machine gun was a "much over-rated weapon."

We have already noted Clausewitz's conviction that defense was the "stronger form" of war, a view which he developed at length and propounded in considerable analytical detail. He meant by "stronger form" that there were inherent advantages to being on the defensive, both strategically and tactically, which to overcome in a successful offensive required adequate compensating advantages, such as marked superiority in numbers. We have seen also that in the wars of the nineteenth century and up to the Russo-Japanese War of 1904–1906, improving firepower made frontal attacks increasingly costly and hazardous. From one decade to the next, firepower had increased to a degree and in a manner that would seem to any detached person—as it did in fact to one Polish scholar writing towards the end of the nineteenth century—to give an enormous advantage to anyone defending, from an entrenched position, against frontal attack.[30] But by 1914 and even up to 1918, such an idea was anathema in the French army, and hardly less so in the British army. Why?

We do not have the space here to attempt to answer this question in depth.[31] Even in Clausewitz's time, his doctrine that the greater strength lay with the defensive met little favor among his colleagues in his profession. Later generations of German soldiers felt quite sure that he would have revised his opinion had he lived longer. On the other hand, they could not quite ignore that opinion, as Foch and his followers did, which may be why the dogma of the offensive never reached the extravagant extremes among the Germans that it did among the French and British. Clausewitz does indeed repeatedly emphasize the need, after a successful defensive, for going over to the offensive to achieve final victory, using some of his most spirited language in the process. Contemporary and later writers on strategy led from the latter point.

Since Napoleon's time, military leaders have always stressed the virtues of initiative and aggressiveness in a commander, in part because they knew that under the stress and hazards of war, human nature tends rather towards caution and timidity.

European wars between 1815 and 1914 were generally short, which meant that the tactical lessons the military would absorb from them were bound to be limited. Such lessons either had to be overwhelming in the demonstrated superiority of some new device or tactic, or they had to be not too uncongenial to preexisting biases. The wars of German unification were special models of brevity and decisiveness. That against Austria in 1866, of which Sadowa was the capstone, is usually called the Seven Weeks' War. And the dates always given for the Franco-Prussian War—1870/1871—are quite deceptive about its duration. Altogether it lasted some six months, but the outcome was decided with the French surrender at Sedan on September 1, 1870, just six weeks after Napoleon III had declared war. French resistance for the remaining months, at the siege of Paris and elsewhere, was bound to be futile except for satisfying the intangibles of French honor.

The disastrous French defeat in that war had much to do with the French military being in the vanguard of offensive religiosity in the period leading up to World War I. A defeat in war is generally traumatic to the nation suffering it, but to the French—with their Napoleonic legend of *la gloire*—it was devastating. The upstart Prussian state, which at that time was no more populous than France, compounded the humiliation by declaring from Versailles the formation of the German Empire, which now displaced France as clearly the first nation on the Continent, and by taking Alsace and half of Lorraine, territories that had been French for over two hundred years. The French military naturally set about determining why they had lost, and naturally, too, the reasons most likely to find favor were those least damaging to the egos of the inquirers.

The French had lost because of some of the worst ineptness in generalship that the world had seen since the Prussians had lost to the French in the Jena campaign of 1806. But those who wrote about the matter with a view to deriving strategic lessons from it tended, rather, to find that, among other things, the French had been too "defensive" in their strategy. After all, it was the Prussians who invaded France, not the reverse; and although that fact had had more to do with the speed of the Prussian mobilization than with ideology, the payoff for Prussian initiative had been handsome indeed.

The French rediscovered the writings of Colonel Ardant du Picq, who had lost his life at the head of his regiment. Ardant du Picq had made scholarly investigations of the psychology of the soldier in combat, dwelling especially on the factors that accounted for the great disparities in casualties between victor and vanquished in some of the battles of antiquity. He had concluded that true bravery in battle is exceedingly rare, that the commander's main task in combat is therefore to give courage to his soldiers in order to keep them from breaking and fleeing. His insightful views were, however, vulgarized into slogans that fitted the needs of the generation of "young Turks," slogans such as: "He will win who has the courage to advance."[32]

The intellectual and social moods of the two or three decades preceding the outbreak of war in 1914 were also exceptionally hospitable to the offensive ideology. It was a period of extraordinary national chauvinism, which was all too compatible with another attitude of the age—namely, "social Darwinism." The latter phrase denotes an attitude that finds in the Darwinian scheme of things an ethic, rather than simply an explanation—the fittest are the most *deserving* of survival—and the fittest among peoples are of course those who win wars rather than those who lose them. The fittest are also those with offensive spirit, for offensive spirit not only makes victory more likely but somehow betokens in itself the superior man. Significantly, the French erected at Sedan, after their defeat, a monument to a futile French attack. On it are inscribed in French the words supposedly uttered (no doubt in German) by the Prussian king as he watched the French cavalry making another hopeless dash against their opponents: *"Ah! Les braves gens!"*

These few speculative observations on why the obvious could be denied before World War I, and could continue to be denied at such great cost during it, may help to establish the point that there is nothing automatic about the influence of weaponry on warfare. That influence has to be exerted initially through the minds of men, who make judgments, first, about the utility of weaponry or other devices and, second, about the tactical and strategic implications of the general adoption of these new weapons or devices. These judgments can be exceedingly stubborn and may long fly in the face of what to succeeding generations will look like the most overwhelming contrary evidence.

Breaking the Stalemate

There were, of course, successful offensives even during World War I. The Eastern Front was always far more fluid than the Western, due to the much greater expanses of territory over which the armies contended and also to the huge technical superiority of the German armies over the Russian ones. The Soviet surrender at Brest-Litovsk on March 3, 1918, was the natural result of some continuing German offensives, which at that time were no longer encountering any resistance. But that was after the Russians had already lost over four million dead or presumed dead, not to mention other casualties—a much higher number than was suffered by any other belligerent. These losses had been largely the result of "human wave" infantry charges against German and Austrian troops, the Russian infantry always being inadequately armed and lacking ammunition. The impressive Brusilov offensive of 1916 had to pay for its temporary gains with the staggering toll of over one million Russian casualties, a loss that contributed directly to the final revolution and collapse.

On the Western Front the German offensive of March 1918 (directly after the Russian collapse) against the pivotal connection between the British and French armies gained initial successes that were greater than any theretofore achieved by any offensive on that front. The reasons are to be found in the new "infiltration tactics" adopted by General Ludendorff and to the considerable local superiority. No doubt the terrible British losses of the Passchendaele offensive, which had ended only a few months earlier, also had much to do with it. In any case, the German offensive was finally contained and defeated, and the now sprawling and disorganized German army had to confront an Allied army that had been made vastly and suddenly more powerful with the addition of one million fresh American troops and virtually unlimited stores of matériel. And so Ferdinand Foch, now a marshal and generalissimo of all the armies of the Western Allies, was at last "vindicated."

After the war the French built their Maginot Line—from the Swiss border north to the edge of the Ardennes Forest, where it stopped. The Ardennes, lying across southern Luxembourg below the tip of Belgium, were supposed to be impassable to German tanks. It was this section of the front, which the French manned with their poorest troops, that Hitler chose for his major thrust in May 1940. He punched through the French lines with seven panzer (armored) divisions, thus outflanking both the Maginot Line to the south and the large force of British and French troops that had moved into Belgium to meet the German invasion of that country and Holland. The Maginot Line itself was penetrated about a week later, but by that time much of its garrison had been removed, and the whole French army was already in an advanced state of demoralization. Whatever the merits or demerits of the Maginot Line, one cannot say that it was ever truly tested under the technological conditions of World War II.

The much greater fluidity of battle lines in World War II, as compared with World War I, was due primarily to the effective use of two military devices that had made their first appearance in World War I. These were the tank and the tactical aircraft. Aircraft had been used from the beginning of World War I for reconnaissance, and subsequently had been used for strafing and bombing troops, but not until 1918 did they play a truly significant part.

Tanks had been developed by the British, under the direct sponsorship of Winston Churchill when he was first lord of the admiralty, the post he held until mid-1915, when the failure of the Gallipoli campaign forced him to resign. Although tanks had been first tested ineffectively in small numbers in 1916, some three hundred were later used in an offensive at Cambrai in November 1917 with enormous success. However, the British were unprepared to exploit their success, having in reserve only some horse cavalry, and the Germans soon won back the ground they had lost.

Between the wars the British and the French developed the tank technically, but they developed no coherent doctrine for its use. That was left for the Germans who, under the leadership of General Guderian, supposedly built upon some of the ideas of two British writers, the civilian Basil Liddell Hart and Gen. J. F. C. Fuller.[33] The central idea was that tanks should be concentrated in "armored divisions," in contrast to the French and British system, which scattered them through the normal infantry divisions. The concept adopted by the Germans borrowed something from naval tactics, for the tanks were handled like so many armored ships, which in concentration are not likely to be bested except by a larger concentration of their own kind. Under World War II conditions, aircraft were not likely to be very effective against moving tanks, and the antitank guns lacked the mobility and the protection that were necessary for effectively massing against armored vehicles.

At the time of the German attack westward in May of 1940, the British and French together seem to have had more tanks than the Germans, and some were of superior quality to any that the Germans had. But those of the Germans were concentrated. In addition, the Germans used their tactical aircraft as a spearhead for the tanks. The combination was novel and effective enough, and the world found itself in a new era of highly mobile warfare. This was to be the pattern followed throughout the war, except when bad weather grounded the aircraft.

However, after the fantastic gains won by the Germans because of their power and the novelty of their tactics—which won them easy victory over the Poles in 1939, a spectacular victory over the French and British in 1940, and great successes against the Russians in the initial onslaughts of 1941—the old rule was restored, namely, that only with marked superiority can one hope to make real advances. The British and the Russians, and subsequently the Americans, showed themselves good pupils with respect to the deployment of tanks and the use of tactical aircraft. And then they made their growing superiority tell.

In the set-piece Battle of El Alamein, which opened in the desert to the west of Egypt in October of 1942, Gen. Bernard Montgomery had accumulated a superiority of at least three to one in aircraft and about four to one in tanks; he also had a marked superiority in infantry. His opponent, Gen. Erwin Rommel, had a spent army, which was operating at the end of an extremely long and difficult line of communications across the North African desert. Even so, success did not come easily to the attacker. In this case the troops led first, clearing corridors through the minefields for the tanks, while being covered by a ferocious artillery bombardment. With all his superiority, Montgomery had what he subsequently called a "stern fight," lasting some twelve days. After that came the pursuit of the defeated German army. In the battle and in the subsequent pursuit, the British had the kind of advantage from their naval superiority that they had enjoyed in the final phase of the Peninsular Campaign. Wellington, moving across northern Spain in 1813/1814 could always depend on the Royal Navy to bring him supplies and reinforcements at each harbor that he seized in his advance, a kind of assistance that the same navy denied to his French opponents. Thus, as warfare changes almost beyond recognition, there still remain some essential patterns, which are modified but not basically changed.

Strategic Air Power and Its Prophet

The idea that a military vehicle that could cruise in the air could also drop bombs needed no great imagination; and the idea that targets behind the front, including cities, might be appropriate targets for such bombing needed only a World War I for its realization. For the concept that modern war is, or tends to be, total—with the "home front" being as critically involved as the troops on the fighting fronts and thus fair game for attack—was almost as necessary to the idea of "strategic bombing" as was the provision of the mechanical means. And World War I was as total as the belligerents knew how to make it. The war at sea, with the British blockading Germany and the Germans attempting a counterblockade with their submarines, effectively wiped out distinctions between civilians and military personnel as ultimate targets. Thus, when the means appeared, neither side showed any compunction about dropping bombs on enemy cities. The Germans attacked London as early as 1915 with bombs dropped from their huge lighter-than-air dirigibles, which had been developed by Count Zeppelin; and the Allies replied in kind as soon as they developed the requisite aircraft.

However, what we now know as strategic bombing follows a well-organized and highly specific body of doctrine that goes far beyond any random dropping of bombs on cities. And although his primacy tends to be disputed by the British, who have their own candidate, the Italian army officer Brig. Gen. Giulio Douhet is without doubt the source of the ideas that animated the United States Army Air Forces in World War II.[34] We know also that German airforce officers studied Douhet, but being committed to the support of huge armies, they were not able to follow his guidance as much as they might have liked.

Douhet was appalled at the useless carnage of World War I, and his writings contain his bitter denunciation of the generals who he thought were responsible. Whether or not he was rationalizing his argument, or whether or not the justification was important to him, Douhet did claim that his method of achieving victory in war was the most humane and the least damaging to the community of nations, because it avoided the senseless bloodshed that had characterized the trench warfare of World War I.

Douhet's argument develops the following major points:

1. The ascendancy of the defensive demonstrated in World War I is permanent; hence the battle fronts along the ground will be static; and hence, too, it will require only small ground forces to hold the lines against much superior ones.
2. The victory is therefore to be won through air attack, and therefore, too, the major military resources of the nation should be concentrated in air power.
3. The decisive air attack is by bombers upon a prescribed group of target systems behind the fronts; it is a total waste of air power to use aircraft tactically in support of the ground forces.

4. The first task of the bombers is the destruction of enemy air power on the ground in order to gain *command of the air*; thus, the enemy's aircraft on his airfields are the first target system, and the enemy's factories for building new aircraft are the second target system. In order to be sure to catch the enemy aircraft on the ground, one should launch a preemptive attack before a declaration of war.
5. The superior efficiency and effectiveness of destroying enemy aircraft on the ground makes it unnecessary to think of destroying them in the air. Hence, one does not need fighter aircraft for escort or for any other purpose. The bomber should be a "battleship of the air," capable of protecting itself against any enemy fighters that initially escape destruction on the ground. Thus, not only are military resources concentrated in air power, but air power is concentrated in bombers.
6. After it has achieved command of the air, the bomber force pursues as its ultimate target system the morale of the enemy civilian population, which is highly vulnerable because civilians are not trained for war. It is useless to attack industries producing for the ground forces, because the latter can do nothing decisive, and anyway the war will be over before such production can matter.

This philosophy is quite distinct from that of, say, Brig. Gen. "Billy" Mitchell, who has been revered by American air officers because of his staunch advocacy of air power, for which, the legend goes, he was martyred.[35] To Mitchell, air power was "anything that flies," and appropriate targets were anything military, whether enemy ground troops, warships, or aircraft. His philosophy, if it can be called such, was quite undifferentiated. He was neither opposed to strategic bombing nor inclined to give it the exclusive role that Douhet did. In any case, he seems to have thought very little about strategy.

Douhet's use of the term "command of the air," which is the title of his major and best-known essay, is obviously a borrowing from Mahan and from contemporary usage with respect to naval power, but his concept really goes far beyond Mahan's. For Mahan, command of the sea was won for the purpose of controlling maritime traffic because of the various military functions that that traffic served. Although Mahan might have conceded it only grudgingly, he conceived of sea power as an important and sometimes decisive adjunct to land power. To Douhet, air power was entirely exclusive and self-sufficient. It gained command of the air, not to serve other branches of the service, but only to carry out its own fundamental purposes; insofar as possible it ignored other forms of military power.

We need not discuss here the development of aircraft from the time of the Wright brothers' first flight in 1903 until Douhet's theories received their great test in World War II. The subject, in its broad outlines, is familiar enough to most readers. The military implications of the flying machine, at least for reconnaissance, were obvious from the beginning of flight. Aircraft were used for reconnaissance in the first month of World War I, some on the French side being responsible for reporting in detail the movements of the German armies that led up to the first Battle of the Marne. Before the war was over, aircraft had been used in virtually every military role in which they were to be used in World War II.

The test of Douhet's theories that was provided by World War II—the "war of the future" that he was writing about—was more than fair to Douhet. Most of his writing dates from the early and middle twenties, and the improvement in aircraft from that time to the beginning of World War II was extraordinary. The bombing aircraft used in that war were capable of much better performance in range, speed, and weight-carrying capacities than any Douhet knew. Also, the numbers that were to take to the air on all kinds of missions, and not least on strategic-bombing missions, were far greater than any Douhet had conceived of. But if one considers his philosophy in its specifics—which is to say as something more than a general advocacy of aircraft in the style of Mitchell—one sees that he was proved wrong in every major aspect of his theory. That is not to say that air power proved ineffective. Quite the contrary. But it was Billy Mitchell's kind of air power that succeeded—anything that flies, and against all kinds of military targets—not Douhet's. Whether or not strategic bombing succeeded in the end in achieving its purposes has been debated heatedly, although in my opinion it has to be answered with a qualified affirmative. But it did not succeed in the way or to the degree that Douhet thought it would.

First of all, battle lines on the ground turned out *not* to be static; one reason for that, as we have seen, was the effective *tactical* use of aircraft. And so long as armies could advance rapidly, they generated a high priority call on aircraft either to support or oppose them. Second, although there were some highly successful attacks of one air force upon the grounded planes of an opponent, it turned out that the total air forces of a great power are not so easily destroyed. One of the reasons for that was the invention and development of radar, which Douhet had not foreseen. Third, the effectiveness of fighters against bombers in air combat turned out to be much greater than Douhet had expected. The American air forces, imbued with Douhet's ideas, came to Europe with their "flying fortresses" (B-17s), which they expected to fly in daylight in close formation for mutual defense, without escorting fighters, and to engage in a "precision bombing" not possible in the night bombing to which the British confined themselves. Their flights over Germany were costly and chastening experiences. Not only the enemy's fighters, but his antiaircraft guns as well, which Douhet had utterly scorned, reaped a grim toll of the invading bombers. Fortunately for the Americans, their devotion to Douhet's theories had not prevented them from developing long-range fighters such as the P-51, which became available in time as escorts to the bombers.

Finally and most important, bombing attacks turned out to be vastly less effective than Douhet had predicted. Civilian morale proved far from vulnerable. So far as war industries were concerned, including aircraft industries, these also turned out to be much less vulnerable than Douhet had supposed. He and his followers had devoted little thought to determining what parts of the plant were physically the most critical or the most vulnerable. What damage was done could often be repaired with a speed that would have been unbelievable before the war. Besides, despite all the talk about "precision bombing," under wartime conditions, bombing turned out to be by orders of magnitude less accurate than the bombing enthusiasts had expected.

The air war against Germany was spent in progressing, largely by trial and error, through various target systems. Some quite effective ones were finally found, especially inland transportation and liquid-fuel production; but by the time these were sufficiently demolished, the Allied armies had brought the war pretty near to its close. To their successes the strategic-bombing attacks had contributed little. Had the war continued six or eight weeks longer, the strategic bombing *might* have proved decisive, but that would have been after years of fighting on the ground and at sea. Douhet had expected "victory through air power" in a matter of days.

Against Japan the American air assault was much more effective, and in much less time. There is strong support for the belief that the Japanese would have surrendered prior to our planned November 1945 landings on their home islands even if the two nuclear weapons had not been used at Hiroshima and Nagasaki. But the air assault could be laid on only after a long, arduous campaign of naval warfare and successive island-landings had won us bases that were close enough to Japan. By that time Japan was already a defeated power, and the terrible air devastation only served to make her government acknowledge this.

The odd aftermath of all this, which should not surprise us in view of prior comparable experience, is that American air officers continued for years after the war to argue what was essentially the Douhet view. Airmen continued to scorn the use of air power for the support of armies or navies; that was "using air power to do the job of artillery." Even "interdiction bombing"— the use of air power to attack enemy supply lines well behind his lines—was not an appropriate mission for air power, because it was still in support of armies. Air power needed to have "an independent mission." Not to understand that was not to "understand air power."

What finally wore down this argument and this point of view was not a reassessment of World War II experience, which was left for the historians, but rather the experience of the wars in Korea and, later, in Vietnam. The opportunity of the Air Force to have a "piece of the action"—and thus an adequate claim upon future budgets—depended upon its becoming more tactically oriented. Also, nuclear weapons had made anachronistic any thought of strategic bombing with conventional bombs, and the use of long-range missiles for such purposes was fast becoming a reality. If airmen wanted to fly airplanes rather than merely tend missiles, and they did most emphatically want to fly airplanes, they simply had to broaden their perspectives about the appropriate use of air power.

It could of course be said that the coming of nuclear weapons finally made Douhet's arguments come true. But in his time, nuclear weapons were totally inconceivable, and he cannot be given credit for anticipating them. All his projections and propositions were in terms of conventional bombing, and he simply failed to measure, or even to attempt to measure, its limitations. Also, with nuclear weapons, we do not need the imagination of a Douhet to tell us what awful destruction they can wreak and in how short a time. With these weapons the whole outlook changes concerning the uses of war itself, not just of strategic bombing. Into this realm we shall not here attempt to penetrate. It has been and is still being done elsewhere, and in the treatment of such questions we move out of history into the present.

Conclusions

We have seen that, *in the long run*, technology has transformed war pretty much in its own fashion. The bumbling ideas of men about the utilities of new weaponry have often caused painful and costly maladjustments, and have even determined at times which side would enjoy the victory; but the mistakes that have been made in the past in these matters seem rarely to have affected the technological conditions in which men found themselves, just as they seem not to have affected the technological conditions in which we find ourselves today. The main reason for this is that the conservatism of the military, about which we hear so much, seems always to have been confined to their adaptation to new weaponry rather than to their acceptance of it. The commander of land, sea, or air forces knows a superior weapon, ship, or aircraft when he sees it, and he has rarely been lacking in eagerness to have it. When he has been unduly lacking in such eagerness, his erroneous decisions have usually been corrected by events. Haig, for example, may have underestimated the effects of the machine gun, and his forces, for that reason, may have had at one time too few of them (and far too many horses carrying lancers). But the British soldier nevertheless did have as good a machine gun as the technology of the time could make available to him, and in time the allocation of two per battalion was raised to a more realistic figure.

On the other hand, in this respect "the long run" can be a pretty long time indeed, and events of grave moment meanwhile have their outcomes determined by gross errors of judgment on the significance of new military techniques. World War I, once it had begun, was bound to cost dearly in casualties to all the participants; but the extraordinary insensitivity that almost all the generals of the time, and some among them in particular, displayed towards the new penalites that technology imposed on offensive ardor made that war far more costly to most of the belligerents than it needed to have been. The effects of that excessive cost were to have great political and strategic consequences also in the next great war, some twenty years later.

Obviously, such mistakes can also determine which side wins the victory in any particular war, and we have seen instances in which such a thing has occurred: for example, the failure of the French to see, prior to 1940, the importance not only of providing tanks but also of concentrating them; or the failure of the Austrians, in 1866, to see that a muzzleloading hand arm was inferior to a breechloading one in important ways. Still, such episodes are much rarer historically than one might expect. There are several reasons for this. For one thing, the conservatism we have referred to follows certain patterns, and these tend to be generalized among the military forces on both sides of a conflict. Military officers tend to be means-oriented rather than object-oriented. Men who have been trained to fly bombers want a bigger, better, and faster bomber; but they do not want to relinquish the bomber type, and they resist arguments that other military means such as missiles will achieve the same object better and cheaper. The same is true of men who have been trained on submarines, or on aircraft carriers, or on tanks. The same was once true of men who were trained to fight on battleships or on horses. Finally, events—or perhaps simple superannuation of individuals—will remove the last effective protests; but in terms of military cost, time is not neutral. These same characteristics tend, however, to affect the military establishments of all nations; and these establishments are also watching each other intently. They have not been given to complete imitation of each other—the forces of the Soviet Union, for example, have passed over bombers in favor of long-range missiles to a much greater extent than the relevant forces of the United States—but it makes a strong argument for getting what one wants from one's government to be able to say that the opponent is building up the same category of weaponry.

Also, when war comes, differences in weaponry between the contestants may appear of modest importance compared with other differences. So long as it was willing to stay the course, the United States was bound to defeat Japan in World War II, because the sheer magnitude of its power was so much greater; the fact that the Japanese at the outset had much better torpedoes turned out to be of no consequence. And, as we have seen, superior generalship has often counted for a great deal more than a marginal superiority in weaponry.

There has been much speculation over the manner and the degree to which certain military inventions or technological developments have favored one nation over another that was its rival. The introduction of ironclad warships and of iron ship construction, we have seen, was supposed to have been of considerable benefit to Britain over its chief naval rival of the nineteenth century, France, because Britain, although it was already having trouble getting the timber it needed for its warships, was the world's leading producer of iron and steel.[36] One has to take such an appraisal with a grain of salt, knowing that historians who write about such things have a bias in favor of finding important consequences from their researches. The proportion of the gross national product of each country that was devoted to naval shipbuilding was relatively small, and one may question whether, in terms of the money it was willing to spend on its navy, France was ever seriously disadvantaged relatively to Britain simply because of its lower level of iron and steel production. The Confederacy in the American Civil War, on the other hand, was so far lacking in heavy industry as compared with the North, and so substantially cut off from European sources by naval blockade, that the difference undoubtedly mattered; but in that special wartime situation there was something approaching a full mobilization condition.

It is clear, however, that some countries have had certain inherent vulnerabilities that were gravely affected by technological developments. The navy that enabled Britain to rule the seas for something like three hundred years gave her both needed security at home and the ability to blockade rivals and to gain vast territories abroad. But the coming of the submarine with its special weapon, the automotive torpedo, gravely qualified Britain's dominion over the seas. A Continental enemy could now imperil her maritime lifelines without first building up a superior navy; and however successful Britain might be in her antisubmarine warfare, it was a challenge that would always be a heavy drain on her resources during wartime and that she might at any time lose, just as she came very close to losing in 1917 and again in 1941/1942. The coming of military aircraft compounded the problem and deprived Britain further of the security that her insular position and her former naval ascendancy had previously given her; and now nuclear weapons mean that, to all practical military purposes, she is no longer an island at all.

The United States has been similarly affected by nuclear weapons. The kind of security that Britain formerly enjoyed was also America's, and to a much greater degree. Maritime communications were not vital to America. Even in a world that knew strategic bombing, with the kinds of bombs used in

World War II the United States was virtually guaranteed against any serious hurt from such attack; for bomb weight always competes with weight of fuel, and the United States was simply too far from any potential opponent's secure aviation bases. And long-range missiles, which are limited to a single mission, are too expensive to be used with chemical-bomb warheads. With nuclear weapons, however, all that is changed. Whether carried by bomber or by missile, the nuclear warhead gives sufficient military payoff to any vehicle that might carry it.

Another recent development that has tended to have still another effect is that of separating further the so-called superpowers from those that were formerly great powers but have now fallen into a decidedly secondary position. As weapons have become more sophisticated in design and performance, their cost per unit has risen accordingly; and since World War II the rise has been extraordinarily steep. The cost of the Grumman F-14, a fighter designed for aircraft-carrier operations, has been steadily mounting since the original contract was written; at this writing, the cost is close to $20 million. It replaces the F-4 Phantom, which cost about $4.5 million; and the Phantom, in turn, replaced an aircraft that cost less than one-tenth its price. The cost of the carrier itself has undergone a similar progression, and at the present writing, the price per unit is already over $1,000 million dollars. There is naturally some trade-off between the performance of units and the numbers of them required to perform any given function; but in many functions there is no substitute for numbers. Two carriers can cover two different locations, which a single carrier cannot do, however superior its performance might be. A country like the United Kingdom or France probably spends today at least as high a proportion of its GNP on military defenses as it has ever done historically in peacetime. And although the GNPs of these countries have risen steadily with the years, both nations have slid from the undoubted great-power status held at the beginning of World War II to something that is militarily much less significant. The reason is mostly the extraordinary rise in unit costs, which applies in greater or lesser degree to virtually every category of military weaponry.

These increases in unit cost and in complexity have helped to further another change that has gained much attention in the years since World War II. This has been the development, especially in the United States, of new institutions that serve the military but are somewhat detached from them. The prototype and best known of these institutions or organizations has been the RAND Corporation at Santa Monica, California, which was originally set up, in 1948, with the United States Air Force as virtually its exclusive client. Similar organizations were set up by the other services; and one (the Institute for Defense Analysis) was later set up by the joint chiefs of staff. Among the techniques developed at RAND, and pursued also at the other organizations, has been that of "systems analysis," which is a refined means of comparing, on a "cost-effectiveness" basis, two or more weapons systems that do not yet exist, in order to determine which, if any, of them should be developed for future use.

The problem dealt with in systems analysis is essentially an old one. Clausewitz, in one fascinating chapter of *On War* (book 5, chapter 4) attempts to analyze the appropriate mix of the three services existing in his time—infantry, cavalry, and artillery—and he understands that the only sensible way to compare them is on the basis of their respective unit costs, on the one hand, and their tactical effectiveness on the other. Determining their costs he finds easy, but determining their comparative effectiveness he finds extremely difficult. The problem of determining appropriate systems became steadily more difficult after his time with the rapid advance of technology, but it was generally handled by senior military officers on an intuitive basis. After World War II, however, the accelerated advances in technology and the large sums of money and long lead times that were required for developing any particular system have made it imperative to think and plan ahead to a degree that was undreamed of prior to that war. To plan ahead means to predict costs as well as effectiveness—costs, not only of a particular weapon like the B-1 bomber, but of the entire *system* of which that weapon is the major component. The system includes all the other components and facilities that are necessary to the use of the contemplated major item, as well as the required manning, training, and maintenance over a given period of time. Thus, predicting the cost side of the equation, which was so easy in Clausewitz's time, can now be at least as difficult as predicting effectiveness. Therefore, the need arises for people of special training and highly developed skills to do the kinds of analysis that will assist the decision-maker in the final exercise of his judgment.

However, although making the appropriate choices and mixes of weapons systems is important enough in modern times, since money is always a scarce resource, these are not the most important problems concerning the national security that a secretary of defense, let alone the president to whom he is responsible, has to deal with. Now as always, the most important problems are not tactical but strategic and political. Over what issues, and where, should we be prepared to threaten the use of military force? What kinds of military judgments are reasonable in a nuclear age? These and other questions of like moment will determine the major parameters within which weapons-systems choices will be made; but far more important are the effects of the pertinent answers upon the life and well-being of the state. The kind of rethinking, for example, of our powers and our interests that has inevitably followed from the failure of our intervention in Vietnam will no doubt leave plenty of room for debate; but very little of that debate will be concerned with questions of weapons and tactics.

Notes

1. A fuller treatment of the subject of this paragraph is contained in chap. 6, "Changing Attitudes Towards War," of my *War and Politics* (New York: Macmillan, 1973).
2. Count Maurice de Saxe (i.e., "of Saxony") wrote his *Mes reveries* during an illness relatively early in his career, but they were not published until 1757, seven years after his death. They are contained in translation (*My Reveries upon the Art of War*) in Thomas R. Phillips, ed., *Roots of Strategy* (Harrisburg, Pa.: Military Service Publishing, 1940), pp. 177–300. The passage quoted is on p. 298. An excellent biography is Jon E. M. White's *Marshal of France* (London: Hamilton, 1962).
3. Frederick's *The Instructions of Frederick the Great for His Generals, 1747*, is contained in Phillips's *Roots of Strategy*, pp. 311–400. See also the excellent chapter on Frederick by R. R. Palmer in *Makers of Modern Strategy*, ed. Edward M. Earle (Princeton, N.J.: Princeton University Press, 1943), pp. 49–74.
4. One of the very few biographies of Clausewitz in English is the recent highly readable though sometimes inaccurate one by Roger Parkinson, *Clausewitz* (New York: Stein & Day, 1971).
5. See Carl von Clausewitz, *On War*, bk. 2, chap. 6. An excellent new translation of *On War* by Michael Howard and Peter Paret, available to me in manuscript, will be published by Princeton University Press, probably in 1976. In the following notes I shall cite the book and chapter numbers. I shall also, where appropriate, put in parentheses the page numbers from the last previous translation, that of O. J. Matthijs Jolles (New York: Modern Library, 1943).
6. Ibid., bk. 4, chap. 12 (pp. 215–16 in the Jolles translation).
7. Ibid., bk. 3, chap. 1 (p. 119 in Jolles).
8. His discussion of that subject is contained mostly in ibid., bk. 1, chap. 2, and in bk. 8, chap. 3.
9. The story of technological change in the navies of the world from the early nineteenth century into World War II forms the subject of my *Sea Power in the Machine Age* (Princeton, N.J.: Princeton University Press, 1941; Greenwood Press ed., 1969). It contains long sections on the changes referred to in this paragraph.
10. In *On War*, bk. 4, chap. 1, Clausewitz says: "A change in the nature of tactics will automatically react on strategy." Jomini was much more persuaded of the eternal character of certain fundamental principles. Jomini's work was voluminous, but is not easily obtainable in the United States. However, his summary work, *The Art of War*, was translated by two officers at West Point in 1862 for the benefit of the Federal generals in the Civil War. They certainly used it, as did the Confederates, no other comparable work being available. This translation, by G. H. Mendell and W. P. Craighill, has been reprinted by the Greenwood Press, Westport, Connecticut, in 1971, 1975.
11. Brodie, *Sea Power*, p. 73.
12. Ibid., chaps. 4 and 5.
13. The classic work on the subject of its title is James P. Baxter, *The Introduction of*

the Ironclad Warship (Cambridge, Mass.: Harvard University Press, 1933). See also my *Sea Power*, chaps. 10 and 11.
14. See, on rifling, Brodie, *Sea Power*, pp. 185–90.
15. The classic work on the subject is by Robert G. Albion, *Forests and Sea Power* (Cambridge, Mass.: Harvard University Press, 1926).
16. Alfred T. Mahan, *From Sail to Steam: Recollections of Naval Life* (New York: Harper, 1907), p. 197.
17. This not unusual case of widespread misinterpretation of the supposed lessons of tactical experience is described at greater length in my *Sea Power*. See index under "ramming."
18. His promotion to rear admiral while on the retired list was due to an act of Congress that granted that title to all surviving naval officers who had reached the rank of captain upon retirement and who were veterans of the Civil War. It had nothing to do with his writings.
19. A virtually complete list of his publications is contained in Allan Westcott, ed., *Mahan on Naval Warfare* (Boston: Little, Brown, 1943), pp. 361–62.
20. Alfred T. Mahan, *Naval Strategy* (Boston: Little, Brown, 1911), p. 269.
21. The British during and after World War I had experimented with some 18-inch guns, mounting two of them on a cruiser, which proved unable to withstand the shock of their firing. They were later mounted as shore batteries at Singapore. They were no doubt shorter in length and generally less powerful than the later Japanese guns of similar caliber. The Japanese guns were measured in millimeters, and "18-inches" is an approximation to what was probably 460 mm.
22. The story of this and other early experiments with submarines is told in my *Sea Power*, chap. 14.
23. Ibid., p. 266.
24. Alfred T. Mahan, *The Influence of Sea Power upon History, 1660–1783* (Boston: Little, Brown, 1890), p. 138.
25. This point was overlooked or ignored by Mr. Colin Simpson in his recent book describing the sinking of the *Lusitania*. The cruiser *Juno*, sent out to escort the *Lusitania* into port, was recalled when it was learned that a U-boat was operating in the Channel along the route that the *Juno* would have to take in meeting the *Lusitania*. Although useful against surface raiders, she would have been utterly helpless against a submarine and would herself have offered a valuable target. Mr. Simpson, however, regards this recall as part of a pattern of presumptive evidence that suggests to him that the British government wanted the *Lusitania* sunk in order to induce American entry into the war. See his *Lusitania* (Boston: Little, Brown, 1973).
26. The substance of this and previous paragraphs is discussed in more detail in Bernard Brodie and Fawn M. Brodie, *From Crossbow to H-Bomb* (rev. and enlarged ed.; Bloomington: Indiana University Press, 1973).
27. Clausewitz, *On War*, chaps. 1–5.
28. All of Wellington's military campaigns are described in the first volume of a recent biography, which contains also one of the best accounts, from the British view, of the Waterloo campaign and of its culminating battle. See Elizabeth Longford, *Wellington: The Years of the Sword* (New York: Harper & Row, 1969).
29. The charge referred to is that of von Bredow at Vionville. See Michael Howard, *The Franco-Prussian War* (New York: Macmillan, 1962), pp. 155–57. This splendid book is the best account in English of that war, and is a classic in the field of military history.

30. The Polish scholar mentioned is Ivan S. Bloch, a retired Warsaw banker, who in the 1880s published in six volumes, based on years of intensive research, a work that with marvelous accuracy predicted the character of World War I. The one-volume abridged translation into English was published in Britain under the title *Is War Now Impossible?* (London: Grant Richards, 1899) and in the United States under the title *The Future of War* (New York: Doubleday & McClure, 1899). The work was treated with great respect by the general staff of the Russian army, who in a memoir to the czar suggested that it be made available to the delegates in the forthcoming Hague Conference of 1899. It seems to have had no influence, however, on people like Foch and his followers.
31. I do not know that this had ever been attempted in real depth, but I made a modest effort in that direction in my *War and Politics*, pp. 262–70; see also my *Strategy in the Missile Age* (Princeton, N.J.: Princeton University Press, 1959), chap. 2.
32. The standard American translation into English of Ardant du Picq's works, by John N. Greely and Robert C. Cotton, has been published in one volume under the title *Battle Studies* (Harrisburg, Pa.: Military Service Publishing Co., 1920, 1947).
33. The late Sir Basil Liddell Hart was most anxious during his lifetime to receive credit for these ideas, even though it was the enemy who used them to advantage, and indeed the Germans do generally credit him with showing them the way. However, a study of his works suggests that he was in fact urging a politically unacceptable idea—that in the event of another war with Germany, Britain refrain from again sending a large conscript army to the Continent in the fashion of World War I. It should send only a small professional army. Such an army, he went on to say, should of course be highly mobile, which is to say highly mechanized and with a high incidence of armored contingents. Thus, with Liddell Hart the idea of armored concentrations was quite incidental to his emphasis on a *small army*, and the British knew that the latter conception was quite unacceptable to the French. See especially his *The Defence of Britain* (New York: Random House, 1939).
34. The British tend to credit the late marshal of the Royal Air Force Hugh M. Trenchard—and especially two members of his staff—as being the fountainhead of their ideas about strategic bombing. Those ideas, however, are suspiciously close in particulars to those of Giulio Douhet, whose principal writings have been translated into English by Dino Ferrari and published in a single volume with the title *The Command of the Air* (New York: Coward-McCann, 1942). For a chapter describing Douhet's ideas in detail and containing a complete bibliography of his and related writings, see my *Strategy in the Missile Age*, chap. 3, "The Heritage of Douhet." In the same book see also chapter 4, which outlines the strategic-bombing experience of World War II.
35. He was court-martialed not for his ideas but for insubordination, of which he was certainly guilty. His ideas may be examined in his *Winged Defense* (New York: Putnam's, 1925).
36. See note 15 above.

The Moral Basis of National Security: Four Historical Perspectives

Thomas L. Pangle

Introduction

In discussing international relations, we are often heard to use the term "national interest." In the past, in similar contexts, men spoke more commonly of the "national good" and even of "the good of the fatherland." It is no accident that these phrases, when applied to international affairs, can immediately bring war to mind. For we tend to speak in these terms when we feel a need to appeal to some overriding moral principle that justifies deeds or intentions that will thwart, sometimes even through violence, the realization of the perceived interests of other nations. The bellicose possibilities implied in this appeal have always raised questions in men's minds. Just what do we mean when we make such an appeal? What is the content of the national interest? What content must it have to become morally preeminent, to justify resolute international competition and, if necessary, great bloodshed? What limits, if any, are there on what can be done for the national interest once it is so understood? What is the ground or source of such limits?

In the late twentieth century these perennial questions might well seem more pressing than ever before. For practical as well as theoretical reasons, we hear more and more men wondering whether this way of speaking and thinking that is so often used is anything more then rhetoric. Increasingly we hear doubts about the morality of war and of many other forms of international competition. Some, proud to call themselves idealists, demand that we cease to take the existence of a "national interest" for granted and begin to question seriously the very need for separate nations and their "interests." Others, sometimes proud to be called realists, ask us to recognize the necessity of the existence of modern nation-states as entities for whom morality in any of its usual meanings is irrelevant: morality may have a certain force, but as something personal, or social, or religious—not as something regulatory of the proper behavior of nations toward one another. In the famous words of de Gaulle, "Un grand pays n'a pas d'amis." The intrusion of "moral values" into international politics is likely to prove only confusing if not dangerous, undermining the security that could arise from the cooperation of shrewdly selfish nations.

In this situation, anyone who seeks to come to terms with the continued existence, in the foreseeable future, of separate, competing nations and yet longs to find some nonarbitrary moral grounding for his attachment to and judgment about the interests of his own country is likely to become ever more perplexed and irresolute.

This impoverishment of contemporary moral discourse makes the study of the history of political thought especially important for those who concern themselves with international affairs. The tradition of political thought presents a rich range of different understandings of the moral basis of foreign policy and war—alternatives that both invite acceptance and provide an immensely fertile stimulus to a broader original reflection.

Moreover, study of the history of thought brings to us a much deeper understanding of ourselves and our situation. For the intellectual apparatus that we accept without question—the key words through which we express ourselves, the conceptual categories by which we divide up and analyze the world, the interpretations, sometimes contradictory, that we impose on things, the ways of thinking that we exclude without realizing it—is not simply given, by nature or by necessity or by God. It is the product of an historical evolution, the evolution of the West. We turn to the history of our philosophic forebears in order to become as conscious as we can of the intellectual forces that shape and predispose our minds. Only in this way, if at all, will we begin to escape from unquestioned tutelage to the past and begin truly to think our way beyond the present.

It is this spirit of thought, rather than the attachment to any particular understanding, that the following essay aims at promoting. In a brief introduction it is necessary to exclude many trends of thought in order to focus on several of the most influential and profound. In making a choice of focus it is most reasonable to concentrate on what the leading thinkers themselves perceived as most important.

Classical Political Philosophy

Political philosophy emerged in ancient Greece as a conscious and daring break with accepted ways of thinking about politics—a break that substituted reflections based on "nature" for reflections based on pious reverence for divine custom and poetic tradition. The fact that it was not the product of any tradition, but rather a challenge to all traditions, would seem to be a key part of the reason that political theory attained, at the very beginning, a high level of sophistication regarding its goal, method, and foundations. The strange, even deadly dangerous, intellectual isolation in which Socrates and his successors found themselves seems to have compelled them to be acutely aware of the need to think and rethink the problematic starting point, the grounding, of all human attempts to be objective or scientific, especially with regard to politics. The Greek political theorists were hence preoccupied with showing how their reflections were derived from the concerns and questions raised by practicing statesmen and citizens—what Aristotle calls the *phainomena* of the political world.

Indeed, modern men may sometimes wonder whether in some respects the Greek thinkers did not remain too close to the world as perceived by common sense. Nowhere does this question pose itself more clearly to us than in their reflections regarding the moral basis of foreign policy. The Greek philosophers exhibit a striking willingness to follow, in a softened but not greatly transformed version, the attitude of the ordinary citizen that considers it just to treat fellow citizens as friends to be helped and to treat noncitizens as potential enemies whom one should not help or should at least avoid helping very much.[1] The reasons that compelled these thinkers to accept so much of the ordinary outlook become fully apparent only when we cast a glance at their understanding of the goals of domestic policy.

The classics begin from the claim that man is evidently and observably a political animal by nature. They do not mean by this merely that man is gregarious or social; they mean that man has a natural need—a drive or longing—to live in a society where he participates directly in the collective, rational determination of his future, ruling and being ruled in turn. Human life remains incomplete, unfulfilled, and therefore unhappy, unless it finds the opportunity to develop and exercise the capacities of care, commitment, and, above all, rational thought or consciousness that are evoked only in active political life. It is this need that is seen as defining man, as distinguishing him from all the other animals. This need is therefore the fundamental need of human nature, the need whose satisfaction serves as the proper goal for political society, the standard of "natural justice" or "natural right" by which each society must be judged.

Accordingly, the Greek theorists articulate very high goals for domestic political life. The "best regime," which is the goal of all political endeavor, is conceived as a "community of friends" whose principal activity is the "liberating education" of themselves and their children to the "love of the beautiful," especially as expressed in bodily grace, music, poetry, and public speech.[2] But following the judgment of experienced statesmen, the Greek thinkers distinguish sharply between what would be the "best regime" that can be elaborated "in speech" and all the actual regimes that they know about or that they expect to appear. The practical advice of the Greek theorists is moderate and even conservative, marked by a spirit of resignation before the power of necessity and chance in human affairs.[3] Nevertheless, reflections about the "best regime" are meant to teach political men the proper direction of their aspiration.

The ancient thinkers were not slow to point out that dedication to such high domestic goals, however qualified by prudential attention to limitations imposed by circumstances, requires great sacrifices. If men are really to care for one another, to respect and cultivate each other's best capacities, they must know one another. Man's capacity for friendship is not unbounded; its natural range has limits within which the size of a healthy political society must be confined—a healthy society can extend only to the size of a city, a *polis*.[4] The community must promote honesty and candor among its members;[5] it must therefore discourage the trappings of luxury and vanity by which men are tempted to hide their characters. Moreover, citizens need to be similar, so that they may sympathize with and understand one another.[6] A healthy city will then prohibit large and unequal accumulations of wealth through commerce and industry. It will provide its citizens with a strict moral education through which all grow up sharing similar delights and sorrows, the same general tastes, common memories, the same heroes and models; and competition in individual excellence must be based on a shared sense of what is noble and important.[7]

As in every relation of intimacy, the attachment to one another goes hand in hand with a sense of exclusion from the rest of the world. Devotion to one's own city and people will necessarily be diluted and reduced in seriousness if the citizens do not restrict the tempting charms of foreign innovation, travel, and cosmopolitanism. Insofar as citizens do regard the outside world, they will emphasize the display of the excellence of their own ways as a model to others rather than admire or adopt the ways of others. Thus, although in Plato's *Laws* the philosophic spokesman encourages a few selected men over fifty years of age to travel, investigating foreign regimes with a view to improvement, for the generality of citizens he legislates as follows:

> Now by nature the mixing of cities with cities blends ways of life indiscriminately, with hosts and guests introducing innovations in one another's lives. This would bring the greatest harm to cities well governed with correct laws. . . . But then again not to welcome others or go visiting is usually impossible, and in addition might be seen by the rest of mankind as beastly and harsh; . . . and reputation ought never to be despised, since the many even though they fall short of real virtue can still judge who among others is noble or wicked. . . . Therefore it is a fine thing to counsel most cities to honor good reputation with the many, . . . and we ought to legislate as follows regarding travel to foreign lands and places and the reception of strangers: First, under no circumstances may anyone under forty years of age leave the country; second, no one may travel abroad in a private capacity, but only as part of an official embassy, mission, or religious delegation . . . and these must be as numerous, splendid, and excellent as possible, composed of men who will make the city illus-

trious in gatherings of peace and religion and who will create a renown that will match the renown we possess in war. And when they return home they will teach the young that the customs and regime of the foreigners are inferior.[8]

Moreover, if the healthy political society is a small society, then it is necessarily endangered. It needs to devote considerable attention to military defense, and its citizens must try to develop a certain waspishness, which will forestall aggression. In the *Republic,* Socrates calls for a citizen army that resembles "the philosophic dogs" who are "as gentle as can be toward their own kind and those they know, and are the opposite with those they don't know."[9] Finally, not only for the sake of defense but even more for the sake of civic virtue, Plato emphasizes the need for encouragement of a human characteristic that he calls "spiritedness."[10] He gives this name to a complex range of psychic phenomena that includes the capacity for anger or righteous indignation, the love of freedom, and the pride or sense of honor that can easily be transformed into elevated loyalty.

Now, unfortunately, training in the art of war involves learning to do many things—some noble, some necessary but surely not noble. The same society that so strives to teach friendship, honesty, and justice among its citizens must make those same citizens adept, with regard to enemies, not only at manly self-defense but also at cruelty, guile, and theft. The Greek theorists were by no means unaware of the potentially dangerous paradox involved in this situation.[11] The desire to dampen its possibly corrupting effects on the interrelations of citizens is another important reason for maintaining the distinction between what is owed to citizens and what is owed to strangers.

But this is not the end of the difficulties. For implicit in the healthy city's encouragement of spirited civic pride combined with military prowess and a love of politics is the danger of inclining toward the imperialistic desire for domination, for demonstrating the community's superiority in international competition and war. Foreign policy is, after all, a magnificent field for the display and exercise of moral and intellectual excellence. Both Aristotle and Plato manifest an acute sensitivity to the danger in this tendency, especially in their attacks on the Spartan political regime; and Aristotle even criticizes Plato for overemphasizing the necessity of being harsh to strangers.[12] The problem and the proposed solution are stated most clearly by Aristotle:

> Some hold that the rule over neighbors, if despotic, is the height of injustice, and if political, a hindrance to well-being. Others hold that the active political life is the only way of life for a real man. . . . And some of these say that the despotic and tyrannical mode of rule is the only happy one; indeed, among some peoples this is the standard for the laws and regime—mastery over neighbors. . . . In fact, where the laws do look to

some one goal they all aim at mastery, even as in Sparta and Crete the education and most of the laws are set up with a view to war. . . . Yet it would seem very strange, perhaps, for those willing to reflect, if this is the activity of a political man, to be able to think in order to rule and exercise mastery over neighbors whether willing or unwilling. For how could it be a political activity? . . . and there might well be a city happy by itself, clearly possessing a fine political life, for it is possible for a city to dwell alone with good laws and with a way of life not ordered toward war or toward mastery over enemies. . . . It is clear then that all preparations for war are to be held noble not as the goal but only as means. . . . Some of the laws will of course vary from place to place; and it must be the duty of the legislator to consider, if there are neighbors, what sort of measures must be taken in regard to each. . . . But the active life need not be, as some think, a life in relation to others . . . and it is not necessary for cities situated in isolation to live lives of inaction, for since the parts of the city can have many dealings with one another, it is possible for the city to be active in that way.[13]

Once again we see a moral posture that is not benevolent but indifferent to outsiders—a posture that emphasizes, not what the city owes to other cities or to mankind, but what it owes to itself, what it requires for its own happiness as experienced in a truly "political" life. Plato surely does not disagree with regard to the desirability of such an isolationist foreign policy,[14] but in the *Republic,* at least, he compels his Socrates to submit to crossexamination by the stern Adeimantus, who demands to know what is to be the foreign policy of the just city if it is faced with some potentially hostile and powerful neighbors. To this Socrates responds:

> You are in happy ignorance if you think any other city but one such as we are building is worthy of the name. . . . Something bigger should be what we call the other places. For each is many cities, not one city; . . . each is two at least, making war on one another—the city of the poor and the city of the rich. And within each of these there are many cities which, if you approach as one, you will make a great mistake; but if you deal with them as many, giving the property or the power or the lives of either side to the other, you will always have many allies and few enemies.[15]

Lying behind Plato's attitude is a greater willingness to make explicit certain harsh realities that stem partly from the brutal fact of economic scarcity.[16] The way of life of a good city requires a great deal of leisure for its citizens;[17] leisure is possible only on a strong economic base. And if the economy is not to depend on preoccupation with acquisitiveness—the corrupting practices and wealth of commerce—the city must be established in a fertile land.[18] Now it is highly unlikely that such land will be found unclaimed or isolated: indeed, it will probably be the scene of age-old struggles for possession. It is therefore likely that in order to have the land it needs, the good city must, at some time in the past, have conquered or stolen it; and the city must be prepared to defend the land often against new invaders or even the earlier possessors, either of whose right to possession may at times seem as strong as that of the present tenants. (Actually, it may well be that the forefathers who conquered it were at the time justified neither by their plans for building a better city nor by their minimum physical needs; it may be that they wanted things like relishes for their food and couches to lie on.)[19] If one goes back very far in the history of even the most just of peoples, one will probably find that they have but a tenuous claim to ownership, a claim that is open to armed attack legitimated by deprivation and scarcity. Plato points to these melancholy facts in a most striking way. In the *Republic*, soon after the origin of what is to become *the* just city in speech, Socrates himself proposes, and with Glaucon carries out, an unprovoked aggressive war for the conquest of a neighboring people's land. Never is it suggested that this land be returned or even that reparation be made; on the contrary, Socrates later promulgates a "noble lie," which is intended to convince all the citizens that they and their forefathers sprang up from the land they now possess.[20]

Plato implies, in other words, that one must not expect to find readily a situation with no economic scarcity or past conflicts to provide at times, on both sides, plausible motives and often even legitimate claims for waging war. It is not sufficient to speak of avoidable wickedness or correctable misunderstanding; it is the above harsh circumstances, not to mention the good society's smallness, its required alienation from foreigners, and its need to encourage in citizens an "indomitable spiritedness," that compel Plato and classical theory in general to doubt the possibility and the naturalness of a very elevated or lasting justice among nations. Yet men do share, as individual human beings, a common nature and even a common good, which can never be entirely forgotten simply because they belong, as citizens, to different cities or nations which do not have any truly common good. The collective rational and political capacities whose fulfillment is the goal of the city are not capacities peculiar to the citizens of any particular nation but are rather natural to men as men. The highest in man transcends his city, even though it be the best city. And this highest or most natural fact is reflected, however dimly, in the way every human being regards every other human being. The moral attitude of citizens toward outsiders must echo in some fashion their attitude toward one another, the more so as they become more self-conscious and refined.[21] It is no accident that later in the *Republic*, after the introduction of philosophy or the fullest use of reason as the true end of politics and political education, Plato has his Socrates plead for a moderation of the strict distinction between citizens and foreigners when it comes to war against cities that are near neighbors.²² Active benevolence toward foreign cities is dangerous to external safety and internal civic health; but absolute indifference, especially given the unlikelihood of true physical isolation, is also potentially damaging to the moral tone of the individuals who form the community. Practically, if not theoretically, international politics will always remain a problematic region of moral uncertainty and hesitation.

It is the Roman thinker Cicero who, more than the Greek originators of political science, is famous for attempts to delineate clear moral limits on foreign relations among nations. Indeed, very often it is said that "the generous conceptions of Cicero show a broader outlook than the rigorous doctrines of Plato and Aristotle" with regard not only to the morality of foreign policy but to the moral basis of politics altogether.²³ For Cicero's writings are clearly under the influence of Stoicism, a school of philosophy that grew up long after Plato's death. Of this school we have only very fragmentary documents, but the evidence seems to indicate that it placed a much greater emphasis than had Plato or Aristotle on duty, purity of intention, and scorn for pleasure and expediency.

Cicero himself, however, failed to sense any fundamental disagreement with Plato, and referred to his thought not as Stoic but as that of a Platonic or "Academic" skeptic.²⁴ On the other hand, it is certainly the case that Cicero, unlike Plato, was not only a political theorist but at the same time a statesman and orator, exercising the highest political responsibilities in an era of civic decay. It is not at all surprising, then, to find this Platonic statesman writing and speaking in such a way as to strengthen and promote the school of philosophy that represented the most decent of the popular contemporary social viewpoints.

Cicero most clearly adopts the Stoic principles in his treatise *De Officiis* (*On Duties*), a work whose style and intention can be characterized by saying that it incorporates what would today be called "an open letter to my son." As a publication it is written primarily for young Romans who are about to begin their careers as rulers in a far-flung imperial system. For the active politician in such a system the principal task is no longer the sharing in the republican rule of citizens over one another, but rather the rule of a few citizens over countless thousands of strangers. Cicero confronts a situation that statesmen and theorists were to face time and again down through the ages: the norms discovered by Plato and Aristotle must be applied in circumstances that are unmistakably "decadent" and to which their writings devote little attention.

Perhaps the most baffling feature of the new imperial political universe is the obscuring or even desuetude of the distinction between domestic and foreign policy.²⁵ How are Romans to understand their moral obligations to the nonslave populations that they rule? They cannot be fellow citizens, sharing in the common good of the "city"; yet neither are they simply "foreigners" anymore. It seems to be this troubling moral dilemma that leads Cicero to adopt, as a potent rhetorical or educational device, the appeal to certain universal rules of conduct that are embodied in the Stoic notion of "natural law" and the kindred Roman conception of *ius gentium* (law of nations).[26] Thus, in the *De Officiis,* Cicero tells his son of the universal norms that regulate the relations of all men:

> That it is not permitted to harm another for the sake of one's own advantage has been established, in truth, not only by nature, i.e., the law of nations, but by the laws of peoples as well—the laws of which the government in individual communities is comprised. . . .
>
> And if nature has prescribed that a human being should want to take care of another human being, whoever he may be, for the reason that he is a human being, then according to the same nature it is necessary that the common interest be the interest of everyone. If this is so, we are all embraced by one and the same law of nature, . . . and are undoubtedly prohibited from doing violence to another by the law of nature. . . . Moreover, those who say that citizens must be taken into account, but not aliens, sunder the common association of human kind. . . . And those who destroy this must be judged undutiful even toward the immortal gods. For by the gods was this association set up.[27]

It is within this framework that Cicero sets down the famous first formulation of the "law of war," a formulation that makes explicit and apparently much more absolute the Greek theorists' advice:

> There are, moreover, certain duties to be observed even toward those by whom you have been done an injustice. In fact there is a limit to taking vengeance and to punishing. . . . In a republic the rightful observances of war are to be kept up to the full. For as there are two ways of deciding an issue, one through discussion, the other through force, and although the former is appropriate for human beings, the latter for beasts, if one is not permitted to use the prior method recourse must be had to the second one. Wherefore wars must be undertaken for this reason: that life may go on in peace without injustice. When, however, victory has been procured, those who were not cruel or monstrous in the war must be given their lives.[28]

A similar statement is presented by Laelius, an old Stoic lawyer and patriot, who appears as a character in Cicero's dialogue *The Republic.*[29]

Now Plato and Aristotle had seldom spoken of "natural law," and almost never in a theoretical context;[30] they had restricted themselves to speaking of what is "just by nature," or of "natural right" (see page 309 above). The difference in terminology points to a very complex difference in understanding.

But, at the cost of considerable oversimplification, it can be said that on a theoretical level, Plato and Aristotle were more concerned than were the Stoics with maintaining the distinction between nature and human or divine convention, and that on a practical level they had greater reservations than did the Stoics regarding the possibility of deducing from the natural goals of man any rules or "laws" that would be binding and naturally sanctioned in all circumstances. As regards Cicero's presentation of the Stoic doctrine of natural law, the theoretical difficulty appears in the reference to the gods, to piety, and to what one is tempted to call supernatural sanction for the natural law. The Stoic conception seems to have depended decisively on a notion of divine rule and providence, a notion that Cicero as a theorist finds it difficult to accept.[31] This would seem to be the reason that, when Cicero turns from what is *prohibited* in dealings with strangers to what is *required* as a part of generosity or humanity, he feels compelled to give considerable weight to the limitations imposed by the harsh scarcity of nature's provisions:

> The association most widely extended to men among themselves, for all and between all, is that of the partnership in all things nature brings forth for the common use of human beings. This fellowship must be watched over, so that the goods regulated by the laws and civil right may be used as those laws dictate, while all other goods should be used in compliance with the proverb of the Greeks, "the things of friends are in common." And these common possessions of all men seem to be things of the kind set down by Ennius: "A man who, to one astray, graciously points out the way does it as one lights a torch from his own torch. No less light does it shed for him when he has lit the other's." From this one example the general lesson is clear enough: let whatever can be given away without detriment be bestowed, even on a stranger—do not check flowing water, allow the lighting of his fire at your fire, if someone asks, give him trustworthy counsel in his deliberations; give whatever is useful to those who get it but not burdensome to the giver. For since the resources of individuals are meager, and the things needed are infinite in multitude, ordinary generosity must be reckoned within the limits prescribed by Ennius: "no less light does it shed for him," so that we may have the means to be generous to our own.[32]

It should also be noted that, while speaking emphatically about the universal friendly ties and duties linking men to one another *as individuals*, Cicero has much less to say, even in the *De Officiis,* regarding the ties and duties that link states or political communities to one another. In fact, Cicero is compelled, just as Plato was, to allude to the harsh exigencies imposed on international relations by natural scarcity and competition. In Cicero's *Republic,* just as in Plato's, there is unmistakable if muted reference to the aggressive war and conquest that is part of the origin of even the "best city."[33] We are hence not completely unprepared to find that in the *De Officiis* the definition of a justifiably "defensive" resort to arms is rather elastic: a city may fight until it possesses a "life in peace," free from "traps."³⁴ In a threatening international environment the maintenance of a people's honor may reasonably be thought to be its first line of defense. Cicero therefore emphasizes (more even than Plato) the need to cultivate civic pride and the legitimacy that such a need may give to wars of national honor or empire. He writes to his son the following passages, which are rich in ambiguity:

> Indeed, seeing that do-or-die struggles for empire occur and that glory is sought after by means of warfare, one is obliged all the same to be entirely supported by those same reasons which I said a little earlier are the just reasons for wars. But those wars in which the objective is the glory of the empire ought to be waged with less asperity. For it is just as when we have contentions in domestic politics: we act one way if we contend with an enemy, differently if with a rival—with the rival the contest is for honor and distinction; with the enemy it is for one's head and good name. . . .
>
> Therefore those who would guard the republic should by whatever means they can, either in war or at home, augment the republic by empire, farmlands, and taxes. These are the things that belong to great men, these are the things that were performed over and over again in our forefathers' time, and those who pursue these kinds of duties will attain, along with the supreme advantage of the republic, both great things and a great glory.³⁵

The sense of the inevitability of tragic armed conflict between cities with equally justifiable claims is partly what leads Cicero to speak so strongly of the respect due to enemies in war. Cicero explicitly distinguishes enemies of the city from criminals, or enemies of mankind; and it is chiefly on this basis that he seeks to erect a code of honor limiting the means to which men may have recourse in war.³⁶

For Cicero, just as for his Greek teachers, the restricted, prudential character of moral limitations on war and on the national interest finds its basis in the view that man's perfection, on the social level at least, is by nature more national and political than cosmopolitan or suprapolitical.

Christian Political Thought: The Doctrine of Just War

When we turn from classical political theory to Christian political theology, we enter a different world. No longer do the leading thinkers strive to remain firmly grounded in the perspective of the unsophisticated citizen; no longer is the morality of foreign policy discussed principally with a view to what is required for the fullest development of the virtues and capacities discovered in domestic political activity. Indeed, politics ceases to possess for the theorist the splendor and fascination that it held for the ancient thinkers, and *the* theme of classical political philosophy—the attempt to articulate the "best regime"—recedes from the center of attention. According to Augustine, that unique classical dedication to the political order was in fact an enchanting delusion, a vice masquerading as virtue.[37]

At the core of Christianity is the commandment "Love thy neighbor." Love of one's neighbor is a charitable love of all human beings as human beings, whether or not they belong to one's family, city, nation, or race. From the beginning, Christians seemed to find a tension between this second-most-sacred commandment and the divisions and deadly competition that characterize political life. The problem appeared most starkly in the areas of foreign policy and the waging of war. Accordingly, the earliest Christians seem to have been hesitant about participating in political affairs; and although the evidence as to the early Church's attitude toward war is conflicting and incomplete, it seems likely that pacifism was the dominant view.[38]

It was St. Augustine, following perhaps the lead of St. Ambrose, who first decisively reversed the apolitical tendencies of Christian thought and elaborated a teaching that has ever since stood at the center of the Christian's attempt to understand his proper political role. Augustine bases his teaching not on the premises of unassisted reason but on reason informed by the revelation of the scriptures. It is this alone, he insists, that can give us a satisfactory explanation of the world as we see it.

When we proceed by this light, we learn that human nature as created by God was and is social; that originally man (Adam and Eve) lived in a familial society that was bound by love of God and love of the neighbor through God. In that state, man's capacity for knowledge of God and the world and man's delight in helping and being helped by his fellow man were unhindered. There was no suffering, competition, injustice, or death, because all lived in obedience to the perfect hierarchy and order created by God.[39]

That blessed situation has been lost forever on earth because of original man's wanton disobedience, which was motivated by pride. The spirit of Adam's wicked revolt has mysteriously contaminated all his offspring, and the world as we now know it is one in which men's souls are dominated by unnatural lust for dominion and luxury and where men are surrounded by the scarcity, threat of death, and physical suffering with which God punished man. It is only through His intercession as the Christ that God has opened for man the possibility of a return to the bliss of a society resembling, or perhaps even more perfect than, the lost original. But this society is never to be seen on earth; indeed, God's grace is conditioned by the test that he imposes on man during his mortal life on earth. And all human beings can be divided into two groups according to their success in passing this test: there are a few who live for the sake of God and in the hope of the life to come (the "city of God"), and there are many more who spurn the proffered grace of God for the sake of earthly loves (the "city of man").[40]

According to this understanding, government and political life lack any elevated goal. Even after the coming of Christ, no nation possesses more than a faint awareness of true justice and the true object of love; every city is "Babylon," and the predominant goal of its way of life is a more or less corrupt attachment to earthly prosperity. Coercion, private property, and slavery characterize every actual regime on earth. Still, though these things are certainly not noble, they are necessary.[41] Government does impose an order that is a faint echo of true order: through coercive penal law and economic arrangements a peace is created that is the precondition for the activity of the pious few and that helps the majority by restraining them from the excesses of their wickedness.[42] The aim of decent government, and of the Christian's participation in it, is not to instill virtue or to cultivate the supposed excellences found in the exercise of office and rule. The aim is, rather, to prevent men from harming one another.[43]

It is from this analysis of politics that Augustine's famous doctrine of "the just war" derives. Although Augustine is recognized as the originator of this classic Christian doctrine, his writings do not contain a sustained and thematic treatment of the subject; it is therefore necessary to gather the teaching from what are, in the main, incidental remarks.[44]

War is a permanent feature of man's fallen state, and most wars are unjust and unnecessary manifestations of man's wicked desires. Yet the high value that Augustine places on order and on obedience ("the mother and guardian of all the virtues")[45] leads him to advise all Christian soldiers to follow, without questioning, the command of their legal rulers:

> The natural condition of mortals, which is suited to peace, demands that the authority and counsel for undertaking war reside with the prince and, moreover, that soldiers owe the service of performing these martial commands. . . . Therefore a just man, who does military service under a king who is an ungodly man, rightly makes war at his command nevertheless, in service to civil peace. For the man given the order, the war is certainly not against God's teaching; and even where it may seem against God's teaching, it is the king, who gives the command, who is accused, while the soldier who follows orders is innocent.[46]

For those Christians who rule, however, it is a duty to wage war only for just causes. Moreover, war is so hideous that even with a just cause, only dire necessity legitimates it. First and clearest of the just causes is defense of the nation against unprovoked threats to its physical safety, its independence, and its integrity. It is true that the command to love thy neighbor denies a Christian the right to kill another human being in self-defense; but government or its agents may kill without sin if they are motivated by love, not of themselves, but of the others in the community, and if they possess no hatred for the enemy.[47] A just national defense is not limited to repulsing or forestalling attack: if an aggressor has stolen or destroyed property, the city may, at once or after a postponement, seek recovery or reparation by waging war. In addition, it is just for a city to seek to *punish* other cities when they do wrong and refuse reparation: "Just wars are usually defined as those which avenge wrongs, when the nation or a city to be the object of war has neglected either to punish what it has itself wrongly done or to return what was taken through its injustices."[48] Augustine seems quite certain that whenever a city justly defends itself, it will have just grounds for punishing its enemy. But even beyond that, a city may punish another city for any grave, unmerited, and unrepaired injury to its property or citizens, whether or not this injury was part of an act of aggressive war. For example, Moses justly punished the Amorites by driving them permanently out of their homeland when they refused his request of innocent passage for his army.[49]

The decent city, in other words, must look upon its war-making power as analogous to the police powers it exercises in domestic affairs.[50] There is a world order of peace, and in the absence of any other temporal government, each decent nation has a duty to try to enforce that just order in its part of the globe. If Christians go to war, they can and must believe that they are like judges and police, while the enemy are like criminals; if they cannot, then they ought not to fight, even in defense:

> For what is blamed in war? Is it that men, who are bound to die some time or other, die instead of living, subjugated, in peace? To make such a reproach is the part of the cowardly, not the religious. What is rightly blamed in war is not death but the desire to do harm, the cruelty of taking revenge, aggressive and implacable enmity, the savageness of resistance, the lust of domination, and the like. Indeed in general it is to punish these things that, by the order of God or of some legitimate authority, and in opposition to the violence of their opponents, good men undertake the wars that have to be fought.[51]

At the same time, the decent city must, in a just war, conduct itself like a judge. Its citizens must chastise with mercy and even love, thinking as much about the true welfare of the enemy as about their own welfare. War that is fought in the spirit of hatred or revenge or even personal anger is worse than death or defeat:

> Precepts of patience . . . and the benevolence of not returning evil for evil must always be fully present in the will. . . . We have to punish

men against their will, with a certain kindly severity. . . . On this account if the earthly republic keeps the Christian precepts, even its wars will be waged with a benevolence, so that counsel may more easily be taken for the benefit of the conquered.[52]

Augustine's profound sense of the mixture of vice in all political affairs prevents him from being as certain as many of his successors were that no war can be just on both sides at the same time;[53] but he is much surer than were the classical writers that the order that encompasses all men never requires unprovoked or judicially questionable acts of war. When exigencies seem to compel a nation to commit such acts, one should realize that those exigencies are due, in the final analysis, not so much to fortune or chance, as to man's aspiring to a kind of earthly grandeur and security that he should know he cannot have.

Intimately connected with this realization is a new attitude toward national pride and its impact on foreign affairs. Augustine cannot help but be moved by the dedication, the sacrifice, the generosity, and the magnanimity that were evoked by the devotion to political greatness in republican Rome.[54] But in the light of the Christian dispensation, with its denigration of the virtues of earthly political participation and rule, the desire to cultivate civic pride cannot legitimately be allowed to have much influence on the decision for peace or war.[55] And Augustine goes further than this: he points to the problematic status of the love of fame among the Greeks and Romans as the key to the decisive weakness in their tradition. The inadequacy of the moral virtue and the political life that they claimed to love for its own sake he finds revealed most clearly in the history of republican Rome and in Cicero's praise of that history. Not the virtues themselves, but recognition for those virtues, was the goal of the Romans. It is in their foreign policy, in their willingness to commit the plainest injustices in pursuit of empire, that one sees unambiguously the rank that they assigned to glory over that of virtue.[56]

Augustine's teaching about the just war was first brought together in systematic form by the canon lawyer Gratian.[57] The most authoritative expression of it is found, however, in St. Thomas Aquinas's *Summa Theologica*.[58] Thomas relies explicitly on the authority of Augustine, and at first the content of his presentation seems to be almost completely unoriginal. But here, as in so many other aspects of Christian doctrine, Thomas's formulation became the influential one, because of the new and far less parochial intellectual basis that he provided for the doctrine.

Thomas placed much more reliance than had any of his Christian predecessors on the natural power of man's unassisted reason. According to Thomas, God has endowed man with a rational faculty that can, even after the Fall and prior to divine revelation, penetrate very far into the truth about the world. God has created a natural order that is almost complete; and natural reason—as exemplified above all in the writings of the pagan philosopher Aristotle—can provide a nearly satisfactory account of that order. In the sphere of politics, man has a natural goal, a happy way of life involving the cultivation and exercise of the moral and political virtues described by Aristotle. God's revelation through Christ has shown a higher goal and higher virtues, but these virtues supplement, without contradicting, the virtues discussed by Aristotle. Political life is not then so full of corrupion and bereft of nobility as Augustine had taught. It is true that after the coming of Christ, the splendor of political life on earth suffers an eclipse; but the eclipse is by no means total.

In other words, Christians can and should provide a moral basis for politics that rests in very large part on the compelling grounds of universally available human reason, rather than on the supernatural revelation of the Scriptures.[59] By apparently transforming the grounding of political morality, Thomas provided the doctrine of just war with a political persuasiveness that has endured even into our secular age. It seems that the doctrine of just war can rest its case on the reason that is available to man as man and not restrict its appeal to those men who are enlightened by the acceptance of Christian revelation.[60] It is crucial, then, that we understand the essentials of Thomas's rational morality.

At the core of this morality is what Thomas calls natural law. Now, as we have seen, natural law does not play a very important role in Aristotle's thought. Thomas implies, however, that such a notion provides the real basis for Aristotle's political theory. The reason appears to be this: in his *Ethics*, Aristotle leaves unclear how men grasp the first principles of morality—the principles from which derive all the duties involved in each virtue that the political community aims to cultivate. Aristotle denies that these principles are based on convention or custom, he denies that they are inborn, and he refuses to say that they come from natural science or theoretical reason.[61] But he does not state unequivocally where they do come from. Thomas supplies an answer by saying that certain laws or commandments (e.g., of the form "Thou shalt ot steal") are known to the human consciousness by means of a natural faculty or habit (*"habitus"*) that Aristotle had not spoken about: *synderesis*, whose act is the conscience. The "primary precepts," which constitute the natural law proper, include commandments such as those found, for instance, in the second table of the Ten Commandments. There are, in addition, "secondary precepts," which are the applications of the primary precepts to various circumstances: for instance, from the prohibition on theft is derived the secondary precept "Return all deposits." The secondary precepts may change in some circumstances; but the primary precepts never change, and it is always wrong to violate them.⁶² Both primary and secondary precepts together are contained in the "law of nations" (*ius gentium*, or *consensus gentium*; by which Thomas does *not* mean international law).⁶³ The moral law is thus "natural," because it is known without divine intervention. It is also "natural," in the sense that its precepts are all aimed at the development of those characteristics that define man's nature—his natural humanity as a familial, political, and rational being.

Thomas's interpretation differs from Aristotle's not only in its legalism but also in its categorical character. For Thomas, the imperatives of morality are not seen as merely means to some further end, and they cannot therefore be changed for the sake of another end. One obeys the natural law, not solely or even chiefly in order to gain something beyond it, but for its own sake, as an expression of one's deepest humanity, and therefore categorically or absolutely. As a result, Thomas's famous formulation of the just basis for war possesses a legal and "absolute" character that is alien to Aristotle's political thought:

> It must be stated that three things are required for any war to be just. First, of course, is the authority of a prince by whose command the war is to be waged. For it does not belong to a private person to begin a war. He can pursue his right through the judgment of his superior. . . . In the second place, a just cause is required: namely, that those who are attacked deserve the attack on account of some wrongdoing of theirs, as Augustine says. . . . In the third place, it is required that the intention of those waging the war be right: namely, an intention that aims at either the promotion of good or the avoidance of evil. . . . Moreover it can happen that, even if the authority for declaring war be legitimate and the cause just, nonetheless a war may be rendered impermissible on account of a wicked intention.⁶⁴

As can be seen, Thomas stresses the policing or punitive character of just war even more than does Augustine. Thomas's commitment to the idea that earthly political life can possess true moral virtue makes him even more certain than was Augustine that there exists a just order governing the relations between nations, an order that must be adhered to and enforced. For the same reason, Thomas insists more on the importance of intention—the purity of the just warrior's intentions and the criminality of his enemy's. The insistence on purity of intention during the course of the war goes with a somewhat stricter restraint on the means that are permissible in war,⁶⁵ and in Thomas's successors, it becomes more and more identified with "laws of war."⁶⁶

It was the combination of the stringency of Thomas's demands and the amazing brevity of his treatment that led the most intelligent of his followers to elaborate at length on the doctrine of just war. The truly significant additions in the two centuries after Thomas are summarized in the course of the systematic expositions of Franciscus Vitoria and his intellectual heir, Franciscus Suarez.[67]

Vitoria's elaboration of the doctrine of just war was in considerable measure a response to his revulsion at the Spanish treatment of the American Indians. Partly because his teaching thus focuses on the relations between a Christian nation and infidel nations, he evinces an unusual interest in delineating precisely the *natural* moral norms that limit war. This leads to considerable change in the emphasis, if not in the content, of the Thomistic doctrine: above all, Vitoria denies that all just wars are punitive. He begins by adopting and refining a classification, derived from Astesanus and others, of the various just causes for war. According to this scheme, just wars are first divided into defensive wars and aggressive wars. A defensive war need not be punitive; it draws its justification from the natural right to self-defense. Vitoria, unlike Thomas, seems to have lost most of the Augustinian reservations against the idea of a natural right to kill in self-defense.[68]

Like defensive war, all just aggressive war is not necessarily punitive war: just aggressive war is divided into war for recuperation of stolen property (or reparation for damage) and punitive war. Vitoria here calls attention to the possibility of an injury that has been done to us through an enemy's excusable ignorance—ignorance, for instance, of the true title to land.[69] In such a case, if aggressive war is required, it should be aimed at the reparation of damages, but not at punishment, since the enemy is "excusably ignorant" and therefore is guilty of no crime or sin.[70] This means that Vitoria, unlike Thomas, admits outright that just war may require the killing of *innocent* enemies. To be excusable, ignorance must be "invincible," that is, it must be such as would remain even after a man who "lives according to natural law" had "bestowed human diligence to learn" the truth about the matter.[71] Although cases of such invincible ignorance happen "frequently," Vitoria remains within the Thomistic horizon in his certainty that among civilized nations most wrongs done in international affairs are avoidable and inexcusable. There remains a strong emphasis on the punitive character of those few aggressive wars that are just.[72]

Pursuing what seems to be the implication of this outlook, Vitoria proclaims the existence, by nature, of a world political order. He goes beyond the letter of Thomas's *Summa* in asserting that a large part of the "law of nations" applies to relations between states, since throughout the world, custom tacitly recognizes a law that specifically defines international, as well as internal, deeds that are deserving of punishment. This international "law of nations" derives its legitimacy, not merely from consent, but from the natural law that is held in the conscience. Partly for this reason, it is binding on all peoples, whether they espouse it or not. The most pertinent aspect of this law is its protection of those possessions, customs, and institutions that all, or almost all, peoples have constructed in order to develop and preserve their human faculties. Punitive war is a justified response whenever one nation gravely injures, or allows its inhabitants to injure, without reparation, any of such things as belong to the citizens of another nation.[73] Key examples of punishable acts are injury to life, injury to property, hindrance of trade and commerce, hindrance of teaching the truth, prevention of the acquisition and use of any natural resource that is considered common property by the nation in which it is found (such as unclaimed gold in America), and injury or affront to the honor and dignity of individuals or nations.[74]

The punishment, like all legal punishment, must suit the crime. The war in itself may be sufficient punishment, but it is not necessarily, or even usually, so. If the arms of the just are blessed with victory, they may then proceed to seek reparation for their war expenses, as well as for the original damage; they may chastise and, if the crime and circumstances merit it, even kill all whom they consider to be guilty, including any who are prisoners of war; they may impose tribute, occupy and fortify land, and on occasion depose the existing regime; in fact, it is not contrary to natural law that they enslave all the inhabitants, the innocent as well as the guilty.[75] Unnecessary cruelty is a serious crime, and the need for vindication should always be overshadowed by the need to secure a lasting peace. Nevertheless, given the absence of a true world government and the consequent weaknesses of the international police system, Vitoria does not shrink from concluding that very harsh measures may sometimes be required in order to deter, through example, future criminal acts.[76]

At the same time, reason dictates strict restraints on what may be done to the innocent during as well as after any sort of just war. Part of Vitoria's attempt to make Thomistic demands enforceable is his substitution of limits on *acts* (the visible manifestations of moderation or self-control) for limits on purity of inward intention (lack of hatred and extreme anger). The innocent civilians, who are generally presumed to be all those who are unable to bear arms and those other adult males who clearly did not participate in the war, must under no circumstances be killed in order to win the war.[77]

Although Vitoria gives more attention than does Thomas to the possibility of unjust aggression done in ignorance, and hence to the possibility of nonpunitive war, he continues to deny that conscious unprovoked aggression is ever necessary, even for defense. He refuses to recognize as real, for example, the dilemma that the Spartans felt they were in when they were compelled to break a treaty and begin war against an enemy whose sheer growth, rather than any particular present offense, implied mortal danger at some future time.[78] Vitoria insists that war can never be truly justified on both sides. Diligent moral investigation is always required, and if there is reason for doubt, war is wrong and unnecessary: in international affairs, as within domestic society, the status quo is to be maintained unless it is clearly unjust.[79] Down through the ages, Vitoria's proponents have argued that insofar as political rulers are awakened to the voice of the natural conscience and the law common to all nations, these strict criteria will dramatically lessen the incidence of war.[80]

But decent opponents have felt compelled to wonder whether the international status quo is always as orderly as Vitoria asserts that it is. Can nations always remain content with existing boundaries, unless they have been manifestly altered by recent aggression? Can all peoples allow foreigners to travel, trade, preach, live, and profit from the common natural resources in their land? Is it always a case of either clear injustice or an acceptable, livable international environment? If it should happen that it sometimes is not, then will not both hypocritical and honest application of the moralism in the doctrine of just war exacerbate the bitterness and widen the scope of the wars that do occur?[81] In response to the latter danger, Vitoria teaches that only the nation that is directly injured and its allies or those that it invites have a right or a duty to enforce punishment.[82] In addition, no nation has the right to intervene in order to punish another nation for allowing crimes against natural law among its own people. Yet the notion that there is a world order to which every ruler has a responsibility induces Vitoria to allow some severe intrusions on the sovereignty of nations. A nation may come unasked to the aid of any other nation that is fighting a just *defensive* war; a government may, when invited by "the people" of another nation, intervene to depose a tyrannical ruler; and there is a right, even a duty, to intervene in the affairs of another nation if innocent human beings are being *murdered,* even if the murder is not against their will or if they refuse assistance.[83]

The possible tendency toward belligerent moralism is strengthened by the influence of Christianity, which supplements the natural law of nations in Vitoria's thought. Christian precepts apply only among Christian states, but they affect all foreign relations; and the role played by Christian divine law may not unreasonably be thought to exemplify the role that other religious or ideological teachings may play in supplementing the doctrine of just war in other places and times. According to Vitoria, once Christianity has entered the world, Christian nations have naturally just causes for punitive war against infidel nations under the following circumstances: (1) if Christian priests are not allowed to preach in those nations, for this is an abridgment of the right to travel and the right to teach the truth; (2) if their fellow Christians who inhabit those nations are persecuted, for they have become allies and friends of those Christians; and (3) if the Christian religion is directly blasphemed, for this, not to speak of the first two offenses, represents a clear affront to the honor and dignity of the Christian nations.[84] In common with both his great predecessors, Vitoria opposes Christian holy war. It is a crime against natural law and a sin against divine law to use force to compel conversion or to injure without cause the lives and property of infidels. But an argument for the moral righteousness of those crusades that did take place in the course of history can be, and by some still is, based on the principles of Vitoria's doctrine of just war, without reference to any notion of a holy war.[85]

Insofar as this danger is found in Vitoria, it continues to exist, in some measure, for Suarez, who makes only one important change in the substantive details of Vitoria's discussion of the just causes and procedure for war. That change concerns the guidelines for a ruler's deliberation over whether a grave crime against the international "law of nations" has been committed. Vitoria had taught that where there is doubt about the validity of a claim, the status quo is not to be disturbed by war: either there is an indubitable injury justifying war, or there is no justification for war. Suarez more candidly faces the fact that in almost every real case some plausible counterclaim can be advanced by the aggressive side in defense of its action; he therefore breaks with the noble simplicity of Vitoria in order to preserve the real effectiveness of the threat of punitive war. According to Suarez, where a claim of grave injury is made questionable by a counterclaim, the relative merits of the opposing claims must be balanced with the aid of prudent counsel. If they are equal, then the status quo must be maintained. But if one side's claim is "more probable," its right must be admitted. If the other side then refuses to acknowledge this necessity, the right may be prosecuted, and the recalcitrant nation may be punished through war.[86]

Suarez's thought on this point has been subject to frequent misinterpretation. He does not mean that war is justified by a merely "probable" claim. He speaks of a good claim that is rendered doubtful because of a counterclaim but that then proves, upon examination, to be better than the counterclaim. The enemy is punished, not because its legitimate claim is not good enough, but because it refuses to recognize the better claim. There is then no question, in principle, of a war that is objectively just on both sides: the war that is waged is a parallel to the police action against a man who refuses to abide by the judicial decision after a hotly contested inheritance suit or a closely fought assault prosecution.[87]

But if there is no weakness in principle, this spelling out of the practical application of the doctrine of just war makes even more evident the dangers of moralism that are already perceived in Vitoria's teaching. It is true that both Vitoria and Suarez stress the need for rulers to consult learned and experienced statesmen or religious leaders of high moral repute. Political power must find its legitimacy in submission to the wise, who do not necessarily rule. This route to restraint notwithstanding, the fact remains that if one is not to interpret the doctrine so as to make the occurrence of legitimate recuperative or punitive war almost impossible, one must allow a state to act with the moral authority and sentiments of a policeman, even when it fights to make good a claim that has been challenged by another state and has not been adjudicated by a third state. Restraint in the war must come not from any respect for the enemy's cause or from any sense of regret at the questionable merit of "our" cause—for to admit that is to admit complete lack of justification—but rather from a belief in the ignorance of the enemy or from our calculation of what will make a lasting peace.

Equally revealing, and of even greater significance, is Suarez's dissatisfaction with Vitoria's conceptualization of the relationship between natural law and the doctrine of just war. He agrees that the moral norms or laws of war must be part of the "law of nations." But he insisted on making explicit the new notion of an international or external law of nations, to which Vitoria implicitly appealed.[88] Suarez says:

> Let me add for greater clarification that something is said to belong to the law of nations in two ways (as far as I can gather from Isidore and other jurists and authorities): in one way, because it is a law that all people and the diverse nations ought to follow in their external relations with one another; in another way because it is a law that individual cities or realms observe internally but which on account of general resemblance and conformity is also called the law of nations. The former way seems to me to preserve the law of nations as something in itself, distinct from civil law, in accordance with our explication here of the law of nations.[89]

As a result of having clarified the meaning of the international type of law of nations, Suarez feels compelled to make sharper the distinction between natural law and this law of nations. The international "laws of nations" are man-made customs that are derived by nations from the premises of natural reason, as conclusions that are appropriate but *not* absolutely necessary; in contrast, natural laws are laws that are independent of man's making and have been derived from the premises of natural reason as conclusions that are inescapably necessary.[90] This new distinction has consequences for practice, consequences that reduce somewhat the danger of exaggerated moralism. For Vitoria, no nation can withhold obedience from the law of nations, because that law, like civil law, is not a product of an implicit pact among the nations;[91] for Suarez, the law of nations is, unlike civil law, an implicit contract, which, once entered into, cannot be broken without mutual consent, but which it is conceivable that a nation has not entered into: "Natural right does not per se oblige [a nation to enter into commercial ties], for it might be possible for a commonwealth to live by itself and not wish to carry on commerce with others, even with no unfriendliness involved."[92] Suarez is perhaps more alive than is Vitoria to the possibility that the Indians or some other people may have good reason to prevent the Spaniards from introducing European commerce and the quest for that "common resource," gold.

Still, if Suarez opens the door to the possibility that most of the law of war must find its basis in a consensus that does not stem from reason but rather from Christian revelation, he does so only to close it again. He remains faithful to Vitoria in asserting the existence of a *natural* "political and moral unity of all nations."[93] He is sure that that order must have some invocable natural sanction, for "it is impossible that the author of nature should have left the human things in such a state . . . that those who possessed the greater might would regularly have the greater right."[94]

It was the problematic dependence of the Thomistic doctrine of just war on divine revelation, combined with the disintegration of the Catholic Christian consensus, that moved Hugo Grotius to attempt a relatively fresh start from a standpoint that was slightly closer to classical rationalism.[95]

Grotius accepted the scholastic idea of natural law, but he drew a distinction even sharper than Suarez's between natural law and the international "law of nations." The latter he termed the "*volitional* law of nations," in order to bring out sharply the fact that this law is the result, not of strict natural inclination or necessity, but rather of human decision and agreement.[96] This human agreement, which is the outcome of many centuries of implicit comity and custom among the civilized nations, represents a semiconscious attempt to extend to international affairs the principles, although not the letter, of natural law. Of course, errors of human will and judgment have crept into this international custom. Grotius made it his great task to show the coherence of the volitional law of nations, and by bringing together and codifying its traditions, he hoped both to make the underlying natural principles clearer and to lead nations to refine the law further in the direction indicated by those principles.[97]

According to Grotius, the most obvious problem in his predecessors' writings is their failure to apply historical research in order to separate out international customs that are peculiar to Christians (and thus dependent on divine law) from those shared by pre-Christian civilized nations as well (and thus reflecting natural law). Hence, whereas Suarez seldom refers to ancient history and tends often to dismiss Roman practices as unreasonable,[98] Grotius begins by saying that he has "preferred examples from the ancient Greeks and Romans to others."[99] He then proceeds to apply an unrivaled encyclopedic learning to the documentation of the universal consensus, the outlines of which Vitoria had delineated. Beyond that, he puts flesh on the bones of the scholastic treatment: he systematically defines and distinguishes every important element of the laws governing war and peace. For example, since so many disputes arise over ownership of property, Grotius devotes over a hundred pages to demonstrating what property is, what its origins are by nature, how title is acquired and transferred, what the nature of inheritance is, how property is controlled through rights over persons, and so forth.

Marshaled before us are the original works of almost every noted philosopher, theologian, historian, poet, orator, and jurist, as well as the Bible and commentaries on it, in order to create an impressive, not to say staggering, refutation of the idea that the human record shows little agreement on moral questions. Still, one cannot help but ask whether the agreement he finds is not in some measure due to his masterful orchestration. The issue over which he explicitly parts company with Vitoria is perhaps the most arresting case. Impelled by his desire to show a truly effective sanction for international law, Grotius argues that it is accepted custom for every government to enforce police powers that extend to every part of the globe. He adds a strong caution against the temptation to misuse this power as an excuse for unjustified expansion; but he is willing to take the risk of asserting that even in international affairs, "it is more decent to avenge the injuries to others than those to oneself."[100] Now, to establish the consensus of mankind on this point, Grotius appeals mainly to what men have written regarding, not other men, but the praiseworthy deeds of demigods like Hercules. Is he bringing out a consensus that exists, or is he building a new consensus, using the present or past consensus as a foundation? This question directs us again to the fundamental question: have the international practices that decent men seem to agree on been perceived by them as *laws,* similar in their binding quality to civil laws, or have they been perceived more as honorable ways, which in general should be followed, but which cannot ever be as simply binding as the laws and the right within each nation? Is there a natural necessity for obeying these laws, comparable to the natural necessity or reason for obeying certain civil laws?

Grotius is convinced that these international practices do have the status of laws, or that at the very least, intelligent men have always aspired to make them laws and to create a true international order—just as Aristotle says societies that antedate the founding of cities visibly strive toward the political life that they as yet do not fully possess. Grotius's conviction is based on a much fuller exploration of the issue involved than we find in his predecessors. In the prolegomena to his great work, he begins by raising the issue of the naturalness of justice altogether. He lucidly restates the Aristotelian position: there is justice by nature, because the good for men by nature is a common good. Men do not cooperate, as Carneades claimed, solely out of the expediency of collective selfishness, or, as Glaucon claimed, like the weak banding together against the strong. Men's ties to their nation are not simply conditional for the sake of private gain, and hence cannot be sacrificed for the sake of private gain. Collective selfishness is a part of the reason for society, but the more important reason is the intrinsic joy of political and social cooperation itself, the engaging in social activity for its own sake and not merely as a means.[101]

With regard to international justice, then, the question is, Does there exist an international common good that is parallel to the national common good? Grotius admits that "many" believe that the only ties among nations are the conditional ties of collective security or selfishness.[102] He counters this in the first place with the argument that even if these were the only ties, they would lead to more lasting obligations than people suppose, because nations are weaker and more threatened than most people think.[103] But this argument, he knows, is inadequate: it leaves an enormous difference between the character and obligatory quality of justice among nations and of justice within each nation. He therefore asserts that there exists beyond any good or activity that is enjoyed by citizens of a nation within the nation itself a higher good, which can only be enjoyed and engaged in through cooperation and even "friendship" between nations.[104] Unfortunately, Grotius never very clearly articulates what that good or activity might be, except for a joy in purity of conscience and moral obedience to law for its own sake.[105] At this point, we must remark that even when he is discussing domestic political society, Grotius explicitly passes over any very concrete treatment of the political activity that is the content of the "common good." That, he says, has been treated by Aristotle, and it concerns what is "useful," or "advantageous," whereas Grotius's subject is what is the lawful or the just (*ius*): he has "in places made mention of the useful, but in passing, and in order that it might be more clearly distinguished from the just."[106] The heavy un-Aristotelian emphasis on this distinction,[107] as well as the implicit strong subordination of the advantageous or useful to the just, helps to explain Grotius's lack of concern at his unsatisfactory articulation of the cosmopolitan common good.

It should of course be remembered that Grotius was striving to find a basis or platform for international agreement in a world riven by sectarian religious war that had been caused by violent disagreement over the nature of the highest good for man. But we are left wondering whether the nobility of obedience to the conscience and to the law is in itself a sufficient theoretical reason for the international structure, or whether in the final analysis it is not, again in Grotius, God's law and heavenly rewards that require men to live by a justice that extends above and beyond one's own nation to all nations.[108]

This suspicion arises because, despite his explicit disavowal of reliance on revelation, Grotius's rationalism still shares a key proclivity of the Thomistic, as opposed to the Aristotelian, version of political theory: Grotius does not find that reason derives normative standards for politics from the ends or goals, from what is required for earthly happiness. The just is not whatever leads to the true good or advantageous. More than for Aristotle, the just or noble has to do with propriety of means, purity of intention, and lawfulness for its own sake.

It is no accident that after Thomas we find a steady growth in concern for foreign policy among political theorists, since this Thomistic perspective, which Grotius adopts, is conducive to a greater preoccupation with international relations at the expense of domestic affairs. International relations can suggest to the moral man the idea of the transnational nature of duty and the moral law. This shift toward a cosmopolitan posture is connected with the turning of attention away from the aspiration for the "best regime" and the "good life" realizable within the political community, and the turning toward obedience to the moral law, regardless of consequences for political goals. The understanding that nature is morally lawful or that there is a natural law that is accessible to all and obeyable by all bespeaks a new and unclassical concern with the actualization of our earthly duties and the certainty of completing them. The medieval tradition, much more than the classical, seems to teach the statesman that it is possible for him to fulfill his earthly work or function, and thus opens up for him the clear possibility of turning to a work that would truly transcend politics.

Modern Political Theory: "Realism"

In the sixteenth and seventeenth centuries there took place a systematic, self-conscious attack on the tradition of political philosophy that had been begun by the Greeks and had been continued in modified form by the Christian, Jewish, and Moslem Aristotelians. The thinker who, more than any other, originated this intellectual break was Machiavelli.

The starting point of Machiavelli's revolution is his assertion that all earlier political theory is decisively flawed by its failure to pay sufficient attention to foreign policy. In attempting to understand man's natural needs and inclinations, previous thinkers had taken their bearings from the behavior that was evident within the city or nation, namely, in the peaceful cooperation under law of fellow citizens. According to Machiavelli, this approach compelled them to distort the sphere of tense, belligerent, and uncooperative international relations. The Christian thinkers had tried to see the international sphere as a decayed and remediable political order (an understanding tenable only on the assumption, which is not rationally justifiable, of rule by a benevolent deity); the pagan thinkers had recognized it for what it is, but had tried to ignore its implications for domestic policy. But, Machiavelli argues, if one pays attention to historians rather than to philosophers, one sees the falseness of all this. The very possibility of any domestic policy depends, not periodically, but constantly on the careful protection of the city from foreign interference. Isolation is always impossible. The more one dwells on this truth, the more one realizes that the need for never-ending vigilance in foreign policy necessarily absorbs almost all a statesman's thought and energy. Foreign policy is, then, not merely an ever-present condition for domestic policy; it overshadows domestic policy. For since we cannot educate or reform foreign peoples, we must adjust our goals so as to be prepared for outrageous aggressions. Otherwise we surrender to a blind trust in the harmonious outcome of unpredictable and uncontrollable external forces.

Indeed, it is necessary to go still further. Truly to anticipate the unprincipled or mad aggressor is not to await him passively but to forestall him by action. The city or nation must keep its friends strong and its enemies weak; it must consider as friends only those whose actions it can control and predict. The city must therefore expand and move to combat every likely potential enemy. Far from believing that war is never just on both sides, we must realize that war is almost always just on both sides. In short, it is inescapably necessary for the most decent and dedicated patriot, the most public-spirited and generous statesman, to imitate the behavior of the shrewdest aggressor. Republican Rome, with its wealth, populous masses, and virile imperialism, must be preferred to the poor, defensive, and isolationist Spartan model of the classical philosophers:

> For the Romans did . . . what all wise princes ought to do, who keep in mind not only present discords but future ones as well, and with great industry prevent them; because being foreseen they can easily be remedied. . . . Thus the Romans, seeing trouble from afar, always found a remedy; and they never allowed them to grow in order to avoid a war, because they knew that war cannot be avoided but only postponed to someone else's advantage. . . . Nor did they ever prefer what is in the mouth of every wise man today, to enjoy the benefits time brings, but they reaped the benefits of their virtue and prudence—because time brings all things, and can bring the good as well as the bad and the bad as well as the good.[109]

This rethinking of the requirements of foreign policy is only the first stage in Machiavelli's comprehensive reflection about the nature of politics. The wolfishness of international politics points to and is rooted in the necessary, rational response of man to his true situation in the world. Nations and men must compete, because they find themselves in an inhuman environment of extreme economic scarcity. For most men the permanent and deepest desire is the desire for security or self-preservation—a necessarily selfish, aggressive, and acquisitive desire in a world where not all can survive. But even more dangerous than the competition for security in which most men are involved is the competition arising from the human desire to win glory or recognition by dominating other men. This latter drive, which is fully manifested in only a few of the strongest and most talented, represents an even more restless and insatiable source of human conflict.[110]

These are the natural needs; satisfaction of them must be understood to be the rational goal of politics. They reveal themselves in the world most clearly in war and foreign affairs; but we will understand how they pervade all human life if we try to imagine or reconstruct the origins, the half-forgotten explanatory causes, of civilization. Once we seriously question the assumption that men are naturally political, we begin to see how unlikely it is that civil society is the outcome of a peaceful, harmonious process. After all, everyone agrees that civil society was preceded by a precivilized epoch, and in that epoch men lived in tribes that were not governed by laws, customs, and political institutions as we know them. It is in foreign policy that we see how groups of men treat one another when they are free from higher legal and political authorities that have full coercive power. The origins, therefore, were probably hideous and terrifying—a state of war. It is likely that political life is not a product of some natural desire to cooperate in friendship for its own sake, but rather exists as the result of an expedient welding together of families and individuals who are driven by collective selfishness and fear. But who did this welding? In the typical case, a civilization is the product of the "armed prophets," men whose sublimely selfish desire for external glory drives them to use imagination and brute strength to persuade and compel lesser men to form stable orders. The deeds and motives of such men are the true core of what all praise as "virtue."[111] Essential to the social permanence that the armed prophets create is a myth, a religion or ideology, that covers both the stark emptiness of nature and the terror—crimes, murders, even fratricides—that must have been part of the armed prophet's forging of a people. Such myths permit most men to believe in the "naturalness" of peace, obedience to law, and civilization.[112]

For a regime to remain strong, however, some men among the ruling class, motivated by the love of glory, must continue to recognize the truth and to act on it. In addition, the multitude that constitutes most of society is in continual danger of "corruption," of forgetting the compulsion to cooperate, of reverting to disorganized selfishness. Good societies, then, are those that are continually "refounded," "restored to their original principles," or made to feel, in moderated form, the harshness of inhuman nature and human competitiveness. An aggressive foreign policy, with all its threats and hardships, proves to be a positive educational blessing, not merely a reluctantly chosen necessity. Moreover, the virile acquisitiveness of a foreign policy like that of republican Rome fosters passions that lead to an explosively tense competition among classes and individuals within the republic. Contrary to what has been traditionally believed, it is precisely this competition, properly structured and channeled by institutions, that promotes the shrewdest leadership, the most alert and energetic populace, and hence the greatest security, glory, and prosperity for almost all members of the society. The enormous task of political science, a task explored in all its rich complexity throughout the *Discourses*, is the delicate balancing of leaders and masses, selfishness and social cohesion, secure order and creative disorder.[113]

Machiavelli is confident that the spread of his new political science will foster a creative competitive struggle, not only within but among states in the international arena. In the world dominated by Christian and classical philosophy, with their unrealistic goals and restraints, men are prevented from unleashing their natural acquisitive energies. International politics has hence decayed into an endless succession of petty, indecisive struggles among small or weak nations that have shifting boundaries and unstable governments: "This way of life seems to me to have made the world feeble, and given it as an easy prey to wicked men."[114] The *Discourses* explicitly claim to found a "new mode and order" of politics,[115] which would bring about a world made more secure by the warlike competition of several great republican or monarchical states.

Machiavelli recognizes one grave problem in his hope or plan: his model is expansionist republican Rome, yet republican Rome was unable to remain a healthy republic after it expanded beyond the Italian peninsula. Eventually, in fact, Rome established a universal tyranny which destroyed everywhere the very possibility of healthy political life, made almost all men effeminate, and created the conditions for the triumph of what Machiavelli regards as the slavish Christian morality. In the light of all this, Machiavellian republicanism appears to be self-destructive or cancerous. This is one important reason for Machiavelli's unwillingness to state a clear preference for republicanism as opposed to monarchy, for monarchy appears to have a more limited capacity for expansion.[116]

It is not certain that Machiavelli ever fully overcomes the problem posed by the history of Rome. He does remind us that in the future, if his teaching is successful, the principles on which Rome built her successful system will be widely known, and leaders in many nations will be liberated from the charms of religion and of classical philosophy.[117] Hence, any "new Rome" will not lack competitors as did the original Rome. Nevertheless, in the final analysis, Machiavelli seems to rely on the malevolence of chance or nature to prevent any single Machiavellian republic from ever achieving such a degree of success as to create a universal and lasting tyranny.[118]

The problematic character of the Roman model is part of the reason for the theoretical innovations of Thomas Hobbes, the most important of Machiavelli's successors. Hobbes's political philosophy literally begins with an attack on the Roman republic.[119] Accepting Machiavelli's premises, Hobbes denies the soundness of the system that Machiavelli had derived from them.

Let us agree, says Hobbes in effect, with Machiavelli's rejection of the unrealistic classical and Christian traditions; let us agree that foreign affairs point to the truth about man's relation to man, and that it is only through reconstructing by that light the original causes of civil society that we will achieve clarity about the fundamental, lasting motives of all political behavior. Let us call that original situation, and its contemporary manifestation in international relations, the "natural" situation, the "state of nature." Our description will be similar to Machiavelli's. The state of nature is a state of war of all against all, which is caused by scarcity, insecurity, and vainglory. In such a condition, every man's need gives him an equal right to all the things that he may judge necessary for his own protection and comfort.[120]

If, however, we now proceed to think through the fundamental stages in man's progress from the natural state to the legal state, reflecting as we go on what is implied regarding the motives or impulses that underlie man's social behavior in general, we necessarily come to see that Machiavelli has vastly overrated the role and value of vainglory. Preoccupation with vainglory is a posture that is based on two false presumptions: the tendency to believe in one's superiority over others and the tendency to believe in one's power to control singlehandedly one's environment. Men possessing such an attitude will be the last to sense their full need to band together with others in order to achieve the only worldly power that is truly secure. The political orders that they create, which reflect their outlook, will have a foreign policy that is dangerously overconfident and a domestic policy that is troubled by the ambitions of willful and erratic men of pride: "No society can be great or lasting, which begins from vainglory."[121] Insecurity, or the fear of violent death, on the other hand, is the reasonable response to the experience of war, an experience that should teach us the natural equality, in weakness and unprotectedness, of all men: "They are equals, who can do equal things one against the other; but they who can do the greatest things, namely, kill, can do equal things. All men therefore among themselves are by nature equal."[122] For all men who understand their situation, for all who are not somehow blinded or crazed, the desire for security must become the strongest of all passions: "For every man is desirous of what is good for him, and shuns what is evil, but chiefly the chiefest of natural evils, which is death; and this he doth by a certain impulsion of nature, no less than that whereby a stone moves downward."[123] The men who fully realize their danger, and hence govern themselves according to a fear-induced defensive mentality, are the ones who are most likely to call a truce, seek one another's assistance, and remain permanently allied to one another. The weak and timorous, not the strong and proud, are the source of peace, order, stability, and civilization.

Only by means of this understanding of the passion or impulse that underlies society can we give a coherent account of the social and political virtues as we know them in everyday life. If we begin from the natural desire for self-preservation, or the "natural right" of self-defense, we can understand all moral and political obligations as deducible means to the guaranteeing of this fundamental selfish drive. Hobbes thus restores the notion of "natural law" on a new basis and with consequent new content: what men call the moral laws of nature "are but conclusions, or theorems concerning what conduceth to the conservation and defence of themselves."[124]

The substance of this new moral teaching is the famous notion of the social contract. Men in the state of nature, having experienced the primordial terror, recognize the first great "conclusion" or "natural law"—"thou shalt seek peace." The mechanism for attaining peace is the creation, through mutual agreement or compact, of a political order that satisfies the four following conditions. First, the number of members must be large enough to wield collectively an irresistible force. Second, each member must voluntarily surrender all his right and power, except the minimal and inalienable right of self-defense, to an "artificial person" or "sovereign representative"—that is, a coercive government, guided by one or more men, which can call on the collective power of all the contracting individuals to enforce the legitimate goal of internal and external security. Third, no part of the power of the "sovereign" may be transferred by those to whom it has been assigned. Fourth, the contract must be permanent and irrevocable. If any of these conditions is lacking, the social contract has no effective force and the state of war remains; for none of the individuals would then gain that lasting security which is the only reason for his surrender of his original right to determine for himself whatever may be the best means to his own preservation.[125]

The consequences of these principles for public policy and a society's way of life are extensive and manifold. The fundamental moral-political fact is no longer duty, or virtue, or happiness, but the freedom of each individual as an independent and anxious being. The purpose of government is, hence, no longer encouragement of the "good life" but the mere protection and securing of life—not happiness but the protection of the means for each individual's pursuit of happiness as he conceives it. This means that political life need not be much concerned with the moral or religious education of citizens or with their having any particular higher faculties or experiences. Government or the coercive state (the public sphere) becomes restricted in its responsibility and permissive in its supervision. The core of life is to be found in the web of spontaneous private relations that constitutes subpolitical society (the private sphere). Here, when unrestricted, men naturally seek to maximize their private security and therefore their health, their comfort, and their wealth. As a result the promotion of economic prosperity—of mercantile and industrial acquisitiveness that is fueled by unrestricted scientific enlightenment and technological advance—replaces Machiavellian imperialism as the chief preoccupation of government: "The benefits of subjects, respecting this life only, may be distributed into four kinds. 1. That they be defended against foreign enemies. 2. That peace be preserved at home. 3. That they be enriched, as much as may consist with public security. 4. That they enjoy a harmless liberty."[126] It is this new understanding of the nature and goals of politics (and not his discussion of the various forms of government and institutions) which marks Hobbes as the founder of what we now call "liberalism," "pluralism," or "the open society."[127]

The implications of this liberal realism for foreign policy are not as clear and unambiguous as its implications for domestic policy. We recall first that the atomistic and hostile individualism of man's natural state is reflected in, and indeed is partly revealed to us by, the atomistic and hostile individualism of nations toward one another. The sovereign nation or "artificial man," not having created through compact with other nations any superior "sovereign representative," remains in a state of war and has no obligation or responsibility to any other nation:

> Concerning the offices of one sovereign to another . . . the same law, that dictateth to men that have no civil government, what they ought to do, and what to avoid in regard of one another, dictateth the same to commonwealths, that is, to the consciences of sovereign princes and sovereign assemblies.
>
> Where there is no common power, there is no law: where no law, no injustice. Force, and fraud, are in war the two cardinal virtues.[128]

On the other hand, the experience of the state of war is supposed to teach the prudent man the need to seek peace and to adopt a defensive posture; certainly the sovereign that is constituted according to Hobbesian principles is the embodiment of his subjects' collective will to peace. Does it not follow that, as Hobbes's principles spread in influence, the Hobbesian sovereigns will look for opportunities to create a new "social contract" among sovereign nations, thus imitating the original contract among individuals which is in principle at the root of all rational political organization? Does not the theory of the social contract point toward the creation of regional and even world federation?

Hobbes himself, as opposed to some of his less sophisticated successors, never even intimates the advisability of such a policy. Some reflection on the foundations of the Hobbesian system shows us why such a policy would be, on Hobbesian principles, prudentially impracticable and morally wrong. Because the "state of nature" among nations is different in crucial respects from the "state of nature" among individuals, the dictates of a reasonable or morally justifiable defensiveness are different in the two cases. Two conditions that are present among individuals but are missing among nations are necessary to make valid the normative conclusion to form a social contract: natural equality and a high degree of geographical mobility (the power to run away). The first creates a reasonable necessity and hence an effective guarantee for each person's adherence to the contract, and the second makes it impractical for anyone to overcome his weakness by enslaving others. In the state of nature, among individual men there are no giants and dwarfs, no lions and rabbits—and no way of becoming like a giant or lion among men. But among nations there are always a few Gullivers and many Lilliputians; and no nation can "run away" from its near neighbors. The equality of men is a natural fact, but the "equality" of sovereigns is merely a convenient legal myth. Among nations the "Gullivers" have no permanently compelling reason to adhere to the contract, and the "Lilliputians" have no way of trusting them to do so.

Apart from these prudential considerations, we must remember the moral fact that the "sovereign representative" has no right to transfer or surrender any of its sovereign power. This famous doctrine of indivisible and inalienable sovereignty follows from the very notion of contract as the fundamental moral-political principle. The "social contract" theory implies that any political authority or government can derive its legitimate powers only from the direct and unanimous consent, in principle, of the governed. Only if the existing sovereign government could be conceived as first somehow dissolved, and the original contract thus abrogated, could a new sovereign be formed, and then only by the individuals. While world government under one untrammeled sovereign is theoretically conceivable according to the principles of the social contract, federation—as anything other than a convenient truce or alliance among sovereign states in the midst of war—is inconceivable. Practically speaking, it seems that the state of war among nations is insuperable.

How is it, then, that despite this necessary consequence of his teaching, Hobbes can assert that the promulgation of his principles would make "mankind enjoy such an immortal peace, that unless it were for habitation, on supposition that the earth should grow too narrow for her inhabitants, there would hardly be left any pretence for war."[129] The reasons seem to be as follows. In the first place, the "Enlightenment," the spread of knowledge of human nature and the true natural law, will gradually lead to a world of nations whose rulers recognize the absurdity of pride or vainglory and the preeminent value of peace and security. At the same time, enlightenment will transform the multitude's religious sectarianism and national vanity into shrewd material self-interest. In addition, since according to Hobbes's principles no man can ever be morally obliged to surrender his life for anything, the "Enlightenment" will undermine the capacity of governments to maintain armies in battle: "A man that is commanded as a soldier to fight against the enemy . . . may nevertheless in many cases refuse, without injustice. . . . When armies fight, there is on one side, or both, a running away; yet when they do it not out of treachery, but fear, they are not esteemed to do it unjustly, but dishonorably."[130] Finally, the engagement in commerce, which is to become more and more the national preoccupation, will make men and nations much less willing to break off peaceful communication and the exchange of goods with one another.[131]

The hopes that Hobbes entertained for changes in the international environment were limited, however, by his judgment that the attachment to glory, honor, domination, and preeminence would always remain a serious temptation to many talented men. This underlying pessimism animates his recommendation that there be a strong and highly centralized police power within the state, as well as a vigorous armed guard against threats from without.[132]

The changes that were brought about by Hobbes's immediate philosophic successors, above all Locke and Montesquieu, can in large measure be traced to their more sanguine view of the possibility of turning men away from the pursuit of glory and honor. Locke and Montesquieu agree with Hobbes's description of the "state of nature" in most important respects, despite the rhetorical impression that they sometimes give to the contrary.[133] But they ascribe the source of man's hostile competitiveness less to vainglory and more to economic scarcity. These thinkers originate the economic interpretation of politics and history, the tracing of much or most of human political behavior to economic motives; as for the power that pride or vanity holds over the human heart, they attribute it mainly to the lack of opportunity to acquire material prosperity.[134] This interpretation implies that the root of the gravest human strife is a more rational, less offensive motive than either Hobbes or Machiavelli had thought: though the desire to gain security through property may be as insatiable or even more insatiable than the desire for dominion and glory, men can be taught to see very clearly that progress toward satisfaction of this desire comes with an economic "system" of peaceful relationships through which all or almost all men must be made more prosperous if anyone is to become more prosperous.

The implications for international affairs are drawn out most clearly by Montesquieu.[135] Nations exist in a condition of permanent war towards one another, but since the state of war arises as the rational outcome of competition for security, it can be regulated by the mutual recognition of certain reasonable limits:

> The law of nations is by nature founded on this principle: that the various nations ought in peace to do the greatest benefit and in war to do the least harm that is possible, without prejudicing their own true interests. The object of war is victory; that of victory, conquest; that of conquest, preservation. From this and the preceding principle ought to be derived all the laws of nations.[136]

As the Enlightenment spreads, peoples will be "softened" and governments will come to see more and more clearly the wastefulness and irrationality of war:

> Knowledge renders men soft; reason brings humanity.
>
> Commerce cures destructive prejudices; and it is almost a general rule that wherever there are soft ways of life there is commerce; and that wherever there is commerce, there are soft ways of life.
>
> The natural effect of commerce is to bring peace. Two nations that negotiate together render themselves mutually dependent.[137]

Nonetheless, rational motives for war will never entirely disappear; the state of war is always immanent.[138] One can hardly expect, therefore, an elaborate code of international law, a "civil law of the universe." True liberty is life under the rule of law enforced by coercive government, and this does not exist among sovereigns: "Princes are not free, they are ruled by force . . . and it follows that treaties which they make under threat of force are as obligatory as those they make by their own free will."[139] International "law" will always be a mixture of prudence, fidelity to covenants, and violence—at best a faint echo of the relation of trust and obligation among citizens.[140] "Whenever a people sees that a continued peace would put another in a situation to destroy it, and that an attack is the sole means to prevent such destruction," it possesses by "strict justice" the right to begin war. On the other hand, when war does break out, Montesquieu argues, the new, loose principles of international justice will go together with a sense of economy and a softness, or even compassion, which will bring less bloodshed and suffering than in the past:

> From the right of war is derived the right of conquest. . . . The latter should follow the spirit of the former. . . . Conquest is acquisition; the spirit of acquisition carries with it the spirit of preservation and usage, not destruction. . . . It is necessary here to render homage to our modern times, to modern reason, modern religion, modern philosophy, and modern customs. The authors who still write about our public law, founding themselves on ancient history, . . . have fallen into grave errors. . . . For

example, they have claimed conquerors have the right, I don't know how, to kill the conquered . . . and from this these political thinkers have drawn a right to reduce the conquered to slavery.[141]

A "law of nations" that is stripped of all policing or punitive spirit, an international environment that does not pretend to comprise a civil community but candidly promotes commercial competitiveness regulated by treaties and the balance of powers, will in the long run create a world that is, if not noble, then at least pacific.

Every reader will recognize the appealing reasonableness and solidity of this sober outlook. It remains today, in one form or another, one of the great guiding lights of foreign policy. Still, in reflecting on this teaching, one encounters troubling obscurities. These gradually resolve themselves into two related questions: First, how much political freedom can we expect in a world based on these principles? Second, can such principles evoke in the hearts of men the attachment and dedication required in order to create a stable world order?

If we look again at Montesquieu with these questions in mind, we find that while he hopes for a stable balance of independent nations within Europe, he frankly welcomes the spread of colonies, spheres of influence, and, in rare cases, even empire over the uncommercial nations outside Europe.[142] He may persuade us that the new conquerors will be in some ways "softer" than any earlier ones; we may grant that the spread of enlightened commercialism will bring greater prosperity and an enlargement of many personal freedoms for individuals. Can we be persuaded, though, that the commercial revolution will bring self-government and political independence? And apart from questions about the fate of uncommercial regimes and civilizations, one can wonder about the fate of the great European powers themselves: has Montesquieu taken sufficient account of the long-range possibilities for war that will arise out of the global competition among nations that possess unprecedented economic power and unheard-of weapons and communications technology?[143]

In giving up the transcendentally based cosmopolitanism of the medieval tradition, the modern realists appear to return in some degree to the classical outlook, divested of its militant or patriotic belligerence. But for classical republicanism the imperial dangers inherent in the necessarily low, blurred ethics of foreign affairs were moderated by the elevated tone and content of domestic policy. In the ancient city the infrequent but still disheartening necessity for harshness or even baseness in international affairs could be overshadowed and justified for the participating citizen by his vision of the goals and way of life pursued within the free city. And the citizen's love for his city's regime—the particular way of life, the character and the virtues inculcated by his political order—opened to him a possible sense of kinship with citizens in foreign cities possessing regimes that resembled his own. Can the modern European find a comparable source of restraint and of international respect, a justification as adequate? Can peoples without such justification and respect summon up the energy and make the sacrifices required from time to time of any people who wish to rule themselves and to rule or guide other peoples? More generally, can men view themselves in the way the modern political philosopher teaches them—can men be "enlightened"?[144]

Given these questions, we should not be surpised to find that from the very beginning, modern realism has been confronted with a rival tradition that dogs its steps with questions and challenges.

Modern Political Theory: Idealism and International Organization

The way of thinking that we have chosen to call "idealist" finds its origins in the now almost-forgotten writings of publicists who hoped to recreate a basis for traditional natural law in the face of the overwhelming intellectual onslaught of Thomas Hobbes. Paradoxically, the century and a half after Hobbes is the high-water mark of the theoretical treatment of international law: treatises on the "natural law of nations" abound during this period. The decline in the importance of religious differences, the growth in trade, and the pacifist and secular cosmopolitan tendencies, which were engendered by Enlightenment thought, brought a new burgeoning of international relations and consequently led many statesmen and lawyers to sense a more pressing need than ever before for clear moral guidelines in international affairs. Few if any of the thinkers who responded to this need were able to resist the temptation to adopt the doctrine of the social contract, with all its persuasive clarity and precision. It is not our business to inquire why the Hobbesian doctrine had such appeal. It is enough to emphasize that the most famous publicists—Samuel Pufendorf, Christian Wolff, and Emmerich de Vattel—attempted to combine eclectically the medieval doctrine of the just war and the notion of the "state of nature." Each of these thinkers claimed to be placing on a "scientific" basis the "unrigorous" teachings of Grotius.

Our brief discussion will center on Vattel, not only because he became the most influential but also because, being the latest, his writings bring out most clearly the overall tendencies of the school. Characteristically, Vattel begins by adopting the notion of a state of nature, while at the same time denying that it has any historical validity. The state of nature is merely a hypothetical construct. This construct is not intended to imply that by envisioning man in a situation of isolated individuality, we will discover man's elemental psychological makeup. On the contrary, man is by nature a social and political being, just as the pre-Hobbesian tradition argues. But the intellectual construct of a state of nature, especially when supplemented by the equally hypothetical social contract, helps us see the principles that impel men to cooperate in political association. The idea of a state of nature reveals more lucidly than any notion of a good political order precisely what duties men have toward one another as the result of natural needs and endowments, apart from conventions that are peculiar to particular societies. The state of nature is therefore a state of peace, not war; a state in which "speech enables men to communicate with each other, to give each other mutual assistance, to perfect their reason and knowledge. . . . Each individual, moreover, is intimately conscious that he can neither live happily nor improve his nature without the intercourse and assistance of others."[145]

But does this construct prove to have the illuminating power that Vattel claims for it? The fact is that despite his frequent and honest reassertions of the classical or medieval doctrine of natural right, the moral basis of politics inevitably takes on a much more individualistic and self-assertive character in Vattel's hands. If rights do not take precedence over duties, then duties to oneself take precedence over duties to others or to the community. The traditional limitations placed upon individual commercial acquisitiveness, universal enlightenment, and freedom of conscience or religon are vastly attenuated. The concern for the "regime," or the promotion, by those who rule, of a morally authoritative way of life, is eclipsed by the concern for efficient administration of the "sovereign" power that protects the lives, property, and freedom of all. In short, one can wonder whether the picture of domestic political life that emerges is not closer to that of Hobbes and Locke than to that of Aristotle or Thomas, although it is clothed with a higher moral tone.[146]

When we turn to international affairs, Vattel's main interest, we find that the new approach gives promise of much more precise guidance than any earlier theoretical treatment. Since the law of nature is conceived of as applying to individuals in a state of independence, it proves to be (as Hobbes taught) directly applicable to international relations. For Grotius, natural law had been addressed primarily to men who were citizens in a political community; it therefore required considerable dilution and restatement in order to be applied as the "law of nations" (*ius gentium*) to sovereign and independent states. This difficult task of application was the work of the consensus of nations, gradually groping its way toward coherence through civilized history. In contrast, for Vattel and his intellectual kinsmen, the law of nations can be almost identical with the law of nature: there emerges the possibility—which becomes a settled project—of articulating a "science," a system of the law of nations derived from natural law.[147] One immediately apparent result is the decreased reliance on history for the derivation of these laws, and the corresponding increased reliance on legalistic deduction. It is Christian Wolff who goes furthest in attempting to make a deductive system out of the natural law of nations.

By positing a "supreme state [*civitas maxima*] which nature has herself established," a state of states, which stands as the not-yet-realized goal of international affairs and which parallels the social contract among men, Wolff can articulate a list of duties of assistance and mutual improvement that are owed by nations to one another: duties to love, to protect, to promote commerce with, to enrich, to educate, and to set good examples of behavior for other nations. On this new basis Wolff adopts almost word for word the doctrine of just war as elaborated by Grotius (see part two of this chapter). A similar line of thought is followed by Vattel.[148]

Our first impression, then, is of a return to an elaborate version of the medieval or Grotian position, based on more clear-cut principles. This impression proves to be deeply misleading. For both Wolff and Vattel admit that among nations, unlike among men, there is not and cannot be any real social pact or state of states. Indeed, so certain of this is Vattel that, although he maintains the looser notion of a "society" among nations and although in general he intends his work as a mere popularized version of Wolff, he feels compelled to begin by rejecting the hypothetical "supreme state." The idea of a supreme state of states is misleading, because states are by their nature much more self-sufficient than are individual men. Indeed, their self-sufficiency is a key part of the purpose for their coming into being. National self-sufficiency provides for human security and ultimately for civilization: it therefore has a sacred moral status. The moral status of national independence only reflects in an emphatic way the modern notion of the elevated moral status of every individual's independence, a notion that is present in the state-of-nature doctrine from the very beginning.

Wolff and Vattel are so impressed with the value of independence, both for individuals and nations, that they create a double standard for the moral guidance of affairs among nations. The natural law of nations that we have outlined and in particular the principles of the doctrine of just war can guide the consciences of leaders only as they plan and judge the policies of their *own* country. With a view to the fact that the strict natural law of nations applies only to each nation in its conscience, as it considers its own policies, Wolff and Vattel call it the "internal" law of nations, as distinguished from the "external" law of nations, which is the law that governs each nation with a view to what conduct it may rightly expect from other nations.[149] This distinction arises for the following reason. Since in the state of nature prior to the establishment of a sovereign arbitrator by means of the social contract no individual can judge another, no sovereign nation can ever judge another nation. In other words, no nation can castigate as unjust the deeds or even the wars of another nation. War must be presumed to be just on both sides. There can then be no punitive war or punishment for deeds done in war: the core of the Grotian

345

or medieval doctrine of just war is lost. Every country must be held to be equally moral in its intention and equally capable of understanding its own needs and proper interests. When war occurs, we must take the position that the enemy is misguided by circumstances beyond its control; we may attempt to persuade it of its mistake, but we may not penalize it or use coercion beyond what is necessary to defend ourselves, to deter further aggression, and, if necessary, to exact reparations for loss. The resulting doctrine of just war can justify only wars of self-defense but can never attribute blame to the other side. The "external" law of nations—what we can expect others to do—is severely limited.

What then is the content of the "external" law of nations if we cannot judge that another nation's warlike (or peaceful) deeds violate it? Though the law continues to enjoin other nations to render duties of peaceful assistance to us, it does not legitimate any enforcement of their performance. Again, in the absence of a higher authority, each country's conscience must be its guide, and our right to assistance is therefore "imperfect," or dependent on the will of others. The only "perfect" rights, or rights which we may coercively secure, are our rights to preservation and independence. Of course, nations do have need of one another in order to survive, and they must have some stronger source of trust than is furnished by the "imperfect" rights of assistance. In order to convert the very loose obligations that are implied in imperfect rights into enforceable or perfect rights, nations must enter into contracts or positive treaties, specifying with one another what is to be given and received. The right to expect fulfillment of contracts is thus presented as another perfect right, and the actual core of external international law comes to be the positive law of treaty and alliance. Yet, here again, in the final analysis it is up to each nation to decide when it has been absolved of its treaty obligations either by another nation's acts or by the absolutely paramount needs of self-preservation. The right to self-preservation proves to be the only completely "perfect" right, for the duty to keep covenants is derived from it.[150]

We can see with special clarity the general thrust of the teaching if we cast a glance at what Vattel has to say about neutrality. Grotius, it may be remembered, had recommended that every nation consider it a duty to intervene with assistance for the just side in any war where the issues are evident. Accordingly, he paid very little attention to the situation of "neutrality," and to some extent he encouraged belligerents to expect or demand aid when they found themselves involved in a just war. Vattel, in contrast, stresses the duty to remain uninvolved unless one is directly attacked or is committed through alliance.[151]

Vattel, like many another eclectic, presents a point of view that proves to be attractive in practical application. His theory seems to allow for complete national independence, while doing justice to the desire for some moral restraints on national behavior. It is altogether possible that national security and international relations constitute a moral area that is so murky as to frustrate any attempt to improve on Vattel's well-intentioned efforts. Nonetheless, reflective citizens may doubt that the moral tone possesses any firm foundation. If there is no coercive social order among nations, what natural sanctions exist for the moral law among nations? Is not the international obligation that is dictated by the conscience or the "internal" law of nations seen as much less important than independence, security, and power? In the long run, will not this restricted idea of international obligation be more and more overlooked, or used merely as a veneer for policy? No doubt, a moral veneer compels men to remember and to do homage to moderation: surely it is not something to be lightly dismissed. But in the case of Vattel the problematic status of the "conscience" that applies "internal law" to foreign affairs goes together with the problematic status of selflessness in the teaching about politics as a whole. The general problem in Pufendorf and Wolff, as well as in Vattel, is this: why does individual independence have such a high moral value if morality for them is constituted above all by one's dedication to a life of participation with others in a political community? If we look to the classics, we see that the elevated status of national independence was not derived from the moral independence of the individual but from the requirements of a tightly knit, highly interdependent civic society. For the medievals, the conscience of the statesman was dedicated to a cosmopolitan community which took precedence over any individual independence, whether of nations or men. How can Vattel combine either of these traditional understandings of morality with the new stress on the value of self-determination that stems from the natural primacy of competitive, self-interested motives?

The inadequacy of the theoretical attempts to give an elevated moral support for the political rights of the individual inspired the epoch-making and innovative thought of Immanuel Kant, with all its far-reaching implications for the moral basis of national security. In order to make intelligible the movement of thought that leads to Kant's reflections on "perpetual peace," it is necessary for us to allude to Kant's philosophic teacher, Jean-Jacques Rousseau. Rousseau thought his way through to what lay behind the dissatisfaction felt by thinkers like Wolff and Vattel. The political problem that Kant later devoted himself to solving is presented most clearly in *The Discourse on the Arts and Sciences*, in which Rousseau unleashes his famous attack on the Enlightenment—on all the most influential and apparently progressive political ideas of his time. The core of the part of his argument that is relevant to our discussion of Kant goes as follows: The new way of thinking claims to show to men for the first time their "nature": to liberate them by means of popular science from the myths of religious and political tradition, to arouse in them an understanding of their self-interest, rightly understood. Its conscious project is the awakening of a kind of anxiety and vanity, which, when channeled by the proper institutions, will lead to free and prosperous commercial rivalry. Modern political theory bases its understanding of right on the original equality of men in regard to their deepest passions or needs, but it intends to foster the development of competitive talents that are by nature unequally distributed. The modern politics nurtures a new kind of inegalitarian society and a highly centralized, quasi-monarchic state. In such a world, men will necessarily lead increasingly atomized lives, having relations with one another only through veils of inauthentic pretension and exploitation. What has been obscured in all modern thought is the moral dimension—the virtue—that constitutes the dignity and happiness of the human race. Virtue is not a product of science; it manifests itself not in thought but in action, and especially in patriotic action—the political deeds of men who participate in small republican regimes. Philosophy is the greatest enemy of this morality: science in general promotes a skepticism that weakens the beliefs that support the selfless dedication that is necessary for a true communal life, and modern science in particular teaches a deterministic approach to human behavior that undermines responsibility and freedom. The only philosophy that could defend itself before the bar of the conscience would be a "Socratic" philosophy, in which scientific skepticism was used to challenge the despotic claims of science itself, thus defending the simple, virtuous man against the unsettling pretensions of the scientist.

Kant explicitly presents himself as carrying out the "Socratic" mission sketched by Rousseau;[152] but in executing that project Kant claims to have discovered a firmer theoretical foundation for morality, a foundation that makes morality safe forever from the attacks of science and that thereby makes it possible to reconcile the new political, economic, and scientific knowledge with the eternal principles of virtue. As a result, Kant rejects much of Rousseau's positive political doctrine, which had in many respects implied a return to the classical ideal of the *polis*, and puts forth a new, cosmopolitan vision of man's secular duty and destiny.

According to Kant, the difficulties in modern attempts to give a theoretical account of morality only make perfectly clear, for the first time, the inadequacy of the entire tradition of moral philosophy. All earlier moral philosophers from Aristotle to Wolff have based morality on the idea of natural right: they have in one way or another understood virtue as man's obedient response to an awareness of a hierarchy of natural needs within himself. This means that they have defined virtue in terms of its contribution to natural satisfaction, or happiness. In doing so, they have demeaned virtue by subordinating it to something less noble. For everyone agrees that virtue cannot be equated with happiness, since happiness requires external goods (health, prosperity, and so forth) which are not produced by virtue. The more one ponders the obvious dependence of happiness on these external goods, which in turn depend on chance circumstances beyond human control, the more the identification of the morally virtuous life with the happy life appears to be tenuous. In addition, in attempting to find the standard for moral virtue in natural needs that determine the individual, the ground is cut from under the freedom of the will necessarily implied in the praise and blame that always accompanies our conception of virtue. In both these respects, the traditional view distorts the phenomena. Do we, asks Kant, in our concrete experience of the moral in ourselves and others, value that nobility in the light of its contribution to happiness? Do we view virtue, the good will, as subordinate to some more fundamental principle and impulse? Or do we not admire it strictly for its own sake, as the uncontingent and unconditioned source of all human dignity? Relying on his certainty with regard to our candid agreement in response to these questions, Kant proceeds to articulate the principle that underlies the universal human experience of what is moral.[153]

He begins by drawing attention to the fact that moral action is one part of conscious, rational action. Insofar as we act rationally, we act not merely in response to stimuli but according to a "maxim"—a general rule or principle, however implicit and crude. Even with regard to sleep, for example, we do not let ourselves fall asleep whenever we feel sleepy; we resist or do not resist, depending on whether the situation satisfies general criteria of appropriateness (the time of day, the work we have to do, and so forth). Insofar as we make these criteria explicit, we make explicit our maxim or general rule ("I shall not fall asleep in church, on the job, etc."). Of course, we humans are not pure reason; our maxims continually encounter resistance from our passions of all kinds (whatever my maxim, I may or may not succeed in staying awake in church, and so forth); the maxims therefore manifest themselves not as automatically applicable principles but as commands or "imperatives."[154] Now Kant understands that all the imperatives that govern our behavior, *except* the moral imperative, are for the sake of some end beyond the imperative itself. Thus, I resist falling asleep while working in order to keep my job, in order to draw my salary, and so forth. All the nonmoral imperatives can be seen as means to my personal happiness—a goal that, according to Kant, is subjective and always shifting but that still gives us rough overall guidance. The imperatives that appear as means have the form "if ———, then ———" ("if I wish to draw my salary, then I must stay awake now"); they can therefore be called "hypothetical" imperatives.

When we seek the principle that governs moral action, Kant says, we are seeking a nonhypothetical imperative, which commands not for the sake of contributing to our personal happiness but for its own sake. What would such a "categorical" imperative be? We can see if we begin from the hypothetical imperatives whose nature is somewhat clearer. Subtract from those imperatives whatever is hypothetical, that is, whatever makes them conditioned by personal happiness—for example, "do x *if you want y.*" What is left is the pure *form* of the imperative itself—("do x" simply) the unrestricted generality or universality of the rule. If we did not limit the generality of our imperatives by making them serve our individual happiness, if we could act for the sake of the form of rational command, we would be acting according to an unconditional or "unconditioned" imperative. What would this mean more concretely? Kant does not mean that to act morally is to cease to be concerned with happiness or to respond to natural need. Rather, the moral man sees his natural needs and his pursuit of happiness as the occasion, the vehicle, for the exercise of his sense of duty. Whenever he acts morally, he asks, "Do I will the maxim of my action not only as a means to my own happiness, but also, and more important to me as a moral person, can I will it as a universal law to be willed by every rational agent confronted with similar circumstances and similar options?" If and only if we subject our maxims to this test of universalization, and consider this test to be the most important thing, will we live for the sake of the form of rational command itself—and not make the imperative of reason a mere means to shifting subjective happiness.[155] Instead of presenting new, specific ends for action, the moral will gives a regulating principle that transforms all the preexisting human goals.

An example will make the meaning of the categorical imperative more vivid. Suppose I have borrowed money and promised to repay it on a given day. In the interval, unforeseen circumstances—perhaps ill health—have arisen; this makes it impossible for me to pay back the money and still have enough to support myself. May I, even without the permission of the lender, postpone payment? The answer is *No*. For when I attempt to will the maxim of this action as universal law, I encounter contradiction or insuperable difficulty: if every man who is in trouble could decide not to repay his debts on time, lenders would soon disappear, and I in effect would will the end of almost all borrowing. Society must have such means of transferring money and resources; without the possibility of borrowing, the social structure that provides the arena in which men may act morally would be endangered. But am I not then willing my own starvation? Not at all: only an inappropriate vanity and sloth prevents me from thinking of the variety of alternatives that are open to me, including selling my belongings, asking help from friends, and, in the last resort, begging. This example brings out another crucial and often misunderstood feature of the test of universality. Kant does not mean the test to be merely that of the logical consistency of a universal extension of our maxim: in the above example, there would be no *logical* inconsistency in willing the disintegration of all society. The real limitation on what maxims can be universalized is the effect on the continued existence of circumstances that allow men to exercise their moral will. Men need society in order to continue to do good deeds. Furthermore, it should be apparent that in universalizing my maxim, I must consider the maxim as applying to men in their average physical and psychic conditions and abilities.

Kant claims to do no more than give a precise statement of the manner of thinking that is shared by all men when they consider what duty dictates: the categorical imperative has been prefigured in such well-known formulae as the Golden Rule. Kant's version, however, seeks to identify better the key elements in our moral experience. First, we experience a moral action as something universal—what any moral man would do under the circumstances. Besides universality, but implied in it, there is in the second place the idea of the moral equality of all men. Insofar as the moral man acts not for the sake of interests that are peculiar to himself but only for the sake of interests belonging to a will that all men can share, his action must treat every other man's will as equal to his own or, more precisely, "not only as a means but also as an end in itself." Thirdly, the moral man takes on responsibility for the whole of humanity, considering himself humanity's representative on every particular occasion when he acts. At the same time, the moral man assigns to every other man full and equal responsibility: fulfillment of duty is not something expected only of some and not of others. In the fourth place, since moral action in obedience to the formal maxim of universality transcends every conscious and unconscious motive that is linked to particular circumstances, the man who acts morally is absolutely free. Every impulse or need that originates outside his rational control becomes binding for him only if and when he wills it as universal law. He obeys only that law which he has given to himself. This autonomy comes to seem the very core of human dignity for Kant.

The political norms derived from the categorical imperative seem at first quite clear: act in such a way as to realize the principle of morality; act in such a way as to bring about a world where men treat one another as free and equal ends in themselves. One might suppose initially that Kant has in mind a reformation of politics in the direction indicated by Rousseau: an increase in direct political participation, government support for rigorous moral education, public regulation of manners and customs through sumptuary laws and censors, and political leadership that provides moral guidance. This is not the case. As it turns out, Kant's unprecedented stress on freedom assumes paramount importance in his political thought. The moral will, to be genuine, must be entirely the result of a man's independent commitment. No one can make another man moral, much less "force him to be free," and habituation and moral education, especially when accompanied by any hint of coercion, are highly suspect. The role of government must be limited to removing the barriers that might impede man's awareness of the possibility for the self-originated moral will. The state can alleviate poverty, sickness, and lack of technical education; it can remove external restraints on freedom of speech and action. But moral enlightenment, the positive effort to elevate man's moral awareness, can take place only in the web of free association and spontaneous communication ("public opinion") that constitutes the liberal *society*. The upshot of all this is a sharp distinction between morality and justice. The categorical imperative, which governs men insofar as they are autonomous individuals in society realizing their inner moral freedom, demands that the motive of action be reverence for the moral law. Justice, which governs men insofar as they are citizens providing for their own external freedom and security, demands only that each man "act externally in such a way that the free use of his will is compatible with the freedom of everyone." Morality demands of men that they be just, but justice cannot demand of men that they be moral or even that they act justly for the sake of justice, "for anyone can still be free, even though I am quite indifferent to his freedom or even though I might in my heart wish to infringe on his freedom, as long as I do not through an external action violate his freedom."[156] It follows that a perfectly just society can be the outcome of pure selfishness: "As hard as it may sound, the problem of setting up a state can be solved even by a nation of devils, so long as they are intelligent."[157]

There is, in regard to domestic policy, a remarkable congruence between Kant's political philosophy and the liberalism of Hobbes and Locke, even though in Kant the liberal state is given a noble raison d'être. The sovereign state, with its rule of law, comes into being and gains its legitimacy through a social contract made by men living in radical independence (the "state of nature"). The purpose of government is to make secure the "natural rights" to life, liberty, property, and the pursuit of happiness.[158] But striking divergences from earlier liberal theory come to sight in foreign policy. The political goal of promoting the conditions that allow for (but do not guarantee) widespread commitments to the *universality* of the categorical imperative implies, from the beginning, a cosmopolitan concern with the human race as a whole. The continued existence of national divisions and war puts mankind in a situation where individuals are often compelled not to recognize the dignity of others. Besides, war diverts human energies from peaceful moral pursuits and self-improvement.[159] The effort to discover means of bringing about "perpetual peace" is therefore a direct moral duty—and perhaps the clearest of all moral duties for men in politics.

Yet at this point a complex question arises: In what sense is this *moral* duty also a duty of *justice* and therefore applicable to governments? Have we not been taught that governments and statesmen, in their official capacity, are to limit themselves to justice, to the protection of the external liberty of their citizens, rather than concern themselves with morality as a whole? Has Kant not reduced even further than did Vattel the scope of morality in affairs between governments? For Vattel, each government was supposed to judge its own policies, internal and external, by the strict criteria of the moral law, even though it was not empowered to pass moral judgment on the policies of other states. For Kant, the state must resist the temptation to look much beyond the criteria of justice (juridical right), lest it begin to impinge on the sacred autonomy of the individual moral sphere. States, as artificial persons, are not so much moral as they are juridical; as such, their behavior towards one another must be guided by the juridical norms that obtain among men living together with no common superior. Following Hobbes, Kant defines the situation among nations as a "state of nature" which is a "state of war":

> The state of peace among men living side by side is not the natural state; the natural state is a state of war . . . unless security is guaranteed to each by his neighbor (which can happen only in a *lawful* state) each may treat his neighbor as an enemy.[160]

> We may consider a threat to exist if another state engages in military preparations, and this is the basis of the right of preventive war. Or even the mere menacing increase of power of another state (e.g. through land-acquisition) . . . can be regarded as a threat, inasmuch as the mere existence of a superior power is itself injurious. . . . On this is founded the right to preserve a balance of power among all states that are contiguous.[161]

Consequently no war can be called unjust,[162] and *a fortiori* there is no such thing as punitive war: "War is only the sad recourse in the state of nature . . . in which neither party can be adjudged unjust. . . . Between states no punitive war is conceivable."[163]

Kant breaks with the Hobbesian perspective, however, when he argues that for states, just as for individuals, the state of nature must be overcome if external freedom is to be made secure. He can therefore assert that it is a duty of justice as well as of morality to endeavor to form a social contract, or some kind of international organization, among states. Because of the curious moral status of the state of nature, no nation can be blamed for going to war, yet at the same time all nations have a duty to seek peace under law. What is more, coercion can be used to compel one's neighbors to enter into the international social contract.[164]

353

In the light of this hoped-for international constitution, states even now—in the state of nature with respect to each other—have an obligation to prepare the way by obeying the following "preliminary articles for perpetual peace":

1. No treaty of peace shall be held valid in which there is secret reservation of matter for future war.
2. No independent states, large or small, shall come under the dominion of another state by inheritance, exchange, purchase or donation.
3. Standing armies shall in time cease to exist.
4. National debts shall not be contracted in such a way as to lead to the external friction of states.
5. No state shall by force interfere with the constitution or government of another state.
6. No state shall, during war, permit such acts of hostility which would make mutual confidence in the subsequent peace impossible: such are the employment of assassins, poisoners, breach of capitulation, incitement to treason, etc.[165]

Beyond the observance of these practices, there is a "definitive" article in support of which all states should exert themselves: "The civil constitution of every state should be republican," or, in other words, "derived from the idea of the original social contract," for only such a government may legitimately speak for its people and bind them permanently to contracts.

One cannot avoid noticing a certain conflict between this definitive article (especially when it is considered in the light of the right to coerce one's neighbors into joining a lasting league of nations) and the fifth preliminary article quoted above.[166] If some recalcitrant "reactionary" regime stands in the way of world government, how much solicitude should be felt for its autonomy? On the other hand, if the "progressive" states intervene to help overthrow a stable regime, where might such a precedent lead? "A league of nations in accordance with the idea of an original social contract is necessary, not, indeed, in order to meddle in one another's internal dissensions, but in order to afford protection against external aggression."[167] But can one feel secure about a neighboring nation's intentions without taking, at the least, an active interest in the spirit and purpose of that nation's regime? This sort of dangerous ambiguity is part of the reason for Kant's visible hesitation in treating the matters that we must now investigate.

The great question left unanswered so far is, What precisely is to be the character of this "league" of nations? Kant seems at first to have in mind a replica of the social contract among men—a "state" of nations. But he immediately shows his awareness of the legal contradiction that we pointed out earlier in our remarks on Hobbes (pp. 338 above): "This would be a league of nations, but it would not have to be a state consisting of nations. That would be contradictory, since a state implies the relation of a superior (legislating) to an inferior (obeying), i.e., the people, and many nations in one state would then constitute one nation. . . . This contradicts the presupposition."[168] Once again, we see that it is part of the very purpose and nature of states that they be more self-sufficient than any natural "person":

> The obligation which men in a lawless condition have under the natural law, and which requires them to abandon the state of nature, does not quite apply to states under the law of nations, for as states they already have an internal juridical constitution and thus have outgrown compulsion from others to submit to a more extended lawful constitution according to their ideas of right. This is true in spite of the fact that reason . . . makes a state of peace a direct duty. . . . For these reasons there must be a league of a particular kind, which can be called a league of peace, and which would be distinguished from a treaty of peace by the fact that the latter terminates only one war, while the former seeks to make an end of all wars forever. This league does not tend to any dominion over the power of the state but only to the maintenance and security of the freedom of the state itself and of other states in league with it, without there being any need for them to submit to civil laws and their compulsion, as men in a state of nature must submit.[169]

Kant appears to favor a "congress" of nations, a "free and essentially arbitrary combination that can be dissolved at any time."[170]

But in the absence of a sovereign authority, how is there to be instituted and enforced the sanctioned rule of law which can alone guarantee the security of each nation's right and hence end the state of war? To highlight a key part of the problem, we need only to observe closely Kant's discussion of the second preliminary article listed earlier. Kant notes that this article—guaranteeing each nation independence—must be "broader . . . , containing permission to delay its execution." What he is getting at will be clear if we remember that it is not enough to forbid in the future the absorption of one nation by another. Many already-existing boundaries represent the arbitrary outcomes of inheritances and conquests that were never ratified by the inhabitants (examples such as Austria-Hungary, Poland, Tibet, and the Baltic States come immediately to mind). It is then necessary to say that the second article "does not authorize . . . delaying until doomsday . . . the reestablishment of states which have been deprived of it—i.e., it does not permit us to fail to do it, but it allows a delay to prevent precipitation which might injure the goal striven for."[171] A plethora of difficult questions arises here: Who is to decide which of the present boundaries are to be changed? Who or what is to enforce the decision? And what criteria are to govern the drawing of new boundaries—how far back in history must we go in righting old wrongs, restoring to nationalities their homelands, and so forth? Is there any nation whose legitimate borders can be specified once this issue is seriously raised and pursued? On the other hand, can we reasonably expect the permanent end of distrust and warfare so long as the heart of a great people or race burns with justified indignation?

The boundary question would become moot if nation-states were replaced by a world state; furthermore, a true world state would guarantee the policing of the peace. The weight of these considerations compels Kant, despite himself,[172] to advocate a true world government, to which the existing nations would surrender sovereignty by a legal mechanism that is left unspecified:

> Only through a union founded on a political constitution which cannot be dissolved can the idea of the kind of public law of nations that should be established become a reality, so that nations will settle their differences in a civilized way by judicial process, rather than in the barbaric way (of savages), namely, through war.[173]

> No state is for a moment secure from the others in its independence and its possessions. . . . And there is no possible way of counteracting this except a state of international right, based on enforceable public laws to which each state must submit (by analogy with a state of civil or political right among individual men). For a permanent universal peace by means of a so-called *European balance of power* is a pure illusion.[174]

But practically in the next breath, Kant withdraws his advocacy, blaming humanity's insuperable weaknesses—avarice, national pride, short-sightedness—for the impossibility of realizing what is in principle correct. In the final analysis, the extreme improbability of world government dooms mankind to a perpetual state of intermittent war:

> For states in their relation to each other, there cannot be any reasonable way out of the lawless condition which entails only war except that they, like individual men, should give up their savage (lawless) freedom, adjust themselves to public coercive laws, and thus establish a continuously growing state consisting of various nations, which will ultimately include all the nations of the world. But under the idea of the law of nations they do not wish to do this, and reject in practice what is correct in theory. If all is not to be lost, there can be, then, in place of the positive idea of a world republic, only the negative surrogate of an alliance which averts war, endures, spreads, and holds back the stream of those hostile passions which fear the law, though such an alliance is in constant peril of their breaking loose again.[175]

Human weakness is not the only thing that militates against the realization of the idea of world government. Even as he paints the pacific splendor of a world under one law and one regime, Kant draws back in trepidation at the possible dire consequences of such a concentration of power and such a homogeneity of ways of life: "The separate existence of many independent but neighboring states . . . is rationally preferable to the amalgamation of states under one superior power, as this would end in one universal monarchy, and laws always lose in vigor what government gains in extent; hence a soulless despotism, after stifling the seeds of the good, falls into anarchy."[176] In reading this last passage, one senses in Kant a sigh of relief at the knowledge that the limitations of human nature make improbable the coming of the universal state on earth.[177] It seems that we may be grateful that the goal can only be approached, perhaps asymptotically.

Nevertheless, we must continue to strive for some kind of international organization that will lengthen periods of peace between wars.[178] Indeed, if the moral man cannot have faith in a progressive movement of history in this direction, his moral fiber may well be sapped. He may quite reasonably suspect that the tension between the commands of morality or of justice and the world reveals the barrenness, the unreality, of his idea of moral freedom. If duty really made no progress in the world, if moral nobility were permanently confronted with a universe in which it was never rewarded and never capable of effecting improvement, then, as Kant himself admits, "reason would have to regard the moral laws as empty figments of the brain."[179] We are thus finally exhorted to live and act in the name of our faith in the existence of a moral order:

> What duty requires is that we act in accordance with the idea of an end in which we have a moral interest, even if there is not the slightest theoretical probability that it is feasible, as long as its impossibility cannot be demonstrated either. . . . We must act as though perpetual peace were a reality, which perhaps it is not, by working for its establishment. . . . Even if the realization of this goal of abolishing war were always to remain just a pious wish, we still would not be deceiving ourselves by adopting the maxim of working for it; . . . to assume that the moral law within us might deceive us would give rise to the disgusting wish . . . to conceive of ourselves and our principles as thrown in together with all the other species of animals under the same mechanism of nature.[180]

Having arrived at this point, we must wonder whether anything supports such hope except "hope against hope." Given the extraordinary ambiguity in Kant's description of the international organization which is the goal, given Kant's own hesitation about the effectiveness of world law as a replacement for vigilant national defense, it can be doubted whether Kant has good grounds for exhorting statesmen to dedicate themselves and their policies to the creation of a league of nations. Are not the "idealists" doomed to come to grief in trying to impose their vision on the real world of competitive states? Will not any congress soon be reduced to paying lip service to an idea of world order while in fact it unwittingly weakens the defensive alliances and balance of power that alone can keep the swords of war sheathed? Will not the practical ineffectiveness of almost everything said at the congress make it possible for its forum to be used as a rhetorical shield for national selfishness, thus increasing the level of hypocrisy and lowering the actual tone of international discourse?

Kant is not unalive to these questions, and much of the persuasiveness of his teaching derives from the surprising hard-headedness with which he attempts to provide "guarantees" for progress toward perpetual peace. As he makes clear, he himself would have grave doubts about the possibility of any progress that depended principally on a change in human intentions, a change of the heart: "We soon realise that the success of this immeasurably long undertaking will depend not so much upon what *we* do (e.g., the education we impart to younger generations) . . . it will rather depend upon what human *nature* may do in and through us, to compel us to follow a course. . . . We must look to Providence alone for a successful outcome."[181] The "providential," or "natural"—that is, from the human point of view, unintentional—process to which Kant refers has as its first "guarantee" commerce and industrialization. A steady increase in the shrewdness of selfish competition will be as productive of peace and order in international affairs as was the "unsocial sociability" that produced a more and more effective rule of law within each nation. Kant's thought here is strikingly reminiscent of Hobbes and Montesquieu:

> Now we come to the question . . . what has nature done to favor man's moral purpose, and how has she guaranteed (by compulsion but without prejudice to freedom) that he shall do that which he ought? . . . Nations which could not have secured themselves against violence and war by means of the law of world citizenship unite because of mutual interest. The spirit of commerce, which is incompatible with war, sooner or later gains the upper hand in every state. As the power of money is perhaps the most dependable of all the powers included under the state power, states see themselves forced, without any moral urge, to promote honorable peace and by mediation to prevent war wherever it threatens to break out. They do so exactly as if they stood in perpetual alliances, . . . and in this manner nature guarantees perpetual peace by the mechanism of the human passions.[182]

The second of Kant's "guarantees" is best understood in the light of this reliance on the spirit of commerce. In giving the reasons for the first "definitive article" of perpetual peace (the article that recommends for every state a republican constitution), Kant says more than that such a constitution is the only legitimate one:

> The republican constitution, besides the purity of its origin . . . also gives a favorable prospect for the desired consequence, i.e., perpetual peace. The reason is this: if the consent of the citizens is required in order to decide that war should be declared . . . nothing is more natural than that they would be very cautious in commencing such a poor game, decreeing for themselves all the calamities of war.[183]

Our first reaction to this asseveration is likely to be incredulous amazement. Kant seems to have utterly forgotten the historical lessons to be learned from Athens, Sparta, Rome, and Florence, among others; he seems blind to the connection established by Rousseau between democratic patriotism and martial vigor or even aggressiveness. Kant's remarks become somewhat more intelligible if we take him to be referring not (as he seems to be) to all republican regimes, but only to those large modern republics where political participation, national glory, and public dedication are emphasized much less than prosperity, family life, and private liberty. Kant's faith in the pacifism of the republican masses leads him to believe that nothing submitted to their approval could be warlike. Hence he arrives at his famous test of "publicity" as a criterion for the justice of any foreign policy (the criterion that came to be known as "open covenants openly arrived at"). Any policy or treaty that cannot be publicly declared and acknowledged can without doubt be counted as wrong. And Kant goes even further: "All maxims which stand in need of publicity in order not to fail their end, agree with politics and right combined," for "if they can attain their end only through publicity, they must accord with the public's universal end, happiness; and the proper task of politics is to promote this."[184] Looked at in the perspective of the twentieth century, with its experience of mass ideology and war hysteria among the most advanced industrialized nations, Kant seems to have been overly sanguine, even if we take him to intend the most limited application of his hopeful analysis of republican citizen bodies and their characteristic modes of threat-perception.[185]

But in a way the most remarkable feature of these Kantian "guarantees" is the degree to which they imply that the achievement of perpetual peace depends on the activation, among entire peoples, of motives lacking in all moral dignity. Some of the very passions that we at first believed to be serious opponents of peace (like commercial acquisitiveness and vanity) turn out to be its guarantors. However much this discovery may lead us to question the beauty of the goal thus achieved, we must admit the wonderful efficaciousness of the process, which brings good from its opposite—if it works as promised.

It is to the credit of Kant's common sense that he never placed complete trust in either of the above "guarantees." He seems, in fact, to be more aware than was Montesquieu of the dire possibilities implied in these new regimes that possess unprecedented mass armies and unheard-of economic and technological power:

> The increasing culture of the states, along with their growing tendency to aggrandise themselves by cunning or violence at the expense of the others, must make wars more frequent. It must likewise cause increasingly high expenditures on standing armies, which must be kept in constant training and equipped with more numerous instruments of warfare. . . . No peace will last long enough for the resources saved during it to meet the expenditure of the next war, while the invention of a national debt, though ingenious, is an ultimately self-defeating expedient.[186]

So the third and firmest guarantee for some kind of international organization is the eventual exhaustion of nations after the experience of repeated debilitating war: "Through war, through the taxing and never-ending accumulation of armament, through the want which even in peacetime any state must suffer internally, nature forces them to take at first inadequate and tentative steps; finally, after devastations, revolutions, and even complete exhaustion, she brings them . . . to step from the lawless condition of savages into a league of nations."[187]

The picture that finally emerges, then, is a future development in which periods of immense economic expansion alternate with more and more horrible wars and revolutions, until at last a point is reached at which the nations must turn to the moral statesmen and opinion leaders who have all along proposed a league of nations. The blind selfishness of the governments will by itself eventually compel them to bow to the guidance of those few whose justice is animated by moral motives and not merely by self-interest.

At times, it is true, Kant gives grounds for doubt as to whether anyone imbued with a truly moral commitment to peace and justice will ever be needed. After all, the "natural guarantees" of progress will in the end persuade even the most narrow and mean of leaders to abandon the state of nature among nations. This doubt regarding the place of moral action or intention in politics reflects a problem that is present throughout Kant's teaching. By making the political goal—the just world order—so independent of moral intention and so exclusively aimed at *external* freedom, by making it a goal that is evolved through the "mechanism of the passions," Kant threatens to remove the moral man from any role in politics:

What profit will progress toward the better yield humanity? Not an ever-growing quantity of morality with regard to intention, but an increase of legality in actions whatever their motives. . . . Gradually violence on the part of the powers will diminish and obedience to the laws will increase. There will arise in the body politic perhaps more charity and less strife in lawsuits, more reliability in keeping one's word, etc., partly out of love of honor, partly out of self interest rightly understood. And eventually this will extend to nations in their external relations toward one another up to the realization of the cosmopolitan society, wihout the moral foundation in mankind having to be enlarged in the least; for that, a kind of new creation (supernatural influence) would be necessary.[188]

Kant remains closer to his own intention, though, when he implies that truly moral, truly cosmopolitan statesmen will be needed in order to create the atmosphere of trust and to take the personal and national risks that will be required in any attempt to replace national sovereignty with an international police.[189]

Still, the question returns when we ask what the moral man is to do in international politics prior to the time when devastation has forced everyone to see the need for world law. If the moral man is convinced by Kant as to the "guarantees," should he not hasten the debacle by supporting the increase of appetitive commerce, grander armaments, and republican revolution? On occasion, Kant comes close to such a recommendation: "With respect to the ideal of perpetual peace, . . . it is our duty to employ the mechanism of nature to that end."[190] In general, however, he resolutely resists any giving-in to the notion that immoral means may be used to further just ends. The use of immoral means will necessarily poison the end if the moral man *himself* is seen to use them. Besides, since the political end is only a just society and not necessarily a moral society, no good man should sully the purity of his own will in order to bring it about. The just order will take on a moral aura and men will obey the law with a moral change of heart only if the moral men have done all that they can to remind the rest of mankind of the inner ideal beyond justice and legality. The moral man must actively oppose or censure the spread of commercialization, the increase in war power, and the revolutionary upheaval, even while he knows in his heart that these movements are the true agents of historical progress. Paradoxically, by opposing the forces that he knows to be the engines of historical change, the moral man injects a spirit that in the long run transforms mere change into progress in a moral sense. And he need not worry about the possibility that his rigidity in speech and deed may thwart the forces moving in the direction of peace and justice, since in the long run even the most wicked will be forced by the historical process to endorse a league of nations. The moral man may rest confident in the inevitable good outcome of his purity.[191]

The intention of Kant's philosophy as a whole was to effect a synthesis, bringing together the ·elevated nobility of classical or Stoic virtue and the prosperity, liberty, and power of modern science and philosophy. The fulcrum of the synthesis was a new interpretation of human freedom and morality as autonomy. This new interpretation implied a lofty status for the individual and for humanity as a whole, but a far less lofty status for the citizen and for the political community. As a direct consequence, international affairs assumed a place of greater importance for Kant than they had had for any previous thinker.

The spirit of Kant's idealism, with all its paradoxical ambiguity and tensions, has increasingly dominated reflections on the moral basis of foreign affairs and of politics altogether. A clear sign of Kant's enormous influence is the fact that since 1800 it has been ever more difficult for "progressive" statesmen to justify their foreign policies in terms of patriotism or simple national interest. The idea of the fatherland or nation has become for many merely a rhetorical cover for the "state," that "cold monster" lacking any high moral calling. It is necessary to add that the reality of the Western state has in some ways grown to resemble the theoretical interpretation given by Kant and Hobbes. For these reasons it is now characteristic of diplomats and national leaders to feel the need to justify their economic expansion, their alliances, and their security arrangements in terms of a contribution to some evolutionary or revolutionary world transformation which will in the long run lessen the spiritual differences among peoples and diminish the power of states. Insofar as we mean by "ideology" this effort to defend political policy on the grounds of some comprehensive theoretical account that integrates our present situation into human nature and history taken as a whole, we may say that Kant is the most important source of the ideological character of foreign policy in both the modern East and West. There is a straight line from Kant's philosophy of history through Hegel to Marx and Marxism. As for Western liberalism, the man who became president of the United States at the time when it stepped forward to assume spiritual and political leadership of the West, the man who in large part set the goals of American foreign policy in the twentieth century, can be said without any exaggeration to have been formed more by Kant than by any other master.[192]

The questions that we must leave the reader with are these. Does Kant's synthesis do justice to both of its elements? Does he succeed in finding in the league of nations an object of aspiration that rivals the republicanism of the classics and of Rousseau? Can the moral man find in world government a satisfying goal when he knows that it will come into being principally through the competition of base motives and when he knows that it runs the risk of becoming a "soulless universal despotism"? Can he expect that his initially vain and ineffective moral exhortations will eventually overcome the immoral habits and ways of life by which nations become aware of the need for world government? Perhaps it is not so strange that Kant from time to time reveals his belief that it is only the action of God (in an afterlife of which we can know nothing except that it exists) that makes possible a future where the wrongs of the world may be righted, where the men of good will may find a society that is worthy of their efforts and that justifies their present devotion to the idea of perpetual peace.[193] On the other hand, if in the face of internal and external threats of unprecedented gravity, the great liberal democracies are to be rescued from a progressive loss of heart and will, is not some version of Kant's interpretation necessary in order to give to liberalism an elevated but not necessarily crusading mission on the world stage?[194]

Notes

1. Cf. Coleman Phillipson, *The International Law and Custom of Ancient Greece and Rome* (2 vols.; London: Macmillan, 1911), 1:41, 124–25; 2:168–70. And see Plato *Cleitophon* 410a8–b1; Xenophon *Memorabilia* 2. 3. 14. Cf. Matthew 5:43.
2. Plato *Republic* 398d–403c, and *Laws* 643e–644b, 653a–654b; Aristotle *Politics* 1295b25–27, 1331b24–1342b34, and *Ethics* 1094a27–b12, 1129b11–26, 1155a 22–31.
3. Plato *Republic* 472d–e, 591d–592b, and *Laws* 739c–d, 769a, 817b, 968e–969a; Aristotle *Politics* 1268b22–1269b27, 1288b10–1289a25, 1301a38–61, 1302a2–3, and *Ethics* 1179b35 ff.
4. Aristotle *Politics* 1325b33 ff.
5. Cf. Plato *Laws* 738d–e.
6. Cf. ibid., 708b–d.
7. It is perhaps necessary to add that the Greek theorists' attachment to the city, or *polis,* as the most fertile soil for a good political life is based on compelling (although surely not indisputable) argumentation such as this, not on some form of Greek ethnocentrism. The free life of the *polis* was not held by them to be essentially or necessarily Greek. On the contrary, according to Aristotle, the *polis* had reached its highest historical development among non-Greek Africans (*Politics* 1272b24–1273b26; compare Plato *Republic* 499c, and *Phaedo* 78a; Xenophon *Education of Cyrus* 1. 2. 2. ff.).
8. Plato *Laws* 949e6–951a4, in *Platonis Opera,* ed. John Burnet (5 vols.; Oxford, Eng.: Clarendon Press, 1899–1907). Here, and throughout this chapter, new, literal translations have been made of all references to works not originally written in English. The texts used are indicated after the first passage quoted from each work. I am grateful to Diane R. Pangle for assistance with translations from Latin and to John Danford for assistance with translations from German.
9. Plato *Republic* 175a2–4.
10. *Thymos*: Plato *Republic* 375a–376c, 410b, 411, 439e–441e, 442c; *Laws* 730c, 731.
11. See especially Xenophon's marvelous presentation of the problem in *Education of Cyrus* 1. 6. 27–34.
12. Aristotle *Politics* 1328a8–12. Cf. Thucydides *History of the Peloponnesian War* 1. 75. 6 (compare especially 1. 75. 3 with 1. 76. 2), 3. 45. 6. For Thucydides' treatment of this problem, see Christopher Bruell's thoughtful and lucid paper "Thucydides' View of Athenian Imperialism," *American Political Science Review,* vol. 68, no. 1 (March 1974), pp. 11–17. See also the reply to this article by Jerome R.

Corsi, *American Political Science Review*, vol. 68, no. 4 (December 1974), pp. 1679–80.
13. Aristotle *Politics*, in *Aristotelis Politica*, ed. William D. Ross (Oxford, Eng.: Clarendon Press, 1957), 1324a25–1325b27.
14. Plato *Laws* 704c–d, 705c.
15. Plato *Republic* 422e3–423a5.
16. The comparable element in Aristotle's thought is his relative candor regarding the necessity and status of slavery, including "naturally just wars" of slave-hunting: compare especially *Politics* 1256b23–26 and 1330a25–33 with Plato *Republic* 469c4–7; cf. Plato *Laws* 776b–778a.
17. Aristotle *Politics* 1328b33 ff.
18. Cf. ibid., 1326b26 ff. and Plato *Laws* 704–705.
19. Cf. Plato *Republic* 372c ff.
20. Ibid., 373d–374a, 414d–e.
21. See, especially, Aristotle *Politics* 1328a8–12.
22. Plato *Republic* 469b–471b.
23. Phillipson, *International Law*, 1:106. Cf. William B. Ballis, *The Legal Position of War: Changes in Its Practice and Theory from Plato to Vattel* (The Hague: Martinus Nijhoff, 1937), pp. 28–29, 31.
24. Cicero *Tusculan Disputations* 5. 4. 10–11. Cf. Leo Strauss, *Natural Right and History* (Chicago: University of Chicago Press, 1953), pp. 146, 153–56.
25. For the line of thought sketched here and in the following sentences, I am indebted to Ernest Fortin.
26. For the Romans, and generally throughout the Middle Ages until Suarez, the "law of nations" was a term referring not so much to international law regulating relations among nations as to that law or body of legal principles that seem to be commonly held by all civilized peoples: for example, the principle that theft is a punishable offense. See Ernest Nys, *Le droit de la guerre et les précurseurs de Grotius* (Brussels: C. Muquardt, 1882), pp. 9–13, as well as James L. Brierly, *The Law of Nations* (Oxford, Eng.: Clarendon Press, 1963), pp. 17, 30; and Phillipson, *International Law*, 1:70–85. Cf. Aristotle *Rhetoric* 1368b1–5.
27. Cicero *De Officiis*, ed. Maurice Testard (Paris: Budé, 1965), 3. 5. 23, 3. 6. 27–28.
28. Ibid., 1. 11. 34–35.
29. Cicero *Republic* 3. 22. 33–3. 23. 35.
30. Consider, as examples, Plato *Laws* 636b4–5 and *Crito* 51c1 and context; Aristotle *Rhetoric* 1368b1–5, 1373b1–24, 1375a27 ff., and *Ethics* 1134b18–1135a.
31. See, for instance, *Laws* 1. 7 and *De Finnibus* 3. 19. 64–3. 20. 67 in the light of *De Natura Deorum* 2. 133 ff. and 3. 66 ff., 3. 95.
32. Cicero *De Officiis* 1. 16. 50–52. Cf. Plato *Laws* 729e–730a and Aristotle *Ethics* 1155a16–22.
33. Cicero *Republic* 2. 8. 14, 2. 17. 31, 2. 18. 33, 2. 20. 36, 2. 14. 44, 3. 15. 24; cf. *De Officiis* 1. 7. 21.
34. Cicero *De Officiis* 1. 11. 35.
35. Ibid., 1. 12. 38, 2. 24. 85; cf. 1. 8. 26.
36. Ibid., 3. 29. 107 ff.; also 1. 12. 37, 1. 13. 39–40.
37. St. Augustine *City of God* 19. 25; hereafter cited as *CG*.
38. See Roland H. Bainton, *Christian Attitudes toward War and Peace* (New York: Abingdon Press, 1960), pp. 57–63, 66–84, 88–89; Joan D. Tooke, *The Just War in Aquinas and Grotius* (London: S.P.C.K., 1965), pp. 2–8, 39–75. The New Testament passages that may seem to lend support to pacifism are Matthew 5:39–

41 and 26:52–53, Romans 12:19, and 2 Corinthians 10:4; while those that seem to oppose pacifism most clearly are Matthew 10:34, Luke 3:14 and 22:36, and Romans 13:4. For St. Augustine's treatment of these passages, see Herbert A. Deane, *The Political and Social Ideas of St. Augustine* (New York: Columbia University Press, 1963), pp. 163–66.
39. *CG* 12. 27; 13. 21; 14. 10, 19, 22–24, 26; 19. 13, 15, 16, 21; *Letter 137* 17.
40. *CG* 5. 16, 24; 11. 1–3; 12. 1, 13–22.
41. *CG* 2. 21; 4. 4; 19. 4–6, 15–17, 21, 23–24, 26.
42. *CG* 19. 14–17.
43. *CG* 5. 17; 19. 27; Augustine *On Free Choice of the Will* 1. 5. See Ernest Fortin, "St. Augustine," in *History of Political Philosophy*, ed. Leo Strauss and Joseph Cropsey (2d ed.; Chicago: Rand McNally, 1972), pp. 155–61.
44. Cf., in this regard, Augustine *Against Faustus*, in *Patrologiae Latina*, ed. J. P. Migne (Paris, 1854–1866), 22. 74 end.
45. *CG* 14. 12.
46. Augustine *Against Faustus* 19. 75.
47. Augustine *On Free Choice* 1. 5; *CG* 1. 21 and 3. 10; *Against Faustus* 22. 74.
48. Augustine *Questions on the Heptateuch*, in *Patrologiae* 6. 10.
49. Ibid., 4. 44.
50. Cf. Alfred Vanderpol, *La doctrine scolastique du droit de guerre* (Paris: Pedone, 1919), pp. 17–18, 64; Robert Regout, *La doctrine de la guerre juste de St. Augustin à nos jours* (Paris: Pedone, 1935), pp. 43–44, 140, and also 66; Deane, *St. Augustine*, p. 161.
51. Augustine *Against Faustus* 22. 74; cf. *CG* 19. 7.
52. Augustine *Letter 138* 14, in *Patrologiae*; cf. *Letter 189* 6 and *Letter 91* 10.
53. See, especially, *CG* 15. 4, and also 5. 4, 19. 7–8. Paul Ramsey rather overstates this point in *War and the Christian Conscience* (Durham, N.C.: Duke University Press, for the Lilly Endowment Research Program in Christianity and Politics, 1961), chap. 2.
54. *GC* 2. 21, 29; 5. 12–15, 18; Augustine *Letter 138* 17.
55. *CG* 5. 14, 20; on political participation see *CG* 19. 19.
56. *CG* 5. 12–14, 17, 20, 22, 25; cf. 3. 16, 21. And see Fortin, "St. Augustine," pp. 163–66.
57. Gratian *Decretum* 2. 38. ques. 1 and 2.
58. St. Thomas Aquinas *Summa Theologica* 2–2. ques. 40; hereafter cited as *ST*.
59. *ST* 1. ques. 1; 1–2. ques. 90. art. 3; 2–2. ques. 47. art. 10; St. Thomas *Commentary on the Politics* 1; *Commentary on the Ethics* 1; Ernest Fortin, "St. Thomas Aquinas," in *History of Political Philosophy*, pp. 223–50.
60. Cf. Heinrich A. Rommen, *The State in Catholic Thought* (St. Louis, Mo.: Herder, 1945), p. 619.
61. Aristotle *Ethics* 1094b11–14, 1134b18–30, 1103a18–19, 1105b2–3; cf. 1095a30–b13 and 1144a6 ff.
62. St. Thomas *Commentary on the Ethics* 1017–18, 1023–25, 1028, and, above all, 1029; also 1072; *ST* 1–2. ques. 91, 93–95, and 2–2. ques. 57. art. 2 and 3. Cf. *ST* 2–2. ques. 66. art. 7.
63. See note 26 above, and *ST* 1–2. ques. 95. art. 4, and 2–2. ques. 57. art. 3.
64. *ST,* ed. Thomas Heath (London: Blackfriars, 1972), 2–2. ques. 40. art. 1.
65. *ST* 2–2. ques. 40. art. 3 and 4.
66. The intimate connection between the un-Augustinian Thomistic natural-law foundation for political ethics, the higher demands consequently placed on men in

political life, and the greater restriction of means permissible in war, is obscured in Ramsey's recent attempt to revive the doctrine of just war in the form of a *synthesis* of Augustine's and Thomas's successors: *War*, especially pp. 32–33.

67. The intervening writers are discussed by Regout, *Doctrine*, pp. 94–108. It is to be noted that Vitoria himself wrote nothing for publication. His thought is available to us only through texts that represent the assiduous collation by his students of notes taken during his lecture courses; what we have lost in accuracy is perhaps compensated for, however, by the opportunity to gain a sense of the charming vigor of this famous lecturer. For details regarding the reliability of the texts, see James B. Scott, *The Spanish Origin of International Law* (Oxford, Eng.: Clarendon Press, 1934), pp. 13a, 73–77, 96–97; and Francisco de Vitoria, *De Indis et De iure belli reflectiones,* ed. Ernest Nys (Washington, D.C.: Carnegie Institution, 1917), pp. 81–84, 191–205.

68. Contrast St. Thomas *ST* 2-2. ques. 64. art. 7 with Vitoria *Theological Lessons* 6, "On the Law of War" 3–5, 15 (hereafter cited as "On War"), and Suarez *On Charity* 1. 4, 2. 1, and 3. 1. See also Ramsey, *War,* chap. 3.

69. Vitoria gives as examples France's refusal to surrender Burgundy to the emperor and the Indians' attacks on innocent Spaniards, attacks that were motivated by excusably ignorant fear of the Spaniards' strange appearance: Vitoria *Theological Lessons* 5, and "On the Indians Lately Discovered" 3. 6 (hereafter cited as "On the Indians"). Cf. Suarez *On Charity* 4. 1 and 7. 19.

70. "On War" 20, 21, 33, 58–59.

71. "On the Indians" 2. 9.

72. "On War" 59; "On the Indians" 2. 11; cf. Regout, *Doctrine*, p. 176.

73. See, however, Suarez *On Charity* 4. 2: "In this connection, however, we must remember that not infrequently a wrong which appears to be slight is in fact serious, if all the circumstances are weighed."

74. Vitoria *Commentary* ad. ques. 57. art. 3; "On the Indians" 1. 7, 2. 7, 3. 1, 2, 3, 4, 5, 6, 9; "On War" 1, 13, 14, 16, 19; cf. Suarez *On Charity* 4. 3, and Msg. Bruno de Solages, *La théologie de la guerre juste* (Paris: Desclée de Brouwer, 1946), pp. 64–68. Even a grave injury, however, does not justify punitive war if the world as a whole would be worse off after the war than it would be if the injustice were to go unpunished; similarly, even a just war should not be prosecuted if its success is very doubtful ("On War" 33; Suarez *On Charity* 4. 10).

75. "On the Indians" 3. 8; "On War" 17–19, 35, 42, 57–59; Vitoria *Commentary* (ad. ques. 40. art. 1) 10, 15, 17–18. Cf. Suarez *On Charity* 7. 7–8, 10, 12, 20. Through the influence of Christianity, enslavement of Christians by Christians is now against the law of nations ("On War" 42; Suarez *On Charity* 7. 13).

76. See, especially, "On War" 48, and Suarez *On Charity* 7. 7.

77. Cf. Suarez *On Charity* 1. 7 and 7. 6, 10–11, 15–16. Innocent civilians may, however, be killed "incidentally," as the unintended (but not necessarily unforeseen) side effect of an act of war such as the seige of a town or a bombardment; Vitoria *Commentary* ad. ques. 40. art. 1. #11; "On War" 35–37, 43, 52; Suarez *On Charity* 7. 17–19. For this famous doctrine of "double effect," see Thomas *ST* 2-2. ques. 64. art. 7; Grotius *On the Law of War and Peace* 2. 1. 4; and Ramsey, *War,* chap. 3.

78. Cf. Thucydides *History* 1. 23. 6, 1. 33. 3, and 1. 33. 88, and Klaus Knorr's chapter in this volume.

79. "On War" 13, 20–24, 27–30, 32.

80. See Vanderpol, *Doctrine*, pp. 304, 125, 145.

81. Compare the unconsciously revealing remarks in Honorio Muñoz, O. P., *Vitoria and War* (Manila: Santo Tomás University Press, 1937), p. 44; see also Regout, *Doctrine*, pp. 204–5; and Nys *Droit*, pp. 132–33. See also Charles Fairbanks's chapter in this volume.
82. "On the Indians" 2. 16; cf. Suarez *On Charity* 4. 3.
83. "By natural law princes can and may defend the whole world," Vitoria *Commentary* ad. ques. 40. art. 1. #6 and #7; "On the Indians" 3. 15; *Theological Lessons* 9, "On Moderation" 5, in *Les leçons de Francisco de Vitoria sur les problèmes de la colonisation et de la guerre,* ed. Jean Baumel (Montpellier: Faculté des Lettres, 1936), pp. 65, 81. Compare also the praise of Roman interventionist policy: "On the Indians" 3. 17, "On War" 56; and cf. also Suarez *On Faith* 18. 1. 4 and 18. 4. 4, and De Solages, *Théologie,* p. 68.
84. "On the Indians" 2. 7, 12 and 3. 9, 12–13. Cf. Suarez *On Faith* 18. 1. 2–4, 7–10 and 18. 4. 4; *On Charity* 5. 7.
85. Vanderpol, although arguing for the strictest possible interpretation of the doctrine of just war, does not hesitate to support the crusades: *Doctrine,* pp. 218 ff., especially 225. See also Muñoz, *Vitoria,* pp. 71, 123–24.
86. Suarez *On Charity* 6. 1–4. Suarez seems really only to develop and make explicit what is implied in some of the cases of Vitoria's "invincible ignorance."
87. About this aspect of Suarez's doctrine of just war there is a longstanding scholarly dispute (Regout's critique of Vanderpol: see their works, cited above, and Yves de la Brière, "Les étapes de la tradition théologique concernante le droit de juste guerre," *Revue générale de droit international public* 44 (1937):156–58). Without even sketching the terms of the contest, let me simply remark that on this point I follow Regout. Suarez opens himself to misunderstanding by committing a surprising blunder. He asserts that the award of satisfaction to the better claim in disputes of this kind is a manifestation of distributive, not corrective, justice. Distributive justice is of course irrelevant to this entire topic and can only lead the reader astray (cf. Aristotle *Ethics* 1130b80 ff.; Grotius *On the Law of War and Peace* 1. 1. 8).
88. Suarez makes a strained and tenuous effort to read this notion of the law of nations back into St. Thomas: see *On Laws and God the Lawgiver* 2. 20. 2 (cf. 2. 19. 3) (hereafter cited as *On Laws*) in contrast to St. Thomas *ST* 1–2. ques. 57. art. 2.
89. *On Laws,* in *Selections from Three Works,* ed. J. B. Scott (2 vols.; Oxford, Eng.: Clarendon Press, 1944), 2. 19. 8.
90. *On Laws* 2. 17–20.
91. Vitoria *On Civil Power* 21.
92. *On Laws* 2. 19. 7; cf. 2. 20. 7–9.
93. *On Laws* 2. 19. 9.
94. Suarez *On Charity* 6. 5.
95. Grotius *On the Law of War and Peace* Prolegomena 11, 30, 37, 50. In the notes immediately following, numbered references without title will be to this work.
96. Prolegomena 40–41, 1. 1. 13–14.
97. 2. 3. 10. 11 and 3. 3. 6. 10.
98. Cf., especially, Suarez *On Charity* 4. 1 and 7. 9, 22.
99. Prolegomena 46; cf. 24–27, especially in contrast to 28.
100. 2. 20. 40; cf. 7–9, 41–51.
101. Prolegomena 5–10, 15–16, 19, and 1. 1. 3, 12; 1. 2. 1; 2. 1. 9. 2.
102. Prolegomena 3, 4, 19, 21, 25.

103. Prolegomena 18, 19, 21, 22.
104. Prolegomena 22–24, 27, 32.
105. Cf. Prolegomena 20.
106. Prolegomena 57. See also Prolegomena 8 (beg.), 10; 1. 1. 3. 1; 1. 2. 1. 3; 2. 9. 8; 3. 12. 8. Cf. Richard H. Cox, "Hugo Grotius," in *History of Political Philosophy*, pp. 364–65.
107. Cf. Prolegomena 45, and 1. 3. 6.
108. See, especially, Prolegomena 20.
109. Niccolò Machiavelli, *The Prince*, in *Tutte le Opere*, ed. Francesco Flora and Carlo Cordié (Milan: Mondadori, 1949—), chap. 3. See also *Discourses on the First Ten Books of Titus Livy* 1. 6: Compare 1. 3–5, 13–15, 19–21; 2. 1–4, 6–7, 9–10, 12–13, 15–21, 23–24, 28, 30, 32; *The Prince*, chaps. 14, 21, and 25; Russell Weigley's chapter in this book (p. 63).
110. Machiavelli *Discourses* 1. 1–2, 5–6, 16, 37, 39–40, 42, 46, and 2. Preface. 8–9; *The Prince*, chaps. 9, 15–16, 25.
111. *The Prince*, chaps. 6, 8, 14, 17, 19 (end)–20 (beg.); consider the movement of thought in chapters 3 through 6; *Discourses* 1. 1–2, 9–10, 16, 18, 19, 26–27, and 2. 5, 8 (cf. 1. 1), 3. 1, 3–4.
112. *Discourses* 1. 11–15, 19–21, 54–56, 2. 2, and 3. 1; *The Prince*, chaps. 6, 18, 26.
113. *Discourses* 1. 3–8, 16–21, 25, 34–35, 37–40, 42–44, 49, 51–58; 2. 7, 15–16, 19; 3. 1, 31, 12–13, 19–22, 25, 27, 38–41, 49.
114. *Discourses* 2. 2: See the context and cf. 2. 6–7, 10, 14, 16–20, 22–24, and 3. 1; *The Prince*, chaps. 3–5, 12–14, 17, 24, 26. For an illustration, see Allan Millett and William Moreland's chapter in this book (pp. 22–23).
115. *Discourses* 1. pref.
116. *Discourses* 1. 10, 2. 1–5, and 3. 24, 49. Cf. Montesquieu, *Considerations on the Greatness of the Romans and Their Decadence*, chaps. 9 and 15.
117. See, especially, *Discourses* 2. 1–3 and cf. 1. 2, 32, 27, 39–42, 46.
118. See, especially, *Discourses* 2. 5.
119. Thomas Hobbes, *On the Citizen*, ed. Bernard Gert (Garden City, N.Y.: Doubleday, 1972), Epistle Dedicatory, pp. 89–90.
120. Hobbes, *On the Citizen*, 1. 12; *Leviathan*, ed. Oakeshott (Oxford, Eng.: Blackwell, 1960), chap. 13, esp. p. 83, chap. 17, pp. 109–10, chap. 30, pp. 231–32. Cf. *On the Citizen*, Preface, p. 98: "You will object perhaps, that there are some who deny this . . . But . . . we see all countries, though they be at peace with their neighbors, yet guarding their frontiers with armed men, their towns with walls and ports, and keeping constant watches. Can men give a clearer testimony of the distrust they have of each other, and all of all?"
121. Hobbes, *On the Citizen*, 1. 2, p. 113.
122. Ibid., 1. 3, p. 114; cf. *Leviathan*, chap. 13, p. 80.
123. *On the Citizen*, 1. 7, p. 115.
124. *Leviathan*, chap. 15, p. 104; *On the Citizen*, 3. 33.
125. *Leviathan*, chaps. 17, 18, 20; *On the Citizen*, 5–6.
126. *On the Citizen*, 13. 6, p. 260. Cf. 13. 4, 9–11 and 14; *Leviathan*, chap. 13, p. 84, chap. 24, and "Review and Conclusion."
127. Cf. Bertrand de Jouvenel, *Sovereignty*, trans. J. F. Huntington (Chicago: University of Chicago Press, 1957), pp. 238–40, 246.
128. *Leviathan*, chap. 30, pp. 231–32, and chap. 13, p. 83.
129. *On the Citizen*, Epistle Dedicatory, p. 91.
130. *Leviathan*, chap. 21, pp. 142–43.

131. See, especially, *On the Citizen*, 13. 14; cf. Raymond Polin, *Politique et philosophie chez Thomas Hobbes* (Paris: Presses Universitaires de France, 1953), p. 88; and Adam Smith, *The Wealth of Nations*, 5. 1. 1.
132. Consider, especially, *Leviathan*, chap. 28, at the end.
133. John Locke, *Second Treatise on Government*, chap. 9, and Montesquieu, *The Spirit of the Laws*, 1. 2–3, 9. 2, 30. 19 (hereafter cited as *S. of L.*). See Richard H. Cox, *Locke on War and Peace* (Oxford, Eng.: Clarendon Press, 1960).
134. Locke, *Second Treatise*, chap. 5; Montesquieu, *S. of L.*, 20–21. An adequate account of Locke's and Montesquieu's complex political psychologies would require a much more extended discussion.
135. Cf. Francis H. Hinsley, *Power and the Pursuit of Peace* (Cambridge, Eng.: Cambridge University Press, 1963), pp. 162–63.
136. Montesquieu, *S. of L.*, in *Oeuvres complètes*, ed. Caillois (2 vols.; Paris: Gallimard, 1949–1951), 1. 3. Cf. 18. 12, 26, and 30. 19.
137. *S. of L.*, 15. 3, 20. 1, and 20. 2.
138. *S. of L.*, 1. 3 and 10. 2.
139. *S. of L.*, 26. 1 and 20.
140. Cf. Morton A. Kaplan and Nicholas de B. Katzenbach, *The Political Foundations of International Law* (New York: Wiley, 1961), p. 66.
141. *S. of L.*, 10. 3.
142. *S. of L.*, 8. 8, 17–20; 9. 5–8; 10. 4–5, 9, 13; 19. 27; 21. 12–16 and 21–22; as for John Locke, cf. Cox, *Locke*, pp. 125–26, 175–77.
143. See Montesquieu, "Discourse on the Motives Which Ought to Encourage Us toward the Sciences," as well as *Reflections on Universal Monarchy in Europe*, in *Oeuvres Complètes*. Cf. Albert Sorel, *Montesquieu* (Chicago: A. C. McClurg, 1888), p. 152; and Klaus Knorr's chapter in this book.
144. "In all the nations of the world, morality is wished for. . . . [H]uman beings, rascals one by one, are when taken all together very honest: they love morality" (*S. of L.*, "Advertisement," and 25. 3).
145. Emmerich de Vattel, *The Law of Nations; or, Principles of the Law of Nature, Applied to the Conduct and Affairs of Nations and Sovereigns* (Washington, D.C.: Carnegie Institution, 1916), 1. 14–15. Also cf. Preface, Preliminaries, 4–5 and 10; 1. 1–2, 14–15, 21, 38–39, and 223; 2. 2–3, 6, and 117; 4. 1. Cf. Pufendorf, *On the Law of Nature and of Nations*, Preface; 1. 1. 7–8, 11, and 16; 1. 4. 6; 2. 2–4; and Wolff, *The Law of Nations Treated According to Scientific Method*, Preface and secs. 2–3, 7–9, 12, 16, 19, 29, 31, 90, 169, 645.
146. Vattel, *Law*, Preliminaries, 3, 10; 1. 13, 24, 74, 85, 87, 111–15, 125, 128, 135, 168–69; 2. 2–3. Cf. Pufendorf, *On the Law*, 1. 1. 20, 1. 2. 6, 1. 4, 1. 6. 4; 2. 3. 4, 2. 4; and Wolff *Law of Nations*, secs. 20, 30, 44, 52–55, 64, 70, 187, 206.
147. Vattel, *Law*, Preface. Cf. Pufendorf, *On the Law*, 2. 3. 23, and Leonard Krieger, *The Politics of Discretion: Pufendorf and the Acceptance of Natural Law* (Chicago: University of Chicago Press, 1965), p. 165. See also Wolff, *Law of Nations*, Preface and secs. 3, 4, 11–12; Cox, *Locke*, pp. 144–47; Polin, *Politique*, p. 202; Brierly, *Law of Nations*, pp. 24–25, 36.
148. Wolff, *Law of Nations*, Preface and secs. 7–10, 13, 15, 19–20, 156, 161, 163, 187, 263, 272, 613, 616, 617, 629, 631, 743, 777. Cf. Vattel, *Law*, Preface, Preliminaries, 11, 2. 4–6, 11–15, 20–22, 53, 168–69, 309, and 3. 26 ff.
149. Vattel, *Law*, Preface, Preliminaries, 9, 16–17, 21–23, 26; 2. 9, 25, 27, 49, 66, 150, 335, 3. 173, 188–95; and Wolff, *Law of Nations*, Preface and secs. 3, 10–12, 20, 22, 25–26, 59, 73, 75, 156–59, 187, 258, 574, 888–91. Cf. Pufendorf, *On the*

Law, 8. 6; and Krieger, *Politics*, p. 166; Brierly, *Law of Nations*, pp. 37–40; Joachim von Elbe, "The Evolution of the Concept of the Just War in International Law," *American Journal of International Law* 33 (1939):682.
150. Vattel, *Law*, Preliminaries, 9, 2. 152 ff., 4. 37. Cf. Pufendorf, *On the Law*, 8. 9, and Krieger, *Politics*, pp. 167–68. See also Wolff, *Law of Nations*, secs. 23–24, 377–78, 388–89; and Patrick Riley, "The Origins of Federal Theory in International Relations Ideas," *Polity* 6 (1973):104.
151. Compare Grotius, *Law of War*, 3. 17. 3, with Vattel, *Law*, 3. 103–35, 188; and see Edward Dumbauld, *The Life and Legal Writings of Hugo Grotius* (Norman: University of Oklahoma Press, 1969), pp. 60, 67.
152. Immanuel Kant, *Critique of Pure Reason*, B 31; *Groundwork of the Metaphysics of Morals*, in *Works* (Berlin: Königliche Preussischen Akademie der Wissenschaften, 1902–1938), 4:404; hereafter cited as *Groundwork*. (All references to works by Kant, except to the *Critique of Pure Reason*, will be to volumes and pages of this standard edition.) Compare the fragment on Rousseau, cited in Carl J. Friedrich, ed., *The Philosophy of Kant* (New York: Modern Library, 1949), pp. xxii–xxiii.
153. For the argument here and in the immediately following paragraphs, see, especially, Kant's *Groundwork*.
154. Cf. Herbert J. Paton, *The Categorical Imperative* (Philadelphia: University of Pennsylvania Press, 1971), chaps. 4, 6, 9, and 11.
155. "There is therefore only a single categorical imperative and it is this: 'Act only on that maxim through which you can at the same time will that it should become a universal law'" (*Groundwork*, 4:421).
156. Immanuel Kant, *The Metaphysical Elements of Justice*, 6:231 (hereafter cited as *Justice*). Cf. pp. 219–20, 230, 232, 237–38, 325–28, as well as *The Metaphysical Elements of Virtue*, 6:449–50, 458–59, 467–68 (hereafter cited as *Virtue*). As for trying to preserve through coercive law a moral tone in society, that would be an unwarranted intrusion, for "the bad example which one free person sets another as a scandal is not an infringement of his rights" (*Perpetual Peace*, 8:346; compare *Virtue*, 6:464, and *Justice*, 6:238).
157. Kant, *Perpetual Peace*, 8:366.
158. Kant, *Justice*, 6:224, 236–37, 239, 242, 255–57, 307, 312–23; and *Perpetual Peace*, 8:348–50.
159. See, especially, Immanuel Kant, "Conjectural Beginning of Human History," 7:121.
160. Kant, *Perpetual Peace*, 8:348–49.
161. Kant, *Justice*, 6:346.
162. Cf., Kant, "Beginning," p. 355: "Hugo Grotius, Pufendorf, Vattel, and the rest (sorry comforters as they are) are still dutifully quoted in *justification* of military aggression, although their philosophically or diplomatically formulated codes do not and cannot have the slightest *legal* force, since states as such are not subject to a common external restraint." See also *Justice*, 6:307, 344, 347–48. But there can be an unjust enemy: *Justice*, 6:349–50, and von Elbe, "Evolution," p. 683*n*.
163. Kant, *Perpetual Peace*, 8:346–47.
164. "Man (or the people) in the state of nature deprives me of security and injures me, if he is near me, by his mere status, even though he does not actively injure me; he does so by the lawlessness of his condition which constantly threatens me. Therefore, I can compel him either to enter with me into a state of civil law or to remove himself from my neighborhood" (Kant, *Perpetual Peace*, 8:349*n*; cf. p. 354 and *Justice*, 6:312–13, 343, 344. On the relation between Kant and Hobbes, see

also Pierre Hassner, "Les concepts de guerre et de paix chez Kant," *Revue française de science politique* 11 (1961):646–51.
165. Kant, *Perpetual Peace*, 8:343–47; cf. *Justice*, 6:347.
166. Cf. Carl J. Friedrich, *Inevitable Peace* (Cambridge, Mass.: Harvard University Press, 1948), p. 48.
167. Kant, *Justice*, 6:344.
168. Kant, *Perpetual Peace*, 8:354; cf. *Justice*, 6:344.
169. Kant, *Perpetual Peace*, 8:355–56.
170. Kant, *Justice*, 6:351.
171. Kant, *Perpetual Peace*, 8:347.
172. Cf. Friedrich, *Inevitable Peace*, pp. 40, 45–46, 184; also Hinsley, *Power*, chap. 2.
173. Kant, *Justice*, 6:351.
174. Immanuel Kant, *Theory and Practice*, 8:312; cf. *Idea for a Universal History with Cosmopolitan Intent*, Seventh Thesis.
175. Kant, *Perpetual Peace*, 8:357; cf. *Idea*, Sixth Thesis.
176. Kant, *Perpetual Peace*, 8:367.
177. Cf. Kant, *Theory and Practice*, 8:310–11: "If such a state of universal peace is in turn even more dangerous to freedom, for it may lead to the most fearful despotism . . . then distress must force men to form a state which is not a cosmopolitan commonwealth under a single ruler, but a lawful federation." See also "Beginning," 8:121, and *Idea*, 8:26.
178. "Only through the establishment of a universal union of states . . . can a true state of peace be achieved. Because, however, such a state . . . would be too large to govern . . . it follows that perpetual peace (the ultimate goal of all of the law of nations) is, of course, an idea that cannot be realized. But the basic political principles that aim at this idea by instructing us to enter such alliances of states as a means of continually approaching it closer are themselves feasible" (*Justice*, 6:350).
179. Kant, *Critique of Pure Reason*, B. 839; cf. *Theory and Practice*, 8:307–10.
180. Kant, *Justice*, 6:354–55; cf. *Perpetual Peace*, 8:386, and *Theory and Practice*, 8:313.
181. Kant, *Theory and Practice*, 8:310.
182. Kant, *Perpetual Peace*, 8:365, 368; cf. *Idea*, Eighth Thesis.
183. Kant, *Perpetual Peace*, 8:351; cf. "An Old Question Raised Again," 7:85–86, and *Theory and Practice*, 8:311.
184. Kant, *Perpetual Peace*, 8:386.
185. See Klaus Knorr's chapter in this book, especially pp. 112–16.
186. Kant, *Theory and Practice*, 8:311.
187. Kant, *Idea*, Seventh Thesis, 8:24. Kant continues in this passage: "All wars are accordingly so many attempts (not in the intention of man, but in the intention of nature) to establish new relations among states, and through the destruction or at least dismemberment of all of them to create new political bodies, which again, either internally or externally, cannot maintain themselves and which thus must suffer like revolutions; until finally, partly by an optimal internal arrangement of the civil constitution, and partly by common external agreement and legislation, a state of affairs is created which can maintain itself like a civil commonwealth, as an *automaton*."
188. Kant, "An Old Question," 7:91–92.
189. See, e.g., Kant, *Perpetual Peace*, 8:367, 370, 372, 376; also "An Old Question," 7:88.
190. Kant, *Perpetual Peace*, 8:362; cf. 373*n*.

191. "Thus may it be said: 'Seek ye first the kingdom of pure practical reason and its righteousness, and your end (the blessing of perpetual peace) will necessarily follow.' For it is the peculiarity of morals, especially with respect to the principles of public law . . . that the less [morality] makes conduct depend on the proposed end, i.e., the material or moral advantage, the more it agrees with [the end] in general. This is because it is the universal will . . . which determines the law among men, and if practice consistently follows it, this will can also, by the mechanism of nature, cause the desired result" (*Perpetual Peace*, 8:378).
192. Woodrow Wilson, "Peace without Victory," "The Fourteen Points Speech," and "Speech Opening Campaign for Fourth Liberty Loan," in Morton J. Frisch and Richard G. Stevens, eds., *The Political Thought of American Statesmen* (Itasca, Ill.: F. E. Peacock, 1973), pp. 286–300. Cf. Hassner, "Concepts," p. 669, and Russell Weigley's chapter in this book (pp. 55–56).
193. Kant, *Critique of Pure Reason*, B. 832–59; "End of All Things," 8:327–39.
194. For a thoughtful exploration in this direction, which perhaps deviates from Wilson (and Kant) more than the author admits, see Daniel P. Moynihan, "Was Woodrow Wilson Right?" *Commentary*, vol. 57, no. 5 (May 1974), pp. 25–31. See also Daniel P. Moynihan, "The United States in Opposition," *Commentary*, vol. 59, no. 3 (March 1975), pp. 31–44.

The Authors

BERNARD BRODIE is professor of political science at the University of California, Los Angeles. His most recent book is *War and Politics* (New York: Macmillan, 1973).

CHARLES FAIRBANKS is assistant professor of political science at Yale University. He works in the areas of political philosophy, Soviet politics, and international relations.

PETER KARSTEN is associate professor of history at the University of Pittsburgh. His first book, *The Naval Aristocracy*, won the Best Book Award for 1973 from Phi Alpha Theta, history honorary society.

KLAUS KNORR is professor of international and public affairs, Woodrow Wilson School, Princeton University. Among his recent books are *The Power of Nations* (New York: Basic Books, 1975) and *Military Power and Potential* (Lexington, Mass.: Heath, 1970).

ALLAN R. MILLETT is professor of history and director of the Mershon Center Force and Polity Program at Ohio State University. His published work is in the field of American military history.

WILLIAM B. MORELAND is adjunct assistant professor of political science and assistant director of the Force and Polity Program at Ohio State University. He has written on policy-making in both the federal bureaucracy and the Congress.

THOMAS L. PANGLE is associate professor of political science at Yale University and is a National Endowment for the Humanities Fellow. He is the author of *Montesquieu's Philosophy of Liberalism* (Chicago: University of Chicago Press, 1973).

PAUL W. SCHROEDER is professor of history at the University of Illinois and author of *The Axis Alliance and Japanese-American Relations, 1941* (Ithaca, N.Y.: Cornell University Press, 1958), *Metternich's Diplomacy at Its Zenith, 1820–1823* (Austin: University of Texas Press, 1962), and *Austria, Great Britain, and the Crimean War* (Ithaca, N.Y.: Cornell University Press, 1972).

RUSSELL F. WEIGLEY is professor of history at Temple University and author of *History of the United States Army* (New York: Macmillan, 1967) and *The American Way of War* (New York: Macmillan, 1973).

Index

Abdul, Hamid, 171
Abruzzi, duke of, 173, 174
Acheson, Dean, 111–12
Adeimantus, 312
Admirals, Generals, and American Foreign Policy, 1898–1914 (Richard D. Challener): quoted, 59
Adriatic Sea, 169, 170, 174, 198, 245
Aegean Sea, 129, 140; during Italo-Turkish War, 169, 181, 191, 194, 195, 197, 198, 206, 207, 208, 209, 210, 211, 212, 213, 214, 216
Aehrenthal, Count Alois, 137, 138, 148, 151, 169
Afghanistan, 247
Africa, 67, 143, 157, 245, 294
Africa, North, 67, 294
aircraft carrier: development of, 282–83
air power: development of, 294–99, 301
Akaba, 192
Akhdar, Jabal al, 170
Alaric the Bold, 144
Alaska, 63
Alaska, 275–76
Albania, 137, 252; during Italo-Turkish War, 173, 174, 175, 185, 191, 195, 215, 218
Albertini, Luigi, 178, 208, 211; quoted, 102
Alexander I, 167, 231, 232, 251
Alexander III (the Great), 140–41, 267
Alexius Comnenus I, 129
Algeciras Act, 155
Algeciras Conference, 155
alliances: defined, 227, 255–57
Allies: during World War I, 62, 183, 185–86, 204, 281–82, 289, 292, 295; during World War II, 11–12, 24–25, 31, 62, 65, 126, 134, 166, 187, 251, 253–54, 282–83, 298
Allison, Graham, 6
Alsace-Lorraine, 245, 291
Ambrose, Saint, 318
America First Committee, 30, 31
American Expeditionary Force, 62
American Revolution, 9–11, 15–17, 23–24, 29–30, 279, 283
Amiens, Peace of, 269

Amorites, 320
Anadarkos, 147
Ankara, 206
Anglo-Japanese Alliance, 246–47
Annam, 121
Antietam, battle of, 47, 49
appeasement: defined, 151, 251
Aquinas, St. Thomas, 321–24, 325, 329, 331, 332, 344; quoted, 323
Aquitania, 143
Arabia, 143, 195–96
Arab League, 172
Arabs, 88, 217; during Italo-Turkish War, 170, 178, 179, 216
Arab states, 190
Arbela, battle of, 140
Ardennes Forest, 293
Argos, 139, 177
Aristotle, 309, 314, 315, 316, 322–23, 330, 331, 332, 344, 348; quoted, 311–12
Arizona Territory, 146
Army War College, U.S., 58
artillery, field: improved, 287–88
ASDIC (SONAR): developed, 282
Asia, 11, 12, 19–20, 24, 245, 246
Astesanus, 324
Atahualpa, 105
Athens, 99, 138–39, 359
Atlanta, 52
atomic bomb: developed, 255
Attica, 139, 140
Aube, Adm., 280
Aubry, Adm., 178
Auerstadt, battle of, 267
Augsburg, Peace of, 22
Augustine, Saint, 318–21, 323, 324; quoted, 320–21
Austerlitz, battle of, 46, 47, 53, 269
Austria, 80, 87, 88, 137–38, 148–49, 151, 155–56, 173, 183, 185, 186; during 19th century, 40, 100, 103, 136, 152, 166, 231, 232, 234, 235, 236, 237, 238, 239, 240–43, 244, 246, 247, 248, 249, 250, 251, 257, 267, 280, 286, 300; during Italo-Turkish War, 168, 169, 173, 174, 175, 188, 192, 193, 194, 196, 198, 201, 206, 207, 208, 210, 211, 212, 218

Austro-Prussian War (Seven Weeks' War), 103, 286, 290
Avni-Illah, 206
Axis powers, 31, 90, 93, 125, 134, 252–53
Aztec empire, 105, 149
Azzam Pasha: quoted, 172

Babylon, 141
Bactrians, 141
Badeau, Adam: quoted, 55
Baden, 241
Bagdad Railway, 247
Baker, Newton D., 62
Baker rifle, 283
balance of trade, Swedish, 127
Baldwin II, 129
Balkan League, 248, 249
Balkans, 156, 185, 247, 249, 253; during 19th century, 129, 148, 242, 243, 246, 257; during Italo-Turkish War, 169, 170, 196, 206, 215, 216
Balkan wars, 188, 217, 218, 248
Ballard, Colin R., *The Military Genius of Abraham Lincoln*, 41, 42, 57
ballistite, 287
balloons, reconnaissance, 284
Balsdon, John P. V. D.: quoted, 99
Baltic Sea, 132
Baltic states, 252
Banque Ottomane, 199
Barbary states, 136
battleship: development of, 268–78, 300
Bavaria, 8, 14, 241
bayonet: refined, 264
Bechuanaland Protectorate, 157
Bedouin tribes, 143
Beirut, 151, 203, 206, 207
Belgium, 89, 176, 183, 204, 234–35, 269, 293
Beloff, Max: quoted, 125
Benes, Eduard, 250
Berbers, 170
Berchtold, Count Leopold von, 208
Bernadotte, Prince, 167
Bernard of Saxe-Weimar, 14
Bessarabia, 124
Best, Werner, 142
"big-stick election," 210, 214
Biscaretti, 173, 174, 175
Bismarck, Prince Otto von, 70, 89, 149, 153, 236, 240–43, 244–45, 248, 256; quoted, 148
Bismarck, 282
Blackfeet, 147
BLACK plan, 62
Black Sea, 168, 193, 234
blitzkrieg, 104
Blücher, Gebhard Leberecht von, 269
Bodenkreditanstalt, 151
Boeotian League, 140
Boers, 157
Boer War, 153–54, 288
Bohemia, 8
Boiotia, 138
Bolshevik Revolution, 110
bomber: development of, 296, 300
bombing, 295–99
Bompard, Louis: quoted, 188
B-1 bomber, 303
Bonnet, Georges, 149–50
Borah, Sen. William E., 30
Bosdari, Count, 196
Bosnia, 137, 149, 151, 152, 155, 182
Boston Massacre, 17
Boxer Protocol, 158
Boxer Rebellion, 107
Bozeman Trail, 147, 148
Brainbridge-Hoff, Comdr. William: quoted, 275
Brazos River, 147
Brecht, Bertolt, *Mother Courage and Her Children*, 14
breechloader: development of, 284, 287, 300
Breitenfeld, battle of, 9, 23
Brest-Litovsk, 292
Brinton, Crane: quoted, 109–10
British Empire, 187, 246, 247, 248
British Grand Fleet, 280–82
British Royal Navy, 16, 270–71, 272, 294
British South Africa Company, 157
"Brown Bess," 264
Browning, John M., 288
Brusilov offensive, 292
B-17 ("flying fortress"), 297
Buford, Gen. John, 285
Bulgaria, 129, 130, 206, 215, 218, 248
Bull Run, first Battle of, 44
Bull Run, second Battle of, 47
Bülow, Prince Bernard von, 148, 149, 156

375

Bunker, Gerald: quoted, 157
Buol, Count, 239
Burma, 11, 145
Burn, A. R.: quoted, 138–40
Bury, J. B.: quoted, 144
Bushnell, David, 279
Butler, Gen. Benjamin F., 48
Butow, Robert: quoted, 94
"Byzantine" diplomacy: defined, 129
Byzantine Empire, 129–30

Caddos, 147
Cadmeia, 140
Caillaux, Joseph, 157
Cajamarca, 105
Cambrai offensive, 293
Cameron, Simon, 44
Canada, 63
Caneva, Gen. Carlo, 179, 205, 206
Canning, George, 233
cap, percussion, 284
Caporetto, battle of, 185
Capponi, Piero, 132
Caribbean Sea, 105
Carneades, 330
Carpathos, 208
Carthage, 99, 152, 166
Carthage, 198
Castlereagh, Lord Robert, 167, 231, 251
Catholicism, 8, 9, 22, 28
Catholic powers, 237
Cato, Marcus, 99
Caux, 216
cavalry: eclipsed, 285–86, 292, 300
Cavour, Count Camillo, 239
Century Group, 31
Cetinje, 137
Chaeronea, battle of, 138, 139
Challener, Richard D., *Admirals, Generals, and American Foreign Policy, 1898–1914*: quoted, 59
Chamberlain, Neville, 82, 152, 157, 188, 251
Chang Chih-tung: quoted, 122–23
Charles of Anjou, 129
Charles VIII, 130, 131, 132
chassepot, 286
Chattanooga, 52
Chiang Kai-shek, 157
China, 105–9, 114, 121–23, 136, 144–46;

Nationalist, 11, 12, 19–20, 31; People's Republic of, 39, 257
Chios, 211
Christian Front, 30
Christianity: and political theory, 317–32
Chungking government, 158
Churchill, Winston, 40, 65, 67, 68, 69, 186, 188, 253, 293; quoted, 134, 187
Cicero, 314–17, 321; quoted, 315, 316, 317
Cilicia, 206
Civil War, U.S., 41–57, 267, 272, 273, 275, 276, 279, 281, 284, 285, 286, 287, 301
Clarendon, earl of, 152
Clausewitz, Karl von, 41, 56, 265–68, 269, 277, 284–85, 289–90, 303; quoted, 38, 70, 266, 267
Clear Fork, Brazos River, 147
Clemenceau, Georges, 40
Cobden, Richard, *The Three Panics*, 271
Cold Harbor, battle of, 285
Cold War, 111, 113, 255
colonial administration: during American Revolution, 15–17, 23–24, 29–30
Colt, Samuel, 288
Comanches, 147
Commandments, Ten, 322
Committee of Union and Progress, 177, 210, 214
"committees of correspondence," 10
Committee to Defend America by Aiding the Allies, 31
Communism, 100
Communist party, U.S., 30
Communists, Chinese, 157
Concord, battle of, 10
Confederacy, 41–57, 137, 272, 301. See also individual armies; Civil War
Congo, 176
Congress, U.S., 17, 32, 42, 44, 48, 50, 53, 61, 147
Conrad, Charles M.: quoted, 146
Constantinople, 130, 143, 234; during Italo-Turkish War, 176, 188, 190, 193, 213, 216, 217
Constitution, 271–72
co-optation: defined, 143
cordite, 287
cordon sanitaire, 250
Corinth, 139, 140
"cost-effectiveness," 303

376

Coughlin, Father Charles E., 30
"counterforce," 174
Crete, 180, 182, 312
Crimea, 239
Crimean War, 103, 237–39, 256, 270, 271, 284
Crittenden Resolution, 44
Croton, 141
Crowe, Eyre, 80, 93, 101; quoted, 78–79, 153–55
Cuba, 88
Cumberland, 275
Cunsolo, Ronald, 200
Cyprus, 88–89
Cyrenaica, 169, 170, 180, 181, 206
Czechoslovakia: during World War I, 186, 250–51; during World War II, 80, 83, 87, 88, 100, 124, 150, 252

Dahlgren guns, 273
Daniels, Josephus: quoted, 61
Dardanelles: during Italo-Turkish War, 168, 191, 192, 193, 196, 206, 207, 208, 209, 210, 211, 213, 215
Darwinism, 113
de Gaulle, Charles: quoted, 307
Daladier, Edouard, 150
Danegeld, the, 151
Darius III, 140
Davis, Jefferson, 43
Declaration of Independence, 10
Delcassé, Théophile, 101, 245, 247
Demologos, 270
Denmark, 9, 89, 132–33, 141–43, 186, 236, 240
De Officiis (Cicero), 314, 315, 316–17
detente, 123, 126, 257
Deutscher, Isaac: quoted, 87
Devastation, 271, 273–74
Dewey, Adm. George, 61
Diesel engine: development of, 280
dirigibles, 295
Disarmament Conference: and Versailles Treaty, 81
Discourse on the Arts and Sciences, The (Jean-Jacques Rousseau), 347
Discourses (Niccolò Machiavelli), 335
Dodecanese: during Italo-Turkish War, 210, 212, 213–14, 216, 217, 219
Donelson, Fort, 52

Douhet, Gen. Giulio, 295–99
Dreadnought, 278
Dual Alliance, 242, 243, 244–45
Dual Monarchy, 242
Dunkerque, 275
Dunkirk, battle of, 142, 187
Dutch East Indies, 11, 25, 93, 172

El Alamein, Battle of, 294
Elba, 231
Elbe River, 267
Elements of Military Art and Science (Henry Wager Halleck), 57
El Hasa, 190
Emancipation Proclamation, 49, 50, 51
Egypt, 88, 182, 190, 198, 233–34, 235, 244, 247, 294
England, 69, 79–86, 98, 102, 136, 153–55, 156, 166, 257, 302; during American Revolution, 9–11, 15–17, 23–24, 29–30; during 19th century, 58, 106, 121, 122, 152, 166, 167, 231, 233, 234, 235, 237–38, 239, 240, 243, 245, 246, 267, 268, 272, 273, 274–75, 278, 279, 280, 283, 288, 301; during Italo-Turkish War, 192, 193, 196, 198, 207, 210, 212; during World War I, 40, 101, 132, 204, 244, 246–48, 249, 250, 278, 289, 290, 292, 295; during interwar years, 63, 80–86, 87, 89, 93, 113, 114, 123, 150, 251–52; during World War II, 30, 40, 65, 66, 68, 83, 88, 90, 96, 124, 125, 126, 158, 184, 186, 187, 188, 253–54, 282–83, 293, 294, 297
Enlightenment, the, 341, 343, 347
English Channel, 271
Entente Cordiale, 101, 102, 125, 155, 198, 247–48
Eritrea, 195
Esthonia, 124
Ethics (Aristotle), 322
Eugenius, 144
Europe, Concert of, 235

fair employment practices program, 32
Falk, Robert A., 228
Far East, 81
Farragut, Adm. David, 277
Farrar, L. L., Jr.: quoted, 102
Fashoda Affair, 125, 154

377

Feng Kuei-fen: quoted, 106–7
Ferdinand II, 8, 9, 14, 22, 28
F-4 Phantom, 302
F-14, Grumman, 302
Fighting for Freedom, 31
Finland, 124, 126, 133–34
"Finlandization": defined, 133–34, 136
firearms: development of, 264, 283–84
"Fish Agreement," 132
flintlock musket, 264, 284
Florence, 130–32, 359
"flying fortress" (B-17), 297
Foch, Col. Ferdinand, 289, 290, 292
Folketing, the, 142
Fontenoy, Battle of, 265
Forrestal, James, 65
Four Policemen, 254
France, 9, 23, 27, 68, 109–10, 130–32, 201, 257, 265–66, 267, 269, 288, 302; during 19th century, 40, 100, 103, 104, 106, 121, 122, 129, 152, 167, 231–45 passim, 271, 274–75, 279, 280, 290, 291, 301; pre–World War I, 101, 102, 125, 153, 156, 157, 246, 247–48, 249; during Italo-Turkish War, 168, 188, 190, 192, 194, 198, 199, 206, 207, 211, 218; during World War I, 40, 185, 289, 290–92, 297; during interwar years, 81, 83, 86, 87, 114, 251–52, 300; during World War II, 30, 69, 89–90, 123, 124, 149–50, 186, 252, 275, 293–94
France, Vichy, 11, 158
Francis Ferdinand, Archduke, 249
Francis Joseph, Emperor, 137, 236
Franco, Francisco, 252
Franco-Prussian War, 165, 267, 276, 286, 290
Frederick II (the Great), 265, 266, 267
Frederick V, 8
Frémont, Gen. John C., 44, 48
French, Sir John, 289
French Revolution, 104, 109–10, 166, 265
"French 75," 288
Fu-k'ang-an, 146
Fuller, Gen. J. F. C., 293
Fulton, Robert, 270, 279
Fusinato, 213

Gage, Gen. Thomas, 10
Gallipoli, 293

Gallup poll, 31, 89
Gathering Storm, The (Winston Churchill): quoted, 134
Gatling, Dr. Richard, 286
Gatling gun, 286, 288
George, David Lloyd, 40, 282
George III, 9–10, 15–17, 23–24, 29–30
George V, 192
German-American Bund, 30
German Confederation, 232, 235, 240, 241
German High Seas Fleet, 281
German Unification, wars of, 290
Germany, 7, 9, 14–15, 80–87, 92, 93–94, 113, 114, 257; during 19th century, 121, 122, 232, 236, 238, 239, 240–43, 244–46, 267, 278, 291; pre–World War I, 62, 79, 101–4, 148–49, 153–55, 156, 157, 247–48, 249, 280; during Italo-Turkish War, 167, 169, 192, 193, 194, 208, 218, 250; during World War I, 40, 104, 132–33, 176, 183, 185, 281–82, 289, 290, 295; during World War II, 11, 66, 68, 87–90, 97, 123–25, 126–27, 134, 141–43, 150, 166, 186, 187, 188, 250, 251–53, 254, 275, 282–83, 292, 293–94, 297, 298
Gettysburg, battle of, 285
Gilbert, Martin, 84, 85; quoted, 80
Giolitti, Giovanni: during Italo-Turkish War, 168, 169, 171, 174, 175, 178, 180, 182, 184, 186, 188, 189, 190, 198, 200, 201, 203, 208, 211, 212, 216, 219; quoted, 179, 181, 195, 205, 213, 214, 217
Girondists, 110
Glaucon, 313, 330
Gloire, 269, 272
Gneisenau, Count August von, 70
Gneisenau, 275
Golden Horde, the, 129
Göteborg, 126
Goths, 143–44
Gott, Richard, 84, 85; quoted, 80
Grand Alliance, 253–55
Grant, Gen. Ulysses S., 42, 52–57, 285; quoted 52–53, 53–54
Gratian, 321
Great Exhibition, the, 287
Great Purge, the, 251

Greece, 129, 210, 213, 232, 233, 248, 251, 252, 270; ancient, 98, 138–41, 308–14, 329
Greek States, League of United, 138, 139
Greeley, Horace, 48
GREEN plan, 62
Greenfield, Kent Roberts, 67; quoted, 65
Gregory X, Pope, 130
Grew, Joseph C., 94
Grey, Sir Edward, 155, 247; quoted, 188, 192–93, 204
Grimmelshausen, Hans Jakob von, *Simplicissimus*, 14
Grotius, Hugo, 329–32, 343, 344, 345, 346
Guderian, Gen., 293
Guisan, Gen., 134
Gulf and Inland Waters, The (Alfred T. Mahan), 276
Gustaf (Gustavus V), 126
Gustavus Adolphus (Gustavus II), 9, 15, 23
Gustav Zede, 280
gyroscopic compass: developed, 280

Habsburgs, 8–9, 22, 23, 28, 103, 149
Haig, Sir Douglas, 40, 289, 299
Halifax, Lord, 82
Halleck, Henry Wager, *Elements of Military Art and Science*, 47, 57, 58
Hamilton, J. R.: quoted, 140
Han dynasty, 136
Hansson, Per Albin, 126, 127
Harper's Ferry Arsenal, 284
Harney, Gen. William, 148
Harriman, Averell, 65
Harrison's Bar Letter, 46, 48, 64; quoted, 45
Hart, Basil Liddell, 293
Hay-Pauncefote Treaty, 101
Hegel, Georg Wilhelm Friedrich, 362
Hemming, John: quoted, 105
Henry, Fort, 52
Herodotus: quoted, 177
Herzegovina, 137
Hiroshima, 298
Hitler, Adolf, 31, 40, 41, 68, 69, 80–85, 87–89, 100, 114, 123, 124, 125, 141, 142, 150, 152, 186, 187, 251, 252, 293
Hoare, Sir Samuel, 82
Hobbes, Thomas, 80, 336–40, 343, 344, 352, 353, 355, 358, 362; quoted, 340

Hodeida, 195
Holborn, Hajo: quoted, 123–24
Holland, 172, 201, 235, 293
Holy Alliance, 231–32, 233, 235, 236, 238, 241, 243
Holy Cities, 192
Holy Roman Empire, 8, 22
Hopkins, Harry, 65
Hotham, Adm. Beaumont, 277
Hötzendorff, Conrad von, 173
Howard, Michael: quoted, 103
Howe, Adm. Richard, 277
Huguenots, 28
Hulagu Khan, 129
Hull, Cordell, 25–26, 64
"Hundred Days," Napoleon's, 267, 269
Hungary, 129, 236, 250
Hunter, Gen. David, 48
Huntington, Samuel P., *The Soldier and the State*: quoted, 66–67
Hussey, J. M.: quoted, 129–30

Iberian Peninsula, 234, 269. See also Spain; Portugal
Ibn Saud, 190
Idris, Sayyid, 195
Ili: treaties over, 122
Imam Yahya, 195
Incas, 105
India, 246
Indians, American, 146–48, 324, 329. See also individual tribes
Indochina, 11, 93
Inflexible, 273
Influence of Sea Power upon History, 1660–1783, The (Alfred T. Mahan), 276
Influence of Sea Power upon the French Revolution and Empire, 1793–1812, The (Alfred T. Mahan), 276–77
Institute for Defense Analysis, 302
interventionists, 30–31, 90
Ionian Sea, 170
Iran, 98
Iriye, Akira: quoted, 91, 92
"ironclad," 269, 272, 301
isolationism, 30–31, 89, 90, 92
Israel, 88, 172, 190
Italian league, 232
Italo-Turkish War, 164, 167–74, 175–76, 177–83, 184–85, 188–99, 201–18

Italy, 92, 123, 150, 152, 167–85, 188–99, 201–19, 249, 251; during 19th century, 232, 235, 236–37, 239, 240, 241, 243, 244, 245
Izvolsky, Alexander, 138, 156

Jakobson, Max: quoted, 134
James River, 47
Janis, Irving, 33
Japan, 63, 90–96, 101, 106, 107, 108–9, 157–58; during Russo-Japanese War, 104–5, 246–47, 272, 288, 290; and attack on Pearl Harbor, 11, 12, 17–20, 24–26, 31, 32; during World War II, 64, 87, 123, 125, 252–53, 254, 278, 298, 300–301
Jellicoe, Adm. John, 280, 282
Jena, battle of, 103, 104, 267, 291
Jervis, Adm. John, 277; quoted, 279
Jews: in Sweden during World War II, 127
Jidda, 192, 195
Joffre, Gen., 289
Johnson, Sen. Hiram W., 30
Johnson, Lyndon Baines, 67
Johnson, Reverdy, 48, 49
Johnson, Sir William, 16
Joint Board, the, 63
Joint Chiefs of Staff: created, 65
Jomini, Antoine Henri, 57, 58, 269, 277
Jones, Arnold: quoted, 143
Jutland, Battle of, 278, 281

Kaffir War, 284
Kant, Immanuel, 80, 347, 348–53, 354–63; quoted, 353, 355, 356, 357, 358, 359, 360, 361
Karelia, 134
Karsten, Peter, *The Naval Aristocracy*, 59
Karteria, 270
Kearney, Fort Phil, 147
Kekkonen, Urho, 133
Kennan, George: quoted, 136
Kennedy, John Fitzgerald, 67
"Kentucky rifle," 283
Kgama III, 157
Khrushchev, Nikita, 39
Kiamil Pasha, 151
King Edward VII, 278
"King's Friends," 24, 29, 30

Kissinger, Henry: quoted, 6, 167
Knorr, Klaus, 127
Konoye, Fumumaro, 158
Korea, 90, 246
Korea, North, 112, 183
Korea, South, 112
Korean War, 96, 112, 183, 184, 299
Koszta, Martin, 152
Krupp munitions, 287
Kunfidah, 194
Kuomintang government, 157, 158
Kynouria, 139

Lacedaemonians, 99
Laelius, 315
Lafore, Laurence, 84, 85, 101; quoted, 83, 149–50, 156
Lam, Trong Buu: quoted 145–46
Langlois, Col., 288
Lansdowne, Lord, 200–201, 247
Laramie, Fort: Treaty of, 148
Latvia, 124
Lausanne, 213
Laws (Plato): quoted, 310–11
Leahy, Adm. William D., 67
Lee, Gen. Robert E., 46, 47, 49, 50, 53, 54, 55, 285
Lend Lease: enacted, 31
Lenin, Nikolai: quoted, 86
Leopold I, 237
Levant, the, 233
Lewis, John L., 32
Lexington, battle of, 10
Leyte Gulf, Battle of, 278
Liaotung, 121, 122
Libya: during Italo-Turkish War, 167–73, 176, 177–86, 188–91, 198–203, 205–7, 209, 210, 213, 215, 216, 218, 219
Lincoln, Abraham, 41–57, 60, 64, 67, 71, 136; quoted, 43, 44, 48, 49, 51, 54, 56
Lincoln and His Generals (T. Harry Williams), 42, 57
Lincoln Finds a General (Kenneth P. Williams), 57
Lindbergh, Charles, 150
Lin Tse-hsu, 106
Liska, George: quoted, 228
Lissa, Battle of, 275
Little Entente, 250
Liu K'un-i: quoted, 121

Lloyd George, David, 40, 282
Locarno treaties, 250
Locke, John, 80, 340, 344, 352
London, 295
Louis IX, 129
Louis XIII, 8, 27–29
Louis XIV, 28, 173
Louis Philippe, 234
Low Countries, 186
Luce, Adm. Stephen B., 58
Ludendorff, Gen. Erich von, 292
Luisitania, 281, 282
Lutheranism, 22
Lützen, battle of, 23
Luxembourg, 123
Lyons, Council of, 129

MacArthur, Gen. Douglas, 25
McClellan, Gen. George B., 42, 44–51, 52, 56, 57, 64; quoted, 45, 46, 49–50
Macedonia: during Italo-Turkish War, 140, 141, 206, 211, 216, 217
Machiavelli, Niccolò, 80, 332–36, 338, 340; quoted, 33, 335
machine gun: development of, 268–88, 299–300
McNamara, Robert S., 67
Magdeburg, 15, 264
"Magic," 17, 18
Maginot Line, 104, 293
Magyars, 242
Mahan, Alfred T., 58, 269, 274, 276–78, 296; quoted, 166, 281
Mahmud Muktar Pasha, 211
Maine, 275
Makaroff, Adm. S. J., *Naval Tactics*, 275
Malaya, 11, 25
Manchu dynasty, 106, 107, 144–46
Manchuria, 92, 101, 121, 246
Manouba, 198
Mansfeld, Ernst von: quoted, 14
Marburg, 15
Marduk, 141
Marne, Battle of the, 297
MAROON plan, 63
Marshall, Gen. George C., 26, 65
Marshall Plan, 133
Marx, Karl, 362
Marxism, 362
Marxism-Leninism, 113

Massaua, 190
Mavia, 143
Maxim automatic gun, 288
Maxim, Hiram, 288
Maximilian, 22
Mazaeus, 141
Meade, Gen. George C., 53, 54
Mecca, 192, 194
Medici Palace, 132
Medici, Pietro, 130, 131, 132
Mediterranean Agreements, 244
Mediterranean Sea, 176
Mehemet Ali, 233, 235
Meiji restoration, 108
Mein Kampf (Adolf Hitler), 82
mercenaries, use of, 14–15, 140, 264
Merrimac, 269, 272, 275
Metternich, Prince Klemens von, 100, 166, 232, 234, 251; quoted, 167
Mexico, 62, 105
Michael VIII, 129–30
Middle Ages, 109
Middle East, 66, 100, 256
Milan, 130
Military Genius of Abraham Lincoln, The (Colin R. Ballard), 41
Millo, Capt., 215
mines, land, 284
"Minié ball," 283–84
Minié, Capt. C. E., 283
Missouri River, 148
Mitchell, Gen. "Billy," 296, 297
mitrailleuse, 286, 288
Modena, 237
Molotov, Vyacheslav M., 133
Moltke, Helmuth von, 70
Monitor, 269, 272, 273, 275
Montenegro, 137–38, 152
Montesquieu, baron de, 80, 340–43, 358, 360; quoted, 341, 342
Montezuma, 149
Montgomery, Gen. Bernard, 294
Morgenthau, Hans, 65; quoted, 6, 151
Morocco, 102, 168, 246, 247
Morse, 280
Mother Courage and Her Children (Bertolt Brecht), 14
Münchengrätz Agreement, 234
Munich, 251, 252
Munich Agreement, 100, 124, 134, 149–50

Muslims, 192, 218
Mussolini, Benito, 252
muzzleloader, 287, 300

Nafusah, Jabal, 170
Nagasaki, 298
Nanking government, 158
Nantes, Edict of, 28
Naples, 130, 131, 233
Napoleon I, 46, 53, 104, 167, 231, 265, 266, 267, 269, 277, 279, 285, 290
Napoleon III, 239, 240, 286, 290
Narvik, 126
Naval Aristocracy, The (Peter Karsten), 59
Naval Tactics (Adm. S. J. Makaroff), 275
Naval War College, 276
Nazi party, Danish, 142
Nazism, 12, 80, 81, 89, 186
Nebraska, 148
needle gun: developed, 286
Neighbors, Robert S., 146–47
Nelson, Adm. Horatio, 268, 277
Netherlands, 89
Neutrality Acts, 30, 31
"New Order," 142
Nguyên Anh, 145
Nguyên Huê, 145, 146
Ngwato, 157
Nice, 240
Nicholas I, 236
Nicholas, Prince, 137, 138
Nile River, Upper, 154
Nivelle, Gen. Robert, 289
Nivelle offensive, 185
Nobel, Alfred, 287
Norden, Heinz, *The Sword and the Scepter*, 69
North, Lord Frederick, 24, 30
Norton, Capt. 283
Norway, 89, 126, 132, 186
nuclear war, 174
nuclear weapons, 263, 299, 301, 302

Oakley, Stewart: quoted, 141–42
On War (Karl von Clausewitz), 265, 285, 303
Open Door policy, 246, 252
Opium War, 106, 109
ORANGE plan, 63, 64
Orchomenos, 138, 140

Orléans, Gaston d', 28, 29
Orôpos, 139, 140
Orthodox church (Greek), 130
Örvik, Nils: quoted, 132, 133
Osgood, Robert E.: quoted, 288
Ottoman Empire, 129, 148, 234; during Italo-Turkish War, 167, 168, 169, 170, 172, 183, 188, 189, 191, 192, 195, 206, 215, 218
OVERLORD, Operation, 69
Oxenstierna, Axel, 23

Paasikivi, Juho Kusti, 133, 134
"Pact of Steel," 252
Paixhans, Henri Joseph, 270, 272
Palatinate, the, 8
Palestine, 143
Palmerston, Lord Henry, 234, 240, 256, 271
Panama, 63
Paris Peace Conference (World War II), 133
Paris, Peace of, 239
Parliament, British, 186; during American Revolution, 9, 16, 23, 24, 29, 30, 137
Parliament, Turkish, 171, 208, 210
Parma, 237
Passchendaele offensive, 292
Peabody-Martini rifle: developed, 287
"Peacemaker," 270
Pearl Harbor, attack on, 11, 12, 17–20, 24–26, 32, 63, 94–96
Peking, 106
Pekkala, Mauno, 133
Peloponnesian War, 99, 139
"People's Defense, The," 156
Peninsular Campaign, 294
Peninsular War, 283
periscope: developed, 280
Perry, Commodore Matthew, 106, 108
Pershing, Gen. John J., 62
Persia, 98, 139, 140–41, 246–47
Persian Gulf, 247
Persian Wars, 141
Peru, 172
Pétain, Gen. Henri: quoted, 289
Peter of Aragon, 129
phainomena, 309
Phayllus, 141
Phelps, Gen. John Wolcott, 48, 49, 54
Philip II, 138–40

Philippines, 11, 19, 24, 25–26, 63, 64, 66
Philoxenus, 141
"phony war," 186
Picq, Col. Ardant du, 291
Pietrasanta, fortress of, 131
Piraeus, 140
Pisa, 131
Pitt, William, 29
Pitt, William, the Younger, 279
Pius IX, Pope, 237
Pizarro, Francisco, 104
Plataia, 138, 140
Plato, 311, 312–14, 315, 316, 317; quoted, 310–11, 312
Platte River, 148
Plevna, Battle of, 287
Plutarch: quoted, 99
Pogue, Forrest C.: quoted, 65
Poincaré, Raymond, 198
Poland, 166, 232, 236, 240, 250; during World War II, 80, 83, 87, 88, 124, 150, 186, 251–52, 294
polis: defined, 310
Politburo, 111
Pollio, Gen., 178
P-151, 298
Pontiac's Rebellion, 16
Pope, Gen. John, 47, 50
Porkkala, 134
Port Said, 176, 192
Portugal, 172, 234, 267
Potomac, Army of the, 45, 46, 47, 53, 54, 55
Powder River, 146, 147, 148
powder, smokeless: developed, 287
Prague, 251
Preveza, 173
Princeton, 270
Principles of War (Col. Ferdinand Foch), 289
Progressive Era, 61
Prussia: during 19th century, 39–40, 103, 104, 123, 136, 152, 167, 231, 232, 234, 236, 238, 240–43, 244, 265, 267, 286, 290, 291
Pufendorf, Samuel, 343, 347
Punic War, first, 99
"Purple," 18

Quadruple Alliance, 231, 233
Queen Elizabeth, 272
Quintuple Alliance, 231, 233
Quisling, Vidkun, 123

RAND Corporation, 302–3
Randolph, A. Philip, 32
rapprochement, 123
realpolitik, 13, 89, 236, 253
Rechberg, Count Johann von, 240–41
recoil mechanism: developed, 287–88
Red Army, 40, 83
Red Cloud, 147, 148
Red Cloud War, 148
RED plan, 63
Red Sea: during Italo-Turkish War, 172, 176, 191, 192, 194, 195, 198, 203, 205, 206, 207
Reflections on the Art of War (Marshal Maurice de Saxe): quoted, 265
refugees: during World War II, 127, 134
Reich, German, 241
Reichstag, the, 153
Reinsurance Treaty, 244
Republic (Plato), 311–12, 313; quoted, 311–12
Republic, The (Cicero), 315, 316
Republican River, 148
reservations, Indian, 146–47
resistance movement (World War II), 142, 150
Restitution, Edict of, 9, 22
Reynaud, Paul, 187
Rhine River, 150, 240
Rhodes, 191, 208, 210, 212
Ribbentrop, Joachim von, 123, 124
Richelieu, duc de, 23, 27–29
Richmond, Battle of, 46–47
rifling: developed, 283, 284, 287
Ripafratta, fortress of, 131
Ritter, Gerhard, *Staatskunst und Kriegshandwerk*: quoted, 69–70
Riza, Achmed, 151
Robinson, Charles A.: quoted, 140–41
Rochelle, La, 28
Rohan, duc de, 28
Roman Empire, 143–44, 335
Rome, 129, 130; ancient, 99, 152, 314–17, 321, 329, 333, 335, 336, 359
Rommel, Gen. Erwin, 294

Roosevelt, Franklin Delano, 11, 12, 24–25, 30–32, 64, 65, 67, 69, 150, 254
Roosevelt, Theodore, 91
Root, Elihu, 61, 63
Roper polls, 31
Rousseau, Jean-Jacques, 347–48, 351, 359, 362
Rowse, A. L., 84, 85, 152; quoted, 82–83
Ruhr Valley, 250
Rumania, 150, 234, 243, 249, 250, 251
Rumbold, Sir Horace: quoted, 81
Russell, John, 240
Russia, 39, 133–34, 185, 249, 250–51, 292; during 19th century, 100, 106, 121–23, 129, 152, 166, 167, 231–38 passim, 242, 243, 244, 245, 266, 267, 271, 272; pre–World War I, 90–94, 101, 102, 104–5, 138, 148–49, 155–56, 188, 246–48; during Italo-Turkish War, 168, 173, 191, 193, 196, 198, 206, 208, 210, 211, 218; during World War II, 19–20, 39, 40, 66, 68, 83, 84, 85, 86–88, 97, 123–25, 133–34, 150, 251, 252, 253–55, 294; post–World War II, 39, 98, 100, 111, 112, 113, 256, 257, 300
Russian Imperial Navy, 275
Russo-Japanese War, 90, 94, 104–5, 272, 288, 290
Russo-Turkish alliance, 233
Russo-Turkish War, 287

Sadowa, Battle of, 286, 290
Said, Sheik, 192
Salonika, 191, 196, 206
Salamis, 141
Salt Fork, Brazos River, 147
Samos, 191, 211
San Giovanni di Medua, 174
San Giuliano, marchese di, 178, 180, 192; quoted, 168
Santisima Trinidad, 268
Saracen tribes, 143
Sardinia, 173, 237, 239, 240
Sarzana, fortress of, 131
Sarzanello, fortress of, 131
Sato, Kojiro, 94
Saudis, 190
"Savior Officers," 214
Savoy, 173, 240

Saxe, Marshal Maurice de, *Reflections on the Art of War*: quoted, 265
Saxony, 8
Scapa Flow, 281
Scavenius, Erik, 142
Scharnhorst, 275
Schelling, Thomas C., 170, 212
Schiller, Johann Christoph Friedrich von, *Wallenstein*, 14
Schleswig-Holstein, 236, 240–41
Schlieffen Plan, 249
Schmitt, Bernadotte: quoted, 137–38, 151, 156
Schroeder, Paul: quoted, 152
Schwartz, Benjamin: quoted, 107–8
Schwarzenberg, Prince Félix, 167, 236, 237
Sciara Sciat, battle of, 178, 179, 180, 182
Scott, Gen. Winfield, 45, 60
Sedan, battle of, 103, 290, 291
Selective Service, U.S., 31
Serbia, 129, 138, 152, 155–56, 206, 215, 218, 243, 248, 249
Seven Weeks' War (Austro-Prussian War), 103, 286, 290
Seven Years' War, 29
Seward, William H., 49
Sforza dynasty, 130
Shanghai, 158
Sharps, Christopher, 284
"sharpshooter," 284
Shenandoah, Army of the, 54
Shenandoah Valley, 55
Sheridan, Gen. Philip H., 54, 55
Sherman, Gen. William Tecumseh, 53, 55, 56, 60; quoted, 55
Shimonoseki, Treaty of, 121
Siam, 145
Siberia, 87, 106
Sicily, 99, 129, 173
"Sick Man of Europe," 167. *See also* Ottoman Empire
Siegfried Line, 150
Signoria, the, 132
Silver Shirts, 30
Simon, Sir John, 82, 83
Simplicissimus (Hans Jakob Christoffel von Grimmelshausen), 14
Singapore, 96
Sino-Russian treaty, 122, 123

Sioux, 147, 148
slavery, 44, 48–51
slaves, fugitive, 44
Smith, Denis Mack: quoted, 188
Smith, Fort C. F., 147
Smyrna, 191, 206, 211, 217
Snell, John L.: quoted, 89
Socrates, 308, 312, 313; quoted, 311
Sogdians, 141
Soldier and the State, The (Samuel P. Huntington): quoted, 66–67
Somalia, 195
Somme, Battle of, 289
SONAR, 282
"Sons of Liberty," 10
South African federation, 157
South African war (Boer War), 153–54, 288
South Carolina, 43
South Dakota, 148
South, U.S., 41–57, 137, 272, 301. *See also* Civil War
Soviet-German Treaty of Non-Aggression, 124
Spain, 8, 9, 22, 29, 105, 124, 149, 150, 166, 172, 173, 201, 232, 234, 324, 329
Spanish-American War, 61
Spanish Armada, 98
Spanish Netherlands, 173
Spanish Succession, War of the, 201
Sparta, 139, 177, 311, 325, 333, 359
Spitamenes, 141
Staatskunst und Kriegshandwerk (Gerhard Ritter): quoted, 69–70
Stalin, Joseph, 39, 40, 68, 69, 84, 86, 87, 88, 124, 125, 133, 253–54
Stamp Act, 137
Stampalia, 208, 210, 212
Stark, Harold R., 26
Stauning, Thorvald, 142
Stimson, Henry L., 65; quoted, 66
Stoicism, 314, 315, 316, 362
Straight, Willard: quoted, 90–91
Straits Convention, 235
Stuart, John, 16
Suarez, Franciscus, 324, 327–29; quoted, 328
submarine: development of, 279–83, 284, 300, 301

Sudetan, 251
Suez Canal, 244
Summa Theologica (St. Thomas Aquinas), 321, 324
Sumter, Fort, 43
Susa, 141
Sweden, 9, 14, 22, 23, 126–27, 186, 267
Switzerland, 127, 134, 152
Sword and the Scepter, The (Heinz Norden), 69
Syria, 88, 143, 194, 206, 207, 240
"systems analysis," 303

Taft, Sen. Robert A., 30
Taiping Rebellion, 106
Taiwan, 121
Talleyrand, Charles Maurice de, 109
Tani, Masayuki, 158
tank, developed: 283, 293–94, 300
Tavignano, 198
Tawakonis, 147
Taylor, A. J. P., 85; quoted, 83, 86
Teheran Conference, 69
telegraph, military use of, 284
Temperley, A. C.: quoted, 81
Tennessee, Army of, 52, 53, 55
"ten-percent plan," 50
Texas, 146, 147
Thebes, 138, 140
Theodosius I, 143–44
Thespiae, 140
Thirty Years' War, 7–9, 14–15, 22–23, 27–29, 264
Thrace, 143–44
Three Emperors Alliance, 243
Three Emperors, League of the, 148
Three Panics, The (Richard Cobden), 271
Thucydides: quoted, 99
Thyrea, 177
Tientsin, 122
Tilly, Count, 14, 15, 264
Tirpitz, Adm. Alfred von, 280
Tocqueville, Alexis de, 200, 202
Tojo, Gen. Hideki, 19, 158
Tokugawa rule, 108, 109
Tonkawas, 147
TORCH, Operation, 67
torpedo: development of, 279–83, 284, 301
Toulouse, 267

Townshend Act, 137
Trafalgar, battle of, 268, 269, 279
trains, armored troop-carrying, 284
trenches, military use of, 285, 287, 290
Tribuna, 191
Triple Alliance, 235, 243, 245, 249; during Italo-Turkish War, 173, 193, 194, 198, 201, 208; quoted, 169
Triple Entente, 149
Tripoli. *See* Libya
Tripoli, Decree of Annexation of, 188
Truman Committee, 32
Truman, Harry S., 32
Tswana, 157
Tukhachevsky, Marshal M. N., 39
Tunis, 198
Tunisia, 190, 198, 243
Turkey, 88–89, 98, 151, 250; during 19th century, 233, 234, 235, 237, 238, 248, 270, 287; during Italo-Turkish War, 167–73, 177–81, 183, 188, 189–202, 206–19
Turkish Straits, 234
Tuscany, 130, 131, 237

U-boat, 24, 281–83
underground, Norweigan (World War II), 126
Union, the, 41–57 passim, 301. *See also* specific armies; Civil War
Union Pacific Railroad, 148
United Nations (U.N.), 183
United States, 62, 63, 91, 92, 101, 112, 122, 146–48, 183, 247, 250, 281–82; and attack on Pearl Harbor, 11, 12, 17–20, 24–26, 32, 63, 94–96; during World War II, 40, 62–69, 89, 90, 93, 94–96, 125, 150, 158, 253–55, 275–76, 283, 294, 297, 298–99, 300–301; post–World War II, 88, 100, 111, 113, 136, 256, 257, 301–4. *See also* American Revolution; Civil War
United States Air Force, 175, 295, 296, 297–99, 302
United States Army, 17, 18, 59, 60, 61, 62, 63
United States Navy, 17, 18, 19, 58–59, 60, 61, 274, 278, 283
Unkiar-Skelessi, 233, 234
Upton, Gen. Emory, 59

Urban VIII, Pope, 22
U.S.S.R. *See* Russia
Utley, Robert: quoted, 146–47, 147–48

Vacca, La, 132
Val Telline, 28
Vandenberg, Sen. Arthur H., 30
Vansittart, Sir Robert: quoted, 81
Vattel, Emmerich de, 343–45, 346–47, 353; quoted, 344
Verdun, Battle of, 289
Versailles, Treaty of, 80–81, 84
Vicksburg, capture of, 52
Victor Emmanuel III, 182, 212, 217; quoted, 181
Victory, 268, 269
Vieille, Paul, 287
Vienna, Congress of, 231
Vietnam, 136, 144–46
Vietnam War, 67, 93, 299, 303–4
Villon, François: quoted, 274
Virginia, 269. See also *Merrimac*
Virginia, Army of, 47, 50
Virginia, Army of Northern, 46, 53, 54
Visigoths, 143–44
Vitoria, Franciscus, 324–27, 328, 329, 330
Voroshilov, K. Y.: quoted, 124–25
Vyshinsky, Andrei, 133

Wacos, 147
Wallenstein, Albrecht von, 9, 14, 22, 23
Wallenstein (Johann Christoph Friedrich von Schiller), 14
Wang Ching-wei, 157–58
War of 1812, 60, 270, 279, 281
Warrior, 269, 272, 273
Warsaw, 251
Warsaw Pact, 257
Waterloo, battle of, 265, 267, 269, 283, 285
Wedemeyer, Gen. Albert C., 65
Wei Yuan, 106
Wellington, duke of, 267, 269, 271, 277, 285, 294
Westphalia, Peace of, 9
Wheeler, Sen. Burton K., 30
Whigs, 29, 30, 240
Whitehead, Robert, 280
Wilkes, John, 24, 30
Wille, Gen., 287

386

William of Villehardouin, 129
William I, 242
Williams, Kenneth P., *Lincoln Finds a General*, 57
Williams, T. Harry, *Lincoln and His Generals*, 42, 57
Wilson, Woodrow, 62, 63, 67
Wohlstetter, Roberta: quoted, 95–97
Wolff, Christian, 343, 344–45, 347, 348
Wood, Sir Charles: quoted, 270
Wood, Gen. Leonard, 62
World War I, 40, 58, 62, 63, 80, 100–104, 132–33, 165, 176, 183, 185–86, 188, 199, 200, 204, 217, 218, 248–50, 280–82, 286, 288, 290–92, 295–96, 297, 300
World War II, 11, 12, 17–20, 24–26, 30–32, 40, 64–69, 80–88, 89–97, 100, 123–25, 126–27, 133–34, 141–43, 166, 186–88, 200, 251, 253–54, 275–76, 278, 282–83, 286, 293–94, 297–99, 300–301
Württemberg, 241
Wyoming, 148

Xerxes I, 139, 141

Yamamoto, Adm. Isoroku, 20
"yellow peril," 90
Yemen, 194
Yen Fu, 107–8
Young, George F.: quoted, 130–32
Ypres, battle of, 185, 289
Yugoslavia, 250

Zeppelin, Count Ferdinand von, 284, 295
Zhukov, Marshal G. K., 39
Zionism, 172
Zollverein, 241
Zuara, 198

ACME
BOOKBINDING CO., INC.

AUG 28 1985

100 CAMBRIDGE STREET
CHARLESTOWN, MASS.